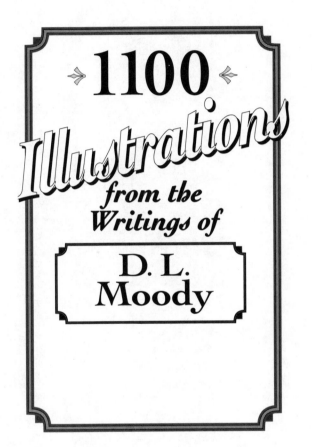

1100 Illustrations

from the
Writings of

D. L. Moody

1100 Illustrations

from the Writings of

D. L. Moody

For Teachers, Preachers, and Writers

John W. Reed, *Compiler*

Baker Books

A Division of Baker Book House Co
Grand Rapids, Michigan 49516

Published by Baker Books
a division of Baker Book House Company
P.O. Box 6287, Grand Rapids, MI 49516-6287

Printed in the United States of America

Library of Congress Cataloging-in-Publication Data

Moody, Dwight Lyman, 1837–1899.
    1100 illustrations from the writings of D. L. Moody : for teachers, preachers, and writers / edited by John W. Reed.
        p. cm.
    Includes index.
    ISBN 0-8010-9022-9 (pbk.)
    1. Homiletical illustrations. I. Reed, John. II. Title.
BV4225.2.M66 1966
252'.08—dc20   96-20563

Contents

Preface   7

Illustrations, Anecdotes, and Quotations   9

D. L. Moody Bibliography   331

Subject Index   335

Scripture Index   345

Preface

It is with great joy that I am privileged to reinvent D. L. Moody for this generation of writers, speakers, and preachers. Mr. Moody was the Billy Graham of the world one hundred years ago. He preached across America, England, and Scotland. Newspapers in the cities where he preached sent stenographers to copy down his sermons and then printed them in the next day's paper. He was a common man who spoke to the person of the street. I have always found him as contemporary as the breath I am currently breathing.

Mr. Moody blessed me in a life-changing way as I read his sermons and went through the task of compiling this edition. This volume could be read devotionally from cover to cover by anyone seeking a fresh word from God. Again and again as I went through the sermons I said to myself, "I wish I had done this at the beginning of my ministry rather than at the end." If you are early in ministry life, God may use Moody's words to mark you as you communicate them to others.

Mr. Moody's illustrations and quotations are up-to-the-current-minute in style because he understood what all writers and speakers must understand. To be effective it is crucial to use concrete examples. This could also be called the specific instance or the case study technique. Ronald Reagan was also a great communicator because he understood and used this principle. This volume is filled with human interest stories of real people resolving crises. In a problem-filled world it is a book of solutions.

Mr. Moody was positive in his emphasis. He told stories of people doing things right in the power of God. He did use negative examples but he preferred to accentuate the positive. He was able to touch people emotionally. People loved to hear and read him because he grabbed them around the heart. He still does. He was skillful in use of comparison and contrast and dynamic imagery.

We can all learn from this master of communication. Often when I am looking for a fresh way to say something, I read some of these illustrations and quotations. I find insight and inspiration and my own style is jump-started.

Mr. Moody's effectiveness was grounded in his deep experience of Holy Spirit–filled servanthood and his profound compassion for the lost masses of the world. In addition he had acquired a mastery of the Bible, particularly in those areas that related to bringing people to saving faith in Christ. He was an example of Cicero's description of the ideal communicator. He was a "good man who spoke well." It was Henry Varley who said, "It remains to be seen what God will do with a man who gives himself up wholly to Him." D. L. Moody said, "By the grace of God I intend to be that man." This volume pulsates with that inspired vision.

John W. Reed

Abstinence, importance of

Lev. 10:9; Num. 6:3–4; Judg. 13:5; Prov. 23:20, 31–32; Jer. 35:6; Dan. 1:8; Luke 1:15; 7:33

I give this word to you who have newly trusted Christ. Be out and out on the Lord's side: and the Lord will help and deliver you. Never touch strong drink as long as you live. Nearly all the new converts who have fallen back in Europe have fallen through strong drink. Even though certain classes of people may drink moderately, don't you touch it. There are some people of personal discipline that drink and do not suffer thereby; but ninety out of every hundred have not this strength and they need the support of your example. Give it up for Christ's sake; give it up for the sake of those who have become the slaves of drink, but now would rather lose their right hand than touch a drop of liquor.

Abstinence, importance of; Temperance, importance of

Lev. 10:9; Num. 6:3–4; Judg. 13:5; Prov. 23:20, 31–32; Jer. 35:6; Dan. 1:8; Luke 1:15; 7:33

I would rather have my right hand cut off than touch beer or liquor before my children. The friends that have been lost to drinking are so many as should rouse us to be as one person in sweeping alcoholic drink from our tables. If you want me to sign a pledge not to drink, I will take any pledge you may bring; I never touch drink, and never intend to do so. Now for the other side. Some temperance people make a grand mistake, and that is they lug in the question every time they get the chance. Everything in its own place! If I go to a prayer meeting I do not want to hear temperance. There is a man who comes to our noonday meetings; no matter what the subject is, he gets up and talks every day on temperance and the higher life. A friend, in going out of the meeting one day, said to me, "I like a fiddle with a thousand strings, not the same one played on every day."

Acceptance, power of

Esther 10:3; Job 42:9; Pss. 44:3; 85:10; Isa. 42:1; Luke 1:28; Acts 4:36; 9:27; 10:35; Rom. 15:31; 2 Cor. 5:9; 6:2; Eph. 1:6; 2 Tim. 4:11

A gentleman came to my office for the purpose of getting me interested in a young man who had just got out of the penitentiary. "He says," said the gentleman, "he doesn't want to go to your office, but I want your permission to bring him in and introduce him." I said, "Bring him in." The gentleman brought the former convict in and introduced him, and I took him by the hand and told him I was glad to see him. I invited him up to my house, and when I took him into my family I introduced him as a friend. When my little daughter came into the room, I said, "Emma, this is papa's friend." And she went up and kissed him, and the man sobbed aloud. After the child left the room, I said, "What is the matter?" "O sir," he said, "I have not had a kiss for years. The last kiss I had was from my mother, and she was dying. I thought I would never have another one again." His heart was broken and opened to the Lord.

Adam's sin, result of; Rebellion against God

Gen. 3:8–9, 15, 17, 21; Job 31:33; Jer. 32:19; Rom. 5:14; 1 Cor. 15:22, 45; 1 Tim. 2:14

Most of us live away from home. We are hiding as Adam did in the bushes of Eden.

There was a time when God's voice thrilled Adam's soul with joy and gladness, and he thrilled God's heart with joy. They lived in sweet fellowship with each other. God had lifted Adam to the very gates of heaven, had made him lord over all creation. I haven't a doubt that he had plans to raise Adam still higher—higher than the angels, higher than seraphim and cherubim, higher than Gabriel, who stands in the presence of Jehovah, and Michael, the archangel. But the man turned and became a traitor to him who wanted to bless him.

Adoration of God

Gen. 28:17, 20–22; 1 Kings 8:23; 2 Chron. 7:14; Neh. 1:5; 9:4, 32; Pss. 29:2; 50:2; 96:6, 9; Dan. 9:4, 7, 16; Micah 7:20; Luke 1:72; Rev. 5:12, 14; 7:12

Adoration has been defined as the act of rendering God honor, including in it reverence, esteem and love. It literally signifies to apply the hand to the mouth, "to kiss the hand." In Eastern countries this is one of the great marks of respect and submission. The importance of coming before God in this spirit is great and is so often impressed upon us in the Bible.

Newman Hall, in his work on the Lord's Prayer, says, "Man's worship, apart from that revealed in the Bible, has been uniformly characterized by selfishness. We come to God either to thank him for benefits already received, or to implore still further benefits: food, raiment, health, safety, or comfort.

"Like Jacob at Bethel, we are disposed to make the worship we render to God correlative with food to eat, and raiment to put on. This style of petition, in which self generally precedes and predominates, if it does not altogether absorb, our supplications, is not only seen in the devotees of false systems, but in the majority of the prayers of professed Christians.

"Our prayers are like the Parthian horsemen, who ride one way while they look another. We seem to go toward God, but, indeed, reflect upon ourselves. And this may be the reason why many times our prayers are sent forth, like the raven out of Noah's ark, and never return. But when we make the glory of God the chief end of our devotion, they go forth like the dove, and return to us again with an olive branch."

Adultery, curse of; Daughter, prodigal; Commandment, seventh

1 Sam. 2:22; 2 Sam. 11:4; 1 Thess. 4:3; Heb. 13:4

I think that the most infernal thing that the sun shines on in America is the way a woman is treated after she has been ruined by a man, often under fair promises of marriage. Someone has said that when the prodigal son came home he had the best robe and the fatted calf, but what does the prodigal daughter get? Although she may have been more sinned against than sinning, she is cast out and ostracized by society. She is condemned to an almost hopeless life of degradation and shame, sinking step by step into a loathsome grave unless she hurries her doom by suicide. But the wretch who has ruined her in body and soul holds his head as high as ever, and society attaches no stain to him.

If he had failed to pay his gambling debts or was detected cheating at cards, he would promptly be dropped by society; but he may boast of his impure life, and his companions will think nothing of it. Parents who would not allow their daughter to become acquainted with a man who is rude in manners, sometimes do not hesitate to accept the society of men who are known to be impure.

Adultery, curse of; Impurity, curse of; Commandment, seventh

1 Sam. 2:22; 2 Sam. 11:4; 1 Thess. 4:3; Heb. 13:4

Talk about stealing—a man who steals the virtue of a woman is the meanest thief that ever was on the face of the earth! One who goes into your house and steals your money is a prince compared with a vile libertine who takes the virtue of your sister, or steals the affection of your wife, and robs you of her; no sneak thief that ever walked the earth is so mean as he. How men pass laws to protect their property, but when that which is far nearer and dearer to them than money is taken, it is made light of!

If a man should push a young lady into the river and she should be drowned, the law would lay hold of him, and he would be tried for murder and executed. But if he wins her affection and ruins her, and then casts her off, isn't he worse than a murderer? There are some sins that are worse than murder, and that is one of them. If someone should treat your wife or sister so, you would want to shoot him as you would a dog. Why do you not respect all women as you do your mother and sister? What law of justice forgives the obscene bird of prey, while it kicks out of its path the soiled and bleeding dove?

Adultery, danger of; Commandment, seventh

Exod. 20:14; Prov. 6:29; 1 Thess. 4:3; Heb. 13:4

This commandment is God's bulwark around marriage and the home. Marriage is one of the institutions that existed in Eden; it is older than the fall of man. It is the most sacred relationship that can exist between human beings, taking precedence even of the relationship of the parent and child. Someone has pointed out that as in the beginning God created one man and one woman, this is the true order for all ages. Where family ties are disregarded and dishonored the results are always fatal. The home existed before the church, and unless the home is kept pure and undefiled, there can be no family religion and the church is in danger.

Adultery and licentiousness have swept other nations out of existence. Did it not bring brimstone from heaven upon Sodom and Gomorrah? What carried Rome into ruin? The obscene statues at Pompeii and Naples tell the tale. Where there is no sacredness around the home, population dwindles; family virtues disappear; the children are corrupt from their very birth; the seeds of sure decay are already planted.

Adultery, danger of; Lust, danger of; Commandment, seventh

Prov. 6:32; 23:27; Hosea 4:11; Matt. 5:28; Rom. 1:27; Gal. 5:16

Lust is the devil's counterfeit of love. There is nothing more beautiful on earth than a pure love and there is nothing so blighting as lust. I don't know of a quicker, shorter way down to hell than adultery and the kindred sins condemned by God's commandments. The Bible says that with the heart man believeth unto righteousness but "whoredom and new wine take away the heart." Lust will drive all natural affection out of a man's heart. For the sake of some vile harlot he will trample on the feelings and entreaties of a mother and a beautiful wife and / or godly sister.

Young man, are you leading an impure life? Suppose God's scales of justice should drop down before you in this moment. What would you do? Are you fit for the kingdom of heaven? You know very well that you are not. You loathe yourself. When you look upon that pure wife or mother, you say, "What a vile wretch I am! The harlot is bringing me down to an untimely and dishonored grave!"

May God show us what a fearful sin adultery is! The idea of making light of it! I do not know of any sin that will make a man run down to ruin more quickly. I am appalled when I think of what is going on in the world; of so many young men living impure lives, and talking about the virtue of women as if it didn't amount to anything. This sin is coming in upon us like a flood at the present day. In every city there is an army of prostitutes. Young men by hundreds are being utterly ruined by this accursed sin.

Adultery, defilement of; Commandment, seventh

Prov. 6:32; 23:27; Hosea 4:11; Matt. 5:28; Rom. 1:27; Gal. 5:16; Eph. 5:3, 5; 2 Peter 2:10

Will anyone deny that the house of the strange woman is "the way to hell, going down to the chambers of death," as the Bible says? Are there not men whose characters have been utterly ruined for this life through this accursed sin? Are there not wives who would rather sink into their graves than live? Many a man went with a pure woman to the altar a few years ago and promised to love and cherish her. Now he has given his affections to some vile harlot and brought ruin on his wife and children!

Young man, young woman, are you guilty, even in thought? Bear in mind what Christ said about adultery of the mind (Matt. 5:27, 28). How many would repent but that they are tied hand and foot, and some vile harlot whose feet are fastened in hell, clings to him and says, "If you give me up, I will expose you!" Can you step on the scales and take that harlot with you? If you are guilty of this awful sin, escape for your life. Hear God's voice while there is yet time. Confess your sin to Christ. Ask him to snap the fetters that bind you. Ask

Christ to give you victory over your passions, and say, "By the grace of God I will not go down to an adulterer's grave."

Adultery, defilement of; Lust, danger of; Commandment, seventh

Gen. 39:12; Judg. 16:1; 1 Sam. 2:22; 2 Sam. 11:4; 1 John 2:17

Lust gave Samson into the power of Delilah, who robbed him of his strength. It led David to commit murder and called down upon him the wrath of God, and if he had not repented he would have lost heaven. I believe that if Joseph had responded to the enticement of Potiphar's wife, his light would have gone out in darkness. Lust ends in one or other of two ways: either in remorse and shame because of the realization of the loss of purity, with a terrible struggle against a hard taskmaster; or in hardness of heart, brutalizing of the finer senses, which is a more dreadful condition.

Adultery, nature of; Commandment, seventh

Prov. 6:26, 32; 9:18; 29:3; Gal. 5:19; 2 Peter 2:14

We hear a good deal about alcoholism these days. That sin advertises itself; it shows its marks upon the face and in the conduct. But the sin of adultery hides itself away under the shadow of the night. A person who tampers with this evil goes on step by step until character is blasted, reputation ruined, health gone and life made as dark as hell. May God wake up the nation to see how this awful sin is spreading!

Adultery, recovery from; Commandment, seventh

2 Sam. 12:13–14; Prov. 5:5, 18; Pss. 32:5; 51:3

If you are guilty of adultery, do not let the day pass until you repent. If you are living in some secret sin or are fostering impure thoughts, make up your mind that by the grace of God you will be delivered. Even in this life adultery and uncleanness bring their awful results, both physical and mental. The pleasure and excitement that lead so many astray at the beginning soon pass away, and only the evil remains. Vice carries a sting in its tail, like the scorpion. The body is sinned against, and the body sooner or later suffers.

Nature herself punishes with terrible diseases and the man goes down to the grave rotten, leaving the effects of his sin to blight his posterity. There are nations whose manhood has been eaten out by this awful scourge. It drags a man lower than the beasts. It stains the memory. I believe that memory is "the worm that never dies," and the memory is never cleansed of obscene stories and unclean acts. Even if a man repents and reforms he often has to fight the past.

Adultery, sin of; Commandment, seventh

Exod. 20:14; 1 Thess. 4:3; Heb. 13:4

An English Army officer who had been living an impure life went around one evening to argue religion with the chaplain. During their talk the officer said, "Religion is all very well, but you must admit that there are difficulties about the miracles, for instance." The chaplain knew the man and his besetting sin, and quietly looking him in the face, answered, "Yes, there are some things in the Bible not very clear, I admit: but the seventh commandment is very plain."

2 Sam. 12:10; Mark 7:22; 2 Cor. 12:21; Gal. 5:19

I would to God I could pass over this commandment without comment, but I feel that the time has come to cry aloud and spare not. Plain speaking about it is not very fashionable. "Teachers of religion have by common consent banished from their public teaching all advice, warning or allusion in regard to love between the sexes," says Dr. Stalker. These themes are left to poets and novelists to handle. In an autobiography recently published in England, the writer attributed no small share of the follies and vices of his earlier years to his never having heard a plain, outspoken sermon on this seventh commandment. But though men are inclined to pass it by, God is not silent or indifferent in regard to it. When I hear anyone make light of adultery and licentiousness, I take the Bible and see how God has let his curse and wrath come down upon it.

Advertising church services

Pss. 40:9–10; 71:15; 119:46; Mark 8:38; Luke 9:26; 2 Tim. 1:8

It is a great mistake not to advertise religious services. I don't see why we shouldn't learn something from the world. They advertise very extensively. A man comes into town from the country or from some other city, and he doesn't know anything about the meetings, and if he sees a notice of them he may attend them. I don't see why the walls should not be placarded also. Many a man has been blest in that way. Some people are sensitive about it, I know; but it seems to me it is a good deal better to advertise and have a full house than to preach to empty pews. Bills are stuck up everywhere for people to go to theaters and places of amusement, and I don't see why we shouldn't give the gospel a chance. If people don't know about the meetings why not advertise them?

Affliction, submission in

Isa. 40:31; Matt. 5:11; 10:19; 1 Cor. 10:13; 2 Cor. 1:4; 3:5; 11:30; 12:5; Eph. 3:16; Phil. 4:13; Col. 1:11; 1 Tim. 1:14; Heb. 4:16; 1 Peter 4:13–14

Rutherford beautifully writes, in reference to the value of sanctified trial and the wisdom of submitting to it in God's will: "Why should I complain at the plough of my

Lord, that maketh deep furrows on my soul? I know that He is no idle husbandman; He purposeth a crop. Oh, what I owe to the file, to the hammer, to the furnace of my Lord Jesus, who hath now let me see how good the wheat of Christ is that goeth through His mill and His oven, to be made bread for His own table!"

Afflictions, blessings of

Isa. 40:31; Matt. 5:11; 10:19; 1 Cor. 10:13; 2 Cor. 1:4; 3:5; 11:30; 12:5; Eph. 3:16; Phil. 4:13; Col. 1:11; 1 Tim. 1:14; Heb. 4:16; 1 Peter 4:13–14

Dyer said, "Afflictions are blessings to us when we can bless God for afflictions. Suffering has kept many from sinning. God had one Son without sin; but he never had any without sorrow. Fiery trials make golden Christians; sanctified afflictions are spiritual promotions."

Aging gracefully

Gen. 15:15; 17:7; 25:8; Deut. 6:2; Job 5:26; 32:7; Pss. 71:9, 18; 91:16; 145:4; Prov. 3:16; 13:22; 22:6; 23:22; Isa. 46:4; Acts 13:36; Rom. 4:20; Heb. 11:11

Some of you with silver locks, I think I hear you saying, "I wish I was young, how I would rush into the battle." Well, if you cannot be a fighter, you can pray and lead on the others. There are two kinds of old people in the world. One grows chilled and sour, and there are others who light up every meeting with their genial presence, and cheer on the workers. Draw near, old age, and cheer on the others, and take them by the hand and encourage them.

Aging gracefully; Children, discipline of

Gen. 15:15; 17:7; 25:8; Deut. 6:2; Job 5:26; 32:7; Pss. 71:9, 18; 91:16; 145:4; Prov. 3:16; 13:22; 22:6; 23:22; Isa. 46:4; Acts 13:36; Rom. 4:20; Heb. 11:11

I want to tell you a secret. There are two classes of old people: some that are getting cross and crabbed in their old age, and some that are growing sunny and bright. You sometimes see an old man who is all the time living in the past, nursing his troubles, and grumbling and finding fault with his lot; and he grows cross and cranky, and keeps things around him uncomfortable for everybody, a man who is looking into the future with dark forebodings and with great anxiety.

You have heard of the boy who didn't want to go to heaven if his grandfather was going there, because he was always saying, "Tut, tut, don't do this, or don't do that." I know a grandfather who fitted up a room with all the toys and things that a child's heart could wish, and then said to his grandchildren, "Go in there and get all you want." If any of you grandfathers and grandmothers find any crossness or crabbiness coming on, just nip it in the bud. There are a good many children like the girl who said her name was "Emma Don't." They nagged her so much with "Emma, don't do this," and "Emma, don't do that," that she thought her name was "Emma Don't."

Alcoholism, healing from

Matt. 4:24; 8:17; 9:2, 6; Luke 4:40; 6:17; 7:21, 47–48; 9:1; Acts 19:12; 28:9; James 5:15–16

Now, some people say they have become so addicted to strong drink, that it has become a disease with them; never mind, bring it to Christ—he will heal all thy diseases. I would not give up a man because his own power over himself is gone; it is the power of God that is going to save him, not his own; and if a person is so given to drink that it is a disease, don't become discouraged and think there is no hope for that man. "He forgiveth all thine iniquities, He healeth all thy diseases, He restoreth thy soul." If a man only brings his disease to Christ, if he only brings this appetite to the Son of God, God is able to forgive him and heal him.

Alcoholism, help in recovery

Matt. 4:24; 8:17; 9:2, 6; Luke 4:40; 6:17–19; 7:21, 47–48; 9:1; Acts 19:12; 28:9; 1 Peter 2:4; James 5:15–16

I said to a Christian Scotchman one day as he stayed to the after-meeting, "Would you speak to that young man there?" He was a great manufacturer. He said, "Mr. Moody, I am very reticent; I don't know that I could do that." I said, "Perhaps you can help him; I wish you would speak to him."

He sat down beside the young man and found him to be a working man. He said that every Saturday noon when he was paid off and went home to get his lunch, a terrible thirst for strong drink came on him, and that by Monday all his wages were drunk up.

The next Saturday noon that great manufacturer was at his home and spent the whole afternoon with him. The next Saturday he came again, and he kept at it until he got that man away from the power of strong drink. That is a good way to confess Christ. If you can't do it with your lips, you can do it in some way. Watch for opportunities to let the world know on whose side you stand.

Alcoholism, recovery from; Forgiveness, repeated

Matt. 4:24; 8:17; 9:2, 6; Luke 4:40; 6:17–19; 7:21, 47–48; 9:1; Acts 19:12; 28:9; 1 Peter 2:4; James 5:15–16

"If an alcoholic has fallen twice, shall we give him up?" The Lord answers that question when he tells Peter "to forgive his brother, not only seven times, but seventy times seven." Suppose a man has stumbled once or twice; you aren't going to cast him off, are you? If a man should, in an unguarded moment, fall, would you say that he had not been reclaimed? How many of us have fallen? Here is a man with a miserable, wretched temper, and, in an unguarded moment, he says some

foolish thing; isn't he just as bad as this man who drinks again? Suppose these men that have been slaves to Satan twenty or thirty years should be tripped up by Satan; would you give them up and say there was no hope?

How many of us have been troubled with besetting sins after our conversion? If Satan gets one of these men down, instead of publishing it to the world, in the name of God let us help him up. If he stumbles a second time, go after him; if he stumbles a third time, go after him; and keep going after him as often as he falls. Why, Dr. Newman Hall's father, I don't know how many times he fell; he kept falling and falling, and rising and rising, and at last he passed through the pearly gates shouting, "Glory to the Lamb." He got victory at last. And so if these new converts fall, let us not go out and publish it to the world, but take them off and talk with them alone and tell them we sympathize with them.

Ambition, controlling

Gen. 3:5–6; 11:4; Num. 12:1; 16:3; 1 Kings 1:5; Pss. 49:11; 16:26; 20:20; 23:6; Luke 4:12; 9:25; 11:43; 22:3; 1 John 2:16; 3 John 9

Now suppose we ask ourselves this question, Have we been working for God with the right motive? Has it been God's work or our own that we have been doing? Has self been crucified, and has God's glory been the uppermost thought in our hearts? I was very much impressed some time ago, in finding this unholy ambition constantly coming out in the lives of those men that Christ chose to follow him; and it seemed very strange that after they had been with him three years they had not got the lesson. It seems about the hardest lesson for us to learn. It seems about the hardest thing to get to the end of self; but when we have got to the end of self, and self is lost sight of, self-seeking and self-glory thrown aside, and

Christ and his cause are uppermost in our hearts, how easy it is for God to use us.

Anger, control of; Temper, control of

Gen. 4:5; 34:25; Ps. 103:8; Prov. 14:17, 29; 15:18; 16:32; 19:11, 19; 25:28; Eccles. 7:9; Matt. 5:22; Mark 6:19; Gal. 5:20; Eph. 4:26; Col. 3:8; James 1:19

With many the temper is a terrible foe. They have hard work to control it. It runs away with them. But if we are going to be Christians we must keep our tempers. God says, in Prov. 16:32, "He that ruleth his spirit is greater than he that taketh a city." If you want, then, to be greater than General Grant, or any of the great generals of the world, rule your spirit. A man without any temper is good for nothing—like untempered steel. The more temper you have, the better, as long as you master it. Have a spirit, but rule your spirit through submission to the Holy Spirit.

Gen. 4:5; 34:25; Ps. 103:8; Prov. 14:17, 29; 15:18; 16:32; 19:11, 19; 25:28; Eccles. 7:9; Matt. 5:22; Mark 6:19; Gal. 5:20; Eph. 4:26; Col. 3:8; James 1:19

You ask, "How am I going to overcome bad temper?" When you find yourself saying or doing a mean thing, say to the one you have wronged that you are sorry. And when you have done that twenty-five times you will stop doing mean things. It takes a good deal of courage to say, "I am wrong." That is "keeping the body under." As Paul said, "I keep under my body, and bring it into subjection." The tempted person may speak of his uncontrolled temper as a misfortune or a weakness. He is mistaken. It is a sin.

But someone says to me, "Moody, you know nothing about it." I do. It was once a word and a blow with me, and the blow came pretty quick, before the word cooled; nothing would satisfy me better than knocking the man down. I was very much

like the Irishman, who said he was "never at peace unless he was fighting somebody."

Anger, control of; Temper, control of; Self-control, need of

Gen. 4:5; 34:25; Ps. 103:8; Prov. 14:17, 29; 15:18; 16:32; 19:11, 19; 25:28; Eccles. 7:9; Matt. 5:22; Mark 6:19; Gal. 5:20; Eph. 4:26; Col. 3:8; James 1:19

I have known a husband to give his wife a good scolding and go out of the house in a mad fit, but before he had gone far his conscience would smite him. Then he would say to himself, "I didn't treat my wife right this morning, and when I go home I will take her a big bouquet." Tons of bouquets won't cover that thing up! If a man wants to conquer that habit let him go to his wife and say, "I feel mean and contemptible for speaking as I did this morning, and I want you to forgive me." After he has done that half a dozen times, he will be cured. You say, "I should like to see you try it yourself!" I have tried it, and I know how it works.

I want to tell you another thing. Some people seem to think that the preachers who have nothing to do but write sermons and preach them ought to be very angelic; but they have the same things to overcome that you have. Preaching isn't going to make me any better, and talking for half an hour isn't going to give me self-control; I must get it as other people do; it is a conflict, it is a battle.

Anxiety, cure of; Worry, answers for; Burdens, provision for

Gen. 32:7; 1 Sam. 1:15; 30:6; 2 Chron. 32:20; 33:12; Pss. 55:17; 127:2; Jer. 17:7; Dan. 3:16; Matt. 6:25; 10:40; 12:11; Phil. 4:6; Heb. 13:5; 1 Peter 5:7

If you go to the world with your cares, your troubles, and your anxieties, all it can do is to put a few more on the top of them. The world is a poor place to go to for sympathy. As someone has said, "If you roll your burdens anywhere but on Christ, they will roll back on you with more weight than ever." Cast them on Christ; and he will carry them for you.

Anxiety, cure of; Worry, lack of; Joy, source of

Gen. 32:7; 1 Sam. 1:15; 30:6; 2 Chron. 32:20; 33:12; Pss. 55:17; 127:2; Jer. 17:7; Dan. 3:16; Matt. 6:25; 10:40; Phil. 4:6; Heb. 13:5; 1 Peter 5:7

Mrs. Sangster says that we hear a good deal in this age, as if it were a novelty, about the futility of being anxious, and people have established "Don't Worry Clubs." But the first "Don't Worry Club" was begun by our blessed Lord himself when he said, "Take no thought for the things of itself. Sufficient unto the day is the evil thereof." He had us consider the lilies growing in their beauty and purity without a thought, and taught us the true way of living without care, without solicitude, bearing all burdens lightly, and having continual joy on our faces. Only those who have the indwelling Christ in their hearts can walk through this world with bright and glad looks, because they know that, let come what may, their Father is leading them safely.

Appetite, spiritual

Job 23:12; Pss. 19:10; 119:103, 111; Isa. 55:1; Jer. 15:16; Hosea 14:7; John 4:14; 6:33; 7:37; 1 Cor. 3:2; Heb. 5:12; 1 Peter 2:2; 2 Peter 3:18; Rev. 22:17

I have heard of artificial bees with springs in them, so that they moved about, and you could hardly tell them from the real live bees when they were put down among them. The maker puzzled a good many people with them, till at last somebody found out how to expose the trick. He just put down a little honey among them, and all the live bees went for it right

away. So it is in the Church, those who have the true life in them have good sharp appetites for the honey of God's word.

Approval, God's; Honor from above

Pss. 50:23; 91:14; Prov. 3:10; Dan. 4:36; 12:3; John 1:12; 8:51; 12:26; 1 Cor. 4:5; 2 Cor. 5:10; Eph. 1:4; Col. 3:4; 2 Thess. 1:7; 2 Tim. 4:8; James 1:12; 1 Peter 5:4; 1 John 3:2

God's honor is something worth seeking. Man's honor doesn't amount to much. Suppose Moses had stayed down there in Egypt. He would have been loaded down with Egyptian titles, but they would never have reached us. Suppose he had been Chief Marshal of the whole Egyptian army, "General" Moses, "Commander" Moses; suppose he had reached the throne and become one of those Pharaohs, and his mummy had come down to our day. What is that compared with the honor God put upon him? How his name shines on the page of history!

The honor of this world doesn't last, it is transient, it passes away; and I don't believe any man or woman is fit for God's service that is looking for worldly preferment, worldly honors, and worldly fame. Let us get it under our feet, let us rise above it, and seek the honor that comes down from above.

Arguments, futility of

Job 15:3; 16:3; Matt. 12:36; Col. 4:6; 1 Tim. 1:4; 4:7; 6:4; 2 Tim. 2:14, 16, 23; Titus 1:14; 3:9

I have offended many people because I will not argue with them in the inquiry room meetings. With honest skeptics I have a great deal of sympathy, and will do all that I can to help them. But I will not waste time on those who come only to cavil, or to ask foolish questions; who want to turn the inquiry meeting into a debating society. An astronomer, after years of study, cannot answer every question that you can ask him about the stars.

And yet some people seem to think that as soon as a man is converted he ought to be able to explain everything in the Bible. And if the old skeptic can puzzle the young Christian with some such question as, "Who was Melchizedek?" he laughs at him, and insinuates that his religion is a sham. Don't have any controversy with such cavilers.

Assurance, basis of; Security, basis of

Pss. 3:8; 9:10; 27:3; 46:11; 73:25; Isa. 12:2; John 5:24; 10:27; 17:12; Rom. 5:5; Phil. 1:20; 2 Tim. 4:18; Heb. 6:19; 1 John 5:13

There is no doubt about assurance in the Word of God. A person said to me some time ago, "I think it is great presumption for a person to say she is saved." I asked her if she was saved. "I belong to a church," she replied. "But are you saved?" 'I believe it would be presumption in me to say that I was saved." "Well, I think it is a greater presumption for anyone to say, 'I don't know if I believe what the Lord Jesus Christ has said.' Because it is written, 'He that believeth on me hath everlasting life.' It is clearly stated that we have assurance."

Job 19:25; Pss. 23:4; 27:3; 56:9; 73:24; John 3:36; 17:11; Rom. 6:23; 2 Cor. 5:1; Phil. 1:6; Heb. 7:25; 1 John 3:2

A great many people say, "Mr. Moody, I would like to know whether or not I am a Christian. I would like to know if I am saved." The longer I live the more I am convinced that it is one of the greatest privileges of a child of God to know—to be able to say, "I am saved." The idea of walking through life without knowing this until we get to the great white throne is exploded. If the Bible doesn't teach assurance it doesn't teach justification by faith; if it doesn't teach assurance it doesn't teach redemption. The doctrine of assurance is as clear as any doctrine in the Bible.

How many people in the Chicago Tabernacle when I ask them if they are Christians, say, "Well, I hope so," in a sort of a hesitating way. Another group says, "I am trying to be." This is a queer kind of testimony, my friends. I notice no man is willing to go into the inquiry room till he has got a step beyond that. Those kinds of Christians don't amount to much.

The assured Christian puts it, "I believe that my Redeemer liveth; I believe that if this building of flesh were destroyed, I have a building not made with hands, eternal in the heavens." No hoping and trusting with them. It is, "I know." Hope is assured to the Christian. It is a sure hope; it isn't a doubting hope. Suppose a man asked me if my name was Moody, and I said, "Well, I hope so." Wouldn't it sound rather strange? "I hope it is"; or, "I'm trying to be Moody." Now, if a man asks you if you are a Christian, you ought to be able to give a reason.

Pss.3:8; 9:10; 27:3; 46:11; 73:25; Isa. 12:2; John 5:24; 10:27; 17:12; Rom. 5:5; Phil. 1:20; 2 Tim. 4:18; Heb. 6:19; 1 John 5:13

"But," a man said to me, "no one has come back from the dead to tell us, and we don't know what is in the future. It is all dark, and how can we be sure?" Thank God! Christ came down from heaven, and I would rather have him, coming as he does right from the bosom of the Father, than anyone else. We can rely on what Christ says, and he says, "He that believeth on Me shall not perish, but have everlasting life." Not that we are going to have it when we die, but we have it right here today.

Pss. 3:8; 9:10; 27:3; 46:11; 73:25; Isa. 12:2; John 5:24; 10:27; 17:12; Rom. 5:5; Phil. 1:20; 2 Tim. 4:18; Heb. 6:19; 1 John 5:13

A person came to me some time ago and said: "Mr. Moody, I wish you would give me a book that preaches assurance, and that tells the children of God it is their privilege to know they are accepted." I said, "Here is a book; it is very orthodox. It was written by John, the most intimate friend of Jesus while he was on earth. The man who laid his head upon Jesus' bosom." Turn to John's Gospel and see that he says in the 5th chapter that if we believe God's word we have eternal life and will not be condemned. I have no book more reliable than that.

2 Sam. 22:3; Job 19:25; Pss. 18:2; 23:4; 27:3; 56:9; 73:24; John 3:36; 17:11; Rom. 6:23; Phil. 1:6; Heb. 7:25; 1 John 3:2

Little Johnny and his sister were one day going through a long, narrow railroad tunnel. The railroad company had built small clefts here and there through the tunnel, so that if anyone got caught in the tunnel when the train was passing, he could save himself. After this little boy and girl had gone some distance in the tunnel, they heard a train coming. They were frightened at first, but the sister just put her little brother in one cleft and she hurried and hid in another. The train came thundering along, and as it passed, the sister cried out, "Johnny, cling close to the rock! Johnny, cling close to the rock!" and they were safe.

The "Rock of Ages" may be beaten by the storms and waves of adversity, but "cling close to the rock, Christians, and all will be well." The waves don't touch the Christian; he is sheltered by the Rock that is higher than he, by the One who is the strong arm, and the Savior, mighty and willing to save.

Job 19:25; Pss. 23:4; 27:3; 56:9; 73:24; John 3:36; 17:11; Rom. 6:23; Phil. 1:6; Heb. 7:25; 1 John 3:2

If anyone should attempt to steal the crown jewels of England, the whole British army would be called out, if necessary, to protect them. The Queen doesn't have to keep them. They are kept for her in the tower, and guarded there day and night. So we don't have to keep our priceless jewel—our soul. God keeps it for us, and would, if need be, summon legions of angels to defend it.

Assurance, example of; Security, basis of

Pss. 42:11; 73:25; Isa. 41:10; 54:4; John 6:40; 10:29; 11:25; Rom. 8:38; 9:33; 1 Cor. 6:15; 2 Cor. 13:5; 2 Tim. 4:17; Heb. 10:22; 1 Peter 4:19; 1 John 2:5; 4:13, 18

After John Wesley had been preaching for some time, someone said to him, "Are you sure, Mr. Wesley, of your salvation?" "Well," he answered, "Jesus Christ died for the whole world." "Yes, we all believe that; but are you sure that you are saved?" Wesley replied that he was sure that provision had been made for his salvation. "But are you sure, Wesley, that you are saved?" It went like an arrow to his heart, and he had no rest or power until that question was settled.

Many men and many women go on month after month, and year after year, without power, because they do not know their standing in Christ; they are not sure of their own footing for eternity. Latimer wrote Ridley once that when he was settled and steadfast about his own salvation he was as bold as a lion, but if that hope wavered he was fearful and afraid and was disqualified for service. Many are disqualified for service because they are continually doubting their own salvation.

Pss. 3:8; 9:10; 27:4; 46:11; 73:25; Isa. 12:2; John 5:24; 10:27; 17:12; Rom. 5:5; Phil. 1:20; 2 Tim. 4:18; Heb. 6:19; 1 John 5:13

It is said of Napoleon that while he was reviewing his army one day, his horse became frightened at something, and the Emperor dropped his reins. The horse went away at full speed, and the Emperor's life was in danger. He could not get hold of the reins. A private in the ranks saw it, and sprang out of the ranks towards the horse, and was successful in getting hold of the horse's head at the peril of his own life. The Emperor was very much pleased.

Touching his hat, he said to him, "I make you Captain of my Guard." The soldier didn't take his gun and walk up there. He threw it away, stepped out of the ranks of the soldiers, and went up to where the bodyguard stood. The Captain of the bodyguard ordered him back into the ranks, but he said, "No! I won't go!" "Why not?" "Because I am Captain of the Guard." "You Captain of the Guard?" "Yes," replied the soldier. "Who said it?" and the man, pointing to the Emperor, said, "He said it." That was enough. Nothing more could be said. He took the Emperor at his word.

My friends, if God says anything, let us take him at his word. "He that believeth on the Lord Jesus Christ shall not perish, but have everlasting life." Don't you believe it? Don't you believe you have got everlasting life? It can be the privilege of every child of God to believe and then know that you have got it.

Assurance, hope of; Security, basis of

Pss. 3:8; 9:10; 27:4; 46:11; 73:25; Isa. 12:2; John 5:24; 10:27; 17:12; Rom. 5:5; Phil. 1:20; 2 Tim. 4:18; Heb. 6:19; 1 John 5:13

Notice the confidence that breathes through Paul's last words to Timothy. It is not a matter of doubt, but of knowledge, "I know," "I am persuaded." The word "hope" is not used in the Scripture to express doubt. It is used in regard to the second coming of Christ, or to the resurrection of the body. We should not say that we "hope" we are Christians. I do not say that I "hope" I am an American, or that I "hope" I am a married man. These are settled things. I may say that I "hope" to go back to my home, or that I "hope" to attend such a meeting. If we are born of God we know it. He will not leave us in darkness if we search the Scriptures.

Pss. 3:8; 9:10; 27:4; 46:11; 73:25; Isa. 12:2; John 5:24; 10:27; 17:12; Rom. 5:5; Phil. 1:20; 2 Tim. 4:18; Heb. 6:19; 1 John 5:13

Many think that assurance is not to be had while traveling through this world. They think they must wait till they get before the terrible judgment seat to know whether they are accepted or not. And I find some ministers preach this terrible doctrine from their pulpits. I heard of a minister who, while on his way to the burial of a man, began to talk upon the subject of assurance. "Why," said he, "if I knew for a certainty that I was saved the carriage couldn't hold me. I would have to jump out with joy." A man should be convinced that he has the gospel, before he preaches it to anyone else. A man is better able to pull another out of the river if he is on the bank than if he is in it himself. A man is better able to lift a man out of a pit if he is out of it than if he is there too. No man can preach salvation till he knows he is saved.

Assurance, importance of; Fitness for service; Security, basis of

Ps. 27:5; Isa. 32:17; Nahum 1:7; John 6:39; 10:28; 14:6; 17:13; Rom. 8:38; 2 Tim. 1:12; Heb. 6:11; 1 Peter 1:5; 1 John 2:16, 17; Jude 24

Someone will ask, "Do all God's people have assurance?" No; I think a good many of God's dear people have no assurance; but it is the privilege of every child of God to have beyond doubt a knowledge of their own salvation. No person is fit for God's service who is filled with doubts. If you are not sure of your own salvation, how can you help anyone else into the kingdom of God? If I seem in danger of drowning and do not know whether I shall ever reach the shore, I cannot assist another. I must first get on the solid rock myself; and then I can lend my brother a helping hand. If being myself blind I were to tell another blind man how to get sight, he might reply, "First get healed yourself, and then you can tell me."

I recently met with a young man who was a Christian, but he had not attained to victory over sin. He was in terrible darkness. Such a one is not fit to work for God, because he has besetting sins; and he has not the victory over his doubts, because he has not the victory over his sins.

Assurance, importance of; Security, basis of

Ps. 27:5; Isa. 32:17; Nahum 1:7; John 6:39; 10:28; 14:6; 17:13; Rom. 8:38; 2 Tim. 1:12; Heb. 6:11; 1 Peter 1:5; 1 John 2:16, 17; Jude 24

Some seem to think that it is presumption not to have doubts; but if anyone were to say that they had known a person for thirty years and yet doubted him, it would not be very creditable; and when we have known God for ten, twenty, or thirty years does it not reflect on his veracity to doubt him. Could Paul and the early Christians and martyrs have gone through what they did if they had been filled with doubts, and had not known whether they were going to heaven or to perdition after they had been burned at the stake? They must have had assurance.

Assurance, lack of; Security, basis of

Pss. 42:11; 73:25; Isa. 41:10; 54:4; John 6:40; 10:29; 11:25; Rom. 8:38; 9:33; 1 Cor. 6:15; 2 Cor. 13:5; 2 Tim. 4:17; Heb. 10:22; 1 Peter 4:19; 1 John 2:5; 4:13,18

There cannot be any peace where there is uncertainty. There is no knowledge like that of a man who knows he is saved, who can look up and see his "title clear to mansions in the skies." I believe hundreds of Christian people are being deceived by Satan now on this point, that they have not got the assurance of salvation just because they are not willing to take God at his word.

Pss. 42:11; 73:25; Isa. 41:10; 54:4; John 6:40; 10:29; 11:25; Rom. 8:38; 9:33; 1 Cor. 6:15; 2 Cor. 13:5; 2 Tim. 4:17; Heb. 10:22; 1 Peter 4:19; 1 John 2:5; 4:13,18

I asked a woman in the inquiry room if she was a Christian, and she said, "You will have to ask my minister." I might have asked him but he was hundreds of miles away. There are a good many people in just that condition. They know just what their minister knows and nothing more.

Assurance, misunderstanding of; Provision of God; Security, basis of

Pss. 3:8; 9:10; 27:4; 46:11; 73:25; Isa. 12:2; John 5:24; 10:27; 17:12; Rom. 5:5; Phil. 1:20; 2 Tim. 4:18; Heb. 6:19; 1 John 5:13

A poor old widow, living in the Scottish Highlands, was called upon one day by a gentleman who had heard that she was in need. The old lady complained of her condition and remarked that her son was in Australia and doing well. "But does he not help you?" inquired the visitor. "No, he does nothing," was the reply. "He writes me regularly once a month, but only sends me a little picture with his letter." The gentleman asked to see one of the pictures that she had received, and found each one of them to be a draft for ten pounds. She was regularly receiving more than enough money to meet her needs and having never seen a pound note she did not realize what she had.

That is the condition of many of God's children. He has given us many "exceeding great and precious promises," which we either are ignorant of or fail to appropriate. Many of them seem to be pretty pictures of an ideal peace and rest, but are not appropriated as practical helps in daily life. And not one of these promises is more neglected than the assurance of salvation. An open Bible places them within reach of all, and we may appropriate the blessing which such a knowledge brings.

Assurance, scope of; Security, basis of

2 Cor. 5:1; Col. 1:12–13

Suppose a man is going to Cincinnati, and he gets on the train but he feels uneasy lest the train will take him to St. Louis instead of his destination. He will not rest till he knows he is on the right road, and the idea that we are on the road to death traveling as fast as time can take us, and do not know our destination, is contrary to Scripture. If we want peace we must know where we are going, and we can know. It is the Word of God. Look what Paul says, "We know we have an incorruptible dwelling." Then in Paul's epistle to the Colossians 1:12, "Giving thanks unto the Father which hath made us meet"—hath made us, not going to—"to be partakers of the inheritance of the saints in light. Who hath delivered us"—not going to deliver us, but he hath delivered us. This is an assurance—"from the power of darkness, and hath translated us into the kingdom of his dear Son."

Assurance, scope of; Shepherd, Christ as

Ps. 23:1; John 10:28–30

John 10:28–30 are precious verses to those who are afraid of falling, who fear that they will not hold out. It is God's work to hold. It is the Shepherd's business to keep the sheep. Whoever heard of the sheep going to bring back the shepherd? People have an idea that they have to keep themselves and Christ too. It is a false idea. It is the work of the Shepherd to look after them, and to take care of those who trust him. He has promised to do it. A sea captain, when dying said, "Glory to God, the anchor holds." He trusted in Christ. His anchor had taken hold of the solid Rock.

Assurance, source of; Security, basis of

Mark 6:7; Luke 10:17; Rev. 20:15

That Mr. Sankey and myself go about and preach the gospel is nothing new. You will find others over these past eighteen hundred years, going off two by two, like Brothers Bliss and Whittle, and Brothers Needham and Stebbins, to different towns and villages. In the time of Christ they had gone out, and there had been great revivals in all the cities, towns, and villages they had entered. Everywhere they had met with the greatest success. Even the very devils were subject to them. Disease had fled before them. When they met a lame man, they said to him, "You don't need to be lame any longer," and he walked. When they met a blind man they but told him to open his eyes, and behold, he could see.

And they came to Christ and rejoiced over their great success, and he just said to them, "I will give you something to rejoice over. Rejoice that your names are written in heaven." Now there are a great many people who do not believe in such an assurance as this, "Rejoice, because your names are written in heaven." How are you going to rejoice if your names are not written there?

While speaking about this some time ago, a man told me we were preaching a very ridiculous doctrine when we preached this doctrine of assurance. I ask you in all candor what are you going to do with this assurance if we don't preach it? It is stated that our names are written there; blotted out of the Book of Death and transferred to the Book of Life.

Assurance, source of; Security, basis of; Faith, fruit of

Mark 5:27; Luke 23:42; Acts 7:56

Bishop Ryle has strikingly said, "Faith is the root, and assurance the flower."

Doubtless you can never have the flower without the root; but it is no less certain you may have the root and not the flower.

Assurance, source of; Security, source of

Pss. 42:11; 73:25; Isa. 41:10; 54:4; John 6:40; 10:29; 11:25; Rom. 8:38; 9:33; 1 Cor. 6:15; 2 Cor. 13:5; 2 Tim. 4:17; Heb. 10:22; 1 Peter 4:19; 1 John 2:5; 4:13,18

Now, a great many people want some token outside of God's Word to give them assurance. That habit always brings doubt. If I made a promise to meet a man at a certain hour and place tomorrow, and he were to ask me for my watch as a token of my sincerity, it would be a slur on my truthfulness. We must not question what God has said. He has made statement after statement, and multiplied figure upon figure.

Atheism, cure for; Conversion, work of God; Salvation, divine activity

Ps. 53:1; Mark 9:24; 16:16; Luke 14:18; 24:39; John 1:12; 3:36; 14:17; 20:27; Rom. 4:20; 10:13; 1 Cor. 1:18; Heb. 4:11; 11:6, 31; James 1:6; 1 Peter 2:7; 1 John 5:10, 12

So we say to you, "Come and see!" I thought, when I was converted, that my Christian friends had been very unfaithful to me, because they had not told me about Christ. I thought I would have all my unbelieving friends converted inside of twenty-four hours. I was quite disappointed when they did not at once see Christ to be the Lily of the Valley, and the Rose of Sharon, and the Bright and Morning Star. I wondered why it was. No doubt many of those who hear me now have had that experience; you thought when you saw Christ in all his beauty that you could soon make your friends see him in the same light. But we need to learn that God alone can do it.

If there is a skeptic now hearing me, I want to say that one personal interview with the Son of God will scatter all your infidelity and atheism. One night, in the inquiry room, I met the wife of an atheist, who had been brought to God at one of our meetings. She had also been an atheist and was converted at the same time. She had brought two of her daughters to the meeting, desiring that they too should know Christ. I said to the mother, "How is it with your skepticism now?" "Oh," said she, "it is all gone." When Christ gets into the heart, atheism must go out; if a man will only come and take one trustful, loving look at the Savior, there will be no desire to leave him again.

Atheism, failure of

Ps. 53:1; Mark 9:24; 16:16; Luke 14:18; 24:39; John 1:12; 3:36; 14:17; 20:27; Rom. 4:20; 10:13; 1 Cor. 1:18; Heb. 4:11; 11:6, 31; James 1:6; 1 Peter 2:7; 1 John 5:10, 12

In the town of Hanover, in Germany, I am told that there is buried a German countess who denied the existence of God and ridiculed the idea of the resurrection. To show her contempt for Christianity she ordered that on her death her grave should be built of solid masonry and covered by large stones bound together by iron clamps. On this tomb was engraved her defiant challenge that through eternity this tomb should never be disturbed.

One day a seed from some tree, either blown by the wind or carried by a bird, became lodged in a small crevice of the tomb, where soon it sprouted and began to grow. And then, as if God's creation mocked the haughty infidel, the delicate roots of that seedling spread under the massive blocks of stone and slowly raised them from their place. Although scarce four generations are passed since the tomb was sealed, that most insignificant seedling has accomplished what God was challenged to accomplish. God cannot be mocked. He will have the last word. You defy God at great risk to your soul.

Atheism, hopelessness of

Ps. 53:1; Mark 9:24; 16:16; Luke 14:18; 24:39; John 1:12; 3:36; 14:17; 20:27; Rom. 4:20; 10:13; 1 Cor. 1:18; Heb. 4:11; 11:6, 31; James 1:6; 1 Peter 2:7; 1 John 5:10, 12

It is related of an atheist who was dying that he appeared very uncomfortable, very unhappy and frightened. Another atheist who stood at his bedside said to him, "Don't be afraid. Hold on, man, hold on to the last." The dying man said: "That is what I want to do, but tell me what I am to hold on to?"

Atonement, importance of; Heaven, way to

Exod. 12:13; 32:30; Lev. 16:22; 17:11; Isa. 53:6; Matt. 8:17; 20:28; John 1:29; 1 Cor. 10:16; 15:3; 2 Cor. 5:21; Gal. 3:13; Eph. 2:13; 5:2; Titus 2:14; Heb. 9:28; 1 Peter 2:24

When God turned Adam out of Eden, he put cherubim at the gate with a sword. Adam could not go back to the tree of life. It would have been a terrible thing if he had gone back and eaten the fruit, and had never died. O, my friends, it is a good thing to be able to die, that in the evening of life we may shuffle off this old Adamic body, and be with the Son of God. There is nothing sad about death for a person that is in Christ Jesus. God put a sword there to guard the tree of life. The Son of Man went into the garden and plucked up the tree, and transferred it into Paradise. The gates of Paradise are ajar, and all we have to do is to walk right in by faith in Christ's shed blood, then pluck the fruit and eat. Men complain because Adam was driven out of the Garden of Eden. I would rather be up there, where Satan cannot go, than to be in the old Eden.

Thanks be to God, Satan cannot go up there! The tree is planted by the throne of God, and there is the crystal stream by the river, and the tree is planted beside it. If God put Adam out of this earthly Eden on account of one sin, do you think he will let us into the Paradise above with our tens of thousands of sins upon us? If he punished one sin in that way, and would not allow him to live in the old garden for one sin, will he permit us to go to heaven, with all our many sins upon us?

There is no sense in the sacred history of the atonement unless our sins have been transferred to another and put away. There is no hope unless God's sword has been raised against sin, and if God finds sin on you and me, we must die. All we have to do is to turn our sins over to him who has borne our sins in his own body on the tree. When Adam was driven out of Eden, all he lost was an earthly garden. God never promised him heaven. What do we get if we are of Christ, the second Adam? We gain a better paradise than Eden. We gain heaven.

Atonement, power of; Passover, power of

Exod. 12:13; 32:30; Lev. 16:22; 17:11; Isa. 53:6; Matt. 8:17; 20:28; John 1:29; 1 Cor. 10:16; 15:3; 2 Cor. 5:21; Gal. 3:13; Eph. 2:13; 5:2; Titus 2:14; Heb. 9:28; 1 Peter 2:24

I have heard people wishing they were as good as this minister or that mother in Israel; but I tell you, my friends, you are just as safe as any of them if you are only sheltered behind the blood. The smallest child in Goshen that night of the Passover was just as safe behind the blood as Moses and Aaron themselves. The blood was the token which God had appointed; nothing else was needed, nothing else was of any use.

Atonement, substitutionary

Exod. 12:13; 32:30; Lev. 16:22; 17:11; Isa. 53:6;
Matt. 8:17; 20:28; John 1:29; 1 Cor. 10:16; 15:3;
2 Cor. 5:21; Gal. 3:13; Eph. 2:13; 5:2; Titus 2:14;
Heb. 9:28; 1 Peter 2:24

When the California gold fever broke out a man went there leaving his wife in New England with his boy. As soon as he was successful he was to send for them. It was a long time before he succeeded, but at last he got money enough to send for them. The wife's heart leaped for joy. She took her boy to New York, got on board a Pacific steamer, and sailed away to San Francisco. They had not been long at sea before the cry of "Fire! Fire!" rang through the ship, and rapidly it gained on them. There was a powder magazine on board, and the captain knew the moment the fire reached the powder, every man, woman, and child must perish.

They got out the lifeboats, but they were too small! In a minute they were overcrowded. The last one was just pushing away, when the mother pled with them to take her and her boy. "No," they said, "we have got as many as we can hold." She entreated them so earnestly, that at last they said they would take one more. Do you think she leaped into that boat and left her boy to die? No! She seized her boy, gave him one last hug, kissed him, and dropped him over into the boat. "My boy," she said, "if you live to see your father, tell him that I died in your place."

That is a reminder of what Christ has done for us. He laid down his life for us. He died that we might live. Now will you not love him? What would you say of that young man if he should speak contemptuously of such a mother! She went down to a watery grave to save her son. Shall we speak contemptuously of such a Savior as Jesus? May God make us loyal to Christ! My friends, you will need him one day. You will need him when you come to the place of death.

Atonement, substitutionary; Passover

Exod. 12:13; 32:30; Lev. 16:22; 17:11; Isa. 53:6;
Matt. 8:17; 20:28; John 1:29; 1 Cor. 10:16; 15:3;
2 Cor. 5:21; Gal. 3:13; Eph. 2:13; 5:2; Titus 2:14;
Heb. 9:28; 1 Peter 2:24

The death of Christ is our life. People say we ought to preach about Christ's life and character. But Christ didn't say we were to preach his life as the source of salvation of sinners. At the time of the Passover God didn't say, "Tie a living lamb to the doorpost, and when I see it I will pass over you." If that had been done, death would have passed over the living lamb and taken the firstborn. It was death that kept death off; the only way to meet death is by death. The sentence has come, and I must either have someone to die for me or die myself. That is the lesson that God is trying to bring out—the great doctrine of substitution. The Passover lambs were typical of the coming of the Lamb of God. They foreshadowed the scene at Calvary; and they continued to be offered until Jesus Christ himself died for us.

Availability to God

Gen. 6:9; 12:4; 35:5; Josh. 24:24; 1 Sam. 17:32;
Job 1:6; Prov. 1:33; Isa. 6:8; Dan. 1:8; Matt. 3:1;
Heb. 1:3; James 2:21

Someone has said, there was not a man in all Saul's army but knew that God could use him to meet Goliath; but there was only one that believed that God would use him, and God used that one. And what we need is not to believe that God can use us, but that God will use us. Forty days had the giant come out and pointed his finger at and defied all Israel. Forty days was Saul trembling from head to foot—and he was head and shoulders taller than anyone else in his army—but he was not the man God had chosen to meet the giant.

It was the little stripling, the youngest son of Jesse, the smallest and the weakest of his sons; and God used him, and went with him, and God delivered the giant into his hands. And God will use the weak ones here if they will only let him. God can take up the learned and the unlearned, and there is not a person living whom God cannot use if that person is willing to be used.

Backsliders, condition of; Prodigal, losses of

Lev. 26:33; Josh. 24:27; 2 Chron. 7:14; Ps. 32:4; 125:5; Prov. 2:17; 26:11; Hosea 4:6; Luke 15:16; 1 Cor. 10:6; Gal. 1:6

Did you ever notice what the prodigal lost? He lost his food. That is what every poor backslider loses. They get no manna from heaven. They see no beauty in the Word of God. Then the prodigal lost his work. They made him take care of swine; that was all loss for a Jew. So every backslider loses his work. He cannot do anything for God; he cannot work for eternity.

The prodigal also lost his testimony. Who believed him? There he stands among the swine, and someone says to another, "Look at that poor wretch." "What?" he says, "Do you call me a poor wretch? My father is a wealthy man; he has more clothes in his wardrobe than you ever saw in your life. My father is a man of great wealth and position." Do you suppose these men would believe him? "That poor wretch, the son of a wealthy man!" "If he had such a wealthy father, surely he would go to him." So with the backsliders: the world does not believe that they are the sons of a King.

Then, the prodigal lost his home. As long as his money lasted, he was quite popular in the public house and among his acquaintants; he had professed friends, but as soon as his money was gone, where were his friends? That is the condition of every poor backslider.

Backsliders, influence of

2 Chron. 7:14; Pss. 32:10; 51:14; Prov. 30:9; Matt. 12:25; 24:12; Mark 9:50; Luke 11:26; John 6:67; 1 Cor. 10:8; 2 Cor. 12:20

I have never seen a father and mother who both were backsliders, that their children haven't gone to ruin. I have talked with a good many backsliders' children, and they asked me this, "If there is so much pleasure in religion, why did my father and mother give it up?" It is an argument I have never been able to answer except to point them to our lovely Lord.

Backsliders, restored

Lev. 26:42; Judg. 16:30; 2 Chron. 7:14; Ezra 6:16; Pss. 32:6; 51:17; John 20:28; Rom. 6:6; Heb. 3:13

I am asked how to account for people losing power who were once used by God mightily. Well, Samson lost his strength, and you know how he lost it—through the lusts of the flesh. The old man isn't dead. We are to reckon him dead. There is a good deal of difference between reckoning a man dead and knowing that he is really dead. I am to put the old man in the place of death, and keep him there, and keep my body under. If I don't keep my body under, sin is going to get me under. That is how it was with Samson. He was a giant—had mighty power; yet he lost it because he fell into sin. But there is one consolation about Samson—they didn't pull his hair out by the roots; it grew again. And there are men who have lost their power, but, thank God, they can get it back.

Peter lost his; but I tell you he got it back before he stood up there and preached to those Jews on the day of Pentecost. He could never have spoken as he did if he hadn't known what it was to be overcome by sin. Bear in mind that greater results followed Peter's preaching than that of any other man. He was a restored backslider. Bear that in mind; and when you see a man that has been used by God, and has fallen back, don't give him up. If he repents, God can use him a thousand times more than before.

Look at David. Probably we would never have had the 32nd Psalm and the 51st Psalm if it hadn't been for David's fall. What a blessing those psalms have been to the people of God all through the ages—written by a restored backslider.

Backsliders, restoring

Lev. 26:40; 2 Chron. 7:14; Pss. 32:5; 51:3; 73:28; Jonah 2:4; Mal. 3:7; Matt. 5:13; 16:24; Mark 8:34; Luke 9:23; Gal. 6:1; 1 John 2:1; Rev. 2:5

If a Christian gets in a backslidden condition, you will find that he has either failed to witness for Christ, refused to forgive somebody that has injured him, or has neglected to make restitution. You can't be a disciple without confession. You must take up your cross and follow him. The cross down here—the crown up yonder. Some are afraid that they shall fall again into sin. Well, suppose you do, you have an advocate. Read 1 John 2:1. It is an advocate's business to take care of his clients, and ours, in the court of heaven, will not neglect us. But if some of those young converts fall into sin, remember the exhortation in Gal. 6:1. Don't trample on them when they are down; that's the devil's work. Try to raise them up, to restore them in the spirit of meekness. Go to that fallen brother; talk with him, pray with him, and you may win him back.

Backsliders, return of

Lev. 26:40; 2 Chron. 7:14; Pss. 32:5; 51:3; 73:28; Jonah 2:4; Mal. 3:7; Matt. 5:13; Rev. 2:5

The devil has been telling you that God won't have anything to do with you, because you have wandered away. If that is true, there would be very few men in heaven. David backslid; Abraham and Jacob turned away from God; I do not believe there is a saint in heaven but at some time of life has backslidden from God. Perhaps not in his action, but in his heart. The prodigal's heart got into the far country before his body got there.

Backsliders, unhappiness of; Prodigals, unhappy

Lev. 26:40; 2 Chron. 7:14; Pss. 32:5; 51:3; 73:28; Isa. 57:20; Jonah 2:4; Mal. 3:7; Matt. 5:13; Luke 15:18; John 20:27; Rev. 2:5

I have traveled a good deal, but I never found a happy backslider in my life. I never knew a man who was really born of God that ever could find the world satisfy him afterward. Do you think the prodigal son was satisfied in that foreign country? Ask the prodigals today if they are truly happy. You know they are not. "There is no peace, saith my God, to the wicked."

Backsliders, unhappiness of; Sin, price of

Gen. 19:14; Lev. 26:40; 2 Chron. 7:14; Pss. 32:5; 51:3; 73:28; Jonah 2:4; Mal. 3:7; Matt. 5:13; John 20:27; Rev. 2:5

I do not exaggerate when I say that I have seen hundreds of backsliders come back, and I have asked them if they had not found it an evil and a bitter thing to leave the Lord. You cannot find a real backslider, who has known the Lord, but will admit that it is an evil and a bitter thing to turn away from God. Look at Lot. Didn't he find it an evil and a bitter thing? He was twenty years in Sodom and never made a convert. Men would have told you that he was one of the most influential and worthy men in all Sodom. But alas! alas! he ruined his family. And it is a pitiful sight to see that old backslider going through the streets of Sodom at midnight, after he has warned his children, and they have turned a deaf ear to him.

Backsliding, cure of

Lev. 26:40; 2 Chron. 7:14; Pss. 32:5; 51:3; 73:28; Jonah 2:4; Mal. 3:7; Matt. 5:13; John 20:27; Rev. 2:5

I went to a physician the other day to tell him that a niece of mine, whom he had been able to cure, as we supposed, had suffered a relapse. "Well," says the doctor, "just increase the remedy." That is just what the relapsed believer must do. Get more of Christ.

Backsliding, process of; Friendship with Christ

Deut. 4:9; 2 Chron. 7:14; Ps. 73:28; Isa. 30:15; Hosea 4:10; Mark 8:38; John 15:6,14; 1 Cor. 10:12; Heb. 3:15; 2 Peter 1:9; Rev. 2:4

A rule I have had for years is to treat the Lord Jesus Christ as a personal friend. It is not a creed, a mere empty doctrine, but it is Christ himself we have. The moment we receive Christ we should receive him as a friend. When I go away from home I bid my wife and children good-bye; I bid my friends and acquaintances good-bye; but I never heard of a poor backslider going down on his knees and saying to God, "I have been near you for ten years. Your service has become tedious and monotonous. I have come to bid you farewell. Good-bye, Lord Jesus Christ!" I never heard of one doing this. I will tell you how they go away; they just run away.

Bad habits, danger of; Excesses, fruit of

Gen. 13:12; 1 Sam. 2:34; Dan. 5:2; John 3:19; Rom. 1:18; 6:13; 1 Cor. 10:6; 2 Thess. 2:10; 1 Tim. 4:1

A leading surgeon performed a critical operation before his class one day. The operation was successful, as far as his part was concerned. But he turned to the class and said, "Six years ago a wise way of living might have prevented this disease. Two years ago a safe and simple operation might have cured it. We have done our best today as the case now stands, but Nature will have her word to say. She does not always repeal her capital sentences." Next day the patient died, reaping the fruit of his excesses.

Bible, denial of; Truth, avoidance of

Isa. 8:20; Matt. 13:22; 22:29; Luke 16:29; 2 Cor. 3:15; Acts 13:27; Rom. 11:8; 2 Cor. 4:4

If I have a right to cut out a certain portion of the Bible, I don't know why one of my friends has not a right to cut out another, and another friend to cut out another part, and so on. You would have a strange kind of Bible if everybody cut out what he wanted to! Every adulterer would cut out everything about adultery; every liar would cut out everything about lying; every drunkard would be cutting out what he didn't like.

Once a gentleman took his Bible around to his minister, and said, "That is your Bible." "Why do you call it my Bible?" said the minister. "Well," replied the gentleman, "I have been sitting under your preaching for five years, and when you said that a thing in the Bible was not authentic, I cut it out." He had about a third of the Bible cut out; all of Job, all of Ecclesiastes and Revelation, and a good deal besides. The minister wanted him to leave the Bible with him. He didn't want the rest of his congregation to see it. But the man said: "Oh, no! I have the covers left, and I will hold on to them." And off he went holding on to the covers.

Bible, depth of

Job 23:12; Ps. 119:100; Matt. 13:23; Luke 16:29; John 5:39; Rom. 11:33; 1 Thess. 2:13; 2 Peter 1:19

I thank God there is a height in the Bible I don't know anything about, a depth I have never been able to fathom, and it makes the Book all the more fascinating.

If I could take that Book up and read it as I can any other book and understand it at one reading, I should have lost faith in it years ago. It is one of the strongest proofs that it must have come from God, that the wisest men who have dug for fifty years have laid down their pens and said, "There is a depth we know nothing of." "No Scripture," said Spurgeon, "is exhausted by a single explanation. The flowers of God's garden bloom, not only double, but sevenfold: they are continually pouring forth fresh fragrance."

Bible, Jesus' endorsement of

Matt. 26:56; Luke 17:29, 32; 18:31; 24:27, 44; John 3:14; 5:39, 46; 19:24

Some people say to me, "Moody, you don't believe in the flood do you? All the scientific men tell us it is absurd." Let them keep on talking. Jesus tells us of the flood, and I would rather take the word of Jesus than that of any other one. I haven't got much respect for those men who dig down for stones with shovels, with the intent to take away the word of God. Men don't believe in the story of Sodom and Gomorrah, but we have it sealed in the New Testament. "As it was in the days of Sodom and Gomorrah." They don't believe in Lot's wife, but Jesus says, "Remember Lot's wife."

So there are things that men reject but the Son of God endorses. They don't believe in the swallowing of Jonah. They say it is impossible that a whale could swallow Jonah because its throat is too small. They forget that the whale was prepared for Jonah; as the black woman said, "Why, God could prepare a man to swallow a whale, let alone a whale to swallow a man."

Bible, knowledge of; Sword of the Spirit

Deut. 11:18; Ps. 119:97; Jer. 36:2; Ezek. 1:3; Acts 1:16; Rom. 15:4

We are told that the Bible is the sword of the Spirit; and what is an army good for

that does not know how to use its weapons? Suppose there was a battle going on, and I were a general and had a hundred thousand men, great, able-bodied soldiers, full of life, but not one of them could handle a sword, and not one of them knew how to use a rifle, what would that army be good for? Why, one thousand well-drilled men, with good weapons, would rout the whole of them. The reason the church can't overcome the enemy is because she doesn't know how to use the sword of the Spirit.

Bible, misjudgment of; Scripture, critics of

Acts 3:17; 13:27; Rom. 11:8; 1 Cor. 2:8; 2 Cor. 4:4; 1 Tim. 1:13

Experience has taught me that most of the men that talk against the Bible are men that never read it. There is no book in the world misjudged like the Bible. A modern book comes out, and people say, "Have you read such a book?" And you say, "Yes, I have just read it." "Well, what is your opinion about it?" "Well, I wouldn't like to give my opinion without reading it more carefully." And yet men are very free to give their opinion about God's Book without reading it. A friend of mine was in Montreal some time ago, and he talked with a man upon the subject of Christ and Christianity. "Well," he said, "the fact is we have got to have a new Bible. That old Book," he said, "was good enough for the Dark Ages, but we have outgrown it. It is of no use to this enlightened age."

My friend said, "Before we give up the old Book let's see how much we know about it. Can you tell me which is the first book in the Bible, Genesis or Revelation?" Well, he said he couldn't just tell that. He didn't quite know, but he knew they had got to have another Bible. That man is typical of all the men that I have ever heard howling and writing against the

Bible. I never met one in my life—yes, I will make one exception, I did meet one man that claimed he had read it through; but I doubted him, because when I pressed him to quote something out of it all he could remember was, "Jesus wept."

Bible, power of

Pss. 19:8; 119:105, 130; Jer. 5:14; 15:16; 23:29; Hosea 6:5; Zech. 1:6; Luke 1:77; Acts 26:18; 2 Peter 1:19

A good many years ago there was a convention held in France, and those who held it wanted to get the country to deny God, to burn the Bible, wanted to say that men passed away like a dog and a dumb animal. What was the result! Not long since, that country was filled with blood. Did you ever think what would take place if we could vote the Bible and the ministers of the gospel and God out from among the people? My friends, the country would be deluged with blood. Your life and mine would not be safe in this city tonight. We could not walk through these streets with safety. We don't know how much we owe God and the influence of his gospel among even ungodly men.

Pss. 19:8; 119:105, 130; Jer. 5:14; 15:16; 23:29; Hosea 6:5; Zech. 1:6; Luke 1:77; Acts 26:18; 2 Peter 1:19

I haven't found the first man who ever read the Bible from front to back carefully who remained an infidel. My friends, the Bible of our mothers and fathers is true.

Pss. 19:8; 119:105, 130; Jer. 5:14; 15:16; 23:29; Hosea 6:5; Zech. 1:6; Luke 1:77; Acts 26:18; 2 Peter 1:19

If you will show me a Bible Christian living on the Word of God, I will show you a joyful man. He is mounting up all the time. He has got new truths that lift him up over every obstacle, and he mounts over difficulties higher and higher, like a man I once heard of who had a bag of gas fastened on either side, and if he just touched the ground with his foot, over a wall or a hedge he would go; and so these truths make us so light that we bound over every obstacle.

Jer. 23:29; Acts 4:31; Heb. 4:12; James 1:18

When I pray I am talking to God; when I read the Bible God talks to me. We need both. They help us to bring our thoughts into captivity. You will never get much of an uplift if you talk with yourself. I heard of a man who thought so much of himself that he shook hands with himself every morning. What is the best sign that I have good healthy lungs? It is that I am not conscious of them. But if I have a diseased lung, I think of that lung all the time. The healthiest Christian is the man or woman who thinks of God, not of himself.

Bible, power of; Holy Spirit's use of Scripture

Pss. 19:8; 119:105, 130; Jer. 5:14; 15:16; 23:29; Hosea 6:5; Zech. 1:6; Luke 1:77; Acts 26:18; 2 Peter 1:19

There was a Christian man witnessing to a skeptic. He kept quoting the Word, and the skeptic said, "I don't believe, sir, in that Book." But the Christian went right on and he gave him more of the Word; and the man again remarked, "I don't believe the Word." But the Christian kept giving him more, and at last the man was reached. And the Christian said, "When I have proved a good sword which does the work, I just keep right on using it." That is what we need. Skeptics and infidels may say they don't believe in the Bible. It is not our work to make them believe in it; that is the work of the Spirit. Our work is to give them the Word of God, not to preach our theories and our ideas about it, but just to deliver the message as God gives it to us.

Ps. 119:18; Matt. 16:17; Acts 26:18; Eph. 1:17–18

We have a great many prayer meetings, but there is something just as important as prayer, and that is that we read our Bibles, that we have Bible study and Bible lectures and Bible classes, so that we may get hold of the Word of God. When I pray, I talk to God, but when I read the Bible, God is talking to me; and it is really more important that God should speak to me than that I should speak to him. I believe we should know better how to pray if we knew our Bibles better.

Bible, relevancy of; Skepticism, weakness of

Jer. 23:29; John 15:3; 20:31; Acts 17:21; 2 Tim. 2:16; 1 Peter 2:2

A great many people seem to think that the Bible is out of date, that it is an old book, that it has passed its day. They say it was very good for the dark ages, and that there is some very good history in it, but it was not intended for the present time; we are living in a very enlightened age and men can get on very well without it; we have outgrown it. Now, you might just as well say that the sun, which has shone so long, is now so old that it is out of date, and that whenever a man builds a house he need not put any windows in it, because we have a newer light and a better light; we have gaslight and electric light.

These are something new; and I would advise people, if they think the Bible is too old and worn out, when they build houses, not to put windows in them, but just to light them with electric light; that is something new and that is what they are anxious for.

Bible study, depth of; Growth, spiritual

Job 23:12; Pss. 1:2; 119:97; Prov 1:5; Isa. 34:16; Matt. 13:23; John 1:45; 5:39; Acts 11:1; 17:11; 1 Thess. 1:6; 2:13; 2 Tim. 3:5; James 1:21; 2 Peter 1:9

Suppose I should send my little boy, five years old, to school tomorrow morning, and when he came home in the afternoon, say to him, "Willie, can you read? Can you write? Can you spell? Do you understand all about algebra, geometry, Hebrew, Latin and Greek?" "Why, papa," the little fellow would say, "how strangely you talk. I have been all day trying to learn the A, B, C's!" Suppose I should reply, "If you have not finished your education, you need not go any more."

What would you say? Why, you would say I had gone mad! There would be just as much reason in that as in the way people talk about the Bible. The men who have studied the Bible for fifty years have never got down to the depths of it yet. There are truths there that the church of God has been searching out for the last nineteen hundred years, but no man has yet fathomed the depths of the ever-living stream.

Bible study, diligence in

Job 23:12; Pss. 1:2; 119:97; Prov 1:5; Isa. 34:16; Matt. 13:23; John 1:45; 5:39; Acts 11:1; 17:11; 1 Thess. 1:6; 2:13; 2 Tim. 3:5; James 1:21; 2 Peter 1:9

The best truths are got by digging deep for them.

Bible study, importance

Job 23:12; Pss. 1:2; 119:97; Prov 1:5; Isa. 34:16; Matt. 13:23; John 1:45; 5:39; Acts 11:1; 17:11; 1 Thess. 1:6; 2:13; 2 Tim. 3:5; James 1:21; 2 Peter 1:9

You know it is always regarded a great event in the family when a child can feed itself. It is propped up at the table, and at first perhaps it uses the spoon upside down: but by and by it uses it all right, and mother, or perhaps sister, claps her hands and says, "Come and see, baby's feeding himself!" Well, what we need as Christians is to be able to feed ourselves. How many there are who sit helpless and listless, with open mouths, hungry for spiritual things and the minister has to try to feed them, while the Bible is a feast pre-pared, into which they never venture.

Bible study, importance of; Peace, a source of

Job 23:12; Pss. 1:2; 119:97, 165; Prov 1:5; Isa. 34:16; Matt. 13:23; John 1:45; 5:39; Acts 11:1; 17:11; 1 Thess. 1:6; 2:13; 2 Tim. 3:5; James 1:21; 2 Peter 1:9

The study of God's Word will secure peace. Take those Christians who are rooted and grounded in the Word of God, and you will find they have great peace; but it is those who don't study their Bible, who are easily offended when some little trouble comes, or some little persecution. Just a little breath of opposition, and their peace is all gone.

Bible study, interest in

Job 23:12; Pss. 1:2; 119:97, 165; Prov. 1:5; Isa. 34:16; Matt. 13:23; John 1:45; 5:39; Acts 11:1; 17:11; 1 Thess. 1:6; 2:13; 2 Tim. 3:5; James 1:21; 2 Peter 1:9

When I was a boy I was taught to believe that all the land west of the Mississippi River was a vast and barren desert of sand. But, later, when they had taken a hundred millions of dollars in silver out of that desert, people began to rub their eyes and wake up to the fact that the land was worth something and that territory was found to be, at that time, the richest in this country. There are some portions of the Bible that you have never explored, yet there is some of the purest gold of heaven there. If you study the Bible you will find it the most interesting book in all the world.

Bible study, method of

Job 23:12; Pss. 1:2; 119:97, 165; Prov. 1:5; Isa. 34:16; Matt. 13:23; John 1:45; 5:39; Acts 11:1; 17:11; 1 Thess. 1:6; 2:13; 2 Tim. 3:5; James 1:21; 2 Peter 1:9

I have found it a good plan to take up one book at a time. It is a good deal better to study one book at a time than to run through the Bible. If we study one book and get its key, it will, perhaps, open up others. Take up the book of Genesis, and you will find eight beginnings; or, in other words, you pick up the key of several books. The gospel was written that man might believe on Jesus Christ, and every chapter speaks of him.

Now, take the book of Genesis; it says it is the book of beginnings. That is the key; then the book of Exodus—it is the book of redemption; that is the key word of the whole. Take up the book of Leviticus, and we find that it is the book of sacrifices. And so on through all the different books; you will find each one with a key. Another thing: We must study it in an unbiased manner. A great many people believe certain things. They believe in certain creeds and doctrines, and they run through the book to get Scripture in accordance with them. If a man is a Calvinistic man he wants to find something in accordance with his doctrine.

But if we go to seek truth the Spirit of God will come. Don't seek it in the light of Presbyterianism, in the light of Methodism, or in the light of Episcopalianism, but study it in the light of Calvary.

Bible study, value of

Job 23:12; Ps. 1:2; Prov. 30:24; Isa. 34:16; Matt. 13:23; John 1:45; 5:39; Acts 11:1; 17:11; 1 Thess. 1:6; 2:13; 2 Tim. 3:5; James 1:21; 2 Peter 1:9

I want to tell you how I was blessed a few years ago, upon hearing a discourse on Proverbs 30:24–28. The speaker said the children of God were like four things. The first thing was, "The ants are a people not strong," and he went on to compare the children of God to ants. They go on steadily preparing for the future.

The next thing he compared them to was the conies. "The conies are but a feeble folk." It is a very weak little thing.

"Well," said I, "I wouldn't like to be as a coney." But he went on to say that it built upon a rock. The children of God were very weak, but they laid their foundation upon a rock. "Well," said I, "I will be like a coney and build my hopes upon a rock." Like the Irishman who said he trembled himself, but the rock upon which his house was built never did.

The next thing the speaker compared them to was a locust. I didn't think much of locusts; and I thought I wouldn't care about being like one. But he went on to read, "They have no king, yet they go forth all of them by bands." There were the Congregationalist, the Presbyterian, the Methodist bands going forth without a king, but by and by our King will come back again, and these bands will fly to him. "Well, I will be like a locust; my King is away," I thought.

The next comparison was a spider. I didn't like this at all, but he said if we went into a gilded palace filled with luxury, we might see a spider holding on to something, oblivious to all the luxury below. It was laying hold of the things above. "Well," said I, "I would like to be a spider." I heard this a good many years ago, and I just put the speaker's name to it, and it makes a sermon. But take your Bibles and mark them. Don't think of wearing them out. It is a rare thing to find a man wearing his Bible out. Bibles are cheap, too. You are living in a land where they are plenty. Study them and mark them, and don't be afraid of using them.

Job 23:12; Pss. 1:2; 119:97, 165; Prov. 1:5; Isa. 34:16; Matt. 13:23; John 1:45; 5:39; Acts 11:1; 17:11; 1 Thess. 1:6; 2:13; 2 Tim. 3:5; James 1:21; 2 Peter 1:9

When we know our Bible, then it is that God can use us. When we find a person meditating on the words of God, my friends, that soul is full of boldness and is successful. When we are filled with the Word of God, you cannot keep us still. If you have the Word in you, you must speak or die.

Job 23:12; Pss. 1:2; 119:97, 165; Prov. 1:5; Isa. 34:16; Matt. 13:23; John 1:45; 5:39; Acts 11:1; 17:11; 1 Thess. 1:6; 2:13; 2 Tim. 3:5; James 1:21; 2 Peter 1:9

One thing I have noticed in studying the Word of God, and that is, when a man is filled with the Spirit he deals largely with the Word of God, whereas the man who is filled with his own ideas refers rarely to the Word of God. He gets along without it, and you seldom see it mentioned in his discourses.

Bible, tried and proven; Promises of God, surety of

Job 23:12; Pss. 1:2; 119:97, 165; Prov. 1:5; Isa. 34:16; Matt. 13:23; John 1:45; 5:39; Acts 11:1; 17:11; 1 Thess. 1:6; 2:13; 2 Tim. 3:5; James 1:21; 2 Peter 1:9

I knew an old lady that marked in the margin of her Bible, opposite the promises, T. P.; T. for "tried," and P. for "proven." What we want is to try the Bible and see if it is not true.

Blood, covering for sin; Passover blood

Exod. 12:13; 32:30; Lev. 16:22; 17:11; Isa. 53:6; Matt. 8:17; 20:28; John 1:29; 1 Cor. 10:16; 15:3; 2 Cor. 5:21; Eph. 2:13; 5:2; Gal. 3:13; Titus 2:14; Heb. 9:28; 1 Peter 1:2,19; 2:24; 3:18; 4:1; 1 John 1:7; 3:5; Rev. 1:5

There was a little child (so runs the legend), the firstborn in the house of an Israelite; and you know God said that, in every house where the blood was not upon the doorpost, the firstborn should be smitten by death. The little girl was sick, but she was afraid that the blood was not upon the doorpost so she asked her father if he was sure he had put the blood upon the doorpost; and the father said, "Yes, I am quite sure; I ordered it to be done." But the little girl said the second time, "Father, are you quite sure that the blood is there?" "Yes, my child," answered the father; "be quiet, and sleep."

But the child could not sleep. She was very sick and very restless; and as night came on, and it grew darker and darker, and nearer and nearer to the time when the angel should pass over Goshen, she got still more nervous and restless and uneasy; and at last she said, "Father, take me in your arms, and let me see the blood upon the doorpost." And the father, to satisfy the child, took her to the door to show her the blood; and lo and behold! It was not there: the man to whom he had given instructions had forgotten to do it. And then the father, in the sight of the child, had the blood sprinkled upon the doorpost, and the child lay down and went to sleep.

Blood of Christ, atonement by

Isa. 53:5; Heb. 9:22; 1 Peter 1:19–20; 2:24

When I was preaching in one of your cities, a gentleman came to me and said, "If you are right, I am wrong; and if I am right, you are wrong." I saw he was a minister, and I said, "Well, I never heard you preach; if you have heard me, you can tell where we differ." "Well, you preach that it is the death of Christ that matters; I preach his life. I tell people his death has nothing to do with it; you tell them his life has nothing to do with their salvation, and that his death only will save them. I do not believe a word of it."

"Well," I said, "what do you do with this passage, 'Who his own self bare our sins in his own body on the tree'?" "Well, I never preached on that text." "What do you do with this, then, 'Ye are not redeemed with corruptible things as silver and gold, but with the precious blood of Christ'?" "I never preached on that text either," was the reply. "Well, what do you do with this, 'Without shedding of blood there is no remission of sins'?" "I never spoke on that," he said. "What do you do with this,

'He was wounded for our transgressions, he was bruised for our iniquities, and the chastisement of our peace was upon him'?" "I never preached on that either."

"What do you preach, then?" I asked. He hesitated for a little, and then said, "I preach moral essays." "You leave out the atonement?" "Yes." "Well," I said, "it would all be a sham to me if I did that; I could not understand it. I would go home tomorrow. I could not preach moral essays on Christ without his death!" The young minister said, "Well, it does seem a sham sometimes." He was honest enough to confess that. Why, the whole thing is a myth without the atonement. The crucifixion of Christ is the foundation of the whole matter. If a person is unsound on the blood, he is unsound in everything.

Exod. 12:13; 32:30; Lev. 16:22; 17:11; Isa. 53:6; Matt. 8:17; 20:28; John 1:29; 1 Cor. 10:16; 15:3; 2 Cor. 5:21; Gal. 3:13; Eph. 2:13; 5:2; Titus 2:14; Heb. 9:28; 1 Peter 2:24

If you cut the crimson thread that binds the Bible, it falls to pieces.

Blood of Christ, atonement by; Sin, remission of

1 Cor. 15:3–4; Heb. 9:22

You ask me what my hope is. It is that Christ died for my sins, in my stead, in my place, and therefore I can enter into life eternal. You ask Paul what his hope was. "Christ died for our sins according to the Scripture." This is the hope in which died all the glorious martyrs of old, in which all who have entered heaven's gate have found their only comfort. Take that doctrine of substitution out of the Bible, and my hope is lost. With the law, without Christ, we are all undone. The law we have broken, and it can only hang over our head the sharp sword of justice. Even if we could keep it from this moment, there remains the unforgiven past. "Without shedding of blood there is no remission."

Blood of Christ, importance of

Exod. 12:13; 32:30; Lev. 16:22; 17:11; Isa. 53:6; Matt. 8:17; 20:28; John 1:29; 1 Cor. 10:16; 15:3; 2 Cor. 5:21; Gal. 3:13; Eph. 2:13; 5:2; Titus 2:14; Heb. 9:28; 1 Peter 1:2,19; 1 Peter 2:24; 4:1; 3:18; 1 John 1:7; 3:5; Rev. 1:5

It is said that old Dr. Alexander, of Princeton College, when a young student used to start out to preach, always gave him a piece of advice. The old man would stand with his gray locks and his venerable face and say, "Young man, make much of the blood of Jesus Christ in your ministry." Now, I have traveled considerably during the past few years, and never met a minister who made much of the blood and much of the atonement but God had blessed his ministry, and souls were born into the light by it. But a minister who leaves out the blood sees his church fall to pieces like a rope of sand, and his preaching barren of good result. And so if you find a man preaching who has covered up this doctrine of blood atonement, don't sit under his ministry. I don't care what denomination he belongs to, get out of it. Fly from it as those who flew from Sodom.

1 John 1:7

I heard of an old minister who had preached the gospel faithfully for fifty years. Many will say, "I wish I was as safe to go to heaven as he." When he was reaching his end he asked that his Bible should be brought to him. His eyes were growing dim in death, and he said to one of those about him, "I wish you would turn to 1 John 1:7," and when it was found, the old man put his dying finger on the passage where it says: "and the blood of Jesus Christ his Son, cleanseth from all sin." He said, "I die in the hope of that." It was the blood of Christ that cleansed him and not his faithful service.

Lev. 14:25; 1 Peter 1:19; Rev. 7:14; 12:11

What are you going to do with the blood of Christ? You must do one of two things—take it or reject it. Trample it under foot or cleanse your sins by it. I heard a lady who told a servant to cook a lamb. She told him how to cook the lamb, but she didn't tell him what to do with the blood. So he went to her and asked, "What are you going to do with the blood of the lamb?" She had been under conviction of the Holy Spirit for some time, and such a question went like an arrow to her soul. She went to her room and felt uneasy. The question kept continually coming to her, "What are you going to do with the blood of the lamb?" Before morning she was on her knees asking for the mercy of the blood of the Lamb.

Blood of Christ, importance of; Scarlet thread

Exod. 12:13; 32:30; Lev. 16:22; 17:11; Isa. 53:6; Matt. 8:17; 20:28; John 1:29; 1 Cor. 10:16; 15:3; 2 Cor. 5:21; Gal. 3:13; Eph. 2:13; 5:2; Titus 2:14; Heb. 9:28; 1 Peter 1:2,19; 1 Peter 2:24; 4:1; 3:18; 1 John 1:7; 3:5; Rev. 1:5

In the British Navy there is said to be a scarlet thread running through every line of cordage, and though a rope be cut into inch pieces it can be recognized as belonging to the government. So there is a scarlet thread running all through the Bible—the whole book points to the blood of Christ.

Blood of Christ, power of

Exod. 12:13; 32:30; Lev. 16:22; 17:11; Isa. 53:6; Matt. 8:17; 20:28; John 1:29; 1 Cor. 10:16; 15:3; 2 Cor. 5:21; Gal. 3:13; Eph. 2:13; 5:2; Titus 2:14; Heb. 9:28; 1 Peter 1:2,19; 3:18; 1 Peter 2:24; 4:1; 1 John 1:7; 3:5; Rev. 1:5

A man who has not realized what the blood has done for him has not the token of salvation. It is told of Julian, the apostate, that while he was fighting he received an arrow in his side. He pulled it out, and, taking a handful of blood threw it into the air and cried, "Galilean, Galilean, thou hast conquered."

Blood of Christ, power of; Impossible task for God, an

Exod. 12:13; 32:30; Lev. 16:22; 17:11; Isa. 53:6; Matt. 8:17; 20:28; John 1:29; 1 Cor. 10:16; 15:3; 2 Cor. 5:21; Gal. 3:13; Eph. 2:13; 5:2; Titus 2:14; Heb. 9:28; 1 Peter 1:2,19; 3:18; 1 Peter 2:24; 4:1; 1 John 1:7; 3:5; Rev. 1:5

In Ireland, some time ago, a teacher asked a little boy if there was anything that God could not do. The little fellow said, "Yes, he can't see my sins through the blood of Christ."

Blood of Christ, power of; Love, crowning act; Grace, crowning act

Exod. 12:13; 32:30; Lev. 16:22; 17:11; Isa. 53:6; Matt. 8:17; 20:28; John 1:29; 1 Cor. 10:16; 15:3; 2 Cor. 5:21; Gal. 3:13; Eph. 2:13; 5:2; Titus 2:14; Heb. 9:28; 1 Peter 1:2,19; 3:18; 1 Peter 2:24; 4:1; 1 John 1:7; 3:5; Rev. 1:5

Look at that Roman soldier as he pushed his spear into the very heart of the God-man. What a hellish deed! But what was the next thing that took place? Blood covered the spear! Oh! thank God, the blood covers sin. There was the blood covering that spear—the very point of it. The very crowning act of sin brought out the crowning act of love; the crowning act of wickedness was the crowning act of grace.

Blood of Christ, power of; Sin, removal of

1 John 1:7

Christ doesn't take some of our sins away; he takes them all away. You may pile up your sins till they rise like a dark mountain, and then multiply them by ten thousand for those you cannot think of; and after you have tried to enumerate all the sins you have ever committed, just let me bring one verse in, and that mountain will melt away: "The blood of Jesus Christ, his Son, cleanseth us from ALL sin."

Blood of Christ, source of salvation; Ark, Noah's; Security of believer

Gen. 6:14; Exod. 12:13; 32:30; Lev. 16:22; 17:11; Isa. 53:6; Matt. 8:17; 20:28; John 1:29; 1 Cor. 10:16; 15:3; 2 Cor. 5:21; Gal. 3:13; Eph. 2:13; 5:2; Titus 2:14; Heb. 9:28; 1 Peter 1:2,19; 3:18; 1 Peter 2:24; 4:1; 1 John 1:7; 3:5; Rev. 1:5

Someone has said that a little fly in Noah's ark was just as safe as an elephant. It was not the elephant's size and strength that made him safe. It was the ark that saved both elephant and fly. It is not your righteousness, your good works, that will save you. Rich or poor, learned or unlearned, you can be saved only by the blood of Christ.

Boasting excluded

John 10:1; Rom. 3:27; 4:2; 11:6; 1 Cor. 1:29; Eph. 2:8–9; 2 Tim. 1:9; Titus 3:5

Remember what Christ says: "He that climbeth up some other way, the same is a thief and a robber." Certainly the attempt to work our way up to heaven is "climbing up some other way," is it not? If ever a man did succeed in working his way into heaven we should never hear the last of it! I have got so terribly sick of these so called "self-made men." There are some men whom you cannot approach without hearing them blow their trumpet, saying, "I am a self-made man. I came here a poor man ten years ago; and now I am rich." It is all I-I-I! They go on boasting, and telling what wonderful beings they are! There is one thing that is excluded from the kingdom of heaven; and that is boasting. If you and I ever get there it will be by the sovereign grace of God. There will be no credit due to ourselves.

Body, temple of Holy Spirit

1 Cor. 3:16; 6:19

Some men were burying an aged saint. He was very poor, like many of God's people, poor in this world, but very rich in the other world, and they were just hastening him off to the grave, wanting to get rid of him, when an old minister, who was officiating the grave, said, "Tread softly, for you are carrying a temple of the Holy Spirit." Whenever you see a believer, you see a temple of the Holy Spirit.

1 Cor. 3:16; 6:19

I never had the advantage of an education, but when God called me into his service, I hungered and thirsted to be used by him, and I wanted to get hold of the Bible. I left this country and went to England, that I might sit at the feet of Charles Spurgeon and George Mueller. Spurgeon said to me something I have never forgotten. He said, "Young man, take good care of your body, because it is a temple for the Holy Spirit to dwell in. God will take care of your soul as you walk with him; but you can take care of the temple it dwells in." If these bodies are the temple of the Holy Spirit, ought we to defile them with liquor and tobacco?

Broken hearts, cure of

Isa. 40:31; Matt. 5:11; 10:19; 1 Cor. 10:13; 2 Cor. 1:4; 3:5; 11:30; 12:5; Eph. 3:16; Phil. 4:13; Col. 1:11; 1 Tim. 1:14; Heb. 4:16; 1 Peter 4:13–14

You will find, my friends, that no group of people are exempt from broken hearts. The rich and the poor suffer alike. There was a time when I used to visit the poor, that I thought all the broken hearts were to be found among them, but within the last few years I have found there are as many broken hearts among the learned as the unlearned, the cultured as the uncultured, the rich as the poor. If you could but go up one of our avenues and down another, and reach the hearts of the people, and get them to turn out their whole story, you would be astonished at the wonderful history of every family.

I remember a few years ago I had been out of the city of Chicago for some weeks. When I returned I started out to make some calls. The first place I went to I found a mother, her eyes red with weeping. I tried to find out what was troubling her, and she reluctantly opened her heart and told me all. She said, "Last night my only boy came home about midnight drunk. I didn't know that he was addicted to drunkenness, but this morning I found out that he has been drinking for weeks and," she continued, "I would rather have seen him laid in the grave than have him brought home in the condition I saw him in last night." I tried to comfort her as best I could when she told me her sad story.

When I went away from that house I didn't want to go into any other house where there was family trouble. The very next house I went to, however, where some of the children who attended my Sunday School resided, I found that death had been there and laid his hand on one of them. The mother spoke to me of her afflictions, and brought to me the playthings and the little shoes of the child, and the tears trickled down that mother's cheeks as she related to me her sorrow.

I got out as soon as possible, and hoped I should see no more family trouble that day. The next visit I made was to a home where I found a wife with a bitter story. Her husband had been neglecting her for a long time "and now," she said, "he has left me and I don't know where he has gone. Winter is coming on, and I don't know what is going to become of my family." I tried to comfort her, and prayed with her, and endeavored to get her to lay all her sorrows on Christ.

The next home I entered I found a woman crushed and brokenhearted. She told me her boy had forsaken her, and she had no idea where he had gone. That afternoon I made five calls, and in every home I found a broken heart. Every one had a sad tale to tell, and if you visited any home in Chicago you would find the truth of the saying, that "there is a skeleton in every house."

I suppose while I am talking, you are thinking of the great sorrow in your own bosom. I do not know anything about you, but if I came round to every one of you, and you were to tell me the truth, I would hear a tale of sorrow. The very last man I spoke to last night was a young mercantile man, who told me his load of sorrow had been so great, that many times during the last few weeks he had gone down to the lake and had been tempted to plunge a knife in his heart and end his existence. His burden seemed too much for him.

Think of the broken hearts in our world tonight! If there is a broken heart here just bring it to the Great Physician. If you break an arm or a leg, you run off and get the best physician. If you have a broken heart, you needn't go to a doctor or minister with it; the best physician is Jesus Christ, the Great Physician.

Broken hearts, healing for; Affliction, comfort in

Isa. 40:31; Matt. 5:11; 10:19; 1 Cor. 10:13; 2 Cor. 1:4; 3:5; 11:30; 12:5; Eph. 3:16; Phil. 4:13; Col. 1:11; 1 Tim. 1:14; Heb. 4:16; 1 Peter 4:13–14

I was thinking today of the difference between those who knew Christ when trouble came upon them and those who knew him not. I know several members of families who are just stumbling into their graves over trouble. I know two widows in Chicago who are weeping and mourning over the death of their husbands, and their grief is just taking them to their graves. Instead of bringing their burdens to Christ, they mourn day and

night, and the result will be that in a few weeks or years at most their sorrow will take them to their graves when they ought to take it all to the Great Physician.

Three years ago a father took his wife and family on board that ill-fated French steamer. They were going to Europe, and when out on the ocean another vessel ran into her and she went down. That mother when I was preaching in Chicago used to bring her two children to the meetings every night. It was one of the most beautiful sights I ever looked on, to see how those little children used to sit and listen, and to see the tears trickling down their cheeks when the Savior was preached. It seemed as if nobody else in that meeting drank in the truth as eagerly as those little ones.

One night when an invitation had been extended to all to go into the inquiry room, one of these little children said, "Mamma, why can't I go in too?" The mother allowed them to come into the room, and some friend spoke to them, and to all appearances they seemed to understand the plan of salvation as well as their elders. When that memorable night came that mother went down and came up without her two children.

Upon reading the news I said, "It will kill her," and I quitted my post in Edinburgh—the only time I left my post on the other side—and went down to Liverpool to try and comfort her. But when I got there I found that the Son of God had been there before me, and instead of me comforting her, she comforted me. She told me she could not think of those children as being in the sea; it seemed as if Christ had permitted her to take those children on that vessel only that they might be wafted to him, and had saved her life only that she might come back and work a little longer for him. When she got up the other day at a mothers' meeting in Farwell Hall and told her story, I thought I would tell the mothers of it the first chance I got.

So if any of you have had some great affliction, if any of you have lost a loving father, mother, brother, husband, or wife, come to Christ, because God has sent him to heal the brokenhearted.

Brotherhood, universal

Matt. 13:38; John 3:3; 6:70; 8:44; Acts 13:10; Rom. 8:15; 1 John 3:8

I want to say very emphatically that I have no sympathy with the doctrine of universal brotherhood; I don't believe one word of it. If a man lives in the flesh and serves the flesh, he is a child of the devil. That is pretty strong language, but it is what Christ said. It brought down a hornet's nest on his head and helped to hasten him to the cross, but nevertheless it is true. Show me a man that will lie and steal and get drunk and ruin a woman— do you tell me he is my Christian brother? Not a bit of it. He must be born into the household of faith before he becomes my brother in Christ. He is an alien, he is a stranger to the grace of God, he is an enemy to God, he is not a friend. Before a man can cry, "Abba, Father," he must be born from above, born of the Spirit.

Burdens, bear one another's; Self-sacrifice, power of

Exod. 23:4; Luke 11:46; John 13:14; Rom. 15:1; Gal. 5:13; 6:2; 1 Thess. 5:14; James 2:8; 1 John 4:21

There is a beautiful tradition connected with the site on which the temple of Solomon was erected. It is said to have been occupied in common by two brothers, one of whom had a family, the other had none. On this spot was sown a field of wheat. On the evening succeeding the harvest—the wheat having been gathered in separate shocks—the elder brother said to his wife, "My younger brother is unable to bear the burden and heat of the day; I will arise, take of my shocks, and place them with his without his knowledge." The younger brother being actuated by the same benevolent motives, said within himself, "My elder brother has a family, and I have none. I will arise, take of my shocks, and place them with his."

Judge of their mutual astonishment, when, on the following day, they found their respective shocks undiminished. This transpired for several nights, when each resolved in his own mind to stand guard and solve the mystery. They did so; and on the following night they met each other halfway between their respective shocks with their arms full. Upon ground hallowed by such associations as this was the temple of Solomon erected—so spacious and magnificent—the wonder and admiration of the world! Alas! in these days, how many would sooner steal their brother's whole shock than add to it a single sheaf!

Burdens, put on God

1 Sam. 1:10; 30:6; Pss. 37:5; 56:3; 27:14; Matt. 6:34; Luke 12:22; Phil. 4:6; Heb. 13:6; 1 Peter 5:7

A man was once traveling along a highway, and he overtook another man carrying a heavy burden on his back, and he asked him to ride. But the man, after he got into the wagon, still kept his bundle on his back, saying, "I am willing to carry it if I can only get a ride." So many are content to be nominal Christians, and go along with great loads and burdens!

Burial of Christians; Resurrection of believers

Ps. 16:10; Luke 20:35; Acts 2:31–34; Rom. 8:21; 1 Cor. 15:42–44, 50, 52; Phil. 3:21; 1 Peter 1:4

As I go into a cemetery I like to think of the time when the dead shall rise from their graves. We read part of 1 Corinthians 15 in what we call the "burial service." I think it is an unfortunate expression. Paul never talked of "burial." He said the body was sown in corruption, sown in weakness, sown in dishonor, sown a natural body. If I bury a bushel of wheat, I never expect to see it again, but if I sow it, I expect to see that bushel replaced many fold. Thank God, our friends are not buried; they are only sown! I like the Saxon name for the cemetery—"God's acre."

Calvary, wonder of

Zech. 12:10; Matt. 27:34; Mark 15:22; Luke 23:33; 24:7; John 3:10; 19:17; Acts 2:23; Gal. 3:13; Heb. 13:12; 1 Peter 2:24

A man once wanted to sell me a "Book of Wonders." I took it and looked it over, and could not find anything in it about Calvary. What a mistake! A book of wonders—and the greatest wonder of all left out!

Character, importance of

Ps. 51:10; Ezek. 11:19; Matt. 12:33; John 15:5; Rom. 8:9; 2 Cor. 5:17, 21; Eph. 1:4; 2:10; Col. 3:1

Some wonder why there are so few conversions. I wonder there are so many with such a low standard of character as Christians have at present. Now let these friends who are concerned that the Lord's work should be revived here ask themselves this question, "Am I right in the sight of God? How is it with me in my private life? What does my family think of me? Have they confidence in my religion and piety?" You know a man who has the smallpox must get rid of it himself before he goes to minister to others. If you are not Christ-like in your home, the least you say about Christ the better.

Character, influence of;
Testimony, power of

Exod. 15:16; 19:6; Deut. 7:6; Acts 9:36; Rom. 14:7–8; 2 Cor. 5:14; Gal. 2:20; Eph. 2:10; 1 Tim. 2:10; 6:18; Titus 2:7, 14; 3:8; Heb. 10:24; 1 Peter 1:22; 2:9, 12

R. A. Torrey, the famed evangelist, gave this report, "When Mr. Moody visited New Haven in 1878 I was a student in Yale University there. The best scholar in the University at the time, if not the best in America, was President Wolsey, Ex-President of Yale. One night a young man went up to hear Mr. Moody preach and President Wolsey sat on the platform, and when they sang the old Gospel hymns, President Wolsey, himself a gray-haired scholar, joined in singing the hymns with all his heart. That young man said, 'Well, if one of the greatest scholars in America can sing those hymns in that way, there certainly must be something in it,' and he was converted, not through Mr. Moody's preaching but through President Wolsey's singing."

Character, proof of confession;
Home life, importance of

Exod. 15:16; 19:6; Deut. 7:6; Acts 9:36; Rom. 14:7–8; 2 Cor. 5:14; Gal. 2:20; Eph. 2:10; 1 Tim. 2:10; 6:18; Titus 2:7, 14; 3:8; Heb. 10:24; 1 Peter 1:22; 2:9, 12

If I wanted to find out whether a man is a Christian, I wouldn't go to his minister. I would go and ask his wife. I tell you, we need more home piety just now. If a man doesn't treat his wife right, I don't want to hear him talk about Christianity. We need a Christianity that goes into our homes and everyday lives. Some men's religion just makes me sick. They put on a whining voice and a sort of a religious tone and talk so sanctimoniously on Sunday that you would think they were wonderful saints. But Monday they are quite different. They put their religion away with their clothes, and you don't see any more of it until the next Sunday. You laugh, but let us look out that we don't belong to that class. My friends, we have got to have a higher type of Christianity or the church is gone.

Character, ruin of; Ten Commandments, breaking of

1 Kings 18:21; 2 Chron. 12:1; Prov. 27:8; Isa. 29:13; Hosea 7:8; Matt. 6:24; James 1:8; 2 Peter 2:14; 3:16

I do not say that all are equally guilty of gross violations of the Ten Commandments. It requires a certain amount of reckless courage openly to break a law, human or divine; but it is easy to crack them. It has been remarked that the life of many who profess religion is full of fractures that result from little sins, little acts of temper and selfishness. It is possible to crack a costly vase so finely that it cannot be noticed by the observer; but let this be done again and again in different directions, and some day the vase will go to pieces at a touch.

When we hear of someone who has had a lifelong reputation for good character and consistent living, suddenly falling into some shameful sin, we are shocked and puzzled. If we knew all, we would find that only the fall has been sudden, that he has been sliding toward it for years. Away back in his life we should find numerous cracked commandments. His exposure is only the falling of the vase to pieces.

Character, vindication of

Gen. 41:42; Esther 8:15; Prov. 29:2; Eccles. 2:26; Dan. 1:17; 5:14; Acts 6:10; 7:10

A young man was employed by a large commission firm in New York City to negotiate with a certain party for a large quantity of damaged beans. The beans were purchased, delivered, and spread out upon the upper floor of the building occupied by the firm. Men were employed to turn them over and over, and to sprinkle them with a solution of soda, so as to improve their appearance and render them more salable. A large lot of the finest quality of beans was then purchased; some of the good beans were first put into barrels, then the barrels were nearly filled with the poor ones; after this the good ones were again put on the top and the barrels headed up for sale.

The employer marked the barrels, Beans-A 1. The clerk seeing this, said: "Do you think, sir, that it is right to mark those beans A 1?" The employer retorted sharply, "Are you head of the firm?" The clerk said no more. The barreling and heading went on. When all was ready, the beans (many hundreds of barrels) were put on the market for sale. Specimens of the best quality were shown in the office to buyers.

At length a shrewd purchaser came in (no man is so sharp in business but he will often meet his equal), examined the samples in the office, inquired the price, and then wished to see the stock in bulk. The clerk was ordered to go with the buyer to the upper loft and show him the stock. An open barrel was shown apparently of the same quality as the sample. The buyer then said to the clerk, "Young man, the samples of beans shown me are of the first quality, and it is impossible to purchase beans anywhere in the market for the price at which you offer them; there is something wrong here. Tell me, are these beans the same quality throughout the entire barrel as they appear on the top?"

The clerk now found himself in a strange position. He thought, "Shall I lie for my employer, as he undoubtedly means I shall; or shall I tell the truth, come what will?" He decided for the truth, and said, "No, sir, they are not." "Then," said the customer, "I do not want them," and he left.

The clerk entered the office. The employer said to him, "Did you sell that man those beans?"

He said, "No, sir." "Why not?" "Well, sir, the man asked me if those beans were of the same quality through the entire barrel as they appeared on the top. I told him they were not. He then said, 'I do not want them,' and left."

"Go to the cashier," said the employer, "and get your wages; we want you no longer."

He received his pay and left the office, rejoicing that he had not lied for the purposes of abetting a sordid greed, and benefiting an unprincipled employer. Three weeks after this the firm sent after the young clerk, entreated him to come back again into their employ, and offered him more salary than they had ever before given him. And thus was his honesty and truthfulness rewarded. The firm knew and felt that the man was right, although apparently they had lost largely by his honesty. They wished to have him again in their employ, because they knew that they could trust him, and never suffer through fraud and deception. They knew that their financial interests would be safe in his custody. They respected and honored that young man.

Chastening, importance of

Deut. 8:5; 2 Sam. 7:14; Pss. 32:4; 119:71, 75; Prov. 3:12; 13:24; Jer. 10:24; Heb. 12:6; James 1:12; 5:11; Rev. 3:19

A lady in England was out riding and she saw a shepherd who had some dogs driving sheep. If the sheep stopped to drink out of the pools in the streets, he would have the dogs after them. She kept saying to herself, "Oh, you cruel man!" But by-and-by the shepherd came to a beautiful park, opened the great iron gate, and let all the sheep in there where the grass was knee-high, sweet, fresh grass, and a beautiful river running right through the park; and she said, "He isn't a cruel shepherd after all. He didn't want them to eat and drink by the roadside where danger

lurked. He was only trying to get them to a better place."

Chastening of God; Submission to God; Correction, divine

Deut. 8:5; 2 Sam. 7:14; Pss. 32:4; 119:71, 75; Prov. 3:12; 13:24; Jer. 10:24; Heb. 12:6; James 1:12; 5:11; Rev. 3:19

When I was a boy my mother used to send me outdoors to get a birch stick to whip me with, when I had to be punished. At first I used to stand off from the rod as far as I could. But I soon found that the whipping hurt me more that way than any other; and so I went as near to my mother as I could, and found she could not strike me so hard. And so when God chastens us let us kiss the rod and draw as near to him as we can.

Child, death of

2 Sam. 12:23; 2 Kings 4:34; Ps. 116:15; Isa. 40:11; Mark 5:41; Luke 8:54; John 11:43; Rev. 14:13

A little child in Chicago, whose parents were unbelievers and had never taught her even the name of God, was dying. She opened her eyes, raised her hands, and said, "Julia is coming, God." Who taught her that there was a God who would receive little children? Her parents learned from her beautiful death to trust in Jesus.

Child, influence of on conversion; Robert Raikes, conversion of

2 Kings 7:9; Isa. 2:3; 11:6; Luke 2:17, 42; John 1:41–42, 45; 4:29; 1 John 1:3

Years ago, when Illinois was but a young State, there were only a few settlers here and there throughout a large portion. One of these was a man who used to spend his Sundays in hunting and fishing. He was a profane and notoriously wicked man. His little girl went to the

Sunday school in the log schoolhouse. There she was taught the way into the kingdom of God. When she was converted the teacher tried to tell her how she might be used of God in doing good to others. She thought she would begin with her father. Others had tried to reach him and had failed to do it, but his own child had more influence with him. It is written, "A little child shall lead them."

She got him to promise to go to the meeting. He came to the door, but at first he would not go in. He had gone to the school when he was young, but one day the boys laughed at him because he had a little impediment in his speech. He would not go back, and so he had never learned to read. However he was at last induced to go to the Sunday school. There he heard of Christ and was converted to God. His little child helped him and others helped him, and he soon learned to read.

This man has since been called to his reward, but about two years ago when I saw him last, he had established on the Western prairies between 1,100 and 1,200 Sunday schools. In addition to all these there are now hundreds of flourishing churches that have grown out of these little mission schools that he planted. He used to have a Sunday school horse, a "Robert Raikes" horse he called him, on which he traveled up and down the country, going into many outlying districts where nothing was being done for Christ.

He used to gather the parents into the log schoolhouses and tell how his little girl led him to Christ. I have heard a great many orators, but I never heard any who could move an audience as he could. There was no impediment in his speech when he began to speak for Christ he seemed to have all the eloquence and fire of heaven. That little girl did what she could. She did a good day's work when she led her father to the Savior.

Everyone of us may do something if we are only willing.

Childhood spiritual education; Satan, influence on children

Exod. 13:8; Deut. 6:6; 11:19; Josh. 8:35; Ps. 34:11; Prov. 22:6; Isa. 28:9–10; Joel 1:3; John 21:25

The story is told that a man once said he would not talk to his son about religion; the boy should make his own choice when he grew up, unprejudiced by him. The boy broke his arm, and when the doctor was setting it, he cursed and swore the whole time. The father was quite grieved and shocked. "Ah," said the doctor, "you were afraid to prejudice the boy in the right way, but the devil had no such prejudice. He has led your son the other way." The idea that a father is to let his children run wild! Nature alone never brings forth anything but weeds.

Children and covenants

Exod. 13:8; Deut. 6:6; 11:19; Josh. 8:35; Ps. 34:11; Prov. 22:6; Isa. 28:9–10; Joel 1:3; John 21:25

I had this question, "Do you think it best to get children to sign a covenant that they will not lie, swear, drink, etc.?" I responded, "Well I did, but I have got over it. I don't think much of covenants. I would not say anything against signing the pledge not to drink, but I think the only hope is in Christ. They must renounce their own strength, give up their own resolutions and lean on Christ. It is a good deal better just to teach them Jesus Christ is the only hope. If they sign the pledge they will come to lean on the pledge. Take Christ as the Savior of the world. Just hold to that. We are holding up almost every substitute except Jesus Christ. We must hold Christ up to them the same as Moses in the wilderness presented the brazen serpent, and it healed them. He didn't have any roots or herbs, but they were healed then. Lean on Christ's strength."

Children, conversion of

Matt. 18:4, 10; 19:14–15; Mark 9:37; 10:16; Luke 18:15–16

Many a father's and many a mother's heart is burdened with anxiety for the salvation of their children. If your own name is there, let your next aim in life be to get the children that God has given you, there also. I have three children, and the greatest desire of my heart is that they may be saved; that I may know that their names are written in the Book of Life. I may be taken from them early; I may leave them in this changing world without a father's care; without a father to watch over them; and I have often said to myself I would rather have them come to my grave after I am dead and gone, and drop a tear upon it, and say, "My father, while he lived, cared for my soul," than I would have them do anything else.

Matt. 18:4, 10; 19:14–15; Mark 9:37; 10:16; Luke 18:15–16

The best thing we can do for children is to bring them early to Christ. Early impressions never, never leave them, and I do not know why they should not grow up in the service of the Lord. I contend that those who are converted early make the best Christians. Take the man who is converted at fifty and has continually to fight against his old habits. But a young person has a Christian character to form and a long life to give to Christ.

Children, prayer for

Gen. 17:18; 2 Sam. 12:16; 1 Chron. 22:12; 29:19; Job 1:5; Isa. 40:11

I received a letter from Scotland. It was from a father. He asked us to look out for his boy, whose name was Willie. That name touched my heart, because it was the name of my own boy. I asked Mr. Sawyer to try and get on the track of that boy some weeks ago, but all his efforts were fruitless. But away off in Scotland that Christian father was holding his son up to God in prayer, and last Friday, in yonder room, among those asking for prayer was that Willie, and he told me a story there that thrilled my heart, and testified how the prayers of that father and mother in that far-off land had been instrumental in affecting his salvation.

Don't you think the heart of that father and mother will rejoice? He said he was rushing madly to destruction, but there was a power in those prayers that saved that boy. Don't you think, my friends, that God hears and answers prayers, and shall we not lift up our voices to him in prayer that he will bless the children he has given to us?

Choice, importance of

Gen. 13:11; Deut. 29:18; Josh. 24:15; Ruth 1:16; 1 Kings 18:21; Ps. 119:111; Ezek. 20:39; John 6:68; Acts 11:23

I would rather go into the kingdom of heaven through the poor house than go down to hell in a golden chariot.

Christ and Adam

Gen. 3:8–9, 15, 17, 21; Job 31:33; Jer. 32:19; Rom. 5:14; 1 Cor. 15:22, 45; 1 Tim. 2:14

You can always tell the difference between the two Adams. When the first Adam sins he begins to make an excuse. Man must have an excuse always ready for his sins. When God came down and said, "Adam, where art thou? What have you been doing? Have you been eating of that tree?" he hung his head and had to own up that he had; but he said, "Lord, it is the woman that tempted me." He had to charge it back upon God, you see. Instead of putting the blame where it belonged, on his own shoulders, he tried to blame God for his sins. That is what the first Adam was like.

We have it right here every day in our inquiry room. Men and women trying to charge their sins back on God instead of getting up and confessing them. They say, "Why did God tempt me? Why did God do this and that?" That was the spirit of the first Adam. But, thank God, the second Adam made no excuse. He took it upon himself to bear our sins upon the tree. The first Adam looked upon the tree and plucked its fruit and fell. The second Adam was nailed to the tree. "Cursed is everyone that is nailed to the tree." He became a curse for us.

The two remarkable events that have taken place in the world are these, that when the first Adam went up from Eden he left a curse upon the earth, but when the second Adam went up from the Mount of Olives he lifted the curse.

Gen. 3:8–9, 15, 17, 21; Job 31:33; Jer. 32:19; Rom. 5:14; 1 Cor. 15:22, 45; 1 Tim. 2:14

When the first Adam was tempted he yielded to the first temptation. When the second Adam was tempted he resisted. Satan gave him a trial. God won't have a Son that he cannot test. Christ was tried; he was tempted; he took upon himself your nature and mine and withstood the temptation. The first Adam was tempted by his bride. The second was tempted for his bride, the church that he might win her for himself.

Gen. 3:8–9, 15, 17, 21; Job 31:33; Jer. 32:19; Rom. 5:14; 1 Cor. 15:22, 45; 1 Tim. 2:14

In 1 Corinthians 15:45 we are told of two federal heads, two Adams. We are all in the first Adam and can be in the second Adam. The first Adam was the chief of all created things; he was intelligent, he gave names to all. The second Adam was the chief of the universe but humbled himself to become "servant of all." The first Adam was conquered by the world. The second Adam conquered the world. The

first Adam charged sin back on God, the second Adam bore our sins in his own body on the tree. The first Adam brought sin in, the second drove it away. The first Adam fell in a garden, the second rose in a garden. This dark world will bloom under the second Adam. The first Adam disobeyed, the second was obedient.

Christ, as Shepherd

Ps. 23:1; Isa. 40:11; Matt. 26:31; John 10:11; Luke 19:10; 1 Peter 2:25

Suppose you had a flock of sheep, and wanted to hire a shepherd to care for them, and someone came to you with his credentials and references. In discussing him with those for whom he had worked before you found that he had lost a good many sheep. You would not want that person to care for your sheep, would you? Christ, our Good Shepherd, will take good care of them that put their trust in him. He will not only give them eternal life, but he will let none of his flock slip out of his hands. Let us trust in him; let us make him our Shepherd and let us say from the heart, "The Lord is my Shepherd, I shall not want."

Christ, burden bearer; Cares, help with

Ps. 55:22; Matt. 6:33; 11:28; John 7:37; 10:11; Phil. 4:6; Heb. 13:6; 1 Peter 5:7; Rev. 22:17

I remember a mother coming to me and saying, "It is easy enough for you to speak in that way; if you had the burden that I've got, you couldn't cast it on the Lord." "Why, is your burden so great that Christ can't carry it?" I asked. "No: it isn't too great for him to carry; but I can't put it on him." "That is your problem," I replied; and I find a great many people with burdens who, rather than just come to him with them, strap them tighter on their backs and go away struggling under their load. They hug their burdens to themselves all the time crying out against them.

I asked her the nature of her trouble, and she told me. "I have an only boy who is a wanderer on the face of the earth. I don't know where he is. If I only knew where he was I would go around the world to find him. You don't know how I love that boy. This sorrow is killing me." "Why can't you take him to Christ? You can reach him at the throne, even though he be at the uttermost part of the world. Go tell God all about your trouble, and he will take away his sin, and not only that, but if you never see him on earth, God can give you faith that you will see your boy in heaven." She went away much comforted, and I believe she ultimately had her wandering boy restored to her!

Christ, comfort from; Trials, ministry of

Isa. 9:6; 32:15; 54:13; 57:19; Luke 2:14; 12:4; John 11:4, 25; 14:3, 27; 16:33; Acts 10:36; Rom. 5:1; Phil. 4:7; Col. 1:20

The communion the sisters of Lazarus had with Jesus brought them so near to his heart that they found great comfort. Many people do not learn that secret when things are going well, and so when the billows of sorrow and testing come rolling up against them, they don't know which way to turn. The darkest and most wretched place on the face of the earth is a home where death has entered, and where Christ is unknown. No hope of a resurrection, no hope of a brighter day coming.

Christ, compassion of

Matt. 9:36; 14:14; 15:32; 20:34; 23:37; Mark 1:14; 6:34; 8:2; Luke 7:13; 13:34; Phil. 2:1; James 5:11

Dr. Roy, Mr. Moody's former pastor at Plymouth Church in Chicago, heard him preach on "The Compassion of Christ," in which he seemed like a man inspired, and under which the great audience was moved like a forest swept by the winds. When it was over the doctor inquired of

him how he had prepared such a sermon. He answered, "I got to thinking the other day about the compassion of Christ; so I took the Bible and began to read it over to find out what it said on that subject. I prayed over the texts as I went along, until the thought of Christ's infinite compassion overpowered me, and I could only lie on the floor of my study, with my face in the open Bible, and cry like a little child."

Christ, confession of

Matt. 10:32; Luke 12:8; 24:9; John 1:41; 4:29; Rom. 10:9; 14:11; 15:9; Phil. 2:11; 1 John 4:15

When I was in Ireland I heard of a man who got great blessings from God. He was a business man—a landed proprietor. He had a large family, and a great many men to work for him taking care of his home. He came up to Dublin and there he found Christ. And he came boldly out and thought he would go home and confess him. He thought that if Christ had redeemed him with his precious blood, the least he could do would be to confess him, and tell about it. So he called his family together and his servants, and with tears running down his cheeks he poured out his soul to them, and told them what Christ had done for him.

He took the Bible down from its resting place and read a few verses of gospel. Then he went down on his knees to pray, and so greatly was the little gathering blessed that four or five out of that family were convicted of sin; they forsook the ways of the world, and accepted Christ and eternal life. It was like unto the household of Cornelius, which experienced the working of the Holy Spirit. And that man and his family were not afraid to follow out their profession.

Matt. 10:32; Luke 12:8; 24:9; John 1:41; 4:29; Rom. 10:9; 14:11; 15:9; Phil. 2:11; 1 John 4:15

I remember while in Boston I attended one of the daily prayer meetings. The meetings we had been holding had been almost always addressed by young men. Well, in that meeting a little towheaded Norwegian boy stood up. He could hardly speak a word of English plainly, but he got up and came to the front. He trembled all over and the tears were all trickling down his cheeks, but he spoke out as well as he could and said, "If I tell the world about Jesus, then will he tell the Father about me?" He then took his seat; that was all he said, but I tell you that in those few words he said more than all of them, old and young together Those few words went straight down into the heart of every one present. "If I tell the world"—yes, that's what it means to confess Christ.

Matt. 10:32; Luke 12:8; 24:9; John 1:41; 4:29; Rom. 10:9; 14:11; 15:9; Phil. 2:11; 1 John 4:15

The blessing of heaven will fall upon you, and you shall have peace and joy if you confess Christ before a scoffing, mocking world. I remember the first time I testified about my faith in Christ my knees smote together. I had a little speech all made up, but when I got on my feet it all went from me. I just stood up for Christ. Satan afterwards said, "What a fool you made of yourself!" I have been making a "fool" of myself ever since.

Matt. 10:32; Luke 12:8; 24:9; John 1:41; 4:29; Rom. 10:9; 14:11; 15:9; Phil. 2:11; 1 John 4:15;

What would you think of a man who wants to be a policeman but is unwilling to put on a policeman's uniform. He doesn't want anyone to know that he is a policeman. Do you think he would be a very effective policeman? Do you think that your life and property would be safe with an officer like that? What would you think of a man who wants to fight for his country, who says, "I am just full of patriotism, but I don't want to put on a soldier's uniform, or have anyone know that I am a soldier." What would you do with an army of such men? Why, a little band of five hundred men whose hearts were truly patriotic, and who lived for their country, would rout an army of five hundred thousand of such cowards.

It takes a hero to be a Christian. Mark that. It takes moral courage to come out and confess Christ, and the lack of it keeps more people out of the kingdom of God than anything else.

Christ, confession of; Lay witness

Matt. 10:32; Luke 12:8; 24:9; John 1:41; 4:29; Rom. 10:9; 14:11; 15:9; Phil. 2:11; 1 John 4:15

A preacher was riding out to a service with a prominent judge who was a mature Christian with a good testimony before his community. The preacher said, "Judge, I want you to speak tonight." "Oh," said the judge, "I can't do that; I have never spoken in a church in my life." When they got to the place they found the room full, and the preacher said, "Judge, let me ask you a few questions. All you will have to do is give answer." "Yes, I could do that," replied the judge. The preacher asked him to tell when he was converted, and something of his experience. The whole audience was under conviction, and many were converted. Let us all be willing to confess Christ before men.

Christ, confession of; Women, ministry of

Matt. 10:32; Luke 12:8; 24:9; John 1:41; 4:29; Rom. 10:9; 14:11; 15:9; Phil. 2:11; 1 John 4:15

I wish we had a few more women like the woman of Samaria, willing to confess what the Lord Jesus Christ had done for their souls.

Christ, confidence in

Heb. 3:1; 1 John 2:28; 1 John 5:14

I hear a new convert get up and say, "I am going to hold out." That is not the way to put it. You will not unless God lets you. He is able to make you stand. He was able to make Joseph stand there in Egypt. He was able to make Elijah stand before Ahab. He was able to make Daniel stand in Babylon. So my friend, you need the same grace and the same power that all these did. They have gone on before you. Your strength lies in God, and not in yourself. The moment you lean on yourself, down you go. The moment we get self-contented and think we are able to stand and overcome, we are on dangerous territory; we are standing upon the edge of a precipice.

Christ, dedication to; Giving to the poor

Prov. 19:17; 22:16; Mark 16:20; Luke 1:16–17; Acts 4:13; 5:42; 8:4; 18:25; Rom. 1:16; Phil. 1:27–28; 2:15; 3:14; Titus 2:14; Heb. 10:34; Rev. 3:19

Mr. Moorehouse told me he was looking down the harbor of Liverpool one day, when he saw a vessel coming up, and she was being towed up by a tug. The vessel was sunk in the water nearly to her edge, and he wondered it did not sink altogether. Upon inquiry he found that it was loaded with lumber. The ship had sprung a leak and was waterlogged. Another vessel came up, her sails set, no tug assisting her, and she soon darted past the waterlogged vessel.

And so it is with some Christians. They are waterlogged. They may belong to a church, and if they find anything in the church disagreeing with them they won't go back. They want the whole church to come out and look for them, and tow them in. If the church doesn't, they think they are not getting the attention due them. When men go up in balloons they take bags of sand with them, and when they want to rise higher they throw out the sand. There are a great many Christians who have got too many bags of sand, and to rise they need to throw some out.

Look at the poor men here in the city—the rich Christians can relieve themselves by giving some of their bags of sand to them. A great many Christians would feel much better if they relieved themselves of their bags of sand. "He that giveth to the poor lendeth to the Lord," and if you want to be rich in eternity, just give to the poor with your heart, and the Lord will bless not only you, but all connected with you.

Christ, dedication to; Zeal, importance of; Dedication, importance of

Mark 16:20; Luke 1:16–17; Acts 4:13; 5:42; 8:4; 18:25; Rom. 1:16; Phil. 1:27–28; 2:15; 3:14; Titus 2:14; Heb. 10:34; Rev. 3:19

I remember when I first went to London, a merchant wanted me to go to Dublin, and I went. He introduced me to an old, white-haired man, who said: "Is this young man all 'O. O.'?" "Yes," said the London merchant, "He is 'O. O.'"I began to blush. I had heard of D. D., but not of "O. O." And he said: "Is he Out and Out for Christ?" I never forgot that expression. "Out and Out." The only way to live a peaceful life, a joyful life, is to live it "Out and Out."

Christ, deity of

Isa. 48:16; Matt. 17:5; 28:19; Mark 3:11; John 1:1–2; 5:23, 26; 8:58; 10:30; 14:9; 17:21; 2 Cor. 13:14; Titus 2:13; 1 John 5:7, 20

Some people, who do not admit Christ's deity, say that he was the best man who ever lived; but if he were not God, for that very reason he ought not to be reckoned a good man, for he laid claim to an honor and dignity to which these very people declare he had no right or title. That would rank him as a deceiver.

Others say that he thought he was God, but that he was deceived. As if Jesus Christ were carried away by a delusion and deception, and thought that he was more than he was! I could not conceive of a lower idea of Jesus Christ than that. This would not only make him out an impostor; but that he was out of his mind, and that he did not know who he was, or where he came from. Now if Jesus Christ was not what he claimed to be, the Savior of the world; and if he did not come from heaven, he was a gross deceiver.

But how can anyone read the life of Jesus Christ and make him out a deceiver? A man has generally some motive for being an impostor. What was Christ's motive? He knew that the course he was pursuing would take him to the cross; and that many of his followers would be called upon to lay down their lives for his sake. If a man is an impostor, he has a motive at the back of his hypocrisy. But what was Christ's object? The record is that "He went about doing good." This is not the work of an impostor.

Christ, deity of; Commandment, first

Isa. 48:16; Matt. 17:5; 28:19; Mark 3:11; John 1:1–2; 5:23, 26; 8:58; 10:30; 14:9; 17:21; 2 Cor. 13:14; Titus 2:13; 1 John 5:7, 20

The first commandment forbids the worship of any one but God. Hence Christ, if not divine, was guilty of a great sin in permitting himself to be worshiped. It will not do to say that he was mistaken—that he imagined that he was divine. That is absurd; it makes the world's Redeemer a lunatic. Jesus wrought miracles and controlled the elements in his own name. He said to the dead, "Arise! Come forth!" and was instantly obeyed.

Isa. 48:16; Matt. 17:5; 28:19; Mark 3:11; John 1:1–2; 5:23, 26; 8:58; 10:30; 14:9; 17:21; 2 Cor. 13:14; Titus 2:13; 1 John 5:7, 20

If Jesus Christ were not the Son of God we are guilty of the very worst sin, because the very first commandment is, "Thou shalt have no other gods before me." Look at the millions of people who would be guilty of idolatry if Christ were not God in the flesh. Think of those who have poured out their blood to establish and maintain this truth! What an impostor he was if he were not God in the flesh!

Christ, description of

Col. 1:18

I do not know where this originally came from; but it was so fresh to my soul that I should like to give it to you: "Christ is our way; we walk in him. He is our truth; we embrace him. He is our life; we live in him. He is our Lord; we choose him to rule over us. He is our master; we serve him. He is our teacher; we follow his instruction. He is our light; we walk in his radiance. He is our prophet; we trust him for the future. He is our priest; we rest in the atonement he made for us. He is our advocate; we find strength in his intercession for us. He is our savior; we know he has saved us to the uttermost. He is our root; we grow up from him. He is our bread; we feed upon him. He is our shepherd; we follow him into green pastures. He is our true vine; we abide in him. He is the Water of Life; we slake our thirst from him. He is the fairest among ten thousand; we admire him above all others. He is the brightness of the Father's glory, and the express image of his person; we strive to reflect his likeness. He is the upholder of all things; we rest upon him. He is our wisdom; we are guided by him. He is our righteousness; we cast all our imperfections upon him. He is our sanctification; we draw all our power for holy life from him. He is our redemption; he redeems us from all iniquity. He is our healer; we put our wounded souls in his care. He is our brother; we are cheered by his presence in all our struggles. He is our friend; we walk with him down life's path."

Christ, fellowship with

Gen. 18:17; John 12:24; 15:15; 17:26; James 2:24; 1 John 1:3

One summer I went up on to the mountain with my brother to visit his farm. He was going to give salt to his sheep; and I noticed one sheep that came right up to him, stood by him, and got all the salt it wanted. Then it put its nose into his pocket and got an apple. But all the other sheep seemed a little afraid of him. I asked him how it was, and he said, "That sheep has been brought up as a pet lamb, and isn't a bit afraid of me." So it is with those Christians who keep close to Christ; they are like the sheep that gets the most salt. But a good many Christians seem a little afraid of the Shepherd; and because they are afraid and keep away from him they never get much salt. It is an old saying, "The sheep that keeps nearest the shepherd gets the most salt."

Christ, God and man

Matt. 26:38; Luke 2:52; John 8:40; 10:30, 33

Some ask why Christ did not come from heaven in glory and grandeur. I suppose he could have done so; he could have come from the throne in a golden chariot, and have gone through the world as an angel of light. But if a man wants to be a mediator he must be a friend of both parties, and how could Christ have been a mediator between us and God if he had not taken upon himself our nature? Some say it was a mystery that God ever permitted sin to come into the world, but it was a greater mystery that God ever sent his Son to bear the brunt of it.

Christ, great physician

2 Chron. 7:14; Job 5:18; Pss. 41:4; 51:2; Isa. 57:19; Jer. 3:22; 17:14; Hosea 6:1; Matt. 8:16; 14:14; 19:2; Mark 3:10; 6:13; Luke 4:18; 5:17; 9:42; John 5:15; 1 Peter 2:24

In the days of Christ they didn't have hospitals or physicians as we have now. When a man was sick he was taken to the door, and the passers-by prescribed for him. If a man came along who had had the same disease as the sufferer he just told him what he had done to get cured. I remember I had a disease for a few months, and when I recovered if I met a man with the same disease I had to tell him what cured me. I could not keep the prescription all to myself. When Jesus came there and found the sick at their cottage door, the sufferers found more medicine in his words than there was in all the prescriptions of that country. He is a mighty physician, who has come to heal every wounded heart. You needn't run to any other physician.

The great difficulty is that people try to get some other physician. They go to this creed and that creed, to this doctor of divinity and that one, instead of coming directly to the Master. He has told us that his mission is to heal the broken hearts, and if he has said this, let us take him at his word and just ask him to heal.

Christ, last act of; Salvation for all

Pss. 32:5; 50:15; Isa. 1:18; 53:11; 55:6; 65:24; Micah 7:18; Matt. 20:16; Luke 15:20; 19:10; 23:43; John 14:3; Heb. 7:25

When a prominent man dies, we are anxious to get his last words and acts. The last act of the Son of God was to save a sinner. That was a part of the glory of his death. He commenced his ministry by saving common sinners, and ended it by saving this poor thief.

Christ, liberty in; Freedom from sin

John 8:32, 36; Rom. 6:18, 22; 8:2; Gal. 5:1; Heb. 2:15

Once the Emperor of Russia had a plan by which he was to liberate the serfs of that country. There were forty million of them. Of some of them, their whole time was sold, of others, only a part. The Emperor called around him his council, and wanted to have them devise some way to set the slaves at liberty. After they had conferred about it for six months, one night the council sent in their decision, sealed, that they thought it was not expedient. The Emperor went down to the Greek Church that night and partook of the Lord's Supper, and he set his house in order, and the next morning you could hear the tramp of soldiers in the streets of St. Petersburg.

The Emperor summoned his guard, and before noon sixty-five thousand men were surrounding that palace. Just at midnight there came out a proclamation that every slave in Russia was forever set free. The proclamation had gone forth, and all the slaves of the realm believed it. They have been free to this day. Suppose they had not believed it? They never would have got the benefit of it. If one man can liberate forty millions, has not God got the power to liberate every captive?

Christ, new creation in

Ps. 51:10; Isa. 45:17; Ezek. 11:19; 18:31; 36:26; Rom. 1:16; 2 Cor. 5:17; Gal. 6:15; Eph. 1:4; 2:10, 15

A man had been carrying on the business of a dogfighter in the East end of London, and had a very valuable dog, called Tiger, which had cost a lot of money. He had won a large amount of money in dogfights. A little child of his died, and it affected him very much. He did not know what to do to get rid of his feelings, and so he was going to a pub to get something to drink to help him to forget his sorrow; but as he was going he thought, "Well, there's this Moody and Sankey, suppose I go and hear them?" He went and heard Mr. Moody speak, and came out thinking it was all very good, but it did not concern

him. His business was very dull, and he had no sport to go to, so he went again.

The man said that it appeared as if the preacher left off speaking to the audience and directed his remarks straight at him. He slid down in the seat that the preacher should not see him, but he only hit him harder than before. The service being over, he felt uncomfortable, and went and made inquiries about the matter, and then found that all men were born in sin. After much conversation, and by the grace of God, he was enabled to trust simply in Jesus, and since that time he had been quite happy.

There was his dog; what was he to do with that? Every time he saw Tiger he saw there was a terrible link between his past life and his present, and he was afraid if he sold the dog he would only lead someone else into sin. So he at last decided to destroy the dog, although it cost a good sum of money, and was a very valuable animal. This he did—he tied the dog in a sack and drowned him in the river.

Christ, new life in

Ps. 51:10; Isa. 45:17; Ezek. 11:19; 18:31; 36:26; Rom. 1:16; 2 Cor. 5:17; Gal. 6:15; Eph. 1:4; 2:10, 15

When Moses commenced to perform his miracles down in Egypt, he turned water into death; but when Christ commenced his miracles at the marriage at Cana, he turned water into life and joy, for such wine is spoken of in the Scripture as the emblem of joy and gladness. That is the difference between the law and the Gospel. The law was, "Thou shalt die." That was the penalty of the law; but the Gospel was life.

Christ, no room for

Luke 2:7; John 1:11; 8:20

The world has no room for the Master, and should the servant be above his Lord?

The cry of the world today is, as it was eighteen hundred years ago, no room. He might have been born in a palace, but he went to the manger in order that he might get his arm under the lowest and bear him up towards heaven. He became poor for our sakes. He occupied a borrowed cradle and a borrowed grave. He had no home. The temple was made for him, and yet it was closed against him.

Christ, not ashamed of

Pss. 40:9–10; 119:46; Mark 8:38; Luke 9:26; Rom. 1:16; 15:19, 29; 1 Cor. 2:2; 2 Tim. 1:8, 12, 16; 1 Peter 4:16

People say, "I am ashamed to speak for Christ because I am such a poor speaker." So am I. Many a time I have wished the floor would open and let me drop out of sight. He is worthy of a better witness than I am. I can honestly say that I have been ashamed of myself a good many times, but I do not remember that I have ever been ashamed of my Lord and Master.

Christ, not ashamed of; Gospel, power of

Pss. 40:9–10; 119:46; Mark 8:38; Luke 9:26; Rom. 1:16; 15:19, 29; 1 Cor. 2:2; 2 Tim. 1:8, 12, 16; 1 Peter 4:16

There was a young man in the middle west who had been more or less interested concerning his soul's salvation. One afternoon, in his office, he said, "I will accept Jesus Christ as my Lord and Savior." He went home and told his wife, who was a nominal professor of religion, that he had made up his mind to serve Christ, and he added, "After dinner tonight I am going to invite our guests to be part of our first family altar worship."

"Well," said his wife, "you know some of the gentlemen who are coming to dinner are skeptics, and they are older than you are. Don't you think you had better wait until after they have gone, or else go out in the kitchen and have your first prayer with the children?"

The young man thought for a few moments, and then he said, "I have asked Jesus Christ into my house for the first time, and I shall keep him in the dining room, and not in the kitchen." So he invited his friends to participate in family worship. There was a little sneering, but he read and prayed. That man afterward became Chief Justice of the United States Court. Never be ashamed of the gospel of Christ; it is the power of God unto salvation.

Christ, our advocate

John 10:15; 14:6; Eph. 2:18; 1 Tim. 2:5; Heb. 7:25; 9:24; 1 John 2:1; Jude 24

Someone may say, "Well, I am a believer; but then I have sinned since I became a Christian." Is there a man or a woman on the face of the earth who has not sinned since becoming a Christian? Not one! There never has been, and never will be, a soul on this earth who has not sinned, or who will not sin, at some time of their Christian experience. But God has made provision for believers' sins. We are not to make provision for them; but God has. Bear that in mind. Turn to 1 John 2:1, "My little children, these things write I unto you, that ye sin not. And if any man sin, we have an Advocate with the Father, Jesus Christ the righteous." He is here writing to Christians. "If any man sin, we"—John put himself in—"we have an Advocate with the Father, Jesus Christ the righteous."

What does an Advocate do? He attends to our interests at the very best place—the throne of God. He went away to become our High Priest, and also our Advocate and plead our cases before God's bar of justice. He has had some hard cases to plead; but he has never lost one: and if you entrust your immortal interests to Christ, he will "present you faultless before the presence of His glory with exceeding joy" (Jude 24).

Christ, our helper; Satan, victory over

Zech. 3:2; Acts 26:18; Rom. 16:20; 1 Cor. 10:13; Phil. 4:13; Heb. 4:16; 1 Peter 5:7; Rev. 20:2

I remember hearing of a little fellow who was met on his way home from school by a great ruffian of a boy, a good deal bigger than he was, who tried to pick a quarrel with him. "I can't fight you," said the little boy, "but you just wait till I go and fetch my big brother," and he ran off as hard as he could to find his big brother; but when they came back the coward wasn't there. Christ is your big Brother. You cannot fight with Satan, for he has more than 6,000 years experience, and is a deal wiser than you are. But the Lion of the Tribe of Judah had a battle with him, and overcame him; and since then Satan always flies when he hears the name of Christ. Our Big Brother is able to help us, and he will always make a way of escape.

Christ, our pioneer leader

Micah 7:7; Matt. 20:28; John 8:56; 12:32; Acts 5:31; Phil. 3:20; Titus 2:13; Heb. 2:10; 5:9; 9:28; 10:14; 12:2–3; 1 Peter 2:21; Rev. 1:8, 11, 17; 2:8

In our western counties, when men go out hunting into dense backwoods, where there are no roads or paths of any kind, they take their hatchet and cut a little chip out of the bark of the trees as they go along, and then they easily find their way by these "blazes," for they call it "blazing the trail." Christ has "blazed the trail." He has traveled the road himself, and knowing the way, he tells us to follow him, and he will lead us safe on high.

If we will take our eyes from one another, and from sects and creeds and doctrines, and follow him we shall be led in the right way. We would be saved many a dark hour, if we were only willing to walk with God, if we would only just let him take us by the hand and lead us. What God wants us to do is to follow in his footsteps. I have been told that scouts sometimes find an Indian trail consisting of only one footprint, as if only one man had passed over the land. The chief goes before, and all the rest of the warriors follow him and put their feet into his footsteps. That is what our Chief wants us to do. He has passed through the heavens, gone up on high, and he wants us to follow.

Christ, personality of

Dan. 2:44; John 3:30; Col. 1:18; Rev. 11:15

You know that some men grow smaller and smaller on an intimate acquaintance; but my experience is, that the more and more you know of Christ, the larger he becomes.

Christ, pleasing; Overcoming the world; Spiritual growth, hindrances to

Gen. 4:7; Acts 10:35; Rom. 8:5; 1 Cor. 9:27; 2 Cor. 5:9; Eph. 1:6; Heb. 12:28; 1 John 3:13; 4:4; 5:4; Rev. 3:21

A lady came to me once and said, "Mr. Moody, I wish you would tell me how I can become a Christian." The tears were rolling down her cheeks, and she was in a very favorable mood. "But," she said, "I don't want to be one of your kind." "Well," I asked, "have I got any peculiar kind? What is the matter with my Christianity?"

"Well," she said, "my father was a doctor, and had a large practice, and he would get so tired that he used to take us to the theater. There was a large family of girls, and we had tickets for the theaters three or four times a week. I suppose we were there a good deal oftener than we were in church. I am married to a lawyer, and he has a large practice. He gets so tired that he takes us to the theater," and she said, "I am far better acquainted with the theater and theater people than with the church and church people, and I don't want to give up the theater."

"Well," I said, "did you ever hear me say anything about theaters? There have been reporters here every day for all the different papers, and they are giving my sermons verbatim in one paper. Have you ever seen anything in the sermons against the theaters?" She said, "No." "Well," I said, "I have seen you in the audience every afternoon for several weeks, and have you heard me say anything against theaters?" No, she hadn't.

"Well," I said, "what made you bring them up?" "Why, I supposed you didn't believe in theaters." "What made you think that?" "Why," she said, "do you ever go?" "No." "Why don't you go?" "Because I have got something better. I would sooner go out into the street and eat dirt than do some of the things I used to do before I became a Christian." "Why!" she said. "I don't understand."

"Never mind," I said. "When Jesus Christ has the preeminence, you will understand it all. He didn't come down here and say we shouldn't go here and we shouldn't go there, and lay down a lot of rules, but he laid down great principles. Now, he says if you love him you will take delight in pleasing him." And I began to preach Christ to her. The tears started again. She said, "I tell you, Mr. Moody, that sermon on the indwelling Christ yesterday afternoon just broke my heart. I admire him, and I want to be a Christian, but I don't want to give up the theaters."

I said, "Please don't mention them again. I don't want to talk about theaters. I want to talk to you about Christ." So I took my Bible, and I read to her about Christ. But she said again, "Mr. Moody, can I go to the theater if I become a Christian?" "Yes," I said, "you can go to the theater just as much as you like if you are a real, true Christian, and can go with his

blessing." "Well," she said, "I am glad you are not so narrow-minded as some."

She felt quite relieved to think that she could go to the theaters and be a Christian. But I said, "If you can go to the theater for the glory of God, keep on going; only be sure that you go for the glory of God. If you are a Christian you will be glad to do whatever will please him." I really think she became a Christian that day. The burden had gone, there was joy; but just as she was leaving me at the door she said, "I am not going to give up the theater."

In a few days she came back to me and said, "Mr. Moody, I understand all about that theater business now. I went the other night. There was a large party at our house, and my husband wanted us to go, and we went; but when the curtain lifted everything looked so different. I said to my husband, 'This is no place for me; this is horrible. I am not going to stay here, I am going home.' He said, 'Don't make a fool of yourself. Everyone has heard that you have been converted in the Moody meeting, and if you go out it will be all through fashionable society. I beg of you don't make a fool of yourself by getting up and going out.' But I said, 'I have been making a fool of myself all of my life.'"

Now, the theater hadn't changed, but she had got something better, and she was going to overcome the world. When Christ has the first place in your heart you are going to get victory. Just do whatever you know will please him. The great objection I have to these things is that they get the mastery, and become a hindrance to spiritual growth.

Christ, redemption by

Exod. 6:6; Ruth 3:9; Ps. 49:15; Jer. 15:21; Hosea 13:14; Micah 4:10; Gal. 3:13; Titus 2:14; Rev. 5:9

A friend of mine once told me that he was going from Dublin one day, and met a boy who had one of those English sparrows in his hand. It was frightened, and just seemed to sit as if it pined for liberty, but the boy held it so tight that it could not get away. The boy's strength was too much for the bird. My friend said, "Open your hand and let the bird go. You will never tame him, he is wild." But the boy replied, "Faith and I'll not; I've been a whole hour trying to catch him, an' now I've got him, I'm going to keep him."

So the man took out his purse and asked the boy if he would sell it. A bargain was made, and the sparrow was transferred to the man's hand. He opened his hand, and at first it did not seem to realize it had liberty, but by and by it flew away, and as it went it chirped, as much as to say, "You have redeemed me." And so Christ has come down and offered to redeem us and give us liberty when we were bound with sin.

Christ saves, not doctrine; Heart deceitful

Gen. 6:5; Prov. 28:26; Jer. 17:9; Matt. 15:19; Mark 7:21; John 3:16

I can believe God better today than I can my own heart. "The heart is deceitful above all things, and desperately wicked: who can know it?" (Jeremiah 17:9). I can believe God better than I can myself. If you want to know the way of life, believe that Jesus Christ is a personal Savior; cut away from all doctrines and creeds, and come right to the heart of the Son of God. If you have been feeding on dry doctrine, there is not much growth on that kind of food. Doctrines are to the soul what the streets which lead to the house of a friend who has invited me to dinner are to the body. They will lead me there if I take the right one; but if I remain in the streets my hunger will never be satisfied. Feeding on doctrines is like trying to live on dry husks; and lean indeed must the soul remain which partakes not of the Bread sent down from heaven.

Christ, second coming of; Return of Christ

Matt. 23:39; 1 Cor. 1:7; 15:23; 1 Thess. 1:10; 2:19; 3:13; 4:15; 2 Thess. 2:1; Jude 14; Rev. 1:7; 19:11

The devil does not want us to see this truth concerning the return of the Lord, for nothing would wake up the Church so much. The moment a person takes hold of the truth that Jesus Christ is coming back again to receive his friends to himself, this world loses its hold upon him. Gas stocks, stocks in banks and in railroads are of much less consequence. The heart is free to look for the blessed appearing of our Lord, who at his coming will take us into his blessed kingdom.

Christ, second coming of; Return of the Lord

Matt. 23:39; 1 Cor. 1:7; 15:23; 1 Thess. 1:10; 2:19; 3:13; 4:15; 2 Thess. 2:1; Jude 14; Rev. 1:7; 19:11

When Christ returns, he will not be treated as he was before. There will be room for him at Bethlehem. He will be welcome in Jerusalem. He will reveal himself as Joseph revealed himself to his brethren. He will say to the Jews, "I am Jesus," and they will reply, "Blessed is he that cometh in the name of the Lord." And the Jews will then be that nation that shall be born in a day.

Matt. 23:39; 1 Cor. 1:7; 15:23; 1 Thess. 1:10; 2:19; 3:13; 4:15; 2 Thess. 2:1; Jude 14; Rev. 1:7; 19:11

If I write to my wife that I am coming home very soon, that she is not to expect any more letters, but to expect me daily until I come, and if when I get home I find that she has gone away, I will feel that she did not believe what I wrote to her. So the Christian who is not listening always for the footsteps of his Lord, shows that he has little faith in his promise. Some think that when Christ comes, everything will be wound up with a whirl of expectation.

But it was not so when he came before. Men were disappointed in some of their expectations then, and they will be at his second coming.

.Matt. 23:39; 1 Cor. 1:7; 15:23; 1 Thess. 1:10; 2:19; 3:13; 4:15; 2 Thess. 2:1; Jude 14; Rev. 1:7; 19:11

When we see how much sin and sorrow there is in the world, must we not long and pray for the speedy coming of Christ? I don't know all that is going to happen when he comes. I have only settled this one thing, that he is surely coming. That my Bible teaches, and I will not give up the glorious hope until convinced by the Bible that I am wrong. I believe that the next great event on the earth will be the coming of Christ. And when he appears, he will draw unto himself those who love him, as the magnet draws particles of steel. They will fly up to meet their Lord in the air, and the graveyards will bloom with the glorified bodies of the saints. Oh! may these blessed truths stimulate us, and may we all listen for the footsteps of our coming Lord as a loving wife listens for the return of her husband!

Christ seeking sinners

Matt. 9:13; 18:11; Luke 5:32; 15:4; 19:10

There was never a sermon which you have listened to but in it Christ was seeking for you. I contend that a man cannot but find in every page of this book that Jesus Christ is seeking him through his blessed Word. This is what the Bible is for—to seek out the lost.

Matt. 9:13; 18:11; Luke 5:32; 15:4; 19:10

Have not some of you heard a sermon in which you were introduced as a sinner to the Lord Jesus Christ, and your conscience was troubled? You went away, but you came back again, and the Spirit of God came upon you again and again, and you were troubled. Haven't you passed through that experience? Don't you remember something like that happening to you? That was the Son of God seeking for your soul. Won't you yield to him now?

Matt. 9:13; 18:11; Luke 5:32; 15:4; 19:10

The parable of the lost coin shows God as the seeker of souls. Someone perhaps had paid the woman a bill that day, giving her ten pieces of silver. As she retires at night, she takes the money out of her pocket and counts it. "Why," she says, "I have only got nine pieces; I ought to have ten." She counts it over again. "Only nine pieces! Where have I been," she asks, "since I got that money? I am sure I have not been out of the house." She turns her pocket wrong side out, and there she finds a hole in it. Does she wait until the money gets back into her pocket? No. She takes a broom, and lights a candle, and sweeps diligently. She moves the sofa and the table and the chairs, and all the rest of the furniture, and sweeps in every corner until she finds it.

And when she has found it, who rejoices? The piece of money? No; the woman who finds it. In these parables of Luke 15 Christ brings out the great truth that God takes the place of Seeker. People talk of finding Christ, but it is Christ who first finds them.

Christ seeking sinners; Christ, good Shepherd

Ps. 23:1; Isa. 40:11; Matt. 9:13; 18:11; Luke 5:32; 15:4; 19:10; John 10:11; 1 Peter 2:25

What do we read in the fifteenth chapter of St. Luke? There is a shepherd bringing home his sheep into the fold. As they pass in, he stands and numbers them. I can see him counting one, two, three, up to ninety-nine. "But," says he, "I ought to have a hundred: I must have made a mistake"; and he counts them over again. "There are only ninety-nine here; I must have lost one." He does not say, "I will let him find his own way back."

No! He takes the place of the Seeker; he goes out into the mountain, and hunts until he finds the lost one, and then he lays it on his shoulder and brings it home. Is it the sheep that finds the shepherd? No, it is the shepherd that finds and brings back the sheep. He rejoiced to find it. Undoubtedly the sheep was very glad to get back to the fold, but it was the shepherd who rejoiced, and who called his friends and said, "Rejoice with me."

Christ seeking sinners; Conversion of older woman

Matt. 9:13; 18:11; Luke 5:32; 15:4; 19:10

I remember, when we were in London, they found one woman who was eighty-five years old, and not a Christian. After the worker had prayed, she made a prayer herself, "O Lord, I thank you for going out of your way to find me." Christ is all the time going out of his way to find the lost.

Christ, sin bearer; Sin, remedy for

Isa. 53:4; Mal. 4:2; Matt. 8:17; Luke 4:18; John 1:29; Acts 5:30; 10:39; Gal. 3:13; Heb. 9:28; 1 Peter 2:24

Dr. Andrew Bonar once said that, although it was a mystery to him how sin should have come into the world it was still a greater mystery how God should have come here to bear the penalty of it himself.

Christ, sinlessness of

Isa. 42:1; Matt. 3:17; 17:5; John 4:34; 5:30; 6:38; 8:29; 17:4; Heb. 4:15; 7:26; 1 Peter 2:21; 1 John 2:1

Christ kept the law. If he had ever broken it, he would have to die for himself; but because he was a Lamb without spot or blemish, his atoning death is effective for you and me. He had no sin of his own to atone for, and so God accepted his sacrifice. Christ is the end of the law for right-eousness to everyone that believeth. We are righteous in God's sight, because the righteousness of God which is by faith in Jesus Christ is applied to all who believe.

Christ spoke clearly

Exod. 33:11; Matt. 7:29; 23:15; 28:18; Mark 1:27; Luke 11:27

An old Welsh woman said Christ was Welsh, and an Englishman said, "No, he was a Jew." She declared that she knew he was Welsh, because he spoke so that she could understand him.

Christ, time of second coming; Return of the Lord, time of

Matt. 23:39; 24:44; 1 Cor. 1:7; 15:23; 1 Thess. 1:10; 2:19; 3:13; 4:15; 5:2; 2 Thess. 2:1; 2 Peter 3:10; Jude 14; Rev. 1:7; 19:11

The doctrine of the second coming of Christ has suffered a good deal from those who claim to be its friends, because they set a time—a certain day—for his coming. But we read in Matthew 24:36 that no man knows when he shall come. Hence, when a man comes and tells you that he knows when Christ is coming—that he is coming next year—or at any particular time, he has got no truth for that assertion. "The day and the hour knoweth no man." Miller said that Christ would come in 1843. Dr. Cumming, of London, said that he would surely come in 1866. But if we knew the day and the hour of his coming, we wouldn't need to be on alert. All through the Scriptures we are told to watch for his coming. "Therefore be ye also ready, for in such an hour as ye think not the Son of Man cometh."

Matt. 23:39; 1 Cor. 1:7; 15:23; 1 Thess. 1:10; 2:19; 3:13; 4:15; 2 Thess. 2:1; 2 Peter 3:3–4; Jude 14; Rev. 1:7; 19:11

A man said to me yesterday, "I don't propose to trouble myself about Christ's second coming, for it won't be in my day."

How does he know that? Is not that the very spirit which Peter speaks of in 2 Peter 3:3–4? We have no right to say when it will not come, any more than we have to say when it will come.

Matt. 24:14

Some tell us that the world must be converted before the second coming of Christ. But this is not what our Savior taught. Matt. 24:14 states: "And this gospel of the kingdom shall be preached in all the world for a witness unto all nations; and then shall the end come." The gospel is to be preached everywhere as a witness. That may be done, and yet the world be far from being converted. All that is prophesied about the knowledge of the Lord filling the whole earth, and holiness to the Lord being written on everything, refers to the next dispensation—to that of Christ's personal reign.

Christ, trust in; Jesus as physician

2 Chron. 32:7–8; Ps. 9:10; Matt. 2:2; 4:22; 9:12, 21; Mark 1:18; 10:48; Luke 5:6; 18:38; John 6:69; 8:56; Acts 6:8; 8:37; James 2:21, 25

Suppose I have a sick boy. I know nothing about medicine; but I call in the doctor, and put that boy's life and everything into his hands. I do not fail to believe in him; and I do not interfere at all. Do you call that trusting in the dark? Not at all! I used my best judgment, and I put that boy's life into the hand of a good physician. You have a soul diseased. Put it into the hand of Christ, the Great Physician! Trust him, and he will take care of it. He has had some of the most hopeless cases! He was able to heal all that came to him while on earth. He is the same today.

Christ, water of life

Isa. 49:10; 55:1; John 4:14; 6:35; 7:38

There was a young woman who lived among the mountains going to a spring for water. When she found it dry she started to go up higher to another spring. On the way a friend met her and learning of her quest asked her what she would do if she found that spring dry too. She answered that she would go up still higher to another spring that she knew always flowed. So, my friends, if the springs we have been drinking out of have got dry, let us go a little higher up. There we will find a fountain that has never yet been dry. It bursts forth from the throne of God; it is the pure stream of the water of life.

Christ, worth hearing

Prov. 8:34; Matt. 7:21; Luke 10:39; John 8:31; James 1:22

I would rather a thousand times be five minutes at the feet of Christ than listen a lifetime to all the wise men in the world. If you want to get heavenly wisdom you must pass through God's college. Do you know where that is? Why, at the feet of Christ. Mary of Bethany found her place there. You may go to Oxford or Cambridge, or anywhere else, but if you have not been to God's seminary you will never be fit for heaven. Christ puts the truth so plain that even the little children can get hold of it.

Christ, wrong views of; Commandment, second

Acts 17:29

Worship involves two things: the internal belief, and the external act. We transgress in our hearts by having a wrong conception of God and of Jesus Christ before ever we give public expression in action. As someone has said, "It is wrong to have sinful opinions as well as to be guilty of sinful practices." The wrong opinions that some people hold about Christ are not in accordance with the Bible and are real violations of the second commandment.

Christ's second coming and evangelism

Matt. 23:39; 1 Cor. 1:7; 15:23; 1 Thess. 1:10; 2:19; 3:13; 4:15; 2 Thess. 2:1; Jude 14; Rev. 1:7; 19:11

The church is cold and formal; may God wake us up! And I know of no better way to do it than to set the church to looking for the return of our Lord. Some people say, "Oh, you will discourage the new converts if you preach that doctrine." Well, my friends, that hasn't been my experience. I have felt like working three times as hard ever since I came to understand that my Lord was coming back again. I look on this world as a wrecked vessel. God has given me a lifeboat, and said to me, "Moody, save all you can." This world is getting darker and darker; its ruin is coming nearer and nearer; if you have any friends on this wreck unsaved you had better lose no time in getting them off.

Christ's second coming, anticipating

Matt. 23:39; 1 Cor. 1:7; 15:23; 1 Thess. 1:10; 2:19; 3:13; 4:15; 2 Thess. 2:1; Jude 14; Rev. 1:7; 19:11

I can't find any place in the Bible where it tells me to wait for signs of the coming of the millennium, as the return of the Jews, and such like; but it tells me to look for the coming of the Lord; to watch for it; to be ready at midnight to meet him, like those five wise virgins. The trump of God may be sounded, for anything we know, before I finish this sermon; at any rate we are told that he will come as a thief in the night, and at an hour when many look not for him.

Christians as lights

Matt. 5:13–14; Eph. 5:8; Phil. 2:15

The eyes of the world are upon us. George Fox, the leader of the Quakers, said every Quaker ought to light up the country for ten miles around him. If we were all brightly shining for Christ, those about us would soon be reached, and there would be a shout of praise going to heaven.

Christlikeness, our opportunity

John 17:19, 23; Rom. 8:29; 2 Cor. 3:18; Eph. 1:11, 18; 4:24; 2 Peter 1:4; 1 John 3:2

A beggar does not enjoy looking at a palace. The grandeur of its architecture is lost upon him. Looking upon a royal banquet does not satisfy the hunger of a starving man. But seeing heaven is also having a share in it. There would be no joy there, if we did not feel that some of it was ours. God unites the soul to himself. As it says in 2 Peter 1:4, we are made partakers of the divine nature. Now if you put a piece of iron in the fire, it very soon loses its dark color, and becomes red and hot like the fire, but it does not lose its iron nature. So the soul becomes bright with God's brightness, beautiful with God's beauty, pure with God's purity, and warm with the glow of his perfect love, and yet remains a human soul. We shall be like him, but remain ourselves.

Church a place for work

1 Cor. 15:58; 2 Cor. 9:8; Eph. 4:12; Phil. 2:20; Col. 1:10; 1 Thess. 1:3; 1 Tim. 3:1; 5:10; 2 Tim. 4:5; Titus 3:1; Heb. 4:9; 6:10; James 1:25

Now, while we all need rest, I fear a great many people make a mistake when they think the church is a place of rest; and when they unite with the church they have a false idea about their position in it. There are a great many that come in to rest. The Bible says, "There remaineth a rest for the people of God," but it doesn't tell us that the church is a place of rest; we have all eternity to rest. We are to rest by and by; but we are to work here, and when our work is finished, the Lord will call us home to enjoy that rest. There is no use in talking about rest down here in the enemy's country. We cannot rest in this world, where God's Son has been crucified and cast out. I think that a great many people are going to lose their reward just because they have come into the church with the idea that they are to rest there.

Church effectiveness, key to

Rom. 12:2; Eph. 4:17

God's line of work is to begin with his own people. It is said that when Mr. Spurgeon went up to London to preach, for six months he preached to the church. For some time he preached to the elders of the church, and when he had preached to them for some time, one of them thought he had better let them alone and get at the outsiders. But his preaching hadn't straightened them out, and he saw he was going to keep at them until they were all right, and then he would go at the church.

When he got the church right, then it began to grow, and it grew for thirty or forty years. When the church gets quickened and is all right, there can be more accomplished in one day than you can accomplish in years when the church is not all right. I believe that it is the experience of most all men that have tried to do God's work when the church is right, then it is very easy to reach those that are wrong.

Church, getting it to work

1 Cor. 15:58; 2 Cor. 9:8; Eph. 4:12; Phil. 2:20; Col. 1:10; 1 Thess. 1:3; 1 Tim. 3:1; 5:10; 2 Tim. 4:5; Titus 3:1; Heb. 4:9; 6:10; James 1:25

People ask me, "How would you get a church to work?" Well, first, I would go to work myself. Some are always telling others to go to work, and they don't go themselves. Get a few people blest, and others will come and want to go to work. I never saw a working Christian yet but what he

was a rejoicing one. When you are working you are not troubled with doubts. Christians wonder why they have so many doubts. It is because they are all the time occupied with themselves. We must work for others, and if we work for others we shall ourselves be blest. "He that watereth shall himself be watered."

Church, how to fill a; Witness, lay

1 Thess. 1:3; 2:4

I don't believe there is a minister but would have a full house if he would just work for it. A few years ago, before I thought I could preach, we built a hall in Chicago for the Young Men's Christian Association, and our plan was to get the different ministers to go there every Sunday night and preach, but we failed in that; we couldn't get many to come, and the ministers didn't like to go there to preach, and so one night they came to me and wanted me to go down there and preach.

It was pretty hard to preach to empty chairs. But I got a few interested in the meeting and then we got out some handbills that cost about sixty cents a thousand. We took some of the young men and got them to come together every night in the hall, and we gave them some tea and they prayed together; and they took these handbills and went out on the street. Every man had a district, and they visited every saloon and billiard hall and bowling alley, and there was not a man who came within a mile of the building but got from one to half a dozen of these invitations to come to that meeting.

And when a man was converted we yoked him up with another, two and two, and sent them out to bring others, and that is the way we did it, and we have always had an audience ever since. Now if people won't come to our churches, let us go for them in that way and keep the church awake. If a man goes out on the street trying to get people to come into the church and he gets another man to come in, he will not go to sleep. He will try to have that man interested in the preaching and if he does not like the sermon, he will go to the minister afterwards and say, "You must make that sermon plainer; that man that I brought didn't understand it."

Church, importance of

Acts 16:5; 1 Thess. 2:14; 2 Thess. 1:4

Let me speak to some of these new converts. I have heard it said that they are not going to unite themselves to any church. They think that they will sustain themselves outside of the church. They can't find a perfect church to go into. Now let me say that if you do not join a church until you find a perfect one, you will never find it. I have got done looking for a perfect church, a perfect minister, or a perfect anything upon earth. But there is nothing so dear to the Son of God as the church. Join one now and start working for your Lord.

A man told me that he would not stay here long, probably not more than a year or two, and it would not be worthwhile to join a church here. Well, can't you move your letter as easily as you can move your trunk? If I was going into fifty different towns I would carry a traveling letter, or take fifty letters. I would belong to fifty churches. Now, if you want to be a useful, happy Christian, just get to work and do not go to sleep. We have enough of sleepy Christians. If a church has nothing for you to do, do not go into it. Find some church where you can find something to do. If you want to be a healthy Christian, you have got to work. Joseph's captivity was turned when he began to work for others.

Church membership, necessity of

Acts 16:5; 1 Thess. 2:14; 2 Thess. 1:4

It is important for a person to be a member of some church. I want to say once

and for all that I have no sympathy whatever for these professing Christians outside the church who are too good to unite with the church. I believe that the best people in this world, and the best people during the last six thousand years, have always identified themselves with God's people, and taken their stand. I believe it is the best institution under heaven. If I have said anything that the enemies of Christ have taken up and that has given the impression that I am not a member of a church, I want them to understand that I am an officer in the church, and that I shall remain an officer in that church until my time expires, and I shall remain a member, unless they turn me out, as long as I live, of some church.

Comfort, source of; Burdens, help for

Isa. 40:1; Rom. 15:5; 2 Cor. 1:3; 1 Peter 5:7

I like to think of Christ as a burden bearer. A minister was one day moving his library upstairs. As he was going up with a load of books, his little boy came in, and was very anxious to help his father. So his father just told him to go and get an armful, and bring them upstairs. When the father came back, he met the little fellow about halfway up, tugging away at the biggest book in the library. He couldn't manage to carry it up. It was too big. So he sat down and cried. His father found him, and just took him in his arms, book and all, and carried him upstairs. So Christ will carry you and all your burdens, if you will but let him.

Commandments for our good; Parental discipline, importance of

Exod. 20:12; Heb. 12:9

Dr. Willie Arnot, one of the greatest Scotch preachers, told me that his mother died when he was a little boy. There was a large family of Arnots. They all missed the tenderness and love of their mother. They got the impression that their father was very stern and rigid, and that he had a great many laws and rules. One rule was, that the children should never climb trees. When the neighbor boys found out that the Arnot children could not climb trees, they told them that climbing trees was just about the best thing a boy could ever do. They told them about the wonderful things they could see from the tops of the trees. Well, tell a boy that he mustn't climb a tree, and he will get up that tree some way. And so the Arnot children were all the time teasing their father to let them climb trees: but their father always said, "No."

One day he was busy reading his paper, and the boys said: "Father is reading his paper. Let's slip down into the lot and climb a tree." Willie stood on the top of the fence to see that father did not catch them. When his brother got up on the first branch, he said, "What do you see?" "Why! I don't see anything." "Then go higher; you haven't got high enough." So up he went higher, and again Willie asked, "Well, what do you see now?" "I don't see anything." "You aren't high enough; go higher."

And the little fellow went up as high as he could go, but he slipped, and down he came, and broke his leg. Willie said he tried to get him into the house, but he couldn't do it. He had to tell his father all about it. He said he was scared nearly out of his wits. He thought his father would be very angry. But he went in and confessed everything. His father surprised him. He just threw aside the paper, and started for the lot. When he got there, he picked the wounded brother up in his arms, and brought him up to the house. Then he sent for the doctor and Willie said, "It seemed like my father was my mother." Willie had got a new view of his father. He found out the reason why he was so stern. The rules were for their protection and guidance.

My dear friends, there is not one of God's commandments that has been given us which has not been for our highest and best interest. There isn't a commandment that hasn't come from the loving heart of God, and what he desires is to have us give up that which is going to mar our happiness in this life, and in the life to come.

Concern for others

Gen. 4:9

Here is a young man. He is the only son of a widowed mother, whose husband died and left her bankrupt. She has toiled hard to give her son an education. She has watched over him with the most tender care, and he leaves home with high hopes of being a comfort and blessing to that mother in her declining years. He has gone down to college, and, as is so often said, he is "easily influenced." If he is easily influenced for bad, why not for good? Somebody has tempted him, and has led him into sins of which he had never dreamed. He has fallen into the depths of wickedness, and is fast reaping the wages of sin. Many a young man has gone from a home like that, and before his college course has closed has been put into his coffin and sent back to his mother.

Some years ago a man living on the banks of a lake, one cold night when the thermometer was below zero, heard a cry of distress. A man out skating had gone through the ice, and it is supposed that he had got hold of the ice, and kept his head above the water, and called for help. The man heard his cries, but said, "It is none of my business. It is a cold night, and I don't want to get up and go out. No one had any business to go out there skating, anyway."

The cries became fainter and fainter, and finally ceased. The next day the body was found. The man was foolish enough to tell what he had heard, and that whole population rose up in indignation and hounded him out of town. They said he wasn't fit to live among them. Everyone would say, "That is true"; and yet is he any worse than one who will see a young man go down through drink, and not lift his hand to help him? Where is thy brother?

Confession, importance of

Luke 15:18; 1 Cor. 11:31; Rev. 2:5

Richard Sibbes quaintly says of confession, "This is the way to give glory to God: let us lay open our souls to God, and lay as much against ourselves as the devil could do. Let us accuse ourselves as he would, and as he will before long. The more we accuse and judge ourselves, and set up a tribunal in our hearts, the more our conscience will receive wonderful ease."

2 Sam. 12:13; Ps. 51:4; Luke 15:21

Thomas Fuller says, "Man's admitting his weakness is the only stock for God thereon to graft the grace of his assistance."

Confession of sin

Dan. 9:4; Ps. 32:5

There may be some confessions we need to make to be brought into close fellowship with God. We must cooperate with God. You may take a bottle and cork it up tightly, and put it under the Niagara Falls, and not a drop of that mighty volume of water will get into the bottle. If there is any sin in my heart that I am not willing to confess and to give up, I need not expect a blessing. The men who have had power with God in prayer have always begun by confessing their sins. Take the prayers of Jeremiah and Daniel. We find Daniel confessing his sin, when there isn't a single sin recorded against him.

Confession, power of

Lev. 16:21; Neh. 1:6; James 5:16

A minister's sister married a lawyer who was a very prominent man, but an unbeliever. She thought that she was going to win her husband to Christ, and she was constantly holding up her brother as a most lovable and beautiful character, a man with a great deal of self-control. This irritated the husband, and he said to himself, "I will bring that man down. I will show my wife that her brother is not so angelic as she thinks he is." So one evening the lawyer accused the brother of doing a very disreputable thing. The minister denied it, but the lawyer insisted that the evidence against him was well supported. The brother flew into a rage and said, "I won't stay in this house if you think that of me!" He got up and went out, and slammed the door after him. After he was gone the lawyer said to his wife, "Your brother is very angelic, isn't he? I tell you, he's no better than the rest of us."

The next morning the minister was at the door of his brother-in-law's house. The minister said, "I want to apologize for speaking to you as I did last night. I am very sorry I lost my temper, and I want you to forgive me." The lawyer had to admit that he had accused him unjustly and when the minister left, he said to his wife, "I believe your brother is a Christian if there ever was one. I never would have done that. I believe in Christianity of that kind." And he, too, soon became a Christian. It takes a hero to confess!

Confession, public

Matt. 10:32; Luke 12:8; Acts 24:14; Rom. 15:9

I remember some meetings being held in a locality where responses did not come very quickly, and bitter and reproachful things were being said about the work. But one day, one of the most prominent men in the place rose and made public confession of his faith in Christ saying, "I want it to be known that I am a disciple of Jesus Christ; and if there is any odium to be cast on his cause, I am prepared to take my share of it." It went through the meeting like an electric current, and a blessing came at once to his own soul and to the souls of others.

Confession vs. profession; Character, importance of

John 12:42; James 2:20; Rev. 3:5

You may very often see dead fish floating with the stream, but you never saw dead fish swimming against it. Well, that is your false believer. Profession is just floating down the stream, but confession is swimming against it, no matter how strong the tide.

Confidence, based on Scripture; Security grounded in Bible

Matt. 7:24; 24:35; Mark 13:31; Luke 21:33

If God has hid me in the secret pavilion, let men slander me and abuse me if they like! If I can say that God is my Father, Jesus is my Savior, and heaven is my home, let the world rail, let the flesh do what it pleases, I will not be afraid of evil tidings, for my trust is in God! Isn't that a good footing for eternity? "Heaven and earth shall pass away, but my word shall not pass away." If you get your feet fair and square on the rock, let the waves beat if they will. A Christian once said that he trembled sometimes, but the foundation never did: he had his feet upon the rock.

Conflict resolution

Prov. 16:32; 18:10; Rom. 14:21

I firmly believe it is much easier to keep railroad cars on the track than to get them back on after they have once been thrown off.

Conflict resolution; Love begets love

Matt. 7:12; Rom. 13:10; Gal. 5:14; 1 Tim. 1:5; James 2:8

You may have heard of the boy whose home was in a forest. One day he thought he heard the voice of another boy not far off. He shouted, "Hallo, there!" and the voice shouted back, "Hallo, there!" He did not know that it was the echo of his own voice, and he shouted again, "You are a mean boy!" Again the cry came back, "You are a mean boy!" After some more of the same kind of thing he went into the house and told his mother that there was a bad boy in the wood. His mother, who understood how it was, said to him: "Oh, no! You speak kindly to him, and see if he does not speak kindly to you."

He went to the wood again and shouted, "Hallo there!" "Hallo, there!" "You are a good boy." Of course the reply came, "You are a good boy." "I love you." "I love you," said the other voice. This little story explains the secret of the whole thing. Some of you perhaps think you have bad and disagreeable neighbors; most likely the trouble is with yourself. If you love your neighbors, they will love you. Love begets love.

Confrontation, spiritual; Witness, consistent

Num. 20:10; 2 Sam. 12:5; Job 2:10; Matt. 16:23; Rev. 3:19

I would rather see people angry than see them go to sleep. I would rather see a man get as angry as possible at anything that I may say than send him to sleep. When a man's asleep there's no chance of reaching him, but if he is angry we may get at him. It is a good thing for a man to get angry sometimes, for when he cools off he generally listens to reason.

Conscience, awaking of

Rom. 2:15; 1 Cor. 8:7; 1 Tim. 1:9; 4:2

When I was in London I went into a wax work there—Tassands—and I went into the Chamber of Horror. There were wax figures of all kinds of murderers in that room. There was Booth who killed Lincoln, and many of that type. But there was one figure I got interested in, who killed his wife because he loved another woman, and the law didn't find him out. He married this other woman and had a family of seven children. And twenty years passed away. Then his conscience began to trouble him. He had no rest; he would hear his murdered wife pleading continually for her life.

His friends began to think that he was going out of his mind: he became haggard and his conscience haunted him till, at last he went to the officers of the law and told them that he was guilty of murder. He wanted to die, life was so much of an agony to him. His conscience turned against him. My friends if you have done wrong, may your conscience be awakened, and may you testify against yourself. It is a great deal better to judge your own acts and confess them, than go through this world with the curse upon you.

Conscience, education of; Bible, standard of truth

Acts 23:1; 24:16; Rom. 2:15; 9:1; 13:5; 2 Cor. 1:12; 1 Tim. 1:15; 1 Peter 3:16

Sometimes we hear men say, "Oh, I don't see any harm in this. My conscience doesn't condemn me." It isn't your conscience, or your consciousness, that is the rule of right and wrong. The word of God is the standard. By the Word is the knowledge of sin. Sin is the transgression of God's Word; not of conscience. Keep teaching your conscience God's Word.

Conscience, nature of

Acts 23:1; 24:16; Rom. 2:15; 9:1; 13:5; 2 Cor. 1:12; 1 Tim. 1:15; 1 Peter 3:16

Conscience is "a divinely implanted faculty in people, telling them that they ought to do right." Someone has said that it was born when Adam and Eve ate of the forbidden fruit, when their eyes were opened and they "knew good and evil." It passes judgment, without being invited, upon our thoughts, words, and actions, approving or condemning according as it judges them to be right or wrong. A person cannot violate conscience without being self-condemned.

But conscience is not a safe guide, because very often it will not tell you a thing is wrong until you have done it. It needs illuminating by God's Word because it partakes of our fallen nature. Many a person does things that are wrong without being condemned by conscience. Paul said: "I verily thought with myself that I ought to do many things contrary to the name of Jesus of Nazareth." Conscience needs to be educated. Conscience is too often like an alarm clock, which awakens a man at first, but after a time the man becomes used to it, and it loses its effect. Conscience can be smothered.

Conscience, power of

Rom. 2:15; 1 Cor. 8:7; 1 Tim. 1:9; 4:2

You often take up the papers and read, "Murder will out." What does that mean? Conscience has become aroused. A minister in Cleveland went to visit a prisoner in the city jail. He was there awaiting his trial. He was accused of murder; but few believed that he was guilty. But in the cell he confessed to the minister that he had done the deed. His friends said it was impossible. He could not have done it. But the man explained how he did it. He said the reason that he made the confession was, "Because I wanted to get away from myself." That is it. He wanted to get away from the cry of his conscience. How it is that men dare to sin, then laugh and mock at sin, with eternity opening up before them, is one of the greatest mysteries of the day. The Bible talks about the mystery of godliness, but that men will trifle with sin, and mock and laugh at sin, is a greater mystery to me.

Conscience, power of; Restitution, example of

Rom. 2:15; 1 Cor. 8:7; 1 Tim. 1:9; 4:2

When I was in Canada a man told me that when he was a boy a man gave him by mistake a piece of money that was called in Canada a "ten shilling" piece. It was just about the size of a quarter of a dollar, and it was gold. Instead of giving the boy a silver shilling, as intended, the man gave him a gold ten shilling piece by mistake, and the boy kept it. The next day the man came back to the boy and said, "When I made change with you yesterday, didn't I give you a ten shilling piece instead of a one shilling piece?" The boy lied, "No, sir, you did not."

For forty-three years that man had that lie on his conscience. At last the Spirit of God got hold of him and he became a Christian. He no longer knew where to find the man so he just figured up the interest and handed principal and interest to an orphanage. So he got it off his conscience at last. If you have anything on your conscience, straighten it out at once. If your mind goes back to some transaction with your neighbor in which you cheated him, pay back every dollar at once.

Consecration, fruit of; Vision, spiritual; Seeking higher life

Matt. 9:13; 18:11; Luke 5:32; 15:4; 19:10

A traveler once made arrangements with a guide to take him to the top of a high mountain to see the sunrise. They had not journeyed long when there arose a terrible thunderstorm. "It's no use to go on," the gentleman said. "We cannot see the sunrise in the midst of this fearful storm." "O, sir," said the guide, "we shall soon get above the storm." They could see the lightning playing about them, and the grand old mountain shook with the thunder, and it was very dark; but when they passed up above the clouds all was light and clear. So if it is dark here, rise higher; it is light enough up around the throne. If I may rise up to the light, I have no business to be in darkness. Rise higher, higher, higher. It is the privilege of the child of God to walk on unclouded.

Contentment, importance of; Provision, God's abundant

Exod. 2:21; Luke 3:14; Phil. 4:11; 1 Tim. 6:8; Heb. 13:5

Ira Sankey, D. L. Moody's song leader, told of an incident that had occurred in his home in Brooklyn one Christmas, while he was in San Francisco. His little boy awoke about 4 o'clock in the morning, and got up to see what was in his stocking. He found a box of paints and a little book. He said, "Santa Claus knew just what I wanted," and went off contentedly to sleep. When he arose at the usual time he was shown in a lower room a whole tree full of presents for him. He was satisfied with the trifles which he thought were all he was to get, and what was the joy of the mother to lead him into the place where greater things were prepared for him. When Christians are grateful for what they have already received, the Lord delights to give them far greater blessings.

Contrition, importance of

Pss. 34:18; 51:17; Isa. 57:15; 66:2

A man may get angry, and if there is not much contrition, the next day he will get angry again. A daughter may say mean, cutting things to her mother, and then her conscience troubles her, and she says, "Mother, I am sorry: forgive me." But soon there is another outburst of temper, because the contrition is not deep and real. A husband speaks sharp words to his wife, and then to ease his conscience he goes and buys her a bouquet of flowers. He will not go like a man and say he has done wrong. What God wants is contrition, and if there is not contrition, there is not true repentance. Many sinners are sorry for their sins, sorry that they cannot continue in sin; but they repent only with hearts that are not broken.

Contrition, importance of; Reverence, importance of

Job 25:6; Isa. 6:3; Rev. 4:8; 15:4

I am sometimes ashamed of myself to think how fluent I am when I go into the presence of God. As if I were on an equal footing with him; as if there were no difference between us. Let us bear in mind that God is holy. The nearer we get to him, the more we should think of his holiness and abhor ourselves. We shall grow smaller and he larger. One of the truest signs that a man is growing great is that God increases and he decreases. Why, some people will talk about themselves by the yard. "I, I, I, I." There will be forty-nine I's in a speech five minutes long. That is a sign that you are not growing in grace, but you are growing in conceit. But when we get near to God, how small we look, and how great God seems. When Isaiah saw God, he cried, "Holy, holy, holy is the Lord of Hosts." And then what did he cry? That he was unclean and dwelt with unclean people, and he wanted his iniquity purged and taken away.

Conversion, example of; Bible, power of; Scripture, power of

Ps. 119:130; Isa. 55:11; Jer. 23:29; 1 Thess. 2:11; Heb. 4:12; 1 Peter 1:23

An infidel had come to one of our meetings and when I talked with him, he replied that he didn't believe one-twelfth part of the Bible, but I kept on quoting Scripture, feeling that if the man didn't believe, God could do what he chose with his Word, and make it quick and powerful, and sharper than a two-edged sword. The man kept saying that he did not believe what the Bible said, and I kept on quoting passage after passage of Scripture, and the man, who, two hours before, had entered the hall an infidel, went out of it a converted man, and a short time after his conversion he left Chicago for Boston, a Christian, to join his family in Europe. Before this gentleman went away, I asked him if he believed the Bible, and his reply was, "From front to back, every word of it."

Conversion, instantaneous; Restitution, importance of

Luke 19:6, 8; Acts 9:6

There are some people who do not believe in sudden conversions. I should like them to tell me when Zacchaeus was converted. He certainly was not converted when he went up into the sycamore tree; he certainly was converted when he came down. He must have been converted somewhere between the branches and the ground. I wish we had a few men converted like Zacchaeus here in London; it would make no small stir. When a man begins to make restitution it is a pretty good sign of conversion. Zacchaeus gave half his goods all at once; and he says, "If I have taken any thing from any man I restore him fourfold." I imagine the next morning one of the servants of Zacchaeus going with a check for $1000, and saying, "My master, a few years ago, took from you wrongfully about $250, and this is restitution money." That would give confidence in Zacchaeus's conversion.

Conversion, meaning of

1 Kings 8:35; 2 Chron. 6:24; 7:14; Ezek. 18:27; Rom. 6:1; 1 John 3:9

Unless our repentance includes conversion, it is not worth much. If a person continues in sin, it is proof of an idle profession. It is like pumping away continually at the ship's pumps without stopping the leaks. Solomon said, "If they pray, and confess thy name, and turn from their sin. . . ." Prayer and confession would be of no avail while they continued in sin.

Conversion of skeptical woman

Acts 9:6

When Mr. Sankey and I were in the north of England, I was preaching one evening, and before me sat a lady who was a skeptic. When I had finished, I asked all who were concerned about their souls to remain. Nearly all remained, herself among the number. I asked her if she was a Christian, and she said she was not, nor did she care to be. I prayed for her there. On inquiry, I learned that she was a lady of good social position, but very worldly. She continued to attend the meetings, and in a week after I saw her in tears. After the sermon, I went to her and asked if she was of the same mind as before. She replied that Christ had come to her and she was happy.

Last autumn I had a note from her husband saying she was dead, that her love for the Master had continually increased. When I read that note, I felt paid for crossing the Atlantic. She worked sweetly after her conversion, and was the means of winning many of her fashionable friends to Christ. Oh, may you seek the Lord while he may be found, and may you call upon him while he is near.

Conversion of skeptics

1 Cor. 15:3–4, 14

It is said of West, an eminent man, that he was going to take up the doctrine of the resurrection, and just show the world what a fraud it was, while Lord Lyttleton was going to take up the conversion of Saul, and just show the folly of it. These men were going to annihilate that doctrine and that incident of the gospel conversion. A Frenchman said it took twelve fishermen to build up Christ's religion, but one Frenchman pulled it down.

West got at it and began to look at the evidence; but instead of his being able to cope with it, he found it perfectly overwhelming—the proof that Christ had risen, that he had come out of the sepulcher and ascended to heaven. The light dawned upon him, and he became an expounder of the Word of God and a champion of Christianity. And Lord Lyttleton, that infidel and skeptic, hadn't been long at the conversion of Saul before the God of Saul broke upon his sight, and he too began to preach.

Conversion of youth; Religious education of children

Matt. 19:14; Mark 10:14; Luke 18:16; Acts 2:39; 2 Tim. 1:5

I have no sympathy with the idea that our children have to grow up before they are converted. Once I saw a lady with three daughters at her side, and I stepped up to her and asked her if she was a Christian. "Yes, sir." Then I asked the oldest daughter if she was a Christian. Her chin began to quiver, and the tears came into her eyes, and she said, "I wish I were."

The mother looked very angrily at me and said, "I don't want you to speak to my children on that subject. They don't understand." And in great rage she took them away from me. One daughter was fourteen years old, one twelve, and the other ten, but they were not old enough to be talked to about religion! Let them drift into the world and plunge into worldly amusements, and then see how hard it is to reach them. Many a mother is mourning today because her boy has gone beyond her reach. In those early days when his mind was tender and young, she might have led him to Christ.

Conversion, work of God; Salvation, divine activity

John 1:46; Rom. 3:23; Eph. 2:5

So we say to you, "Come and see!" I thought, when I was converted, that my friends had been very unfaithful to me, because they had not told me about Christ. I thought I would have all my friends converted inside of twenty-four hours, and I was quite disappointed when they did not at once see Christ to be the Lily of the Valley, and the Rose of Sharon, and the Bright and Morning Star. I wondered why it was. But we need to learn that God alone can do that.

Converts, work of

Isa. 25:1; Matt. 10:32; Luke 12:8; Acts 24:14; 1 John 4:15

When a man is converted let us have him in these meetings giving his testimony. Some are afraid of that. I believe the secret of John Wesley's success was that he sent every man to work as soon as he was converted. Of course you have to guard that point. Some say new converts become spiritually proud—no doubt of that but if they don't go to work they become spiritually lazy, and I don't know what's the difference.

Conviction, importance of

Heb. 2:1; 1 Peter 3:15

I like a man to be able to give a reason for the faith that is in him. Once I asked a man what he believed, and he said he believed what his church believed. I asked him what his church believed, and he said he supposed his church believed what he did, and that was all I could get out of him. And so men believe what other people believe and what their church believes, without really knowing what their church and other people do believe.

Conviction, lack of; Denial of spiritual need

Gen. 3:10; Prov. 13:7; Hosea 12:8; Luke 6:24; 18:11; John 9:10; 1 Cor. 4:8; 2 Peter 1:9; Rev. 3:17

A black preacher once said that a good many of his congregation would be lost because they were too generous. He saw that the people looked rather surprised, so he said, "Perhaps you think I have made a mistake, and that I ought to have said you will be lost because you are not generous enough. That is not so; I meant just what I said. You give away too many sermons. You hear them, as it were, for other people." There are a good many who listen for those behind them; they say the message is very good for neighbor so-and-so; and they pass it over their shoulders, till it gets clear out of the door.

Conviction of sin, importance of; Conversion, thorough

Num. 12:11; Josh. 7:20; Ps. 51:4; Micah 7:9; Luke 15:18

One thing I have noticed, that some conversions don't amount to anything; that if a man professes to be converted without conviction of sin, he is one of those stony-ground hearers who don't bring forth much fruit. The first little wave of persecution, the first breath of opposition, and the man is back in the world again. Let us pray that God may carry on a deep and thorough work, that people may be convicted of sin so that they cannot rest in unbelief. Pray that this conviction and confession may begin in our own church. I would a great deal rather see a hundred men thoroughly converted, truly born of God, than to see a thousand professed conversions where the Spirit of God has not convicted of sin.

Covetousness, control of; Commandment, tenth

Ps. 49:16–17; Acts 20:33; Col. 3:5; 1 Tim. 6:6, 8; Heb. 13:5–6

You ask me how you are to cast the unclean spirit of covetousness out of your heart? In the first place, make up your mind that by the grace of God you will overcome the spirit of selfishness. You must overcome it, or it will overcome you. In the next place, cultivate the spirit of contentment. Contentment is the very opposite of covetousness, which is continually craving for something it does not possess (Heb. 13:5). "Be content with such things as ye have," not worrying about the future, because God has promised never to leave or forsake you. What does the child of God need more than this? I would rather have that promise than all the gold of the earth.

Would to God that we might be able to say with Paul, "I have coveted no man's silver, or gold, or apparel" (Acts 20:33). The Lord had made Paul partaker of his grace, and he was soon to be a partaker of his glory, and earthly things looked very small. "Godliness with contentment is great gain," he wrote to Timothy, "having food and raiment therewith let us be content" (1 Tim. 6:6, 8). Observe that he puts godliness first. No worldly gain can satisfy the human heart. Roll the whole world in, and still there would be room.

May God tear the scales off our eyes if we are blinded by this sin of covetousness. Oh, the folly of it, that we should set our heart's affections upon anything below! For we brought nothing into this world, and it is certain we can carry nothing out (Ps. 49:16–17).

Covetousness, danger of; Commandment, tenth

Job. 1:21; Pss. 73:19; 78:30; Jer. 17:11; Dan. 5:1; Luke 12:20; 16:22; 1 Tim. 6:7; James 4:14

An English clergyman was called to the death bed of a wealthy parishioner. Kneeling beside the dying man the pastor asked him to take his hand as he prayed for his upholding in that solemn hour, but the man declined to give his hand. After the end had come, and they turned down the coverlet, the rigid hands were found holding the key to his safe in their death grip. Heart and hand, to the last, clinging to his possessions, but he could not take them with him.

Prov. 1:19; 15:27; Isa. 56:11; 1 Tim. 3:3; 1 Peter 5:2

I have read of a millionaire in France who was a miser. In order to make sure of his wealth, he dug a secret cave in his wine cellar so large and deep that he could go down into it with a ladder. The entrance had a door with a spring lock. After a time, he was missing. Search was made, but they could find no trace of him. At last his house was sold, and the purchaser discovered this door in the cellar. He opened it, went down, and found the miser lying dead on the ground in the midst of his riches. The door must have shut accidentally after him, and he perished miserably.

Covetousness, danger of; Commandment, tenth; Character, importance of

Exod. 18:21, 24; Ps. 10:3; 1 Thess. 2:5

Isn't it extraordinary that Jethro, the man of the desert, should have advised Moses to appoint men of character who were free of covetousness to positions of authority in Israel? How did he learn to beware of covetousness? We honor men today if they are wealthy and covetous. We elect them to office in church and state. We often say that they will make better treasurers because we know them to be covetous. But in God's sight a covetous man is as vile and black as any thief or drunkard. David said, "The wicked boasteth of his heart's desire, and blesseth the covetous, whom the Lord abborreth." I am afraid that many who profess to have put away wickedness also speak well of the covetous.

Covetousness, danger of; Hearts, searcher of; Commandment, tenth

1 Sam. 16:7; 1 Chron. 28:9; Ps. 7:9; Luke 16:15; Acts 1:24; 2 Cor. 10:7; Heb. 4:13

It would be absurd for such a law as the tenth commandment to be placed upon any human statute book. It could never be enforced. The officers of the law would be powerless to detect infractions. The outward conduct may be regulated, but the thoughts and intents of a man are beyond the reach of human law.

But God can see behind outward actions. He can read the thoughts of the heart. Our innermost life, invisible to mortal eye, is laid bare before him. We cannot deceive him by external conformity. He is able to detect the least transgression and shortcoming, so that no man can shirk detection. God cannot be imposed upon by the cleanness of the outside of the cup and the platter.

Surely, we have here another proof that the Ten Commandments are not of human origin, but must be divine. This tenth commandment, then, did not, even on the surface, confine itself to visible actions, as did the preceding commandments. Even before Christ came and showed their spiritual sweep, men had a commandment that went beneath public conduct and touched the very springs of action. It directly prohibited—not the wrong act, but the wicked desire that prompted the act. It forbade the evil thought, the unlawful wish. It sought to prevent—not only sin, but the desire to sin. In God's sight it is as wicked to set covetous eyes as it is to lay thieving hands upon anything that is not ours.

And why? Because if the evil desire can be controlled, there will be no outbreak in conduct. Desire has been called "actions in the egg." The desire in the heart is the first step in the series that ends in action. Kill the evil desire, and you successfully avoid the ill results that would follow upon its hatching and development. Prevention is better than cure.

Covetousness, deceitfulness of; Commandment, tenth

Gen. 13:11; 2 Sam. 11:3; Matt. 13:22; Mark 4:19; 2 Thess. 2:10; Heb. 3:13

The Bible speaks of the deceitfulness of two things—"the deceitfulness of sin" and "the deceitfulness of riches." Riches are like a mirage in the desert which has all the appearance of satisfying and lures the traveler on with the promise of water and shade; but he only wastes his strength in the effort to reach it. So riches never satisfy: the pursuit of them always turns out a snare.

Lot coveted the rich plains of Sodom, and what did he gain? After twenty years spent in that wicked city, he had to escape for his life, leaving all his wealth behind him. What did the thirty pieces of silver do for Judas? Weren't they a noose about his neck? Didn't David fall into foolish and hurtful lusts? He saw Bathsheba, Uriah's wife, and she was "very beautiful to look upon," and David became an adulterer and a murderer. The guilty longing hurled him into the deepest pit of sin. He had to reap bitterly as he had sowed.

Covetousness, defilement of; Commandment, tenth

2 Sam. 11:2; Luke 16:14; Rom. 1:29; Phil. 3:19

Notice that in 1 Corinthians 6:9–10 the covetous are named between thieves and drunkards. We lock up thieves and have no mercy on them. We loathe drunkards and consider them great sinners against the law of God as well as the law of the land. Yet there is far more said in the Bible against covetousness than against either stealing or drunkenness. Covetousness and stealing are almost like Siamese twins—they go together so often. In fact we might add lying, and make them triplets. The covetous person is a thief in the shell. The thief is a covetous person out of the shell. Let a covetous person see something that he desires very much; let an opportunity of taking it be offered; how very soon he will break through the shell and come out in his true character as a thief.

The Greek word translated covetousness means "an inordinate desire of getting." When the Gauls tasted the sweet wines of Italy, they asked where they came from and never rested until they had overrun Italy.

Matt. 13:22; Mark 4:19; 1 Tim. 6:10

"For the love of money is the root of all evil . . ." The Revised Version translates it— "a root of all kinds of evil." The tenth commandment has therefore been aptly called a "root extractor," because it would tear up and destroy this root. Deep down in our corrupt nature it has spread. No one but God can rid us of it.

Matthew tells us that the deceitfulness of riches chokes the Word of God out of the human heart. Like the Mississippi River which chokes up at its mouth by the amount of soil it carries down. Isn't that true of many businessmen today? They are so engrossed with their affairs that they have not time for God. They lose sight of their soul and its eternal welfare in their desire to amass wealth. They do not even hesitate to sell their souls to the devil. How many a man says, "We must make money, and if God's law stands in the way brush it aside."

Covetousness, evil of; Commandment, tenth

Exod. 20:17; Eph. 5:3; Col. 3:5; 1 Thess. 2:5; 1 Tim. 6:9; Heb. 13:5; 2 Peter 2:14

Dr. Boardman has shown how covetousness leads to the transgression of every one of the commandments, and I can't do better than quote his words: "Coveting tempts us into the violation of the first commandment, worshiping mammon in addition to Jehovah. Coveting tempts us into a violation of the second commandment, or idolatry. The apostle Paul expressly identifies the covetous man with an idolater: 'Covetousness, which is idolatry.' Again: Coveting tempts us into violation of the third commandment, or sacrilegious falsehood: for instance, Gehazi, lying on the matter of his interview with Naaman the Syrian, and Ananias and Sapphira perjuring themselves in the matter of the community of goods.

"Again: Coveting tempts us into the violation of the fourth commandment, or Sabbath breaking. It is covetousness which encroaches on God's appointed day of sacred rest, tempting us to run trains for merely secular purposes, to vend tobacco and liquors, to hawk newspapers. Again: Coveting tempts us into the violation of the fifth commandment, or disrespect for authority; tempting the young man to deride his early parental counsels, the citizen to trample on civic enactments.

"Again: Covetousness tempts us into violation of the sixth commandment, or murder. Recall how Judas' love of money lured him into the betrayal of his divine Friend into the hand of his murderers, his lure being the paltry sum of, say, fifteen dollars in today's money.

"Again: Covetousness tempts us into the violation of the seventh commandment, or adultery. Observe how Scripture combines greed and lust. Again: Covetousness tempts us into the violation of the eighth commandment, or theft. Recall how it tempted Achan to steal a goodly Babylonish mantle, two hundred shekels of silver, and a wedge of gold of fifty shekels weight.

"Again: Covetousness tempts us into the violation of the ninth commandment, or bearing false witness against our neighbor. Recall how the covetousness of Ahab instigated his wife Jezebel to bear blasphemous and fatal testimony against Naboth, saying, 'Thou didst curse God and the king.'"

Covetousness, example of; Commandment, tenth

Num. 22:7; 2 Peter 2:15; Jude 11; Rev. 2:14

Think of Balaam. He is generally regarded as a false prophet, but I do not find that any of his prophecies that are recorded are not true; they have been literally fulfilled. Up to a certain point his character shone magnificently, but the devil finally overcame him by the bait of covetousness. He stepped over a heavenly crown for the riches and honors that Balak promised him. He went to perdition backwards. His face was set toward God, but he backed into hell. He wanted to die the death of the righteous, but he did not live the life of the righteous. It is sad to see so many who know God miss everything for riches.

Josh. 7:25; 2 Kings 5:23, 27; Hosea 10:13; Matt. 27:3; Acts 5:5, 10

Consider the case of Gehazi. There is another man who was drowned in destruc-

tion and perdition by covetousness. He got more out of Naaman than he asked for, but he also got Naaman's leprosy. Think how he forfeited the friendship of his master Elisha, the man of God! So today lifelong friends are separated by this accursed desire. Homes are broken up. Men are willing to sell out peace and happiness for the sake of a few dollars.

Prov. 1:9; Isa. 1:3; 1 Tim. 6:10; Jude 11; Rev. 2:14

I heard of a wealthy man out West who owned a lumber mill. He was worth nearly two million dollars, but his covetousness was so great that he took a job as a common laborer carrying railroad ties all day in order to gain a few more dollars. It was the cause of his death.

Josh. 7:1; Ps. 119:36; 2 Peter 2:14

Achan saw—he coveted—he took—he hid! The covetous eye was what led Achan up to the wicked deed that brought sorrow and defeat upon the house of Israel. We know the terrible punishment that was meted out to Achan. God seems to have set a danger signal at the threshold of each new age. It is remarkable how soon the first outbreaks of covetousness occurred. Think of Eve in Eden, Achan just after Israel had entered the Promised Land, Ananias and Sapphira in the early Christian church.

Covetousness, extent of; Commandment, tenth

Gen. 3:6; Exod. 20:17; Josh. 7:21; Luke 12:15; Rom. 7:7; 13:9

We must not limit covetousness to the matter of money. The commandment is not thus limited; it reads, "Thou shalt not covet. . . anything." The word "anything" is what will condemn us. Though we do not join the race for wealth, have we not sometimes a hungry longing for our neighbor's good lands, fine houses, beautiful clothes, brilliant reputation, personal accomplishments, easy circumstance, comfortable surroundings? Have we not had the desire to increase our possessions or to change our lot in accordance with what we see in others? If so, we are guilty of having broken this law.

Covetousness, folly of; Commandment, tenth

Jer. 5:8; Luke 12:18; Acts 5:4; 1 Tim. 6:9; James 3:15

The folly of covetousness is well shown in the following extract: "If you should see a man that had a large pond of water, yet living in continual thirst, nor suffering himself to drink half a draught for fear of lessening his pond; if you should see him wasting his time and strength in fetching more water to his pond, always thirsty, yet always carrying a bucket of water in his hand, watching early and late to catch the drops of rain, gaping after every cloud, and running greedily into every mire and mud in hopes of water, and always studying how to make every ditch empty itself into the pond; if you should see him grow gray in these anxious labors, and at last end a thirsty life by falling into his own pond, would you not say that such a one was not only the author of his own disquiet, but was foolish enough to be reckoned among madmen? But foolish and absurd as this character is, it does not represent half the follies and absurd disquiets of the covetous man."

Covetousness, greed of; Commandment, tenth

Ezek. 22:25; Matt. 23:25; Luke 11:39; John 12:6

Covetousness has more than once led nation to war against nation for the sake of gaining territory or other material resources. It is said that when the Spaniards came over to conquer Peru, they sent a message to the king, saying,

"Give us gold, for we Spaniards have a disease that can only be cured by gold."

Covetousness, sin of; Commandment, tenth

Jer. 7:11; John 12:6; 1 Cor. 5:11; 6:10

Notice that the covetous who are greedy are named between thieves and drunkards in 1 Corinthians 6:10. We lock up thieves, and have no mercy on them. We loathe drunkards, and consider them great sinners against the law of God as well as the law of the land. Yet there is far more said in the Bible against covetousness than against either stealing or drunkenness.

Gen. 3:6; 2 Cor. 11:3; 1 Tim. 2:3

We may say that covetous desire plunged the human race into sin. We can trace the river back from age to age until we get to its headwaters in Eden. When Eve saw that the forbidden fruit was good for food and that it was desirable to the eyes, she partook of it, and Adam with her. They were not satisfied with all that God had showered upon them, but coveted the wisdom of gods which Satan deceitfully told them might be obtained by eating the fruit. She saw, she desired, then she took! Three steps from innocence into sin.

Covetousness, sin of; Greed, nature of; Commandment, tenth

1 Sam. 8:3; Isa. 56:11; 1 Tim. 3:3; Titus 1:11

The word "lucre" occurs five times in the New Testament, and each time it is called "filthy lucre." "A root of all kinds of evil." Yes, because what will not men be guilty of when prompted by the desire to be rich? Greed for gold leads men to commit violence and murder, to cheat and deceive and steal. It turns the heart to stone, devoid of all natural affection, cruel, unkind. How many families are wrecked over the father's will! The scramble for a share of the wealth smashes them to pieces. Covetous of rank and position in society, parents barter sons and daughters in ungodly marriage. Bodily health is no consideration.

The uncontrollable fever for gold makes men renounce all their settled prospects and undertake hazardous journeys—no peril can drive them back. Covetousness destroys faith and spirituality, turning men's minds and hearts away from God. It disturbs the peace of the community by prompting to acts of wrong.

Creation, evidence of God

Pss. 8:3; 19:1; Isa. 40:26; Rom. 1:19–20

Suppose we knew nothing of the sun except what we saw of its light reflected from the moon? Would we not wonder about its immense distance, about its dazzling splendor, about its life-giving power? Now all that we see, the sun, the moon, the stars, the ocean, the earth, the flowers, and above all, man, are a grand mirror in which the perfection of God is imperfectly reflected.

Creation, old and new

Ps. 51:10; Isa. 45:17; Ezek. 11:19; 18:31; 36:26; Rom. 1:16; 2 Cor. 5:17; Gal. 6:15; Eph. 1:4; 2:10, 15

A friend of mine said that when he was converted and began preaching, he talked a good deal about himself. He said one day he saw in one of the hymnbooks left by a godly woman who had a seat in the church, a flyleaf on which was written these words: "Dear Harry: not I, but Christ; not flesh, but spirit; not sight, but faith." These words my friend pasted in his Bible, and never preached or thought anymore about himself. He kept himself out of the way. That is just what the old man does not

do. With him it is self, self, self. If it is the new man, it is not I, but Christ.

If it is the new man, it is not flesh, but spirit. If it is the new man, it is not sight but faith. In the old Adam it is death; in the new Adam, it is eternal life. We all come under the two heads. Which, my friend, do you belong to, the old creation or the new? Let us pray that we may stand by the throne of God clothed in the righteousness of the second Adam.

Creator, God as; Doubt, futility of

Num. 22:28

A friend of mine was going back to Scotland, and he heard a couple of these modern philosophers discussing the Bible. One said, "The Bible says that Balaam's donkey spoke. Now, I am a scientific man, and have taken the pains to examine an ass's mouth, and it is so formed that it couldn't speak." He was going to toss the whole Bible over because Balaam's donkey couldn't speak.

My friend said he stood it just as long as he could and finally he said, "Ah, man, if you could make a donkey, you could make him speak." The idea that the God who made the donkey couldn't speak through his mouth! Did you ever hear such stuff? And yet this was one of your modern philosophers?

Criticism, danger of; Complaint, danger of

Dan. 6:5; Rom. 15:1; Col. 3:13; James 2:13

Very often a man will hear a hundred good things in a sermon, but there may be one thing that strikes him as a little out of place, and he will go home and sit down at the table and talk right out before his children and magnify that one wrong thing, and not say a word about the hundred good things that were said. That is what people do who criticize.

75

Cross, importance of

Isa. 8:14; Rom. 1:16; 9:33; 1 Cor. 1:8, 23

A minister who covers up the cross of Christ in his preaching, though he may be an intellectual man, and draw large crowds, will have no life in his congregation, and his church will be but a gilded sepulcher.

Culture inadequate to regenerate

Gen. 1:11; Isa. 55:10; Matt. 13:3; Luke 8:5; 2 Cor. 9:10

Culture is all right in its place, but culture won't regenerate a human heart. Suppose I commence the first day of May and plow an acre of ground crosswise, and the next day I plow it lengthwise, and every day in the week except Sunday I plow that acre of land. I begin the first day of May and plow all through May and June and July. Once in a while I put a cultivator in and cultivate it, and I harrow it, and brush it, and roll it. I have been harrowing, brushing, rolling and cultivating for months, and you come along and say, "Moody, what are you doing?" "Doing! I am cultivating this acre of land." "Well, I should say so! I was around here last May, and you were plowing that acre of land. Been at it ever since?" "Yes." "What are you going to put in it?" "Well, I am not going to put anything in it, but I believe in a high state of culture."

You would say I was a first-class lunatic! But that is what is going on all the while in spiritual things. Put the seed in, and then pray God that the dew of heaven may rest upon it, and you will have some results. There isn't a sower that goes forth and sows that kind of seed, but there are results.

Death as gain; Resurrection, hope of; Citizenship in heaven

1 Cor. 15:49; Phil. 1:21; 3:20; Heb. 11:21

Thank God, we are to gain by death! We are to have something that death cannot touch. When this earthly body is raised, all the present imperfection will be gone. Jacob will leave his lameness. Paul will have no thorn in the flesh. We shall enter a life that deserves the name of life, happy, glorious, everlasting—the body once more united to the soul, no longer mortal, subject to pain and disease and death, but glorified, incorruptible, "fashioned like unto his glorious body," everything that hinders the spiritual life left behind. We are exiles now, but then we who are faithful shall stand before the throne of God, joint-heirs with Christ, kings and priests, citizens of that heavenly country.

Death, certainty of

Gen. 3:19; Job 30:23; Ps. 89:48; Eccles. 3:20; Rom. 5:12; Heb. 9:27

There is a legend that I read some time ago of a man who made a covenant with Death; and the covenant was this: that Death should not come on him unawares—that Death was to give warning of his approach. Well, years rolled on, and at last, Death stood before his victim. The old man blanched and faltered out, "Why, Death, you have not been true to your promise, you have not kept your covenant. You promised not to come unannounced. You never gave me any warning." "Not so!" came the answer. "Every one of those gray hairs is a warning; every one of your lost teeth is a warning; your eyes growing dim is a warning; your natural power and vigor abated—that is a warning. Aha! I've warned you—I've warned you continually." And Death would not delay, but swept his victim into eternity.

That is a legend; but how many in the past year have heard these warning voices? Death has come very near to many of us. What warnings have come to us all? The preacher's calls to repentance, how again and again they have rung in our ears. We may have one or two more calls yet, this year, in the next few hours. Then how many of us in the last twelve months have gone to the bedside of some loved friend, and kneeling in silent anguish unable to help, have whispered a promise to meet that dying one in heaven?

Oh why delay any longer? Before these few lingering hours have gone, and the year rolls away into eternity, I beg of you, see to it that you prepare to make that promise good. Some of you have kissed the marble brow of a dead parent this year, and the farewell look of those eyes has been, "make ready to meet thy God." In a few years you will follow, and there may be a reunion in heaven. Are you ready, dear friends?

Death, Christ's victory over; Gospel, source of liberty

Ps. 23:4; John 11:25; Acts 26:23; Rom. 8:11; 1 Cor. 15:22, 55; Col. 1:18; 1 Peter 1:3; Rev. 1:5

I think Psalm 23 is more misquoted than any other portion in the whole Bible. It is known in all the Catholic churches; it is known in the Greek church; it is in the Jewish synagogue; they chant it in a great many denominations burying the dead. Armies went to battle chanting the Twenty-third Psalm. People will weave it into their prayers, and conversation, and chapel services. They will say, "Yea, though I walk through the dark valley." They will emphasize the word "dark," and send the cold chills running down your back. "Yea, though I walk through the dark valley of the shadow of death." I want to tell you, my dear friends, the word "dark" isn't there at all. The devil sticks that in to confuse believers. It is, "Yea, though I walk through the valley of the shadow of death."

What is the difference? Must not there be light where there is shadow? Can you get a shadow without light? If you doubt it, go down into the cellar tonight without a light, and find your shadow if you can. All that death can do to a true believer is to throw a shadow across his path. Shadows never hurt any one. You can walk right through shadows as you can through fog, and there is nothing to fear. Must not there be light where there is shadow?

I pity down deep in my heart any man or woman that lives under the bondage of death! If you are under it, may God bring you out today! May you come right out into the liberty of the blessed gospel of the Son of God!

Death, conquered by Christ; Funeral sermons

Ps. 23:4; John 11:25; Acts 26:23; Rom. 8:11; 1 Cor. 15:22, 55; Col. 1:18; 1 Peter 1:3; Rev. 1:5

When a young man in Chicago, I was called upon suddenly to preach a funeral sermon. A good many Chicago businessmen were to be there, and I said to myself, "Now, it will be a good chance for me to preach the gospel to those men, and I will get one of Christ's funeral sermons." I hunted all through the four Gospels trying to find one of Christ's funeral sermons, but I couldn't find any. I found he broke up every funeral he ever attended! He never preached a funeral sermon in the world. Death couldn't exist where he was. When the dead heard his voice they sprang to life. He has taken the sting from death for all his people.

Death of Christian

Job 19:25

Bishop Heber has written of a dead friend:

Thou art gone to the grave, but we will not deplore thee,

Though sorrow and darkness encompass the tomb;

Thy Savior has passed through its portals before thee,

And the lamp of His love is thy guide through the gloom;

Thou art gone to the grave; we no longer behold thee,

Nor tread the rough paths of the world by thy side,

But the wide arms of Mercy are spread to enfold thee,

Thus sinners may die, since the Sinless has died.

Death, victory over

Isa. 25:4; Hosea 13:14; Rev. 21:4

Someone said to a person dying: "Well, you are in the land of the living yet." "No," said he, "I am in the land of the dying, but I am going to the land of the living; they live there and never die." This is the land of sin and death and tears, but up yonder they never die. It is perpetual life; it is unceasing joy.

1 Kings 17:21; 2 Kings 4:33; Mark 5:41; Luke 8:54; John 11:43

It has been said that others besides Christ have raised dead people to life. That is true, but they did it very differently from the way he did it. In the seventeenth chapter of the first book of Kings we read of Elijah raising the son of the widow. But just hear what he says: he cried unto the Lord, "O Lord, my God, let this child's soul come into him again." Then, when Elisha did the same thing, we find that he went in and shut the door, and prayed unto the Lord.

Now just notice the difference between these accounts and the account of Christ raising Jairus's daughter. He didn't pray to anybody, but he just took her by the hand and said to her, on his own account, "Maid, arise!" And she that was dead sat up, and began to speak. Take

the case of his raising the widow's son. Death had got hold of his captive, and was dragging him off to the grave; but Christ stopped him, and commanded him to come back. "Young man, I say unto thee, Arise!" And the young man arose, and Christ delivered him again to his mother.

He does not ask help or permission of anybody, but of his own authority he calls back the dead to life. See him there at the grave of Lazarus. Jesus thanks his Father for hearing him but he calls forth the dead man in his own power. He just calls the dead man, and Lazarus comes forth, bound hand and foot with grave clothes. Even the dead must obey when Christ commands.

Death, victory over; Vision, power of

Isa. 25:8; Hosea 13:14; 1 Cor. 15:26; 2 Tim. 1:10

Jesus Christ is a great deal nearer and dearer to me than he was twenty years ago. I do not now regard death as an enemy, but I look right through death to glory.

Death, view of

Rev. 21:18

I received some time ago a letter from a friend in London, and I thought as I read it, I would take it and read it to other people, and see if I could not get them to look upon death as this friend does. He lost a loving mother. In England it is a very common thing to send out cards in memory of departed ones, and they put upon them great borders of black—sometimes a quarter of an inch of black border. But this friend had put on gold; he did not put on black at all. She had gone to the golden city, and so he just put on a golden border; and I think it a good deal better than black.

Deception, futility of

Eccles. 12:14; Dan. 12:2; John 5:29; 1 Cor. 4:5; Rev. 20:12

It is impossible for deception to last forever. Lincoln said, "You may be able to deceive all the people some of the time, and some of the people all of the time, but you will not be able to deceive all the people all of the time." Death will uncover the deception, if it has not been detected sooner; and the unfortunate victim will stand in the presence of the God who cannot be mocked.

Decision, importance of

1 Kings 18:21; Matt. 6:24; Rom. 6:16; 1 Cor. 10:21; 2 Cor. 6:14

People are always going to become Christians some time or other. It is hard to get them to act now. But this is just what the Bible tells them to do. We ought to settle this most important of all matters today. We can't claim or be sure of a day in the future. Now is the day of salvation. Every person who has made a mark in the world has been a person of decisiveness. The people who are always waiting and putting off are failures. Today the Savior calls. Today harden not your hearts. If the old prophet Elijah could rise from the dead and stand in my place, he would repeat the sermon he preached on Mount Carmel, "How long halt ye between two opinions?" If you are infidel, say so; if you are not, and want to be a Christian, come out on the side of the Lord today.

Dedication, evidence of; Commitment, power of

Acts 26:25; 2 Cor. 5:13

In my opinion no one is fit for God's service until he is willing to be considered mad by the world. They said Paul was mad. I wish we had many more who were bitten with the same kind of madness. As someone has said, "If we are mad, we have a good Keeper on the way and a good Asylum at the end of the road."

Dedication, example of; Enthusiasm, example of; Zeal, example of

Isa. 42:13; John 2:17; 2 Cor. 9:2

As I was leaving New York to go to England in 1867, a friend said to me: "I hope you will go to Edinburgh and be at the General Assembly this year. When I was there a year ago I heard such a speech as I shall never forget. Doctor Duff made a speech that set me all on fire. I shall never forget the hour I spent in that meeting."

Doctor Duff had been out in India as a missionary; he had spent twenty-five years there preaching the gospel and establishing schools. He came back with a broken-down constitution. He was permitted to address the General Assembly, in order to make an appeal for men to go into the mission field. After he had spoken for a considerable time, he became exhausted and fainted away. They carried him out of the hall into another room. The doctors worked over him for some time, and at last he began to recover.

When he realized where he was, he roused himself and said, "I did not finish my speech; carry me back and let me finish it." They told him he could only do it at the peril of his life. He cried, "I will do it if I die." So they took him back to the hall. My friend said it was one of the most solemn scenes he ever witnessed in his life. They brought the white-haired man into the Assembly Hall, and as he appeared at the door every person sprang to his feet; the tears flowed freely as they looked upon the grand old veteran.

With a trembling voice, he said, "Fathers and mothers of Scotland, is it true that you have no more sons to send to India to work for the Lord Jesus Christ? The call for help is growing louder and louder, but there are few coming forward to answer it. You have the money put away in the bank, but where are the laborers who shall go into the field? When Queen Victoria wants men to volunteer for her army in India, you freely give your sons. You do not talk about their losing their health, and about the trying climate. But when the Lord Jesus is calling for laborers, Scotland is saying, 'We have no more sons to give.'"

Turning to the President of the Assembly, he said, "Mr. Moderator, if it is true that Scotland has no more sons to give to the service of the Lord Jesus Christ in India, although I have lost my health in that land and came home to die, if there are none who will go to those who know not Christ, then I will be off tomorrow, to let them know that there is one old Scotchman who is ready to die for them. I will go back to the shores of the Ganges, and there lay down my life as a witness for the Son of God."

Thank God for such a man as that! We need men today who are willing, if need be, to lay down their lives for the Son of God. Then we shall be able to make an impression upon the world. When they see that we are in earnest, their hearts will be touched, and we shall be able to lead them to the Lord Jesus Christ.

Dedication, need of all

Acts 16:15; 1 Cor. 4:2, 17; Col. 4:7; 1 Tim. 3:1

I believe in what John Wesley used to say, "All at it, and always at it," and that is what the church needs today.

Dedication, power of; Zeal, power of

John 6:39; 10:28; Rom. 8:34, 39; Gal. 2:20; Col. 3:3; Heb. 7:25; 1 Peter 1:3

In the second century they brought a Christian before a king, who wanted him to recant and give up Christ and Chris-

tianity, but the man spurned the proposition. But the king said, "If you don't do it, I will banish you." The man smiled and answered, "You can't banish me from Christ, for he says he will never leave me nor forsake me."

The king got angry, and said, "Well, I will confiscate your property and take it all from you." And the man replied, "My treasures are laid up on high; you cannot get them."

The king became still more angry, and said, "I will kill you." "Why," the man answered, "I have been dead forty years; I have been dead with Christ, dead to the world, and my life is hid with Christ in God, and you cannot touch it." "What are you going to do with such a fanatic?" said the king.

Despair, victory over; Depression, victory over; Repentance, example of

Pss. 30:5; 126:1; 137:4; Eccles. 3:4; John 16:20

Some years ago, a man who is a very dear friend of mine was engaged to be married to a very beautiful girl. As he looked into the future he had everything which heart could desire; money, grand business prospects, health, and in the immediate future a wife and a very happy home. He forgot all his past and in his imagination he lived in the castles which he built in the air. Every castle had a golden minaret, for when we build with the imagination we do not count the cost. All at once, as though a flash of lightning had come out of a clear, cloudless sky, sickness fell upon this lady, and she died at once.

The shock, of course, was terrible. He was a man of large heart and generous sympathies, and those are they who make the best or worst men in the world. And my poor friend, thrown down by his despair, rushed into every sort of dissipation which New York life affords, and New York life is very rich in that sort of material;

and he spent an immense amount of money—nearly all he had. What he wanted was forgetfulness, and he went on from bad to worse until he reached low tide and the mud of moral iniquity; and one day in the midst of all this, by one of those instincts you and I know, he was led to open his safe and take from it a bundle containing a little silver key, which he had turned in the casket of his beloved. Next to it was a tress of her auburn hair.

As he looked at her hair he started back in horror as he reflected upon the gulf that now separated him from her. He turned to his friend and asked if he thought he should ever see her again, and was answered, "I don't think you ever will. I don't see how you can. The life you and I have been living these last twelve months doesn't lead that way. It leads down the other side, and you and I can never look a pure woman in the face again."

And then the poor fellow burst into tears, and wringing his hands he cried, "Oh, I must see her again, and I will meet her again; if there is anything in religion by which I can get rid of my past life I am going to get rid of it, and I am going to right about face, and keep my face forward and my eyes upon heaven. And if she is in heaven, I am going there too."

In due course he came to see me, and wrung my hand in a way I cannot describe, but there was great resolution in his heart. With the memory of that golden tress and silver key, George, for that was his name, trusted Christ and joined the church, and being asked if he would like to go back to the past, he exclaimed, "I have found a home and I cannot go back to despair." He is marching on that journey tonight to the tune of glory, glory, hallelujah.

Devotional life, importance of

Pss. 42:1; 63:1; 84:2; 143:6; Isa. 26:9; Luke 10:39

It is a good deal better, my friends, if you are going to work for God, to be con-

stantly alone with him. There are two lives for the Christian, one before the world, and one alone with God. If you dwell constantly at the feet of Jesus, it will save you many a painful hour. The sweetest thoughts of God I ever got were not found in a great assembly like this, but when alone, sitting at the feet of Jesus.

Diligence, reward of

1 Cor. 3:14; 1 Tim. 5:18; Heb. 11:26; Rev. 22:12

An insurance case was brought to Daniel Webster when he was a young lawyer in Portsmouth. Only a small amount was involved, and a twenty-dollar fee was all that was promised. He saw that to do his client full justice, a journey to Boston would be desirable, in order to consult the law library. The trip would be costly, and for the time involved he would receive no adequate compensation. But he determined to do his best, cost what it might. He accordingly went to Boston and looked up the authorities, and won the case.

Years after, Webster, who had meanwhile become famous, was passing through New York. An important insurance case was to be tried that day, and one of the counsel had suddenly been taken ill. Money was no object, and Webster was begged to name his terms and conduct the case. "I told them," said Mr. Webster, "that it was preposterous to expect me to prepare a legal argument at a few hours' notice. They insisted, however, that I should look at the papers; and this I finally consented to do. It was my old twenty-dollar case over again; and as I remembered the details well, I had all the authorities at my fingers' ends. The court knew that I had no time to prepare, and were astonished at the range of my acquirements. So you see, I was handsomely repaid both in fame and money for that journey to Boston; and the moral is that good work is rewarded in the end."

Discipline, based on love

Deut. 8:5; 2 Sam. 7:14; Prov. 3:12; 13:12; Heb. 12:6; Rev. 3:19

In the little country district where I went to school there were two parties. One party said that boys could not possibly be controlled without the cane, and they kept a schoolmaster who acted on their plan; the other party said they should be controlled by love. The struggle went on, and at last, on one election day, the first party was put out, and the other ruled in their stead. I happened to be at the school at that time, and we said to each other that we were going to have a grand time that winter. There would be no more corporal punishment, and we were going to be ruled by love.

The new teacher was a lady, and she opened the school with prayer. We hadn't seen it done before, and we were impressed, especially when she prayed that she might have grace and strength to rule the school with love. The school went on for several weeks, and we saw no cane. I was one of the first to break the rules of the school. The teacher asked me to stay behind. I thought the cane was coming out again, and I was in a fighting mood. She sat down and began to talk to me kindly. That was worse than the cane; I did not like it. She said: "I have made up my mind that if I cannot control the school by love, I will give it up. I will have no punishment. If you love me, try to keep the rules of the school."

I felt something right here in my throat, and never gave her any more trouble. She just put me under grace. And that is what God does. God is love, and he wants us all to love him. God wants us to obey him in response to his love.

Discord, danger of; Dispute, danger of

Prov. 6:14, 19; 16:28; Hosea 8:7

We are told that one time just before sunrise, two men got into a dispute about what part of the heavens the sun would first appear in. They became so excited over it that they fell to fighting, and beat each other over the head so badly that when the sun did come up neither of them could see it. So there are persons who go on disputing about heaven until they dispute themselves out of it, and more who dispute over hell until they dispute themselves into it.

Doctrines, limits of; Communion with God

Rom. 4:4; Gal. 3:24

Doctrines are to the soul what the streets which lead to the house of a friend who has invited me to dinner are to the body. They will lead me there if I take the right one; but if I remain in the streets my hunger will never be satisfied. Feeding on doctrines is like trying to live on dry husks; and lean indeed must the soul remain which will not partake of the Bread sent down from heaven.

Doubt, cure for; Fear, cure for; Laziness, problem of

John 20:27; Titus 3:1; Heb. 6:10; 1 Peter 1:17; 3 John 5

People say, "If I could only get rid of these doubts and fears, I think I would be ready to work." Go to work, and these doubts will disappear. There is work to be done. Life is short at the longest, so let us be about our Master's business. While you are engaged in his work, these doubts will not assail you so much. I believe any Christian would have doubts in less than six months if he did nothing.

Doubt, danger of

Matt. 14:31; 21:21; Mark 11:23

I notice if a man goes to cut up the Bible and comes to you with one truth and says, "I don't believe this, and I don't believe that." I notice when he begins to doubt portions of the Word of God he soon doubts it all.

Doubts, remedy for

Heb. 11:10; 1 John 4:18

Suppose a man, in directing me to the post office, gives me ten landmarks; and that, in my progress there, I find nine of them to be as he told me; I should have good reason to believe that I was coming to the post office. And if, by believing, I get a new life, and a hope, a peace, a joy, and a rest to my soul, that I never had before; if I get self-control, and find that I have a power to resist evil and to do good, I have pretty good proof that I am in the right road to the "city which hath foundations, whose builder and maker is God." And if things have taken place, and are now taking place, as recorded in God's Word, I have good reason to conclude that what yet remains will be fulfilled.

And yet people talk of doubting. There can be no true faith where there is fear. Faith is to take God at his word, unconditionally. There cannot be true peace where there is fear. "Perfect love casteth out fear." How wretched a wife would be if she doubted her husband! How miserable a mother would feel if after her boy had gone away from home she had reason, from his neglect, to question that son's devotion. True love never has a doubt.

Dreams, unable to save

Job 20:8; Ps. 73:20; Jer. 29:8

In New Orleans, when they were examining candidates for church membership once, a lady wanted to be admitted because she had a dream about a beautiful lamb, but she didn't know a verse of scripture. They instructed her in the truth. Another person applied to Pastor Rowland Hill's church for membership on account of his having had a religious dream. The pastor wisely said, "Let us see how you can get on for a while when you're awake."

Earnestness, importance of; Zeal, importance of

Exod. 3:1; Judg. 6:11; 1 Kings 19:19; 2 Cor. 7:7

In all ages God has used those who were in earnest. Satan always calls idle men into his service. God calls active and earnest—not indolent—men. When we are thoroughly aroused and ready for his work, then he will take us up and use us. You remember where Elijah found Elisha; he was ploughing in the field—he was at work. Gideon was threshing grain. Moses was away in Horeb looking after the sheep. None of these eminent servants of God were indolent men; what they did, they did with all their might. We need such men and women today. If we can't do God's work with all the knowledge we would like let us at any rate do it with all the zeal that God has given us.

Earnestness, importance of; Zeal, power of; Dedication, importance of

Ps. 64:9; Isa. 51:11; Jer. 51:10; Hosea 14:9

I heard of someone who was speaking of something that was to be done, and who said he hoped zeal would be tempered with moderation. Another friend very wisely replied that he hoped moderation would be tempered with zeal. If that were always the case, Christianity would be like a red hot ball rolling over the face of the earth. There is no power on earth that can stand before the onward march of God's people when they are in dead earnest.

Election, doctrine of; Invitation to salvation

Matt. 24:22; Acts 9:15; Rom. 8:33; Rev. 22:17

I have an idea that the Lord Jesus saw how men were going to stumble over the doctrine of election, so after he had been thirty or forty years in heaven he came down and spoke to John. One Lord's day in Patmos, he said to John: "Write these things to the churches." John kept on writing. His pen flew very fast. And then the Lord, when it was nearly finished, said, "John, before you close the book, put in one more invitation. 'The Spirit and the bride say, Come. And let him that heareth say, Come. And let him that is athirst, come. And whosoever will, let him take the water of life freely.'" If you want to know if you are among the elect just come to Christ.

Election, proof of

1 Thess. 1:4; 2 Tim. 2:19; 2 Peter 1:10

Do you think that God offers the cup of salvation to all people, and then, just as a person is about to drink snatches it away, and says, "Oh, but you are not one of the elect." God doesn't do anything of the kind. All who trust in Jesus are of the elect.

Encouragement for service

Acts 4:36; 9:27; Rom. 15:4; 2 Cor. 1:6; Philem. 7

On one of my rounds of meetings in the state of Indiana, I was riding in the wagon of a quiet Christian brother, who was taking me to my next appointment, when we passed a little schoolhouse which was closed for the day. Telling my friend to stop at the dwelling nearest to it, I stood up in the wagon and hailed at the house. A woman came to the door, and I asked her if there were any religious meetings held in that schoolhouse. "No, indeed," answered the woman; "we haven't any meetings anywhere about here." "Well," said I, "tell all your neighbors there will be prayer meetings in that schoolhouse every night next week." At the next house we found the teacher of the school, to whom I gave the same announcement, and bade her send the notice by all her scholars.

As we rode on the brother who was conveying me seemed lost in amazement. He knew that I had a long list of appointments in advance, and could not attend those meetings I was giving

notice of. At length he said, "You are telling these people there are to be prayer meetings in that schoolhouse every night next week. I should like to know who is going to conduct them?" "You are," said I. "I!" said the man in astonishment. "I never did such a thing in my life." "It's time you had, then," said I. "I have made the appointment, and you will have to keep it"; and so the good brother actually went and held the meetings, which filled the little schoolhouse to overflowing, and resulted in a great revival throughout all that neglected region of the country.

Encouragement, importance of; Peace, source of

Ps. 91:1

Psalm 91 might have been written by Moses after some terrible calamity had come upon the children of Israel. It might have been after that terrible night of death in Egypt, when the firstborn from the palace to the hovel were slain; or after that terrible plague of fiery serpents in the wilderness, when the people were full of fear and in a nervous state. Perhaps Moses called Aaron and Miriam, and Joshua and Caleb, and a few others into his tent and read this psalm to them first. How sweet it must have sounded, and how strange!

I can imagine Moses asking, "Do you think that will help them? Will that quiet them?" They all thought that it would. And then, (it may be), on one of those hilltops of Sinai, at twilight, this psalm was read. How it must have soothed them, how it must have helped them, how it must have strengthened them!

Encouragement, power of; Discouragement, overcoming

Gen. 6:8; Heb. 11:7; 1 Peter 3:2

I remember a few years ago I got discouraged, and could not see much fruit of my work; and one morning, as I was in my study, cast down, one of my Sunday school teachers came in and wanted to know what I was discouraged about, and I told him because I could see no result from my work; and speaking about Noah, he said, "By the way, did you ever study the character of Noah?" I felt that I knew all about that, and told him that I was familiar with it, and he said, "Now, if you never studied that carefully, you ought to do it, for I cannot tell you what a blessing it has been to me."

When he went out I took down my Bible and commenced to read about Noah, and the thought came stealing over me, "Here is a man that toiled and worked a hundred and twenty years and didn't get discouraged; if he did, the Holy Spirit didn't put it on record," and the clouds lifted, and I got up and said, if the Lord wants me to work without any fruit I will work on. I went down to the noon prayer meeting, and when I saw the people coming to pray I said to myself, "Noah worked a hundred and twenty years and he never saw a prayer meeting outside of his own family."

Pretty soon a man got up right across the aisle where I was sitting, and said he had come from a little town where there had been a hundred uniting with the Church the year before. And I thought to myself, "What if Noah had heard that! He preached so many, many years, and didn't get a convert, yet he was not discouraged." Then a man got up right behind me, and he trembled as he said, "I am lost. I want you to pray for my soul." And I said, "What if Noah had heard that! He worked a hundred and twenty years, and never had a man come to him and say that; and yet he didn't get discouraged." And I made up my mind then, that, God helping me, I would never get discouraged. I would do the best I could, and leave the result with God, and it has been a wonderful help to me.

Encouragement, power of; Hope, power of

Pss. 16:9; 22:9; 31:24; 2 Cor. 1:4; Heb. 6:18; 1 Peter 1:3

Someone tells of an incident that happened in a New England town the other day. All the boys were sledding on the snow-packed streets. A big sleigh—we call it a "pung" up there—was being driven through the streets by an old man who looked like Santa Claus. He was calling out to the small boys to hitch on and slide along behind the sleigh, for a pung is like a bus, it always holds one more.

There were already about twenty rollicking boys hitched on, when one little fellow dropped off behind. He tried, but couldn't catch up again, and pretty soon he began to look out for another chance for a ride. A man's sleigh was standing nearby, and the boy began to eye the man. When the man in the sleigh started off, the little fellow hitched on behind, and the man grabbed his whip and struck him directly in the eye. It looked as if the eye had been put out, but it wasn't.

Now, that's the way we go through this world. Some say, "Hitch on, hitch on," others, "Get away, get away." The hitch-on people fill the churches, and the get away ones empty them.

Encouragement, power of; Prayer for workers

Acts 12:5; Rom. 15:30; 2 Cor. 1:11; Phil. 1:19; Col. 4:3

A child was rescued from the fire that was raging in a house up on the fourth story. The child came to the window and as the flames were shooting up higher and higher it cried out for help. A fireman started up the ladder of the fire escape to rescue the child from its dangerous position. The wind swept the flames near him, and it was getting so hot that he wavered, and it looked as if he would have to return without the child. Hundreds looked on, and their hearts quaked at the thought of the child having to perish in the fire, as it must do if the fireman did not reach it.

Someone in the crowd cried, "Give him a cheer!" Cheer after cheer went up, and as the man heard them he gathered fresh courage. Up he went into the midst of the smoke and the fire, and brought down the child in safety. If you cannot go and rescue the perishing yourself, you can at least pray for those who do, and cheer them on. If you do, the Lord will bless the effort. Do not grumble and criticize; it takes neither heart nor brains to do that.

Encouragement, power of; Service, vision for

Josh. 1:6; Acts 21:5; 28:15; Heb. 10:24

If you are not able to go and invite the people to hear the gospel, you can give a word of cheer to others, and wish them Godspeed. Many a time when I have come down from the pulpit, some old man, trembling on the very verge of another world, living perhaps on borrowed time, has caught hold of my hand, and in a quavering voice said, "God bless you!" How the words have cheered and helped me! You can speak a word of encouragement to younger friends, if you are too feeble to work yourselves.

End times, faithfulness in; Worldliness, danger of

1 Sam. 17:37; 23:25; 2 Chron. 32:7–8; 2 Tim. 3:4

The world is not growing better, but worse. By the world, I mean those who are outside of the church. The church will grow. But the church is not the world. The church is like a ship at sea. The water may be all around the ship, and dash over it, yet the ship is safe. It is only when the water gets into the ship that it is in danger. So the peril of the church is not from the opposition of the world, but from its own conformity to the world.

Paul, in his letter to Timothy, says men shall be "lovers of pleasure" in the last days. How true that is now, and especially in California. Apply the test to yourselves. Do you prefer the dance and the theater to the house of God? Do you prefer the novel and the magazine to the Bible? The church is retrograding in spirituality and in power. She is losing her testimony. Ungodly men have come in, and have turned God's house into a place of amusement. Is it any wonder, then, that the children of the church are going to ruin? The demand is for preachers who can tickle men's ears, and draw crowds, and not for godly ministers full of the Holy Ghost.

Enthusiasm, need of

Ps. 142:7; Acts 24:14; 26:25

Someone has said to me, "When are you going to preach to the unconverted?" Well, I don't know that I shall preach to them at all. I will get you to preach to them. We need five or six or seven thousand sermons preached to the unconverted every day. We need thousands of men and women going out to tell the story of the cross. It is very easy when we get enthusiasm and are full of love for God and his work. A great many will cry out, "He has zeal without knowledge." I would a good deal rather have zeal without knowledge than knowledge without zeal. If we are enthusiasts for Christ as we ought to be, there will be some who will call us fanatics and say we are mad. I don't believe a man is worth much for Christ until he is mad. And when we hear that cry raised it is a sure sign we are getting into the footsteps of the Master.

2 Cor. 11:22; 12:11

Well, my friends, the question is, have you got it? Have you got enthusiasm for

Christ? Has the Spirit of God moved on your heart yet? Are you ready to be called a fool for Christ's sake? Are you ready to be called beside yourself? Are you ready to hear the scoffs and jeers of the world for Christ's sake? Remember, my friends, God cannot use you until you are willing to have the world point the finger of scorn at you. If the world hasn't got anything to say against us it is pretty sure that Christ won't have much to say for us. Because, if we love God in Jesus Christ we shall surely suffer persecution, and if we are afraid of our dignity, and reputation, and standing, we are not fit for Christ's service.

Enthusiasm, power of; Selflessness, power of; Dedication, power of

Isa. 53:6; Rom. 5:8; 1 Peter 3:18; 1 John 4:10

I did not agree with Garibaldi's judgment in all things, but I did admire his enthusiasm. I never saw his name in the papers, or in a book, but I read all I could find about him. There was something about him that fired me up. I remember reading of the time when he was on the way to Rome in 1867, and when he was cast into prison. I read the letter he sent to his comrades, "If fifty Garibaldis are thrown into prison, let Rome be free!" He did not care for his own comfort, so long as the cause of freedom in Italy was advanced. If we have such a love for our Master and his cause that we are ready to go out and do his work whatever it may cost us personally, depend upon it the Lord will use us building up his kingdom.

Enthusiasm, power of; Zeal, power of

Acts 20:24; Col. 4:13; 1 Thess. 2:11; 1 John 4:14

When we went to London there was an eighty-five-year-old woman, who came to the meetings and said she wanted a hand in the evangelistic work. She was appointed to a district and called on all classes of people. She went to places where we would probably have been put out, and told the people of Christ. There were none that could resist her. When the eighty-five-year-old woman came to them and offered to pray for them, they all received her kindly—Catholics, Jews, Gentiles—all. That is enthusiasm. That is what we need.

Eternal life, importance of; Aging, proper perspective

Pss. 21:4; 91:16; Prov. 3:2

I was down in Texas some time ago, and happened to pick up a newspaper, and in it they called me "Old Moody." Honestly, I never got such a shock from any paper in my life before! I had never been called old before. I went to my hotel, and looked in the looking glass. I can't conceive of getting old. I have a life that is never going to end. Death may change my position but not my condition, not my standing with Jesus Christ. Death is not going to separate us.

Old! I wish you all felt as young as I do here tonight. Why, I am only sixty-two years old! If you meet me ten million years hence, then I will be young. Read that ninety-first Psalm, "With long life will I satisfy him." That doesn't mean seventy years. Would that satisfy you? Did you ever see a man or woman of seventy satisfied? Don't they want to live longer? You know that seventy wouldn't satisfy you. Would eighty? Would ninety? Would one hundred? If Adam had lived to be a million years old, and then had to die, he wouldn't be satisfied. "With long life will I satisfy him"—life without end! Don't call me old. I am only sixty-two. I have only begun to live.

Eternal life, nature of

John 6:54; 17:7; Rom. 5:21

Eternal life is life without end. The government was trying to make a treaty with the Indians, and in one place put in the word "forever." The Indians did not like that word, and said, "No; put it, 'As long as water runs and grass grows.'" They could understand that.

Eternity, length of

Ps. 90:4; 2 Peter 3:8

How little we realize the meaning of the word eternity! The whole time between the creation of the world and the ending of it would not make a day in eternity. In time, eternity is like the infinity of space, whose center is everywhere and whose boundary is nowhere.

Evangelism, call to

Luke 24:48; John 15:27; Acts 1:8; 3:23

I was on the steamship *Spree* when the shaft broke and knocked a hole in the ship's bottom. The stern sank thirty feet in mid ocean, and for a whole week, if a storm had burst upon us, we would have gone down. One man was so bewildered and terrified that he jumped overboard. I remember how wretched I felt to think I couldn't help him, to see him left out there in mid-ocean, head above the waves, looking at us.

The passengers took life preservers and whatever they could find, and threw them to him, but all fell short. He was gone before lifeboats could be lowered to save him. I never forgot the look of that man; it has followed me all these years. But what would you have said of me, if the lifeline had laid right at my feet and I had refused to throw it to him? What would you say? Oh, friends, the lifeline of the gospel message lies at our feet. People are sinking all around us. Let us throw out the lifeline!

Evangelism, church-wide; Lay witness, importance of

Isa. 62:7; Ezek. 3:17; Acts 21:8; 2 Tim. 4:5

It is a great thing to get a church stirred. I think if I was a settled pastor I would reach the unconverted as a general thing through the people of the church. There isn't any agency on earth so powerful as a quickened church. But if the minister does all the preaching and nearly all the praying, and all the visiting, he hasn't got much of the church after all. If he is sick or taken away, the whole thing goes down.

Evangelism, individual

Acts 8:35; 17:3; 1 Cor. 1:23

A pastor stated in a sermon that handpicked fruit was the best kind of fruit. The orchard worker does not pick up the fruit that falls on the ground and put it away to keep late in the season, but he saves the fruit that is picked one by one, apple by apple, taken from the bough carefully. So we ought to be handpicking the Lord's harvest. A woman who had been going to my church a great while, when she heard this, began to work. The next night she brought her husband to the meeting. He said, "For twenty years I have not darkened the door of a church but my wife has been urging me so much all day to come here tonight, I had to come." "Yes," the woman said, "I thought I would try to do some of the work you told us about last night. My husband was the nearest to me; and I thought I would begin at home and pick him."

Evangelism, kindness in

Luke 24:45; Acts 8:30; 1 John 1:3

A few years ago as I stood at the door of a church giving out invitations to a meeting to take place that evening, a young man to whom I offered one said, "I want something more than that. I want something to do!" I urged him to come into the meeting, and after some remonstrance he consented. After the meeting I took him home, and after dinner I told him there was a room which I called the "Prophet's Room," and upstairs was another which I called the "Unbeliever's Room," and I would give him till night to decide which he would take. He was able by night to take the first, and the next day was at work urging young men to attend the noonday prayer meeting.

When I was burned out in the great Chicago fire and was left perfectly destitute, I received a letter with some money from this young man in Boston, who said, "You helped me and took me in your home, keeping me six weeks and refused to take anything for it, and I have never forgotten your kindness." I had lost sight of him, but he had remembered that as a turning point in his existence.

Evangelism, lay; Watching for souls

Isa. 62:7; Ezek. 3:17; Acts 21:8; 2 Tim. 4:5

If the ministers would encourage their members to be scattered among the audience, to never mind their pews, but sit where they can watch the faces of the audience, it would be a good thing. In Scotland, I met a man who with his wife would sit, as they said, so as to watch for souls. When they saw any one who seemed impressed, they would go to those persons after the meeting and talk with them. Nearly all the conversions in that church during the last fifteen months had been made through that influence. Now, if we could only have from thirty to fifty members of the church whose business it is just to watch, and you laymen and laywomen to afterwards clinch them in. The best way in our regular churches

is to let the workers all help pull the net in. You will get a good many fishes; it won't be now and then one, but scores and scores.

Evangelism, lostness of men

Matt. 10:6; 18:11; Luke 15:4, 24; 19:10; 2 Cor. 4:3; 2 Peter 3:9

I heard of a Christian who did not succeed in his work so well as he used to, and he got homesick for heaven and wished himself dead. One night he dreamed that he had died, and was carried by the angels to the Eternal City. As he went along the crystal pavement of heaven, he met a man he used to know, and they went walking down the golden streets together. All at once he noticed everyone looking in the same direction, and saw One coming up who was fairer than the sons of men. It was his blessed Redeemer.

As the chariot came opposite, the Lord beckoning him, placed him in his own chariot seat, and pointing over the battlements of heaven, said, "Look over yonder, what do you see?" "It seems as if I see the dark earth I have come from." "What else?" "I see men as if they were blindfolded, going over a terrible precipice into a bottomless pit." "Well," said he, "will you remain up here, and enjoy these mansions that I have prepared, or go back to yon dark earth, and warn these men, and tell them about me and my kingdom, and the rest that remaineth for the people of God?" That man never wished himself dead again. He yearned to live as long as ever he could, to tell men of heaven and of Christ.

Evangelism, necessity of

Isa. 65:24; Acts 10:19; 11:12; Rom. 10:14

One day I saw a steel engraving that I liked very much. I thought it was the finest thing I ever had seen, at the time, and I bought it. It was a picture of a woman coming out of the water, and clinging with both arms to the cross. There she came out of the drowning waves with both arms around the cross perfectly safe. Afterwards, I saw another picture that spoiled this one for me entirely, it was so much more lovely. It was a picture of a person coming out of the dark waters, with one arm clinging to the cross and with the other she was lifting someone else out of the waves. That is what I like. Keep a firm hold upon the cross, but always try to rescue another from the drowning.

Evangelism, need for

Jer. 50:6; Ezek. 34:16; Matt. 10:6; Luke 15:4; 19:10

One minister said to another: "How are you getting on at your church?" "Oh, splendidly." "Many conversions?" "Well, well, on that side we are not getting on so well. But," he said, "we have rented all our pews and are able to pay all our running expenses. We are getting on splendidly." That is what the godless call "getting on splendidly." They rent the pews, pay the minister, and meet all the running expenses.

Evangelism of children; Education, early childhood

Ps. 131:2; Matt. 18:3; Mark 10:14–15; Luke 18:16–17

It is a masterpiece of the devil to make us believe that children cannot understand religion. Would Christ have made a child the standard of faith if he had known that it was not capable of understanding his words? It is far easier for children to love and trust than for grown-up persons, and so we should set Christ before them as the supreme object of their choice.

Evangelism of peers

Mark 5:20; John 4:29; Acts 8:26; 1 Cor. 1:17

The demoniac who was healed in the country of the Gadarenes went and told of it all over Decapolis. He was only a new convert. But such was the effect of his telling his experience, that the next time Christ went over there everybody crowded to hear him and be healed by him. The woman at Jacob's well, as soon as she received the living water into her heart, ran to tell the news in Sychar; and the whole town came out to see Jesus, and to invite him to visit them.

You businessmen can reach many that the ministers cannot, and some of them are waiting for you to come and tell them about Christ. If religion is such a good thing they wonder at you for not commending it to them. If you are afraid to because you have not lived right, go and confess your sins first and then confess Christ. My rule is to speak to someone about his or her soul every day. So I preach the gospel to at least 365 persons every year; and have had many blessed experiences in doing this.

Mark 5:20; John 4:29; Acts 8:26; 1 Cor. 1:17

I would not give much for a man's Christianity if he is saved himself and is not willing to try to reach others. It seems to me the basest ingratitude if we do not reach out the hand to others who are down in the same pit from which we were delivered. Who is able to reach and help drinking men like those who have themselves been slaves to the intoxicating cup? Will you not go out this very day and seek to rescue these men? If we were all to do what we can, we should soon empty the drinking saloons.

Evangelism, patience in

Ezek. 33:31; Mark 10:17; Acts 24:25; 26:28; 2 Cor. 4:2

I remember a family in Chicago that used to hoot at me and my students as we passed their house. One day one of the boys came into the Sunday school and made light of it. As he went away, I told him I was glad to see him there and hoped he would come again. He came and still made a noise, but I urged him to come the next time, and finally one day he said, "I wish you would pray for me, boys." That boy came to Christ. He went home and confessed his faith, and it wasn't long before that whole family had found the way into the kingdom of God.

Evangelism, united effort; Enthusiasm, power of

Matt. 28:19; Acts 14:27; 20:28; 1 Cor. 10:30

In York, England, although I preached with as much earnestness and apparent effectiveness as anywhere, yet there were only a few people to hear, and it was a long time before any results were evident. The trouble in York was that the church people were not interested, and didn't care. But when there were only two or three hundred persons at our meeting, we went to work on them, and they told others, and then the meetings became crowded. As soon as the church people got interested, the blessing came.

Evangelism, vision for

Ps. 22:27; Matt. 28:19; Mark 16:15; Luke 24:47; Acts 1:8

It seems to me after I am dead and gone, I would rather have a man come to my grave and drop a tear, and say, "Here lies the man who led me to the Savior: who brought me to the cross of Christ." I would rather have this than a column of pure gold reaching to the skies, built in my honor. If a man wants to be useful, follow Christ and lead others to him.

Evangelism, work of all; Witnessing, work of all; Mission, work of all

Ps. 22:27; Matt. 28:19; Mark 16:15; Luke 24:47; Acts 1:8

If the lost are to be reached by the gospel of the Son of God, Christianity must be more aggressive than it has been in the past. We have been on the defensive long enough; the time has come for us to enter on a war of aggression. When we as children of God wake up and go to work in the vineyard, then those who are living in wickedness all about us will be reached but not in any other way. You may go to mass meetings and discuss the question "How to reach the masses." But when you have done with discussion you have to go back to personal effort. Every man and woman who loves the Lord Jesus Christ must wake up to the fact that he or she has a mission in the world, in this work of reaching the lost.

Evangelistic meetings, time of

Prov. 15:23; Isa. 50:4; Ezek. 34:26; Matt. 24:25; Gal. 6:9; 2 Tim. 4:2

God is always ready for evangelistic meetings; just as ready in August as in January. A good many people fail in evangelism because they are waiting for a set time. This idea that we have got but a few months in the year to work is a false one. We should reach out with the gospel every day.

Evangelize your world of influence

Ps. 22:27; Matt. 28:19; Mark 16:15; Luke 24:47; John 1:45; Acts 1:8; 8:5

I remember when in London a friend asked me to go down to the dog market and preach. It is a part of the city where men come to sell dogs and cats and birds. They had fighting cocks there, and were trying to get up a fight. The streets were literally crowded with this class of men, but traffic went right on. My friend said he wanted someone to preach who could get the attention of these men and he thought I could since I was an Ameri-

91

can. Some of them stopped a little while to listen, but I did not get into sympathy with them.

One man came up to me with a fighting cock, but I did not succeed in getting any hold on him; but one of their own number, who had been converted a short time before, stood up on a chair and immediately all traffic stopped, a crowd gathered round to hear him, and this man, in fifteen minutes, did more than all of us put together. What we need is every person who comes to Christ reaching out to his own folks.

Evil, association with

Josh. 23:12; Ps. 1:1; 1 Cor. 5:9; 2 Cor. 6:14; Eph. 5:11; 2 Thess. 3:14

I am judged by the company I keep. If I walk with a burglar to a bank, and wait while he robs it, and walk away with him, I am considered a partner with him in crime.

Exaggeration, sin of; Lying, sin of; Character, importance of

Matt. 18:15, 35; Luke 17:3; Acts 19:18; Col. 3:13; James 5:16

A lady once said to me, "I have got so in the habit of exaggerating that my friends accuse me of exaggerating so that they don't believe me." She said, "Can you help me? What can I do to overcome it?" "Well," I said, "the next time you catch yourself lying, go right to that party and say you have lied, and tell him you are sorry. Say it is a lie; stamp it out, root and branch; that is what you want to do." "Oh," she said, "I wouldn't like to call it lying." But that is what it was. Christianity isn't worth a snap of your finger if it doesn't straighten out your character.

Example, importance of

Ezra 7:10; Prov. 11:30; Dan. 12:3; 1 Cor. 9:19; James 5:20

Some people say, "I would follow Christ, but I am as good as the majority of Christians." Suppose I went to a man to buy some cloth and he gives me thirty-three inches to the yard. I won't take it, and then he says the man over the way gives only thirty-two. One is measuring by the standard of the other, and he should not do it. He should give thirty-six inches to the yard. But even now I would appeal to you, haven't you ever known one, who has so shone out into your life, who you are willing to say was a Christian whom you would wish to be like? We should not take the poorest specimens—we should take the best.

Excuses, abundance of

Luke 8:14; 14:18–19; 18:24

When a man prepares a feast, men rush in, but when God prepares one they all begin to make excuses, and don't want to go.

Excuses, inadequacy of; Judgment, nature of

1 Cor. 4:5; Rev. 20:12

If you have a good excuse, don't give it up for anything any preacher says; don't give it up for anything your mother may have said; don't give it up for anything your friend may have said. Take it up to the bar of God and state it to him. But if you have not got a good excuse—an excuse that will stand in eternity—let it go now and flee to the arms of a loving Savior.

Excuses, weakness of

Jer. 17:13; Matt. 7:23; 25:41

It is easy enough to excuse yourself to hell, but you cannot excuse yourself to heaven.

Existence of God, evidence of

Isa. 40:26; John 1:9; Rom. 1:19–20

Someone asked an Arab: "How do you know that there is a God?" "How do I know whether a man or a camel passed my tent last night?" he replied. God's footprints in nature and in our own experience are the best evidence of his existence and character.

Faith and works; Belief, and works; Fruit, source of

Matt. 7:16–17; 12:33; Luke 6:43; John 8:39; 1 Cor. 3:2; Heb. 11:31; James 2:18; 3:12

I believe in a faith that you can see, a living, working faith that prompts to action. Faith without works is like a man putting all his money into the foundation of a house; and works without faith is like building a house on sand without any foundation. You often hear people say, "The root of the matter is in him." What would you say if I had a garden and nothing but roots in it?

Suppose I hire two men to set out some trees and at night I go to see how they are getting on. I find that one has set out a hundred trees, and the other only ten. The first man says to me, "Look at my trees! Don't they look as well as that man's, and he has set out only ten?" I say to the other: "How's this?" "Well," he says, "wait a short time, and you will see how it is. That man doesn't believe in roots, and has cut off the little roots and stuck the trees in like sticks. I have set out ten trees roots and all." What roots are to the tree, faith is to the child of God. If we are to have eternal life, if we are to bear fruit, we must be rooted and grounded in Christ Jesus.

Faith, aspects of; Belief, aspects of

John 17:3

There are three things indispensable to faith—knowledge, assent, and appropri-ation. We must know God. "And this is life eternal, that they might know Thee the only true God, and Jesus Christ, whom Thou hast sent" (John 17:3). Then we must not only give our assent to what we know, but we must lay hold of the truth. If a man simply gives his assent to the plan of salvation, it will not save him: he must accept Christ as his Savior. We must receive and appropriate him.

Faith before works; Belief before works

Phil. 2:12

We work because we are saved. We do not work to be saved. We work from the cross and not toward it. I imagine some of you say, "Why does Paul say, then, 'Work out your own salvation with fear and trembling'?" You must have salvation before you can work it out. I must give my boy a garden before he can work the weeds out of it. If I said to him: "Be careful how you spend that hundred dollars," he would say, "Give it to me first."

Faith, bond of society

Gen. 15:6; Deut. 31:8; 2 Sam. 22:31; Neh. 4:14; Pss. 5:11; 7:1; 118:8–9; Isa. 26:4; Rom. 4:3; 1 Thess. 2:13; 1 Peter 2:6; James 2:23

Faith is the bond which holds family with family. If once this bond is dissolved, there would exist a state of barbarism and anarchy like that which marked the close of the eighteenth century in Paris. With everyone distrusting his neighbor, and fearing his nearest friends, progress is impossible and civilization inconceivable.

Faith, childlike

Matt. 6:25, 34; 8:2; 9:20; 17:8, 19–20; Mark 1:40; 5:12, 28; 11:23–24; Luke 8:44; 12:32; 17:6

A family in a Southern city were stricken down with yellow fever. It was raging there, and there were very stringent sanitary rules. The moment anybody died, a cart went around and took the body away. The father was taken sick and died and was buried, and the mother was at last stricken down. The neighbors were afraid of the plague, and none dared go into the house. The mother had a little son and was anxious about her boy, and afraid he would be neglected when she was called away, so she called the little fellow to her bedside, and said, "My boy, I am going to leave you, but Jesus will come to you when I am gone." The mother died, the cart came along and she was laid in the grave.

The neighbors would have liked to take the boy, but were afraid of the pestilence. He wandered about and finally went up to the place where they had laid his mother and sat down on the grave and wept himself to sleep. Next morning he awoke and realized his position—alone and hungry. A stranger came along and seeing the little fellow sitting on the ground, asked him what he was waiting for. The boy remembered what his mother had told him and answered, "I am waiting for Jesus," and told him the whole story.

The man's heart was touched, tears trickled down his cheeks and he said, "Jesus has sent me," to which the boy replied, "You have been a good while coming, sir." He was provided for. So it is with us. To wait for results, we must have courage and patience and God will help us.

Matt. 6:25, 34; 8:2; 9:20; 17:8, 19–20; Mark 1:40; 5:12, 28; 11:23–24; Luke 8:44; 12:32; 17:6

A little child, whose father and mother had died, was taken into another family. The first night she asked if she could pray, as she used to do. They said, "Oh, yes." So she knelt down, and prayed as her mother taught her; and when that was ended she added a little prayer of her own, "Oh, God, make these people as kind to me as father and mother were." Then she paused and looked up, as if expecting the answer, and added, "Of course you will." How sweetly simple was

that little one's faith; she expected God to "do," and of course she got her request.

Matt. 6:25, 34; 8:2; 9:20; 17:8, 19–20; Mark 1:40; 5:12, 28; 11:23–24; Luke 8:44; 12:32; 17:6

Let the same confidence motivate us that was in little Maggie, as related in the following simple but touching incident which I read in *The Bible Treasury*.

"I had been absent from home for some days, and was wondering, as I again drew near the homestead, if my little Maggie, just able to sit alone, would remember me. To test her memory, I stationed myself where I could see her, but could not be seen by her, and called her name in the familiar tone, 'Maggie!' She dropped her playthings, glanced around the room, and then looked down upon her toys. Again I repeated her name, 'Maggie!' Then she once more surveyed the room; but, not seeing her father's face, she looked very sad, and slowly resumed her employment.

"Once more I called, 'Maggie!' Then dropping her playthings, and bursting into tears, she stretched out her arms in the direction from whence the sound proceeded, knowing that, though she could not see him her father must be there, for she knew his voice."

Matt. 6:25, 34; 8:2; 9:20; 17:8, 19–20; Mark 1:40; 5:12, 28; 11:23–24; Luke 8:44; 12:32; 17:6

There is a man who works in the city of New York who has a home on the Hudson River. His daughter and her family went to spend the winter with him: and in the course of the season the scarlet fever broke out. One little girl was put in quarantine, to be kept separate from the rest. Every morning the grandfather used to go in to bid his grandchild, "Good-by," before going to his business.

On one of these occasions the little girl took the man by the hand, and, leading him to a corner of the room, without saying a word she pointed to the floor where she had arranged some small crackers so they would spell out, "Grandpa, I want a box of paints."

He said nothing. On his return home he hung up his overcoat and went to the room as usual: when his little grandchild, without looking to see if her wish had been complied with, took him into the same corner, where he saw spelled out in the same way, "Grandpa, I thank you for the box of paints." The old man would not have missed gratifying the child for anything. That was faith.

Matt. 6:25, 34; 8:2; 9:20; 17:8, 19–20; Mark 1:40; 5:12, 28; 11:23–24; Luke 8:44; 12:32; 17:6

The best illustration of faith is a little child. Take that little girl—she lives a life of faith. She never bothers her head where her breakfast or supper are coming from. Her elbow peeps out of a hole in her sleeve; don't bother her a bit; she knows mother will get her another dress. Now, we are to have that same childlike faith.

Faith, content of; Belief, content of

Gen. 17:7; Exod. 15:2; 2 Sam. 7:28; 2 Chron. 32:7–8; Jer. 31:1; John 13:35; 3:16; Acts 2:24; Rom. 8:24; 9:26; Heb. 11:1–2, 13; 2 Peter 1:1, 8

People have an idea now that it makes very little difference what a man believes if he is only sincere, if he is only honest in his creed. I believe that is one of the greatest lies that ever came out of the pit of hell. Why, they virtually say you can believe a lie just as well as you can believe the truth, if you are only in earnest, and stick to it.

Suppose I go to a bank in Boston and present a request for $10,000, and the cashier says, "Have you any money in this bank?" I say, "No, nor in any other bank." "What are you drawing this request on?" "Earnestness. I really need that money! There isn't a man in Massachusetts who wants to get $10,000 as much as D. L. Moody."

They would have me in a madhouse inside of thirty days, if not inside of thirty hours; and you people who say it doesn't make any difference what a man believes, you are deluded by Satan!

Faith, courageous

Gen. 24:7; Josh. 1:9; 1 Sam. 17:37; 2 Kings 18:5; 2 Chron. 32:8; Jer. 24:7; Ezek. 36:24; Matt. 21:21; Luke 8:48; Rom. 6:17; 1 Tim. 1:19; James 1:6, 25

The trouble is that a lot of people are satisfied with a little. I believe God will fill every cup, but I believe there are some awful small cups. It wouldn't take a long while to fill some cups here, they are so small. There's a little cup, a dainty one, and it won't hold much. If you are very thirsty, it will not satisfy you; it's too small. "My cup runneth over," said one; and you are satisfied with a cup that won't run over. Be a man and be thirsty! There are hundreds of small cups. I would say to you: "Get the biggest cup you can find." You can have a good big cup, if you will. Pray God to increase your capacity. Don't be satisfied with small things. I honor God when I ask for great and mighty things. Ask for great things here today.

Faith, courageous; Vision, importance of

Gen. 24:7; Josh. 1:9; 1 Sam. 17:37; 2 Kings 18:5; 2 Chron. 32:8; Jer. 24:7; Ezek. 36:24; Matt. 21:21; Luke 8:48; Rom. 6:17; 1 Tim. 1:19; James 1:6, 25

We need the courage that will compel us to move forward. We may have to go against the advice of lukewarm Christians. There are some who never seem to do anything but object, because the work is not carried on exactly according to their ideas. They are very fruitful in raising objections to any plans that can be suggested. If any onward step is taken they are ready to throw cold water on it and suggest all kinds of difficulties. We want to have such faith and courage as shall enable us to move forward without waiting for these timid unbelievers.

Faith, credentials of; Christianity, proof of

Gen. 17:7; Exod. 15:2; 2 Sam. 7:28; 2 Chron. 32:7–8; Jer. 31:1; Acts 2:24; John 13:35; 3:16; Rom. 8:24; 9:26; Heb. 11:1–2; 2 Peter 1:1, 8

How are you going to tell whether or not you are a Christian? Not by the fact that you are a Catholic or a Protestant, not that you subscribe to some creed that man has drawn up. We must have something better than that. What did Christ say? "By this shall all men know that ye are My disciples, if ye have love one to another."

When I was first converted, I used to wish that every Christian would wear a badge, because I would like to know them; my heart went out toward the household of faith. But I have got over that. If Christianity should become popular, every hypocrite would have a badge inside of thirty days. We have no badge to wear outside; but God gives us a badge in the heart. The man that hasn't any love in his creed may let it go to the winds; I don't want it. Love is the fruit of the Spirit. "If any man have not the Spirit of Christ, he is none of His."

Faith, definition of; Belief, definition of

Gen. 17:7; Exod. 15:2; 2 Sam. 7:28; 2 Chron. 32:7–8; Jer. 31:1; Acts 2:24; John 13:35; 3:16; Rom. 8:24; 9:26; Heb. 11:1–2, 13; 2 Peter 1:1, 8

Hebrews 11:1 is the Bible definition of Faith. The best definition I ever saw outside the Bible is: Dependence on the veracity of another. In other words, faith says Amen to everything that God says. Faith takes God without any "If's." If God says it, Faith says, "I believe it"; Faith says "Amen" to it.

Faith, elements of; Belief, elements of

Ps. 33:6; Isa. 40:26; John 1:3; Acts 17:24; Rom. 1:19; 8:25; Gal. 5:6; Heb. 10:22, 39; 11:3, 6; 1 Peter 1:7; 2 Peter 3:5;

Faith is very important. It is the link that binds us to every promise of God—it brings us every blessing. I do not mean a dead faith, but a living faith. There is a great difference between the two. A man may tell me that ten thousand dollars are deposited in a certain bank in my name. I may believe it, but if I don't act upon it and get the money it does me no good. Unbelief bars the door and keeps back the blessing.

Someone has said there are three elements in faith—knowledge, assent, laying hold. Knowledge! A man may have a good deal of knowledge about Christ, but that does not save him. I suppose Noah's carpenters knew as much about the ark as Noah did, but they perished miserably nevertheless, because they were not in the ark. Our knowledge about Christ does not help us if we do not act upon it. But knowledge is very important. Many also assent and say "I believe"; but that does not save them. Knowledge, assent, then laying hold: it is that last element that saves, that brings the soul and Christ together.

Faith, enemies of

1 John 2:15

There are three terrible foes that oppose the believer: the world, self, and Satan. We read in 1 John 2:15, "Love not the world, neither the things that are in the world. If any man love the world, the love of the Father is not in him." To some people that is a difficult passage. But it doesn't mean that you must not admire the wonders of creation, the beautiful rivers, the lofty mountains, etc., but that you do not set your heart upon those things. We are only pilgrims upon this earth; our true home is heaven. Hence it is that anything that would tend to win our hearts from God should be regarded as an enemy.

But I don't mean that you are to give up your business. It is necessary that everybody be engaged in some legitimate business to earn an honest living. The fashions and pleasures of this world draw away the hearts of many. During the summer months in California Christians will be greatly exposed to temptations, for amusements and excursions will surround them on all sides. Every true disciple of the cross must adopt the motto of Martin Luther: "I yield to none."

Faith, example of; Belief, example of

2 Chron. 32:7–8; Ps. 9:10; Matt. 2:2; 4:22; 9:21; Mark 1:18; 10:48; Luke 5:6; 18:38; John 6:69; 8:56; Acts 6:8; 8:37; James 2:21, 25

I remember, while in Mobile attending meetings, a little incident occurred which I will relate. It was a beautiful evening, and just before the meeting some neighbors and myself were sitting on the front porch enjoying the evening. One of the neighbors put one of his children upon a ledge eight feet high, and put out his hands and told him to jump. Without the slightest hesitation he sprang into his father's arms. Another child was lifted up, and he, too, readily sprang into the arms of his father.

He picked up another boy, larger than the others, and held out his arms, but he wouldn't jump. He cried and screamed to be taken down. The man begged the boy to jump, but it was of no use; he couldn't be induced to jump. The incident made me curious, and I stepped up to him and asked, "How was it that those two little fellows jumped so readily into your arms and the other boy wouldn't?" "Why," said the man, "those two boys are my children and the other boy isn't, he doesn't know me."

Faith, example of; Belief, nature of

2 Chron. 32:7–8; Ps. 9:10; Matt. 2:2; 4:22; 9:21; Mark 1:18; 10:48; Luke 5:6; 18:38; John 6:69; 8:56; Acts 6:8; 8:37; James 2:21, 25

We have heard a great deal about the faith of Abraham, and the faith of Moses; but the thief on the cross seems to me to have had more faith than any of them. He stands at the head of the class. God was twenty-five years toning up the faith of Abraham; Moses was forty years getting ready for his work; but this thief, right here in the midst of men who rejected Christ— nailed to the cross, and racked with pain in every nerve, overwhelmed with terror, and his soul in a perfect tempest—still manages to lay hold upon Christ, and trust in him for a swift salvation.

Faith, example of; Conversion of infidel

Luke 5:20

When I was in Edinburgh, at the inquiry meeting in Assembly Hall, one of the ushers came around and said, "Mr. Moody, I'd like to put that man out; he's one of the greatest infidels in Edinburgh." He had been the chairman of an infidel club for years. I went around to where he was and sat down by him. "How is it with you, my friend?" I asked, and then he laughed and said, "You say God answers prayer; I tell you he doesn't. I don't believe in a God. Try it on me." "Will you get down with me and pray?" I asked him; but he wouldn't. So I got down on my knees beside him and prayed.

Next night he was there again. I prayed, and quite a number of others prayed for him. A few months after that, away up in the north of Scotland, at Wick, I was preaching in the open air, and while

I stood there I saw the infidel standing on the outskirts of the crowd. I went up to him at the close of the meeting and said, "How is it with you, my friend?" He laughed and said, "I told you your praying is all false; God hasn't answered your prayers; go and talk to these deluded people." He had just the same spirit as before, but I relied on faith.

Shortly after I got a letter from an attorney who is a Christian. He was preaching one night in Edinburgh, when this infidel went up to him and said, "I want you to pray for me; I am troubled." The barrister asked, "What is the trouble?" He replied, "I don't know what's the matter, but I don't have any peace, and I want you to pray for me." Next day he went around to that lawyer's office and he said that he had found Christ.

This man now is doing good work, and I heard that out of thirty inquirers there, ten or twelve of his old associates and friends were among them. So, if you have God with you, and you go to work for him, and you meet infidels and skeptics, just bear in mind that you can win through faith. When Christ saw the faith of those four men, he said to the man, "Thy sins are forgiven you." My friends, if you have faith all things are possible.

Faith, exercise of; Belief, exercise of

2 Chron. 32:7–8; Ps. 9:10; Matt. 2:2; 4:22; 9:21; Mark 1:18; 10:48; Luke 5:6; 18:38; John 6:69; 8:56; Acts 6:8; 8:37; James 2:21, 25

The first sign of a dawning intelligence in the mind is the exercise of the infant's faith toward those it knows, and its fear toward those it does not know. We cannot even remember when we first began to have faith.

Faith, fervent; Prayer, power of

Gen. 24:7; Josh. 1:9; 1 Sam. 17:37; 2 Kings 18:5; 2 Chron. 32:8; Jer. 24:7; Ezek. 36:24; Matt.

21:21; Luke 8:48; Rom. 6:17; 1 Tim. 1:19; Heb.11:11; James 1:6, 25

God's best gifts, like valuable jewels, are kept under lock and key, and those who want them must, with fervent faith, importunately ask for them; for God is the rewarder of them that diligently seek him.

Faith, grounds of; Belief, grounds of

Gen. 17:7; Exod. 15:2; 2 Sam. 7:28; 2 Chron. 32:7–8; Jer. 31:1; John 13:35; 3:16; Acts 2:24; Rom. 8:24; 9:26; Heb. 11:1–2, 13; 2 Peter 1:1, 8

What grounds do you have for not believing God?

Faith in testimony; Belief in testimony

Num. 23:19; Acts 27:25; Rom. 4:20

Faith is a belief in testimony. It is not a leap in the dark. God does not ask any person to believe without giving something to believe. You might as well ask a person to see without eyes, as to demand belief without giving something to believe.

Faith, lack of; Belief, lack of

Ps. 95:10; Matt. 13:58; 16:8; Mark 9:19; 16:14; Luke 9:41; 24:25; John 16:9; 20:27; Acts 13:18; 1 Tim. 1:5,19; Heb. 4:2; 10:35, 38

I said to a man, "We know that the Son of God hath come." He replied, "I don't believe that." I talked with him a little, and made another statement from the Bible. He didn't believe that. Finally, I said, "Man, will you tell me what you do believe?" and he didn't believe anything except that he didn't believe.

Faith, lack of; Unbelief, danger of

John 20:28

Some men seem to think it is a great misfortune that they do not have faith. They seem to look upon it as a kind of infirmity, and they think they ought to be sympathized with and pitied. Bear in mind it is not a misfortune; it is the most damning sin of the world. The greatest enemy God and man have got is unbelief. Christ found it on both sides of the cross. It was the very thing that put him to death. The Jews did not believe him. They did not believe God had sent him. They took him to Calvary and murdered him. And the first thing we find after he rose from the grave was unbelief again. Thomas, one of his own disciples, did not believe he had risen. He said, "Thomas, feel these wounds"; and Thomas believed, and said, "My Lord and my God."

Faith, little; Humility, example of

Matt. 17:20; Mark 4:31; Luke 13:19; 17:6

A Scotch woman was once introduced as "Mrs.—, a woman of great faith." "No," she said, "I am a woman of little faith, but with a great God."

Faith, naturalness of

Matt. 6:25, 34; 8:2; 9:20; 17:8, 19–20; Mark 1:40; 5:12, 28; 11:23–24; Luke 8:44; 12:32; 17:6; Acts 5:15

To many people the very term of faith, used in connection with man's relation to God, implies something mysterious. They will speak of having implicit confidence in a friend, of trusting a servant with their last cent, or being willing to credit a customer with any amount, considering his word as good as his note; yet they do not realize that God simply asks of them the same trust and confidence, which they are using in the affairs of their everyday life.

Faith, nature of; Belief, joy of; Testimony, importance of

Ps. 33:6; Isa. 40:26; John 1:3; Acts 17:24; Rom. 1:19; 8:25; Gal. 5:6; 1 Peter 1:7; 2 Peter 3:5; Heb. 10:22, 39; 11:3, 6

People will not trust strangers. I want to get acquainted with a man before I put my confidence in him. I have known God for forty years, and I have more confidence in him now than I ever had before; it increases every year. In the Bible, some things that were dark ten years ago are plain today; and some things that are dark now will be plain ten years hence. We must take things by faith. You take the existence of cities on the testimony of men that have been in those cities; and we ask men to take our testimony, who have found joy in believing.

Faith, nature of; Belief, nature of; Unbelief, danger of

John 20:28; Rom. 3:4

I have a great admiration for the old black woman who said if God told her to jump through a stone wall she would jump at it; getting through the wall was God's work, not hers, and she would do whatever God told her to do.

Christians that have learned to trust God in past years will bear me out that the more they know of God the more they can trust him. Why? They have found God to be true. When man has failed, God never has failed; and when everyone else has disappointed them, God has proven true.

Faith, nature of; Unbelief, nature of

Ps. 33:6; Isa. 40:26; John 1:3; Acts 17:24; Rom. 1:19; 8:25; Gal. 5:6; 1 Peter 1:7; 2 Peter 3:5; Heb. 10:22, 39; 11:3, 6

Have faith in God! Take him at his word! Believe what he says! Believe the record God has given of his Son! I can imagine some of you saying, "I want to, but I have not got the right kind of faith." What kind of faith do you want? Now, the idea that you need a different kind of faith is all wrong. Use the faith you have got; just believe on the Lord Jesus Christ. Not only that, you can't give any reason for not believing. If a man told me he couldn't believe me, I should have a right to ask him why he couldn't believe me. I should have a right to ask him if I had ever broken my word with him; and if I had not broken my word with him, he ought to believe me. I would like to ask you, has God ever broken his word? Never. My friends, he will keep his word.

God condemns the world because they believe not on him; that is the root of all evil. A man who believes in the Lord Jesus Christ won't murder, and lie, and do all these awful things. Don't get caught up by that terrible delusion that unbelief is a misfortune. Unbelief is not a misfortune, but is the sin of the world. Christ found it on all sides of the world. When he first got up from the grave, he found that his disciples doubted. He had reason to cry out against unbelief.

Faith, not feelings

Gen. 3:12; 16:2; Rom. 4:10; 5:1; Gal. 3:3

I was preaching in Illinois in an area where I had never been before. When I crossed a bridge and went down along the river, I said, "I am sure this is the road to Quincy." But after traveling a while it occurred to me that I had better ask because I was going by my feelings altogether. So I shouted to a man, and said, "Hello! Am I on the right road to Quincy?" "No, sir, you are going right away from it." And I concluded that man had probably been to Quincy, and was acquainted with the way. So I turned my horse around and went on to Quincy. Before I turned I had traveled according to my feelings; but I was now traveling against my feelings. When you come to Christ, don't trust your feelings but the sure word of the Bible.

Faith, not feelings; Belief, object of

Gen. 3:12; 16:2; Isa. 26:3–4; Rom. 4:10; 5:1; Gal. 3:3; Heb. 12:2

As long as our mind is stayed on our dear selves, we will never have peace. Some people think more of themselves than of all the rest of the world. It is self in the morning, self at noon, and self at night. It is self when they wake up, and self when they go to bed. They are all the time looking at themselves and thinking about themselves, instead of "looking unto Jesus." Faith is an outward look. Faith does not look within, it looks without. It is not what I think, or what I feel, or what I have done but it is what Jesus Christ is and has done that is the important thing for us to dwell upon.

Faith, object of

Rom. 10:17

When first entering Christian work, my one ambition was to be a man of faith. I prayed for faith; I worked for faith; I fasted for faith. All the useful men I had ever heard of had been men of faith, and I realized that it was a necessity for anyone who was to devote his life to God's service. I looked for some wonderful, miraculous gift that should suddenly come to me. One day I was reading the Epistle of Romans when I came to the verse: "So then faith cometh by hearing, and hearing by the word of God" (Rom. 10:17). That one passage gives the direction for receiving faith in Christ, and that is simply by trusting the scriptural revelation about him.

Faith is not some mysterious feeling that we discover within ourselves, but simply the natural results of knowing Christ, both through the Scriptures, and in our lives. Faith is an outward look and not an inward view. It is not important to examine the nature of faith, but it is all-important to study the object of faith.

Faith, object of; Confidence in God

Gen. 15:6; Deut. 31:8; 2 Sam. 22:31; Neh. 4:14; Pss. 5:11; 7:1; 118:8–9; Isa. 26:4; Rom. 4:3; 1 Thess. 2:13; James 2:23; 1 Peter 2:6

Some men in Scotland made it a business to get a certain kind of egg, and they made considerable money. They tried to get a man into a basket and lower him over a cliff to collect the eggs from birds' nests. They would pay him a good deal of money, and he needed the money. He declined to do it. They told him, "We are strong, and we'll hold the rope." The man replied, "If you'll wait until I go and get my father, I'll let him hold the rope, and I'll go down in the basket." They said, "We are stronger than your father." "Yes," he answered, "but I don't know you." He knew that his father wouldn't let go of the rope. He could trust his father, but these strangers he could not trust. I want to get acquainted with a man before I put my confidence in him. I have known God for forty years, and I have more confidence in him now than I ever had before; it increases every year.

Faith, object of; Temptation, strength in; Trials, strength in

Gen. 15:6; Deut. 31:8; 2 Sam. 22:31; Neh. 4:14; Pss. 5:11; 7:1; 118:8–9; Isa. 26:4; Rom. 4:3; 1 Thess. 2:13; James 2:23; 1 Peter 2:6

How often we hear a man say, "There is a member of the church who cheated me out of five dollars, and I am not going to have anything more to do with people who call themselves Christians." But if the man had had faith in Jesus Christ you do not suppose he would have had his faith shattered because some one cheated him out of five dollars, do you? What we need is to have faith in the Lord Jesus Christ. If

a man has that, he has something he can anchor to, and the anchor will hold; and when the hour of temptation comes to him, and the hour of trial, the man will stand firm. If we are only converted to man and our faith is in man, we will certainly be disappointed.

Faith, pilgrim nature of; Strangers on earth

Gen. 23:4; 47:9; Lev. 25:23; 1 Chron. 29:15; Pss. 39:12; 119:19; 146:9; Heb. 11:13, 34; 13:2; 1 Peter 1:1; 2:11

I was going to New Orleans from Chicago a few years ago, and there were two ladies on the train near me. They got well acquainted with one another by the time they reached Cairo, Illinois, where one lived; the other was going on to New Orleans. The one who had to get out at Cairo said to the other, "I wish you would stay here with me for a few days, I like your company so much." "I should like to stay," replied the other, "but my things are all packed and have gone on before; I have no clothes but those I am wearing. They are good enough to travel in, but I would not like to be seen in company with them."

Now that is the way with the Christian. We are away from home here, our treasure has gone on before, and anything is good enough to travel in. If things don't go smoothly down here we need not be too particular, they're good enough to travel in. If our treasures are in heaven our hearts will be there, and we shall be living as pilgrims and strangers on the earth. That is what I think of the journey of this world. A very little is good enough for us to travel in. We are all travelers, and this is good enough for traveling. We have raiment and mansions up there, waiting for us. Let us have our hearts and affections set on things above, and not on things on the earth.

Gen. 23:4; 47:9; Lev. 25:23; 1 Chron. 29:15; Pss. 39:12; 119:19; 146:9; Heb. 11:13, 34; 13:2; 1 Peter 1:1; 2:11

You must learn to be like a rock in the stream, past which the current flows rapidly, but it is unmoved. You are still in the world, but you are not of the world. You are citizens of another world, and only strangers and pilgrims here.

Faith, power of; Belief, power of

Acts 16:25

Listen to Paul in the jail at Philippi. "If God wants me to go to heaven by way of this prison," he says, "it is all the same to me; rejoice and be exceeding glad, Silas. I thank God that I am accounted worthy to suffer for Jesus' sake." And as they sang their praises to God, the other prisoners heard them; but, what was far more important, the Lord heard them, and the old prison shook. Talk about Alexander the Great making the world tremble with his armies. Here is a little tentmaker who makes the world tremble without any army!

Matt. 6:25, 34; 8:2; 9:20; 17:8, 19–20; Mark 1:40; 5:12, 28; 11:23–24; Luke 8:44; 12:32; 17:6

We get life by believing. In fact we get more than Adam lost; for the redeemed child of God is heir to a richer and more glorious inheritance than Adam in Paradise could ever have conceived; yea, and that inheritance endures forever— it is inalienable. I would much rather have my life hid with Christ in God than have lived in the Garden of Eden; for Adam might have sinned and fallen after being there ten thousand years. But the believer is safer, if these things become real to him. Let us make them a fact, and not a fiction. God has said it; and that is enough. Let us trust God even where we cannot trace him.

Faith, power of; Courage, source of; Fruitfulness, source of

Matt. 9:29

I remember a man telling me he preached for a number of years without any result. He used to say to his wife as they went to church that he knew the people would not believe anything he said; and there was no blessing. At last he saw his error. He asked God to help him, and took courage, and then the blessing came.

"According to your faith it shall be unto you." This man had expected nothing and he got just what he expected. Dear friends, let us expect that God is going to use us. Let us have courage and go forward, looking to God to do great things.

Faith, power of; Unbelief, danger of

Pss. 18:30; 125:1; Prov. 28:5; 29:25; Isa. 26:3; 57:13; Jer. 17:7–8; Matt. 9:22; 21:21–22; Luke 8:48; Acts 3:16; Heb. 3:19; James 1:6

When the Israelites first came out of Egypt, God would have led them right up into the land of Canaan if it had not been for their accursed unbelief. But they desired something besides God's word; so they were turned back, and had to wander in the desert for forty years. I believe there are thousands of God's children wandering in the wilderness still. The Lord has delivered them from the hand of the Egyptian, and would at once take them through the wilderness right into the Promised Land, if they were only willing to follow Christ. Christ has been down here, and has made the rough places smooth, and the dark places light, and the crooked places straight. If we will only be led by him right into the land of promise, all will be peace, and joy, and rest.

Faith, power of; Unbelief, failure of; Belief, power of

Pss. 18:30; 125:1; Prov. 28:5; 29:25; Isa. 26:3; 57:13; Jer. 17:7–8; Matt. 9:22; 21:21–22; Luke 8:48; Acts 3:16

So faith is the golden key that unlocks the treasures of heaven. It was the shield that David took when he met Goliath on the field; he believed that God was going to deliver the Philistine into his hands. Someone has said that faith could lead Christ about anywhere; wherever he found it he honored it. Unbelief sees something in God's hand, and says, "I cannot get it." Faith sees it, and says, "It is mine."

Faith, practical; Reverence, false

Isa. 58:8; Matt. 5:16; Mark 4:21; Luke 11:33; Eph. 2:8; 5:8; Phil. 2:15; 1 Peter 2:9

Phillips Brooks told a story about a primitive tribe to whom was given a sundial. So desirous were they to honor and keep it sacred that they housed it in and built a roof over it. Is your belief in God so reverent that you put it to one side carefully as being too sacred for daily use? Learn to use it. Let God in on your life. Let your faith inspire you to good works.

Faith, prayer of

Matt. 17:21; Rom. 8:26; James 1:6; 5:15

I remember hearing of a boy brought up in an English orphanage. He had never learned to read or write, except that he could read the letters of the alphabet. One day a man of God came there, and told the children that if they prayed to God in their trouble, he would send them help. After a time, this boy was apprenticed to a farmer. One day he was sent into the fields to look after some sheep. He was having great difficulty with the task; so he remembered what the preacher had said, and he thought he would pray to God about it. Someone going by the field heard a voice behind the hedge.

They looked to see whose it was, and saw the little fellow on his knees, saying, "A, B, C, D," and so on. The man said, "My boy, what are you doing?" He looked up, and said he was praying. "Why, that is not praying; it is only saying the alphabet." He said, "I don't know just how to pray, but a man once came to the orphanage, who told us that if we called upon God, he would help us. So I thought that if I named over the letters of the alphabet, God would take them and put them together into a prayer, and give me what I need." The little fellow was really praying.

Faith, reasonableness of

Gen. 17:7; Exod. 15:2; 2 Sam. 7:28; 2 Chron. 32:7–8; Jer. 31:1; John 13:35; 3:16; Acts 2:24; Rom. 8:24; 9:26; Heb. 11:1–2, 13; 2 Peter 1:1, 8

A couple of commercial travelers went to hear a minister preach. He explained that men don't find out God; that it is God who has to reveal his nature to man; that it is all a matter of revelation; that God reveals Christ to man. When they went back to the hotel they began to talk the matter over, and both maintained that they could not believe anything except they could reason it out. An old man there heard the conversation, and remarked, "I heard you say you could not believe anything except you could reason it out. Now, when I was coming down on the train, I noticed in the fields some geese and sheep and swine and cattle eating grass. Can you tell me by what process that grass is turned into hair and bristles and feathers and wool?"

They could not. "Well, do you believe it is a fact?" "Oh yes, we can't help but believe that." "Well, then, I can't help but believe in the revelation of Jesus Christ. I have seen men who have been reclaimed and reformed through it, and who are now living happy, when before they were outcasts from society." The two commercial men were silenced by that old man's outspoken faith.

Faith, reasonableness of; Belief, reasonableness of

Gen. 17:7; Exod. 15:2; 2 Sam. 7:28; 2 Chron. 32:7–8; Jer. 31:1; John 13:35; 3:16; Acts 2:24; Rom. 8:24; 9:26; Heb. 11:1–2, 13; 2 Peter 1:1, 8

We ought in these days to have far more faith than Abel, or Enoch, or Abraham had. They lived away on the other side of the cross. We talk about the faith of Elijah, and the patriarchs and prophets but they lived in the dim light of the past, while we are in the full blaze of Calvary and the resurrection. When we look back and think of what Christ did, how he poured out his blood that men might be saved, we ought to go forth in his strength and conquer the world. Our God is able to do great and mighty things.

Faith, result of; Belief, result of

Pss. 18:30; 125:1; Prov. 28:5; 29:25; Isa. 26:3; 57:13; Jer. 17:7–8; Matt. 9:22; 21:21–22; Luke 8:48; Acts 3:16; Eph. 2:8–9; Heb. 3:19; James 1:6

Before my conversion, I worked toward the cross, but since then I have worked from the cross. Then I worked to be saved, now I work because I am saved.

Faith, reward of; Belief, reward of

Matt.14:20; Mark 6:43; 8:19; Luke 9:17; John 6:13

There was a little boy probably with his satchel and the five loaves and two fishes that he brought himself, but he comes and lays it down for the feeding of that multitude. Andrew was almost put to the blush and said, "What are they among so many?" He forgot that Christ was behind them, who took them and multiplied them for the thousands. The motive power is not in the railway car, but in the engine. So if you and I are coupled to Christ by a living faith, he works through us and it is in this way that one can chase a thousand. The issue will be far more than you can accomplish because Christ is working through you.

There is also a lesson of piety. Christ took the bread, and gave thanks to the great Giver of bread, that he might teach you and me to do the same. Let us thank God over our meals. There is an old story of the Covenanters when they were being persecuted, that a man came among them and passed himself off as one of themselves, until the girl came from the faraway farm with food. With their usual hospitality, they served the stranger first, but they noticed he began to eat without a blessing. That revealed the spy, and they escaped before the soldiers came to arrest them.

There is also a lesson of reward. God never encourages us to work for nothing. Here twelve baskets of fragments were taken up. The most frugal Christians are often those who give the most for Christ's cause. Never forget, if you work for Christ a return blessing comes to your own heart.

Faith, saving

Isa. 35:4; 43:2; Jer. 42:11; Zeph. 3:17; Acts 26:18; Rom. 1:16; 4:2; 5:1; 9:32; Gal. 3:24; 2:8; Eph. 2:8–9

While I was in New York, an Irishman stood up in a young converts' meeting and told how he had been saved. He said in his broken Irish brogue that I used an illustration, and that illustration showed him the light. He said I used an illustration of a wrecked vessel, and said that all would perish unless some assistance came. Presently a lifeboat came alongside and the captain shouted, "Leap into the lifeboat. Leap for your lives, or you will perish," and when I came to the point and said, "Leap into the lifeboat; Christ is your lifeboat of salvation," he made the leap of faith in Christ and was saved.

Faith, saving; Feelings, unable to save

Job 13:15

"I can't feel," says one. That is the very last excuse people use. When a man comes with that excuse he is getting pretty near the Lord. With some people it is feel, feel, feel all the time. What kind of feeling have you got? Have you got a desire to be saved? Suppose a gentleman asked me to dinner, and I say, "I will see how I feel." "Sick?" he might ask. "No; it depends on how I feel." That is not the question—it is whether I will accept the invitation or not. The question with us is, will we accept salvation—will you believe? There is not a word about feelings in the Scriptures.

When you come to your end, and you know that in a few days you will be in the presence of the Judge of all the earth, you will remember this excuse about feelings. You will be saying, "I went up to the Chicago Tabernacle, I remember, and I felt very good, and before the meeting was over I felt very bad, and I didn't feel I had the right kind of feeling to accept the invitation." Satan will then say, "I made you feel so."

Suppose you build your hopes and fix yourself upon the Rock of Ages, the devil cannot come to you. Stand upon the Word of God and the waves of unbelief cannot touch you, the waves of persecution cannot assail you; the devil and all the fiends of hell cannot approach you if you only build your hopes upon God's Word. Say, I will trust him, though he slay me—I will take God at his word.

Faith, simplicity of; Belief, possibility of

Matt. 6:25, 34; 8:2; 9:20; 17:8, 19–20; Mark 1:40; 5:12, 28; 11:23–24; Luke 8:44; 12:32; 17:6

God has put the offer of salvation in such a way that the whole world can lay hold of it. All men can believe. A lame man might not perhaps be able to visit the sick; but he can believe. A blind man, by reason of his infirmity, cannot do some things; but he can believe. A deaf man can believe. A dying man can believe. God has put salvation so simply that young and old, wise and foolish, rich and poor, can all believe if they will.

Faith vs. feeling

Gen. 3:12; 16:2; Rom. 4:10; 5:1; Gal. 3:3

But it is not feeling God requires, but faith; and faith comes by hearing. It is taking God at his word, receiving what he has said as true. It is better to know a thing than to feel it. I would rather build my hopes on God's word than on my own feelings. They often deceive me. When I am in Cleveland, I lose the points of the compass, because the water is on a different side of the city from that I have been accustomed to in Chicago. If I went by my feelings, I would walk into the lake. I have to use my knowledge to correct and control my feelings. If I take a wrong road and find it out, I don't feel like turning back; but I do so, in spite of my feelings; I do so on the testimony of someone whom I meet. And should we not turn when God tells us that we are going in the wrong direction?

Faith vs. feeling; Religion, sensual; Commandment, second

Gen. 3:12; 16:2; Exod. 20:4; Isa. 42:8; Acts 17:29; Rom. 1:23; 4:10; 5:1; Gal. 3:3

The tendency of the human heart to represent God by something that appeals to the senses is the origin of all idolatry. It leads directly to image worship. At first there may be no desire to worship the thing itself, but it inevitably ends in that. As Dr. MacLaren says, "Enlisting the senses as allies of the spirit is risky work. They are apt to fight for their own hand when they once begin, and the history of all symbolical and ceremonial worship shows that the experiment is much more likely to end in sensualizing religion than in spiritualizing sense."

False witness, danger of; Commandment, ninth

Prov. 21:6; Isa. 59:4; Hosea 4:2; John 8:44; Col. 3:9; Rev. 21:8

The most dangerous thing about the lies of false witness is that such a word once uttered can never be obliterated. Someone has said that lying is a worse crime than counterfeiting. There is some hope of following up bad coins until they are all recovered; but an evil word can never be overtaken. The mind of the hearer or reader has been poisoned, and human devices cannot reach in and cleanse it. Lies can never be called back.

A woman who was well known as a scandalmonger went and confessed to the priest. He gave her a ripe thistle top, and told her to go out and scatter the seeds one by one. She wondered at the penance, but obeyed; then she came and told the priest. He next told her to go and gather again the scattered seeds. Of course she saw that it was impossible. The priest used it as an object lesson to cure her of gossip.

False witness, dealing with; Gossip, dealing with; Commandment, ninth

Prov. 12:19; Jer. 9:3; John 8:44; Col. 3:9

Hannah More's method was a sure cure for scandal. Whenever she was told anything derogatory about another, her invariable reply was, "Come, we will ask if it be true." The effect was sometimes ludicrously plain. The tale bearer was taken aback, stammered out a qualification or begged that no notice might be taken of the statement. But the good lady was inexorable. Off she took the scandal-monger to the scandalized to make inquiry and compare accounts. It is not likely that anybody ventured a second time to repeat a gossipy story to Hannah More.

False witness, sin of; Commandment, ninth

Isa. 9:15; John 8:44; Acts 5:3; Col. 3:9; 1 Tim. 4:2

"Thou shalt not bear false witness against thy neighbor." Love will not slander or lie. How often we have felt the sting of the slanderer's tongue, and our lives have been made bitter by some lie. I think one of our national sins is the way that people in public office are abused. There's not a person that's not slandered. I believe as a general rule our public servants have been good people. The Presidents in my day have been good men. But what false and slanderous reports have been started about them. Let us keep in mind that if we hear evil or false reports of a person, and we take them up, and start them along, and push them on, we are equally guilty.

Prov. 6:17; John 8:44; Eph. 4:25; Col. 3:9

Two out of the Ten Commandments deal with sin that finds expression by the tongue—the third commandment, which forbids taking God's name in vain, and this ninth commandment, which forbids false witness against our neighbor. This twofold prohibition ought to impress us as a solemn warning, especially as we find that the pages of Scripture are full of condemnation of sins of the tongue. The Psalms, Proverbs, and the epistle of James deal largely with the subject.

Organized society of a degree higher than that of the herding of animals and flocking of birds depends so much upon the power of speech, that without it society would be impossible. Language is an essential element in the social fabric. To fulfill its purpose speech must be trustworthy. Words must command confidence. Anything which undermines the truth takes (as it were) the mortar out of the building, and if widespread will bring ruin. All community, all union and fellowship would be shattered if a man did not know whether to believe his neighbor or not.

Family altar, example of; Dedication, example of; Father as leader

Gen. 18:19; Exod. 12:26; Deut. 6:7; 11:29; 2 Sam. 24:10; Pss. 32:5; 74:8; Prov. 28:13; 1 John 1:8

A businessman in Edinburgh, Scotland, came to our meeting. He had made up his mind that he ought to live right as a Christian, and he ought to have a family altar. And as he hurried his wife and children up the next morning his wife said, "George, what's your hurry?" He replied, "I have a confession to make this morning, and I want all of you to forgive me. You have never heard me say any words in prayer. I am going to start this morning. I want you and the children to help me." And he got down on his knees and confessed his soul as well as he could. I do not know of a man who was ever more blessed of God than that man. God responded to the urgent desire of his heart. Do you need to make a similar decision of commitment to God for yourself and your family? God will meet you and bless you.

Family altar, importance of

Gen. 18:19; Exod. 12:26; Deut. 6:7; 11:29; Ps. 74:8

It seems to me that every man should have a family altar in his house. And if we cannot deliver prayers, let us take up each of our children by name; let us ask that Johnny, while playing with his schoolmates, may be kept from temptation. Why, we forget that a child's temptations are just as difficult for him as ours are to us. The boy at school has just as heavy trials as we have. And then pray for Mary. If she is in trouble bring it out and pray that God may give her power to overcome any besetting sin that she may have in her heart.

I believe the day has come when we should have more religion in our families, more family altars. I believe that the want of this is doing more injury to the growth of our children than anything else. Why, long before the church was in a building, it was in the homes of the people. We can make the family altar a source of happiness. By it we can make the home the pleasantest place in the world. Let us, when we get up in the morning, bright and fresh, have some family devotions. If a man runs downtown immediately on getting up, and doesn't get home until late, and then has family devotions, the children will be tired and so go sound asleep.

It seems to me that we should give a little more time to our children and call them around the altar in the morning. Or suppose we ask them to recite a verse, to recite a portion of a hymn—it must not necessarily be a long one—and, after that, have some singing, if the children can sing. Do not be in a hurry to get it out of the way, as if the service was a nuisance; take a little time. Let them sing some religious hymns. The singing need not be all psalms, but there should be a few hymns and gospel songs. Then pray for each of them by name. The time needn't be long but sincere.

Family altar, significance of; Conviction, power of

Gen. 18:19; Exod. 12:26; Deut. 6:7; 11:29; 2 Sam. 24:10; Pss. 32:5; 74:8; Prov. 28:13; 1 John 1:8

When I was in Edinburgh, Scotland, last winter I heard a good thing. A young man left a praying home and went up to Edinburgh to live. He had been there for a short time when he met some young men. Needing friends he spent time with them. One night his friends were urging him to go with them to a house of prostitution. They were walking up Princes Street, the great thoroughfare of Edinburgh, when the nine o'clock bell struck, and the young man said to himself, "This is the hour my father is taking down the Bible to have family worship; this will be the hour my father will be praying for me." He stopped and said: "I cannot go with you." "Why not?" "Well, I can't go to that kind of place." Then they began to laugh at him. He said, "You may laugh, but I can't go with you."

He turned round. He went to his room and got his Bible down and read. He got on his knees and cried to his father's God to have mercy upon him. He found heaven, and today he is one of the most eminent merchants in the city of Edinburgh. He has a fine family and a ringing testimony for Christ. The other young men went down to ruin and were lost. How important it is to act on conviction even if others laugh.

Family, time with; Fathering, importance of

Gen. 18:19; Exod. 12:26; Deut. 6:7; 11:29; 2 Sam. 24:10; Pss. 32:5; 74:8; Prov. 28:13; 1 John 1:8

I heard of a father who was very busy with work and other activities so that he was rarely home when his young son was awake. On one occasion the child said to his mother, "Mamma, that man that comes to our house on Sundays has been scolding me." He called his own father "that man."

Father, honoring; Commandment, fifth

Matt. 15:4–5; Mark 7:10; Eph. 6:2

A poor farmer was toiling hard to keep his son at school. One day he went up to the city in his old work clothes to sell a load of wood. The boy was about finishing his course and the father was trying hard to raise money to pay the bills. As he was going up the street he came suddenly upon his son, who was with some other young men, dressed in the height of fashion. The father eagerly rushed up to him and said, "I am so glad to see you, my boy." But the son rudely pushed him aside, and said, "Get away, old man, I don't know you." The father went home heartbroken, because his son was ashamed of him. God pity a young man who would treat his father that way!

Father, responsibility of; Family altar, importance of

Deut. 6:7

It may be that some father or mother is saying, "I have not been living right myself in God's sight; so how can I talk to my children of Christ?" It seems to me the best thing to do under those circumstances is to make a confession. I knew a father who a few days ago told his children that he had not been living right. The tears rolled down his cheeks as he asked their forgiveness. "Why," said one child, "do you ask us for forgiveness? Why, father, you have always been kind to us." "I know I have, my child," he answered, "but I have not been doing my whole duty toward you. I've never had a family altar. I have paid more heed to your temporal welfare than to your spiritual: but I am going to have a family altar now."

He took down his Bible and began there, and it wasn't long before his children were touched. Suppose you haven't been living in accordance with the gospel. Why not make an open confession to your wife—to your children—set up a family altar, and pray for your children, and it will not be long before you are blessed.

Father's example, power of

Gen. 44:21; Matt. 17:17; Mark 9:19; Luke 9:41

Not long ago a young man went home late. He had been in the habit of going home late and the father began to mistrust that he had gone astray. He told his wife to go to bed, and said he would sit up till his son came home. The boy came home drunk, and the father in his anger gave him a push into the street and told him never to enter his house again, and shut the door. He went into the parlor and sat down, and began to think, "Well, I may be to blame for that boy's conduct, after all. I have never prayed with him. I have never warned him of the dangers of the world."

And the result of his reflections was that he put on his overcoat and hat, and started out to find his boy. The first policeman he met he asked eagerly, "Have you seen my boy?" "No." On he went till he met another. "Have you seen anything of my son?" He ran from one to another all that night, but not until the morning did he find him. He took him by the arm and led him home, and kept him till he was sober. Then he said, "My dear boy, I want you to forgive me; I've never prayed for you; I've never lifted up my heart to God for you; I've been the means of leading you astray, and I want your forgiveness."

The boy was touched, and what was the result? Within twenty-four hours that son became a convert, and gave up drinking. It may be that some father here has a wayward son. Go to God, and on your knees confess it. Let the voice of Jesus sink down in your heart, "Bring him unto me."

Father's influence

Gen. 24:5; Matt. 9:9; 1 Thess. 5:15; 2 Thess. 3:9

A father started for his office early one morning after a light fall of snow. Turning, he saw his two-year-old boy endeavoring to put his tiny feet in his own great footprints. The little fellow shouted, "Go on, I'se comin', papa, I'se comin' right in ure tracks." He caught the boy in his arms and carried him to his mother, and started again for his office. His habit had been to stop on the way at a saloon for a glass of liquor. As he stood upon the threshold that morning he seemed to hear a sweet voice say, "Go on, I'se comin', papa, I'se comin' right in ure tracks." He stopped, he hesitated, he looked the future squarely in the face. "I cannot afford to make any tracks I would be ashamed or sorry to have my boy walk in," he said decidedly, and turned away.

Father, mother, neighbor are your tracks true? Are they straight? Can you turn to any walking behind you and say, "Follow me as I follow Christ"?

Fault-finders, cure of

Mark 7:2; 1 Cor. 6:7; 4:21; 2 Cor. 10:1; Gal. 5:23; 6:1; 2 Tim. 2:25

Let me tell you how to cure a chronic, fault-finding church member. Pray for the person. Pray God to cast that devil out. Many people hinder the Word of God by just finding fault. They do not like the way revivals are conducted. They say it was not so in the days of our fathers. They say they did things then in such and such a way and they want it so now. But because God acted in a certain way, years ago, is that any reason that it should be so now? These people who find fault do more harm in the church than twenty do good.

When I first began to preach, I thought it was my duty to find fault everywhere, and so I went round scolding, and I got to be looked upon in a little while as a public bore and a great nuisance, and then I stopped finding fault and began to preach Christ and people liked to hear me. There are a good many men who have great talents and might do a good deal of good, who are continually finding fault. Their hands, Ishmael-like, are against everybody. Look at Stephen and Barnabas and the early Christians. We don't find them finding fault! They were holding up and preaching Christ, and that is what this world needs.

Fault-finding, futility of; Prayer, power of

Ezek. 34:16; Mark 7:2; Rom. 15:1; 1 Cor. 6:7; 4:21; 2 Cor. 10:1; Gal. 5:23; 6:1; 1 Thess. 5:28; 2 Tim. 2:25; Heb. 12:13; 13:18; 1 John 5:19

If things don't always please you, don't complain—just pray!

Feed people well

Isa. 40:11; Jer. 3:15; John 21:16–17; Acts 20:28; 1 Peter 5:2

A story is related of a little boy in a country town, who could catch pigeons when no other boy could catch a single one, and somebody asked him how he did it; said he, "I will tell you, but I don't care about anybody else knowing it: I feed them well." That, my friends, is just what we must do, we must feed them well.

Feelings, unable to save; Salvation, basis of; Christ our Rock

Gen. 3:12; 16:2; Deut. 32:15; 2 Sam. 22:47; Pss. 18:2; 62:7; 89:26; 95:10; Isa. 17:10; Rom. 4:10; 5:1; Gal. 3:3

Don't be watching your feelings. There is not one verse from Genesis to Revelation about being saved by feeling. When the devil sees a poor soul in agony in the waves of sin, and getting close to the Rock of Ages, he just holds out the plank of "feeling" to him, and says, "There, get on that. You feel more comfortable now, don't you?" And, while the man starts getting breath again, out goes the plank from under him, and he is worse off than ever.

Accept no refuge but the Rock—Christ our Everlasting Strength.

Fellowship, encouragement of

Gen. 31:49; 1 Sam. 7:5; 2 Chron. 29:30; Ps. 7:17

When we were in Glasgow there were about one thousand men converted who had been slaves of strong drink, and the question was, how to hold them together. They organized, and called themselves the Mizpah Band, and met every Saturday. That is the day of peculiar temptation in the old country, for men are generally paid off on Saturday, and the week's wages often go for whiskey. These men knew they would be strongly tried and tempted on Saturday; so they agreed to meet every Saturday afternoon. Then the question came up, "What will bind us together?"

They decided to start a male choir. They began with a choir of four hundred and out of these there were not more than a dozen who could sing. If you could have heard them you wouldn't have thought it was singing. The noise sounded as though it came from cracked kettles and tin pans. But these choir meetings kept them off the street corners and out of the whiskey shops. They went on practicing and improving, and six months later, when Mr. Sankey and I returned to Glasgow, I never heard such inspiring singing.

They kept on growing in numbers until there were over eleven hundred of them. They went out every week to the different parts of Glasgow, some to preach the best they knew how, others to tell what God had done for them, and others to sing; and thus in one way or another, they declared the gospel. I mention this to bring out the fact that a great deal of talent in all our churches lies buried. Let's utilize it.

Fellowship of believers; Heaven, nature of

Acts 2:42; Gal. 2:9; 1 John 1:3, 7

A Methodist minister, on his way to a camp meeting, through some mistake took passage on the wrong boat. He found that instead of being bound for a religious gathering, he was on his way to a horse race. His fellow passengers were betting and discussing the events, and the whole atmosphere was foreign to his nature. He besought the captain that he would stop his boat and let him off at the first landing, as the surroundings were distasteful to him.

The story also goes on to relate how, on the same occasion a sporting man, intending to go to the races by some mistake found himself on the wrong boat, bound for the camp meeting. The conversation about him was no more intelligible to him than to the man in the first instance, and he, too, besought the captain to stop and let him off the boat.

Now what was true in these two cases is practically true with everyone. A true Christian is wretched where there is no fellowship, and an unregenerate man is not at ease where there are only Christians. A man's future will be according to what he is here prepared for. If he is not regenerate, heaven will have no attractions for him. Heaven is a prepared place for a prepared people.

Fellowship with God

Gen. 3:8–9, 15, 17, 21; Job 31:33; Jer. 32:19; Rom. 5:14; 1 Cor. 15:22, 45; 1 Tim. 2:14

When Adam fell he fell out of a communion with God and he didn't want to walk with God. What we need is to bring men back into fellowship and communion with God. When we walk with God, then we are going to have power, and not only with God, but with our fellowmen.

Finishing, importance of; Patience, example of

Matt. 26:56; Luke 9:62; 17:32; 2 Tim. 1:15; 4:10, 16; 2 Peter 2:15; 1 John 5:4

Two men were digging in California for gold. They had worked a good deal and got nothing. At last one of them threw down his tools and said, "I will leave here before we starve," and he left. The next day his comrade's patience was rewarded by finding a gold nugget that supported him until he made a fortune.

Finishing well; Vision, importance of

Ps. 45:7; Matt. 25:4; Acts 17:11; Rom. 8:9; 1 John 5:5

There was a game in Athens. The competitors would all start with blazing torches. He who reached the goal before his torch burned out won the prize. So let us run, keeping our lights trimmed and burning. And then, as we come in with our torches burning, we shall obtain our crowns.

Flesh, struggling against; Natures, two

2 Cor. 6:17; Eph. 4:24; Col. 3:10; James 4:1; 2 Peter 1:4

I never had a conflict with myself until I found God. I had a good opinion of myself, but as soon as I found God, a conflict sprung up between the old nature and the new. When a man has no conflict in himself you may know that he is not a Christian. But when a man or a woman is struggling with a mean, contemptible disposition, you may know that he or she is a partaker of the Divine nature. I have got a good deal more respect for a woman who is trying to overcome and gain the victory over a mean, contemptible disposition, than for those who are naturally pretty good and don't want to be any better. These people come into the world with these mean, contemptible dispositions and they try to conquer them and they succeed in becoming quite respectable, so that we can get along with them. A fish cannot live out of the water, and we cannot live in the water, and so the natural man cannot live for God.

Flesh, walking after the

Rom. 8:4, 13; 2 Cor. 10:3; Gal. 5:16, 24; Phil. 3:3

If it never troubles a man's conscience to spend a great deal of his time in questionable places of amusement, and to take his family into places where there are degraded people, if he drives like Jehu all the week to make a dollar and moves like a snail on Sunday toward spiritual things, I believe that man is following the flesh; the divine nature is not in him; he is not walking after the Spirit, but after the flesh.

Flesh, weakness of; Sin, power of

2 Kings 8:13; Matt. 26:41; Mark 14:38; John 6:63; Rom. 6:19; 7:18

The flesh is weak. Is there anyone on earth that dares to dispute that statement? Is there anything weaker under the sun than the human flesh? The spirit is willing. Most men would rather do the right thing, and think they will do it. Tell them that they will do certain things inside of twelve months, and they would say, as the king did, "Is thy servant a dog that he should do such a thing? No, never." But they will do it just the same.

Focus, positive; Desire, object of

1 Cor. 9:24; Phil. 3:13; Heb. 12:2

My wife told me one day that she had just come from a friend's house where one of the children, a little boy, had been cutting something with a knife, and it had slipped upward and put out his eye, and his mother was afraid of his losing the other.

Of course, after that my wife was careful that our little two-year-old boy shouldn't get the scissors, or anything by which he could harm himself. But prohibit a child from having any particular thing, and he's sure to want it; so one day our little fellow got hold of the scissors. His older sister seeing what he had, and knowing the rule, tried to take the scissors from him, but the more she tried the more he clung to them.

Then she remembered how much he liked oranges, and that there was one in the next room. Away she went and back she came: "Willie, would you like an orange?" The scissors were dropped, and he clutched the orange. God sometimes takes away the scissors, but he gives us an orange. Get both your feet into the narrow way—it leads to life and joy; its ways are ways of pleasantness, and all its paths are peace. It is the way of victory, of peace; no gloom there; all light.

Followers of Christ or Satan

Zech. 3:2; Matt. 4:10; Mark 4:15; Acts 5:3; 26:18; Rom. 16:20; 2 Cor. 6:15

If you should take the most faithful follower that Satan has in all your city, the man that has served the devil most faithfully for the last two decades, and then take the one who has served Jesus Christ for the last twenty years, keeping nearer to Christ than anyone else in the city, and let the two stand here, do you think they would have to speak to show who and what they were? Let that electric light shine so that it will reflect their bodies and their faces. Wouldn't that light reveal the story?

Instead of taking two men, I'll take two women; for when a woman falls, she often falls lower than a man. Why? Because when God created woman, it was his last, his highest workmanship. She falls lower; and you take the one who falls lowest in all Boston, and let her stand here tonight, and then the purest woman in all Boston, and let the two stand here. Would you not say that the devil is a hard master, and the Lord of Glory a good Master?

Forgiveness, accepting; Confession of sin

Rom. 4:7; 8:33; 2 Cor. 2:10; Eph. 4:32; Col. 2:3; 1 John 1:9; 2:12

If we have confessed our sins, it is distrusting God not to believe that they are put away. Suppose that I have a little boy, and when I go home he comes to me and says: "Papa, I did that naughty thing you told me not to do." I see there are signs of contrition, and say, "I am sorry you did it, but I am thankful you confessed it. I forgive you." He goes off lightly. He has been forgiven. But the next day he comes and says, "Papa, do you know that yesterday while you were away I did that naughty thing that you told me not do. I am very sorry. Won't you forgive me?" I say, "My son, was not that forgiven yesterday?" "Well," he says, "I wish you would forgive me again."

Don't you see how dishonoring it is? It is very disheartening to a father to have a child act in that way. And it is distrusting God, and dishonoring him for us to be constantly lugging up the past. If God has forgiven us, that is the end of it. "Who will lay anything to the charge of God's elect? It is God that justifieth." God has justified me, will he lay any charge against me? But, dear friend, if you are not already forgiven, do not sleep until you are. Have this question of sin forever settled for time and eternity. God wants to forgive you, and he will, if you will confess your sins and ask his pardon.

Forgiveness and church growth

Matt. 6:15; 18:18; Mark 11:26; 2 Cor. 2:10; 5:20

A man said to me some time ago, "We have a magnificent organ in our church, a wealthy and cultured preacher, but we haven't had any people converted. Can you tell me why?" I replied, "Yes, I know your congregation well. There are half a dozen families in your church who are not on speaking terms, and the Holy Spirit cannot work." If there is anyone you are not willing to forgive, don't you see that you have broken down the communication bridge between yourselves and God? You can't force yourself into God's presence. Now, if you have had trouble with someone and have not forgiven that person, go and have it settled before the sun goes down. God delights to answer prayer. But you can't deceive yourself. If you are living a dishonorable life, God hides his face and will not hear you.

Forgiveness and retribution

2 Sam. 12:13–14; Neh. 5:9; Matt. 18:7; 1 Cor. 11:22; Rev. 3:19

I believe that God forgives sin fully and freely for Christ's sake; but he allows certain penalties to remain. If a man has wasted years in debauchery, he can never hope to live them over again. If he has violated his conscience, the scars will remain through life. If he has soiled his reputation, the effect of it can never be washed away. If he shatters his body through indulgence and vice, he must suffer until death. As Talmage says, "The grace of God gives a new heart, but not a new body."

2 Sam. 12:13–14; Neh. 5:9; Matt. 18:7; 1 Cor. 11:22; Rev. 3:19

"John," said a father to his son, "I wish you would get me the hammer." "Yes, sir." "Now a nail and a piece of pine board." "Here they are, sir." "Will you drive the nail into the board?" It was done. "Please pull it out again." "That's easy, sir." "Now, John," and the father's voice dropped to a lower key, "pull out the nail hole." Every wrong act leaves a scar. Even if the board be a living tree the scar remains.

Forgiveness before service

Matt. 5:24; 18:15; Luke 12:58; Rom. 12:18; 1 Cor. 6:7

When we were in Chicago there was a businessman who was going to take lunch with me; he came in late. I said, "How is this? I thought you were coming in right after the noon meeting." "Well," said he, naming another prominent businessman, "I had trouble with him six months ago, and I could not eat my lunch until I went down and asked his forgiveness." There was a good deal of that in Chicago, and that is one reason why I think the work was so great.

Let us have that in every community. If there is anybody that any of you ought to forgive go and do it right away. I can imagine some of you saying, "They won't forgive me." But go to them and ask their forgiveness. I cannot make others forgive me, but I can forgive them. We must have nothing but love in our hearts. If they hate us and their hearts are filled with the fire of hell against us, we will forgive them in spite of that. We can love others whether they love us or not, and when we are right with God, he will speak through us and use us and not till then.

Forgiveness, extent of

Matt. 6:12; 18:21–22; Col. 3:13

Peter asked Jesus how many times he should forgive a brother that sinned against him. Peter did not seem to think that he was in danger himself of falling into sin; his question was, "How often should I forgive my brother?" But very soon we hear that Peter has fallen. I can imagine that when he did fall, the sweet thought came to him of what the Master had said. The voice of sin may be loud, but the voice of forgiveness is louder.

Forgiveness, importance of

Matt. 5:24; 1 Peter 3:7

My little boy had some trouble with his sister one Saturday, and he did not want to forgive her. That night he was going to say his prayers, and I wanted to see how he would say his prayers. He knelt down by his mother and said his prayers, and then I went to him, and I said, "Willie, did you pray?" "I said my prayers." "Yes, but did you pray?" "I said my prayers." "I know you said them, but did you pray?" He hung his head. "You are angry with your sister?" "Well, she had no business to do thus and so." "That has nothing to do with it; you have the wrong idea, my boy, if you think that you have prayed tonight." You see he was trying to get over it by saying, "I said my prayers tonight."

I find that people say their prayers every night, just to ease their conscience. And then I said, "Willie, if you don't forgive your sister, you will not sleep tonight. Ask her to forgive you." He didn't want to do that. He loves the country, and he has been talking a great deal about the time when he can go into the country and play outdoors. So he said, "Oh, yes, I will sleep well enough; I am going to think about being out there in the country." That is what we are trying to do; we are trying to think of something else to get rid of the thought of these sins, but we cannot.

I said nothing more to him. I went on studying, and his mother came downstairs. But soon he called his mother, and said, "Mother, won't you please go up and ask Emma if she won't forgive me?" Then I afterwards heard him murmuring in bed, and he was saying his prayers. And he said to me, "Papa, you were right, I could not sleep, and I cannot tell you how happy I am now." Don't you think there is any peace until your sins are put away. My dear friends, the gospel of the Lord Jesus Christ is the gospel of peace.

Matt. 5:24; 18:15; 23:23; 1 Cor. 6:8

There was one place we were in and we were trying to find out the obstacles that were in the way of God's working, and we were trying to put the plough down into the city—some of you who have ploughed where the ground is full of rocks and stumps know that the plough will not stay in when it hits against a rock or stump—so we were trying to plough and kept running against obstacles. At last we found that two prominent ministers in the place hadn't spoken together for a number of years. We went to work and tried to bring about a reconciliation, and these men didn't see how they could forgive one another.

It seems to me—if you will allow me to use the word—a perfect farce to preach for forgiveness if the minister is not ready to forgive, especially when the public know, and the public say, "It is very well for him to talk about my forgiving my enemies, but he will not forgive his." If we are going to preach forgiveness let us begin to forgive others ourselves.

Forgiveness of son

Esther 8:2; Isa. 61:10; Ezek. 16:9; Luke 15:22; Rom. 8:15

I can give you a little experience of my own family. Before I was fourteen years old the first thing I remember was the death of my father. He had been unfortunate in business, and failed. Soon after his death the creditors came in and took everything. My mother was left with a large family of children. One calamity after another swept over the entire household. Twins were added to the family, and my mother was taken sick. The eldest boy was fifteen years of age, and to him my mother looked as a stay in her calamity, but all at once that boy became a wanderer. He had been reading some of the trashy novels, and the belief had

seized him that he had only to go away to make a fortune. Away he went.

I can remember how eagerly she used to look for tidings of that boy; how she used to send us to the Post Office to see if there was a letter from him, and recollect how we used to come back with the sad news, "No letter." I remember how in the evenings we used to sit beside her in that New England home, and we would talk about our father; but the moment the name of that boy was mentioned she would hush us into silence. Some nights when the wind was very high, and the house, which was upon a hill, would tremble at every gust, the voice of my mother was raised in prayer for that wanderer who had treated her so unkindly.

I used to think she loved him more than all the rest of us put together, and I believe she did. On a Thanksgiving Day—you know that is a family day in New England—she used to set a chair for him, thinking he would return home. Her family grew up and her boys left home. When I got so that I could write, I sent letters all over the country, but could find no trace of him. One day while in Boston the news reached me that he had returned.

While in that city, I remember how I used to look for him in every store—he had a mark on his face—but I never got any trace. One day while my mother was sitting at the door, a stranger was seen coming toward the house, and when he came to the door he stopped. My mother didn't know her boy. He stood there with folded arms and great beard flowing down his breast, his tears trickling down his face. When my mother saw those tears she cried, "Oh, it's my lost son," and entreated him to come in. But he stood still. "No, mother," he said, "I will not come in till I hear first you have forgiven me."

Do you believe she was not willing to forgive him? Do you think she was likely to keep him long standing there? She rushed to the threshold and threw her arms around him, and breathed forgiveness. Ah, sinner, if you but ask God to be merciful to you a sinner, ask him for forgiveness, although your life has been a long trail of sin—ask him for mercy, and he will not keep you waiting for an answer.

Forgiveness, true

Deut. 15:7; 2 Kings 10:31; Prov. 16:1; Isa. 29:13

As Matthew Henry says: "We do not forgive our offending brother aright nor acceptably, if we do not forgive him from the heart, for it is that God looks at. No malice must be harbored there, nor ill-will to any; no projects of revenge must be hatched there, nor desires of it, as there are in many who outwardly appear peaceful and reconciled. We must from the heart desire and seek the welfare of those who have offended us."

Formalism, danger of

Matt. 26:45; Mark 14:37; Luke 22:46; Rom. 11:8; 13:11; 1 Thess. 5:6

When every person that belongs to the Lord is willing to speak for him, is willing to work for him, and, if need be, willing to die for him, then Christianity will advance, and we shall see the work of the Lord prosper. I fear more than anything else, the dead, cold formalism of the Church of God. Talk about the false isms! There is none so dangerous as this dead, cold formalism which has come right into the heart of the Church. So many of us just sleep while souls all around are perishing.

Freshness, spiritual; Intimacy with God

John 4:10; 7:38

We must have spiritual freshness. Haven't you ever preached or ministered in some other way and found it hard work—like hard pumping without bringing any water? Though you love to preach the Gospel, and it is easy and delightful most of the time, yet haven't you sometimes found it hard work? I have, though not lately. The trouble is we often preach on the strength of old experiences. If a man has been for twenty years cultivating an acquaintance with Christ, he will have a richer experience than he had twenty years before. He will have a new testimony all the time. He will have freedom in speaking. It is hard to preach without a fresh supply of the Spirit. That is why so many ministers have hard work getting up their sermons.

Friendliness, church

John 13:34–35

Strangers coming into a church like to have someone speak to them. They do not feel insulted at all. If a person comes to New York a stranger and goes to church, if someone asks that person to go into the inquiry room it brings happiness and cheer. Two young men came into our inquiry room here the other night. After a counselor had talked with them and showed them the way to Christ, the light broke in upon them. They were asked, "Where do you go to church?" They gave the name of the church where they had been going. The counselor said, "I advise you to go and see the minister of that church." They said, "We don't want to go there anymore; we have gone there for six years and no one has spoken to us."

Friendship, Christian

Gal. 6:2

A gambler told me one day that he gambled away all his money, and then gambled away some of his employer's money, and he knew that if he did not replace it, he would be dismissed and perhaps arrested. He told his friends, as he thought them, that he wanted to borrow money enough to replace his employer's money. But his supposed friends laughed at him, so he went to a Christian man and told him all, and he lent him the money, and he gave his heart to Christ: he has never gone near those gamblers since. If you want friends you want the friends of Christ.

Fruit bearing, importance of

Matt. 7:20; Rom. 14:1; 15:1; Gal. 6:2; Col. 1:10; Heb. 12:13; James 5:19; Jude 12

I once asked a lady to go and speak to a woman who sat weeping, about her soul. "Oh!" said the lady, "I am afraid I am not qualified for the work. Please send someone else." "How long," I said, "have you been a Christian?" "Twenty years." Twenty years on the Lord's side, and not qualified to point a soul to Christ! I am afraid there will be a great many starless crowns in glory.

Fruit of the Spirit

Gal. 5:22; Eph. 5:9

The lawyers would soon be bankrupt, taxes would be down, there would be no need of the police, if all had the fruit of the Spirit.

Fruit of the Spirit; Love, importance of

Gal. 5:22–23

The fruit of the Spirit begins with love. There are nine graces spoken of, and of these nine Paul puts love at the head of the list; love is the first thing, the first in that precious cluster of fruit. Someone has said that all the other eight can be put in terms of love. Joy is love exulting; peace is love in repose; longsuffering is love on trial; gentleness is love in society; goodness is love in action; faith is love on the battlefield; meekness is love at school; and temperance is love in training. So it is love all the way; love at the top, love at the bottom, and all the way along down this list of graces. If we only just brought forth the fruit of the Spirit, what a world we would have! People would have no desire to do evil.

Fruitfulness, importance of; Call to preach

John 15:8,16

How is a man to know whether he is called and anointed to preach? Go out to preach and watch the results. If the people go to sleep, then you are not called. A man might go through forty seminaries and yet not be called to preach. We are to look for fruit. If there is no fruit, then you are not sent. I pity the man who preaches year after year without fruit.

Fruitfulness, source of

Pss. 1:3; 92:14; Jer. 17:8; Rev. 22:2

Suppose a minister has been laboring for twenty years without fruit, and yet everyone says he is a very good man, and is in the right occupation? That is like saying there is a fruit tree out there in the field, and someone told you, "That tree has not borne anything for twenty years, and yet it is a grand old tree." I like to see a tree bearing all the time. They say that when you look at a lemon tree, you can see fruit in all stages of growth, and you can get ripe lemons every month in the year. Let us be like the lemon tree.

Men that deal in oranges say that the best oranges from Florida or California come from those trees that send a taproot forty feet down into the ground. Trees that send down the root only ten or twenty feet have oranges that are not so good. When a tree sends down its taproot so far as to strike water, its fruit is delicious. So with the Christian. He has a hidden source of life that the world knows nothing about, and the more he receives of that life, the more and better fruit he will bring forth.

Future, glorious; Vision, eternal; Values, eternal

2 Cor. 4:18; 2 Thess. 2:14; 1 Peter 5:4; 2 Peter 1:3

There is glory for the time to come. A great many people seem to forget that the best is before us. Dr. Bonar once said that everything before the true believer is "glorious." This thought took hold on my soul, and I began to look the matter up, and see what I could find in Scripture that was glorious hereafter. I found that the kingdom we are going to inherit is glorious; our crown is to be a "Crown of glory"; the city we are going to inhabit is the City of the glorified; the songs we are to sing are the songs of the glorified; we are to wear garments of "glory and beauty"; our society will be the society of the glorified; our rest is to be "glorious"; the Country to which we are going is to be full of "the glory of God and of the Lamb."

There are many who are always looking on the backward path, and mourning over the troubles through which they have passed; they keep lugging up the cares and anxieties they have been called on to bear, and are forever looking at them. Why should we go reeling and staggering under the burdens and cares of life when we have such glorious prospects before us?

Generosity, nature of; Samaritan, true

Prov. 3:27; Rom. 13:7; Gal. 6:10

After the Chicago fire I came to New York for money, and I heard there was a rich man in Fall River who was very liberal. So I went to him. He gave me a check for a large amount, and then got into his carriage and drove with me to the houses of other rich men in the city, and they all gave me checks. When he left me at the train I grasped his hand and said, "If you ever come to Chicago, call on me, and I will return your favor." He said, "Mr. Moody, don't wait for me; do it to the first man that comes along." I never forget that remark; it had the ring of the true good Samaritan.

Gifts, use of

1 Cor. 12:1; 14:1, 12

I remember hearing of a man's dream, in which he imagined that when he died he was taken by the angels to a beautiful temple. After admiring it for a time, he discovered that one stone was missing. All finished but just one little stone; that was left out. He said to the angel, "What is this stone left out for?" The angel replied, "That was left out for you, but you wanted to do great things, and so the stone is missing." He was startled and awoke, and resolved that he would become a worker for God, and that man always worked faithfully after that.

Rom. 12:6; 1 Cor. 12:7; 14:12; Eph. 4:7; 1 Peter 4:10

Mr. Reynolds, of Peoria, visited the humble mission in Chicago where D. L. Moody began his work. His description of the service is invaluable, as illustrating the progressive growth of Mr. Moody as an evangelist in strength and usefulness by the grace of God. "The first meeting I ever saw him at," he said, "was in a little old shanty that had been abandoned by a saloon-keeper. Mr. Moody had got the place to hold the meetings in at night. I went there a little late, and the first thing I saw was a man standing up, with a few tallow candles around him, holding a black boy, and trying to read to him the story of the prodigal son; and a great many of the words he could not make out, and had to skip. I thought, if the Lord can ever use such an instrument as that for his honor and glory, it will astonish me.

"After that meeting was over, Mr. Moody said to me, 'Reynolds, I have got only one talent. I have no education, but I love the Lord Jesus Christ, and I want to do something for him. I want you to pray for me.' I have never ceased from that day to this, morning and night, to pray for that devoted Christian soldier. I have watched him since then, have had counsel with him, and know him thoroughly; and, for consistent walk and conversation, I have never met a man to equal him. It astounds me when I look back and see what Mr. Moody was, and then what he is under God today as one of the leading evangelists in the world. It astounds me to look back and see what Mr. Moody was thirteen years ago, and then what he is under God today, shaking Scotland to its very center, and reaching now over to Ireland. The last time I heard from him, his injunction was, 'Pray for me every day; pray now that God will keep me humble.'"

Gifts, use of; Abilities, use of

Josh. 6:5; Rom. 12:6; 1 Cor. 12:9, 31

Look at Joshua with his men walking around the walls of Jericho. Suppose you had met him on the seventh day and asked him, "Joshua, what does all this performance mean? You have been walking around here for a week. What are you going to do?" "I am going to take down the walls of Jericho and sack the city." "You are?" "Yes; we will have them down before night." "Where are your battering rams? Where is your artillery?" "We are using these rams' horns."

And they went on blowing their rams' horns and down went the walls of Jericho. If we cannot blow a fine trumpet let us take what we have, and with a stammering tongue, but with a heart on fire for God, we can be used.

Gifts, use of; Obedience, power of

Eph. 4:12

If we were all of us doing the work that God has got for us to do, don't you see how the work of the Lord would advance?

Gifts, use of; Unity, working in

Ezra 4:3; Neh. 2:20; Eph. 4:13; Heb. 2:4

If this world is going to be reached, I am convinced it must be done by men and women of average talent. After all, there are comparatively few people in the world who have great talents. Here is a man with one talent; there is another with three; perhaps I may have only half a talent. But if we all go to work with the gifts we have, the Lord will prosper us, and we may double or triple our talents. What we need is to be up and about our Master's work. The more we use the means and opportunities we have, the more will our ability and our opportunities be increased.

Gifts, variety of

Jer. 3:15; Matt. 25:15; 1 Cor. 12:28; Eph. 4:11

There is great variety in God's kingdom. You have seen those little tin soldiers, haven't you, that all come out alike? I suppose if we were making men we would make all alike. We'd make them in one mold, and if they didn't fit we'd break every bone in them to make them fit the mold. God's way is to bless you according as you use what he has given you already. Use what you have got, and keep looking for more, and it will just increase. That is brought out, I think, in the parable of the talents.

Giving, blessing of

1 Cor. 16:2; 2 Cor. 8:1; 9:5; Phil. 4:15

I once heard of a man who had his leg broken, and he was obliged to stay in the house, and someone brought him in the first cluster of grapes from his vine, and he told his wife, "I can't eat that cluster. I am going to send it to a neighbor of mine who is sick." I will call him neighbor Jones. That's a good name. So he sent them to neighbor Jones, but neighbor Jones said, "I can't eat these grapes. It was very kind of my neighbor to send them. I will send them to neighbor White, as he is sick." So the grapes were sent on from one to another, and they all got wonderfully blessed in sending them on in that way. And the last man they were sent to said, "I hear that Mr. So-and-so has got his leg broken. Poor fellow; I think I'll send these grapes to him." And so he sent them back to the one who sent them first. So he got his grapes back again and a blessing too.

Giving, joy of

Deut. 15:7; 2 Cor. 8:12; 9:7; James 5:9; 1 Peter 4:9

When I was preaching in Baltimore a friend came to me and said, "I want to tell you of an unusual dinner party I had recently. Two bachelors that I have known for many years were my guests for dinner as they had been many times before. Their names were George Peabody and Johns Hopkins. They had been clerks together at a store in Baltimore and had decided to see which of them could make the most money. They both had become extremely wealthy.

"During dinner Johns Hopkins said to me, 'I hear that George Peabody has been giving his money away. I don't give money to people who ask and very rarely to some who don't ask.' I turned to George Peabody and asked, 'Is it true that you have been giving your money away?' He replied, 'Yes, it is true and you tell Johns Hopkins that he had better get his will prepared. He has nobody left but nieces and nephews and they don't need his money.'"

My friend said that he did not want to miss out on such an excellent opportunity so he asked George Peabody, "Would you rather make money or give money?" He replied, "You know that I enjoy making money and having money gives a power that can't be achieved otherwise. But I came to realize that I couldn't take it with me. I have seen many estates utterly destroyed by those that came after. I have gained much wealth in commerce between America and England and wanted to do something for the poor of London. I didn't want to give them money. That would not help them.

"Therefore I assembled a board of trustees to build housing for the London poor. The hardest thing I ever did was to let that money go. Later I went to visit the completed project. I saw the flowers growing and the children playing in the quadrangle rather than in the street. A feeling came over me that I had never had before. I will say that for me there is more pleasure in giving than in getting."

My friend told me that within forty-eight hours Johns Hopkins had completed his will and from that will came Johns Hopkins University and the Johns Hopkins Hospital. My friend you do not have to be wealthy to discover that giving is a more satisfying experience than merely getting.

Giving, treasures in heaven; Commandment, eleventh

Matt. 6:20; 19:21; Luke 12:33; 18:22; 1 Tim. 6:17; 1 Peter 1:4

There are a great many people who forget that there are eleven commandments. They think there are only ten. The eleventh commandment is: "Lay up for yourselves treasures in heaven." How few of our people pay any heed to these words. That's why there are so many broken hearts among us; that's why so many men and women are disappointed and going through the streets with shattered hopes; it's because they have not been laying up treasures in heaven.

God as seeker; Holy Spirit striving

Ezek. 34:16; Matt. 9:13; 18:11; Luke 5:32; 15:4; 19:10

I don't believe there is a person that the Spirit of God has not striven with at some point in time. Bear in mind, Christ takes the place of the seeker. Every person who has ever been saved through these six thousand years was sought after by God. No sooner did Adam fall, than God sought him. He had gone away frightened, and hid himself away among the bushes in the garden, but God sought him; and from that day to this, God has always had the place of the seeker.

God is love

Rom. 8:39; Eph. 2:4; 1 John 4:8, 16

There is no truth that Satan has tried so hard to blot out as the fact that God is love. He has gone up and down in the earth, trying to make men believe that God is full of malice and envy and hate. But this is false. John perhaps knew as much about God as anybody that has ever lived, and John says that God is love! John was the beloved disciple of Jesus. He used to lean on Jesus' breast, and no doubt he asked him about God, and Jesus told him, and he tells us what Jesus said. So that we know Satan is a liar, and that this record is true—that God is love.

In all lands and in all ages God has shown his love for men. And why? Because he can't help it. His very nature is love. He loves because he must; loves because he is love. The trouble with us is, that we measure God by ourselves. We love people while they are lovable and love us. But when they cease to love us we sometimes cast them off. It is not so with

God. Christ, we are told by John, "having loved His own that were in the world, loved them to the end."

God the Father's love

John 3:16

There was a time when I used to think more of the love of Jesus Christ than of God the Father. I used to think of God as a stern judge on the throne, from whose wrath Jesus Christ had saved me. It seems to me now I could not have a falser idea of God than that. Since I have become a father I have made this discovery: that it takes more love and self-sacrifice for the father to give up the son than it does for the son to die. Is a father on earth a true father that would not rather suffer than to see his child suffer? Do you think that it did not cost God something to redeem this world? It cost God the most precious possession he ever had. When God gave his Son, he gave all, and yet he gave him freely for you and me.

God, view of

Job 29:12, 16; 42:6

Job, in talking with his three friends, tried to justify himself. He told how good he had been to the poor, and so on. It was all "I," "I," "I." He was like many in this city, who tell how much better they are than us Christians. But when God came and talked with him, Job said, "I abhor myself." He saw himself in God's mirror; and so must we.

God works through people

Matt. 28:19; Mark 16:15; Luke 24:48; Acts 13:46

If a great and mighty work is not done, it will not be God's fault, but our own. I find a class of people saying: "Well, we must wait until God works, and when he is ready we will see a great work." If I read the Bible correctly, God is always ready,

121

and will work through us when we get busy. Someone will say, "Let the Lord do it all." He could have sent down ten legions of angels to do his work if he wanted to, but God doesn't work in that way. He works through us, and if there are to be any spiritually dead raised the disciples of Jesus must do their part. There has got to be a deep work of grace among God's own people. We must get right to God before he is going to use us.

God's abundant love

Luke 7:47; 1 John 4:10,19; Rev. 1:5

We say that Columbus discovered America; but how much did he know about it? Nothing, hardly, of its mountains, rivers, valleys and plains. So with God's love. Oh, how little we know about it; as little as we know about the Pacific Ocean, when we stand on its shore or bathe in its waters. I stand in the sunshine and am warm; but how little of the sunshine can I enjoy! But I can have all that I want, and all that I can receive, and have it freely. And so it is with God's love. We can't force ourselves to love God, but if we ask him, he will give us love. And it is the nature of love to beget love.

God's mercy, false view

Exod. 20:6; Luke 18:7; 2 Thess. 1:9; Jude 7, 21

There are those who believe God is too merciful to punish sin. He is so full of compassion and love that he can't punish sin. The drunkard, the harlot, the gambler, the murderer, the thief, and the libertine will all share alike with the saints at the end. Supposing the governor of your state was so tenderhearted that he could not bear to have a man suffer, could not bear to see a man put in jail, and he set all the prisoners free. How long would he be governor? You would have him out of office before the sun set. These very people that talk about God's mercy would be the first to raise a cry against a governor who would not have a man put in prison when he had done wrong.

God's will, doing

Gen. 18:14; Mark 14:36; Luke 22:42; 2 Tim. 2:13; Heb. 5:7

Whenever God has been calling me to higher service, there has always been a conflict with my will. I have fought against it, but God's will has been done instead of mine. When I came to Jesus Christ, I had a terrible battle to surrender my will, and to take God's will. When I gave up business, I had another battle for three months; I fought against it. It was a terrible battle. But how many times I have thanked God that I gave up my will and took God's will.

God's will, importance of; Heaven without tears

Ps. 40:8; Mark 14:36; Luke 22:42; Rev. 21:4

There are no tears in heaven, and there would be few on earth if the will of God was only done.

God's will, surrender to

Ps. 40:8; Mark 14:36; Luke 22:42; John 4:34; Rev. 21:4

A great many people are afraid of the will of God, and yet I believe that one of the sweetest lessons that we can learn in the school of Christ is the surrender of our wills to God, letting him plan for us and rule our lives. If I know my own mind, if an angel should come from the throne of God and tell me that I could have my will done the rest of my days on earth and that everything I wished should be carried out, or that I might refer it back to God, and let God's will be done in me and through me, I think in an instant I would say: "Let the will of God be done." I cannot look into the future. I do not know what is going to happen tomorrow; in fact, I do not know what may happen before night; so I cannot choose for myself as well as God can choose for me, and it is much better to surrender my will to God's will.

Good works, encouragement to; Willingness, advantages of

Ruth 1:17; 1 Kings 5:5; Dan. 1:8; 1 Cor. 7:37

We have too many of those men who are always faint and discouraged. I know of a family of boys who, if they did not get more than the regular wages, would never go to work. The result was they only worked about one quarter every year. I know another family of boys who would work for fifty cents a day—would be willing to take anything. The one family of boys was ruined and the other succeeded. So some are willing to work for wages if they have fruit immediately, but if they have only fifty cents a day, perhaps no fruit, they just get discouraged. What we want is to work right on and leave the result to God. A Christian might win one soul to Christ and that convert might win a thousand.

Gospel, good news

1 Cor. 15:1; 1 Thess. 1:6; 2:13

It is said that the poet Tennyson once asked an old Christian woman if there was any news. "Why, Mr. Tennyson," she replied, "there's only one piece of news that I know, and that is—Christ died for all men." "That is old news, and good news, and new news," Tennyson responded.

Gospel, need for clarity

1 Cor. 1:24; 15:1; Gal. 1:6; 1 Peter 5:12

Another idea that is very prevalent, is that people will not hear the old gospel, and that the old gospel has lost some of its power. I don't believe one word of it. There is a lot of stuff that men call the gospel that has no more gospel in it than there is wheat in sawdust; but some people don't seem to know the difference. I heard some time ago of a young wife who had a certain amount given her every week, from which she was to pay all the household bills and keep an account. After a few months the husband said, "Darling, I will stay at home this evening, and we will look over the accounts and see how we are getting along."

They looked them over carefully, and he saw that every week she had balanced her accounts by charging something to "G. K. W." The husband began to wonder who this man was, and asked, "Who is this G. K. W.?" She explained that she could never balance the account, so she always put something down to "Goodness knows what." When we hear some people preach, we have to put it down, "G. K. W.—goodness knows what."

I honestly say that I have heard some able men preach, and I didn't know what they were talking about. I suppose I am about the average; and if I couldn't understand, what about the rest? I want to say, if you put the old gospel straight and square, it has as much effect as it ever had. It is a false idea that people want a new kind of gospel, and that the preaching has lost its power. Man is the same as he has been for six thousand years. Sin leaped into the world full grown. The first-born of woman was a murderer. We are a bad lot; and what we need is to tell men so—not flatter them, and tell them how angelic they are because they have some education. An educated rascal is the meanest kind of a rascal.

Gospels, simplicity of

Matt. 18:3; 19:14; Mark 10:14; Luke 18:16

The Word of God may be darkened to the natural man, but the way of Salvation is written so plain, that the little six-year-old child can understand it if she will.

Grace, abundance of

1 Sam. 1:18; Isa. 55:6; Rom. 5:15; Phil. 4:6; Heb. 4:16; 1 Peter 2:10

Many are satisfied to go into the stream of grace ankle deep, when God wants them to swim in it.

Josh. 1:9; Rom. 5:15; 2 Cor. 3:5; 12:9; Phil. 4:13; Heb. 4:16

What would you say if I were a millionaire with an income of several hundred thousand dollars a year, and I really lived on a few cents a day? You would say that I was the meanest, closest man you ever met, and you would have the utmost contempt for me. We have a rich banker, but if we get a "little" we are perfectly satisfied. God says, "Come boldly unto the throne of grace that we may obtain mercy and find grace to help in time of need." We can have all the grace we want. It is a question of simply taking what God offers us.

Grace, abundance of; Favor, unmerited

1 Sam. 1:18; Isa. 43:2; Rom. 5:15; 1 Cor. 10:13; 15:10; 1 Tim. 1:14

Rowland Hill used to tell a good story of a rich man and a poor man in his congregation. The rich man desired to do an act of benevolence, and so he sent a sum of money to a friend to be given to this poor man as he thought best. The friend just sent him five pounds, and said in the note, "This is yours. Use it wisely. There is more to follow." After a while he sent another five pounds, and said, "more to follow." Again and again he sent the money to the poor man, always with the cheering words, "more to follow." So it is with the wonderful grace of God. There is always "more to follow."

Grace, abundance of; Needs, supply of

Isa. 53:4; Rom. 5:15; 2 Cor. 12:9–10; Phil. 4:19; Col. 1:11

I pity those people who are all the time looking to see what they will have to give up. God wants to bestow his marvelous grace on his people; and there is not a soul who has believed on Jesus, for whom God has not abundance of grace in store. What would you say of a man dying of thirst on the banks of a pure river, with the stream flowing past his feet? You would think he was mad! The river of God's grace flows on without ceasing; why should we not partake of it, and go on our way rejoicing?

Grace, abundant

Gen. 6:8; Isa. 41:13; Matt. 5:11–12; Rom. 5:15; 2 Cor. 11:30; 12:5; Eph. 3:16; Titus 2:11

What would you think of a man who had $1,000,000 in the bank and only drew out a penny a day? That's you and I, and the sinner is blinder than we are. The throne of grace is established, and there we are to get all the grace we need. Sin is not so strong as the arm of God. He will help and deliver you if you will come and get the grace you need.

Grace and glory contrasted

Gen. 6:8; Ps. 84:11; Matt. 5:11–12; Rom. 5:2; 2 Cor. 11:30; 12:5; Eph. 1:6

There is not such a great difference between grace and glory after all. Grace is the bud, and glory the blossom. Grace is glory begun, and glory is grace perfected. It will not come hard to people who are serving God down here to do it when they go up yonder. They will change places, but they will not change employments.

Grace, availability of

Ezra 9:8; Isa. 35:4; John 1:17; Titus 2:11; Heb. 3:13–14;

God has a throne which he has set up for the express purpose of giving aid to those who are in need. To that throne we ought to go boldly—go with large requests—not satisfied with asking for and receiving drops when we might have buckets full. Many Christians fail—as many merchants do—by trying to do too much on too small a capital. Suppose some friend places a million of dollars to my credit in the Nevada Bank, and I don't draw out the interest, but only a dollar a week, and try to live on that, half starving myself: wouldn't you think I was a mean, penurious fellow? So, many Christians like starving themselves, though God tells them to come boldly to the throne of grace. No matter what my necessities, trials, or temptations, I can go to that throne and get all that I need.

Grace, available

1 Sam. 1:18; John 1:17; Phil. 4:19; Titus 2:11

We are asked to come boldly to the throne of grace—as a child to its father—that we may find grace. You have noticed that a son is much more bold in his father's house than if he were simply a servant. A good many Christians are like servants in the house. If you go into a house, you can soon tell the difference between the family and the servants. A son comes home in the evening; he goes all over the house—perhaps talks about the letters that have come in the mail, and wants to know all that has been going on in the family during his absence. It is very different with a servant, who perhaps does not leave the kitchen or the servants' hall all day except when duty requires it.

Prov. 3:4; Isa. 40:29; Phil. 4:19; Titus 2:1

I heard of a man who went into business out in one of these western towns, where people said he was sure to fail; but he didn't. After he had been getting along very well for some years, and showing no signs of failing, it was discovered that the man had a brother from the East who was

very rich, and who helped him along from time to time. Just so with you, sinner; you have a Brother who is very rich, and, if you are joined in partnership with him, he will help you to hold out. It is those who are not joined to Christ who fail but they who are joined to him have power and grace. "They that trust the Lord shall not want any good thing."

Grace, daily; Provision, daily

Matt. 28:20; John 6:34; 2 Cor. 4:15–16; Heb. 12:15

I cannot but believe that the reason for the standard of Christian life being so low, is that we are living on stale manna. You know what I mean by that. So many people are living on their past experience—thinking of the grand times they had twenty years ago, perhaps when they were converted. It is a sure sign that we are out of communion with God if we are talking more of the joy and peace and power we had in the past, than of what we have today. We are told to "grow in grace"; but a great many are growing the wrong way.

The Israelites used to gather the manna fresh every day. They were not allowed to store it up. There is a lesson here for us. If we would be strong and vigorous, we must go to God daily. A man can no more take in a supply of grace for the future than he can eat enough today to last him for the next six months, or take sufficient air into his lungs at once to sustain life for a week to come. We must draw upon God's boundless stores of grace from day to day as we need it.

Grace, dying

Isa. 40:30; John 1:17; 2 Cor. 4:17; Phil. 4:19

I find that many Christians are in trouble about the future; they think they will not have grace enough to die by. It is much more important that we should have grace enough to live by. It seems to me that death is of very little importance in the meantime. When the dying hour comes there will be dying grace but you do not require dying grace to live by. If I am going to live perhaps for fifteen or twenty years, what do I need with dying grace? I am far more anxious about having grace enough for my present work.

Grace, for forgiveness

John 1:17; Rom. 5:20–21; Titus 2:11

Grace not only frees you from payment of the interest you owe on your debt of sin, but of the principal also.

Grace for living; Trials, strength for; Needs, supply of

Deut. 33:25; Isa. 40:29; Rom. 6:14; Phil. 4:19; James 4:6; 1 Peter 5:5

Philippians 4:19 does not say God will supply our wants. There are many things we want that God has not promised to give. It is our needs, and all our needs. My children often want many things they do not get; but I supply all they need, if it is in my power to do it. I do not supply all their wants by any means. And so, though God may withhold from us many things that we desire, he will supply all our needs. There can come upon us no trouble or trial in this life, but God has grace enough to carry us right through it, if we will only go to him and get it. But we must ask for it day by day. "As thy days, so shall thy strength be."

Grace for needs; Death, facing; Affliction, strength for

Gen. 6:8; Isa. 41:13; Rom. 6:14; Titus 2:11; James 4:6; 1 Peter 5:5

I have sometimes been asked if I had grace enough to enable me to go to the stake and die as a martyr. No; what do I want with martyrs' grace? I do not like suffering; but if God should call on me to die a martyr's death, he would give me martyrs' grace. If I have to pass through some great affliction, I know God will give me grace when the time comes; but I do not want it till it comes.

Grace for service

Gen. 6:8; Esther 2:17; Isa. 42:1; Jer. 1:8; Acts 4:33; 6:8; 13:43; Rom. 12:6; 1 Cor. 15:10

I have had three red-letter days in my experience: the first was when I was converted; the next was when I got my lips opened, and I began to confess Christ; the third was when I began to work for the salvation of others. I think there are a great many who have got to the first stage; some have got to the second; very few have got to the third. This is the reason, I believe, that the world is not reached.

Many say they are anxious to "grow in grace." I do not think they ever will, until they go out into the harvest field and begin to work for others. We are not going to have the grace we need to qualify us for work until we launch out into the deep, and begin to use the abilities and the opportunities we already possess. Many fold their arms, and wait for the grace of God to come to them; but we do not get it in that way. When we "go forward," then it is that God meets us with his grace.

Grace, free

Gen. 6:8; Ruth 2:2; John 1:17; Rom. 3:24; 2 Cor. 8:9; Titus 2:11; James 4:6; 1 Peter 5:5

Men talk about grace, but, as a rule, they know very little about it. Let a businessman go to one of your bankers to borrow a few hundred dollars for sixty or ninety days; if he is well able to pay, the banker will perhaps lend him the money. His chances are better if he has collateral or can get another responsible man to sign the note with him. They give what they call "three days' grace" after the sixty or ninety days have expired; but they will make the borrower pay interest on the money during these three days, and if he does not return principal and interest at the appointed time, they will sell his goods; they will perhaps turn him out of his house, and take the last piece of furniture in his possession.

That is not grace at all; but that fairly illustrates man's idea of it. Grace not only frees you from payment of the interest, but of the principal also. The grace of God frees us from the penalty of our sin without any payment on our part. Christ has paid the debt, and all we have to do is to believe on him for our salvation.

Grace, free; Sin, debt of paid

Ruth 2:2; John 1:16; Rom. 3:24; 4:16; 12:6; Titus 3:15; James 4:6; 1 Peter 5:5

Doctor Arnot, my friend in Scotland, told me a story of a poor woman who was in great distress because she could not pay her landlord his rent. The doctor put some money in his pocket, and went round to her house, intending to help her. When he got there he knocked at the door. He thought he heard some movement inside; but no one came to open the door. He knocked louder and louder still; but yet no one came. Finally he kicked at the door, causing some of the neighbors to look out and see what was going on, but he could get no entrance. At last he went away, thinking his ears must have deceived him, and that there was really no one there.

A day or two afterward he met the woman in the street, and told her what had happened. She held up her hands and exclaimed, "Was that you? I was in the house all the while; but I thought it was the landlord, and I had the door locked!" Many people think the grace of God is coming to smite them. My dear friends, it is coming to pay all your debts!

Grace, free to all

Ruth 2:2; John 1:16; Rom. 3:24; 12:6; Titus 3:15; Heb. 13:9

When Moses took his rod and struck the flinty rock in the wilderness, out of it there came a pure crystal stream of water, which flowed on through that dry and barren land. All that the poor thirsty Israelites had to do was to stoop and drink. It was free to all. So the grace of God is free to all. God invites you to come and take it: will you come?

Grace, growing in

Luke 2:40; Acts 20:32; Rom. 6:14; Titus 3:15; Heb. 13:9; 2 Peter 3:18

When I was at Mr. Spurgeon's house he showed me the photographs of his two sons who were twins, and whose photographs had been taken every year since they were twelve months old until they were seventeen years old. For the first two years they did not seem to have grown much, but when we compared the first with those of the age of seventeen they seemed to have grown amazingly. So it is with the children of God—they grow in grace. A great many people talk about others being unsound in faith. I believe that one of the graces which require cultivation is more love to the Master, more love to one another, more love for a perishing world, and more love for the lost.

There are two lives that every Christian should live. One life he should live alone with God—a life that nobody but God and himself knows—that inner life, that constant communion whereby he draws strength from God; and the other the outer life before the world, adorning the doctrine of Jesus Christ.

Grace, growth in

Luke 2:40; Acts 20:32; Rom. 6:14; Titus 3:15; Heb. 13:9; 2 Peter 3:18

People make the same prayer that they made twenty years ago; they tell over and over the same old experience. They go back to the past, instead of getting fresh supplies. Suppose I should say to my wife: "Emma, I did love you when we were married, eighteen years ago." Why, talking so would break her heart. She wants me to love her now; and I do love her a great deal better than I did eighteen years ago. We ought to grow in grace. Everything else grows. Sin grows. Our children grow. We would be sad enough if they didn't—if they remained dwarfs.

But there are Christians who are no larger spiritually than they were years ago. They are stunted, because they have starved themselves. The early Christians grew. And each of us should examine ourselves—should ask, "Am I growing?" I have a picture of my child. It was a good likeness once, but not now, for the child has outgrown it. But there are some in the churches whose spiritual photographs, if taken a dozen years ago, would be just like them now. They haven't grown a bit. Rowland Hill said a good many people's activity was like that of a child on its rocking horse—motion, but no progress.

Grace, obtaining

Exod. 33:17; John 1:16; Rom. 3:24; 11:6; Titus 3:15; Heb. 13:9

Grace means undeserved kindness. It is the gift of God to man the moment he sees he is unworthy of God's favor. A man does not get grace till he comes down to the ground, till he sees he needs grace. When a man stoops to the dust and acknowledges that he needs mercy, then it is that the Lord will give him grace.

Grace overflowing; Self-discipline, importance of

Gen. 6:8; Deut. 33:25; John 1:16; Rom. 4:16; 11:6; Titus 3:15; Heb. 2:9

Take a tumbler, and get it so full of water that you can't get another drop in, and

then touch it, and it will overflow. So Christ, when that woman touched him, overflowed with virtue, and she was healed. That is the privilege of every child of God—to be so full of grace as to have a surplus. If a Christian hasn't got grace enough to regulate self, there isn't enough to go and work for others.

Grace, sufficient for need

Gen. 6:8; Deut. 33:25; Isa. 41:13; Rom. 6:14; 1 Cor. 12:9; Heb. 2:9

Paul had a thorn in the flesh. It is well we don't know just what it was; for if we did, we would all think our thorns sharper than his. But Paul learned to thank God for that thorn, because he got more grace by it. People pray to have their thorns taken away, when they ought to pray for grace to bear them. God will give us grace according to our day. I have not grace to die by now. I don't need it. I don't ask for it. What I want is grace to serve God in California for three or four months; that is what I am praying for now. God is not going to waste his grace. I like to go right on, knowing that as my day is, so shall my strength be. God has plenty of grace, and I have only to go and get it just as I need it.

Grace, sufficient; Satan, strategy of; Temptation, resisting

Deut. 33:25; Isa. 41:13; Rom. 6:14; 1 Cor. 12:9; Heb. 2:9

One of the happiest men I ever knew was a man in Dundee, Scotland, who had fallen and broken his back when he was a boy of fifteen. He had lain on his bed for about forty years, and could not be moved without a good deal of pain. Probably not a day had passed in all those years without acute suffering. But day after day the grace of God had been granted to him, and when I was in his chamber it seemed as if I was as near heaven as I could get on earth. I can imagine that when the angels passed over Dundee, they had to stop there to get refreshed.

When I saw him, I thought he must be beyond the reach of the tempter, and I asked him, "Doesn't Satan ever tempt you to doubt God, and to think that he is a hard Master?" "Oh, yes," he said, "he does try to tempt me. I lie here and see my old schoolmates driving along in their carriages, and Satan says, 'If God is so good, why does he keep you here all these years? You might have been a rich man, riding in your own carriage.' Then I see a man who was young when I was walk by in perfect health, and Satan whispers, 'If God loved you, couldn't he have kept you from breaking your back?'"

"What do you do when Satan tempts you?" "Ah, I just take him to Calvary, and I show him Christ, and I point out those wounds in his hands and feet and side, and say, 'See how much he loves me?' and the fact is, he got such a scare there eighteen hundred years ago that he cannot stand it; he leaves me every time." That bedridden saint had not much trouble with doubts; he was too full of the grace of God.

Grace to the Gentiles; Grace, abundant

John 1:16; Rom. 9:30; Eph. 2:8–9; 3:8; Heb. 2:9

A friend of mine in England told me this story. Suppose that a man had a beautiful farm on the side of a mountain. Everything was in an enclosure. He had a great wall all around it. Everything within the walls was bright and green, while everything outside was hot and dried up. One day there came a messenger to the man that had the farm, and he said to him: "Sir, you have a fine, flourishing farm, but I want to make it better. I will increase its fertility; I will make it a thousand times better than it now is." "No," says the

farmer, "my farm is good enough; you can do nothing to better it"; and drove him away.

He wouldn't have his farm made better, and the farmer built his walls still higher to keep all men out. Up in the mountain near the house was a fountain. Its stream was used to irrigate and beautify the farm, and from it the crystal waters came to the fields and gardens. The man that had gone to him was the owner of the fountain. He said to himself, "This man won't let me make his farm more beautiful; he won't accept my kindness. I will build up a barrier, cut the stream off from him and let it flow to all the other farms on the mountain."

When the barrier arose around the fountain's head the waters ceased to flow to the farm; the flowers began to fade and wither, and soon the farm became a scene of desolation and ruin.

God's people of Israel spurned the offer of Jesus their Messiah feeling that what they had in the old way was good enough. God's grace flowed out to the Gentiles and what a blessing it has been to us. So the Lord of Glory comes and wants to give us his grace, but we spurn it, refuse to accept his blessing, and we perish. Christ had the hardest work of his ministry to teach this subject to his disciples. Rejecting God's grace offered in Christ is just what the sinner is doing now. But if you'll only let the grace flow, nothing can hinder you from getting a blessing.

Grace, unlimited

Exod. 33:13; John 1:16; Rom. 4:16; Phil. 4:19; Heb. 2:9

In London there are signs, "Limited Capital." The parties doing business there assume only a limited responsibility. But God's grace is not limited. In temporal matters, it is prudent to live within one's income. But not so in the spiritual life. There we may spend freely. There we cannot be too extravagant, "for our God will supply all our needs." God is more willing to give than we are to receive. I pity those who are satisfied with crumbs, when they might have loaves. Let us be grateful to God for what we have asked and received; but let us keep asking for more and more.

Grace, using daily; Obedience, continual

Gen. 6:8; Deut. 33:25; Luke 2:40; Heb. 13:9

It is said by travelers that in climbing the Alps the houses of far distant villages can be seen with great distinctness, so that sometimes the number of panes of glass in a church window can be counted. The distance looks so short that the place to which the traveler journeying appears almost at hand, but after hours and hours of climbing it seems no nearer. This is because of the clearness of the atmosphere. By perseverance, however, the place is reached at last, and the tired traveler finds rest.

So sometimes we dwell in high altitudes of grace; heaven seems very near. At other times the clouds and fogs caused by suffering and sin cut off our sight. We are just as near heaven in the one case as we are in the other, and we are just as sure of gaining it if we but keep in the path that Christ has pointed out.

Gray areas, test of

Deut. 12:7; 1 Cor. 10:31; Col. 3:17; 1 Peter 4:11

In Europe in a place where there was a good deal of whisky distilled, one of the men in the business was a church member, and got a little anxious in his conscience about his business. He came and asked me if I thought that a man could be an honest distiller. I said, "You should do whatever you do for the glory of God. If you can get down and pray about a barrel of whisky, and say, for instance, when you sell

it, 'Oh, Lord God, let this whisky be blessed to the world,' it is probably honest."

Greatness, path to; Service, self-sacrificial

Matt. 20:20; Mark 9:34–35; 10:37, 44; Luke 9:46; 22:24; John 13:4; Phil. 2:3; James 4:6; 1 Peter 5:6

To me, one of the saddest things in all the life of Jesus Christ was the fact that just before his crucifixion, his disciples should have been striving to see who should be the greatest. It was his last night on earth, and they never saw him so sorrowful before. He knew Judas was going to sell him for thirty pieces of silver. He knew that Peter would deny him. And yet, in addition to this, when going into the very shadow of the cross, there arose this strife as to who should be the greatest. He took a towel and girded himself like a slave, took a basin of water and stooped and washed their feet. That was another object lesson of humility. He said, "Ye call me Master and Lord, and ye say well. If you want to be great in my kingdom, be servant of all." If you serve, you shall be great.

Greatness, true

Matt. 20:20; Mark 9:34–35; 10:37, 44; Luke 9:46; 22:24; John 13:4; Phil. 2:3; James 4:6; 1 Peter 5:6

How quickly the glory of this world fades away! Over one hundred years ago the great Napoleon almost made the earth to tremble. How he blazed and shone as an earthly warrior for a little while! A few years passed, and a little island held that once proud and mighty conqueror; he died a poor brokenhearted prisoner. Where is he today? Almost forgotten. Who in all the world will say that Napoleon lives in their heart's affections? Earth's nobility are soon forgotten. John Bunyan, the Bedford tinker, has outlived the whole crowd of those who were the nobility in his day. They lived for self, and their memory is blotted out. He lived for God and for souls, and his name is as fragrant as ever it was.

Growth, Christian; Humility, spirit of

1 Sam. 18:4; John 3:30

Doctor Bonar once remarked that he could tell when a Christian was growing. In proportion to his growth in grace he would elevate his Master, talk less of what he was doing, and become smaller and smaller in his own esteem, until, like the morning star, he faded away before the rising sun. Jonathan was willing to decrease that David might increase; and John the Baptist showed the same spirit of humility.

Grumblers, church of

Exod. 16:2; 17:3; Num. 11:1; 1 Cor. 10:10; 1 Thess. 5:17; Heb. 12:29; Jude 16

There are a good many people that are always grumbling. I wish that we could have a great national church and call it a church for grumblers. These grumblers, instead of going into the church and reforming it, stand outside and find fault with the church and throw stones at it. They would do better to spend their energy praying for the church and trying to make it better.

Grumbling, cure of; Fault-finding, cure of

Matt. 24:9; 26:67; 27:29–30; Mark 15:17, 19; John 19:2; Heb. 12:3

A pastor of a little church in a small town became exceedingly discouraged, and brooded over his trials to such an extent that he became a perpetual grumbler. He found fault with his brethren because he imagined they did not treat him well. A brother minister was invited to assist him a few days in a special service. At the close of the Sunday morning service our unhappy brother invited the visiting minister to his house to dinner. While they were waiting alone in the parlor he began his doleful story by saying, "You have no idea of my troubles; and one of the greatest is that my brethren in the church treat me very badly."

The other asked the following questions, "Did they ever spit in your face?" "No; they haven't come to that." "Did they ever hit you?" "No." "Have they ever crowned you with thorns?" This last question he could not answer, but bowed his head thoughtfully. The other replied, "Your Master and mine was thus treated, and all his disciples fled and left him in the hands of the wicked. Yet he did not complain."

This conversation had a healing effect. Both ministers bowed in prayer and earnestly sought to possess the mind which was in Christ Jesus. During the ten days' meetings the discontented pastor became wonderfully changed. He labored and prayed with his friend, and many souls were brought to Christ. Some weeks after, a deacon of the church wrote and said, "Your recent visit and conversation with our pastor have had a wonderful influence for good. We never hear him complain now, and he labors more prayerfully and zealously."

Grumbling, uselessness of; Thanksgiving, blessing of; Praise, blessing of

Job 35:10; Pss. 77:6; 119:62; Isa. 30:29; Luke 6:32; Acts 16:25; Rom. 5:3

An old gentleman got up once in a meeting and said he had lived nearly all his life on Grumble Alley, but not long ago he had moved over on Thanksgiving Street. He didn't have to pay any more rent than he had on Grumble Alley. The new neighbors were delightful, and he had made the best friends he had ever known. The man showed in his face that he lived there; it was full of praise and thanksgiving. You can tell these people as soon as you see them. I like to see them in my meetings; I like to hear them pray. It is a great thing to meet people full of praise and thanksgiving.

Guilty, all people

Rom. 3:9, 23; Gal. 3:22; 1 John 1:8

The people before the flood would not believe Noah. "What! Do you mean to tell us that there is a flood coming, and that we shall all perish alike? Statesmen, great and mighty men and rulers, rich and poor, all perish alike?" "Yes, every one of you that is not in the ark when the flood comes will perish." Did they believe? No, on the contrary. The Son of God tells us that when the flood came it swept them all away.

And so it was even in Jesus' days. On one side of the cross of Christ was the thief, penitent and believing, and on the other the unbelieving thief. You see many different classes of people may come together; there will be the educated and the ignorant; the churchman and the nonchurched; Sunday school teachers and Sunday school scholars. But arrange them as you will, God sees them all; God draws the line between them.

And God has drawn the line between two classes here tonight, believers and unbelievers, those who have been saved from under the curse of the law, and those who remain guilty. The verdict is given against you—Guilty. And why? Because all have sinned and come short of the glory of God.

Rom. 3:4; 5:12; 6:23; 7:7; Gal. 3:10; 6:14; James 1:5

There is a woman in our country who was hoping to be saved, because she thought she was a respectable sinner. Some sinners don't think they are like other sinners. When people talk to me like this, I know they are great sinners. She heard a sermon, which showed her clearly that Christ died for the ungodly; and she said, "I must be ungodly; he died for the ungodly." She awoke to the fact that she was unlike God, and the light of eternity flashed into her soul. My friends, take your place among the ungodly. I am tired of people making out that they are not bad sinners whereas they are bad from the crown of the head to the sole of the foot. They are bad, and God says it: and let God be true and every man a liar.

Rom. 3:4; 5:12; 6:23; 7:7; Gal. 3:10; 6:14; James 1:5

In Chicago, when our City Constitution was new, a bill was passed that no man should be a policeman that was not a certain height—five feet six. The commissioners advertised for men to come round and be examined, and they must bring good letters of recommendation with them. Now as they are passing from one man to another, examining their letters, and trying their height, suppose there are two of us who want to get in, and I say to my friend, "There is no man has a better chance than I have; I have got letters from the supreme judge, from the mayor and leading citizens of Chicago; no man can have better letters." He says, "Ah, my friend, my letters are as good as yours."

Well, the chief commissioner says, "Look here, Moody, these letters are all right, but you must be up to the standard"; so he measures me, and I am only five feet, and he says, "You are half a foot too short." My friend looks down on me and says, "I have got a better chance than you." Well, he stands up and is measured, and is only one-tenth of an inch short, but he goes with me. He has come short. I admit some men have come shorter than others, but that is the verdict God has brought in—all are guilty.

Guns, use of; Self-protection, basis of

Pss. 42:11; 43:5; 59:1; 62:6; Isa. 12:2; 25:4; Jer. 17:7; 2 Tim. 2:19; Heb. 6:19

I don't think a man gains much by loading himself down with weapons to defend himself. There has been life enough sacrificed in this country to teach men a lesson in this regard. There is better protection than the revolver. We had better take the Word of God to protect us, by accepting its teaching, and living out its precepts.

Habit, power of

Jer. 12:5; Luke 11:4; 22:32, 46; 1 Cor. 10:13; Eph. 6:13; 2 Thess. 3:3; 1 Peter 1:6–7; 2 Peter 2:9

Beware of your habits. A recent writer has said: "Could the young but realize how soon they will become mere walking bundles of habits, they would give more heed to their conduct while young. We are spinning our own fates, good or evil, and never to be undone. Every smallest stroke of virtue or of vice leaves its little scar. The drunken Rip Van Winkle, in Jefferson's play, excuses himself for every fresh dereliction by saying, 'I won't count this time.' Well, he may not count it, and a kind heaven may forgive it, but it is being counted none the less. Down among his nerve cells and fibers the molecules are counting it, registering and storing it up, to be used against him when the next temptation comes. Nothing we ever do is, in strict scientific literalness, wiped out. Of course, this has its good side as well as its bad one. As we may become permanent drunkards by so many separate drinks, so we become saints in the moral sphere, and authorities and experts in the practical and scientific spheres of life, by so many separate acts and hours of work."

We are weak and sinful by nature, and it is a good deal better for us to pray for avoidance of temptation rather than for strength to resist when temptation has overtaken us.

Habit, power of; Self-control, need of

Jer. 12:5; Luke 11:4; 22:32, 46; 1 Cor. 10:13; Eph. 6:13; 2 Thess. 3:3; 1 Peter 1:6–7; 2 Peter 2:9

When I was speaking to five thousand children in Glasgow, Scotland, some years ago, I took a spool of thread and said to one of the largest boys, "Do you believe I can bind you with that thread?" He laughed at the idea. I wound the thread around him a few times, and he broke it with a single jerk. Then I wound the thread around and around, and by and by I said, "Now get free if you can." He couldn't move head or foot. If you are slave to some vile habit, you must either slay that habit, or it will slay you.

Habits, sinful; Satanic strategy; Sin, freedom from

Jer. 12:5; Luke 11:4; 22:32, 46; 1 Cor. 10:13; Eph. 6:13; 2 Thess. 3:3; 1 Peter 1:6–7; 2 Peter 2:9

Mr. Spurgeon once made a parable. He said, "There was once a tyrant who summoned one of the subjects into his presence, and ordered him to make a chain. The poor blacksmith—that was his occupation—had to go to work and forge the chain. When it was done, he brought it into the presence of the tyrant, and was ordered to take it away and make it twice the length. He brought it again to the tyrant, and again he was ordered to double it. Back he came when he had obeyed the order. The evil tyrant looked at it, and then commanded his servants to bind the man hand and foot with the chain he himself had made and cast him in prison.

"That is what the devil does with men," Mr. Spurgeon said. "He makes them forge their own chain, and then binds them hand and foot with it, and casts them into outer darkness." My friends, that is just what drunkards, gamblers, blasphemers—that is just what every sinner is doing. But thank God, we can tell them of a deliverer. The Son of God has power to break every one of their fetters if they will only come to him.

Harvest, result of sowing; Reaping, result of sowing

Job 4:8; 15:31; Prov. 1:31; 11:18; 1 Cor. 6:9; Gal. 6:7; Eph. 5:6

This law is just as true in God's kingdom as in man's kingdom; just as true in the spiritual world as in the natural world. If I sow tares, I am going to reap tares; if I sow a lie, I am going to reap lies; if I sow adultery I am going to reap adulterers; if I sow whisky, I am going to reap drunkards. You cannot blot this law out, it is in force. No other truth in the Bible is more solemn.

Hearing for others; Application to self

Ps. 51:1

I have noticed that in the fifty-first Psalm the word "me," or its equivalent, occurs thirty-three times. I much fear that nowadays nine-tenths of the sermons preached are lost through the habit of hearing, not for ourselves, but for others. The application is passed over from one to another, until both text and sermon are passed out of the place of worship altogether. We must not think that the sermon is for others rather than ourselves.

Hearing, spiritual; Satan, strategy of; Soul, ear of

Gen. 3:6; Pss. 78:1; 119:130; Matt. 11:15; Mark 4:9; Luke 8:8; John 6:63; 12:50; Rom. 10:17; 2 Cor. 3:6

Man lost spiritual life and communion with his Maker by listening to the voice of the tempter, instead of the voice of God. We get life again by listening to the voice of God. The Word of God gives life. "The words that I speak unto you," says Christ, "they are spirit, and they are life." So, what people need is to incline their ear, and hear. It is a great thing when the preacher gets the ear of a congregation—I mean the inner spiritual ear, for a man has not only two ears in his head; he has what we may call the outer ear and the inner ear— the ear of the soul. You may speak to the outward ear, and not reach the ear of the soul at all. Many in these days are like the "foolish people" to whom the prophet Jeremiah spoke: "Which have eyes, and see not; which have ears, and hear not." "He that hath ears to hear, let him hear."

Heart, cleansing of

Ps. 51:2, 7; Ezek. 36:25; Zech. 13:1; 1 Cor. 6:11; Heb. 9:14; 1 John 1:9

We must commence with our own hearts. God wants truth there. It is not people who are making outward profession and yet living out of communion with God that are going to accomplish much. God looks down into our hearts. He wants truth there. We cannot deceive God. If we attempt to wash ourselves we shall make very poor work of it. What we need is for God to wash us, and then we will be clean. We must let God cleanse us. That is his work.

Heart, deceitful

Jer. 17:9; John 3:19

Some years ago a remarkable picture was exhibited in London. As you looked at it from a distance, you seemed to see a monk engaged in prayer, his hands clasped, his head bowed. As you came nearer, however, and examined the painting more closely, you saw that in reality he was squeezing a lemon into a punch bowl! What a picture that is of the human heart! Superficially examined, it is thought to be the seat of all that is good and noble and pleasing in a man; whereas in reality, until regenerated by the Holy Ghost, it is the seat of all corruption.

Prov. 28:26

How many times we have said that we never would do a certain thing again, and then have done it within twenty-four hours. A man may think he has fathomed his heart's depths, but he finds there are further depths he has not reached. "He that trusteth in his own heart is a fool," said Solomon. Luther once said, "I fear my own heart more than the Pope and all the cardinals."

Heart, deceitful; Corruption, inner

Mark 7:21–22

If a man should advertise that he could take a correct photograph of people's inner thoughts and hearts, do you believe he would find any customers? There is not a person among us who would ask to have such a photograph taken, if it were possible to photograph the inner thoughts. We go to have our faces photographed, and carefully arrange ourselves, and if the picture flatters us, we say, "Oh, yes, that's a first-rate likeness," and we pass it around among our friends. But let the real person be revealed, the photograph of the heart, and see if we will pass that around among our neighbors! Why, we would not want our own wives, husbands or parents to see it! We would be frightened even to look at it ourselves.

Heart, hardening of; Conscience, searing of

Gen. 6:5; Prov. 28:26; Eccles. 9:3; Jer. 17:9–10; Matt. 5:19; Mark 7:21; Luke 2:35; 16:15; 1 Tim. 4:2; Heb. 3:12; 1 John 2:19

Do you know that the gospel of Jesus Christ proves either a savior of life unto life, or of death unto death? You sometimes hear people say, "We will go and hear this man preach. If it does us no good, it will do us no harm." Don't you believe it! Every time one hears the gospel and rejects it, the hardening process goes on. The same sun that melts the ice hardens the clay. The sermon that would have moved to action a few years ago makes no impression now.

There is not a true minister of the gospel who will not say that the hardest people to reach are those who have been impressed, and whose impressions have worn away. It is a good deal easier to commit a sin the second time than it was to commit it the first time, but it is a good deal harder to repent the second time than the first.

Heart, preparation of

Josh. 22:5; 2 Chron. 12:14; 19:3; Ezra 7:10; Prov. 4:23; Jer. 4:3; Hosea 10:12

My experience is that the work among the unconverted is in proportion to the work in the church. If it is superficial with us and does not take hold of us and go down deep in our hearts, and if we have not had tender consciences and have not dealt honestly with God, the work is superficial. If the work in your city is superficial it will be because we Christians are not right ourselves.

Heart searching, need of

Pss. 44:21; 139:23; Jer. 17:10; Zeph. 1:12; Acts 17:21

Listen to the confession of a minister, sensible of his tendency to neglect spiritual things, and especially of the difficulty of this duty: "I have lived," said he, "more than forty years and carried my heart in my bosom all this while, and yet my heart and I are as great strangers, and as utterly unacquainted, as if we had never come near one another. Nay, I know not my heart; I have neglected my heart. We are fallen into an Athenian age, spending our time in nothing more than in telling or hearing news. How go things here? How there? How in one place? How in another? But who is there that is inquisitive concerning the inner life? How are things with my poor heart? Oh, the days, months, years, I bestow upon sin, vanity, the affairs of this world, while I afford not a minute to converse with my own heart concerning its need!"

Heart, value of a good

Pss. 51:10; 73:1; Prov. 4:23; 20:9; Ezek. 11:19; Matt. 5:8; 15:9; Mark 7:21; 2 Cor. 5:17

A Jewish rabbi once asked his scholars what was the best thing a man could have in order to keep him in the straight path. One said a good disposition; another, a good companion; another said wisdom was the best thing he could desire. At last a scholar replied that he thought a good heart was best of all. "True," said the rabbi, "you have comprehended all that the others have said. For he that has a good heart will be of a good disposition, and a good companion, and a wise man. Let everyone, therefore, cultivate a sincerity and uprightness of heart at all times, and it will save him an abundance of sorrow." We need to make the prayer of David, "Create in me a clean heart, O God, and renew a right spirit within me."

Heaven, a place of triumph

2 Cor. 2:14; Rev. 20:10; 21:5; 22:3

Heaven is the place of victory and triumph. This is the battlefield; heaven is the place of triumphal procession. This is the land of the sword and the spear; that is the land of the wreath and the crown. Oh, what a thrill of joy will shoot through the hearts of all the blessed when their conquests will be made complete in heaven; when death itself, the last of foes, shall be slain, and Satan dragged as captive at the chariot wheels of Christ!

Heaven and service

Rev. 22:3

It won't come hard to people who are serving God down here to do it when they go to heaven. They will change places, but they won't change employment.

Heaven as home

Rev. 21:4

What a home is that of the Christian! This is not our home, this is only our training place. We look for a city eternal in the heavens. Just think of it! A city in God's universe that has no cemetery, whose streets never see a hearse, and where a funeral procession is never seen. A city where nothing that defiles ever enters, and weeping and mourning are gone. No jails nor hospitals are there, no want nor sickness, for God shall supply all needs. And there, in the glorious light of his face, we may serve him whom we love, for ever and ever. Seeing we are citizens of such a home, how lightly should we count every trifle here, and how earnestly should we lay up treasures where we shall ever live to enjoy them.

Heaven, certainty of

Matt. 11:28; 19:14; Mark 10:14; Luke 12:32; 18:16; John 5:24; 14:23; Rom. 8:17; Gal. 3:26; 4:7; Eph. 3:6; Titus 3:7; Rev. 22:17

To the Christian heaven is a sure promise, and there is no room for doubt. The heir to some great estate, while a child, thinks more of a dollar in his pocket than all his inheritance. So even some professing Christians sometimes are more delighted by a passing pleasure than they are by their title to eternal glory. In a little while we will be there. How certain is the thought that everything is prepared. That is what Christ went up to heaven to do. In a little while we will be gone. We are

"Only waiting till the shadows
Are a little longer grown,
Only waiting till the glimmer
Of the day's last beam is flown:
Then from out the gathered darkness,
Holy, deathless stars shall rise,
By whose light our souls shall gladly
Tread their pathway to the skies."

Heaven, description of

Rev. 21:4; 22:3

Think of a city without a cemetery—they have no dying there. If there could be such a city as that found on this earth what a rush there would be to it! You can't find one on the face of this earth. A city without tears—God wipes away all the tears up yonder. This is a time of weeping, but by-and-by there is a time coming when God shall call us where there will be no tears. A city without pain, a city without sorrow, without sickness, without death. There is no darkness there. The Lamb is the light thereof. It needs no sun, it needs no moon.

The paradise of Eden was as nothing compared with this one. The tempter came into Eden and triumphed, but in that city nothing that defiles shall ever enter. There will be no tempter there. Think of a place where temptation cannot come. Think of a place where we will be free from sin; where pollution cannot enter, and where the righteous shall reign forever. Think of a city that is not built with hands, where the buildings do not grow old with time; a city whose inhabitants no census has numbered except the Book of Life, which is the heavenly directory. Think of a city through whose streets runs no tide of business, where no hearses creep slowly with their burdens to the tomb; a city without griefs or graves, without sins or sorrows, without marriages or mournings, without births

or burials; a city which glories in having Jesus for its king, angels for its guards, and whose citizens are saints!

We believe this is just as much a place and just as much a city as New York is, or London or Paris. We believe in it a good deal more, because earthly cities will pass away, but this city will remain forever. It has foundations whose builder and maker is God.

Heaven, hope of

John 14:2; 2 Cor. 5:1; Phil. 3:20; Heb. 11:10; 12:22, 28; 13:14; Rev. 21:22

What has been, and is now, one of the strongest feelings in the human heart? Is it not to find some better place, some lovelier spot, than we have now? It is for this that men are seeking everywhere; and yet, they can have it, if they will; but instead of looking down, they must look up to find it. As men grow in knowledge, they vie with each other more and more to make their homes attractive, but the brightest home on earth is but an empty barn, compared with the mansions that are in the skies.

What is it that we look for at the decline and close of life? Is it not some sheltered place, some quiet spot, where if we cannot have constant rest, we may at least have a foretaste of what is to be? What was it that led Columbus, not knowing what would be his fate, across the unsailed western seas, if it was not the hope of finding a better country? This it was that sustained the hearts of the Pilgrim Fathers, driven from their native land by persecution, as they faced an iron-bound, savage coast, with an unexplored territory beyond. They were cheered and upheld by the hope of reaching a free and fruitful country, where they could be at rest and worship God in peace.

Somewhat similar is the Christian's hope of heaven, only it is not an undiscovered country, and in attractions cannot be compared with anything we know on earth.

Heaven, identity retained in

Matt. 8:11; 17:2; Mark 9:2; Rev. 3:5; 20:15

Many are anxious to know if they will recognize their friends and loved ones in heaven. In the 8th chapter of Matthew and the 11th verse, we read: "And I say unto you, that many shall come from the east and west, and shall sit down with Abraham and Isaac and Jacob, in the kingdom of heaven." Here we find that Abraham, Isaac and Jacob who lived so many hundreds of years before Christ had not lost their identity. Moses and Elijah retained their identity on the Mount of Transfiguration. God says in Isaiah, "I will not blot your names out of the Lamb's Book of Life." We have names in heaven; we are going to bear our names there; we will be known.

Heaven, information concerning

Matt. 6:20; Luke 12:23; John 14:3; Eph. 1:18; Col. 1:5

A great many persons imagine that anything said about heaven is only a matter of speculation. They talk about heaven much as they would about the air. Now there would not have been so much in Scripture on this subject if God had wanted to leave the human race in darkness about it. What the Bible says about heaven is just as true as what it says about everything else. The Bible is inspired. What we are taught about heaven could not have come to us in any other way than by inspiration. No one knew anything about it but God, and so if we want to find out anything about it we have to turn to his Word.

Heaven, interest in

John 14:3; Phil. 3:20; Heb. 11:10; 12:22; 13:14

Surely it is not wrong for us to think and talk about heaven. I like to locate it, and find out all I can about it. I expect to live there through all eternity. If I were going to dwell in any place in this country, if I were going to make it my home, I would inquire about its climate, about the neighbors I would have, about everything, in fact, that I could learn concerning it. If soon you were going to emigrate, that is the way you would feel. Well, we are all going to emigrate in a very little while. We are going to spend eternity in another world, a grand and glorious world where God reigns. Is it not natural that we should look and listen and try to find out who is already there, and what is the route to take?

Heaven, nature of; Mother, importance of

John 14:3; Rev. 21:3; 22:3

Once I heard of a little sick child, whose mother was seriously ill; and so, in order that she might have quiet, and that the sick child might be no trouble to her, the little one was taken away to a friend's house, and placed in care of a kind lady for a time. The mother grew worse, and at length died. The father said, "We'll not trouble the child about it; she is too young to remember her mother; just let her remain where she is until the funeral is over."

This was done, and in a few days the little girl was brought back to the house. No mention was made of her mother or of what had occurred; but no sooner was she taken to the house than she ran first into one room, then into another, into the parlor, the dining room, and all over the house, and then away into a little room where her mother used to go to pray alone. "Where is mother?" she cried. "I want mother!" And when they were compelled to tell her what had happened, she cried out, "Take me away, take me away; I don't want to be here without mother."

It was the mother who made it home to her. And so it is in heaven. It is not so much the white robes, the golden crown, or the harps of gold, but it is the society we shall meet there. Who, then, are there? What company shall we have when we get there? Jesus is there, the Holy Father is there, the Spirit is there—our Father, our elder Brother, our Comforter.

Heaven, only way to

John 10:9; 14:6; Acts 4:12; Rom. 5:2; Rev. 22:17

I heard of a man who was going to get into heaven in his own way. He did not believe in the Bible or the love of God, but was going to get in on account of his good deeds. He was very liberal, gave a great deal of money, and he thought the more he gave, the better it would be for him in the other world. I don't, as a general thing, believe in dreams, but sometimes they teach good lessons.

This man's dream was the acting out of the way he had chosen to get to heaven. Well, this man dreamed one night that he was building a ladder to heaven, and he dreamed that every good deed he did put him one round higher on this ladder, and when he did an extra good deed, it put him up a good many rounds; and in his dream he kept going, going up, until at last he got out of sight, and he went on and on doing his good deeds, and the ladder went up higher and higher, until at last he thought he saw it run up to the very throne of God.

Then in his dream he thought he died, and that a mighty voice came rolling down from above: "He that climbs up some other way, the same is a thief and a robber," and down came his ladder, and he woke from his sleep, and thought, "If I go to heaven, I must go some other way." My friends, it is not just by another way but the only way. It is only by the way of the blood of Christ that we are to go to heaven. If a man has got to work his way to heaven, who will ever get there?

Heaven, place of God's presence

Rev. 5:6; 21:3; 22:17

When the angel Gabriel came down to tell Zachariah that he was to be the father of John the Baptist, the forerunner of Jesus Christ, Zachariah doubted him. Gabriel had never been doubted before; and that doubt is met with the declaration: "I am Gabriel, that standeth in the presence of the Almighty." What a glorious thing to be able to say! If you belong to Christ one day you will be able to say those words.

Heaven, place of joy

2 Cor. 12:7; Heb. 11:21; Rev. 21:3–4

It is an exhaustless store of comfort in the thought that the resurrected body will be free from all that mars it here on earth. Then will Jacob come forth from the tomb no longer leaning heavily upon his staff; Paul will never again experience a thorn in the flesh. The fevered brow and wasted form will give place to health and strength, and the moan of the little sufferer will give place to the joyous song of the redeemed. Why, then, should we ever be reminding ourselves of death when just beyond are strength and joy. Alexander MacLaren has well said: "The grave has a door on its inner side, and when the outer access is closed the inner portal opens on Heaven."

Heaven, place of song

Rev. 5:9; 14:3

In heaven we will have a new song. It is the song of Moses and the Lamb. I don't know just who wrote it or how, but it will be a glorious song. I suppose the singing we have here on earth will be nothing compared with the songs of that upper world. Do you know the principal thing we are told we are going to do in heaven is singing, and that is why men ought to sing down here. We ought to begin to sing here so that it won't come strange when we get to heaven. I pity the professed Christian who has not a song in his heart—who never feels like singing. It seems to me if we are truly children of God, we will want to sing about it. And so, when we get to heaven, we can't help shouting out loud hallelujahs.

Heaven, society of; Fellowship, importance of

John 8:21

One sentence from the lips of the Son of God in regard to the future state has forever settled it in my mind. "Ye shall die in your sins; whither I go, ye cannot come." If a man has not given up his drunkenness, his profanity, his licentiousness, his covetousness, heaven would be hell to him. Heaven is a prepared place for prepared people. What would a man do in heaven who cannot bear to be in the society of the pure and holy down here?

Heaven, treasures in

Matt. 6:20; 11:11; Luke 7:28

By laying up treasures in heaven we also leave behind us a memorial more lasting than marble or granite. Anything we do for our own selfish gratification is sure to perish; but what we do for Christ, that is eternal. And thus it is that we may live as much in the future as in the present—indeed, we may live more. John Wesley's influence is greater today a thousand fold than when he lived; Horatius Bonar lives today in the hymns he wrote, and through them preaches to more people than ever heard him preach. Herod thought to silence that eloquent preacher by the banks of the Jordan, but the unselfish beauty of the character of John the Baptist has preached and is preaching to millions of Christians in every quarter of this world. Now while it is day we must work to lay up treasures above,

and when our course is ended we shall enter into rest, while the works done in the name of Christ shall follow us.

Matt. 6:20; 19:21; Luke 12:32; 18:22; 2 Cor. 5:7; Heb. 10:34

An acquaintance of mine was very fond of investing his money in real estate, and when I asked him the reason he said, "Oh, I like to have my property where I can see it." And this is one reason why people don't like to lay up treasure in heaven. They forget what the apostle says, "The things which are seen are temporal, but the things which are not seen are eternal."

Heaven, way to; Resurrection, hope of

Eph. 1:13; 1 Thess. 2:3; 1 Peter 2:10

A poor woman once told Rowland Hill that the way to heaven was simple; comprising only three steps—out of self, into Christ, and into glory. We have a shorter way now—out of self and into Christ. That is heaven begun below—a little of what waits us over there. As a dead person can't inherit an estate, no more can a dead soul inherit heaven. The soul must be resurrected in Christ.

Heaven without hypocrites

Rev. 21:8; 22:11, 15

"I won't become a Christian because of hypocrites in the churches." My friend, you will find very few there if you get to heaven. There won't be a hypocrite in the next world, and if you don't want to be associated with hypocrites in the next world, you will take this invitation. You find hypocrites everywhere! One of the apostles was himself the very prince of hypocrites, but he didn't get to heaven. You will find plenty of hypocrites in the church. They have been there from the beginning, and will probably remain there. But what is that to you? This is an individual matter between you and your God.

Heaven, worth living for

Matt. 25:46; Rom. 8:25; 2 Cor. 4:17–18; Heb. 11:25

It is because there is no real happiness down here, that earth is not worth living for. It is because it is all above, that heaven is worth dying for. In heaven there is all life and no death. In hell there is all death and no life. Here on earth there is both living and dying, which is between the two. If we are dead to sin here we will be in heaven, and if we live in sin here we must expect eternal death to follow.

Heaven's certainties

Isa. 33:17; Matt. 5:8; John 12:26; 17:24; Heb. 12:14; 1 John 3:2; Rev. 22:4

There are two things that the Bible makes as clear and certain as eternity about heaven. One is that we are going to see Christ, and the other that we are going to be like him. God will never hide his face from us there, and Satan will never show his.

Heaven's inhabitants

1 Cor. 15:49; Heb. 12:23–24; Rev. 7:14; 14:14

A friend told me not long ago of a young lady who argued herself into the belief that God would never close the gates of heaven against a human soul. This young lady was entertaining a little niece one day by telling her the story of the "Babes in the Wood." As she finished the story the child asked anxiously, "And did the children go to heaven?" "Yes," replied the aunt. "And what became of the wicked uncles?" asked the child. "Well, I suppose God took them to heaven too." "But, won't they kill the babes again?" anxiously asked the little one. The practical nature of the question was too much for the aunt's philosophy, and the very impossibility of such a government under a righteous God appeared to her as it never had before.

1 Cor. 15:49; Heb. 12:23–24; Rev. 7:14; 14:14

Among the good whom we hope to meet in heaven, we are told, there will be every variety of character, taste, and disposition. There is not one mansion there; but many. There is not one gate to heaven, but many. There are not only gates on the north; but on the east three gates, and on the west three gates, and on the south three gates. From opposite quarters of the theological compass, from opposite quarters of the religious world, from opposite quarters of human life and character, through different expressions of their common faith and hope, through different modes of conversion, through different portions of the Holy Scripture, will the weary travelers enter the Heavenly City, and meet each other—"not without surprise" on the shores of the same river of life.

And on those shores they will find a tree bearing, not the same kind of fruit always and at all times, but "twelve manner of fruits," for every different turn of mind, for the patient sufferer, for the active servant, for the holy and humble philosopher, for the spirits of just men now at last made perfect; and "the leaves of the tree shall be for the healing," not of one single church or people only, not for the Scotchman or the Englishman only, but for the "healing of the nations"—the Frenchman, the German, the Italian, the Russian—for all those from whom it may be, in this, its fruits have been farthest removed, but who, nevertheless, have "hungered and thirsted after righteousness," and who therefore "shall be filled."

Heaven's new song

Pss. 33:3; 40:3; 96:1; 98:1; 144:9; Isa. 42:10; Rev. 5:9

There was a Wesleyan preacher in England, Peter Mackenzie, full of native humor, a most godly man. He was once preaching from the text, "And They Sang a New Song," and he said, "Yes, there will be singing in heaven, and when I get there I will want to have David with his harp, and Paul, and Peter and other saints gather around for a sing. And I will announce a hymn from the Wesleyan Hymnal. 'Let us sing hymn No. 749'—

My God, my Father, while I stray—

"But, someone will say, 'That won't do. You are in heaven, Peter; there's no straying here.' And I will say, 'Yes, that's so. Let us sing No. 651'—

Though waves and storms go o'er my head,

Though friends be gone and hopes be dead—

"But another saint will interrupt, 'Peter, you forget you are in heaven now; there are no storms here.' 'Well, I will try again, No. 536'—

Into a world of ruffians sent—

"'Peter! Peter!' someone will say, 'we will put you out unless you stop giving out inappropriate hymns.' I will ask—what can we sing? And they will all say: 'Sing the new song, the song of Moses and the Lamb.'"

Heaven's people

1 Cor. 15:49; Heb. 12:23–24; Rev. 7:14; 14:14

I remember after being away from home some time, I went back to see my honored mother, and I thought in going back I would take her by surprise, and steal in unexpectedly upon her, but when I found she had gone away, the old place didn't seem like home at all. I went into one room and then into another, and I went all through the house, but I could not find that loved mother, and I said to some member of the family, "Where is mother?" and they said she had gone away. Well, home had lost its charm to me; it was that mother that made home so sweet to me, and it is the loved ones that make home so sweet to every one; it is the loved ones that are going to make

heaven so sweet to all of us. Christ is there; God, the Father, is there; and many, many that were dear to us that lived on earth are there—and we shall be with them by and by.

Heaven's perfections

John 12:26; 14:3; 17:24; Phil. 1:23; 1 Thess. 4:17; 1 John 3:3; Rev. 3:12

We are amazed at ordinary perfections now. Few of us can look the sun square in the face. But when that which is corruptible shall have put on incorruption, as Paul says, the powers of the soul will be stronger. We will be able to see Christ in his glory then. Though the moon be confounded and the sun ashamed, yet shall we see him as he is. This is what will make heaven so happy.

We all know that great happiness cannot be found on earth. Reason, revelation, and the experience of six thousand years, all tell us that. No human creature has the power to give it. Even doing good fails to give it right away, for owing to sin in the world even the best do not have perfect happiness here. They have to wait for heaven; although they may be so near it sometimes that they can see heralds of its joy and beauty, like Columbus saw the strange and beautiful birds hovering around his ships long before he caught sight of America.

All the joys we are to know in heaven will come from the presence of God. This is the leading thought in all that the Scripture has to say on the subject. What life on this earth is without health, life in heaven would be without the presence of God. God's presence will be the very light and life of the place. It is said that one translation of the words describing the presence of God is "a happy making sight." It will be a sight like the return of a long-lost boy to his mother, or the first glimpse of your home after you have been a long time away. Some of you know how a little sunshine on a dark day, or the face of a kind friend in trouble, often cheers us up. Well, it will be something like that, only a thousand times better. Our perceptions of God will be clearer then, and that will make us love him all the more.

Heaven's surprises

Matt. 7:22–23; Rev. 3:5

It has been said that there will be three things which will surprise us when we get to heaven—one, to find many whom we did not expect to find there; another, to find some not there whom we had expected; a third, and perhaps the greatest wonder, to find ourselves there!

Heavenly-minded; Hypocritical spirit

1 Chron. 22:19; Luke 16:9; Col. 3:1–2; 1 John 2:15

You may very often see dead fish floating with the stream, but you never saw a dead fish swimming against it. Well, that is your false believer; that is the hypocrite. Profession of faith is just floating down the stream, but confession is swimming against the current, no matter how strong the tide. The person in the process of sanctification and the unsanctified one look at heaven very differently. The unsanctified person simply chooses heaven in preference to hell, thinking that if one must go to either one heaven is the better choice.

It is like a man with a firm who has a place offered him in another country, where there is said to be a gold mine. He hates to give up all he has and take any risk. But if he is going to be banished, and must leave, and has his choice of living in a wilderness or digging in a coal pit, or else take the gold mine, then there is no hesitation. The unregenerate man likes heaven better than hell, but he likes this world the best of all. When death stares him in the face, then he thinks he would like to get to heaven. The true believer prizes heaven above everything else, and is always willing to give up the world. Everybody wants to enjoy heaven after they die, but some don't want to be heavenly-minded while they live.

Heavenly perspective

1 Chron. 22:19; Luke 16:9; Col. 3:1–2; 1 John 2:15

When people going up in a balloon have ascended a little height, things down here begin to look very small indeed. What had seemed very grand and imposing now seem as mere nothings; and the higher they rise the smaller everything on earth appears; it gets fainter and fainter as they rise, till the railway train, dashing along at fifty miles an hour, looks like a thread, and scarcely appears to be moving at all, and the grand piles of buildings seem now like mere dots. So it is when we get near heaven; earth's treasures, earth's cares, look very small.

Hell, despair of

Matt. 18:9; Mark 9:47; Luke 12:5; 16:23; 2 Peter 2:4; Rev. 1:18; 20:14

Mr. Moody closed his sermon on hell by reading the following piece of poetry which, he said, had affected him deeply.

I sat alone with my conscience,
In a place where time was o'er,
And we talked of my former living
In the land of the evermore
And I felt I should have to answer
The question it put to me,
And to face the answer and question
Throughout an eternity.

The ghosts of forgotten actions
Came floating before my sight,
And things that I thought had perished
Were alive with a terrible might.

And the vision of life's dark record
Was an awful thing to face—
Alone with my conscience sitting
In that solemnly silent place.

And I thought of a far-away warning,
Of a sorrow that was to be mine,
In a land that then was the future,
But now is the present time.
And I thought of my former thinking
Of the judgment day to be,
But sitting alone with my conscience
Seemed judgment enough for me.

And I wondered if there was a future
To this land beyond the grave;
But no one gave me an answer,
And no one came to save.
Then I felt that the future was present,
And the present would never go by.
For it was but the thought of a future
Become an eternity.

Then I woke from my timely dreaming,
And the vision passed away,
And I knew the far-away warning
Was a warning of yesterday;
And I pray that I may not forget it,
In this land before the grave,
That I may not cry in the future,
And no one come to save.

I have learned a solemn lesson
Which I ought to have known before,
And which though I learned it dreaming,
I hope to forget no more.

So I sit alone with my conscience
In the place where the years increase,
And I try to fathom the future
In the land where time will cease;
And I know of the future judgment,
How dreadful soe'er it be,
That to sit alone with my conscience
Will be judgment enough for me.

Help, source of

Ps. 34:15; Matt. 6:33; Luke 12:30; Heb. 13:6;
1 Peter 5:7

I remember one time my little girl was teasing her mother to get her a muff, and so one day her mother brought a muff home, and, although it was snowing, she very naturally wanted to go out in order to try her new muff. So she tried to get me to go out with her. I went out with her, and I said, "Emma, better let me take your hand." She wanted to keep her hands in her muff, and so she refused to take my hand. Well, by and by she came to an icy place, her little feet slipped, and down she went.

When I helped her up she said, "Papa, you may give me your little finger." "No, my daughter, just take my hand." "No, no, papa, give me your little finger." Well, I gave my finger to her, and for a little way she got along nicely, but pretty soon we came to another icy place, and again she fell. This time she hurt herself a little, and she said, "Papa, give me your hand," and I gave her my hand, and closed my fingers about her wrist, and held her up so that she could not fall. Just so God is our keeper. He is wiser than we.

Holiness, influence of

Matt. 26:73; John 7:15; Acts 4:13; 2 Cor. 3:7;
Eph. 5:15

Walk circumspectly, because you don't know who will be influenced by your words and actions. I have heard of a canary that was taught to sing, "Home, Sweet Home," by being placed in a room, when young, with a musical box that played only that tune. Moses' face shone after he had been on the mount with God forty days. They took knowledge of the disciples "that they had been with Jesus." And it is said of Lord Peterborough after spending a night with Fenelon, the great French preacher, he was so impressed with his holy character that he said to him on leaving, "If I stay here any longer, I shall become a Christian in spite of myself."

Holy Spirit and prayer

Rom. 8:26

There is much praying that is not honored by the Holy Spirit. In former years I was very ambitious to get rich; I used to pray for one hundred thousand dollars; that was my aim, and I used to say, "God does not answer my prayer; he does not make me rich." But I had no warrant for such a prayer; yet a good many people pray in that way; they think that they pray, but they do not pray according to the Scriptures.

Holy Spirit as fire

Matt. 3:11; Acts 2:3

"I indeed baptize you with water unto repentance," said John the Baptist, "but Jesus shall baptize you with the Holy Ghost and with fire." Until the fire came the disciples were not qualified to work for God. They were all the time making blunders. The disciples never did or said a thing that was worth recording until the fire of Pentecost came and took the impurities out of them. There are some things that water cannot do. It may cleanse the outside, but fire searches not only the outside but the inside: it is penetrating. Take a lump of quartz, filled with beautiful pieces of gold which you can see sparkle. If dust gets on it and covers up the gold, you can wash the dust away and restore the glitter.

But there is one thing you cannot do with water. You cannot get the gold away from the impurities. There is only one way to do that—put it into fire and melt it. Then the pure gold will come out and the impurities may be thrown away. What we need is to have the Holy Spirit fire kindled that shall burn up all impurities and let the pure gold shine forth.

Holy Spirit brings hope; Conversions, impact of

Rom. 14:17; 15:13

Wherever I have found a worker in God's vineyard who has lost hope, I have found a man or woman not very active in the work of God. It is very important to have hope in the church; and it is the work of the Holy Spirit to impart hope. Let the power of the Holy Spirit come into some of the churches where there have not been any conversions for a few years, and let him convert a score of people, and see how hopeful the church becomes at once. He imparts hope. A man filled with the Spirit of God will be very hopeful. He will be looking out into the future, and he knows that it is all bright, because the God of all grace is able to do great things.

Holy Spirit, convicting power of

Zech. 12:10; John 16:8

There are more people ruined by flattery than by telling them their faults. We once found a man in Chicago sleeping on the sidewalk. It was one of the coldest days of the season, and we knew he would freeze to death if we didn't wake him. So we woke him, and he got mad at us. That was just what we wanted—to get his blood stirred, and then he would be all right. So sometimes the Holy Ghost wakes up men, and they wake up mad. But that is a good sign: it is better to have them wake up cross than sleepy, because the devil can't easily rock them to sleep again. Oh that we may have preaching that will wake people up and set their consciences at work!

Holy Spirit, conviction; Witnessing, cost of

Zech. 12:10; John 16:8; Acts 13:14; 14:2; 17:5, 13; 18:12

John Wesley used to ask his young men whom he had sent out to preach on trial two questions, "Has anyone been converted?" and "Did anyone get mad?" If the answer was "No," he told them he did not think the Lord had called them to preach the gospel, and sent them about their business. When the Holy Spirit convicts of sin, people are either converted or they don't like it, and get mad.

Holy Spirit-filled woman

1 Sam. 1:15; Luke 1:15, 41, 44; Acts 21:9

When we were in Philadelphia a lady said to me, "Mr. Moody, can women have the filling of the Holy Spirit?" I told her I saw no reason why anyone should not have it that wanted to work for God. Women need it as much as men. "Well," said she, "if I can have it I want it. I have a husband who is not a Christian. I have also a Sunday school class and they are unconverted." A week from that time she came to me and said, "I have got it. The Lord has blessed me. My husband has been converted and five of my Sunday school class." That was the result of that woman's receiving the power of the Holy Spirit. It spread all through the church of which she was a member, and the people seeing that she had something which they had not got began to inquire, and as a result of the quickening of that woman five hundred members were added to the church.

Holy Spirit filling, availability of; Praise, source of; Christians, classes of

Isa. 59:21; John 4:14; 7:38–39; Eph. 5:9

Every believer can experience the filling of the Spirit referred to in John 7:38–39, "He that believeth in Me, out of his inmost heart shall flow rivers of living water." God is able to do a great deal for us if we will only thirst for it. The trouble is, that a great many Christians don't thirst. They believe on Christ, and forget about the Holy Spirit in them. They are satisfied to stay where they are, and just rest there. The rivers that flow out of the believing soul may be rivers of praise to the Lord, pouring out in song and the language of grateful adoration; so that there may be rivers that flow upward, as well as flow over upon our fellowmen.

That is the highest type of Christian life—a river. Now, there are just those three classes of Christians. The first class gets life, but doesn't flow out; the second class is like a well of water, springing up. But I think it is the privilege of every believer to move into the seventh chapter of John, and live there. We should be river Christians.

Holy Spirit filling, commanded; Earnestness, need for; Dedication, need for

Acts 11:24; 2 Cor. 7:7; Eph. 5:8; Heb. 2:1

I wish we were all dead in earnest. What does the hungry man want? Money? Not at all. Fame? No. Good clothes? Not a bit. He wants food. What does the thirsty man want? Reputation? Bonds and stocks? No! He wants water. When we are dead in earnest and want the bread of heaven and water of life, we shall not stop till we get them. God has commanded us to be filled with the Holy Spirit. We have his promise that he will pour water on him that is thirsty. Claim that promise now in faith, fulfill the conditions laid down in the Word, and God will not disappoint you.

Holy Spirit filling, evidence of

Eph. 5:9, 18–20

You can tell a man who is filled by the Holy Spirit: he is all the time talking about Christ; he has nothing to say of himself, but is constantly holding Jesus Christ up as an all-sufficient Savior.

Holy Spirit filling, experience of

Gal. 5:22, 25

I can go back almost twenty years and remember two holy women who used to come to my meetings. It was delightful to see them there. When I began to preach I could tell by the expression of their faces that they were praying for me. At the close of the Sunday evening meetings they would say to me, "We have been praying for you." I said, "Why don't you pray for the people?" They answered, "You need the power." "I need power?" I said to myself. "Why, I thought I had the power." I had a large Sabbath school and the largest congregation in Chicago. There were some conversions at that time. I was, in a sense, satisfied.

But right along these two godly women kept praying for me, and their earnest talk about "anointing for special service" set me thinking. I asked them to come and talk with me, and we got down on our knees. They poured out their hearts that I might receive the anointing from the Holy Spirit, and there came a hunger into my soul. I did not know what it was. I began to cry as I never did before. The hunger increased. I really felt that I did not want to live any longer if I could not have this power for service.

Then came the Chicago fire. I was burned out of house and home at two o'clock in the morning. This did not so much affect me. My heart was full of the yearning for divine power. I was to go on a special mission to raise funds for the homeless, but my heart was not in the work for begging. I could not appeal. I was crying all the time that God would fill me with his Spirit.

Well, one day in the city of New York— ah, what a day! I cannot describe it; I seldom refer to it; it is almost too sacred an experience to name. Paul had an experience of which he never spoke for fourteen years. I can only say that God revealed himself to me, and I had such an experience of his love that I had to ask him to stay his hand. I went to preaching again. The sermons were not different; I did not present any new truths, and yet hundreds were converted.

I would not now be placed back where I was before that blessed experience if you would give me all Glasgow—it would be as the small dust of the balance. I tell you it is a sad day when a convert goes into the church and that's the last you hear of him. If, however, you want this power for some selfish end, as, for example, to gratify your own ambition, you will not get it. "No flesh," says God, "shall glory in my presence."

Holy Spirit filling for service

Ezek. 3:9; Acts 2:4; 4:8; 6:5; 8:39; Eph. 5:18

We must keep going to the Fountainhead to get filled. We must have fresh supplies. We don't get enough of Christ at once to carry us through life. The manna came down fresh six days a week, but it wouldn't keep: and the reason we have so many lean, half-starved Christians is because they live on stale manna. We are leaky vessels and lose the power. We find that the disciples were several times filled with the Holy Spirit, and we should profit by their experience.

Hundreds of men lose the power without knowing it, and they go on with their forms of preaching, and are astonished at their lack of success. A minister came to me and asked, "How can I keep free, and not be trammeled when I attempt to preach?" If a man is filled with the Holy Ghost he isn't trammeled; he has perfect freedom. The Lord gave Ezekiel a forehead of brass, and he went before the rebellious people fearlessly. When a man is filled with God he doesn't care about public opinion. He is simply a mouthpiece to declare the word and will of God. "A trumpet isn't afraid of its own sound."

I remember many a time I have gone from one place to another, and I have said, "God gave me success in that place, and now I shall have the same here." I have tried to carry on the work with the former grace and failed utterly, and I found I had to come right back and get fresh power. I believe that for every work we have to do for God we should get new power. The strength God gave me for Chicago won't do for Boston. I must have a fresh supply for the meetings here.

Holy Spirit filling, importance of

Exod. 28:3; 31:3; 35:31; Luke 2:41; Eph. 5:18

I make a distinction between the Spirit of God in a man and the Spirit of God on him. I may have the Spirit of God dwelling in me, but I can't have unction in service till I have the Spirit of God on me. What we want is not to be satisfied till we get power. Get this power, and you will do more good in one week than you could do without it in many years. Jonathan Edwards said there was more done in Northampton in one week than there had been in seven years before when the Holy Spirit came in power and Christians were quickened.

Luke 4:14; Acts 1:8; 4:8, 31

When I first went to Scotland I was a little troubled about my theology, for fear it wouldn't jibe with theirs. I hadn't my forehead covered with brass then. At one of the early meetings I saw one man with his head covered with his hands, and I thought he was mortified about my theology. When the meeting was over he grabbed his hat, and away he went. I gave him up, and thought he wouldn't come again. He was absent the next few days; but one day he came to the prayer meeting, and there was such a change in him that I scarcely knew him. He said he was so thoroughly convinced that what I had said about the importance of being filled with the Holy Spirit was true; that he felt he had been preaching without the power.

He had made up his mind to get it. So he locked himself in his closet, and God revealed himself to his soul. It was not a month before the people couldn't get into that man's church it was so full of people. I met him before I sailed for this country, and he told me that he hadn't preached a sermon since without someone being converted.

Holy Spirit filling, method of

Eph. 5:18

I have been asked, "How can I empty myself?" That is impossible. You can't do it, any more than you can fill yourself. I think a great many people make a mistake there. They go to work trying to empty themselves, and then when they can't do it they get discouraged. If, when this building was put up, the builder hadn't put any windows in, it would have been folly for the trustees of this institution to have got a hundred men to come here with buckets and try to bale out the darkness. The quickest way to get the darkness out is to let the light in. Just let in the light.

[Here Mr. Moody took a glass in his hand.] Say that tumbler is filled with jealousy, selfishness, pride, arrogance and every enemy to righteousness—and we go to work trying to get selfishness out, and pride out; and we work on and on, and find we can't do it. God's way isn't for us to try to get those things out. But here is the way. [Taking a pitcher in his hand, Mr. Moody filled the glass.] We get those things out by letting God's Spirit fill our lives.

Holy Spirit filling, method of; Yieldedness to God

Exod. 40:34–35; Acts 2:4; 1 Cor. 3:16

In Exodus we read that when Moses had finished the tabernacle in the desert, the Shekinah came and filled it with the presence of God—that was the Holy Spirit. The moment the tabernacle was ready it was filled. And when the temple was built, and the priests and the Levites were there singing with one accord, the cloud came and filled the temple; the moment the temple was ready it was filled.

These were two of his dwelling places; but where does he dwell now? Ye are the temples for the Holy Spirit to dwell in, and the moment the heart is ready, the Spirit of God will fill it.

Holy Spirit filling, need of

John 4:14, 23

I remember the first time I was in California I stood in a valley and noticed that in one section vegetation was green and vigorous. But just over the fence everything was dried up. On that side of the fence was another ranch, and there was scarcely a bit of vegetation there. I thought that was very curious, and I said to a farmhand, "Can you explain why on one side of the fence vegetation is fresh and green, and on the other side it is all dried up?" "Oh, yes," said he, "one man irrigates—he brings water down from the mountain and thoroughly waters his farm. The other doesn't." I think that is the way with a good many Christians in our churches. Some are dried up; but others have a secret communication between their souls and heaven, and God sends the water to them and keeps them always fresh. Drink deeply; don't be satisfied with merely "getting water."

Holy Spirit filling, need of; Renewal, spiritual; Service, power of

John 4:14, 23

We must constantly seek renewal of the filling of the Holy Spirit for service. We are very leaky vessels. We need to keep under the fountain all the time; then we will be kept full.

Holy Spirit filling, power of

Isa. 54:17; Matt. 10:20; Luke 1:17; 12:11–12; Acts 6:10; 1 Cor. 2:4

A lady in Philadelphia came to me and said: "You described me exactly when you said you pitied down deep in your soul any man or woman who never had the luxury of leading a soul to Jesus Christ. My husband is not a Christian. None of the people who work for me are Christians. I have a Bible class, and not one of them has been converted. I don't know what the trouble is." I said, "Are you in the habit of getting angry with your workers and scolding them?" "Yes," she said. "Then," I said, "when you think you would like to talk to them about their souls, your own life comes up and condemns you." "Yes," she said; "that is my difficulty."

Said I, "Sometimes you get out of patience with your husband, and scold him; and then when you want to talk with him about his soul, your own life comes up before you." "Yes," she said. "What should I do?" "Why," I said, "instead of praying for them, pray for yourself. Pray that you may be endued with power and grace to overcome your own inconsistencies." I prayed for that lady. After a while she came back to me and said, "I really don't know whether I am in the flesh or out of it. Why, I am the happiest mortal on the face of the earth. When I prayed for myself, and asked for power to live better, it seemed as if I was a different person. There came such a blessing to my soul that I went direct to my husband and I said that I hadn't lived as I should have done, and that I had professed what I hadn't possessed; and I wanted him to forgive me. He broke right down, and he was the first soul that God gave me. Three of my employees have been converted, and eight of my Bible class are converted, and I have accomplished more by my Christian life these last few days than I ever did before with all my talking."

Isa. 54:17; Matt. 10:20; Luke 1:17; 12:11–12; Acts 6:10; 1 Cor. 2:4

About four years ago I got into a cold state. It did not seem as if there was any unction resting upon my ministry. For four long months God seemed to be just showing me myself. I found I was ambitious. I was not preaching for Christ; I was preaching for ambition. I found everything in my heart that ought not to be there. For four months a wrestling went on within me, and I was a miserable man.

But after four months the anointing came. It came upon me as I was walking in the streets of New York. Many a time I have thought of it since I have been here. At last I had returned to God again, and I was wretched no longer. I almost prayed in my joy, "Oh, stay Thy hand." I thought this earthen vessel would break. He filled me so full of the Spirit. If I have not been a different man since, I do not know myself. I think I have accomplished more in the last four years than in all the rest of my life.

But, oh, it was preceded by a wrestling and a hard struggle! I thought I would never get out of this miserable selfishness. There was a time when I wanted to see my little vineyard blessed, and I could not get out of it; but I could work for the whole world now. I would like to go round the world and tell the perishing millions of a Savior's love.

Isa. 54:17; Matt. 10:20; Luke 1:17; 12:11–12; Acts 6:10; 1 Cor. 2:4

When we are filled with the Spirit of God and the Word of God, we must speak. We must shine. A lighthouse doesn't need to make itself shine; it can't help it. You don't have to put up a notice, "This is a lighthouse." The light tells its own story. I pity a person who goes around with a little light saying, "Look at my light; I shine." If you are filled with the Spirit of God you will shine so that no one will need to be told.

Holy Spirit filling, power of; Self-sacrifice, strength for

Isa. 54:17; Matt. 10:20; Luke 1:17; 12:11–12; Acts 6:10; 1 Cor. 2:4

When the Spirit came to Moses, the plagues came upon Egypt, and he had power to destroy men's lives; when the Spirit came upon Elijah, fire came down from heaven; when the Spirit came upon Gideon, no man could stand before him; and when it came upon Joshua, he moved around the city of Jericho and the whole city fell into his hands; but when the Spirit came upon the Son of Man, he gave his life so that the world might live eternally.

Holy Spirit filling, price of

1 Cor. 2:10; Eph. 4:30; 1 Thess. 5:19

It is the privilege of every one of us to have power or unction that comes from the filling of the Holy Spirit. But we have got to pay the price. Do you know what the price is? It is a complete and unconditional surrender to God for anything. If God wants me to leave my home and start for Africa, I am to go. That is what it means. I have lived long enough to make this discovery—I don't know my own heart, but I think I have got this far—I think if Gabriel should come and tell me that I could have my own will in everything, and I might have my own will to the end of my life, I would say in an instant, "No! Let the Lord's will be done." If the Lord wanted me to go to Africa I would start this afternoon. I'd rather a thousand times be in Africa with God than to be in America without him.

Holy Spirit filling, significance of

Ezek. 3:9; Acts 2:4; 4:8; 6:5; 8:39; Eph. 5:18

Ministers ask, "How can I keep my church out of the world?" My reply is, "Get them filled with the Spirit, and they are out at once."

Holy Spirit filling; Spurgeon's power

Ezek. 3:9; Acts 2:4; 4:8; 6:5; 8:39; Eph. 5:18

A few years ago a young man was living in a small town in England, and the Lord said to him: "Charles, go up to London, and rivers of living water will flow from you." Up he went, and for forty years he preached in that great metropolis, and brought thousands to Christ. Every Wednesday sermons were printed and translated into different languages and sent all over the earth. He founded a home for the poor. He was editor of *The Sword and Trowel*. He had an orphan asylum for two hundred and fifty boys, and another for two hundred and fifty girls. I can't begin to tell the streams that flowed forth from that man. He got the secret, as a young man, of being filled with the Spirit of God; and God let living waters flow through him.

Holy Spirit, guidance

John 14:26; 15:26; 16:13; Acts 2:14; 1 Cor. 2:10; 1 John 2:20, 27

I am told by people who have been over the Alps, if they are going in a dangerous place that the guide fastens them to himself, and goes on before them. And so should the Christian be linked to his unerring Guide, and be safely upheld. Why, if a man was going through the Mammoth Cave, it would be death to him if he strayed away from his guide; if separated from him, he would certainly perish. There are pitfalls in that cave and a great river, and there would be no chance for a man to find his way through that cave without a guide or a light.

So there is no chance for us to get through the dark wilderness of this world alone. It is folly for a man or woman to think they can get through this evil world without the light of the Divine Spirit through the Bible. God sent him to guide us through this great journey, and if we seek to work independent of him, we shall stumble into the deep darkness of eternity's night.

Holy Spirit, guidance; Conscience, weakness of

John 14:26; 15:26; 16:13; Acts 2:14; 1 Cor. 2:10; Heb. 13:18; 1 John 2:20, 27

Let us ever remember the Spirit has been sent into the world to guide us into all truth. We don't need any other guide; he is enough. Some people say, "Is not conscience a safer guide than the Word and the Spirit?" No, it is not. Some people don't seem to have any conscience, and don't know what it means. Their education has a good deal to do with conscience. There are persons who will say that their conscience did not tell them that they had done wrong until after the wrong was done; but what we need is something to tell us a thing is wrong before we do it. Very often a man will go and commit some awful crime, and after it is done his conscience will wake up and lash and scourge him, and then it is too late, the act is done.

Holy Spirit, guidance of

John 14:26; 15:26; 16:13; Acts 2:14; 1 Cor. 2:10; 1 John 2:20, 27

There is not a truth that we ought to know but the Spirit of God will guide us into it if we will let him. It would have saved us from a great many dark hours if we had only been willing to let the Spirit of God be our counselor and guide. Lot never would have gone to Sodom if he had been guided by the Spirit of God. David never would have fallen into sin and had all that trouble with his family if he had been guided by the Spirit of God. There are many Lots and Davids nowadays. The churches are full of them. Men and women are in total darkness, because they have not been willing to be guided by the Spirit.

Holy Spirit, illumination of

John 16:13

When I was in Baltimore, my window looked out on an Episcopal Church. The stained glass windows were dull and uninviting by day, but when the lights shone through at night, how beautiful they were! So when the Holy Spirit touches the eyes of your understanding, and you see Christ shining through the pages of the Bible, it becomes a new book to you.

Holy Spirit, illumination of; Hypocrisy, danger of

Matt. 5:16; John 16:13

We see very few illuminated Christians now. If every one of us was illuminated by the Spirit of God how we could light up the churches! But to have a lantern without any light, that would be a nuisance. Many Christians carry along lanterns and say, "I wouldn't give up my religion for yours." They talk about religion. The religion that has no fire is like painted fire. They are artificial Christians. Do you belong to that class? You can tell. If you can't, your friends can.

There is a fable of an old lantern in a shed, which began to boast because it had heard its master say he didn't know what he would ever do without it. But the little candle within the lantern spoke up and said: "Yes, you'd be of little comfort if it wasn't for me! You are nothing. I'm the one that gives the light." We are nothing, but Christ is everything, and what we need is to keep communion with him and let Christ dwell in us rich and shine forth through us.

I have a matchbox with a phosphorescent front. It draws in the rays of the sun during the day and then throws them out in the dead hours of the night, so that I can always see it in the dark. Now, that is what we ought to be, constantly drawing in the rays of the Son of Righteousness and then giving them out. Someone said to some young converts, "It is all moonshine being converted." They replied, "Thank you for the compliment.

The moon borrows light from the sun, and so we borrow ours from the Son of Righteousness." That's what takes place when we have this illumination.

Holy Spirit, illumination of; Regeneration, power of

Matt. 5:16; John 16:13

I happened to be in Palestine some years ago. In the south part of the land, we had to go through some dry spots—fields quite dry; but we were told that if you were only to flood that ground with water, it would spring into verdure. There are plenty of seeds lying in the ground, dropped at various times—some of them dropped by the birds of the air—so that you have only to let a flood of water upon the field, and in a short time you will have a rush of life.

Now, it may be just like that in the case of some people. You have been taught the Word of God; you know the doctrines of the Word; you know them in your head, and, perhaps, approve of them, too; but they have no power over you, and you have no feeling. When, however, the Spirit comes, floods are poured over the dry field. What you knew before blossoms in new meaning. You wonder, "How did I not feel that before?" Or, you say, "I knew that, but I never saw the application of it before." It is because the Spirit has come. A flood of water has been poured into your heart. You are born of the Spirit— the Spirit being represented in the Old Testament by water.

The seeds of truth may have lain dormant in your heart a long while, but now they shall come to some grand harvest. After I left the country parish where I was, there was a lad awakened some months after in a remarkable way; and he told me the next time I was in the neighborhood, "Wasn't this a remarkable thing? No sooner had I got my eyes opened, than all the lessons I used to get at the Sunday school began to come back to me immediately." He said, "I cannot explain it, but things I hadn't thought of for eight years came back to me immediately." It was the flood poured over the dry field.

Holy Spirit, leadership of

Acts 8:39; 10:19; 11:12, 28; 13:4; 15:28; 16:7; 18:5; 19:21; 21:4; Gal. 5:18

Every child of God ought to be led by the Spirit, and as long as they are led by him they are led into light, and not into darkness. Perhaps many of you have been talking with souls that have been struggling and praying to get into liberty, and into God's kingdom, and you have watched their countenances as the light broke upon them and their faces have shone with a glorious light. Now that takes place when a person is willing to let the Spirit lead; that is, at the time of conversion.

A Scotchman once said, it took two to bring him to God—it took the Lord and himself. A friend asked him what he did, and he said, "I fought against God, and the Lord did all the rest." That is the great trouble; people are not willing to give up their own way, but when they are ready to surrender and be led by the Spirit of God, he leads them unto life eternal. If you will be led by the Spirit you will have an Instructor who will throw light on many questions you don't now understand.

Those who are led by the Spirit don't know what darkness is; but when we want our own way, and are led by the flesh and the motives of the flesh—when the world and the influences of the world lead us—then it is that we get into darkness. Let us ask ourselves today, "Am I led by the Spirit?"

Holy Spirit, leadership of; Alcoholism, recovery from

Acts 8:39; 10:19; 11:12, 28; 13:4; 15:28; 16:7; 18:5; 19:21; 21:4; Gal. 5:18

An old citizen came to me last night, and said, "I hope you won't speak without having just a word for the poor drunkard." I do want to hold out a hope to the drunkards. If they will only accept God they will get the world under their feet, and God will give them power to hurl the cup from their lips. No other power can do it. If you are led by the Spirit of God you can be saved. Now just give yourself up while I am talking, and say, "Spirit of God, lead me; I give up all to you; I make a complete surrender. God's will shall be my will, and his Spirit shall lead me from this day and hour," and see how quick he will come to your help. If you get your hand in God's he will lead you safely to the light. Don't think that he will desert you. He knows your life, your wants, your temptations. No soul ever went wrong when led by the Holy Spirit.

Holy Spirit, need for; Child rearing, strength for

Micah 3:8; Zech. 4:6; Luke 1:35; Acts 6:8

When asked about the need of the power of the Holy Spirit for ministry, Dr. Bonar agreed that such power was essential. He also said that a mother needed it for the proper upbringing of her family. Mr. Moody remarked that a mother with several children needed it more than preachers.

Holy Spirit, need of; Leaders, failure of

Micah 3:8; Zech. 4:6; Luke 1:35; Acts 6:8

Why do so many workers break down? Not from overwork, but because there has been friction of the machinery; there hasn't been enough of the oil of the Spirit. Great engines have their machinery so arranged that where there is friction there is oil supplied to it all the time. It is a good thing for Christians to have plenty of oil. Many people are full of vinegar instead of oil.

153

Holy Spirit power, importance of; Waiting on God

Acts 1:8

If these early Christians had gone out and commenced preaching after Christ's ascension without the promised power of the Spirit, do you think that scene would have taken place on the day of Pentecost? Peter would have stood up and beat against the air, while the Jews would have gnashed their teeth and mocked at him. But they tarried in Jerusalem; they waited ten days.

"What!" you say, "with the world perishing and men dying! Shall I wait?" Do what God tells you. There is no use in running before you are sent; there is no use in attempting to do God's work without God's power. A man working without this unction, a man working without this anointing, a man working without the Holy Spirit upon him, is losing time after all. We shall not lose anything if we tarry till we get this power.

Holy Spirit power, need of

Exod. 40:34–35; Acts 2:4; 1 Cor. 3:16; 6:19–20

I think it is clearly taught in the Scripture that every believer has the Holy Spirit dwelling in him, that there is a divine resident in every child of God. He may be quenching the Spirit of God, and he may not glorify God as he should, but if he is a believer on the Lord Jesus Christ, the Holy Spirit dwells in him. But I want to call attention to another fact. I believe today that though Christian men and women have the Holy Spirit dwelling in them, he is not dwelling within them in power; in other words, God has a great many sons and daughters without power.

Holy Spirit, quenching of

1 Thess. 5:19

Anything that comes between me and God—between my soul and God—is quenching the Spirit. It may be my family. You may say: "Is there any danger of my loving my family too much?" Not if we love God more; but God must have the first place. If I love my family more than God, then I am quenching the Spirit of God in me; if I love wealth, if I love fame, if I love honor, if I love position, if I love pleasure, if I love self more than I love God, who created me, then I am committing a sin; I am not only grieving the Spirit of God, but quenching him, and God cannot bless.

Holy Spirit quickening; Renewal, spiritual; Witnessing, need of

Exod. 40:34–35; Acts 2:4; 1 Cor. 3:16; 6:19–20

Nine-tenths, at least, of our church members never think of speaking for Christ. If they see a man, perhaps a near relative, going right down to ruin, going rapidly, they never think of speaking to him about his sinful course and of seeking to win him to Christ. Now, certainly there must be something wrong. And yet when you talk with them you find they have faith, and you cannot say they are not children of God; but they have not the power, the liberty, the love that real disciples of Christ should have. A great many think that we need new measures, new churches, new organs, new choirs, and all these new things. That is not what the church of God needs today. It is the old power that the apostles had. If we have that in our churches, there will be new life.

I remember when in Chicago many were toiling in the work, and it seemed as though the car of salvation didn't move on, when a minister began to cry out from the very depths of his heart, "Oh, God, put new ministers in every pulpit." Next Monday I heard two or three men stand up and say, "We had a new minister last Sunday—the same old minister, but he had got new power," and I firmly believe that is what we need today all over America—new ministers in the pulpit and new people in the pews. We want people quickened by the Spirit of God.

Holy Spirit, sealing of

2 Cor. 1:22; Eph. 1:13; 4:30; 2 Tim. 2:19

One purpose of sealing is for safety. Every summer the Connecticut river is full of logs that are floated down from the mountains up north. If I should take one of those logs out of the river, I might be put into prison, because every log is stamped with the seal of the owner. So the seal of the Spirit is upon every child of God; they are sealed for the day of redemption.

Holy Spirit, witness of; Witnessing, importance of; Testimony, need of

John 16:14

The world can get on very well without you and me, but the world cannot get on without Christ, and therefore we must testify of him. The world today is just hungering and thirsting for this divine, satisfying portion. Thousands and thousands are sitting in darkness, knowing not of this great Light, but when we begin to preach Christ honestly, faithfully, sincerely and truthfully; holding him up, not ourselves; exalting Christ, and not our theories; presenting Christ, and not our opinions; advocating Christ, and not some false doctrine; then the Holy Spirit will come and bear witness. He will testify that what we say is true.

Holy Spirit, work of

John 16:14

The Holy Spirit's work is not to speak of himself, but to speak of Christ. Supposing I had an only son out in California, and a man came to me this afternoon and said,

"Mr. Moody, I am going out to California, and I will see your son; would you like to send any message?" and I sent a message to my absent boy; and when the man gets out there he talks to my son about himself! That wouldn't be what my boy would want to hear, but of his absent parents. And so the Holy Spirit comes to testify of Christ. That is his work. When we preach Christ, the Holy Spirit has got something to do—to carry home the message to the hearts of the people; but if a man preaches himself, his sermons have no power.

John 16:14

The Holy Spirit's work is to testify of Christ. You know that when Abraham wanted to get a bride for his son Isaac he sent his servant to Haran to get Rebecca. He told her all about Isaac's inheritance, and gave her the magnificent presents, and wanted her to go with him at once. Her parents wanted her to wait ten days; but no, she went at once, and was led through the wilderness by the messenger, to Isaac. It is these ten days that are the great fault with people. The work of the Holy Spirit is to lead us through the wilderness to Christ at once. The Holy Spirit is to tell us of God. If a man gets up in a prayer meeting and talks about his love for God it chills me; but if he talks about God's love for him, that fires my heart.

Home, importance of

Gen. 18:19; Exod. 12:26; Deut. 4:9; 6:7; Ps. 78:4; Prov. 4:1; Eph. 6:4; Col. 3:21; 2 Tim. 1:5; 3:15; Heb. 12:7

After being superintendent of a Sunday school in Chicago for a number of years, a school of over a thousand members—children that came from godless homes, having mothers and fathers working against me, taking the children off on excursions on Sunday and doing all they could to break up the work I was trying to do—I used to think that if I should ever stand before an audience I would speak to no one but parents; that would be my chief business. It is an old saying—"Get the lamb, and you will get the sheep." I gave that up years ago. Give me the sheep, and then I will have someone to nurse the lamb; but get a lamb and convert him, and if he has a godless father and mother, you will have little chance with that child. What we need is godly homes. The home was established long before the church.

Home, importance of; Parental influence; Commandment, fifth

Gen. 18:19; Exod. 12:26; Deut. 4:9; 6:7; Ps. 78:4; Prov. 4:1; Eph. 6:4; Col. 3:21; 2 Tim. 1:5; 3:15; Heb. 12:7

The first four commandments deal with our relations to God. They tell us how to worship and when to worship; they forbid irreverence and impiety in word and act. In the fifth commandment God turns to our relations with each other, and isn't it significant that he deals first with family life? God is showing us our duty to our neighbor. How does he begin? Not by telling us how kings ought to reign, or how soldiers ought to fight, or how merchants ought to conduct their business, but how boys and girls ought to behave at home. We can see that if their home life is all right, people are almost sure to fulfill the law in regard to both God and man.

Parents stand in the place of God to their children in a great many ways until the children arrive at years of discretion. If the children are true to their parents, it will be easier for them to be true to God. God used the human relationship as a symbol of our relationship to him both by creation and by grace. God is our Father in heaven. We are his offspring.

On the other hand, if people have not learned to be obedient and respectful at home, they are likely to have little respect for the law of the land. It is all in the heart.

The heart is prepared at home for good or bad conduct outside. The tree grows the way the twig is bent.

Humanism, danger of

Dan. 12:4; 1 Cor. 2:14; James 1:23

Now there are three stumbling stones in the way of every person—human religion, human wisdom, and human righteousness. In a great many of our colleges they are leaving the Bible out entirely. They are trying to get wisdom without the Word of God and without the mind of God and without any knowledge of God. Daniel tells us that men shall run to and fro and knowledge shall be increased. I believe that day has come. There never has been a day when knowledge has been sweeping over the earth as it is at the present time. We are living in a most marvelous age. A boy sixteen years old knows more than his father did at the same age. He has more advantages. But this doesn't mean that righteousness is increasing. Therefore, let us be wary.

Humility, based in holiness

2 Kings 22:19; Isa. 57:15; James 1:9; 4:10

As the lark that soars the highest builds her nest the lowest; as the nightingale that sings so sweetly sings in the shade when all things rest; as the branches that are most laden with fruit bend lowest; as the ship most laden sinks deepest in the water; so the holiest Christians are the humblest.

Humility before God

2 Chron. 12:7; Isa. 2:11; James 4:10

The London *Times* told the story of a petition that was being circulated for signatures. It was a time of great excitement, and this petition was intended to have great influence in the House of Lords; but there was one word left out. Instead of reading, "We humbly beseech thee," it read, "We beseech thee." So it was ruled out. My friends, if we want to make an appeal to the God of heaven, we must humble ourselves; and if we do humble ourselves before the Lord, we shall not be disappointed.

Humility, detection of

2 Chron. 32:26; Dan. 5:22; 1 Peter 5:6

A man can counterfeit love, he can counterfeit faith, he can counterfeit hope and all the other graces, but is very difficult to counterfeit humility. You soon detect mock humility. They have a saying in the East among the Arabs, that as the tares and the wheat grow they show which God has blessed. The ears that God has blessed bow their heads and acknowledge every grain, and the more fruitful they are the lower their heads are bowed. The tares which God has sent as a curse lift up their heads erect, high above the wheat, but they are only fruitful of evil.

Humility, evidence of

2 Chron. 33:12; Isa. 2:17; James 4:10

A farmer went with his son into a wheat field, to see if it was ready for the harvest. "See, father," exclaimed the boy, "how straight these stems hold up their heads! They must be the best ones. Those that hang their heads down, I am sure cannot be good for much." The farmer plucked a stalk of each kind and said, "See this, my son! This stalk that stood so straight is light-headed, and almost good for nothing; while this that hung its head so modestly is full of the most beautiful grain."

Prov. 29:23; Matt. 17:2; Mark 9:2; 2 Cor. 3:13; James 4:10

We read of the three men in Scripture whose faces shone, and all three were noted for their humility. We are told that the face of Christ shone at his transfiguration; Moses, after he had been on the mount for forty days, came down from his communion with God with a shining face; and when Stephen stood before the Sanhedrin on the day of his death, his face was lighted up with glory. If our faces are to shine we must get into the valley of humility; we must go down in the dust before God. John Bunyan says that it is hard to get down into the valley of humiliation. The descent into it is steep and rugged but that it is very fruitful, fertile and beautiful when once we get there.

Humility, example of

Dan. 4:37; John 3:30; James 4:10

One of the most humble characters in history was John the Baptist. You remember when they sent a deputation to him and asked if he was Elijah, or this prophet, or that prophet, and he said, "No." Now he might have said some very flattering things of himself. He might have said, "I am the son of the old priest Zacharias. Haven't you heard of my fame as a preacher? I have baptized more people than any man living. The world has never seen a preacher like myself."

I honestly believe that in the present day most men standing in his position would do that. On the railroad train some time ago, I heard a man talking so loudly that all the people in the car could hear him. He said that he had baptized more people than any man in his denomination. He told how many thousand miles he had traveled, how many sermons he had preached, how many open-air services he had held, and this and that, until I was so ashamed that I had to hide my head. This is the age of boasting. It is the day of the great "I."

Humility, examples of

1 Sam. 17:49; Matt. 23:12; James 4:10

My attention was recently called to the fact that in all the Psalms you cannot find any place where David refers to his victory over the giant Goliath. If it had been in the present day, there would have been a volume written about it at once; I don't know how many poems there would be telling of the great things that this man had done. He would have been in demand as a lecturer, and would have added a title to his name: G.G.K.—Great Giant Killer. That is how it is today; great evangelists, great preachers, great theologians, great bishops. "John the Baptist," they asked, "who are you?" "I am nobody. I am to be heard, not to be seen. I am only a voice." He hadn't a word to say about himself.

Humility, fruit of

Luke 14:11; John 5:35; James 4:10

See what Christ says about John the Baptist. "He was a burning and shining light." Christ gave him the honor that belonged to him. If you take a humble position, Christ will see it. If you want God to help you, then take a low position. I am afraid that if we had been in John's place, many of us would have said, "What did Christ say? I am a burning and shining light?" Then we would have had that recommendation put in the newspapers and would have sent them to our friends, with that part marked in blue pencil.

Sometimes I get a letter just full of clippings from the newspapers, stating that this man is more eloquent than all the other preachers. And the man wants me to get him some church. Do you think that a man who has such eloquence would be looking for a church? No, the churches would all be looking for him.

My dear friends, isn't it humiliating? Sometimes I think it is a wonder that any man is converted these days. Let another praise you. Don't be around praising yourself. If we want God to lift us up, let us get down. The lower we get, the higher God will lift us. It is Christ's eulogy of John the Baptist, "Greater than any man born of

woman." The top position has already been filled but there is still room at the bottom.

Humility, importance of

Luke 18:14; James 4:10

Someone asked Augustine what was the first of the religious graces, and he said, "Humility." They asked him what was the second, and he replied, "Humility." They asked him the third, and he said, "Humility." I think that if we are humble, we have all the graces.

Luke 14:11; 1 Cor. 15:9; Eph. 3:8; 1 Tim. 1:15; James 4:10

Some time ago I heard a man in the pulpit say that he should take offense if he was not addressed by his title. My dear friend, are you going to take that position that you must have a title, and that you must have every letter addressed with that title or you will be offended? John the Baptist did not want any title, and when we are right with God, we shall not be caring about titles. In one of his early epistles Paul calls himself the "least of all of the apostles." Later on he claims to be "less than the least of all saints," and again, just before his death, humbly declares that he is the "chief of sinners." Notice how he seems to have grown smaller and smaller in his own estimation. So it was with John. And I do hope and pray that as the days go by we may feel like hiding ourselves and letting God have all the honor and glory.

Luke 18:14; 1 Peter 5:5

"When I look back upon my own religious experience," says Andrew Murray, "or around upon the church of Christ in the world, I stand amazed at the thought of how little humility is sought after as the distinguishing feature of the discipleship of Jesus. In preaching and living, in the daily interaction of the home and social life, in the more special fellowship with Christians, in the direction and performance of work for Christ—alas! how much proof there is that humility is not esteemed the cardinal virtue, the only root from which the graces can grow, the one indispensable condition of true fellowship with Jesus."

Matt. 3:3; 23:12; Mark 1:3; Luke 3:4; John 1:23; 1 Peter 5:6

When the committee of official men from Jerusalem went down to see who John the Baptist was, he said: "I am nobody. I am nothing but a voice." When Christ came John began to preach himself down and Christ up. When we, who are nothing, want to work for Christ, he will use us.

Humility, nature of

2 Chron. 32:26; James 1:9; 1 Peter 5:6

Some years ago I saw what is called a sensitive plant. I happened to breathe on it, and suddenly it drooped its head; I touched it, and it withered away. Humility is as sensitive as that; it cannot safely be brought out on exhibition. A man who is flattering himself that he is humble and is walking close to the Master, is self-deceived. It consists not in thinking meanly of ourselves, but in not thinking of ourselves at all. Moses was not aware that his face shone when he came down from the mountain after being with God. If humility speaks of itself, it is gone.

Humility, nature of; Obedience, source of

2 Chron. 33:12; Matt. 23:12; Luke 1:52; 1 Peter 5:6

There is a story told of William Carey, the great missionary, that he was invited by the Governor-General of India to go to a dinner party at which were some military officers belonging to the aristocracy, and who looked down upon missionaries with scorn and contempt. One of these officers said at the table: "I believe that Carey was a shoemaker, wasn't he, before he took up the profession of a missionary?" Mr. Carey spoke up and said: "Oh, no, I was only a cobbler. I could mend shoes, and wasn't ashamed of it." The one prominent virtue of Christ, next to his obedience, is his humility; and even his obedience grew out of his humility.

Humility, power of; Holy Spirit filling

2 Chron. 32:27; Ps. 138:6; Matt. 10:3; 1 Peter 5:6

To me, one of the saddest things in all the life of Jesus Christ was the fact that just before his crucifixion, his disciples should have been striving to see who among them should be the greatest. But when the Holy Spirit came and those men were filled, from that time on mark the difference: Matthew takes up his pen to write, and he keeps Matthew out of sight. He tells what Peter and Andrew did, but he calls himself "Matthew the publican." He tells how they left all to follow Christ but does not mention the feast he gave.

Jerome says that Mark's Gospel is to be regarded as memoirs of Peter's discourses and to have been published by his authority. Yet here we constantly find that damaging things are mentioned about Peter, and things to his credit are not referred to. Mark's Gospel omits all allusion to Peter's faith in venturing on the sea but goes into detail about the story of his fall and denial of our Lord. Peter put himself down, and lifted others up.

If the Gospel of Luke had been written today, it would be signed by the great Dr. Luke, and you would have his photograph as a frontispiece. But you can't find Luke's name; he keeps out of sight. He wrote two books, and his name is not to be found in either. John covers himself always under the expression "the disciple whom Jesus loved." None of the four men whom history and tradition assert to be the authors of the Gospels lays claim to the authorship in his writings. I would that I had the same spirit, that I could just get out of sight—hide myself.

My dear friends, I believe our only hope is to be filled with the Spirit of Christ. May God fill us, so that we shall be filled with meekness and humility. Let us take the hymn "O, to Be Nothing, Nothing" and make it the language of our hearts. It breathes the spirit of him who said: "The Son can do nothing of himself."

Humility, source of fruitfulness

Prov. 3:34; 15:33; 1 Peter 5:6

I have a pear tree on my farm which is very beautiful; it appears to be one of the most beautiful trees on my place. Every branch seems to be reaching up to the light and stands almost like a wax candle, but I never get any fruit from it. I have another pear tree that is not attractive but was so full of fruit last year that the branches almost touched the ground. It is not how attractive we are but how humble that matters. If we only get down low enough, my friends, God will use every one of us to his glory.

Humility, source of peace; Sin, conviction of

Prov. 22:4; 29:23; Isa. 57:15; 1 Peter 5:6

William Dawson once told this story to illustrate how humble the soul must be before it can find peace. He said that at a revival meeting a little lad who was used to Methodist ways went home to his mother and said: "Mother, John So-and-so is under conviction and seeking for peace, but he will not find it tonight, mother." "Why, William?" she asked. "Because he is only down on one knee, mother, and he will never get peace until he is down on both knees." Until conviction of sin brings us down on both knees, until we are completely humbled, until we have no hope in ourselves left, we cannot find the Savior.

Hunger, spiritual; Worship, human need for

Jer. 23:24; Acts 14:17; 15:17; 17:27; Rom. 1:20

Anthropologists are agreed that even the most primitive races of mankind reach out beyond the world of matter to a superior Being. It is as natural for man to feel after God as it is for the ivy to feel after support. Hunger and thirst drive people to seek for food, and there is a hunger of the soul that needs satisfying, too. People don't need a command to worship, as there is not a race so high or so low in the scale of civilization but has some kind of a god. What people need is to be directed in the right direction in his worship.

Husbands, sensitivity of

Gen. 2:24; Prov. 5:15; 1 Cor. 7:3; Eph. 5:25; Col. 3:19; 1 Peter 3:7

I know how it is with that mother who has a large family of children. I know how she is pulled this way and that. James comes in and says, "Mother, where's my coat?" John comes along and asks, "Mother, what have you done with my shoes?" And Mary comes and says, "Mother, where's my purse?" Mother is pulled this way and that, and she gets out of patience and frets, and the children fret, and the husband isn't much better. Sunday morning he says, "Helen, why are you not ready for church?" He hasn't done a thing to help get the children ready for church. The mother must get all of them ready on time, and get herself ready, and all he has to do is to put his hat on and go.

Hymns, singing new

Pss. 33:3; 40:3; 96:1; 98:1; 144:9; 149:1; Isa. 42:10; Rev. 5:9; 14:3

Now, I have come to this conclusion, that if we are going to have successful gospel meetings, we have got to have a little more life in them. Life is found in singing new hymns, for instance. I know some churches that have been singing about a dozen hymns for the last twenty years, such hymns as "Rock of Ages," "There Is a Fountain Filled with Blood," etc. These hymns are always good, but we need a variety; we need new hymns as well as the old ones. I find it wakes up a congregation very much to bring in now and then a new hymn. And if you can't wake them up with preaching let us sing it into them. I believe the time is coming when we will make a good deal more of just singing the Gospel.

Hypocrisy, danger of

Ps. 78:37; Ezek. 33:31; John 3:3; 6:26, 64; Acts 8:18; Rom. 16:18; Phil. 3:9

It was just as it used to be when I had a Sunday school over on the north side of Chicago. Just advertise a picnic or a festival, where there was going to be something to eat, and the school would be out in full force. We would find people there who had hardly been inside the church for a whole year. Now Christ accuses these people of just this very thing, "Ye seek me, because ye did eat of the loaves"; and that is just the way with a great many people, who are standing round on the edges of the church, and saying to themselves, "Can't we make some money out of this thing for ourselves?"

Hypocrisy, problem of; Family leadership

Ps. 78:37; Ezek. 33:31; John 3:3; 6:26, 64; Acts 8:18; Rom. 16:18; Phil. 3:9

A friend of mine was talking to a young man about his soul. The young man turned up his nose, and said, "Christianity is all a farce." "Why?" said my friend. "Are you in earnest?" "Yes," said he, "I believe that Christians are hypocrites." My friend knew that the young man had a mother that professed to be a Christian, and he said, "You would not call your own

mother a hypocrite, would you?" "No, sir, I would not; that would sound very disrespectful. But I will say that my mother doesn't believe what she professes. If my mother did, don't you think she would talk to me about my soul? My mother never got down and prayed with me. If my mother believes what she professes don't you think she would be concerned about my eternal welfare? I tell you there is no reality in it." And that young man had reason to doubt his mother's profession. Have you asked yourself what your family and friends think of the quality of your spiritual life?

Hypocrisy, source of

Ps. 78:37; Ezek. 33:31; John 3:3; 6:26, 64; Acts 8:18; Rom. 16:18; Phil. 3:9

Christianity is not responsible for the deception that exists among its professing disciples. You might just as reasonably hold the Cunard Ship Company responsible for the suicide of a passenger who jumps overboard one of their vessels at sea. Had the person remained on the vessel, he would have been safe; and had the disciple remained true to his principles, he would never have turned out a hypocrite. Was anybody ever more severe in denouncing hypocrisy than Christ? Do you want to know the reason why, every now and then, the church is scandalized by the exposure of some leading pastor or church member? It is not their Christianity, but lack of it. Some secret sin has been eating at the heart of the tree, and in a critical moment it is blown down and its rottenness revealed.

Idol worship; Commandment, second

Exod. 20:4–6; Isa. 40:18; 46:5; Acts 17:29; 19:26; Rom. 1:23

You need not go to a distant country to find men worshiping idols. How many there are everywhere who bow down to the idols of Business, Pleasure, Children, Wealth, Dress. How many have their minds continually on the question, "What shall I wear?" I was in a meeting once when a lady came in and took a seat near the front. I handed her a hymnbook but she was so taken up with herself, looking at her dress, and admiring herself generally—you could see it in her eyes—that she had no thought of anything else. She worshiped herself. That was her god. You can make a god of yourself as well as of some image that people make with their hands.

Impure thoughts, control of

Ezek. 36:25; Zech. 13:1; John 3:5; 17:17; 1 Cor. 6:11; Eph. 5:26; Titus 2:14; 3:5

People ask, "How can I keep impure thoughts out of my mind?" The Bible tells us (Eph. 5:26) that there is no way except to let this living water flow constantly through your mind. We are cleansed "with the washing of water by the Word." Let clean water flow through a pipe that is full of dirt, and it will soon clear the pipe and come out as pure and clean as when it passed into the pipe.

Indifference, danger of

Rev. 2:5; 3:16

Beware of indifference. You cannot afford to neglect your soul. There is too much at stake. I never knew an idle man to be converted. Until he wakes up and realizes his lost and hopeless condition, God Almighty will not reach down and take him by the hand. A ship was once in great danger at sea, and all but one man were on their knees. They called to him to come and join them in prayer, but he replied: "Not I; it's your business to look after the ship. I'm only a passenger."

Infallibility of Bible, proof of

Pss. 34:8; 119:103; 1 Peter 2:3; 1 John 1:1

"The highest proof of the infallibility of Scripture," said the late A. J. Gordon, "is the practical one that we have proved it so. As the coin of the realm has always been found to buy the amount of its face value, so the prophecies and promises of Scripture have yielded their face value to those who have taken the pains to prove them. If they have not always done so, it is probable that they have not yet matured. There are multitudes of Christians who have so far proved the veracity of the Bible that they are ready to trust it without reserve in all that it pledges for the world yet unseen and the life yet unrealized."

Influence, enduring nature of; Character, enduring power of

Ps. 99:6; Heb. 11:32; James 5:10; 2 Peter 3:2

But there is one thing you cannot bury with a good person; the influence of such an individual still lives. They have not buried Daniel yet; his influence is as great today as ever it was. Do you tell me that Joseph is dead? His influence still lives and will continue to live on and on. You may bury the frail tenement of clay that a good person lives in, but you cannot get rid of the influence and example of a life lived for God. Paul was never more powerful than he is today.

Influence, evil, danger of; Testimony, loss of

Judg. 2:11; 3:7; 4:1; 6:1; 10:6; 13:1; 1 Kings 11:6; 2 Chron. 21:6; 2 Tim. 4:14

A friend of mine said he had a beautiful canary bird; he thought it was the sweetest singer they had ever had. Spring came, and he felt it was a pity to keep the poor bird in the house, so he put it under a tree right in front of his house. He said before he knew it a lot of these little English sparrows got under that tree (and you know they cannot sing any more than I can, and I don't know one note from another), and went, "Chirp, chirp, chirp." Before he knew it, that little canary had lost all its sweet notes. It had got into bad company.

After he found out that he had made a mistake, he took the bird into the house, but it kept up that, "Chirp, chirp, chirp." He bought another bird, but the canary nearly ruined it. He said that bird never got back its song. Now, don't you know lots of Christian people who had a fine testimony several years ago, but they have lost their witness, and all they do now is talk, talk, talk, talk? Why? Because they are out of communion with God, and have lost their witness.

Influence, power of

Ps. 99:6; Heb. 11:32; James 5:10; 2 Peter 3:2

On a trip back from Europe on an ocean liner, there were a number of ministers on board. A young man who had evidently crossed several times before and knew the captain, stepped up to him, and in a loud tone of voice, intending doubtless to insult some of the ministers, said he was sorry he had taken passage on the boat, as it would be unlucky to travel with so many parsons.

The captain was himself a pretty rough fellow, and turning to him, he said, "If you'll show me a town in England where there are five thousand people and not one parson, I'll show you a place a mile nearer hell than ever you've been." The young man slunk away. I'd like to take all these people who do not believe in the things of God and put them on an island by themselves. Why, they'd sink the first boat that touched there in their efforts to get on board and get away!

Influence, power of; Reaps more than sows

Ps. 99:6; Heb. 11:32; James 5:10; 2 Peter 3:2

We cannot control our influence. If I plant thistles in my field, the wind will take the thistledown when it is ready, and blow it away beyond the fence; and my neighbors will have to reap with me. So my example may be copied by my children or my neighbors, and my actions reproduced indefinitely through them, whether for good or evil.

Influence, power of; Witness, importance of

Luke 24:28; Acts 3:15; 5:32; 2 Tim. 2:2

I do not know anything that would wake up Chicago better than for every man and woman here who loves the Lord to begin to talk about him to their friends, and just to tell them what he has done for you. You have got a circle of friends. Go and tell them of him.

Inheritance of the saints; Wealth of Christians; Values, eternal

Prov. 3:35; Zech. 8:8; Matt. 19:29; 25:34; 1 Cor. 9:25; 2 Tim. 4:8; 1 Peter 1:4; 5:4; Rev. 2:11; 21:7

I used to have my Sunday school children sing "I want to be an angel" but I have not done so for years. We shall not be angels: we shall be sons of God. Just see what a kingdom we shall come into. We shall inherit all things! Do you ask me how much I am worth? I don't know. The Rothschilds cannot compute their wealth. They don't know how many millions they own. That is my condition—I haven't the slightest idea how much I am worth. God has no poor children. If we overcome we shall inherit all things.

Inner city evangelism

Luke 14:13, 21; 24:27; 1 Tim. 1:15; James 2:5; Rev. 19:9

In reaching out to the urban community you can have a children's prayer meeting and tell Bible stories. I used to be wonderfully blessed that way. Some of the happiest nights I ever had I had in these children's meetings. Some people do not believe in early conversion. "If they have a father and mother let them take care of them." But many of these fathers and mothers can't or won't take care of them. Take these little street urchins that have no one to take care of them and look after them and teach them to love Christ.

But these people say: "If you do get them, and they are converted, they will not hold out." Well, that is not my experience. Some of the most active men that I had to help me in Chicago were little barefooted boys once picked up in the lanes and the byways. Some of the most active men in the church there today were boys that went to that church then.

There is a boy with a drunken father and mother—who is going to lead him to the cross of Christ? Are we going to let these boys and girls go down to death? Are we going to let these boys fill our penitentiaries, and these daughters go into our houses of ill-fame? Here is a work for you. Take these children by the hand and lead them to Christ. They can be gathered into our churches, and be a blessing to the church of God.

Inner city evangelism; Willingness to work

Luke 14:13, 21; 24:27; 1 Tim. 1:15; James 2:5; Rev. 19:9

I have been asked, "How can we promote revivals in the dark and crowded portions of our large cities?" I think that the best way to reach people of that kind is by cottage prayer meetings. You take thousands of those mothers that are poor, with large families perhaps—it is out of the question for them to go to church. They can't go. I noticed last week a lady come in here with a baby, and the baby cried. That's the kind of music I like to hear; but all the people were looking, and I saw the lady take the baby away. It made her uncomfortable, and I suppose she said, "I will not go again." Now, this class of people is a very easy one to reach. They have large hearts.

Go right down into those cottages, and get the mothers and the babies together. Let the babies cry; it will not matter. I had a meeting in London where each mother had to bring a baby. That was the ticket. A woman couldn't get in unless she brought a baby. You never heard such crying, but it was a blessed meeting. One godly woman can do a great deal of good by starting cottage prayer meetings in those homes. Go right down into those cottages in the spirit of the Master: go into the kitchen, and while the housewife is working, talk and sing, and get her to join you in prayer, and you cannot tell what will be the result. This is something many of you can do. I don't believe there is a man or woman that can't help in the Lord's work if willing.

Inner city ministry

Luke 14:13, 21; 24:27; 1 Tim. 1:15; James 2:5; Rev. 19:9

When I was in London I got acquainted with one of the most remarkable men I ever met. He was a young man brought up in the best society, as the world called it. His father was one of the knights and moved in what the world calls the upper circle. This young man was well acquainted with the Royal family, but when he was converted he went down into the Seven Dials, a locality where there were dark alleys and the lowest dens of infamy. He would go out on those dark narrow streets until midnight, and often-times stay until 2 and 3 o'clock in the morning.

Here he met ragged boys, without any homes, lying around on boxes, barrels and stairways, and he would gather them together, give them supper, good shelter and a bed, and stay there with them. He left his beautiful mansion, and seven nights in a week that young man went down to what I might call the very borders of hell, for it seemed to me the darkest sight I ever saw. He went not only one or two weeks, but for eight or nine years, spending every night among the most abandoned people, trying to bring them up out of their degradation.

When I was there he had upwards of three hundred young men, whom he had brought from those slums, some of whom were now in China, others in Canada and Australia, and some in this country. When he would take them from the horrible pit he would have their photographs taken in their rags and dirt. Then they were taken to a bath and given new clothes. They were put into an institution, taught a trade, and taught not only the rules of life but every one of them was taught to read his Bible.

After keeping them a few years and educating them, before they left they were taken to a photograph gallery and had their pictures taken. Then the two pictures were given to them. This was to show them the condition in which the institution found them, and that in which it left them. In 1872 he had eighty-five boys in Canada, all of whom have been converted, corresponded with them, and found they were all doing well.

When I was there the last time, it was my privilege to stop at his house. He has since married, and his wife tells me that he gives several nights out of the week to that work at the Seven Dials. He has put up a large building. Not only has he spent his money, but his time. A good many people are willing to help the Lord in a patronizing way, by giving a hundred dollars or so to the church, and let others do the work, but this man was willing to go right down among them, and get hold of them, and I don't know a man so blessed as he.

I speak of this to encourage someone else in this audience to go and do likewise. You may not be rich, but thank God we don't need money to work for God if our hearts are full of love for him. He has got plenty of work for all. He can use all kinds of talent, great and small, those of great ability and those of little, if we are willing just to go to work. So, my friends, remember where God found you and praise him for saving you.

Inspiration, spiritual; Enthusiasm in preaching

Ps. 104:4; Heb. 1:7

I was once preaching in Scotland, and when I got to the church it was so cold that I could see my breath three feet away. I said to the janitor, "Aren't you going to have any heat in this building?" He said, "There are no stoves or any other provision for heat." "Well, how do you expect people to get warm?" "Oh!" he said, "we expect the preacher to warm us up."

Integrity, power of

Ruth 1:18; Ps. 119:106,115; Dan. 1:8; Acts 11:23; 1 Cor. 7:37

A young man in our Bible Institute in Chicago got onto the street car, and before the conductor came around to take the fare, he had reached the Institute, and jumped off without paying his fare. In thinking over that act, he said: "That was not walking circumspectly; that was not right. I had my ride, and I ought to pay that fare." He remembered the face of the conductor, and he went to the car barns and paid him the five cents. "Well," the conductor said, "you are a fool not to keep it."

"No," the young man said, "I am not. I got the ride, and I ought to have paid for it." "But it was my business to collect it." "No, it was my business to hand it to you." The conductor said, "I think you must belong to that Bible Institute."

I have not heard anything said of the Institute that pleased me so much as that one thing. Not long after that the conductor came to the Institute, and asked the student to come to see him. A cottage meeting was started in his house; and not only the conductor, but a number of others around there were converted as a result of that one act.

Introducing others to God

John 1:45; 12:22; Acts 3:6; 8:30

I would not think of introducing a man to another man when two or three blocks off from him. The first thing is to draw near, then the introduction may take place. When we seek to introduce the unsaved to God, we need to be close to God and to the lost person being introduced to him.

Jealousy, cure of; Rivalry, cure of; Conflict resolution

Job 5:2; Prov. 14:30; 23:17; Matt. 27:18; Mark 15:10; Acts 13:45; 1 Cor. 13:4; James 4:5

Are you jealous? Go and do a good turn for that person you are jealous of. That is the way to cure jealousy. It will give it a blow right over the head. There were two businessmen, merchants across the street from each other, and there was great rivalry between them. One of them was converted, and there was a great deal of bitter feeling between them. The man who had been converted came to me and said, "I am still jealous of that man, and I do not know how to overcome it."

"Well," I said, "if a man comes into your store to buy goods, and you cannot supply him, just send him over to your neighbor." "Oh," he said, "I wouldn't like to do that." "Well," I said, "you do it, and you will kill jealousy." He said he would, and when a customer came into his store for goods which he did not have, he would tell him to go across the street to his neighbor. And by-and-by the other began to send his customers over to this man's store and they reconciled.

Jealousy, danger of; Envy, danger of; Resentment, danger of

Job 5:2; Prov. 14:30; 23:17; Matt. 27:18; Mark 15:10; Acts 13:45; 1 Cor. 13:4; James 4:5

There is a fable of an eagle which could outfly another and the other didn't like it. The latter saw a sportsman one day, and said to him, "I wish you would bring down that eagle." The sportsman replied that he would if he only had some feathers to put into his arrow. So the eagle pulled one out of his wing. The arrow was shot, but didn't quite reach the rival eagle; it was flying too high. The envious eagle pulled out more feathers, and kept pulling them out until he lost so many that he couldn't fly, and then the sportsman turned around and killed him. My friend, if you are jealous, the only man you can hurt is yourself.

Jesus, importance of name; Eternal life, gate to

Matt. 1:21; John 10:1, 7; 14:6; Acts 4:12; 1 Cor. 3:11; 1 Tim. 2:5

If there is one word above another that will swing open the eternal gates, it is the name of JESUS. There are a great many passwords and bywords down here, but that will be the Countersign up above. Jesus Christ is the "Open Sesame" to heaven. Anyone who tries to climb up some other way is a thief and a robber. And when we get in, what a joy above every other joy we can think of, will it be to see Jesus himself, and to be with him continually!

Joint-heirs with Christ

Matt. 11:28; 19:14; Mark 10:14; 18:16; John 5:24; 7:37; 14:23; Rom. 8:17; Gal. 3:26; 4:7; Eph. 3:6; Titus 3:7; Rev. 22:17

When Frederick of Germany was dying, his own son wouldn't have been allowed to sit with him on the throne. Yet we are told that we are joint-heirs with Jesus Christ, that we are to sit with him in glory! What a prospect!

Matt. 11:28; 19:14; Mark 10:14; 18:16; John 5:24; 7:37; 14:23; Rom. 8:17; Gal. 3:26; 4:7; Eph. 3:6; Titus 3:7; Rev. 22:17

There is a fable that a kind-hearted king was once hunting in a forest, and found a blind orphan boy, who was living almost like the beasts. The king was touched with pity and adopted the boy as his own, and had him taught all that can be learned by one who is blind. When he reached his twenty-first year the king, who was also a great physician, restored the youth his sight, and took him to his palace, where surrounded by his nobles and all the majesty and magnificence of his court, he proclaimed him one of his sons, and commanded all to give him their honor and love.

The once friendless orphan thus became a prince and a sharer in the royal dignity, and of all the happiness and glory to be found in the palace of a king. Who can tell the joy that overwhelmed the soul of that young man, when he first saw the king of whose beauty and goodness and power he had heard so much! Who can tell the happiness he must have felt when he saw his own princely attire, and found himself adopted into the royal family—honored and beloved by all!

Now, Christ is the great and mighty King who finds our souls in the wilderness of this sinful world. He finds us wretched and miserable, and poor and blind and naked. He washes us from our sins in his own blood, clothes us with a spotless robe of righteousness and makes us joint-heirs with himself.

Joint-heirs with Christ; Exultation of believers

Matt. 11:28; 19:14; Mark 10:14; Luke 12:32; 18:16; John 5:24; 7:37; 14:23; Rom. 8:17; Gal. 3:26; 4:7; Eph. 3:6; Titus 3:7; Rev. 22:17

God is able to set us on high. Up above the angels, up above the archangels, up above the cherubims and seraphims, on the throne with his own Son. We are called to be sons and daughters of the eternal God. Do you know, the Prince of Wales couldn't sit on the throne with Queen Victoria? But it is not so yonder. Christ has gone up and taken his seat at the right hand of the Father, and every son and daughter of God is to be lifted up to the throne. Think of the promise. Isn't it rich, isn't it sweet?

Joint-heirs with Christ; Salvation, rewards of

Matt. 11:28; 19:14; Mark 10:14; Luke 12:32; 18:16; John 5:24; 7:37; 14:23; Rom. 8:17; Gal. 3:26; 4:7; Eph. 3:6; Titus 3:7; Rev. 22:17

There was a clerk in a store in Chicago. One day she could not have bought five dollars' worth of anything; the next day she could go and buy a thousand dollars' worth of whatever she wanted. What made the difference? Why, she had married a rich husband; that was all. She had received him, and of course all he had became hers. And so we can have all, if we only receive Christ. And I have Scripture authority to say that Christ will receive every soul that will only come to him.

When a bride marries a bridegroom, it is generally love that prompts her. If anyone is here that really loves a man, is she thinking of how much she will have to give up? No; that wouldn't be love. Love doesn't feed upon itself, it feeds upon the person who is loved. So, my friends, it is not by looking at what you will have to give up, but by looking at what you will receive, that will enable you to accept the Savior.

Joint-heirs with Christ; Vision, importance of; Values, eternal

Matt. 11:28; 19:14; Mark 10:14; Luke 12:32; 18:16; John 5:24; 7:37; 14:23; Rom. 8:17; Gal. 3:26; 4:7; Eph. 3:6; Titus 3:7; Rev. 22:17

After the Chicago fire I met a man who said, "Moody, I hear you lost everything in the Chicago fire." "Well," I said, "you understood it wrong; I didn't." He said, "How much have you left?" "I can't tell you; I have got a good deal more left than I lost." "You can't tell how much you have?" "No." "I didn't know that you were ever that rich. What do you mean?"

"I mean just what I say. I got my old Bible out of the fire; that is about the only thing. One promise came to me that illuminated the city a great deal more than the fire did. 'He that overcometh shall inherit all things; and I will be his God and he shall be My son.' You ask me how much I am worth. I don't know. You may go and find out how much the Vanderbilts are worth, and the Astors, and Rothschilds, but you can't find out how much a child of God is worth. Why? Because he is a joint-heir with Jesus Christ."

Why are you going around with your head down, talking about your poverty? The weakest, poorest child of God is richer than a Vanderbilt, because he has eternal riches. The stuff that burned up in Chicago was like the dust in the balance.

Joy, continuing

Luke 6:22; Acts 20:24

But you may say: "How can I rejoice when I have opposition at home; when my husband persecutes me because I am a Christian?" Well, if you want to see that husband saved, you must be a joyful Christian. The grace of God is for just such cases. Take your burden to the Lord and leave it there. Read in Luke 6:22, what Christ says: "Blessed are ye when men shall hate you." We must get our eyes on the reward. Paul suffered more than all the rest of the disciples, and yet he was always rejoicing. In Acts 20:24, we read that he wanted to finish his course with joy. He didn't want to get cross or peevish in his old age, like that pious aunt whose nephews and nieces said they didn't want to go to heaven if she was to be there, for she would be scolding them all the time.

Joy, definition of

Neh. 8:10; Matt. 25:21, 23; Acts 20:24; 1 Thess. 1:6; 1 Peter 5:7

There is a difference between mirth and cheerfulness. Mirth flashes and is gone. Cheerfulness is calm and steady. It comes from God, and is closely allied with the spirit of praise. Some people keep their houses shut up and dark. Everything is in perfect order, but the atmosphere is that of gloom—of death. So, many keep their hearts. They exclude the sunlight of God's love. We read that there were three stories in the Ark. But Noah and his family did not stay down in the lowest one, below the waterline, where all was dark. Many Christians, however, live spiritually down in the cellar.

We ought to go into the highest story, and get as near God as we can. Joy is deeper and more abiding than happiness. Joy sings in the dark like the nightingale. The Christian can have joy, even in adversity. We ought to rejoice always.

Unless we are joyful, we cannot be useful. We read in Nehemiah 8:10, "The joy of the Lord is your strength." A joyful Christian will have power. If we are occupied with ourselves and our own burdens, we can't help others. But if we cast our burden on the Lord, then we are ready to work for him. We get joy by trying to make others joyful. A farmer who kept all his grain and would not sell any, or sow any, wouldn't do any good or get any good. There is nothing on earth so powerful as a church full of joy. Such was the apostolic church.

Joy of Christianity

Neh. 8:10; Matt. 25:21, 23; Acts 20:24; 1 Thess. 1:6; 1 Peter 5:7

There is another class of people who say, "I love the world very much and if I become a Christian I shall have to give up all pleasure and go through the world with a long face." I want to say here, that no greater lie was ever forged than that. The devil started it away back in Eden; but there is not one word of truth in it; it is a libel upon Christianity. It does not make a man gloomy to become a child of God. See! there is a man going to execution. In a few moments he will be launched into eternity. But, flashing over the wires, comes a message, a reprieve. I run in haste to the man. I shout, "Good news! good news! You are not to die!" Does that make him gloomy? No! No! No! It is the want of Christ that makes men gloomy.

Take a man who is really thirsty, dying for want of water, and you go and give him water. Is that going to make him gloomy? That is what Christ is—water to the thirsty soul. If a man is dying for want of bread, and you give him bread, is that to make him gloomy? That is what Christ is to the soul—the bread of life. You will never have true pleasure or peace or joy or comfort until you have found Christ.

Joy, source of; Holy Spirit, fulness of

Prov. 23:24; Jer. 15:16; Gal. 5:22; 3 John 4

But, how are we to get joy? Just as we get the other Christian graces—by receiving Christ. Love, Peace, and Joy are the three divine sisters who stand at the threshold of the kingdom. They are the gifts of the Holy Spirit. How shall we keep joy when we get it? By feeding on the words of God. See Jeremiah 15:16. The more we learn of Christ in his Word, the more joy we will have. It is our privilege to be as full of joy and of the Holy Spirit, as were the early disciples. There are three things for the Christian to specially rejoice in: first, his own salvation; second, the salvation of others; third, seeing Christians walking in the truth.

Matt. 5:40; Luke 6:35; Gal. 6:10; 1 Tim. 6:18; Heb. 13:16; James 4:17; 1 Peter 3:11

There are two mountains in this world—one of joy, the other of sorrow. If we take a little every day from the latter and add it to the former, it will amount to a good deal in a year. We must get outside of ourselves and live for others. We must be dead unto the world, and alive unto God. Let's say these young ladies here in the front seat resolve that they will try to brighten some life every day, and forty years hence they will each have cheered and helped 14,600 people. And there is plenty of this work for us all. It seems to me that right at this moment I could use a thousand lives for Christ if I had them. It is the little acts of kindness that tell. A physician's prescription to a hypochondriac patient was, "Do good to somebody."

Joy, strength of; Happiness, nature of

1 Sam. 15:22; Isa. 35:2; 1 Thess. 2:20; Heb. 13:17

I think there is a difference between happiness and joy. Happiness is caused by things which happen around me, and circumstances will mar it, but joy flows right on through trouble; joy flows on through the dark; joy flows in the night as well as in the day; joy flows all through persecution and opposition; it is an unceasing fountain bubbling up in the heart, a secret spring which the world can't see and doesn't know anything about. The Lord gives his people perpetual joy when they walk in obedience to him.

Judgment, accuracy of; Cheating, danger of

Neh. 9:13; Micah 6:8

The merchant's measure may be wrong, but God's measure is just right. The merchant measures a gallon of oil or a pound of tea and does not give full measure. God says to the recording angel, "So many drops too few; so many grains short. Write it down." We may cheat man, but we cannot cheat God.

Judgment, certainty of; Change, resistance to; Reaping what was sown

Acts 24:25; Rom. 1:32; 2:5; Heb. 9:27; 2 Peter 2:9

A man died in the Columbus penitentiary some years ago who had spent over thirty years in his cell. He was one of the millionaires of Ohio. Fifty years ago when they were trying to get a trunk railroad from Chicago to New York, they wanted to lay the line through his farm near Cleveland. He did not want his farm divided by the railroad, so the case went into court, where commissioners were appointed to pay the damages and to allow the road to be built. One dark night, a train was thrown off the track, and several were killed. This man was suspected, was tried and found guilty, and was sent to the penitentiary for life. The farm was soon cut up into city lots, and the man became a millionaire, but he got no bene-

fit from it. It may not have taken him more than an hour to lay the obstruction on the railroad, but he was over thirty years reaping the result of that one act!

Judgment, nearness of; Unbelief, danger of

Acts 24:25; Rom. 1:32; 2:5; Heb. 9:27; 2 Peter 2:9

I read of a young man who had just come out of a saloon, and had mounted his horse. As a certain deacon passed on his way to church, he followed and said, "Deacon, can you tell me how far it is to hell?" The deacon's heart was pained to think that a young man like that should talk of spiritual things so lightly; but he passed on and said nothing. When he came round the corner to the church, he found that the horse had thrown that young man, and he was dead. You, too, may be nearer the judgment than you think.

Justice, nature of; Reaps more than sows

Gen. 18:19; 1 Kings 10:9; Prov. 1:3; 21:3; Eccles. 5:8; Isa. 1:17; 9:7; Micah 6:8

In the history of France we read that a certain king wanted some new instrument with which to torture his prisoners. One of his favorites suggested that he should build a cage, not long enough to lie down in, and not high enough to stand up in. The king accepted the suggestion; but the first one put into the cage was the very man who suggested it, and he was kept in it for fourteen years. It did not take him more than a few minutes, perhaps, to suggest that cruel device; but he was fourteen long years reaping the fruit of what he had sown.

Justification, meaning of; Debt of sin, canceled

Rom. 4:25; 5:16,18; 8:33

That word "justifieth" seems too good to be true. No wonder that Martin Luther shook all Germany when that truth dawned upon him, "the just shall live by faith." Do you know what "justified" means? I will tell you. It is to stand before God without spot or wrinkle, without a sin. It is to be put back beyond Eden. God looks over his ledger, and says: "Moody, I have no account against you. Your debt has all been wiped out by my Son Jesus Christ."

Kindness, power of

1 Cor. 13:4; Eph. 4:32; Titus 1:8; Heb. 7:26

You do not know how far a loving word will go. When I went to Chicago years ago I remember how I walked up and down the streets trying to find a job; and I recollect how, when they roughly answered me, their treatment chilled my soul. But when someone would say: "I would like to help you, but I can't; but you will find a job soon," I went away happy and light-hearted. That man's sympathy did me good. I believe there are thousands who are waiting for someone to come and offer a little sympathy. They need someone to take them by the hand and help them.

Knowledge, act on

James 1:23; 1 John 2:3

If I put a loaf of bread in front of this pulpit you can look at it, believe it is bread, and that it will satisfy your hunger; but if you don't take it, you can look at it till you die, and it won't do you any good. If the doctor gives me medicine, and I believe it will do me good, what good is my belief if I don't take it? And so the knowledge of Jesus Christ is no good unless you act on it.

Knowledge, partial on earth

1 Cor. 13:12; 2 Cor. 3:18; 5:7; Phil. 3:12

Dr. Talmage tells the story that one day while he was bothering his theological professor with questions about the mysteries of the Bible, the latter turned on

him and said: "Mr. Talmage, you will have to let God know some things you don't."

Law and grace contrasted

John 1:4, 17

Some contrasts between law and grace:

THE LAW was given by Moses.
GRACE and truth came by Jesus Christ.

THE LAW says—This do, and thou shalt live.
GRACE says—Live, and then thou shalt do.

THE LAW says—Pay me that thou owest.
GRACE says—I frankly forgive thee all.

THE LAW says—The wages of sin is death.
GRACE says—The gift of God is eternal life.

THE LAW says—The soul that sinneth, it shall die.
GRACE says—Whosoever believeth in Jesus, though he were dead, yet shall he live; and whosoever liveth and believeth in him shall never die.

THE LAW pronounces—Condemnation and death.
GRACE proclaims—Justification and life.

THE LAW says—Make you a new heart and a new spirit.
GRACE says—A new heart will I give you, and a new spirit will I put within you.

THE LAW says—Cursed is every one that continueth not in all things which are written in the book of the law to do them.
GRACE says—Blessed is the man whose iniquities are forgiven, whose sin

is covered; blessed is the man to whom the Lord will not impute iniquity.

THE LAW says—Thou shalt love the Lord thy God with all thy heart, and with all thy mind, and with all thy strength.

GRACE says—Herein is love: not that we love God, but that he loved us, and sent his Son to be the propitiation for our sins.

THE LAW speaks of what man must do for God.

GRACE tells of what Christ has done for man.

THE LAW addresses man as part of the old creation.

GRACE makes a man a member of the new creation.

THE LAW presses down on a nature prone to disobedience.

GRACE creates a nature inclined to obedience.

THE LAW demands obedience by the terror of the Lord.

GRACE beseeches men by the mercies of God.

THE LAW demands holiness.
GRACE gives holiness.

THE LAW says, Condemn him.
GRACE says, Embrace him.

THE LAW speaks of priestly sacrifices offered year by year continually, which could never make the comers thereunto perfect.

GRACE says—But this Man, after he had offered one sacrifice for sins forever . . . by one offering hath perfected forever them that are sanctified.

THE LAW declares—That as many as have sinned in the law, shall be judged by the law.

GRACE brings eternal peace to the troubled soul of every child of God, and proclaims God's salvation in defiance of the accusations of the adversary. "He that heareth my word, and believeth on him that sent me, hath everlasting life, and shall not come into judgment (condemnation), but is passed from death unto life."

Law and grace, differences

John 1:17; Rom. 5:21; 6:14; Gal. 5:18

When Moses was in Egypt to punish Pharaoh, he turned the waters into blood. When Christ was on earth he turned the water into wine. That is the difference between law and grace. The law says, "Kill him"; grace says, "Forgive him." Law says, "Condemn him"; grace says, "Love him." When the law came out of Horeb three thousand men were destroyed. At Pentecost, under grace, three thousand men found life. What a difference! When Moses came to the burning bush, he was commanded to take the shoes from off his feet. When the prodigal came home after sinning he was given a pair of shoes to put on his feet. I would a thousand times rather be under grace than under the law.

Law, perfect nature of

Ps. 19:7; Acts 22:3

It is related of a clever infidel that he decided to become acquainted with the truths of the Bible so he could argue against it, and began to read at the books of Moses. He had been in the habit of sneering at the Bible, and in order to be able to refute arguments brought by Christian men, he made up his mind, as he knew nothing about it, to read the Bible and get some idea of its contents.

After he had reached the Ten Commandments, he said to a friend: "I will tell you what I used to think. I supposed that Moses was the leader of a horde of bandits; that, having a strong mind, he acquired great influence over a superstitious people; and that on Mount Sinai he played off some sort of fireworks to the amazement of his ignorant followers, who imagined in their fear and superstition that the exhibition was supernatural. I have been looking into the nature of that law. I have been trying to see whether I could add anything to it, or take anything from it, so as to make it better. Sir, I cannot! It is perfect!

"The first commandment directs us to make the Creator the object of our supreme love and reverence. That is right. If he be our Creator, Preserver, and supreme Benefactor, we ought to treat him, and none other, as such. The second forbids idolatry. That certainly is right. The third forbids profanity. The fourth fixes a time for religious worship. If there be a God, he ought surely to be worshipped. It is suitable that there should be an outward homage significant of our inward regard. If God be worshipped, it is proper that some time should be set apart for that purpose, when all may worship him harmoniously, and without interruption. One day in seven is certainly not too much, and I do not know that it is too little.

"The fifth commandment defines the peculiar duties arising from family relations. Injuries to our neighbor are then classified by the moral law. They are divided into offenses against life, chastity, property, and character; and I notice that the greatest offense in each class is expressly forbidden. Thus the greatest injury to life is murder; to chastity, adultery; to property, theft; to character, perjury. Now the greatest offense must include the least of the same kind. Murder must include the least of the same kind. Murder must include every injury to life; adultery every injury to purity, and so of the rest. And the moral code is closed and perfected by a command forbidding every improper desire in regard to our neighbors.

"I have been thinking. Where did Moses get that law? I have read history. The Egyptians and the adjacent nations were idolaters; so were the Greeks and Romans; and the wisest or best Greeks or Romans never gave a code of morals like this. Where did Moses obtain that law, which surpasses the wisdom and philosophy of the most enlightened ages? He lived at a period comparatively barbarous; but he has given a law in which the learning and sagacity of all subsequent time can detect no flaw. Where did he obtain it? He could not have soared so far above his age as to have devised it himself. I am satisfied where he obtained it. It came down from heaven. It has convinced me of the truth of the religion of the Bible."

The former infidel remained to his death a firm believer in the truth of Christianity.

Law, power of

Rom. 7:10–11; 2 Cor. 3:7

A friend in England was telling me that an acquaintance of his, a minister, was once called upon to officiate at a funeral in the place of a chaplain of one of Her Majesty's prisons, who was absent. He noticed that only one solitary man followed the body of the criminal to the grave. When the grave had been covered, this man told the minister that he was an officer of the law whose duty it was to watch the body of the culprit until it was buried out of sight; that was "the end" of the British law. And that is what the law of God does to the sinner; it brings him right to death, and leaves him there. I pity deep down in my heart those who are trying to save themselves by the law. It never has, it never will, and it never can save the soul.

Law, power of; Sin, penalty of; Commandment, tenth

Deut. 27:26; Matt. 5:19; Gal. 3:10; James 2:10

If I have an orchard, and two apple trees in it which both bear some bitter apples, perfectly worthless, does it make any difference to me that the one tree has got perhaps five hundred apples, all bad, and the other only two, both bad? "Whosoever shall keep the whole law, and yet offend in one point, he is guilty of all." Suppose you were to hang up a man to the roof with a chain of ten links; if one were to break, does it matter that the other nine are all sound and whole? Not in the least. One link breaks, and down comes the man. But is it not rather hard that he should fall when the other nine are perfect, when only one is broken? Why, of course not; if one is broken, it is just the same to the man as if all had been broken: he falls. So the man who breaks one commandment is guilty of all. He is a criminal in God's sight.

Law reveals sin; Blood of Christ, cleansing power

Lev. 16:22; 17:11; Isa. 53:6; Matt. 8:17; 20:28; John 1:29; 1 Cor. 10:16; 15:3; 2 Cor. 5:21; Gal. 3:24; Eph. 2:13; 5:2; Titus 2:14; Heb. 9:28; 1 Peter 1:2, 19; 2:24; 3:18; 4:1; 1 John 1:7; 3:5; Rev. 1:5

I said to my little family, one morning, a few weeks before the Chicago fire, "I am coming home this afternoon to give you a ride." My little boy clapped his hands, "Oh, papa, will you take me to see the bears in Lincoln Park?" "Yes." I had not been gone long when my little boy said, "Mamma, I wish you would get me ready." "Oh," she said, "it will be a long time before papa comes." "But I want to get ready, mamma."

At last he was ready to have the ride, face washed and clothes all nice and clean. "Now, you must take good care, and not get yourself dirty again," said mamma. Of course, he was going to take care; he wasn't going to get dirty! So off he ran to watch for me. However it was a long time yet until the afternoon, and after a little he began to play.

When I got home, I found him outside, with his face all covered with dirt. "I can't take you to the park that way, Willie." "Why, papa? You said you would take me." "Ah, but I can't; you're all over mud. I couldn't be seen with such a dirty little boy." "Why, I'se clean, papa; mamma washed me." "Well, you've got dirty again." But he began to cry, and I could not convince him that he was dirty. "I'se clean; mamma washed me!" he cried.

Do you think I argued with him? No. I just took him up in my arms, and carried him into the house, and showed him his face in the mirror. He would not take my word for it; but one look at the mirror was enough; he saw it for himself. He didn't say he wasn't dirty after that!

Now, the mirror showed him that his face was dirty—but I did not take him to the mirror to wash it; of course not. Yet that is just what thousands of people do. The law is the mirror to see ourselves in, to show us how vile and worthless we are in the sight of God; but they take the law and try to wash themselves with it, instead of being washed in the blood of the Lamb.

Law still current

Mark 12:30–31; Rom. 3:31; 13:10

People must be made to understand that the Ten Commandments have not been canceled, and that there is a penalty attached to their violation. We do not need a gospel of mere sentiment. The Sermon on the Mount did not blot out the Ten Commandments. When Christ came he condensed the statement of the law into this form: "Thou shalt love the Lord thy God with all thy heart, and with all thy soul, and with all thy mind and with all thy strength . . . [and] thy neighbor as thyself" (Mark 12:30–31).

Paul said: "Love is the fulfilling of the law" (Rom. 13:10). But does this mean that the detailed precepts of the Ten Commandments are superseded and have become back numbers? Does a father cease to give children rules to obey because they love him? Does a nation burn its statute books because the people have become patriotic? Not at all. And yet people speak as if the commandments do not hold for Christians because they have come to love God. Paul said: "Do we then make void the law through faith? God forbid: yea, we establish the law" (Rom. 3:31). It still holds good.

The Commandments are necessary. So long as we obey, they do not rest heavy upon us; but as soon as we try to break away, we find they are like fences to keep us within bounds. Horses need bridles even after they have been properly broken in.

Law vs. grace

John 1:17; Rom. 4:16; 5:20; 6:14; Gal. 5:4

I pity those who are always hanging around Sinai, hoping to get life from the law. I have an old friend in Chicago who is always lingering at Sinai. He is a very good man; but I think he will have a different story to tell when he gets home to heaven. He thinks I preach free grace too much; and I must confess I do like to speak of the free grace of God. This friend of mine feels as though he has a kind of mission to follow me and whenever he gets a chance he comes in with the thunders of Sinai. The last time I was in Chicago, I said to him, "Are you still lingering around Sinai?" "Yes," said he, "I believe in the law." I have made inquiries, and I never heard of anyone being converted under his preaching: the effects have always dwindled and died out. If the

law is the door to heaven, there is no hope for any of us.

Law vs. grace; Profanity, cure for

John 1:17; Rom. 4:16; 5:20; 6:14; Gal. 2:21; 5:4

I believe there is no man so far gone but the grace of God will melt his heart. It is told of Isaac T. Hopper, the Quaker, that he once encountered a profane black man, named Cain, in Philadelphia, where at that time there was a law against public profaning of God's name. He took him before a magistrate, who fined him for blasphemy. Twenty years after, Hopper met Cain, whose appearance was much changed for the worse. This touched the Quaker's heart. He stepped up, spoke kindly, and shook hands with the forlorn Cain, "Dost thou remember me," said the Quaker, "how I had thee fined for swearing?"

"Yes, indeed, I do. I remember what I paid as well as if it was yesterday." "Well, did it do thee any good?" "No, never a bit: it made me mad to have my money taken from me." Hopper invited Cain to reckon up the interest on the fine, and paid him principal and interest too. "I meant it for thy good, Cain; and I am sorry I did thee any harm." Cain's countenance changed; the tears rolled down his cheeks. He took the money with many thanks, became a quiet man, and was not heard to swear again. Even so there is a great deal of difference between the powers of law and of grace.

Lay ministry, importance of

Matt. 28:18–20; Acts 1:8

A man was preaching about Christians recognizing each other in heaven, and someone said, "I wish he would preach about recognizing each other on earth." In one place where I preached, I looked over the great hall of the old circus building where it was held, and saw men talking to other men here and there. I said to the Secretary of the Young Men's Christian Association who got up the meeting, "Who are these men?" He said, "They are a band of workers." They were all scattered through the hall, and preaching and watching for souls. Out of the fifty of them, forty-one of their number had got a soul each and was talking with the person. We have been asleep long enough. When the laity wake up and try and help the minister the minister will preach better.

Lay volunteers, work of

Luke 15:11

A man came into the inquiry room and found Christ, and I felt curious and asked him what it was that first impressed him. He said some lady offered him a card at one of the meetings, which he took from his pocketbook and showed me. It was an announcement of the "Gospel Meetings of Moody and Sankey," etc., and on the back was a verse reading, "A certain man had two sons," etc. And he said when he read that the thought came to him that he was that son that had wandered away.

I knew those cards had been printed, and on inquiry as to who did it I learned that a certain young man had printed 15,000 of them at his own expense. I asked this gentleman if he would let me have that one. He replied he would like to accommodate me, but said he valued it as too precious to do so, and he put it back in his pocket. I found out the printer and got two or three to keep for myself. A person had paid for the printing of the cards and had organized people to hand them out. I wish we had ten thousand such workers just trying to find some work to do for the Master.

Lay witness, importance of

Mark 16:15; Luke 10:19; Acts 2:32; 4:33; 5:32; 6:8; 10:39; 22:15

We have to get rid of this idea that the world is going to be reached by ministers alone. All those who have drunk of the cup of salvation must pass it around.

Laziness, danger of

Prov. 6:6, 9; 13:4; 19:24; 20:4; 21:25; 22:13

I believe there is a great deal more hope for a drunkard or a murderer or a gambler than there is for a lazy man. I never heard of a lazy man being converted yet, though I remember talking once with a minister in the backwoods of Iowa about lazy men. He was all discouraged in his efforts to convert lazy men, and I said to him, "Did you ever know of a lazy man being converted?" "Yes," said he, "I knew of one, but he was so lazy that he didn't stay converted but about six weeks." And that is as near as I ever heard of a lazy man being converted.

Prov. 6:6, 9; 13:4; 19:24; 20:4; 21:25; 22:13

I once read of the founder of the Russian Empire going down to a Dutch seaport as a stranger, in disguise, that he might learn how to build ships; that he might go back and teach it to his own subjects. People have wondered at that; but this is a greater wonder, that the Prince of Glory should come down here and learn the carpenter's trade. He was not only the son of a carpenter, but he was a carpenter himself. And right here is one lesson that we ought to learn, and that is, when Christ was here he was an industrious man, and I have often said on this platform that I never knew yet a lazy man to be converted. If he was, he soon gave up his laziness.

I tell you, laziness does not belong to Christ's kingdom. I don't believe a man would have a lazy hair in his head if he was converted to the Lord Jesus Christ. If a man has really been born of the Spirit of Christ, he isn't lazy; he desires something to do. Let us be willing to go out and work. If we can't find what we want, let us do what we can find until something better comes our way. A good many people are always waiting for something to turn up, instead of going out and turning up something. Look for something and you will likely find it.

Laziness, danger of; Work, spirit of

Prov. 6:6, 9; 13:4; 19:24; 20:4; 21:25; 22:13; Phil. 2:12–13

I have very little sympathy with any man who has been redeemed by the precious blood of the Son of God, and who has not got the spirit of work. If we are children of God we ought not to have a lazy drop of blood in our veins. If a man tells me that he has been saved, and does not desire to work for the honor of God, I doubt his salvation. Laziness belongs to the old creation, not to the new. In all my experience I never knew a lazy man to be converted—never. I have more hope for the salvation of drunkards, and thieves, and harlots than of a lazy man.

Laziness, problem of; Reaping not fainting

Prov. 6:6, 9; 13:4; 19:24; 20:4; 21:25; 22:13

Laziness doesn't belong to the new creation; it belongs to the old, and if a man professes to be converted, and is not stirred up to work for God, I doubt his conversion. He may make great professions, but when he has no desire to work for God, that is a true sign that he has not been born of God. I was for twelve or fifteen years superintendent of a Sunday school in the mission district of Chicago, and you know it isn't easy work in these districts. It is sometimes very dark and discouraging, when you have doubtless been pulling seven days in the week one way to get children in when perhaps their parents have been doing all they could to prevent you from prosecuting your work.

It is sometimes pretty dark, like toiling all night and catching nothing.

I noticed that the people who got discouraged, and gave up their classes, and went from one school to another, from one field to another, were never successful; but those that persevered and held on, day after day, week after week, month after month, held right on, have always been blessed.

When I was in Chicago the last time, I saw a young man in the school who had been toiling for months and years without having many results, as far as conversions were concerned. Last spring he took his boys out into the country, as was often his custom, for a week or two. There were about fifty, and only five or ten of them that were Christians. When I was there last spring he came right into our meetings, was one of the ushers, and every once in a while there would be a request for prayer for that class. After awhile their hearts began to be moved, and out of one hundred and eighty in that class over one hundred had been converted and were working for the Savior. "We shall reap if we faint not."

Laziness, problem of; Welfare

Prov. 6:6, 9; 13:4; 19:24; 20:4; 21:25; 22:13; Eccles. 10:18

I had charge of the relief in Chicago for a number of years, and I was brought into contact with these lazy men. I say there is no hope of a man that will not work. Talk about their conversion, it is only just put on to get a little money out of you without work. They are willing to do anything to get on, but they will not work, and those men are the ones we have so much difficulty with in these cities.

There was a man I knew in Chicago; he did not drink, but he was always poor. What kept him down I could not tell. He had five beautiful children. I do not believe his furniture was worth five dollars, and he had no beds. One cold day in November he came to see me. He said, "My landlord has put my family out on the prairie." I said: "McDonald, you are a mystery to me; I have known you for years; what do you do with your money? I begin to think, McDonald, you are lazy." "I think you hit it there," he said. "Well, you must go," I said. "I pity your wife and children, but I am not going to take care of a lazy man all winter." "That's pretty hard," he said. "I know it is. But I cannot help you."

That was in the morning. About five o'clock in the afternoon he came back. He knew I wouldn't let those children stay out all night; he knew he had me. He asked for a place for his children to sleep. I said: "What have you been doing all day?" He used a great many big words, and said he had been studying the philosophy of pauperism. There he is now, I suppose, starving his family because he will not work. We have got to take care of these children, but these men, if they will not work, must starve. Some of you ladies think you are doing God's service by giving them money, but you are really injuring them and their children, for as long as they can get along they will go on that way without work.

Leadership, lay

Gal. 5:7; Heb. 12:25; 1 Peter 4:17

When Spurgeon went up to London to preach, he said, "You could fire a cannonball right through the church and not hit anyone." So he preached, Sunday after Sunday, right to the elders. Finally they said, "Don't you think you had better leave us alone and preach to the unconverted?" And he said, "I must preach to you first, and get you right with God." And when he got them stirred up, he went to the church members, and then his work began with the unconverted, and it has been going on ever since. You must get the church thor-

oughly alive first, and then you can have power over the unconverted.

Life, brevity of

Job 14:1; Pss. 39:5; 89:47; 90:5; 102:3; James 1:10; 4:14; 1 Peter 1:24

Now death may take us by surprise. That's the way it has taken our dear friends, Mr. and Mrs. Bliss. You know what a blessing they have been to us with their singing and the wonderful songs Mr. Bliss has written. Little did they know as they rode toward Cleveland last Friday night what was to be the real end of the journey. About this time I was giving out notice last Friday night of their being here this afternoon to sing for us, they were then struggling with death in that terrible train wreck. That was about the time they passed into glory land. It was a frightful death, by surprise. But, beautiful salvation; star of hope in that time of gloom, darkness and death; they both were ready. They were just ripened for the kingdom of God.

Life, brevity of; Salvation, importance of

Job 14:1; Pss. 39:5; 89:47; 90:5; 102:3; James 1:10; 4:14; 1 Peter 1:24

In one of the mining districts of England, a young man attended one of our meetings and refused to go from the place till he had found peace in the Savior. The next day he went down into the pit, and the coal fell in upon him. When they took him out he was broken and mangled, and had only two or three minutes of life left in him. His friends gathered about him, saw his lips moving, and, bending down to catch his words, heard him say, "It was a good thing I settled it last night." Settle it now, my friends, once for all. Begin now to confess your sins, and pray the Lord to remember you. He will make you an heir of his kingdom, if you will accept the gift of salvation.

Life, purpose of; Vision, lack of

Num. 13:30; 1 Chron. 22:19; 29:2; Eccles. 9:10; Rom. 12:11; 1 Cor. 9:26; Eph. 5:16; Col. 3:23

I have lived long enough to know that if I can't have the power of the Spirit of God on me to help me to work for him, I would rather die, than live just for the sake of living. How many are there in the church today, who have been members for fifteen or twenty years, but have never done a solitary thing for Jesus Christ? They cannot lay their hands upon one soul who has been blessed through their influence; they can't point today to one single person who has ever been lifted up by them.

Life, wasted

Ps. 6:5; Isa. 38:18; John 9:41

In Glasgow there lay a young man who was dying, and who cried out, "Lost! lost! lost!" His mother heard him, and asked, "Is it possible that you have lost your faith in God?" "No," said he, "I have a hope of heaven, but I have lost my life. I have lived twenty-four years and have done nothing for the Lord." How many Christians are there in this house, who, if they were to die, would die as this man did, having done nothing for the Lord?

Love, active

Isa. 60:1; Matt. 22:39; Rom. 13:8; Gal. 5:14; Col. 3:14; 1 Tim. 1:5; James 2:8

Love must be active, as light must shine. As someone has said, "A man may hoard up his money; he may bury his talents in a napkin; but there is one thing he cannot hoard up, and that is love." You cannot bury it. It must flow out. It cannot feed upon itself; it must have an object.

Love and God's law

Rom. 13:10

If the love of God is shed abroad in your heart, you will be able to fulfill the law. Paul reduced the commandments to one: "Love is the fulfilling of the law" (Rom. 13:10). Someone has written the following:

Love to God will admit no other God.

Love resents everything that debases its object by representing it by an image.

Love to God will never dishonor his name.

Love to God will reverence his day.

Love to parents makes one honor them.

Hate, not love, is a murderer.

Lust, not love, commits adultery.

Love will give, but never steal.

Love will not slander or lie.

Love's eye is not covetous.

Love, badge of Christian

John 13:34–35

Love is the badge that Christ gave his disciples. Some put on one sort of badge and some another. Some put on a strange kind of dress, that they may be known as Christians, and some put on a crucifix, or something else, that they may be known as Christians. But love is the only badge by which the disciples of our Lord Jesus Christ are known. "By this shall all men know that ye are my disciples, if ye have love one toward another."

Love, brotherly; Unity, source of

Rom. 12:10; 1 Thess. 4:9; Heb. 13:1

There are two ways of being united—one is being frozen together, and the other is by being melted together. What Christians need is to be united in brotherly love, and then they may expect to have power.

Love, Christ's forgiving; Grace, redeeming

Song of Sol. 2:4; Matt. 27:29–30; Mark 15:17,19; Luke 23:34; John 19:2, 34; Col. 3:13; 1 John 1:9

I can imagine Jesus saying, "Go search out the man who put that crown of thorns on my brow; tell him I will have a crown for him in my kingdom, if he will accept salvation; and there shall not be a thorn in it. Find out that man who took the reed from my hand, and smote my head, driving the thorns deeper into my brow. Tell him I want to give him a scepter. Go, seek out that poor soldier who drove the spear into my side; tell him that there is a nearer way to my heart than that. Tell him I want to make him a soldier of the cross, and that my banner over him shall be love."

Love covers sins

1 Cor. 13:7; James 5:20; 1 Peter 4:8

When an eminent painter was requested to paint Alexander the Great so as to give a perfect likeness of the Macedonian conqueror, he felt a difficulty. Alexander, in his wars, had been struck by a sword, and across his forehead was an immense scar. The painter said: "If I retain the scar, it will be an offense to the admirers of the monarch, and if I omit it, it will fail to be a perfect likeness. What shall I do?" He hit upon a happy expedient; he represented the Emperor leaning on his elbow, with his forefinger upon his brow, accidentally, as it seemed, but covering the scar upon his forehead. Might not we represent each other with the finger of love upon the scar, instead of representing the scar deeper and blacker than it really is?

Love, dimensions of; Adversity, strength for

2 Cor. 5:14; Eph. 3:18–19; 5:2; 1 John 4:9

Many of us think we know something of God's love, but centuries hence we shall admit we have never found out much about it. Columbus discovered America; but what did he know about its great lakes, rivers, forests, and the Mississippi valley? He died, without knowing much about what he had discovered. So, many of us have discovered something of the love of God, but there are heights, depths, and lengths of it we do not know. That love is a great ocean, and we must plunge into it before we really know anything of it.

Among the many victims of the Paris Commune during the Inquisition was a Catholic bishop. He was a man who knew something of the love of God in his own experience. In the little cell where he was confined, awaiting execution, was a small window in the shape of a cross. After his death there was found written above the cross "height"; below it, "depth"; and at the end of each arm of the cross, "length" and "breadth." He had learned that God's love was unfailing in the hour of adversity and death.

Love for God; Holy Spirit, source of love

Rom. 5:5; 2 Cor. 6:6; 13:4

Some time ago, in an inquiry meeting, I said to a young woman who said that she could not love God, that it was very hard for her to love him, "Is it hard for you to love your mother? Do you have to learn to love your mother?" She looked up through her tears, and said, "No; I can't help it; that is spontaneous." "Well," I said, "when the Holy Spirit kindles love in your heart, you cannot help loving God; it will be spontaneous." When the Spirit of God comes into your heart and mine, it will be easy to love and serve God.

Love, generosity of; Satisfaction, true

Ps. 112:5; Prov. 19:17; 22:9; Luke 6:35

Love never looks to see what it is going to get in return. I have generally found that those workers who are all the time looking to see how much they are going to get from the Lord are never satisfied. But love does its work and makes no bargain.

Love, God's for sinners

John 3:16

I want to tell you how I got my eyes open to the truth that God loves the sinner. When I went over to Europe I was preaching in Dublin, when a young fellow came up to the platform and said to me that he wanted to come to America and preach. He had a boyish appearance; did not seem to be over seventeen years old. I measured him all over, and he repeated his request, and asked me when I was going back. I told him I didn't know; probably I should not have told him if I had known. I thought he was too young and inexperienced to be able to preach.

In course of time I sailed for America, and hadn't been here long before I got a letter from him, dated New York, saying that he had arrived there. I wrote him a note and thought I would hear no more about him, but soon I got another letter from him, saying that he was coming soon to Chicago, and would like to preach. I sent him another letter, telling him if he came to call upon me, and closed with a few commonplace remarks. I thought that would settle him, and I would hear no more from him.

But in a very few days after he made his appearance. I didn't know what to do with him. I was just going off to Iowa, and I went to a friend and said: "I have got a young Irishman—I thought he was an Irishman, because I met him in Ireland—and he wants to preach. Let him preach at the meetings—try him, and if he fails, I will take him off your hands when I come home."

When I got home—I remember it was on Saturday morning—I said to my wife: "Did that young man preach at the meetings?" "Yes." "How did they like him?" "They liked him very much," she replied. "He preaches a little different from you; he preaches that God loves sinners." I had been preaching that God hated sinners; that he had been standing behind the sinners with a double-headed sword ready to cut the heads of the sinners off.

So I concluded if he preached different from me, I would not like him. My prejudice was up. Well, I went down to the meeting that night, and saw them coming in with their Bibles. I thought it was curious. It was something strange to see the people coming in with Bibles, and listen to the flutter of the leaves. The young man gave out his text, saying: "Let us turn to the third chapter of John, and sixteenth verse: 'For God so loved the world that He gave His only begotten Son that whosoever believeth in Him should not perish but have everlasting life.'" He didn't divide up the text at all. He went from Genesis to Revelation, giving proof that God loved the sinner, and before he got through two or three of my sermons were spoiled. I have never preached them since.

The following day—Sunday—there was an immense crowd flocking into the hall, and he said, "Let us turn to the third chapter of John, sixteenth verse: 'For God so loved the world that He gave His only begotten Son, that whosoever believeth in Him shall not perish, but have everlasting life'"; and he preached the fourth sermon from this verse. He just seemed to take the whole text and throw it at them, to prove that God loved the sinner, and that for six thousand years he had been trying to convince the world of this.

I thought I had never heard a better sermon in my life. It seemed to be a new revelation to all. Ah, I notice there are some of you here who remember those times; remember those nights. I got a new idea of the blessed Bible. On Monday night I went down and the young man said, "Turn to the third chapter of John, sixteenth verse," and he seemed to preach better than ever. Proof after proof was quoted from Scripture to show how God loved us.

I thought sure he had exhausted that text, but on Tuesday he took his Bible in his hand and said: "Turn to the third chapter of John, sixteenth verse," and he preached the sixth sermon from that verse. He just seemed to climb over his subject, while he proved that there was nothing on earth like the love of Christ, and he said, "If I can convince men of God's love, if I can but bring them to believe this text, the whole world will be saved."

On Thursday he selected the same text, John 3:16, and at the conclusion of the sermon he said: "I have been trying to tell you for seven nights now, how Christ loves you, but I cannot do it. If I could borrow Jacob's ladder and climb up to heaven, and could see Gabriel there and ask him to tell me how much God loves me, he would only say, 'God so loved the world that He gave His only begotten Son, that whosoever believeth in Him should not perish, but have everlasting life.' How a man can go out of this tabernacle after hearing this text, saying, 'God does not love me' is a mystery to me."

Love, God's unchangeable; Love, power of

Mal. 3:6; Heb. 13:8; James 1:17

Spurgeon went down into the country to visit a friend who had built a new barn, and on the peak of the barn roof they had put a weather vane with this Scripture text on it: "God is love." Spurgeon said to the man, "What do you mean by putting that text of Scripture on the weather vane? Do you mean that God's love is as changeable as the wind?" "Oh, no," was the reply, "I mean to say that God is love which ever way the wind blows."

Love, importance of

Gen. 3:1; 2 Cor. 11:3; Gal. 2:20; Eph. 2:4; 5:2; 2 Thess. 2:16; 1 John 4:10; Rev. 12:9

There is nothing in this world that people prize so much as they do love. Show me a person who has no one to care for or love him, and I will show you one of the most wretched beings on the face of the earth. Why do people commit suicide? Very often it is because this thought steals in upon them—that no one loves them; and they would rather die than live. I know of no truth in the whole Bible that ought to come home to us with such power and tenderness as that of the love of God; and there is no truth in the Bible that Satan would so much like to blot out. For more than six thousand years he has been trying to persuade men that God does not love them. He succeeded in making our first parents believe this lie, and he too often succeeds with their children.

Love, importance of; Care, pastoral

John 21:16–17

There was a young minister who went to take charge of a church that had been under the care of an old pastor. He began scolding the people, and he kept that up for six months. One day one of the old deacons asked him home to dinner with him. After dinner, the old deacon asked the young pastor if he had read the twenty-first chapter of John. "Read it! I hope I have read every chapter in the Bible. Read it! Why, of course I have."

So the old deacon got his Bible, and began to read it. He got down to when the Lord is sifting Peter and testing him. "Peter, lovest thou me more than these? Beat my sheep." "Peter, lovest thou me more than these? Maul my sheep." "Lovest thou me more than these? Wallop my sheep." "Why," said the minister to the deacon, "that isn't there." "Well, I thought I would read it to you, as you have been at us for the last six months and see how it sounded." You never make a sheep fat in that way. Feed them well if you want them to work and grow fat spiritually.

Ps. 78:72; Isa. 40:11; Ezek. 34:2; Acts 20:28; 1 Peter 5:2

I honestly believe we have too much preaching in the exhorting line. Exhort! Exhort! Exhort! I believe that the church needs to be fed; and where there is one sermon preached to the unconverted, I wish we had one hundred preached to the church members. People watch the church members and say, "Look at that man and woman; they are members of the church. If that is religion, I don't want any of it." And I don't blame them. Do you? Scolding the sheep won't feed them. A man said he could take a fat sheep and make it lean in a week. There was a bet on that statement, and they put up the money. He took a sheep and put it in a cage, and got a dog. That dog kept barking at the sheep and worried it so that it was quite poor in a week. Some pastors are just like that barking dog.

Love in action; Brotherly love

Rom. 12:10; 1 Thess. 4:9; Heb. 13:1

I read in one of the daily papers a thing that pleased me very much. When the new administration of President McKinley went into office some clerks in one of the departments were promoted. One young lady was offered a promotion, but she went to see the secretary, General Butterworth, and said that there was a girl sitting next to her that had a family to support. A brother who had been supporting the family had died, or sickened, and it had fallen upon her, and she asked the general to let her friend that sat next to her have the promotion in her place.

The general said that he had heard of such things in other generations, but he didn't know that it would ever happen in his generation. He was amazed to find a person on duty in Washington that was willing to give up her position and take a lower one, and let someone else have it that she might be able to help her family.

In Colorado the superintendent of some works told me of a miner that was promoted, who came to the superintendent, and said, "There is a man here that has seven children, and I have only three, and he is having a hard struggle. Don't promote me, but promote him." I know of nothing that speaks louder for Christ and Christianity than to see a man or woman giving up what you call your rights for others, and "in honor preferring one another."

Love, language of; Love, power of

John 13:34–35; 17:21; Acts 4:32; 1 John 3:10

In the late Professor Drummond's book "The Greatest Thing in the World," he tells of meeting with a primitive tribe in the interior of Africa who remembered David Livingstone, the famous pioneer missionary. They could not understand a word he uttered, but they recognized the universal language of love through which he appealed to them. It had been many years since that Christian hero had passed their way, but the very remembrance of his presence among them would kindle a friendly smile. It is this universal language of love, divine, Christlike love, that we must have if we are going to be used of God. The world does not understand theology or dogma, but it understands love and sympathy. A loving act may be more powerful and far-reaching than the most eloquent sermon.

Love, nature of; Fatherhood of God

Matt. 6:8, 32; 16:23; Luke 12:30

If you ask me why God should love us, I cannot tell. I suppose it is because he is a true Father. It is his nature to love; just as it is the nature of the sun to shine.

183

Love, nature of God

1 John 4:8,16

We were once erecting a tabernacle in Chicago, and a businessman said to me, "I would like to put up a text on the wall of that building." I supposed he was going to put up a motto in fine fresco. But I soon found the gas fitter was working back of the pulpit. "What are you doing?" I said. "Putting in gas jets," he replied. And, to my amazement, I found he was putting up the motto "GOD IS LOVE" in gas jets so that it was impossible to light the church without lighting that text.

One night a man was going by and he saw the gas-lighted text "GOD IS LOVE," and he said to himself, "God is love, God is love." By and by he came back, and he looked at it again. I saw him come in and take a seat by the door. Soon he put his hands up to his face, and once in a while I would see tears running down his cheeks, and I was foolish enough to think they were caused by my preaching.

I went to him and said, "What is the trouble?" "I don't know." "What was there in the sermon that made you cry?" "I didn't know you had been preaching." "Well, what was it that troubled you; was it anything in the songs?" "I don't know anything about the songs." "Well," I said, "what is the matter?" "That text up there," he replied. "My man," I said, "do you believe that God loves you?" "I am not worth loving." "That's true," I said, "but he loves you all the more." And I sat there a half hour, and the truth of God's love shone into his soul and he became a new man.

Love, not duty

Song of Sol. 8:7; 2 Cor. 5:14

I have an old mother away down in the Connecticut mountains, and I have been in the habit of going to see her regularly for twenty years. Suppose I go there and say, "Mother, you were very kind to me when I was young. You were very good to me; when father died you worked hard for us all to keep us together, and so I have come to see you because I feel it is my duty." I went then only because it was my duty.

Then she would say to me, "Well, my son, if you only come to see me because it is your duty, you need not come again." And that is the way with a great many of the servants of God. They work for him because it is their duty not for love. Let us abolish this word duty, and feel that it is only a privilege to work for God, and let us try to remember that what is done merely from a sense of duty is not acceptable to God.

Song of Sol. 8:7; 2 Cor. 5:14

I remember once, after speaking on the subject of love being more important than duty, a minister got hold of me and said, "Moody, you're all wrong—why, if you talk like that you will empty our prayer meetings." "Well, then," said I, "the quicker they are emptied the better." "Well," says he, "Moody, I'm sure you're wrong." "Well, see here," says I, "you're married, aren't you? Well, suppose you go home and take a beautiful book to your wife and say, 'Well, wife, there is a book—a present I thought it my duty to bring you. There take it.' Do you think she would accept it? I don't think she would." She wants you to bring it out of love.

Love of God

John 3:16

Suppose a mother should come in here with a little child, and after she has been here awhile the child begins to cry, and she says, "Keep still," but the child keeps on crying, and so she turns him over to the police and says, "Take that child, I don't want him." What would you say of such a mother as that? Teach a child that God loves him only so long as he is good, and that when he is bad the Lord does not love him, and you will find that when he grows up, if he has a bad temper he will have the idea that God hates him because he thinks God doesn't love him when he has got a bad temper, and as he has a bad temper all the time, of course God does not love him at all, but hates him all the time. Now God hates sin, but he loves the sinner, and there is a great difference between the love of God and our love.

Love of God; Satan, strategy of; Children, instruction of

Rom. 5:8

I know of no truth in the whole Bible that ought to come home to us with such power and tenderness as that of the love of God. There is no truth in the Bible that Satan would so much like to blot out. For more than six thousand years he has been trying to persuade men that God does not love them. He succeeded in making our first parents believe this lie; and too often he succeeds with their children.

The idea that God does not love us often comes from false teaching. Mothers make a mistake in teaching children that God does not love them when they do wrong, but only when they do right. That is not taught in Scripture. You do not teach your children that when they do wrong you hate them. Their wrongdoing does not change your love to hate; if it did, you would change your love a great many times. Because your child is fretful, or has committed some act of disobedience, you do not cast him out as though he did not belong to you! No! He is still your child; and you love him. And if men have gone astray from God it does not follow that he hates them. It is the sin that God hates.

Love, power of

Isa. 63:9; Hosea 11:4; 14:4; Luke 7:47; John 8:42; 12:32; 13:35; 17:24; Rom. 13:8; 1 Cor. 13:3; 2 Cor. 5:14; James 2:8; 1 John 4:18; Rev. 12:11

An Arab proverb runs thus: "The neck is bent by the sword, but the heart is only bent by love." Love is irresistible.

Love, power of; Evangelism through love

Isa. 63:9; Hosea 11:4; 14:4; Luke 7:47; John 8:42; 12:32; 13:35; 17:24; Rom. 13:8; 1 Cor. 13:3; 2 Cor. 5:14; James 2:8; 1 John 4:18; Rev. 12:11

Show me a church where there is love, and I will show you a church that is a power in the community. In Chicago a few years ago a little boy attended a Sunday school with which I am acquainted. When his parents moved to another part of the city the little fellow still attended the same Sunday school, although it meant a long, tiresome walk each way. A friend asked him why he went so far, and told him that there were plenty of others just as good nearer his home. "They may be as good for others, but not for me," was his reply. "Why not?" she asked. "Because they love a fellow over there," he replied. If only we could make the world believe that we love them there would be fewer empty churches, and a smaller proportion of our population who never darken a church door. Let love replace duty in our church relations and the world will soon be evangelized.

Love, power of; God is love

1 John 4:8, 16

If I could only make men understand the real meaning of the words of the apostle John—"God is Love"—I would take that single text, and would go up and down the world proclaiming this glorious truth. If you can convince a man that you love him you have won his heart. If we could make people believe that God loves them, how we should find them crowding into the kingdom of heaven! The trouble is that people think God hates them; and so they are continually turning their backs on him.

Love, power of; Trials, strength in

John 13:34; 15:12; 1 Cor. 13:13; Gal. 5:14; 1 John 3:14

Napoleon tried to establish a kingdom by the force of arms. So did Alexander the Great, and Caesar, and other great warriors; but they utterly failed. Jesus founded his kingdom on love, and it is going to stand. When we get on this plane of love, then all selfish and unworthy motives will disappear, and our work will stand the fire when God shall put it to the test.

Love produces love; Knowing Christ intimately

Eph. 1:18; Phil. 3:8, 10; 1 John 2:3, 5

There is no power like love. I loved my little boy long before he loved me. One night I heard him say to his mamma, when he thought me asleep, "I love papa." What a thrill of joy that gave me. I had loved him from infancy, but now he was beginning to love me. A few weeks before, he might have seen me carried out of the house in a coffin, and, perhaps, not knowing better, have thoughtlessly laughed about it. But now my love for him had found a response.

Something like this is the feeling which God has when a sinner melts under his love. Love produces love. What a power it might become in our pulpits and Sunday school classes and meetings! The reason we have so little love for Jesus Christ is that we are so little acquainted with him. The more intimately we get acquainted with the Son of God, the more shall we love him; and we may get acquainted with him by reading about him in the Word. If you can read the life of Jesus Christ without having your heart kindled with love toward him, the devil has surely blinded you, and you ought to pray God to open your eyes.

Love, real (negative example)

Rom. 12:9; 2 Cor. 6:6; James 3:17; 1 Peter 1:22

I remember, I was talking with a man one day and an acquaintance of his came in, and he jumped up at once and shook him by the hand—why I thought he was going to shake his hand out of joint, he shook so hard—and he seemed to be so glad to see him and wanted him to stay, but the man was in a great hurry and could not stay, and he coaxed and urged him to stay, but the man said no, he would come another time; and after that man went out my companion turned to me and said, "Well, he is an awful bore, and I am glad he's gone." Well I began to feel that I was a bore too, and I got out as quickly as I could! That is not real love.

Love, sign of new birth; Regeneration, evidence of

1 John 4:7

The first impulse of a new convert is to love. Do you remember the day you were converted? Was not your heart full of sweet peace and love? I remember the morning I came out of my room after I had first trusted Christ. I thought the old sun shone a good deal brighter than it ever had before. I thought that the sun was just smiling upon me. I walked out upon Boston Common, and heard the birds in the trees, and I thought that they were all singing a song for me. Do you know I fell in love with the birds? I never cared for them before, but now it seemed to me that I was in love with all creation. I had not a bitter feeling against any man, and I was ready to take all men to my heart. If a man has not the love of God shed abroad in his heart, he has never been regenerated.

Lying, sin of; Commandment, ninth

Exod. 20:16; Eph. 4:31; 1 Tim. 1:10; James 4:11

We have got nowadays so that we divide lies into white lies and black lies, society lies, business lies, etc. The Word of God knows no such lowering of the standard. A lie is a lie, no matter what are the circumstances under which it is uttered, or by whom. I have heard that in Siam they sew up the mouth of a confirmed liar. I am afraid if that was the custom in America, a good many would suffer. Parents should begin with their children while they are young and teach them to be strictly truthful at all times. There is a proverb, "A lie has no legs." It requires other lies to support it. Tell one lie and you are forced to tell others to back it up.

Lying, sin of; Transparency, importance of

Prov. 19:22; 1 Tim. 4:2; Titus 1:2

Lying is just as bad as drinking. Don't think that because you have given up drinking that you can go on lying. God hates it. What we want is to be real. Let us not appear to be more than we are. Don't let us put on any assumed humility, but let us be real; that is the delight of God. If we profess to be what we are not, God knows all about us. God hates a sham.

Marriage to unbeliever

2 Cor. 6:14; Eph. 4:17; 1 Peter 2:9; 1 John 3:12

A Christian should never marry an unbeliever. I have heard many a woman say, "When I was married I thought I could lead my husband and be the means of his conversion. He drank some, but he promised me when we were married he would give it up. He didn't get drunk on our wedding trip, but he was drunk very soon after." There is many a mother whose life is as dark as hell, and many a family that has been wrecked because a woman went directly against the Word of God.

It is not for you, young people, who have not seen as much of life and the world as some others, to dispute this. You can see it is plain. There is not a mother that would not feel badly to have a daughter marry a man who would abuse her and make her life wretched. There is not a father who would not be made miserable by such a probability. Do you suppose God does not feel it to have one of his sons or daughters marry an unregenerate and unconverted person who hates him and would misrepresent and abuse him? You say, "Yes, but I shall influence my husband after we are married." Well, influence him before you are married.

Materialism, danger of; False god, business; Commandment, second

Matt. 6:33; Luke 12:20

There are some people who are business blind. It is business, business, business with them all the time. In the morning they haven't time to worship. They must attend to business; must get down to the store. Down they run, and haven't time to get home to dinner. They mustn't let anyone get ahead of them; and they get home late at night and their families have gone to bed. They scarcely ever see their children. It is all business with them. A man told me not long ago, "I must attend to my business. That is my first consideration, and see that none gets ahead of me." That is his god. I don't care if he is an elder or a deacon in the church. That is his god. The god of business has blinded him.

Look at the famous merchant who died the other day. Men called him a clever, shrewd man. Call that shrewdness—to pile up wealth for a lifetime and leave no record behind so that we know he has gone to heaven? He rose above men in his business; he devoted his whole soul to it, and the world called him a power among men; the world called him great. But let the Son of God write his obituary; let him put an epitaph on his tombstone, and it would be, "Thou fool." Man says, "I must attend to business first"; God says, "Seek first the kingdom of God." I don't care what your business may be; it may be honorable, legitimate, and all that, but if you think you must attend to it first it has become your god.

Maturity, spiritual

1 Chron. 29:28; Pss. 34:12; 128:5; Eccles. 5:18; 1 Peter 3:10

When I was at Wellesley College the other day, a young lady said: "Is it true, Mr. Moody, as so many tell us, that these are the best days of our lives?" I said, "No, not if you are children of God walking with him." I have served Christ for twenty-one years and this last year has been the best. It grows better and better. I mount up higher and higher every year. I have had more peace, more strength, more rest the past year, than I ever had in my life. When I was converted I thought I got a great boon, the greatest I had ever received. I wondered if it would seem as pleasant to me after a few years, and if these things would not come to be old things. But Christ is a thousand times more to me now than he was then. You know that some men grow smaller and smaller on an intimate acquaintance; but my experience is that the more and more you know of Christ the larger he becomes.

Meditation, importance of

Josh. 1:8; Ps. 119:97; Luke 10:39; Col. 3:16

The longer I live and the older I grow, the more convinced I am that there are times when we must sit quietly at the feet of Jesus, and only let God speak to our souls. Just keep quietly alone, and learn of Jesus. It is when a man is alone with his wife that he tells her the precious secrets of his soul. It is not when the family members are around or when there is company near. So, when we want to learn the secrets of heaven we should be alone with Jesus, and listen, that he may come and whisper to our souls. The richest hours I have ever had with God have not been in great assemblies, but sitting alone at the feet of Jesus.

Memory, power of

Gen. 4:8; Matt. 26:14; Mark 14:10; Luke 22:48

Do you think that Judas, after nearly 1,900 years, has forgotten that he betrayed his Savior for thirty pieces of silver? Do you think that Cain, after 6,000 years, has forgotten the pleading look of his brother Abel when he slew him?

Luke 16:25

We hear people talk about certain men having wonderful memories. It is said of Cyrus, the Persian general, that he had such a memory that he could call by name all the private soldiers in his army. I have read of a literary man that could repeat everything that he had ever written. Some of us complain about our short memories, but I think memory will be long enough when God says, "Son remember!" When conscience is thoroughly aroused and we are thoroughly awakened, then we cannot help but remember. Memory will do its work.

Memory is God's officer, and when God touches the secret spring and says, "Son, daughter, remember," tramp, tramp, tramp will go the whole life before us. You may plunge into the world, and into amusements; you may drink and drown your consciences, and drown memory; but the time is coming when you cannot forget; the time is coming when memory will do its work, and you cannot for a moment forget the past.

We talk about the recording angel that is keeping men's records. I think we are keeping our own record. God makes us keep our own records. Day after day that record is being written. Some are very anxious that their biography should be written, but we are all writing our own biography. I don't believe that God will need to condemn us; I think we will condemn ourselves. Our own records will condemn us.

Memory, power of; Gospel, danger of rejecting

Lam. 1:7; Matt. 26:75; Mark 14:72; Luke 16:25; 22:61; 24:8

I have been twice at the point of death. I was drowning once, and just as I was going down the third time I was rescued. In the twinkling of an eye my whole life came flashing across my mind. I cannot tell you how it was. I cannot tell you how a whole life can be crowded into a second of time; but everything I had done from my earliest childhood—it all came flashing across my mind. And I believe that when God touches the secret spring of memory, every one of our sins will come back, and if they have not been blotted out by the blood of the Lord Jesus Christ, they will haunt us as eternal ages roll on.

There is a man in prison. He has been there five years. Ask that man what makes the prison so terrible to him. Ask him if it is the walls and the iron gates—ask him if it is his hard work, and he will tell you no; he will tell you what makes the prison so terrible to him is memory; and I have an idea that if we got down into the lost world, we would find that is what makes hell so terrible—the remembrance that they once heard the gospel, that they once had Christ offered to them, that they once had the privilege of being saved, but

they made light of the gospel, they neglected salvation, they rejected the offer of mercy, and now if they would accept it they could not.

Mercy, cry for

Pss. 57:1; 119:132; Luke 18:13

Let our cry be that of the publican: "Be merciful to me!"—not to someone else. A mother was telling me some time ago that she had trouble with one of her sons, because he had not treated his brother rightly. She sent him upstairs; and after awhile she asked him what he had been doing. He replied that he had been praying for his brother! Although he had been the naughty one, he was acting as if the fault lay with his brother instead of himself. So many of us can see the failings of others readily enough; but when we get a good look at ourselves, we will get down before God as the Publican did and cry for mercy: and that cry will bring an immediate answer.

Message more than ministers

Deut. 16:19; 2 Chron. 19:7; Rom. 2:11; Eph. 6:19

A good many people say, "Oh, I don't like such and such a minister; I should like to know where he comes from, and what he has done, and whether any bishop has ever laid his hands on his head." My dear friends, never mind the minister; it's the message you want. Why, if someone were to send me a message, and the news were important, I shouldn't stop to ask about the messenger who brought it; I should want to read the news; I should look at the letter and its contents, and not at the person who brought it. And so it is with God's message. The good news is everything, the minister nothing. Why, if I got lost in London, I should be willing to ask anybody which way to go. It is the way I want, not the person who directs me.

Millennium, views of

1 Thess. 4:16; Rev. 20:4

There are two opinions in the church in regard to the millennium. Some think that the thousand years of holiness and peace will precede the return of Christ to the earth; others think that they will follow his return, and that he will reign here in person during the thousand years. The former class of interpreters are called postmillenarians, and the latter are called premillenarians. Those who differ on that point ought to have charity for each other. There is no reason that I should denounce a brother because he doesn't see this thing just as I do. I believe that when Christ comes the saints then on the earth will be changed. They will not have to die and go into the grave, but will be caught up to meet their Lord in the air, and that he will then set up a visible kingdom on the earth.

Ministers, prayer for

Rom. 12:10; Gal. 5:13; Eph. 4:2; 6:19; 1 Thess. 4:9

You go into a church that is all aglow with love, and into another where there is a lack, and mark the difference. In the latter the people get as far away from the pulpit as possible; and mark the coldness, and see how quick they get out of the church. Their hearts are cold to one another, and they have no sympathy. But when their hearts are all aglow they crowd round and are genial toward one another, and "God bless the sermon," however poor the minister who preaches.

The reason that we have so many poor ministers is because we have so few praying people. Look at Joshua: while he was fighting for the Lord, Moses was up on the mountain praying. So we need everyone to pray for their ministers while they are fighting for the Lord. When a man comes to me and grumbles and complains about his minister, I ask him, "Do you ever pray for your minister?" He runs away. It spikes his guns. They do not work with the minister: never think of praying for him.

We want to see every man red-hot for the Savior, and he will wake up the church. If he had got his heart red-hot, sparks will kindle in the little circle, and the whole church will be ablaze. Every soul will be filled with the glory of Christ. There is not a man—I do not care what he is; he may be an Atheist, a Pantheist, a drunkard, or a gambler—I do not believe that a man's heart is so hard but that God can break it.

Ministry, call to; Fruitfulness, evidence of call

Ps. 39:3; Isa. 50:4; Jer. 15:16; 20:9; 23:29

No man ought to give up his business and enter the ministry unless he feels that he can't help it. There are a great many men in the pulpit who ought never to have been there. They have mistaken their vocation. They might have been much more useful as businessmen, or lawyers, or doctors, or mechanics. A man should only enter the ministry when he is constrained to do so by love to God and love to man. It cost me the hardest struggle of my life to abandon business and give myself entirely to the Lord's work. I was driven into it. The best evidence that a man is called to the ministry is the actual consequence of his efforts. A man should see souls saved as the fruit of his work before he concludes that his entire time ought to be given to that kind of work.

Ministry, lay

Isa. 43:10; 44:8; Acts 1:8; 17:23; 1 John 1:2

There's not a man or woman here, not one, that loves Jesus Christ, if the record is clean and the heart's all right, but can do good work. If you can't open a hall, go out on the streets. When I was in Edinburgh, they told me that one of the worst places was in Cow Court, one of the darkest streets of Edinburgh. But, rain or shine, Sundays and cloudy days, every night right along for twenty-nine years, there has been a religious meeting there. One man took it on Monday, and another on Tuesday, and another on Wednesday, and so on through the week.

I like the Scotch grit; there's no cessation in the meetings. Just at a quarter to eight a man came and backed himself up against a lamppost. In a few minutes he had a crowd; and then they marched up to the building—it was a miserable-looking building. I had the pleasure of trying to get the people of Edinburgh to put him up a good building; but without this they have had a meeting right along every Sunday for between thirty and forty years.

Some of the finest men today in Scotland who are standing for the Son of God were converted at Cow Gate near to that lamppost. There are many of these laymen, not only willing to go there nights, but at other times. And so it can be today if the Christian men and women will rise up and say: "I'll not wait any longer for any Christian committee to put me to work!"

Ministry, power for; Holy Spirit power

Luke 4:18; John 1:33; Acts 2:4

Jesus didn't commence his ministry until the Spirit of God came upon him. I can't conceive of a greater mistake than for any man to attempt to do the Lord's work without first receiving an anointing of the Holy Spirit. Education is very good—all you get in your college is a great help; but yet your life will be a failure unless you get an anointing of the Spirit. Jesus Christ lived for thirty years without preaching. It was only when the Spirit of God came upon him that he began to preach.

If Peter had commenced the sermon he preached on the day of Pentecost before the Pentecostal power came, it would have been a stupendous failure. I have no doubt those Christians would have been exterminated. But they waited for the unction—for the power—and when the power came, they began to preach the glorious gospel of the Son of God with great power.

Ministry, worthless without love

1 Cor. 13:1

What is the worth of a sermon, however sound in doctrine it may be, if it be not sound in love and in patience? What are our prayers worth without the spirit of love? People say, "Why is it that there is no blessing? Our minister's sermons and prayers are very good." Most likely you will find it is because the whole thing is done professionally. The words glisten like icicles in the sun, and they are just as cold. There is not a spark of love in them. If that is the case there will be very little power. God says such sermons are as sounding brass and a tinkling cymbal.

Money, use of

Acts 24:26; 1 Cor. 3:9; 2 Cor. 6:1; 1 Tim. 3:3, 8; Titus 1:7; Heb. 13:5

God is rich, and I am working for him. When this question was settled, money became my servant, while to most men it is the master. A man in London offered me a thousand pounds sterling just to sit for his photograph, but I refused. The thing did not seem right, and the money was of no possible consequence.

Mother, honoring; Commandment, fifth

Exod. 20:12; Prov. 1:8; 20:20; 30:11, 17; Matt. 15:4

Dr. John Hall once told of a boy who had been sent by his mother off to school, and when the time came for him to graduate he wrote home that he wanted his timid, old, widowed mother to be there on graduation day. She wrote back that she could not come; she hadn't a new dress, and had turned the skirt of her old one once and she couldn't turn it again. The boy said he could not graduate without her; she must come. He persuaded her to come. She wasn't dressed very well. When the people had assembled, it was discovered that the best seat in the hall was reserved for somebody.

Soon that young man came proudly down the broad aisle with his aged, widowed mother leaning on his arm, and he escorted her to that seat. She did not know that he had carried everything before him, that he was Valedictorian of his class, and the most popular man in the whole school. When he won the prize and the medal was placed upon his breast, he slipped down and put it on his mother, and kissed her, and said, "I should never have had it but for you."

Exod. 20:12; Prov. 1:8; 20:20; 30:11, 17; Matt. 15:4

There was nothing in President Garfield's life that touched me so much as when, the moment after his inauguration, he turned and kissed his aged mother. I say that man is a miserable, contemptible wretch who speaks sneeringly of his parents. A man ashamed of his old mother! God forgive him. If you have a mother, treat her kindly. She is the best friend you have. If she is alive, make her last days as sweet as you can. When she is gone you will realize that about half the world is gone.

Exod. 20:12; Prov. 1:8; 20:20; 30:11, 17; Matt. 15:4

When I see drinking saloons full of young men I think of the white-haired mother back home somewhere; I think of the father whose head is bowed with grief and shame. You who live in the city ought to do all you can to save these young men. Give them a kind word, a helping hand. I can't tell you how lonely I felt when I first came to the city. I didn't know where to go. The stores were closed at night, and I was out on the streets, and my feet almost slipped. I remember the first time a young man asked me to drink with him. I said "No." I told him I had promised my mother that I would never drink. He said, "You are tied to your mother's apron strings." I turned round and gave him a blow that almost knocked him down.

I am now over sixty years old, and I am not ashamed to say that I thank God I obeyed my mother. She had seven sons, and not one of us ever drank. The last influence a man forgets is the teaching of his mother.

Mother, honoring; Mother, faithfulness of; Commandment, fifth

Exod. 20:12; Deut. 5:16; Prov. 1:8; 20:20; 30:11, 17; Matt. 15:4

Young man, young woman, how do you treat your parents? Tell me that, and I will tell you how you are going to get on in life. When I hear a young man speaking contemptuously of his gray-haired father or mother, I say he has sunk very low indeed. When I see a young man as polite as any gentleman can be when he is out in society, but who snaps at his mother and speaks unkindly to his father, I would not give the snap of my finger for his religion. If there is any man or woman on earth that ought to be treated kindly and tenderly, it is that loving mother or that loving father. If they cannot have your regard through life, what reward are they to have for all their care and anxiety?

Think how they loved you and provided for you in your early days. Let your mind go back to the time when you were ill. Did your mother neglect you? When a neighbor came in and said, "Now, mother, you go and lie down; you have been up for a week; I will take your place for a night"—did she do it? No; and if the poor worn body forced her to it at last, she lay watching, and if she heard your voice, she was at your side directly, anticipating all your wants, wiping the perspiration away from your brow. If you wanted water, how soon you got it!

She would gladly have taken the disease into her own body to save you. Her love for you would drive her to any lengths. No matter to what depths of vice and misery you have sunk, no matter how profligate you have grown, she has not turned you out of her heart. Perhaps she loves you all the more because you are wayward. She would draw you back by the bands of a love that never dies.

Mother, influence of; Discipline, parental

Ruth 3:1; 1 Sam. 2:19; Matt. 2:11; Luke 1:15; 2:23; 2 Tim. 1:5

I remember blaming my mother for sending me to church on Sunday. On one occasion the preacher had to send someone into the balcony to wake me up. I thought it was hard to have to work in the field all the week, and then be obliged to go to church and hear a sermon I didn't understand. I thought I wouldn't go to church anymore when I got away from home; but I had got so in the habit of going that I couldn't stay away. After one or two Sundays, back again to the house of God I kept going. There I first found Christ, and I have often said since: "Mother, I thank you for making me go to the house of God when I didn't want to go."

Mother's heart

2 Tim. 1:5

I have great respect for that old woman who with ribbons flying ran into a crowded thoroughfare and rescued a child from under a wagon. She was asked,

"Is it your child?" "No," she replied, "but it is someone's child." She had a mother's heart. God has given us a charge, not only in looking to the salvation of our own children, but we should see to the salvation of the children of others.

Mother's influence

Ruth 3:1; 1 Sam. 2:19; Matt. 2:11; Luke 1:15; 2:23; 2 Tim. 1:5

I was urging the early conversion of children in a meeting, and a man got up at the close and said, "I want to endorse every word. Sixteen years ago I was a missionary in another country, and my wife died and left three little children. On the Sunday after her death my eldest girl came to me and said, 'Papa, shall I take the children into the bedroom and pray with them as mother used to?'" The mother was dead, and little Nellie, ten years old, wanted to follow in her footsteps. The father agreed, and she led them off to the bedroom to pray.

When they came out he noticed that they had been weeping and asked what about. "Well, father," said the little girl, "I prayed just as mother taught me, and then"—naming her little brother—"he prayed the prayer that mother taught him; but little Susie, she was too young, mother had not taught her a prayer so she made a prayer of her own, and I couldn't help but weep to hear her pray." "Why," said the father, "what did she say?"

"Why, she put up her little hands, and closed her eyes, and said, 'O God, you have come and taken away my dear mamma, and I have no mamma to pray for me now—won't you please make me good just as my dear mamma was, for Jesus' sake, Amen.'" And God heard that prayer. That little child before she was four years old gave evidence of being a child of God, and for sixteen years she was by her father's side leading little children to the Lamb of God that taketh away the sin of the world.

Ruth 3:1; 1 Sam. 2:19; Matt. 2:11; Luke 1:15; 2:23; 2 Tim. 1:5

John Wesley's mother did a great work when she led her boy to Christ. Whitefield's mother did a great work when she led her son to Christ. Train that boy of yours for eternity. God may use him to turn thousands and tens of thousands to Christ.

Ruth 3:1; 1 Sam. 2:19; Matt. 2:11; Luke 1:15; 2:23; 2 Tim. 1:5

A murderer was to suffer the penalty of his crime. Speaking of his reckless career, he said, "How could it be otherwise, when I had such bad training? I was taught these things from my youth. When only four years old my mother poured whisky down my throat to see how I would act." On the morning of his execution, the wretched mother bade good-bye to the son whom her influence had helped to that shameful end.

Mother's love

Ruth 3:1; 1 Sam. 2:19; Matt. 2:11; Luke 1:15; 2:23; 2 Tim. 1:5

There was a lady that came down to Liverpool to see us privately; it was just before we were about to leave that city to go to London to preach. With tears and sobs she told a very pitiful story. She said she had a boy nineteen years of age who had left her. She showed me his photograph, and asked me to put it in my pocket. "You stand before many and large assemblies, Mr. Moody. My boy may be in London, now. Oh, look at the audience to whom you will preach; look earnestly. You may see my dear boy before you. If you see him, tell him to come back to me. Oh, implore him to come to his sorrowing mother, to his deserted home. He may be in trouble; he may be suffering; tell him for his loving mother that all is for-

given and forgotten, and he will find comfort and peace at home."

On the back of this photograph she had written his full name and address; she had noted his complexion, the color of his eyes and hair; why he had left home, and the cause of his so doing. "When you preach, Mr. Moody, look for my poor boy," were the parting words of that mother. That young man may be in this hall tonight. If he is, I want to tell him that his mother loves him still. I will read out his name, and if any of you ever hear of that young man, just tell him that his mother is waiting with a loving heart and a tender embrace for him. His name is Arthur P. Oxley, of Manchester, England.

Mother's love, example of

1 Kings 3:27

The closest tie on earth is a mother's love for her child. There are a good many things that will separate a man from his wife, but there isn't a thing in the wide, wide world that will separate a true mother from her own child. I will admit that there are unnatural mothers, that there are mothers that have gone out of their heads, mothers that are so steeped in sin and iniquity that they will turn against their own children, but a true mother will never, never turn against her own child. I have talked with mothers when my blood boiled with indignation against the sons for their treatment of their mothers, and I have said, "Why don't you cast him off?" They have said, "Why, Mr. Moody, I love him still. He is my son."

I was once preaching for Dr. G. in St. Louis, and when I got through he said that he wanted to tell me a story. There was a boy who was very bad. He had a very bad father, who seemed to take delight in teaching his son everything that was bad. The father died, and the boy went on from bad to worse until he was arrested for murder. When he was on trial, it came out that he had murdered five other people, and from one end of the city to the other there was a universal cry going up against him. During his trial they had to guard the courthouse, the indignation was so intense.

The white-haired mother got just as near her son as she could, and every witness that went into the court and said anything against him seemed to hurt her more than her son. When the jury brought in a verdict of guilty a great shout went up, but the old mother nearly fainted away; and when the judge pronounced the sentence of death they thought she would faint away. After it was over she threw her arms around him and kissed him, and there in the court they had to tear him from her embrace.

She then went the length and breadth of the city trying to get men to sign a petition for his pardon. And when he was hanged, she begged the governor to let her have the body of her son, that she might bury it. They say that death has torn down everything in this world, everything but a mother's love. That is stronger than death itself. The governor refused to let her have the body, but she cherished the memory of that boy as long as she lived.

A few months later she followed her boy in death, and when she was dying she sent word to the governor, and begged that her body might be laid close to her son. That is a mother's love! She wasn't ashamed to have her grave pointed out for all time as the grave of the mother of the most noted criminal the State of Vermont ever had. The prophet takes hold of that very idea. He says, "Can a mother forget her child?" But a mother's love is not to be compared to the love of God.

Motivation, inner; Sincerity

Luke 22:47

Judas got near enough to Christ to kiss him, and yet went down to damnation.

Motives, nature of; Service, reasons for; Rewards, desire for

Matt. 6:2; 23:5; Luke 16:15; John 12:43; Rom. 2:29; Rev. 22:12

If I understand things correctly, whenever you find men or women who are looking to be rewarded here for doing right, they are unqualified to work for God. If they are looking for the applause of men and reward in this life, it will disqualify them for the service of God.

Murder, by evil conduct; Commandment, sixth

Gen. 27:41; 1 John 3:15

When I was in England in 1892, I met a man who claimed that the English are ahead of Americans in the respect they have for the law. "We hang our murderers," he said. "But there isn't one out of twenty in your country that is hung." I said, "You are greatly mistaken, for there are a multitude of murderers who walk about both countries unhung." "What do you mean?" "I will tell what I mean," I said; "the man that comes into my house and runs a dagger into my heart for my money is a prince compared with a son that takes five years to kill me and the wife of my bosom. A young man who comes home night after night drunk, and when his mother remonstrates, curses her gray hairs and kills her by inches, is the blackest kind of a murderer."

That kind of thing is going on constantly all around us. One young man at college, an only son, whose mother wrote to him protesting against his gambling and drinking habits, took the letters out of the post office, and when he found that they were from her, he tore them up without reading them. She said, "I thought I would die when I found I had lost my hold on that son." If a boy kills his mother by his conduct, you can't call it anything else than murder, and he is as truly guilty of breaking this sixth commandment as if he drove a dagger to her heart. If all young people in this country who are killing their parents and their wives or husbands by inches should be hung this next week, there would be a great many funerals.

Murder, definition of; Animal rights; Self-defense; Commandment, sixth

Gen. 9:6; Exod. 22:2; Matt. 24:43; Luke 12:39

Let us see what the sixth commandment does not mean. It does not forbid the killing of animals for food and for other reasons. Millions of rams and lambs and turtledoves must have been killed every year for sacrifices under the Mosaic system. Christ himself ate of the Passover lamb, and we are told definitely of cases where he ate fish and provided it for his disciples and the people to eat.

It does not forbid the killing of burglars or attackers in self-defense. Directly after the giving of the Ten Commandments, God laid down the ordinance that if a thief be found breaking in and be smitten that he die, it was pardonable. Did not Christ justify this idea of self-defense in Matthew 24:43? It does not forbid capital punishment. God set the death penalty upon violations of each of the first seven commandments, as well as for other crimes. God said to Noah after the deluge, "Whoso sheddeth man's blood, by man shall his blood be shed" (Gen. 9:6); and the reason given is just as true today as it was then—"for in the image of God made he man."

Murder, from carelessness; Commandment, sixth

Exod. 20:13

But I want to speak of other classes of murderers that are very numerous in this country, although they are not classified as murderers. The man who is the cause of the death of another through criminal carelessness is guilty. The man who sells diseased meat, the saloonkeeper whose drink has maddened the brain of a criminal; those who adulterate food; the employer who jeopardizes the lives of employees and others by unsafe surroundings and conditions in dangerous occupations—they are all guilty of blood where life is lost as a consequence.

Murder, nature of; Commandment, sixth

Gen. 27:41; 1 John 3:15

I used to say "What is the use of talking about a law like this in an audience where, probably, there isn't a man who ever thought of, or ever will commit, murder?" But as one gets on in years, he sees many a murder that is not outright killing. I need not kill a person to be a murderer. If I get so angry that I wish a man dead, I am a murderer in God's sight. God looks at the heart and says he that hates his brother is a murderer.

Nature, old

Rom. 6:6; Eph. 4:22; Col. 3:9

If you took a man right from the dirtiest streets of your city and placed him in the crystal streets of heaven, he wouldn't want to stay there long. He would immediately become homesick. In such a place he would be a natural man, and a natural man who can't find any whisky or anything of a worldly character in heaven wants to get out of that beautiful place as soon as possible.

Nature, witness to God; Creation, revelation of deity

Ps. 19:1; Isa. 40:26; Rom. 1:20; 1 Cor. 13:12

The word Paul used in 1 Cor. 13:12, properly translated, is "mirror." Now, we see

God, as it were, in a mirror, but then, face to face. Suppose we knew nothing of the sun except what we saw of its light reflected from the moon? Would we not wonder about its immense distance, about its dazzling splendor, about its life-giving power? But all that we see, the sun, the moon, the stars, the ocean, the earth, the flowers, and above all, human beings, are a grand mirror in which the perfection of God is imperfectly reflected.

Natures, two

Rom. 6:6; Eph. 4:22; Col. 3:9

You will often find the best Christians doing strange things. Why? Because they have given way to the old nature. The horse has but one nature, and he is true to it. The sheep, the ox, are true to their natures. But a child of God has two natures, one a deceitful, corrupt, and carnal nature, the other a heavenly nature, received when we are born of God, and are made partakers of the divine nature. Now I never had any serious conflict with myself until I got the new nature; then the warfare began. I agree with the man who said it was as if one foot wanted to go one way and the other foot the other way, and he couldn't get on. I found that I had to crucify one nature. Men either give way to their corrupt and deceitful nature, or else they put off the old man and put on the new man by faith.

Neglect, danger of

Heb. 2:3; 10:28

How watchful we should be of our thoughts, practices, and feelings. Deception in moral life is, for the most part, neglect. We do not stop to examine ourselves, to lay our hearts and minds bare in the sight of God, and judge ourselves by God's most holy will. A man need not shoot himself in order to commit suicide: he need only neglect the proper means of

sustenance, and he will soon die. Where an enemy is strong and aggressive, an army is doomed to sure defeat and capture unless a sharp lookout is kept, every man wide awake at his post of duty.

It has been noticed that there are more accidents in the mountains of Switzerland in fair weather than in stormy seasons. People are apt to undertake expeditions that they would not take under less favorable conditions, and they are less careful in their conduct. And so it is that moral and spiritual disaster usually overtakes us when we are off our guard and careless against temptation. We may become proud and self-reliant in seasons of prosperity, whereas adversity drives us to the living God for guidance and comfort.

New birth, fruit of; Children of God

Rom. 8:15; Gal. 3:16; 4:6; 1 John 3:1–2; 5:1

God has not only adopted us, but we are his by birth. We have been born into his kingdom. My boy was as much mine when he was a day old as now that he is fourteen. He was my son; although it did not appear what he would be when he attained manhood. He is mine; although he may have to undergo probation under tutors and governors. The children of God are not perfect; but we are perfectly his children.

New birth, importance of; Regeneration, doctrine of

John 3:3

The doctrine of the new birth is of the highest importance. We can afford to be deceived about many things rather than about this one thing. Christ makes it very plain. He says, "Except a man be born again, he cannot see the kingdom of God"—much less inherit it. This doctrine of the new birth is therefore the foundation of all our hopes for the world to

197

come. It is really the A B C of the Christian religion. My experience has been this—that if a man is unsound on this doctrine he will be unsound on almost every other fundamental doctrine in the Bible. A true understanding of this subject will help a man to solve a thousand difficulties that he may meet with in the Word of God. Things that before seemed very dark and mysterious will become very plain.

New converts, advice to

Ezek. 33:7; 2 Tim. 4:5

A young man came to me and said, "Mr. Moody, I have been converted, shall I give up all my old friends?" I said, "No, go for them. Keep telling them about Christ and they will either come to God or give you up."

New converts, witness of

Ps. 107:2; 2 Thess. 3:1

If the Lord has redeemed us let us say so. I was very much encouraged last night at the new converts' meeting to hear what was said by that man who was converted here a week ago after having been a drunkard for thirty years. After he had gone home, he said, an old companion came to his house in Cambridge, weeping and wanting to get power over his appetite. He prayed with him and showed him the way to Christ, and both were there last night rejoicing. When you find Christ, go right out and tell your friends!

New converts, work of

Isa. 52:7; 66:19; Rom. 10:14; 1 Thess. 1:8

If the church will only set the young converts to work, we can reach a great many homes; but if we just take them into the church and leave them there, and not teach them how to work, the homes are never going to be reached. Some young converts during the past weeks have been

to work, and they have already brought, some eight, some ten, and some twelve of their friends to Christ. If we keep on in that way how long will it be before we have hundreds and thousands of converts in this city?

New man, example of

2 Cor. 5:17

A man got up in one of our meetings in New York, who had been pretty far down, but a wonderful change had taken place when he trusted Christ, and he said he hardly knew himself. He said the fact was, he was a new man in his old clothes. That was just it. Not a man in new clothes, but a new man in old clothes.

I saw an advertisement which read like this, "If you want people to respect you, wear good clothes." That is the world's idea of getting the world's respect. Why! A leper may put on good clothes, but he is a leper still. Mere profession doesn't transform a man. It is the new nature spoken of in 2 Corinthians 5:17, "Therefore if any man be in Christ, he is a new creature; old things are passed away; behold, all things are become new."

No, just say

Ps. 1:1; Prov. 9:6; Isa. 52:11; 2 Cor. 6:17; 7:1

I believe there are more young people who are lost because they cannot say no, than for any other reason.

Nourishment, spiritual; Bible, value of

John 6:51; Heb. 4:12

If you go out to your garden and throw down some sawdust, the birds will not take any notice; but if you throw down some crumbs, you will find they will sweep down and pick them up. The true child of God can tell the difference (so to speak) between sawdust and bread.

Many so-called Christians are living on the world's sawdust, instead of being nourished by the Bread that comes down from heaven. Nothing can satisfy the longings of the soul but the Word of the living God.

Obedience, examples of; Pleasing God, process of

2 Kings 5:14; Hag. 1:12; Luke 17:12; John 9:7

Do you know every man who was blessed while Christ was on earth, was blessed in the act of obedience? Ten lepers came to him, and he said, "Go and show yourselves to the priest." They might have said, "What good is that going to do us? It was the priest that sent us away from our families." But they said nothing; and it came to pass, that, as they went, they were healed. Do you want to get rid of the leprosy of sin? Obey God. You say you don't feel like it. Did you always feel like going to school when you were a child? Supposing a man only went to business when he felt like it; he would fail in a few weeks.

Jesus said to another man, "Go to the Pool of Siloam and wash," and as he washed, he received his sight. He was blessed in the act of obedience. The prophet said to Naaman, "Go and dip seven times in Jordan," and while he was dipping he was healed. Simple obedience pleases God.

Obedience, fruit of; Peace, source of

Ps. 89:15; Isa. 2:5; John 8:12; Eph. 5:8; 1 John 1:7

When I was a little boy I tried to catch my shadow. I don't know if you were ever so foolish; but I remember running after it, and trying to get ahead of it. I could not see why the shadow always kept ahead of me. Once I happened to be racing with my face to the sun, and I looked over my head and saw my shadow behind me, and it kept behind me all the way. It is the same

with the Son of Righteousness. Peace and joy will go with you while you go with your face toward him, but those who turn their backs on the Son are in darkness all the time. Turn to the light of God and the reflection will flash in your heart.

Obedience, importance of

Matt. 13:5; Mark 4:5; Luke 8:6

In the country there are sometimes seen great trees blown over and torn up by the roots, and the reason for it was the shallow soil. So it is with many people who profess to be Christians. They believe for a while, but in time of temptation they fall away, because they had not been rooted in Christ. We must grow inwardly as well as in outward appearance. The only way to keep from falling is to send our roots deeply into obedience to God's Word.

Isa. 1:19; Acts 6:7; Rom. 6:17; Phil. 2:10; 1 Peter 1:14

You know that when you were a child and were disobedient to your parents you not only made them unhappy, but were unhappy yourself. There will be no peace in any soul until it is willing to obey the voice of God. I believe that the great reason there is so much trouble in this world is because we are living in disobedience to God's laws, God's commands, and God's Word. Luther said, "I would rather obey than work miracles."

Obedience, importance of; Submission, importance of; Will, power of

Isa. 1:19; Acts 6:7; Rom. 6:17; Phil. 2:10; 1 Peter 1:14

The battle is fought on that one word of the will; the door hangs on that one hinge of the will. Will you obey? That is the question! Will you obey the voice of God and do as he commands you? No man can obey for you any more than he can eat and drink for you. You must eat and drink for yourself, and you must obey God for yourself.

Obedience, joy of; Disobedience, danger of

1 Sam. 9:2; 15:26; Matt. 26:42; Mark 14:36; Acts 8:3; 9:6

Take the two Sauls. They lived about one thousand years apart. One started out well and ended poorly, and the other started out poorly and ended well. The first Saul got a kingdom and a crown; he had a lovely family (no father ever had a better son than Saul had in Jonathan); he had the friendship of Samuel, the best prophet there was on the face of the earth; and yet he lost the friendship of Samuel, lost his crown, his kingdom, his son and his life, all through an act of disobedience.

Now take the Saul of the New Testament. When God called him he was obedient to the heavenly vision, and he was given a heavenly kingdom. One act of obedience, one act of disobedience. The act of obedience gained all, and the act of disobedience lost everything. I believe the wretchedness and misery and woe in this country today come from disobedience to God. If people won't obey God as a nation, let us begin individually. Let us make up our minds that we will do it, cost us what it will; and we will have peace and joy.

Obedience pleases God; Submission, importance of

1 Sam. 15:22; Ps. 51:17; Prov. 21:3; Jer. 7:23; Hosea 6:6

Suppose I say to my boy, "Willie, please bring me a glass of water." He says he doesn't want to go. "Willie, I asked you politely but now I am telling you to go." "But I don't want to go," he says. "I tell you, you must go and get me a glass of water." He does not like to go. But he

knows I am very fond of grapes, and he is very fond of them himself, so he goes out, and someone gives him a beautiful cluster of grapes. He comes in and says, "Here, papa, here is a beautiful cluster of grapes for you." "But what about the water?" "Won't the grapes be acceptable, papa?" "No, my boy, the grapes are not acceptable; I won't take them; I want you to get me a glass of water."

The little fellow doesn't want to get the water, but goes out, and this time someone gives him an orange. He brings it in and places it before me. "Is that acceptable?" he asks. "No, no, no!" I say, "I want nothing but water; you cannot do anything to please me until you get the water." And so, my friends, to please God you must first obey him.

Obedience, power of

Exod. 15:26; Jer. 7:23; Heb. 5:8–9

There is a story told about Girard, one of the first millionaires this country ever had. A green Irishman came over to this country, and he had been walking around the streets of Philadelphia for a long time unable to get anything to do. One day he went into Girard's office, and asked him if he couldn't give him something to do to keep soul and body together. Girard said, "Yes; do you see that pile of bricks down there?" "Yes." "Well, pile it up at the other end of the yard."

The Irishman went to work. Night came on, and he had the work all done, and he went up into the office, touched his hat, got his pay, and asked if Girard had any work for him the next morning. Girard told him he had. The next morning he came along. Girard said, "You go and take that pile of bricks and carry it back where you found it." The Irishman went at the work without a word. He wasn't a Yankee, you better believe.

Night came on, he got his pay, and wanted to know if there would be work for him the next morning. Girard kept him marching up and down there for a number of days, until he found he was just the man he wanted. One day he said, "You go down and bid sugar off at the commodities auction in precisely the way I tell you." When the auctioneer put the sugar up, here was a green Irishman bidding. The people laughed and made sport of him, and finally it was sold to him. The auctioneer said in a gruff tone, "Who is going to pay for this sugar?" "Girard, sir." "Are you Girard's agent?" "Yes, sir."

Girard had found a man he could trust; God wants to find people he can trust. Obedience is literal, prompt, cheerful, willing action. Do what God wants you to do without asking any questions. When God finds such people, I believe they become the mightiest power on this earth.

Obedience, source of harmony; Unity, source of

1 Sam. 15:22; Ps. 51:17; Prov. 21:3; Jer. 7:23; Hosea 6:6

Did you ever notice all but the heart of man obeys God? If you look through history, you will find that this is true. In the beginning God said, "Let there be light," and there was light. "Let the waters bring forth," and the water brought forth abundantly. And one of the proofs that Jesus Christ is God is that he spoke to nature, and nature obeyed him. At one time he spoke to the sea, and the sea recognized and obeyed. He spoke to the fig tree, and instantly it withered and died; it obeyed literally and at once. He spoke to devils, and the devils fled. He spoke to the grave, and the grave obeyed him and gave back its dead. But when he speaks to man, man will not obey him. That is why man is out of harmony with God, and it will never be different until men learn to obey God. God desires obedience, and he will have it, else there can be no harmony.

Obstacles, look beyond the; Vision, power of

Isa. 45:22; John 8:56; 2 Tim. 4:8; Heb. 2:10; 12:2–3; Jude 21

The great trouble with the church is that it is all the time looking at the obstacles. I have yet to find successful men and women in God's service that are looking at the obstacles.

Old man vs. New Man

Rom. 6:6; Eph. 4:22; Col. 3:9

A man was once brought into court, and he said he hadn't done the thing he was charged with; it was the old man in him that had done it. "Well," the judge said, "I'll send the old man to prison, and the new man can go where he has a mind to."

Opinions of others

Jer. 23:16; Matt. 24:24; Luke 12:5; Eph. 5:6; Col. 2:4, 8

There is an old stone building that belongs to the University of Aberdeen, and upon it is inscribed a motto that has been there for many years. I wanted to see it with my own eyes, and I went up to look at it. It is this, "They say. What do they say? Let them say." That's a pretty good motto for a person who wants to be a Christian, isn't it? I took that for my motto.

Opportunity, lost; Education, early youth

Gal. 6:10; Phil. 1:3; 4:10

If a farmer neglects to plant in the springtime, he can never recover the lost opportunity; no more can you, if you neglect yours. Youth is a seedtime, and if it is allowed to pass without good seed being sown weeds will spring up and choke the soil. It will take bitter toil to uproot them. An old minister said that when a good farmer sees a weed in his field he pulls it up. If it is taken early enough, the blank is soon filled in, and the crop waves over the whole field. But if allowed to run too late, the bald patch remains. It would have been better if the weed had never been allowed to get root.

Opportunity, nature of

1 Cor. 10:31; Gal. 6:10; Phil. 1:3; 4:10; 1 Thess. 1:5; 2:2

A sculptor once showed a visitor his studio. It was full of statues of gods. One was very curious. The face was concealed by being covered with hair, and there were wings on each foot. "What is his name?" said the visitor. "Opportunity," was the reply. "Why is his face hidden?" "Because men seldom know him when he comes to them." "Why has he wings on his feet?" "Because he is soon gone, and once gone can never be overtaken."

It becomes us, then, to make the most of the opportunities God has given us. It depends a good deal on ourselves what our future shall be. We can sow for a good harvest, or we can do like the Sioux Indians, who once, when the United States Commissioner of Indian Affairs sent them a supply of grain for sowing, ate it up. Men are constantly sacrificing their eternal future to the passing enjoyment of the present moment; they fail or neglect to recognize the dependence of the future upon the present.

1 Cor. 10:31; Gal. 6:10; Phil. 1:3; 4:10; 1 Thess. 1:5; 2:2

Do not neglect opportunities. Napoleon used to say: "There is a crisis in every battle—ten or fifteen minutes—on which the issue of the battle depends. To gain this is victory; to lose it is defeat."

Opposition to work

Rom. 13:2; 1 Tim 6:10; Titus 3:1; Heb. 12:3

No real work was ever done for God without opposition. If you think that you are going to have the approval of a godless world, and of cold Christians, as you launch out into the deep with your net, you are greatly mistaken. A man said to me some time ago, that when he was converted he commenced to do some work in connection with the church; he was greatly discouraged because some of the older Christians threw cold water on him, so he gave up the whole thing. I pity a man who cannot take a little cold water without being any the worse for it. Why, many of the Christians in old times had to go through the fire, and did not shrink from it. A little cold water never hurts anyone.

Matt. 11:12; 14:11; Mark 6:28

A man may go into a town and preach for ten years with all the eloquence of Demosthenes, and draw great crowds, and if there are no conversions the papers will applaud him, and there will be a great many fine things said about him. But let there be a few hundred conversions, and the opposition will grow as hot as hell can make it. It always has been, and always will be. The nearer a man lives to Christ, and the more truth he has, the more bitter and vile will be the things that are said against him by the enemies of God.

Did this world ever have such a preacher as John the Baptist, except the Master himself? See how bitter the opposition was, not only among bad people, but among the so-called good men of that time. His ministry was very short; but it was like a breath of Spring after a long dark winter's night. Then came Christ with his apostles, and they did a great work, and yet met opposition everywhere. Opposition can be a clear sign that God is at work.

Opposition to work; Enemies of righteousness

Job 2:2; Matt. 21:23; Rom. 8:38–39; 2 Cor. 4:4; Eph. 6:12

I want to call your attention to this fact, that there never has been anything good from the time God put Adam and Eve into Eden that didn't have enemies—bitter enemies. We must expect opposition. If a work has no enemies, God is not in it. Everything that has been good in this world has had its bitter enemies.

Organization, importance of

Exod. 18:21; 1 Cor. 11:34; 14:40; Titus 1:5

It should be understood that anyone who joins the church joins with the expectation of going to work, and something suitable to them must be given them to do.

Parables, teaching in; Illustrations, use of

Luke 15:11

We must imitate the mode of teaching of Jesus Christ. He taught in parables; and travelers say that there is hardly a natural object in Palestine that he did not make use of to illustrate some truth. He spoke so that even the little children could understand him. There isn't an unrepentant prodigal in this country that would not like to get the story of the prodigal son out of his mind, but he can't. Stories and object lessons help to fix truths in the mind. Often I have heard a speaker trying to explain some truth, and thought, "Oh, if he would only give us an illustration!" What is addressed to both the eye and ear makes more impression than what is addressed to the ear alone. Use the imagination. Weave in illustrations. Illustrations are to truths like windows that let in the light on them.

Pardon for sins

Exod. 34:9; Ruth 3:9; 4:14; Ps. 25:11; Rom. 3:24; Eph. 1:7

I remember, while in England, I was told of a man who was to be hung at 8 o'clock upon a certain morning. The black flag was waving from the prison in the heart of the town where he was incarcerated. A great many of the ministers in the churches had for their subject this condemned man. Everybody was talking about the execution, and the whole town was excited. The black flag raised upon the prison told them that a man was to be launched into eternity. Thousands were praying for him, a great many were weeping, for he was a man who had been very much liked by some. They had sent petitions to the Queen, but without any effect so far.

The poor captive heard the carpenters at work building the scaffold, and as they struck blow upon blow it seemed to be upon his very breast, for every nail driven in brought him nearer to his doom. Now the hour is approaching. The day preceding his execution passes into night, and darkness hangs over that prison. How dark it must have been in that cell that night! Next morning he knew he was to die upon the gallows. That night about midnight he heard the footfalls of the sheriff coming near his door. He knew the hour had not yet arrived, and he began to tremble. "Is he coming before my time to take me out and execute me?"

The door was unlocked, and the sheriff said to the condemned man, "I bring you good news. I bring you a pardon from the Queen." What do you think would be the feelings of that man? Wouldn't he rejoice? My friends, the black flag of death may be waving over you, and hell rejoicing that you will soon be there, but Christ comes with a pardon today by which your sins are blotted out; by which all your iniquities are taken away; by which you will become a child of God and be made meet for his kingdom. Is not this good news? If anyone here is living under sin, you are condemned, but you can receive Christ's pardon.

Pardon, joy of

Luke 15:24; 1 Cor. 1:30; Eph. 1:14

How much of mankind is deluded with the false idea that God is a hard Master and Satan is an easy one. I believe there are tens of thousands who would become Christians, within ten miles of here in the next twenty-four hours, if they believed that God is an easy Master and Satan a hard master. But men are under the power of the awful delusion that it is an easy thing to serve the god of this world and hard to serve the God of heaven.

People have the mistaken idea that if they become Christians it will make them gloomy. If I see a man dying for the want of bread, and I give him bread, is that making him gloomy? If I see a man dying of thirst, and give him a glass of clear, cold water, is that going to make him gloomy? The gospel is bread to the hungry, water to the thirsty, and clothes to the famishing.

For many years I've been trying to get a man out of prison. We tried on New Year's Day (Jan.1,1897) to get the President to grant our request and God gave us success. I can't tell you what delight came to me when I heard of the joy of that father and husband when he went back to the bosom of his family. Did it make that man gloomy to get a pardon? That's the gospel, a pardon for all sins, going out from under the service of Satan.

Parental correction

Prov. 13:24; 19:18; 22:15; 23:13; 29:17; Jer. 46:28; Heb. 12:7

I remember my little girl had a habit of getting up in the morning very cross. I don't know whether your children are like that. She used to get up in the morning speaking crossly, and made the family very uncomfortable. So I took her aside one morning and said to her, "Emma, if you go on that way, I shall have to correct you; I don't want to do it, but I will have

to." She looked at me for a few moments—I had never spoken to her that way before—and she went away. She behaved herself for a few weeks all right, but one morning she was as cross as ever, and when she came to me to be kissed before going to school, I wouldn't do it.

Off she went to her mother, and said, "Mamma, Papa refused to kiss me: I cannot go to school because he won't kiss me." Her mother came in, but she didn't say much. She knew the child had been doing wrong. The little one went out and as she was going downstairs, I heard her weeping, and it seemed to me as if that child was dearer to me than ever she had been before. I went to the window and saw her going down the street crying, and as I looked on her I couldn't suppress my tears.

That seemed to be the longest day I ever spent in Chicago. Before the closing of the school I was at home, and when she came in her first words were: "Papa, won't you forgive me?" and I kissed her and she went away singing. It was because I loved her that I corrected her. My friends, don't let Satan make you believe when you have any trouble, that God does not love you.

Parental influence

2 Kings 17:14; 2 Chron. 30:7; Ps. 78:57; Luke 6:23

A lady once told me she was in her pantry on one occasion, and she was surprised by the ringing of the doorbell. As she whirled round to see who it was, she broke a tumbler. Her little child was standing there, and she thought her mother was doing a very correct thing. The moment the lady left the pantry, the child commenced to break all the tumblers she could get hold of. You may laugh, but children are very good imitators. It is very often by imitation that they utter their first curse word, that they tell their first lie, and then they grow upon them, and when they try to quit the habit, it has grown so strong upon them that they cannot do it.

Parents, honor of; Christ and his parents; Commandment, fifth

Exod. 20:12; Prov. 1:8; Matt. 15:5; Mark 7:11; Luke 2:51

The one glimpse the Bible gives us of thirty out of the thirty-three years of Christ's life on earth shows that he did not come to destroy the fifth commandment. The secret of all those silent years is embodied in that verse in Luke's Gospel, "And he went down with them and came to Nazareth, and was subject to them." Did Christ not set an example of true family love and care when in the midst of the agonies of the cross he made provision for his mother? Did he not condemn the miserable evasions of this law by the Pharisees of his own day?

Parents, honor of; Commandment, fifth

Judg. 9:5; 2 Sam. 18:33

There was a very promising young man in my Sunday school in Chicago. His father was a confirmed drunkard, and his mother took in washing to educate her four children. This was her eldest son, and I thought that he was going to redeem the whole family. But one day a thing happened that made him go down in my estimation. The boy was in the high school, and was a very bright scholar. One day he stood with his mother at the cottage door—it was a poor house, but she could not pay for their schooling and feed and clothe her children and hire a very good house too out of her earnings. When they were talking a young man from the high school came up the street, and this boy walked away from his mother. Next day the young man said, "Who was that I saw you talking to yesterday?" "Oh, that was my washer woman." I said: "Poor fellow! He will never amount to anything."

That was a good many years ago. I have kept my eye on him. He has gone down, down, down, and now he is just a miserable wreck. Of course, he would go down! Ashamed of his mother that loved him and toiled for him, and bore so much hardship for him! I cannot tell you the contempt I had for that one act.

Prov. 20:20; 23:22; Eph. 6:1–3

Disobedience and disrespect for parents are often the first steps in the downward track. Many a criminal has testified that these are the points where he first went astray. I have lived over sixty years, and I have learned one thing if I have learned nothing else—that no man or woman who dishonors father or mother ever prospers, in the long run.

Prov. 30:17; Matt. 15:4; Col. 3:20; 2 Tim. 3:2

We are living in dark days on the issue of honoring parents. If Paul were alive today, could he have described the present state of affairs more truly (2 Tim. 3:1–3)? There are perhaps more men in this country that are breaking the hearts of their fathers and mothers and trampling on the law of God than in any other civilized country in the world. How many sons treat their parents with contempt and make light of their entreaties? A young man will have the kindest care from parents; they will watch over him and care for all his wants, and some bad companion will come in and sweep him away from them in a few weeks. How many young ladies have married against their parents' wishes and have gone off and made their own lives bitter! I never knew one case that did not turn out badly. They invariably bring ruin upon themselves unless they repent.

Matt. 15:6; Mark 7:11; Luke 2:51; Rom. 1:30

"Honor thy father and thy mother." That word honor means more than mere obedience—a child may obey through fear. It means love and affection, gratitude, respect. We are told that in the East the words "father" and "mother" include those who are "superiors in age, wisdom and in civil or religious station," so that when the Jews were taught to honor their father and mother it included all who were placed over them in these relations, as well as their parents. Isn't there a crying need for that same feeling today? The lawlessness of the present time is a natural consequence of the growing absence of a feeling of respect for those in authority.

Exod. 20:12; Prov. 1:8; Matt. 15:5–6; Mark 7:11; Luke 2:51

"Honor thy father and thy mother: that thy days may be long upon the land which the LORD thy God giveth thee." I believe that we must get back to the old truths. You may make light of it and laugh at it, but remember that God has given this commandment, and you cannot set it aside. If we get back to this law, we shall have power and blessing. I believe it to be literally true that our temporal condition depends on the way we act upon this commandment.

It would be easy to multiply texts from the Bible to prove this truth. Experience teaches the same thing. A good, loving son generally turns out better than an obstinate son. Obedience and respect at home prepare the way for obedience to the employer and are joined with other virtues that help toward a prosperous career, crowned with a ripe, honored old age. Disobedience and disrespect for parents are often the first steps in the downward track. Many a criminal has testified that this is the point where he first went astray. I have lived over sixty years, and have learned one thing if I have learned nothing else—that no man or woman who dishonors father or mother ever truly prospers. He may gain material wealth but his hard heart will ultimately betray him and bring him down.

Exod. 20:12; Prov. 1:8; Matt. 15:5–6; Mark 7:11; Luke 2:51

I have read of a custom in China, which would do us credit in America. On every New Year's morning each man and boy, from the emperor to the lowest peasant, is said to pay a visit to his mother, carrying her a present varying in value according to his station in life. He thanks her for all she has done for him and asks a continuance of her favor another year. Abraham Lincoln used to say: "All I have I owe to my angel mother."

Gen. 46:29; 47:12

I would rather die a hundred deaths than have my children grow up to treat me with scorn and contempt. I would rather have them honor me a thousand times over than have the world honor me. I would rather have their esteem and favor than the esteem of the whole world. And any man who seeks the honor and esteem of the world, and doesn't treat his parents right, is sure to be disappointed. Young person, if your parents are still living, treat them kindly. Do all you can to make their declining years sweet and happy. Bear in mind that this is the only commandment that you may not always be able to obey. What bitter feelings you will have when the opportunity has gone by if you fail to show them the respect and love that is their due!

Gen. 46:29; 47:12; Judg. 9:5; 2 Sam. 18:33

Which would you rather be—a Joseph or an Absalom? Joseph wasn't satisfied until he had brought his old father down into Egypt. He was the great man in Egypt, next to Pharaoh; he was arrayed in the finest garments; he had Pharaoh's ring on his hand, and a gold chain about his neck. Yet when he heard his father Jacob was coming, he hurried out to meet him. He wasn't ashamed of the old man with his shepherd's clothes. What a contrast we see in Absalom. That young man broke his father's heart by his rebellion and the Jews are said to throw a stone at Absalom's pillar to the present day, whenever they pass it, as a token of their horror of Absalom's unnatural conduct.

Parents, treatment of

Luke 18:20; Eph. 6:2

Tell me how you treat your parents, and I will tell you how your children will treat you. A man was making preparations to send his old father to the poorhouse, when his little child came up and said, "Papa, when you are old shall I have to take you to the poorhouse?"

Do you never write home to your parents? They clothed you and educated you, and now do you spend your nights in gambling? You say to your godless companions that your father crammed religion down your throat when you were a boy. I have a great contempt for a man who says that of his father or mother.

They may have made a mistake; but it was of the head, not of the heart. If a telegram was sent to them that you were down with smallpox, they would take the first train to come to you. They would willingly take the disease into their own bodies and die for you. If you scoff and sneer at your father and mother you will have a hard harvest; you will reap in agony. It is only a question of time. There is a saying—

The mills of God grind slowly,
But they grind exceeding small.
With patience He stands waiting,
With exactness grinds He all.

Peace, benediction; Tranquility, source of

Num. 6:23; Ps. 119:165; Isa. 44:8; Matt. 14:27; Mark 4:39; 6:50; John 6:20

I think the priestly blessing God gave to Aaron in Numbers 6:22–27 are about the sweetest verses to be found in the Old Testament. I marked them years ago in my Bible, and many times I have turned to this chapter and read them. They remind us of the loving words of Jesus to his troubled disciples, "It is I; be not afraid." The Jewish salutation used to be, as a man went into a house, "Peace be upon this house," and as he left the house the host would say, "Go in peace." God is our only reliable source of peace.

Peace, enemies of

Esther 10:3; Ps. 119:165; Prov. 16:7

It has been said that peace has five enemies: Envy, avarice, ambition, anger and pride. But all sin disturbs our peace. If I turn from sin, however, and try to please God, he promises that he will make even my enemies to be at peace with me.

Peace, gift of Christ

John 14:27; 16:33; 20:21; Rom. 5:1; 15:13; 1 Cor. 1:3; Eph. 2:14; Phil. 4:7; Col. 1:20

Did you ever think that when Christ was dying on the cross, he made a will? Perhaps you have thought that no one ever remembered you in a will. If you are in the kingdom, Christ remembered you in his. He willed his body to Joseph of Arimathea, he willed his mother to John, the son of Zebedee, and he willed his Spirit back to his Father. But to his disciples he said, "My peace, I leave that with you; that is my legacy. My joy, I give that to you." "My joy," think of it. "My peace"—not our peace, but his peace!

They say a man can't make a will now that lawyers can't break. I will challenge them to break Christ's will; let them try it. No judge or jury can set that aside. Christ rose to execute his own will. If he had left us a lot of gold, thieves would have stolen it in the first century; but he left his peace and his joy for every true believer, and no power on earth can take it from him who trusts.

207

John 14:27; 16:33; 20:21; Rom. 5:1; 15:13; 1 Cor. 1:3; Eph. 2:14; Phil. 4:7; Col. 1:20

A great many people are trying to make their peace with God, but that has already been done. God has not left it for us to do; all that we have to do is to enter into it, to accept it. It is a condition, and instead of our trying to make peace and to work for peace, we need to cease all that, and simply enter into the peace that has been purchased for us.

Peace, marred by sin; Wickedness, fruit of

Pss. 72:3; 85:10; Isa. 32:17; 57:20; Rom. 14:17; James 3:18

The only thing that can keep us from peace is sin. God turns the way of the wicked upside down. There is no peace for the wicked, says my God. They are like the troubled sea that cannot rest, casting up filth and mire all the while; but peace with God by faith in Jesus Christ—peace through the knowledge of forgiven sin— is like a rock; the waters go dashing and surging past, but it abides.

Peace, source of

Isa. 26:3–4; 27:5; 57:19; Luke 14:32; Rom. 5:1; Eph. 2:17; Col. 1:20

There is little comfort in looking at ourselves. That is the way to be miserable. Love must have an object outside of itself. He who loves himself only cannot be happy. True satisfaction is found, not in thinking what I am to the Lord, but what the Lord is to me. I like that word "perfect." That is the kind of peace the world can't give, and that it can't disturb. When you go to the communion table, don't think about your unworthiness. None of us are worthy. Think of the infinite worthiness of Christ. There is no peace until we forget ourselves and look to him. We cannot make peace with our own strength. A little child will go to sleep when clasping its mother's or father's hand, thinking "I feel safe because you are so strong." And so feels the child of God. May he help us to lay hold of his strength.

Peculiar people

Exod. 19:5; Deut. 14:2; 26:18; Titus 2:14; 1 Peter 2:9

Now I think you know that we don't like to be considered peculiar. We are so afraid of it, that we want to be like the world, and just mingle with the world so that people won't consider us peculiar. Very often we hear people say, "Yes, she is a very good woman but she is very peculiar; yes, he is a very good man—oh, yes, but he's very peculiar." I tell you I'd be willing to make a journey around the world to find one church full of peculiar people. Why, that church would stir the world. The very thing we consider peculiar is the thing we lack today.

I believe Elijah was the most peculiar man in his day, but he was better than those thousands who followed Baal; he held the keys of heaven and could stand fearlessly before Ahab because God was with him. Enoch was a peculiar man in his day, but of course he was different from other people; and undoubtedly Daniel was the most peculiar man Babylon ever had. Why, if we had only just a few peculiar people in our churches we should have a wonderful result.

Perfectionism, danger of; Progress, importance of

Matt. 6:34; Acts 14:22; 1 Thess. 3:3–4; Heb. 13:5

A good many people are afraid of doing anything out of the regular lines—of doing anything out of order. Now, you will find perfect order in a cemetery. You will find perfect order where there is death. Where there is life you will find something out of order.

Perseverance, basis of

Ruth 1:18; Pss. 55:22; 119:11; Luke 2:19; 1 Cor. 15:58; 2 Peter 1:4; 3:4

Now I am no prophet, nor the son of a prophet, but one thing I can predict; that every one of our new converts that goes to studying his Bible, and loves this book above every other book, is sure to hold out. The world will have no charm for him; he will get the world under his feet, because in this book he will find something better than the world can give him.

Perseverance, example of

1 Cor. 15:58; Gal. 6:9; 2 Thess. 3:13

Paul says, "Let us not be weary in well doing; in due season we shall reap if we faint not." In a chat with an interviewer Thomas Edison quite unconsciously preached a most powerful sermon on perseverance and patience. He described his repeated efforts to make the phonograph reproduce the aspirated sound and added, "From eighteen to twenty hours a day for the last seven months I have worked on this single word 'specia.' I said into the phonograph, 'specia, specia, specia,' but the instrument responded, 'pecia, pecia, pecia.' It was enough to drive one mad! But I held firm, and I have succeeded."

Perseverance, example of; Optimism, example of

Phil. 2:3; Col. 2:5, 7; 2 Thess. 1:3; Heb. 3:14

A child once said to his mother, "Mamma, you never speak ill of anyone. You would speak well of Satan." "Well," said the mother, "you might imitate his perseverance."

Perseverance, importance of; Persistence, importance of

Ruth 1:18; Pss. 55:22; 119:11; Luke 2:19; 1 Cor. 15:58; 2 Peter 1:4; 3:4

Spurgeon used to call perseverance "Stick-to-it-ive-ness." That's what we need. If we don't succeed today, we will go at it all the stronger tomorrow. If we don't succeed on Sunday, we'll try again on Monday; if we don't get it in February, we will go at it in March and if we fail in March, we will try it in April, and we will not let up all summer. There's no calendar in heaven. The church should not stop work in summer. Saloons and all the haunts of vice are wide open every day and every night in the week, and while we are sleeping Satan is doing his work.

Persistence, example of

Luke 19:7; 20:35; Acts 5:41; 1 Thess. 1:3

As I was preparing to leave London the last time I was there, I called on a celebrated physician, who told me my heart was weakening and that I had to let up on my work, that I had to be more careful of myself; and I was going home with the thought that I would not work quite so hard. I was on that ill-fated steamer, the *Spree*, when the announcement came that the vessel was sinking and that there was no hope. The stern had sunk thirty feet, and we were there forty-eight hours in that helpless condition. No one on earth knew what I passed through during those hours, as I thought that my work was finished, that I would never again have the privilege of preaching the gospel of the Son of God.

And on that dark night, the first night of the accident, I made a vow that if God would spare my life and bring me back to America I would come back to Chicago and at this World's Fair preach the gospel with all the power that he would give me; and God has enabled me to keep that vow during the past five months. It seems as if I went to the very gates of heaven during those forty-eight hours on the sinking ship, and God permitted me to come back and preach Christ a little longer.

Personal holiness, power of; Witness of a pure life

2 Cor. 3:2; 1 Thess. 1:7–8; Rev. 22:11

I remember reading of a blind man who was found sitting at the corner of a street in a great city with a lantern beside him. Someone went up to him and asked what he had the lantern there for, seeing that he was blind, and the light was the same to him as the darkness. The blind man replied, "I have it so that no one may stumble over me."

Where one man reads the Bible, a hundred read you and me. That is what Paul meant when he said we were to be living epistles of Christ, known and read of all men. I would not give much for all that can be done by sermons, if we do not preach Christ by our lives. If we do not commend the gospel to people by our holy walk and conversation, we shall not win them to Christ.

Power, inner

Isa. 40:29; John 15:4; Acts 1:8; 2 Cor. 3:5; Eph. 3:16; Phil. 4:13

The hands on the clock move because they can't help it. The power within constrains them.

Praise for health

Pss. 22:26; 42:5; 71:6; 74:21; 115:17–18

There was a poor afflicted man living in Chicago, and I never came out of his house without praising God. He was deaf, dumb, blind, and had lockjaw. He had a hole between his teeth, and all the food he took was put through that hole. My friend, do you ever thank God for your senses? Do you ever thank God for your eyes, by which you can read the Bible? Think of the millions of people in this world who haven't any sight at all. Hundreds of thousands of them never saw the mother who gave them birth; never saw their own offspring; never saw nature in all its glory; never saw the beautiful sun and the stars. Do you ever praise God for the ears by which you can hear the voice of man, by which you hear the gospel preached, by which you hear the songs of God's praise? Do you ever praise God for your reason?

Praise, heaven's occupation

Pss. 116:19; 118:19; 137:2; Rev. 5:13; 19:5

Praise is an occupation of heaven, and I pity the man who does not learn how to praise God before he goes there. A selfish man can't praise God. He praises only himself. Neither can an envious man, an ambitious man, a lazy man, an ungrateful man or a backslider. We read in the 137th Psalm that the Jews, when in captivity, hung their harps upon the willows. They could not praise God then. The prodigal son did not feel much like singing when he was in the fields feeding swine.

Praise, importance of

Ps. 57:9; Isa. 61:11; Rom. 15:11; 1 Cor. 4:5

There was a little boy converted and he was full of praise. When God converts boy or man his heart is full of joy—he can't help praising. His father was a professed Christian. The boy wondered why he didn't talk about Christ, and didn't go down to the special meetings. One day, as the father was reading the papers, the boy came to him and put his hand on his shoulder and said, "Why don't you praise God? Why don't you sing about Christ? Why don't you go down to these meetings that are being held?" The father opened his eyes, and looked at him and said, gruffly, "I am not carried away with any of these doctrines. I am established."

A few days after they were getting out a load of wood. They put it on the cart. The father and the boy got on top of the load, and tried to get the horse to go. They used the whip, but the horse wouldn't move. They got off and tried to roll the wagon along, but they could move neither the wagon nor the horse. "I wonder what's the matter?" said the father. "He's established," replied the boy. You may laugh at that, but this is the way with a good many Christians.

Ps. 74:21; Jer. 20:13

I have found people who were poor in this world's goods, in bad health, and yet continually praising God. I can take you to a poor, burdened one who has not been off her bed for ten years, and yet she praises him more than hundreds of thousands of Christians. Her chamber seems to be just the anteroom of heaven. It seems as if that woman had just all the secrets of heaven. Her soul is full of the love of God, full of gladness, and she is poor. Like Elijah at the brook of Cherith, she is fed by the Almighty; God provides for all her wants.

Any person that knows God can trust him and praise him. He knows that the word of God is true, and he knows that God will care for him. God cares for the lilies of the field; without his knowledge not a sparrow can fall to the ground. He knows every hair of our heads; any person that knows this can rejoice. Is there anyone here, who, although poor, can find no reason to praise God? Some of those Christians who are so poor, but who have the love of God, would not give up their place for that of princes.

Praise, importance of; Thanksgiving, value of

Dan. 2:23

We don't thank and praise God half enough. That is one reason why so many of our churches are so dull and gloomy. When churches get into a backslidden state, they hire singers to stand away up in some organ loft and praise God for them. How can we expect God to give us further blessings if we don't thank him for what he has given us? There ought to be more of thanksgiving in our prayers, and there ought to be more of thanksgiving from the heart in our singing. One of the best ways to wake a church up and start a revival is to hold a praise meeting.

Praise in church; Praise, power of

2 Cor. 8:18; Phil. 1:11; Heb. 2:12; 13:15; 1 Peter 4:11

If we have a praise church we will have people converted. I don't care where it is, what part of the world it's in, if we have a praise church we'll have successful Christianity.

Praise, naturalness of

Pss. 33:1; 146:1; 147:1; Rev. 19:6

The first impulse of a newborn Christian is to praise God; and the last utterance of a dying saint is praise. The spirit of true piety is praise. The nearer we are to God, the more we will feel like praising him. And our heavenly Father loves praise, just as we love to hear our children tell how much they love us. Praise is speaking well of God. A living church is a praising church. Praise is paying rent to God. Read the 146th Psalm; how full of praise it is.

Pray, too busy to; Priorities of life; Values, primary

Dan. 6:10

There is many a businessman today who will tell you he has no time to pray: his business is so pressing that he cannot call his family around him, and ask God to bless them. He is so busy that he cannot ask God to keep him and them from the temptations of every day. "Business is so pressing." I am reminded of the words of an old Methodist minister, "If you have so much business to attend to that you have no time to pray, depend upon it you

211

have more business on hand than God ever intended you should have."

But look at Daniel. He had the whole, or nearly the whole, of the king's business to attend to. He was Prime Minister, Secretary of State, and Secretary of the Treasury, all in one. He had to attend to all his own work, and to give an eye to the work of lots of other men. And yet he found time to pray: not just now and then, nor once in a while, not just when he happened to have a few moments to spare, but "three times a day."

Prayer, answer to

Matt. 26:42; Mark 14:36; Luke 22:42; John 12:27

My little boy, when he was eight years old, wanted a pony. He got his answer. It was "No." Was his prayer answered? Of course it was. I got him a goat. A pony might have kicked his head off. A goat was a good deal better for a boy eight years old than a pony. It is a foolish idea to think that God has got to do everything you ask. You will notice that the people whose prayers are recorded in the Bible didn't always have their prayers answered just as they wanted them to be, but often in some other way. In all true prayer you will say, "Not my will, but Thine, be done." All true prayer will be answered if you have made it in that spirit.

John 15:16; 16:23

I was on the disabled ocean steamer *Spree* in 1892, when for forty-eight hours it seemed certain that we would go down. After great personal struggle, I had prepared to meet my destiny in peace and was asleep. About 2:15 that morning my son, who was with me on the voyage, came to my stateroom and awakened me, telling me to come on deck. There he pointed out in the dim distance a tiny light that we could occasionally catch a glimpse of as it shone over the waves as our ship rolled heavily from side to side.

"It is our star of Bethlehem," I said, "and our prayers are answered." Before daylight the *Huron*, whose masthead light it was, had reached us, and the waves were stilled and the winds were hushed as by divine command, while we were drawn out of the direst peril to a safe haven. God answered our prayer. He sent us a rescuing ship, and he calmed the ocean. It was a grand test of prayer.

Many of you are shipwrecked in your life. There is a redeemer, a rescuer who will respond to your distress call. Lift your heart in earnest prayer right now.

James 4:3

I want to have my children on such terms with me that they will come to know that I love them too well to give them everything they ask for instantly on their request. One of my boys went through all my sermons to turn what I had said about answering prayer into an argument that he ought to have a bicycle. Now faith believes that if God is to answer your prayers for your highest, best interests, he is going to answer them in his own way according to his own timetable and not yours. Keep praying in faith and have patience to wait on God.

Prayer, answered

John 15:16; 16:23

In the city of Philadelphia there was a mother that had two sons. They were just going as fast as they could to ruin. They were breaking her heart, and she went into a prayer meeting and got up and presented them for prayer. They had been on a drunken spree and she knew that their end would be a drunkard's grave, and she went among these Christians and said, "Won't you just cry to God for my two boys?" That afternoon several godly women went to her home to join in praying for those two boys.

The next morning the boys had made an appointment to meet each other on the corner of Market and Thirteenth Streets—though not that they knew anything about our meeting or the women praying—and while one of them was there at the corner, waiting for his brother to come, he followed the people who were flooding into the building for our meeting, and the Spirit of the Lord met him, and he was convicted and found his way to Christ.

After his brother came he found the place too crowded to enter, so he too went curiously into another meeting and found Christ, and went home happy; and when he got home he told his mother what the Lord had done for him, and the second son came with the same tidings. I heard one of them get up afterwards to tell his experience in the new converts' meeting, and he had no sooner told the story than the other got up and said, "I am that brother, and there is not a happier home in Philadelphia than we have got."

Prayer, asking

Matt. 7:7; Luke 11:9

Importunity has three names—asking, seeking, and knocking—and if the blessing doesn't come by asking, we are to seek and find out the reason; and if it doesn't come by seeking, we are to knock and knock and knock till the door is opened. The door may seem to be made of granite, and no one hears us inside, but we have the promise that if we keep knocking it will be opened.

I think a great many of us can learn lessons from children. I have. You have sometimes been in the house when the children were playing, rolling a hoop around the room, or playing with a ball or some toy, and they would cry out: "Mamma, I am thirsty. I want some water"; but they go on rolling their hoop, and their mother thinks they are not very thirsty, and doesn't get them any water. In a little while they say: "Mamma, I am hungry; I want something to eat." But the child goes on playing with its hoop, and the mother does not trouble herself.

By and by they repeat their request, with the same result; but at last they leave everything—they are done asking and going to seek and to find out why their mother does not give them the bread or water. There are a great many people who ask and never wait for an answer. In fact, they would be greatly surprised if the answer came. You often hear of people who have been praying fifteen or twenty years, and when the answer came they would say, "Isn't that a wonderful thing?" When we pray let us ask and expect that we are going to get that for which we asked.

Prayer, asking; Provision, God's abundant

John 16:24

It is said that Alexander the Great had a favorite general to whom he had given permission to draw upon the royal treasury for any amount. On one occasion this general had made a draft for such an enormous sum that the treasurer refused to honor it until he consulted the emperor. So he went into his presence and told him what the general had done. "Did you not honor the draft?" said the emperor. "No; I refused until I had seen your majesty, because the amount was so great." The emperor was indignant. His treasurer said that he was afraid of offending him if he had paid the amount. "Do you not know," replied the emperor, "that he honors me and my kingdom by making a large draft?" Whether the story be authentic or not, it is true that we honor God when we ask for great things.

Prayer, attitude in

Dan. 9:4

I believe that we get a good many blessings just by asking; others we do not get, because there may be something in our lives that needs to be brought to light. When Daniel began to pray in Babylon for the deliverance of his people, he sought to find out what the trouble was, and why God had turned away his face from them. So there may be something in our lives that is keeping back the blessing; if there is, we need to find it and deal with it. Someone, speaking on this subject, has said, "We are to ask with a beggar's humility, to seek with a servant's carefulness, and to knock with the confidence of a friend."

Prayer, conditions for answers

Ps. 37:7; John 15:16; 16:23

Before I was converted I used to ask God to give me $100,000, and because he didn't do it, I thought that he didn't keep his promise to answer prayer. But I didn't abide in him. Now he answers all my prayers, for I say: "Thy will be done," and so I know that if he doesn't give me just what I ask for, he gives me just what I ought to have. People curse God because they do not prosper. But he has never said that he would bless the disobedient and rebellious. If your child refuses to obey you, do you give it presents or do you punish it? If I do not try to please God, I cannot claim any of his promises.

Prayer, delayed answers; Petition, persistence in

Neh. 1:4; 1 Thess. 5:17

It was in November or December when the men of Judah arrived at Shushan to tell Nehemiah of the plight of Jerusalem, and Nehemiah prayed on until March or April before he spoke to the king. If a blessing doesn't come tonight, pray harder tomorrow, and if it doesn't come tomorrow, pray harder, and even then, if it doesn't come, keep right on, and you will not be disappointed. God in heaven will hear your prayers, and will answer them. He has never failed, if a person has been honest in petitions and honest in confessions. Let your faith beget patience. "God is never in a hurry," said St. Augustine, "because he has all eternity to work."

Prayer, earnestness in

Matt. 7:7; Luke 11:9

"Teacher," said a bright, earnest-faced boy, "why is it that so many prayers are unanswered? I do not understand. The Bible says, 'Ask, and ye shall receive; seek, and ye shall find; knock, and it shall be opened unto you'; but it seems to me a great many knock and are not admitted." "Did you never sit by your fireplace," said the teacher, "on some dark evening, and hear a loud knocking at the door? Going to answer the knock, have you not sometimes looked out into the darkness, seeing nothing, but hearing the pattering feet of some mischievous boy, who knocked but did not wish to enter, and therefore ran away? It is often so with us. We ask for blessings, but do not really expect them; we knock, but do not mean to enter; we fear that Jesus will not hear us, will not fulfill his promises, will not admit us; and so we go away."

"Ah, I see," said the earnest-faced boy, his eyes shining with the new light dawning in his soul, "Jesus can't be expected to answer runaway knocks. He has never promised it. I mean to keep knocking, knocking, until he can't help opening the door."

Prayer, fervency

Matt. 7:7; Luke 11:9; James 5:16

Bishop Hall, in a well-known extract, thus puts the point of earnestness in its relation to the prayer of faith. "An arrow, if it be drawn up but a little way in the bow, goes not far; but, if it be pulled up to the head, flies swiftly and pierces deeply. Thus prayer, if it be only dribbled forth from careless lips, falls at our feet. It is the strength of strong desire which sends it to heaven, and makes it pierce the clouds. It is not the arithmetic of our prayers, how many they are; nor the rhetoric of our prayers, how eloquent they be; nor the geometry of our prayers, how long they be; nor the music of our prayers, how sweet our voice may be; nor the logic of our prayers, how argumentative they may be; nor the method of our prayers, how orderly they may be; nor even the divinity of our prayers, how good the doctrine may be;—which God cares for. He looks not for the callused knees which James is said to have had through the persistence of prayer. Fervency of spirit is that which availeth much."

Matt. 7:7; Luke 11:9; James 5:16

Archbishop Leighton says: "It is not the gilded paper and good writing of a petition that prevails with a king, but the moving sense of it. And to that greater King who discerns the heart, heart-sense is the sense of all, and that which he only regards. He listens to hear what that speaks, and takes all as nothing where that is silent. All other excellence in prayer is but the outside and fashion of it. This is the life of it."

Prayer, focus in; Giving to the poor

Mark 11:24

One woman said to me, "I always think of a new dress, or something, whenever I kneel down to pray." You laugh, but how many of you are guilty of just such sin and folly? If you fashionable people would get along with fewer dresses, and spend some of your

pocket money relieving the poor, you would show a great deal more wisdom than in spending your lives like so many butterflies.

Prayer for ministers

Exod. 17:11–12

When Joshua was down there with his mighty army fighting Amalek, Moses was praying while Aaron and Hur held up his hands. What we want is men like Aaron and Hur to hold up the minister's hands. You hear men talking against their ministers. When a man comes to me talking about his minister, I say, "How many times a day do you pray for your minister?" They don't pray for the ministers. They have not got the love of God for their ministers. One man with his heart red-hot with his Savior's love will work up cold ministers. The sparks will just fly out and get people in this circle and that circle, and the whole church will be in a blaze.

Prayer for unbelieving husband

James 1:6; 5:16–18

In one of the towns in England there is a beautiful little chapel, and a very touching story is told in connection with it. It was built by an unbeliever who had a praying wife, but he would not listen to her. He would not allow her pastor even to take dinner with them; would not look at the Bible; would not allow religion even to be talked of. She made up her mind, seeing she could not influence him by her voice, that every day she would pray to God at twelve o'clock noon for his salvation. She said nothing to him, but every day at that hour she told the Lord about her husband. At the end of twelve months there was no change in him.

But she did not give up. Six months more went past. Her faith began to waver, and she said, "Will I have to give him up at last? Perhaps when I am dead God will answer my prayers." When she had got to that point, it seemed just as if God had got her where he wanted her. The man came home to lunch one day. His wife was in the dining room waiting for him, but he didn't come in. She waited some time, and finally looked for him all through the house. At last she thought of going into the little room where she had prayed so often. There he was, praying at the same bed with agony, where she had prayed for so many months, asking forgiveness for his sins. And this is a lesson to you wives who have unbelieving husbands. The Lord saw that woman's faith and answered her prayers.

Prayer, importance of

Luke 11:1

Jesus' disciples came to him, and said, "Lord, teach us to pray." It is not recorded that Jesus taught them how to preach. I have often said that I would rather know how to pray like Daniel than to preach like Gabriel. If you get love into your soul, so that the grace of God may come down in answer to prayer, there will be no trouble about reaching the people. It is not by eloquent sermons that perishing souls are going to be reached; we need the power of God in order that the blessing may come down.

Prayer, importunity in

Luke 11:8

There is a story told of a governor in New Jersey, that he was sought by an Irish woman to release her husband who was to be hung. She came day after day, until he was so troubled that he gave orders not to let her in his office; he could not be troubled anymore with her. But one day he went into his office, and she had got in there by some strategy, and she brought her ten children with her. The ten children fell on their knees and cried: "Governor, pardon our father!" The mother said, "For the sake of these ten children, spare the life of my husband." It touched his heart, and the life of her husband was spared. Let us have faith to pray. Oh, may God increase our faith!

Prayer in crisis

Job 27:9; Ps. 107:19, 28

I was on the steamship *Spree*, on that terrible night when no stars could be seen, and the word came that we were going to sink. I tell you the Jews, Catholics, Protestants, and the Gentiles, all, prayed there; skeptics, infidels, everyone. I had had a discussion with a man the night before and he said, "Prayer is a good exercise for the man who makes it." But, he added, "The Lord really doesn't hear it. It is just a healthy exercise, and teaches us submission." But when he thought we were going down, there was a different feeling, and he too prayed. Some of you might have discussed prayer; but if you had been there on the *Spree*, you would have stopped discussing and gone to praying. Thank God we were rescued!

Prayer, influence of; Service, willingness for

Neh. 1:6

When Nehemiah began to pray I have no idea that he thought he himself was to be the instrument in God's hand of building the walls of Jerusalem. But when a man gets into sympathy and harmony with God, then God prepares him for the work he has for him. No doubt he thought the Persian king might send one of his great warriors and accomplish the work with a great army of men; but after he had been praying for months, it may be, the thought flashed into his mind, "Why shouldn't I go to Jerusalem myself and build those walls?" Prayer for the work will soon arouse your own sympathy and effort.

Prayer, influence of unconfessed sin

Prov. 28:9; Isa. 1:15; James 5:16

It may shock some of us to think that our prayers are an abomination to God, yet if any are living in known sin, this is what God's Word says about them. If we are not willing to turn from sin and walk in obedience to Christ, we have no right to expect that he will answer our prayers. Unconfessed sin is unforgiven sin, and unforgiven sin is the darkest, foulest thing on this sin-cursed earth. You cannot find a case in the Bible where a man has been honest in dealing with sin, but God has been honest with him and blessed him. The prayer of the humble and the contrite heart is a delight to God. There is no sound that goes up from this sin-cursed earth so sweet to his ear as the prayer of the man who is walking uprightly.

Prayer, intensity in

Pss. 22:1; 61:1; 130:1; Eph. 6:18; Heb. 5:7

Dr. Austin Phelps, in his "Still Hour," says, "The prospect of gaining an object will always affect the expression of intense desire. I come to my devotions this morning on an errand of real life. This is no romance, and no farce. I do not come here to go through a form of words. I have an object to gain; I have an end to accomplish. This is a business in which I am about to engage. An astronomer does not turn his telescope to the skies with a more reasonable hope of penetrating those distant heavens, than I have of reaching the mind of God by lifting up my heart at the throne of grace. This is the privilege of my calling of God in Christ Jesus. Even my faltering voice is now to be heard in heaven; and it is to release a new power there, the results of which only God can know, and only eternity can reveal."

Ps. 88:1; Luke 18:1; 22:44; 2 Cor. 12:8

Jeremy Taylor says, "Lack of desire is a great enemy to the success of a good man's prayer. It must be an intent, zealous, busy, operative prayer; for consider what a huge indecency it is that a man should speak to God for a thing that he values not! Our prayers upbraid our spirits when we beg tamely for those things for which we ought to die, which are more precious than imperial scepters, richer than the spoils of the sea, or the treasures of far off lands."

Prayer, mother's

1 Sam. 1:11; Acts 1:14

I remember a man leaping to his feet in one of our meetings and shouting, "Oh, mother, I am coming!" The mother had been fruitless in her endeavors to bring her son to Christ while she was on earth. The influence of her prayers had touched his heart and he decided for Christ.

Prayer, mother's influence

Luke 2:51; John 2:5; 2 Tim. 1:5

A young man went home from one of our meetings some time ago. He had been converted. He had previously been a dissipated young man. His mother had made it a rule, she told me, that she would not retire till he came home. That was her rule, she said. "I never went to bed until my boy was at home. I just prayed for him. If he did not come home till five o'clock in the morning, I sat up. When he was out all night, I got no sleep; but when he came home I always met him with a kiss. I threw my arms around his neck. I treated him just as if he was kind, attentive and good. Sometimes he would be out all night. Those nights I would not go to bed. He knew that I did not.

"One night he came home. I looked to see if he was under the influence of liquor. He came up to me, and he said, 'Mother,

I have been converted.' And then I fell on his neck and embraced him, and wept over him tears of joy.

"Why," said she, "Mr. Moody, you don't know what joy it gave me. I can't tell you. You don't know what a load it took off my heart. You don't know how I praised God that my prayers had been answered."

Prayer, of Christ

Matt. 26:42; Mark 1:35; 14:35; Luke 5:16; 22:41

Christ's prayer on the cross was a short one, "Father, forgive them for they know not what they do." I believe that prayer was answered. You find that right there in front of the cross, a Roman centurion was converted. It was probably in answer to the Savior's prayer. The conversion of the thief, I believe, was in answer to that prayer of our blessed Lord. Saul of Tarsus may have heard it, and the words may have followed him as he traveled to Damascus; so that when the Lord spoke to him on the way, he may have recognized the voice. One thing we do know; that on the day of Pentecost some of the enemies of the Lord were converted. Surely that was in answer to the prayer, "Father, forgive them!"

Prayer, partnership with God

John 11:39

God chooses to do his work through people. Jesus did not himself roll away the stone from Lazarus' grave; he said to his disciples surrounding him, and to his disciples in all times, "You take away the stone." Now I find a great many men and a great many wives, and a great many Christians, too, who ask God to roll away some stone in their lives, and because he does not answer their prayer, they throw the blame on God. Why, the blame is not his; it is theirs. God works in partnership. When he is asked to do a thing he first wants to see an active disposition in the asker to help get the blessing.

This failure to second God's work for us comes from unbelief. Such a half-hearted man does not believe God will grant his prayer, and so fails to carry out his own part of the program. The mother that prays for the reclaiming of a drunken son or a dissolute husband must faithfully do her part to this end, and then must have full belief that God will do the rest.

Prayer, petitions

Matt. 21:22; John 16:24

There was a man in England who got up in a meeting, and made one of those wonderful prayers, but there was no petition in it. And there was a poor, godly saint who could not stand it any longer, and she cried out, "Ask God for something." Now, that is just it. "Ask, and ye shall receive; knock, and it shall be opened unto you." That is a promise; now let's lay hold of it.

Pss. 55:17; 65:2; Luke 11:5; 18:1, 5

Some people think God does not like to be troubled with our constant coming and asking. The only way to trouble God is not to come at all. He encourages us to come to him repeatedly, and press our claims.

Prayer, power of

2 Kings 19:19; 20:1–2; Acts 9:40

At the close of one of the afternoon meetings we had in the Berkeley Street Church a few weeks ago, a little child brought me a note. I put it in my pocket and read it when I got home. It was this, "Won't you pray that my mother may come home?" On inquiry I found that the child was a little waif, her father was dead, and that her mother had deserted her and gone out to San Francisco and had been gone more than a year. Well, I must confess it staggered me to be asked to pray that her mother might come back.

But another note was handed to me a few days later, "You will remember the little child who asked prayers for her mother to return home, having been absent a year? This mother has returned, and was at the meeting with her little child on Friday night." The little child now wants us to pray that her dear mother may be converted.

Matt. 7:7; Luke 11:9; James 1:5

Prayer holds a high place among the exercises of a spiritual life. All God's people have been praying people. Look, for instance, at Baxter. He stained his study walls with praying breath; and after he was anointed with the unction of the Holy Ghost, sent a river of living water over Kidderminster, and brought hundreds to Christ. Luther and his companions were men of such mighty pleading with God, that they broke the spell of ages, and laid nations subdued at the foot of the Cross.

John Knox grasped all Scotland in his strong arms of faith; his prayers terrified tyrants. Whitefield, after much holy, faithful closet-pleading, went to the Devil's fair, and took more than a thousand souls out of the paw of the lion in one day. See a praying Wesley turn more than ten thousand souls to the Lord! Look at the praying Finney, whose prayers, faith, sermons, and writings have shaken this whole country, and sent a wave of blessing through the churches on both sides of the sea.

Rom. 8:34; Heb. 4:15; 7:25

Bishop Ryle has said of Christ's intercession as the ground and sureness of our faith, "The banknote without a signature at the bottom is nothing but a worthless piece of paper. The stroke of a pen confers on it all its value. The prayer of a poor child of Adam is a feeble thing in itself, but once endorsed by the hand of the Lord Jesus, it availeth much. There was an officer in the city of Rome who was appointed to have his doors always open, in order to receive any Roman citizen who applied to him for help. Just so the ear of the Lord Jesus is ever open to the cry of all who want mercy and grace. It is his office to help them. Their prayer is his delight."

Prayer, power of; Conversion of saloonkeeper

Matt. 8:2;15:25; Mark 1:40; Luke 5:12

Almost the last family that was converted before we finished the Chicago campaign was a saloon keeper that I had held up in prayer twelve long years. We were out riding, and just making a few calls on New Year's day and I said, "Let us go in and see my friend," mentioning a man that had kept a bar for a long time. I went in and sat with him, and at last I said, "Shouldn't we have prayer?" and he said he should have no objection. Then we asked him up to the meeting that night, and he came and God met him. Then his wife came and found peace; then his son, then his daughter and ultimately the whole family.

Prayer, power of; Doubter converted

Luke 5:24

There was a man, while we were in London, who got out a little paper called "The Moody and Sankey Humbug." He used to have it to sell to the people coming into the meeting. After he had sold a great many thousand copies of that number, he wanted to get out another number; so he came to the meeting to get something to put into the paper; but the power of the Lord was present. It was like Christ's experience described in Luke 5 when the Pharisees, scribes, and doctors were watching the words of Christ in that house in Capernaum, and the power of the Lord was present to heal.

It doesn't say they were healed. They didn't come to be healed. If they had, they would have been healed. But sometimes there is a prayer of faith going up to God from someone, that brings down blessings. And so this man came into that meeting. The power of the Lord was present, and the arrow of conviction went down deep into his heart. He went out, not to write a paper, but to destroy the paper that he had written, and so to tell what the Holy Spirit had done for him.

Prayer, public

Matt. 6:9; Luke 11:2; John 17:1

The prayer our Lord taught his disciples is commonly called the Lord's Prayer. I think that the Lord's Prayer, more properly, is that in the seventeenth of John. That is the longest prayer on record that Jesus made. You can read it slowly and carefully in about four or five minutes. I think we may learn a lesson here. Our Master's prayers were short when offered in public; when he was alone with God that was a different thing, and he could spend the whole night in communion with his Father. My experience is that those who pray most in their closets generally make short prayers in public. Long prayers are too often not prayers at all, and they weary the people.

How short the publican's prayer was, "God be merciful to me a sinner!" The Syrophenician woman's was shorter still: "Lord help me!" She went right to the mark, and she got what she wanted. The prayer of the thief on the cross was a short one, "Lord, remember me when you come into your kingdom!" Peter's prayer was, "Lord save me, or I perish!" So, if you go through the Scriptures, you will find that the prayers that brought immediate answers were generally brief. Let our prayers be to the point, just telling God what we want.

Prayer, sinner's

Luke 18:13

There was a man at one of our meetings in New York City who was moved by the Spirit of God. He said, "I am going home, and I am not going to sleep tonight until Christ takes away my sins, if I have to stay up all night and pray. I'll do it." He had a good distance to walk, and as he went along he thought, "Why can't I pray now as I go along, instead of waiting to go home?" But he did not know a prayer. His mother had taught him to pray, but it was so long since he had uttered a prayer that he had forgotten. However, the publican's prayer came to his mind. Everybody can say this prayer. "God be merciful to me a sinner." May God write it on your hearts tonight. It is a very short prayer, and it has brought salvation to many a soul. Well, this prayer came to the man, and he began, "God be merciful to me a—" but before he got to "sinner" God blessed him with assurance of salvation.

Prayer, submission in

Matt. 6:10; 26:42; Luke 11:2

As one has well put it: "Depend upon it, prayer does not mean that I am to bring God down to my thoughts and my purposes, and bend his government according to my foolish, silly, and sometimes sinful notions. Prayer means that I am to be raised up into feeling, union and design with God; that I am to enter into his counsel, and carry out his purpose fully. I am afraid sometimes we think of prayer as altogether of an opposite character, as if by it we persuade or influence our Father in heaven to do whatever comes into our own minds, and whatever would accomplish our foolish, weaksighted purposes. I am quite convinced that God knows better what is best for me and for the world than I can possibly know; and even though it were in my power to say, 'My will be done,' I would rather say to Him, 'Thy will be done.'"

Prayer, submission in; Faith, submission in

Ps. 121:1; Matt. 6:10; 26:42; Luke 11:2

Mr. Spurgeon remarked, "The believing man resorts to God at all times, that he may keep up his fellowship with the Divine mind. Prayer is not a soliloquy, but a dialogue; not an introspection, but a looking toward the hills, whence cometh our help. There is a relief in unburdening the mind to a sympathetic friend, and faith feels this abundantly; but there is more than this in prayer. When an obedient activity has gone to the full length of its line, and yet the needful thing is not reached, then the hand of God is trusted in to go beyond us, just as before it was relied upon to go with us. Faith has no desire to have its own will, when that will is not in accordance with the mind of God; for such a desire would at bottom be the impulse of an unbelief which did not rely upon God's judgment as our best guide. Faith knows that God's will is the highest good, and that anything which is beneficial to us will be granted to our petitions."

Prayer, unanswered

1 Kings 19:4

A man was shaving himself once with his straight razor, and his little four-year-old boy came up to him and said, "Father, let me have the razor." And his father said, "Why, my boy, what do you want it for?" "Oh, I just want to whittle a little with it; I just want to play with it." The father said, "No, I can't let you have it, my boy. You will cut yourself." The boy said, "No, I won't. I want it, it shines so!" The father said, "You cannot have it." Then that little fellow just sat down and cried as if his heart would break.

Do you say the father did not love the boy? He loved him too well to let him have the razor. Now there are a great many of God's people who are just like this little boy. They are praying for razors. Elijah prayed for a razor—he wanted his throat cut. But his prayer wasn't answered that way. God wasn't going to take his life, or let him take it. He had something better for him.

Prayer, unanswered; Sin, unconfessed

Ps. 66:18; Prov. 15:8; Isa. 1:15; James 4:3

I sometimes tremble when I hear people quote promises, and say that God is bound to fulfill those promises to them, when all the time there is some sin in their lives they are not willing to give up. It is well for us to search our hearts, and find out why it is that our prayers are not answered.

Prayer understood by God

Pss. 6:9; 10:17; Rom. 8:26; Eph. 6:18; Jude 20

Sometimes when your little child talks your friends cannot understand what he says; but you, the mother, understand very well. So if our prayer comes right from the heart, God understands our language.

Prayer, vital nature of

Gen. 30:1

Dr. Guthrie thus speaks of prayer and its necessity: "The first true sign of spiritual life, prayer, is also the means of maintaining it. Man can as well live physically without breathing, as spiritually without praying. There is a class of animals—the cetaceans, neither fish nor seafowl—that inhabit the ocean. It is their home, they never leave it for the shore; yet, though swimming beneath its waves, and sounding its darkest depths, they must regularly rise to the surface that they may breathe the air. Without that, they could not exist in the dense element in which they live, and move, and have their being.

"And something like what is imposed on them by a physical necessity, Christians have to live by a spiritual one. It is by regularly ascending up to God, by rising through prayer into a loftier, purer region for supplies of Divine grace, that we maintain our spiritual life. Prevent these animals from rising to the surface, and they die for want of breath; prevent the Christian from rising to God, and he dies for want of prayer. 'Give me children,' cried Rachel, 'or else I die.' 'Let me breathe,' says a man gasping, 'or else I die.' 'Let me pray,' says the Christian, 'or else I die.'"

Luke 21:36; Rom. 12:12; Col. 4:2; 1 Thess. 5:17; 1 Peter 4:7

"Since I began," said Dr. Payson when a student, "to beg God's blessing on my studies, I have done more in one week than in the whole year before." Luther, when most pressed with work, said, "I have so much to do that I cannot get on without three hours a day praying." "A great part of my time," said McCheyne, "is spent in getting my heart in tune for prayer. It is the link that connects earth with heaven."

Prayers, a mother's

1 Sam. 1:11; Acts 1:14

The other day I read of a mother who died, leaving her child alone and very poor. She used to pray earnestly for her boy, and left an impression upon his mind that she cared more for his soul than she cared for anything else in the world. He grew up to be a successful man in business, and became very well off. One day not long ago, after his mother had been dead for twenty years, he thought he would remove her remains and put her into his own lot in the cemetery, and put up a little monument to her memory.

As he came to remove them and to lay her away the thought came to him, that while his mother was alive she had prayed for him, and he became concerned her prayers were not answered concerning his salvation. That very night he trusted Christ and was saved. After his mother had been buried so long a time, the act of removing her body to another resting place, brought up all the recollections of his childhood, and he became a Christian. Oh, you mothers!

Prayers, cold

Prov. 1:28; 21:13; Jer. 11:11; James 1:6; 4:3

Brooks says: "As a painted fire is no fire, a dead man is no man, so a cold prayer is no prayer. In a painted fire there is no heat, in a dead man there is no life; so in a cold prayer there is no power, no devotion, no blessing. Cold prayers are as arrows without heads, as swords without edges, as birds without wings; they pierce not, they cut not, they fly not up to heaven. Cold prayers do always freeze before they get to heaven. Oh that Christians would chide themselves out of their cold prayers, and chide themselves into a better and warmer frame of spirit, when they make their supplications to the Lord!"

Preach the text

Rom. 10:8; 2 Tim. 4:2

Many men use the Bible as a repository of texts, and preach about everything else—go up among the stars, off among the rocks, down into the bed of the sea, everywhere. They take a text then preach from it—away from it. What we need to do is to preach the text.

Preach to be understood

Rom. 11:14; 1 Cor. 9:22

I once read of a lawyer who used to pick out the dullest-looking man in the jury and talk to him, believing that what that man could understand the others could.

He was generally successful. It helps me a great deal to pick out one person, a young man or a young girl, and talk as if to that one alone. Of course you shouldn't keep your eye on one person all the time; he might become embarrassed; but if you talk as if to one person you will have more effect on the mass.

Preach to convict

Eph. 5:11; 1 Tim. 5:20; Titus 1:9,13; Jude 15; Rev. 3:19

Don't be afraid to say things that will make people mad. That may be the only way to bring them to a conviction of sin. When a baby has to be awakened, it often wakes up cross. Don't be discouraged if people wake up mad. If they are unforgiven sinners, it's better to give them the truth and wake them up mad than to let them sleep.

Preaching for effect

Eph. 5:11; 1 Tim. 5:20; Titus 1:9, 13; Jude 15; Rev. 3:19

I have been asked, "Shouldn't a minister be careful not to be too personal in preaching?" On the contrary. It seems to me that is what we need. Some men cover up points so that people won't see them. I think it is better to bring them out. Personal preaching is effective. It is not a bad thing for a man who is sound asleep; it wakes him up. When Dr. Taylor was preaching the other night so powerfully, I was annoyed at seeing a man sound asleep near the platform. I asked Dr. Gordon to wake him up and he looked at me in amazement. I think it is a religious duty to wake them up. It is terribly annoying to a man to be preaching and have a man sound asleep right in front of him. A little punch of the elbow may save that man.

I remember I used to go up in the gallery, when I was a boy, and get into a comfortable place and go to sleep. And when I went to Mt. Vernon Church I used to go to sleep there. And one day when I was up there in the gallery, sound asleep, a young man from Harvard College, and I shall always feel very grateful to him—I wish I knew his name—gave me a punch with his elbow and I looked up and I said to myself, "Who has been telling Dr. Kirk about me?"

I woke up just at the right time. It was just the place in the sermon that hit my case. The perspiration stood out all over me. I never felt so cheap in my life, and I thought if I only got out of that church, I would never go there again. It did me a great deal of good to wake me up because it moved me nearer to Christ. So when you see a man asleep near you, wake him up.

In my opinion, the bulk of the preaching goes over the heads of the people. What we need is preaching for effect. Some people say, "Oh, that sermon is all preached for effect." Of course it is; that is what we must do to wake people up. Be personal! Be direct!

Preaching, maintain interest

Prov. 7:24; Isa. 28:23; Jer. 6:17; 1 Cor. 7:35

Don't talk to men when they are asleep. How some ministers can do this is to me a mystery. If you find people getting drowsy, make yourself more interesting, or tell them a story about something right in that neighborhood; at all events, do something to wake them up. If you can't wake them up in any other way, get them to sing. Dr. Bonar tells us that in a certain part of Scotland it used to be the custom for a man when he got sleepy to stand up. I don't know but we might adopt that custom now.

Preaching, naturalness in

Josh. 1:7; 1 Kings 2:2; Eph. 6:10

If a man is going to preach, he wants to be himself. Let him be perfectly natural. If he tries to be like anybody else, people will soon see it, and his vanity will be exposed. Such a man can do no good.

Preaching, power in

Rom. 10:8; 2 Tim. 4:2

Harry Moorehouse, the English Bible preacher, said to me when visiting the church I pastored in Chicago, "If you will stop preaching your own words and preach God's Word, he will make you a great power for good." This prophecy made a deep impression on me, and from that time I devoted myself to the study of the Bible as I had never done before. I had been accustomed to draw my sermons from the experiences of Christians and the life of the streets, but now I began to follow the counsel of my friend and preach the Word.

My first series of sermons on characters in the Bible was preached the summer before the great Chicago fire, and I was surprised by the attention received. I also began to compare scripture with scripture. "If I don't understand a text," I said to my friend Moorehouse, "I ask another text to explain it, and then if it is too hard for me, I take it to the Lord and ask him about it." I have learned that the best source for sermons that help people is the Bible.

Preaching to inspire

Prov. 7:24; Isa. 28:23; Jer. 6:17; 1 Cor. 7:35

It is said of Cicero, the great Roman orator, that when he had spoken, everyone would go out of the building saying: "What a magnificent address! What an orator!" But when Demosthenes, the Greek orator, had finished, the people would say, "Let us go and fight Philip!" They wanted to fight right away. It was Demosthenes' love for his country that stirred him, and then he stirred the people. He had fired them up with the cause; and what we need, dear friends, is

to get the attention of the people away from ourselves and on the subject. If they will go asleep, it is a good thing to stop and say, "Won't you open the window and let a little air in? Here is a gentleman that has gone asleep." That'll wake up the whole of them. You can't reach a man when he is asleep. Men may talk in their sleep, but you can't talk to a man when he is asleep.

Preaching, use of humor

Prov. 17:22; Eccles. 9:7

Some object to bringing in things that make people laugh. I don't know that I ever intended to make people laugh. If a man tries to make people laugh—makes a study of it—he will be sure to make a fool of himself. But if your way of illustrating a truth happens to raise a laugh, there is no harm in it, and it may do a great deal of good. You know, when you are carrying a pan of milk if the milk moves to one side, how easily it moves to the other side. When people have laughed at something, then is the time when you can get at their deepest feelings. At all events, it is a great deal better to have them laugh or smile now and then than to have them go to sleep.

Preaching, use of surprise

Judg. 7:20

I have heard men say, "Now, my friends, I have got a very striking incident; it is a very striking one, very thrilling"; and then go on four or five minutes without telling it. If you have an impressive story or thought, don't tell the people that it is impressive. Let them find that out themselves. Let it take them by surprise.

Preaching, word choice

Matt. 6:5

Don't use big words. Remember that the great majority of people can't understand them. Two ministers, discussing this point, asked a man if he could draw an inference. "I don't know that I could," said he, "but I have a strong team of horses, and I am pretty sure they could." And don't be all the time saying, "It doesn't mean that in the original," just to show that you know Hebrew and Greek. Plain people don't like that. If you have to refer to the original to explain a point, do it in such a way that it will not look as if you wanted to parade your learning. And then don't strive for smooth-sounding phrases. Some men try hard to be eloquent. Any man that does that makes a fool of himself. He can have no influence. Men will say of him, "He cares more for his reputation than he does for my soul."

Pride, danger of; New converts, treatment of

Esther 3:5; Prov. 16:18; Isa. 2:11; Dan. 4:30; 5:22; Obad. 1:3; Matt. 26:74; Rom. 11:20; 1 Tim. 3:6

If you tell a new convert that you'd rather hear him speak than the minister, you'll spoil him. Many have been spoiled in that way. And when he thinks he is strong, down he goes—he backslides. A man who hasn't humility is in a backslidden state. If he wants to puff himself up, and he says I, I, I, I, and the "I" goes forward, and he thinks more of himself than of anyone else, he is in a backslidden state; I don't care who he is. I got a letter from a man who had his photograph on the outside of the envelope—on the outside. He advertised himself as a prominent worker, which I think he was. Then the paper had another big photograph of him; and he had two printed notices with his photograph. I got four photographs of him in one letter. Yes, I felt as if the man had backslidden. What does the Bible say? It says: "Pride goeth before a fall."

Pride, deceitfulness of

2 Sam. 12:5; Matt. 7:3–5; Luke 6:41–42; 18:11; John 8:7; Gal. 6:1

When I became a Christian I thought God would change my old nature, banish all the evil out of sight; but I have had more trouble with D. L. Moody than with anyone else; he is my worst enemy. I have had no time to throw stones at others—too much trouble with my own pride and deceit.

Pride, futility of

Esther 3:5; Prov. 16:18; Isa. 2:11; Dan. 4:30; 5:22; Obad. 1:3; Matt. 26:74; Rom. 11:20; 1 Tim. 3:6

People that haven't any money are just as proud as those that have it. We have got to crush it out. It is an enemy. You needn't be proud of your beautiful face, for there is not one of you but that after ten days in the grave the worms would be eating your body. There is nothing to be proud of, is there? Let's ask God to deliver us from pride.

Profanity, cure of; Commandment, third

Exod. 20:7; Deut. 5:11

I used to swear before I was converted; it didn't seem to trouble me then. But after I was converted if I got an oath halfway out I bit it in two with my teeth. It caused me more agony than all the oaths I had ever sworn before. Once I knew what a terrible thing cursing was, I could no longer do it. Christians must never take the name of their Lord in vain. It is an awful thing for a person to know the truth and then act against it.

Exod. 20:7; Deut. 5:11; Rom. 5:5; 2 Cor. 5:17

There will be no swearing people in the kingdom of God. They will have to drop that sin, and repent of it, before they see the kingdom of God. Men often ask, "How can I keep from swearing?" I will tell you.

If God puts his love into your heart, you will have no desire to curse him. If you have much regard for God, you will no more think of cursing him than you would think of speaking lightly or disparagingly of a mother whom you love. But the natural man is at enmity with God and has utter contempt for his law. When that law is written on his heart, there will be no trouble in obeying it.

Profanity, excuses for; Swearing, excuses for; Commandment, third

Exod. 20:7; Deut. 5:11; Rom. 5:5; 2 Cor. 5:17

I was greatly amazed in talking to a man who thought he was a Christian, to find that once in a while, when he got angry, he would swear. I said, "My friend, I don't see how you can tear down with one hand what you are trying to build up with the other. I don't see how you can profess to be a child of God and let those words come out of your lips."

He replied, "Mr. Moody, if you knew me, you would understand. I have a very quick temper. I inherited it from my father and mother, and it is uncontrollable; but my swearing comes only from the lips." When God said, "I will not hold him guiltless that takes my name in vain," he meant what he said, and I don't believe anyone can be a true child of God who takes the name of God in vain.

Promises of God, availability of; Laziness, cure for

2 Cor. 1:20; 7:1; 2 Peter 1:4; 1 John 2:25

Let people feed for a month on the promises of God and they will not be talking of their "leanness." It is not leanness, it is laziness. There is an abundant supply for us if we will only rouse ourselves to take it.

Promises of God, best of; Rest in Christ

Matt. 11:28

Some years ago a gentleman asked me which I thought was the most precious promise of all those that Christ left. I took some time to look over the promises, but I gave it up. I found that I could not answer the question. Like a man with a large family of children, he cannot tell which he likes best, he loves them all. But if not the best, one of the sweetest is Christ's promise of rest in Matt. 11:28.

Promises of God, faithfulness of

Ps. 33:6; Isa. 40:26; John 1:3; Acts 17:24; Rom. 1:19; 8:25; Gal. 5:6; Heb. 10:22, 39; 11:3, 6; 1 Peter 1:7; 2 Peter 3:5;

God is always true to what he promises to do. He made promises to Abraham, Jacob, Moses, Joshua, and the others, and did he not fulfill them? He will fulfill every word of what he has promised; yet how few take him at his word! When I was a young man I was a clerk in the establishment of a man in Chicago, whom I observed frequently occupied sorting and marking bills. He explained to me what he had been doing; on some notes he had marked B, on some D, and on others G; those marked B, he told me, were bad, those marked D meant they were doubtful, and those with G on them meant they were good; and, said he, you must treat all of them accordingly. And thus people endorse God's promises, by marking some as bad and others as doubtful; whereas we ought to take all of them as good, for he has never once broken his word, and all that he says he will do, will be done in the fullness of time.

Promises of God, number of

2 Cor. 1:20

A Scotchman found thirty-one thousand distinct promises of God in the Bible.

There is not a despondent soul but God has a promise just to suit that person.

Promises of God, trusting; Faith, childlike

Matt. 6:25, 34; 8:2; 9:20; 17:19–20; Mark 1:40; 5:28; 11:23–24; Luke 8:44; 12:32; 17:6; Acts 5:15

A little child believes everything that you tell it. And if we always kept our word with our children, they would grow up confiding. But even mothers tell lies to their little ones, and no wonder that the children grow up believing that everybody is false. Satan never keeps a promise. He is a liar and deceiver. But God's promises can be depended on for three reasons: (1) He is never rash in making them, as men are. (2) He is never sick, and thus delayed in carrying them out. (3) He never dies.

Promises of man, unfulfilled

Jer. 23:16; Eph. 5:6

If we go to the world we shall be disappointed. Its promises are vain. Even when the world tries to keep its promises it fails. A man drifted out into the Niagara River. He got upon a rock just above the falls. There he clung for life in the swift current. The whole country was excited. Thousands gathered on the shore to try to save him. They printed on canvass the words, "We will save you," and put them upon the shore, and then kindled fires, and planned and toiled all night. But in the morning the man was gone. They could not reach him in time. They could not keep their promise to him.

Prostitute, salvation of; Mother's heart

Luke 7:37; John 4:18; 8:11

Not long ago, in Edinburgh, an earnest Christian lady found a woman whose feet had taken hold of hell, and who was pressing onwards to a harlot's grave. The lady begged her to go home, but she said, "No, my parents would not receive me." This Christian woman knew what a mother's heart was. So she wrote a letter to the mother, telling her how she had met her daughter, who was sorry and wanted to return. The next post brought an answer back, and on the envelope was written, "Immediately—immediately!" They opened the letter: yes, she was forgiven. They wanted her back, and they sent money for her to come immediately. That is what the great and loving God is saying to every wandering sinner—immediately.

Prostitutes, ministry to

Luke 7:37; John 4:18; 8:11

I remember in Birmingham a lady who said: "Well, now, I don't see why I can't do something. I have means and I've no family, nor family ties, so I can't see why I shouldn't be worth something to somebody." She obtained a house; then she hunted up prostitutes and told them if they would come around to her house—she didn't call it a Place of Refuge—she would be very glad to help them in any way she could. When they came, she made the place as cheerful and cozy as possible. She had pleasant books for them to read; she had a sewing machine, everything indeed to take their minds off of their past lives. That woman rescued four hundred of these fallen sisters who were going to ruin, and she made such an impression upon that town that when she died, the Mayor and the Council said, "This work must not stop"; and they've kept that work up ever since. That's what one woman did!

Providence, consequences of

Gen. 50:20; Rom. 8:28

The parsonage at Epworth, England, caught fire one night, and all the family was rescued except one son. The boy came to a window, and was brought safely to the ground by two farmhands, one standing on the shoulder of the other. The boy was John Wesley. If you would realize the consequences of that rescue, ask the millions of Methodists who look back to John Wesley as the founder of their denomination.

Providence of God; Circumstances, victory over

Gen. 50:20; Rom. 8:28

There is one passage of Scripture which has always been a great comfort to me. In the eighth chapter of Romans Paul says: "All things work together for good to them that love God." Some years ago a child of mine had scarlet fever. I went to the druggist's to get the medicine which the doctor had ordered, and told him to be sure and be very careful in making up the prescription. The druggist took down one bottle after another, in any one of which there might be what would be rank poison for my child; but he stirred them together and mixed them up, and made just the medicine which my child needed. And so God gives us a little adversity here, a little prosperity there, and all work for our good.

Provision, God's abundant

Exod. 3:14; John 7:29

And when Moses said, "If they ask me who sent me, what shall I tell them?" God said, "Say I AM sent me"; and as someone has said, that was a blank check, and God told him to fill it out; and when they were in the desert and wanted water he filled out the check and drew water from the rock. When he needed bread he filled out the check and God gave him bread from heaven.

Purpose of life; Values, importance of; Vision, importance of

Matt. 6:21; 12:35; 12:34

You can soon tell where a man's treasure is by his talk. If it is in heaven, he will not be long with you before he's talking about heaven; his heart is there, and so his speech isn't long in running there, too. If his heart is in money, he will soon have you deep in talk about mines, speculation, stocks, bank rate, and so on. If his heart is in lands, it won't be long before he's talking about real estate, improvements, houses, and so on. Always the same, wherever a man's heart is, there his tongue will be sure to go.

Someone in England said, if you see a man's goods and furniture come down by the luggage train, you're pretty sure he'll be down by the next passenger train; he won't be long after; he'll follow his goods. And so it is with heaven; if your treasure has gone on before you, you'll be wanting to follow it; you'll be glad to be on the road thither as soon as possible.

Purpose, spiritual; Vision, spiritual

Matt. 6:21; 12:35; Luke 12:34

I was visiting a friend a few years ago, and he took me to call on his brother, whose estate was one of the most beautiful in that region. There was a fernery which had been built at an enormous cost, and I have never seen anything of the kind that could equal it in beauty and interest. In this hothouse were the most beautiful variety of ferns, and at one end of the building was an artificial waterfall; its music, together with the beautiful surroundings, seemed to transform a bleak, wintry day into the most ideal June weather.

My friend noted my admiration, and when we left his brother's house he turned to me and said, "Now we will see my fernery." When we returned to the town he took me away to a mission he was supporting, in which he was rescuing orphan children from a schooling of vice and sin, and teaching them of a better life while equipping them for the present one. These two brothers were laying up treasures, and both were enthusiastic over them; but one's treasures made heaven no nearer, while the other's made heaven a familiar place.

Questionable practices, guidelines

Ezek. 36:25; 2 Cor. 6:17; Eph. 4:24; Col. 3:10; 1 Peter 4:2; 2 Peter 1:4

Concerning questionable practices I ask "Would Jesus do so and so?" If he wouldn't, then I won't. We can't afford to live so that we have no contact with God in time of trouble. Have God, and we have no taste for the things that are wrong. Cold Christians who say, "What's the harm?" ought to say, "What's the good?" Old habits will fall away as the old leaves are pushed off by the new ones. It is easier to be an out-and-out Christian. People who are afraid to be "too religious" have a contest all the time. We want a victory all the time.

Questionable practices, handling

Ezek. 36:25; 2 Cor. 6:17; Eph. 4:24; Col. 3:10; James 1:5; 1 Peter 4:2; 2 Peter 1:4

I fancy someone saying, "I wish Mr. Moody would give us something practical." And you are asking, "Is it right to go to the theater? Is it right to drink moderately? Is it right to read novels?" Well, I can't carry your conscience. Christ does not lay down rules for our lives; he lays down principles; and wherever there seems a room for any doubt as to which is right, I give Christ the benefit of it rather

than seek to live up to the very outside limit. I could not go to the theater myself because I would not like my children to go. I could not smoke because I do not want my boy to smoke. I do not read those miserable flashy novels because I have no desire to do so; but then I can't carry your conscience.

Just be men and women of the Bible. Live near to God and these things will regulate themselves. Then if you have any doubt, ask for direction. "If any man lack wisdom, let him ask of God." Carry the whole matter to God; pray over it, and don't do anything about which you cannot ask God's blessing.

Rebellion, God's love in spite of

Titus 1:6

A great many people wonder why it is that they don't prosper, and are not blessed in the world. It is no wonder to me. The wonder is that God blesses them as he does. If I had a child in constant rebellion toward me, I wouldn't want that child to prosper until that spirit of rebellion would be swept away, because prosperity would ruin him.

Reconciliation, extent of; Peace, source of

Isa. 9:6; Luke 2:14; 2 Cor. 5:18–19; Eph. 2:13; Col. 1:20

When we had war in this country with England, and everything looked dark for the people of these shores, you remember how some commissioners sailed to see if they could not bring about a reconciliation. They had been absent six months and you know we hadn't any cable in those days, or fast steamers sailing every few days. When the people heard no news from the commissioners, things began to look very dark. It looked as if they were not going to have a reconciliation, and peace, but a long war. You know the colonies were very weak, and they dreaded to have a continuance of the war.

At last the news came that the vessels were off Sandy Hook, and the people were anxious for the commissioners to arrive, so that they could learn whether the war was ended. The news spread through the colonies that day that they were coming. But the day passed into the night, and it looked as if the vessels would not be able to reach port before morning. So the people went to bed. But the vessels sailed on in, and the men had good news. The boats were lowered. The commissioners stepped into the boats, and the sailors, in the darkness, pulled for the shore.

When they got within hearing distance they could not contain themselves, and cried, "Peace, peace!" Men took up the glad news and ran up one street and down another shouting, "Peace, peace!" Men, women and children came from their homes and took up the cry, and it echoed through the city. The cannon were booming, bells were ringing, and all New York was full of the joy of that peace.

It was what the people wished. The war was over, peace was brought, and the English army was withdrawn, and we had peace in this blessed land for nearly a century. If we have been at war with God, here is reconciliation today. Yes, my friends, it is goodwill to men. If you have been at enmity with him, bear in mind that our enmity can cease today. We can be reconciled unto him, we can have peace for time and eternity.

Reconciliation to others

Gen. 4:8; Matt. 5:24; 18:15

I knew of two brothers who had a quarrel—a regular Cain and Abel over again. The mother could not get them reconciled. She could not sleep. Her prayers went up night after night. One of the brothers saw how his mother felt, and

was sorry for her. To please her he bought a very costly gift and took it to her. "I don't want a gift," she said. "I want you to be reconciled to your brother." If he had been reconciled first then brought the gift to his mother, it would have been all right. So it is with God. You take your gifts to the altar and keep in your heart hatred toward your brother. God doesn't want your gift until you are reconciled.

Redemption, power of; Deliverance from sin

Ruth 3:13; Ps. 44:26; Gal. 3:13; Titus 2:14; Rev. 5:9

A few years ago, I was going away to preach one Sunday morning, when a young man drove up in front of us. He had an aged woman with him. "Who is that young man?" I asked. "Do you see that beautiful meadow," said my friend, "and that land there with the house upon it?" "Yes." "His father drank that all up," he said. "His father was a great drunkard, squandered his property, died, and left his wife in the poorhouse. And that young man has toiled hard and earned money, and bought back the land. He has taken his mother out of the poorhouse, brought her home and now he is taking her to church."

The first Adam sold us to sin in the Garden of Eden, but the Messiah, the second Adam, came and bought us back again. The first Adam brought us to the poorhouse; the second Adam makes us kings and priests unto God.

Regeneration by faith alone

Isa. 35:4; 43:2; Jer. 42:11; Zeph. 3:17; Acts 26:18; Rom. 1:16; 4:2; 5:1; 9:32; Gal. 3:24; Eph. 2:8–9

I freely admit salvation is worth working for. It is worth a man's going round the world on his hands and knees, climbing mountains, crossing valleys, swimming rivers, going through all manner of hardship in order to attain it. But we do not get it in that way. It is to him that believeth.

Regeneration, evidence of

Matt. 7:20; Gal. 5:22; James 1:27

I do not believe that there are many people who feel that they are living as God intended them to live. Of course there are many self-satisfied people, but the testimony of their neighbors would give good reason for questioning their confidence in their own perfection. Jesus disclosed to his early disciples the only means for self-examination when he said, "Wherefore by their fruits ye shall know them" (Matt. 7:20). Paul, in writing to the Galatians, enumerates the virtues of the true Christian in the passage: "The fruit of the Spirit is love, joy, peace, long-suffering, gentleness, goodness, faith, meekness, temperance" (Gal. 5:22).

If a man has none of these virtues, or if they are not increasing in his character, he may well doubt the reality of his regeneration. If there is no love for those who are overcome by sin, and no joy in the return of a wanderer, be assured there is in the heart no life from above. If there are no pangs of grief for yielding to sin, and no victory over temptation, his religion is vain.

Regeneration, importance of; Heaven, residents of

John 1:13; 3:3; James 1:18; 1 Peter 1:3, 23

The only way to get into the kingdom of God is to be "born" into it. The law of this country requires that the President should be born here. When foreigners come to our shores they have no right to complain against such a law, which forbids them from ever becoming president. Now has not God stated that the heirs of eternal life must he "born" into his kingdom?

An unregenerated man would rather be in hell than in heaven. Take a man whose heart is full of corruption and wickedness, and place him in heaven among the pure, the holy and the redeemed; and he would not want to stay there. Certainly, if we are to be happy in heaven we must begin to make a heaven here on earth. Heaven is a prepared place for a prepared people. If men were taken to heaven just as they are by nature, without having their hearts regenerated, there would be another rebellion in heaven. Heaven is filled with a company of those who have been twice born.

Regeneration, nature of

John 1:13; 3:3; James 1:18; 1 Peter 1:3, 23

When I was born of my mother, I got a nature from my mother, and I got a life from her; but in Boston seventeen years afterward, I was born from above; I got life from God; a new life, distinct and separate from the natural life, everlasting as God's life. How did I get it? By receiving the Word of God into my heart. Christ says, "The words that I speak unto you, they are spirit, and they are life." You take the Word of God into your heart, and there is the germ that produces life. If I should take my watch and plant it, I wouldn't get any little watches, would I? Why? Because the germ of life isn't there. If I should plant a bushel of gravel, I wouldn't get any more gravel, would I?

But let me plant a bushel of corn at the proper time, let me get the seed and put it into the ground in the spring of the year, and let the dews of heaven come upon the land, and the rain and the sun, and out of the death of that corn will come a new life.

Regeneration, nature of; New birth; Culture, importance of

John 1:13; 3:3; James 1:18; 1 Peter 1:3, 23

We hear much about "culture." Culture's all right when you have something to cultivate. If I should plant a watch, I shouldn't get any little watches, would I? Why? Because the seed of life is not there. But let me plant some peas or potatoes, and I will get a crop. Don't let any man or woman rest short of being born of the Spirit of God. First make sure that you have that divine nature, then you have something to cultivate.

Regeneration, nature of; Salvation, instantaneous

John 5:24

Salvation is instantaneous. I admit that a man may be converted so that he cannot tell when he crossed the line between death and life, but I also believe a man may be a thief one moment and a saint the next. I believe a man may be as vile as hell itself one moment, and be saved the next. Christian growth is gradual, just as physical growth is; but a person passes from death unto everlasting life quick as an act of the will in believing.

Religious education of children

Deut. 4:9; 6:7; 1 Sam. 1:24; Prov. 22:6; Eph. 6:4

One of Coleridge's friends once objected to prejudicing the minds of the young by selecting the things they should be taught. The philosopher-poet invited him to take a look at his garden, and took him to where a luxuriant growth of ugly and pungent weeds spread themselves over beds and walks alike. "You don't call that a garden!" said his friend. "What!" said Coleridge, "would you have me prejudice the ground in favor of roses and lilies?"

Have you never noticed the same thing about the mind and the heart? Let a child be idle, and Satan will soon lead him into mischief. He must be looked after. Those things that will help to develop character must be selected for him. Hurtful things must be kept out, just as industriously as the farmer cultivates the useful products of the soil, but wages continual war on weeds and all unwholesome growths.

Renewal, spiritual

Ps. 51:10; Isa. 40:31; 41:1; Lam. 5:21

I have sometimes been in a place where the very air seemed to be charged with the breath of God, like the moisture in the air. I remember one time as I went through the woods near Mount Hermon school I heard bees, and asked what it meant. "Oh," said one of the men, "they are after the honey dew." "What is that?" I asked. He took a chestnut leaf and told me to put my tongue to it. I did so, and the taste was sweet as honey. Upon inquiry I found that all up and down the Connecticut valley what they call "honey dew" had fallen, so that there must have been altogether hundreds of tons of honeydew in this region. Where it comes from I don't know.

Do you suppose that this earth would be worth living on if it were not for the dew and the rain? So a church that hasn't any of the dew of heaven, any of the rain that comes down in showers, will be as barren as the earth would be without the dew and rain.

Ps. 51:10; Isa. 40:31; 41:1; Lam. 5:21

Our churches need to be irrigated, and God says: "I will pour water upon him that is thirsty." Let us seek him. Let us not live on the arid desert. As the colonists in Africa sought a place to settle where the clouds were pierced, and poured out abundant rain, so let the church get near to Christ, near to him who was pierced for our sins, and then it will receive the refreshing from on high.

Repentance and faith

Isa. 35:4; 43:2; Jer. 42:11; Zeph. 3:17; Acts 26:18; Rom. 1:16; 4:2; 5:1; 9:32; Gal. 3:24; Eph. 2:8–9

One night in the inquiry room there were four persons together and I found that three of them were Christians. They had come to seek a blessing upon the fourth, a fine-looking businessman. After talking a little with him, I said, "Now, my friend, what is the difficulty? What is it that keeps you from Christ?" His young wife, who was one of the party, said, "Mr. Moody, I can tell you what the trouble is; it is his business; he is in the liquor business." I said, "Well, can't you give it up?" The man thought he would not give it up just at once; in three or four years he would make his way out of the business. But I said, "You can't afford to wait that time, you may be dead in less than three or four years."

And then I turned to his wife and said, "Have you faith to pray that your husband may repent now and find the Savior?" She said, "Yes, I do!" I asked his two other friends, "Have you faith for him?" They said, "Yes!" We knelt down around the man, surrounding him with prayer. The talk we had with him seemed to have little effect, but when we talked to God about him, he broke down; there and then. He repented, resolved to give up the liquor business, and found peace and salvation.

Repentance is not conviction

Isa. 6:10; Zech. 7:11; Matt. 13:15; Acts 3:19; 28:27

Repentance is not conviction of sin. That may sound strange to some. I have seen men under such deep conviction of sin that they could not sleep at night; they could not enjoy a single meal. They went on for months in this state; and yet they were not converted; they did not truly repent. Do not confound conviction of sin with repentance.

Repentance is not praying

Isa. 6:10; Zech. 7:11; Matt. 13:15; Acts 3:19; 28:27

Repentance is not praying. That may sound strange. Many people, when they become concerned about their soul's salvation, say, "I will pray, and read the Bible" and they think that will bring about the desired effect. But it will not do it. You may read the Bible and cry to God a great deal, and yet never repent. Many people cry loudly to God, and yet do not repent.

Repentance, lack of

2 Sam. 14:1; 18:33

David made a woeful mistake with his rebellious son, Absalom. He could not have done his son a greater injustice than to forgive him when his heart was unchanged. There could be no true reconciliation between them when there was no repentance. But God does not make these mistakes. David got into trouble on account of his error of judgment. His son soon drove his father from the throne.

Repentance, nature of

Jonah 1:5; Matt. 27:5

Repentance is not fear. There may be a great deal of fear, and no repentance at all. Sailors in a storm at sea are all at once very good saints, but the moment the storm is over, they are the same blaspheming set again. Repentance is not feeling. Men may have feeling when they repent, or they may not. When a thief is caught, he feels bad because he got caught, but that isn't repentance.

Whether you have feeling or not, repent, and the feeling will come afterward. Repentance isn't remorse. Judas had remorse and went away and committed suicide. If he had repented, no doubt he would have been forgiven. Repentance is not conviction.

Many a person is convicted of sin for years. A man may want to go to Boston. Suppose I tell him he is on the train for Vermont. He may believe me, but he has got to do something. He must pick up his suitcase and go into the other train. Repentance is turning right-about-face. Again, it is not fasting, nor praying, nor lopping off particular sins. If I have a vessel full of holes, and stop only part of them, the vessel will still leak. We must break off from sin, and turn unto God.

Gen. 6:7; 1 Sam. 15:11; Ezek. 14:6; 18:30; Acts 26:18; 1 Thess. 1:9

What is repentance? Someone says it is a "godly sorrow for sin." But I tell you a man can't have a godly sorrow, or a godly anything else, till after he repents. Repentance means right-about-face! Someone says, "Man is born with his back towards God, and repentance is turning square round."

Repentance, need of; Confession, importance of

Job 42:6; Ezek. 18:30; Luke 17:3; Rev. 2:5,16; 3:3,19

If you have lied about a person, if you have slandered someone, if you have abused someone, go and tell them what you have done, and ask for forgiveness. I felt much encouraged one night when a man came into the inquiry room and said, "Mr. Moody, I want you to forgive me." "Why," said I, "I have nothing to forgive you for. I never met you before." "Well," said the man, "I have been saying bad things about you for about a year. I was here last night and I got converted, and I want to ask your forgiveness." What a joy to grant that man his wish.

Repentance, not breaking from sin

Prov. 28:13; 30:20; Hosea 6:1; Luke 16:15

Repentance is not breaking off some one sin. A great many people make that mistake. A man who has been a drunkard signs the pledge, and stops drinking! Breaking off one sin is not repentance. Forsaking one vice is like breaking off one limb of a tree, when the whole tree has to come down. A profane man stops swearing; very good: but if he does not break off from every sin it is not repentance—it is not the work of God in the soul! When God works he hews down the whole tree. He wants to have a man turn from every sin.

Supposing I am on a ship out at sea, and I find the ship leaks in three or four places. I may go and stop up one hole; yet down goes the vessel. Or, suppose I am wounded in three or four places, and I get remedy for one wound: if the other two or three wounds are neglected, my life will soon be gone. True repentance is not merely breaking off this or that particular sin.

Repentance, true

Matt. 3:2; 4:17; Mark 1:15; Luke 13:3, 5; Rom. 10:9–10

There are five things that flow out of true repentance:

1. Conviction

When a man is not deeply convicted of sin, it is a pretty sure sign that he has not truly repented. Experience has taught me that people who have very slight conviction of sin sooner or later lapse back into their old life.

2. Contrition

The next thing is contrition, deep godly sorrow and humiliation of heart because of sin. If there is not true contrition, a person will turn right back into the old sin. That is the trouble with many Christians.

3. Confession of sin

If we have true contrition, that will lead us to confess our sins. I believe that nine-tenths of the trouble in Christian lives comes from failing to do this. We try to hide and cover up our sins; there is very little confession of them.

4. Conversion

Confession leads to true conversion, and there is no conversion at all until these three steps have been taken. Now the word conversion means two things. We say a man is "converted" when he is born again. But it also has a different meaning in the Bible. Peter said, "Repent, and be converted." The Revised Version reads: "Repent, and turn." Paul said that he was not disobedient unto the heavenly vision, but began to preach to Jews and Gentiles that they should repent and turn to God.

5. Confession of Jesus Christ

If you are converted, the next step is to confess openly. Listen: "If thou shalt confess with thy mouth the Lord Jesus Christ, and shalt believe in thine heart that God hath raised Him from the dead, thou shalt be saved. For with the heart man believeth unto righteousness, and with the mouth confession is made unto salvation." Confession of Christ is the culmination of the work of true repentance. We owe it to the world, to our fellow Christians, to ourselves. He died to redeem us, and shall we be ashamed or afraid to confess him? Religion as an abstraction, as a doctrine, has little interest for the world, but what people can say from personal experience always has weight.

Repentance, true; Failure, recovery from

1 Sam. 15:14; Ps. 51:1

A man said to me some time ago, "Don't you think David fell as low as King Saul?" Yes, he fell lower, because God had lifted him up higher. The difference is that when Saul fell there was no sign of repentance, but when David fell, a wail went up from his broken heart, there was true repentance.

Repentance, true; Seeking God

1 Kings 3:11; 2 Chron. 31:21; Ps. 34:10; Matt. 5:6; 6:33; Luke 12:31; 18:29; John 6:27; Rom. 14:17

Someone has defined repentance as a "change of mind." Man was born with his heart at enmity with God, and when, tired of sin, he turns from it and seeks God, his act is that of repentance. But there is a fuller meaning in the act than a change of mind. Action also is implied. A soldier defined it as including three commands: halt, right-about-face, forward march. Christ illustrated repentance most simply in the parable of the man having two sons, whom he told to go and work in his vineyard. One rebelled against his command and refused to go; but later he repented. First, he gave up his own plans; second, he assented to his father's will; and third, he did as commanded.

Repentance, true; Sin, confession of

2 Sam. 12:13; 24:10; Pss. 32:5; 38:18

We are good at confessing other people's sins, but if it is true repentance, we shall have as much as we can do to look after our own. When a man or woman gets a good look into God's mirror, the Bible, he is not finding fault with other people: he is fully occupied at home.

Rest, in heaven

Matt. 11:28; Heb. 4:9,10

Our rest is in heaven as well as our treasure. Many think that our rest is here. They want to go into the church to rest. But God says, "A rest remaineth." This is an enemy's country. It is the world in which Jesus was crucified. How, then, can we rest in it?

Rest, lack of

Gen. 9:21; 19:32; Prov. 23:29; Isa. 5:11; Gal. 5:21; Eph. 5:18

To find rest I would not go among the pleasure seekers. They have a few hours' enjoyment, but the next day there is enough sorrow to counterbalance it.

They may drink a cup of pleasure today, but the cup of pain comes tomorrow.

Rest, seeking

Matt. 11:28

A lady in Wales told me this little story: An English friend of hers, a mother, had a child that was sick. At first they considered there was no danger, until one day the doctor came in and said that the symptoms were very unfavorable. He took the mother out of the room, and told her that the child could not live. It came like a thunderbolt. After the doctor had gone the mother went into the room where the child lay and began to talk to the child, and tried to divert its mind.

"Darling, do you know you will soon hear the music of heaven? You will hear a sweeter song than you have ever heard on earth. You will hear them sing the song of Moses and the Lamb. You are very fond of music. Won't it be sweet, darling?" And the little tired, sick child turned its head away, and said, "Oh, mamma, I am so tired and so sick that I think it would make me worse to hear all that music."

"Well," the mother said, "you will soon see Jesus. You will see the seraphim and cherubim and the streets all paved with gold"; and she went on picturing heaven as it is described in Revelation. The little tired child again turned its head away, and said, "Oh, mamma, I am so tired that I think it would make me worse to see all those beautiful things!"

At last the mother took the child up in her arms, and pressed her to her loving heart. And the little sick one whispered: "Oh, mamma, that is what I want. If Jesus will only take me in his arms and let me rest!" Dear friend, are you not tired and weary of sin? Are you not weary of the turmoil of life? You can find rest on the bosom of the Son of God.

Rest, source of

Prov. 23:5; Eccles. 5:10; Luke 10:41; 12:17; 21:34; 1 Tim. 6:9

Money cannot buy rest. Many a millionaire would gladly give millions if he could purchase it as he does his stocks and shares. God has made the soul a little too large for this world. Roll the whole world in your soul, and still there is room. There is care in getting wealth, and more care in keeping it. It never satisfies.

Restitution, help from

Exod. 22:1; Lev. 6:4; Num. 5:7; Prov. 6:31; Ezek. 33:15

There was a friend of mine who had come to Christ and was trying to consecrate himself and his wealth to God. He had formerly had transactions with the government, and had taken advantage of them. This came to memory, and his conscience troubled him. He had a terrible struggle. His conscience kept rising up and smiting him. At last he drew a check for the amount he had underpaid, and sent it to the Treasury of the government. He told me he received great blessing after he had done it. That is bringing forth fruits meet for repentance. I believe a great many men are crying to God for light; and many are not getting it because they are not honest.

Exod. 22:1; Lev. 6:4; Num. 5:7; Prov. 6:31; Ezek. 33:15

A man came to one of our meetings, when the subject of restitution was touched upon. The memory of a dishonest transaction flashed into his mind. He saw at once how it was that his prayers were not answered, but "returned into his own bosom," as the Scripture phrase puts it. He left the meeting, took the train, and went to a distant city, where he had defrauded his employer years before. He went straight to this man, confessed the wrong, and offered to make restitution.

Then he remembered another transaction, in which he had failed to meet the just demands upon him; he at once made arrangements to have a large amount repaid. He came back to the place where we were holding the meetings, and God blessed him wonderfully in his own soul. I have not met a man for a long time who seemed to have received such a blessing.

Restitution, necessity of

Exod. 22:1; Lev. 6:4; Num. 5:7; Prov. 6:31; Ezek. 33:15

Finney, the evangelist, makes one grand mark of genuine repentance to be restitution. "The thief has not repented who keeps the money he stole. He may have conviction, but no repentance. If he had repentance, he would go and give back the money. If you have cheated anyone, and do not restore what you have taken unjustly; or if you have injured anyone, and do not set about to undo the wrong you have done, as far as in you lies, you have not truly repented."

Restitution, requirement for; Confession, importance of

Exod. 22:1; Lev. 6:4; Num. 5:7; Prov. 6:31; Ezek. 33:15

If you have ever taken money dishonestly, you need not pray God to forgive you and fill you with the Holy Spirit until you make restitution. If you have not got the money now to pay back, will to do it, and God accepts the willing mind. Many people are kept in darkness and unrest because they fail to obey God on this point. If the plough has gone deep, if the repentance is true, it will bring forth fruit. What use is there in my coming to God until I am willing, like Zacchaeus, to make it good, if I have done any person wrong or have taken anything falsely? Confession and restitution are the steps that lead up to forgiveness.

Resurrection body, nature of; New creation, law of

Ps. 51:10; Ezek. 18:31; 36:26; John 12:24; Rom. 1:16; 2 Cor. 5:17; Gal. 6:15; Eph. 1:4; 2:10, 15

Take a little black flower seed and sow it; after it has been planted some time, dig it up. If it is whole you know that it has no life; but if it has begun to decay, you know that life and fruitfulness will follow. There will be a resurrected life, and out of that little black seed will come a beautiful fragrant flower.

Here is a disgusting grub, crawling along the ground. By and by old age overtakes it, and it begins to spin its own shroud, to make its own sepulcher, and it lies as if in death. Look again, and it has shuffled off its shroud, it has burst its sepulcher open, and it comes forth a beautiful butterfly, with different form and habits.

So with our bodies. They die, but God will give us glorified bodies in their stead. This is the law of the new creation as well as of the old: light after darkness: life after death: fruitfulness and glory after corruption and decay.

Resurrection, disbelief in

Matt. 26:32; 27:63; Mark 14:28; 1 Cor. 15:14

It has always been a mystery to me why every disciple of Jesus Christ who was anywhere near Jerusalem, was not at the sepulcher on the morning of the third day after the crucifixion. Over and over again he told them that he would arise. One of the last things he said to them, as they were on their way to the Mount of Olives, was, "After that I am risen, I will go before you into Galilee." But there is not one solitary passage that tells us that they had any expectation of his resurrection. It seems as if his enemies had better memories than his friends. When Jesus' body was laid away in the tomb, the Jews went to Pilate, and wanted him to make it secure because, they said, "We remember that that deceiver said, while he was yet alive, After three days I will rise again."

Resurrection, doctrine of

1 Cor. 15:14

A lady once asked me why I did not fellowship with a certain preacher. I said, "You ask him if he believes that Christ rose from the grave." She returned and said, "Yes, he believes it." "You ask him if he believes his body rose." She came back and reported that he did not think that the doctrine of the bodily resurrection of Christ was essential to Christianity. If a man is unsound on the resurrection, he is unsound on the atonement and justification, and everything else that matters. 1 Corinthians 15:14: "If Christ be not risen, then is our preaching vain, and your faith is also vain." If I didn't believe this doctrine, I would not preach anymore.

Resurrection, hope of

John 11:25; Rom. 6:5; 1 Cor. 15:42; 1 Peter 1:3; Rev. 20:6

A bright young girl of fifteen was suddenly cast upon a bed of suffering, completely paralyzed on one side and nearly blind. She heard the family doctor say to her parents as they stood by the bedside—"She has seen her best days, poor child!" "No, doctor," she exclaimed, "my best days are yet to come, when I shall see the King in his beauty." That is our hope. We shall not sink into annihilation. Christ rose from the dead to give us a pledge of our own rising.

John 11:25; Rom. 6:5; 1 Cor. 15:42; 1 Peter 1:3; Rev. 20:6

Upon Dean Alford's tomb in England is inscribed, "The inn of a traveler on the way to the New Jerusalem."

John 11:25; Rom. 6:5; 1 Cor. 15:42; 1 Peter 1:3; Rev. 20:6

In the north of Scotland there are many miles where there are no trees. Suppose a boy who had never seen a tree should be told that if an acorn is put in the ground and dies, a great tree would come forth. He wouldn't believe it. A worm, of which you are afraid, becomes a butterfly. A little black seed dies, and a beautiful flower is the result. The resurrection is the sweetest doctrine in the Bible. Paul says the body is "sown" in corruption—we say "buried." We ought to abolish that word. We don't say we "bury" the wheat, we "sow" it. 1 Corinthians 15:42–44. Thank God for this chapter. You say good-bye to friends in the grave; but we shall soon meet again. Jacob will lose his lameness, Paul his thorn in the flesh, and you all your blemishes in the resurrection. A glorious day is before us.

John 11:25; Rom. 6:5; 1 Cor. 15:42; 1 Peter 1:3; Rev. 20:6

You know the merchants generally put the best specimens of their wares in the window to show us the quality of their stock. And so, when Christ was down here, he gave us a specimen of what he could do. He raised three from the dead, that we might know what power he had. There was (1) Jairus's daughter, (2) the widow's son, and (3) Lazarus of Bethany. He raised all three of them, so that every doubt might be swept away from our hearts.

How dark and gloomy this world would be if we had no hope in the resurrection; but now, when we lay our little children down in the grave, although it is in sorrow, it is not without hope. We have seen them pass away, we have seen them in the terrible struggle with death; but there has been one star to illumine the darkness and gloom—the thought that though the happy circle has been broken on earth, it shall be completed again in yon world of heavenly light.

Resurrection, hope of; Death, victory over; Transfiguration of Christ

Ps. 23:4; Matt. 17:2; Mark 9:2; John 8:51; 11:25; Acts 26:23; Rom. 8:11; 1 Cor. 15:22, 55; Col. 1:18; 1 Peter 1:3; Rev. 1:5

Someday you will read in the papers that D. L. Moody, of East Northfield, Massachusetts, is dead. Don't you believe a word of it! At that moment I shall be more alive than I am now. I shall have gone up higher, that is all; gone out of this old clay tenement into a house that is immortal, a body that death cannot touch, that sin cannot taint, a body like unto his own glorious body. I was born of the flesh in 1837. I was born of the Spirit in 1856. That which is born of the flesh may die. That which is born of the Spirit will live forever. Moses wouldn't have changed the body he had at the transfiguration for the body he had at Pisgah. Elijah wouldn't have changed the body he had at the transfiguration for the body he had under the juniper tree. They got better bodies; and I too am going to make something out of death. I turn my back on death, and journey toward life from this time on, and away into the eternity beyond the grave I see LIFE.

Resurrection, hope of; Unbelief, cruelty of

John 11:25; Rom. 6:5; 1 Cor. 15:8, 12-23, 42; 1 Peter 1:3; Rev. 20:6

To deny the resurrection is to say that we will never see more of the loved ones whose bodies have been committed to the clay. If Christ has not risen, this life is the only one, and we are as the brutes. How cruel it is to have anyone love you if this be true! How horrible that they should let the tendrils of your heart twine around them, if, when they are torn away in death, that is to be the end! I would rather hate than love if I thought there would be no resurrection, because then I would feel no pangs at losing the hated thing. Oh, the cruelty of unbelief! It takes away our brightest hopes.

Resurrection, importance of

1 Cor. 15:3–4

I was once talking with an atheist in my hometown, and I got him to read the New Testament. He came back in a few days and said, "Mr. Moody, I have taken your advice and read the life of Jesus Christ, and I have come to the conclusion that John the Baptist was a greater character than Jesus Christ. Why don't you preach John the Baptist?" "Well," I said, "you go through the countries and preach in the name of John the Baptist, and I will follow, and preach in the name of Jesus Christ, and I venture to say that I will win more converts than you." "Oh, well," he said, "of course you would, because people are very superstitious." "No, that's not the reason," I replied. "When they buried John the Baptist he hasn't gotten out of the grave yet. But when they buried the Son of God the grave could not hold him. He rose again. We don't worship a dead Christ. He is a glorified Christ."

Resurrection power; Holy Spirit, power of

Rom. 8:11; 1 Peter 3:18

Christ was raised up from the grave by the Spirit, and the power exercised to raise Christ's dead body must raise our dead souls and quicken them. No other power on earth can quicken a dead soul but the same power that raised the body of Jesus Christ out of Joseph's sepulcher. And if we want that power to quicken our friends who are dead in sin, we must look to God, and not be looking to man to do it. If we look alone to ministers, if we look alone to Christ's disciples to do this work, we shall be disappointed; but if we look to the

Spirit of God and expect it to come from him and him alone, then we shall honor the Spirit, and the Spirit will do his work.

Resurrection, power of

Jonah 2:10; Matt. 12:39–40; 16:4; 20:19; Mark 9:31; 10:34; Luke 11:29–30; 18:33; 24:7

Jesus taught his disciples and said unto them, "The Son of Man is delivered into the hands of men, and they shall kill him, and after he is killed, he shall rise the third day." Then when the Pharisees came to him wanting a sign, he would have no other but the sign of Jonah. That sign was resurrection. Undoubtedly when the captain of that boat in which Jonah sailed had got ashore he reported the wonderful thing which had taken place, how Jonah had been swallowed up by a great fish. He had no more than noised it abroad when this very man appeared in the streets of Nineveh. The message of the resurrection has always had a powerful impact.

Retribution, certainty of; Harvest, certainty of; Sowing and reaping

Prov. 22:8; Eccles. 11:6; 2 Cor. 9:6; Gal. 6:7–8

You may go out here tonight laughing at everything I say, but it is true as the God in heaven that the day of retribution will come. It is only a question of time. See that false-hearted libertine! The day is coming when he will reap what he's sowing. He may not be called to reap it in this world, but he will be brought up before that bar of heaven, and there the harvest will be seen. These men who have got smooth, oily tongues go into society and play their part, and still walk around. If a poor woman falls, she's ruled out, but these false-hearted libertines still go up and down the world.

The eyes of justice may not find them out. They think themselves secure, but they are deceiving themselves. By and by the God of heaven will summon them to give an account. They say that God will not punish them, but the decree of heaven has gone forth, "Whatsoever a man soweth so shall he reap."

Prov. 22:8; Eccles. 11:6; 2 Cor. 9:6; Gal. 6:7–8

Dr. Chalmers has drawn attention to the difference between the act of sowing and the act of reaping. "Let it be observed," he says, "that the act of indulging in the desires of the flesh is one thing and the act of providing for the indulgence of them is another. When a man, on the impulse of sudden provocation, wreaks his resentful feelings upon the neighbor who has offended him, he is not at that time preparing for the indulgence of a carnal feeling, but actually indulging it. He is not at that time sowing, but reaping (such as it is) a harvest of gratification. This distinction may serve to assist our judgment in estimating the ungodliness of certain characters.

"The rambling sensualist who is carried along by every impulse, and all whose powers of mental discipline are so enfeebled that he has become the slave of every tendency, lives in the perpetual harvest of criminal gratification. A daughter whose sole delight is in her rapid transitions from one scene of expensive brilliancy to another, who dissipates every care and fills every hour among the frivolities and fascinations of her ever-changing society, leads a life than which nothing can be imagined more opposite to a life of preparation for the coming judgment or coming eternity. Yet she reaps rather than sows.

"It lies with another to gather the money with which to purchase all the things, and with her to taste the fruits of the purchase. It is the father who sows. It is he who sits in busy and brooding anxiety over his speculations, wrinkled, perhaps, by care, and sobered by years into an utter distaste for the splendors and insignificances of fashionable life." The father sows, and he reaps in his daughter's life.

Retribution, certainty of; Reap what is sown

Prov. 28:8; Eccles. 11:6; 2 Cor. 9:6; Gal. 6:7–8

If I should tell you that I sowed ten acres of wheat last year and that watermelons came up, you wouldn't believe it. It is a fixed law that you reap the same kind of seed you sow. One day, the master of Lukman, an Eastern fable teller, said to him, "Go into such a field, and sow barley." Lukman sowed oats instead. At the time of harvest his master went to the place, and, seeing the green oats springing up, asked him: "Did I not tell you to sow barley here? Why, then, have you sown oats?" He answered, "I sowed oats in the hope that barley would grow up." His master said, "What foolish idea is this? Have you ever heard of the like?"

Lukman replied, "You yourself are constantly sowing in the field of the world the seeds of evil, and you expect to reap in the resurrection day the fruits of virtue. Therefore I thought, also, I might get barley by sowing oats." The master was convicted in his heart at the reply and set Lukman free.

Retribution, certainty of; Reap what you sow

Prov. 22:8; Eccles. 11:6; 2 Cor. 9:6; Gal. 6:7–8

The fact of reaping what you sow is a tremendous argument against selling liquor. Leaving out the temperance and religious aspects of the question, no man on earth can afford to sell strong drink. If I sell liquor to your son and make a drunkard of him, some man will sell liquor to my son and make a drunkard of him. Every man who sells liquor has a

drunken son or a drunken brother or some drunken relative. Where are the sons of liquor dealers? To whom are their daughters married? Look around and see if you can find a man who has been in that business twenty years who has not a skeleton in his own family.

I threw that challenge down once, and a man said to me the next day, "I wasn't at your meeting last night, but I understand you made the astounding statement that no man could have been in the liquor business twenty years who hadn't the curse in his own family." "Yes," I said, "I did." "It isn't true," he said, "and I want you to take it back. My father was a liquor seller, and I am a liquor seller, and the curse has never come into my father's family or into mine." I said, "What! Two generations selling that infernal stuff, and the curse has never come into the family! I will investigate it, and if I find I am wrong, I will make the retraction just as publicly as I did the statement."

There were two prominent citizens of the town in the room, on whose faces I noticed a peculiar expression as the man was talking. After he left, one of them said, "Do you know, Mr. Moody, that man's own brother was a drunkard and committed suicide a few weeks ago and left a widow with seven children. They are under his roof now. He was a terrible drunkard himself until the shock of his brother's suicide cured him. I don't know how you can account for it unless he thought his brother wasn't a relative. Perhaps he was a sort of a Cainite, saying, 'Am I my brother's keeper?'"

Retribution, certainty of; Sowing and reaping

Prov. 22:8; Eccles. 11:6; 2 Cor. 9:6; Gal. 6:7–8

A widow woman had an only son, and this son was in the habit of going to a hotel bar. The pleadings of the mother were in vain, and the hotel keeper said he would sell liquor to anyone who asked it.

This son died, and the mother soon followed, and afterwards a terrible retribution was that hotel keeper's, for his only son became a drunkard and one night blew out his brains. "Whatsoever a man soweth he shall reap." This picture is not overdrawn; there are hundreds of similar cases. Judgment is sure to come. God is a God of goodness, but also a God of equity, a God of justice, and he will sit in judgment upon us.

Prov. 22:8; Eccles. 11:6; 2 Cor. 9:6; Gal. 6:7–8

If you will read the Bible you will find that the sacred record shows that the people of the Bible have reaped what they sowed. It is the same today. I was in a town where a wealthy man had built a handsome house in a very respectable part of the city, and when the house was finished, someone offered him a very large rent for it to be used for a brothel. He had four promising sons, and every one of them was ruined in that house. How much did he make? Sit down and reckon it up. Sow brothels and you will reap adultery and it will come into your family. You can't put temptation in the way of young men, but it will come back to you.

Retribution, degree of; Reap more than sow

Prov. 22:8; Eccles. 11:6; 2 Cor. 9:6; Gal. 6:7–8

If I sow a bushel, I expect to reap ten or twenty bushels. The Spaniards have this proverb, "Sow a thought and reap an act. Sow an act, and reap a habit. Sow a habit, and reap a character. Sow a character and reap a destiny." I have heard of a certain kind of bean that reproduces itself a thousand fold. One thistledown which blew from the deck of a vessel is said to have covered with thistles the entire surface of a South Sea island. The oak springs from an acorn, the mighty Mississippi from a little spring.

One glass of whisky may lead to a drunkard's death. One lie may ruin a man's career. One error in youth may follow a man all through life. Someone has said that many a Christian spends half his time trying to keep down the sprouts of seed sown in his young days. Unless it is held in check, the desire to "have a drink" will become a consuming thirst; the desire to "play a game of cards" an irresistible gambler's passion.

Retribution, examples of; Reap what you sow

Prov. 22:8; Eccles. 11:6; 2 Cor. 9:6; Gal. 6:7–8

But you say you don't believe the Bible when it says we reap what we sow. Then look at history, and see if this law is not true. Maxentine built a false bridge to drown Constantine, but was drowned himself. Maximinus put out the eyes of thousands of Christians; soon after a fearful disease of the eye broke out among his people, of which he himself died in great agony. Valens caused about eighty Christians to be sent to sea in a ship and burnt alive: he was defeated by the Goths and fled to a cottage, where he was burnt alive.

Alexander VI was poisoned by wine he had prepared for another. Henry III of France was stabbed in the same chamber where he had helped to contrive the cruel massacre of French Protestants. Marie Antoinette, riding to Notre Dame Cathedral for her bridal, bade the soldiers command all beggars, cripples and ragged people to leave the line of the procession. She could not endure the sight of these miserable ones. Soon after, bound in the executioner's cart, she was riding toward the place of execution amidst crowds who gazed on her with hearts as cold as ice and hard as granite.

When Foulon was asked how the starving populace was to live, he said: "Let them eat grass." Afterward, the mob, maddened with rage, caught him in the streets of Paris, hung him, stuck his head upon a pike and filled his mouth with grass.

Retribution, nature of; Reap what is sown

Prov. 22:8; Eccles. 11:6; 2 Cor. 9:6; Gal. 6:7–8

If I sow tares, I am going to reap tares; if I sow a lie, I am going to reap lies; if I sow adultery I am going to reap adulterers; if I sow whisky, I am going to reap drunkards. You cannot blot this law out, it is in force. No other truth in the Bible is more solemn. Suppose that a neighbor, whom I don't want to see, comes to my house and I instruct my son to tell him, if he asks for me, that I am out of town. He goes to the door and lies to my neighbor; it will not be six months before that boy will lie to me; I will reap that lie.

A man said to me some time ago, "Why is it that we cannot get honest clerks now?" I replied, "I don't know, but perhaps I can imagine a reason. When merchants teach clerks to say that goods are all wool when they are half cotton, you will not have honest clerks. Dishonest merchants make dishonest clerks. It is not poetry, but solemn prose that a man must reap the same kind of seed that he sows."

Revival, cost of; Commandment, second

Gen. 35:2; Deut. 7:25; Josh. 24:15; Judg. 10:16; 1 Sam. 7:3

One reason people don't like revivals is, that they don't want to put away their idols. Jacob down there at Shechem, when the Lord told him to arise and go to Bethel, had to call his family together and bury their household gods under an oak tree. They had to have a funeral of those household gods. The trouble with us sometimes is, that we are down at Shechem, and we want to stay there. The church has strange gods. It has a great many idols. The sons and daughters of Jacob put away their strange gods so that God could visit them, and then came the breath of heaven, and they were revived.

Revival, importance of

Pss. 85:6; 138:7; Isa. 57:15; Ezek. 37:4; Hab. 3:2; Rom. 13:12; Eph. 5:14

There is nothing I am more concerned about just now than that God should revive his church in America. I believe it is the only hope for our country, for I don't believe that a democracy can last without righteousness. It seems to me that every patriot, every man who loves his country, ought to be anxious that the church of God should be quickened and revived. Perhaps "awakening" is a better word than "revival," but the term "revival" is better known today.

Revival, need for

1 Kings 19:4; Rev. 11:15; 20:6

When God has revived his work there has always been great need; it is darkest just before the dawn. I think it is getting very dark, but don't think for a moment that I am a pessimist. If I should live ten thousand years I couldn't be a pessimist. I haven't any more doubt about the final outcome of things than I have of my existence. I believe Jesus is going to sway his scepter to the ends of the earth, that the time is coming when God's will is to be done on earth as it is done in heaven, and when man's voice will be only the echo of God's. I believe the time is coming when every knee will bow and every tongue confess Christ. I am no pessimist, and I am not under the juniper tree, either. If I look on the dark side it is to stir you up and get you to fighting. But it is getting dark; there is no doubt about that.

Revival, time of; Laziness brings leanness

2 Chron. 7:14; Prov. 28:13; Rom. 13:11–12; James 4:8

I have been asked when to expect revival to come. If you wait for a revival and do nothing you will never get it. Revival will come when we are ready to go to work. Spiritual leanness is the result of spiritual laziness.

Revivals, effectiveness of

2 Chron. 7:14; Prov. 28:13; Rom. 13:11–12; James 4:8

I was in a town not very long ago. The people didn't go to church, and the pastor was very much grieved about it. He didn't know what to do. Something ought to be done, and yet he was in doubt whether there would be any real benefit from a revival. One day, he took the church record, and looked over the names of the church members, and to his surprise he found that over four-fifths of his church membership had been converted in time of revival. I think that a great many members will find the same experience, if they will only just look into it carefully. I think, if we would just look over this audience, and ask those that were converted in time of revival to rise, a great many would spring to their feet and say, "I was converted in time of revival."

Revivals, Jonathan and David

1 Sam. 7:3–6

When I was in Scotland a few years ago, Dr. Bonar threw out this idea. It is quite possible that Jonathan and David might have been converted at the revival under Samuel the prophet. They showed very good signs of being converted, and they must have been converted somewhere. Why not in that time, when the whole nation was turning to God? Jonathan, who was afterward the King Saul's son, and David, who was to be anointed king over Israel.

Revivals, necessity of; Christ, reign of

Josh. 5:4; Ps. 51:1; Dan. 2:44–45; 7:14; Luke 1:33; Rom. 5:17; Heb. 1:8; Rev. 11:15

I don't like to look at the dark side. That little hymn helps me a great deal: "The Crowning Day Is Coming." Only a little while and Jesus will be crowned. Infidels and skeptics may howl as much as they have a mind to. "He must increase"; and neither devils nor men can help it. Christ's kingdom is rolling on like the little stone cut out of the mountain; and it will grind to dust all that opposes it. Don't let us be afraid of revivals. God often works in ways that are out of the regular order. I dare say it looked very strange to see those Israelites marching around Jericho blowing rams' horns; but the walls fell. I myself was converted during a revival, in Dr. Kirk's church, in Boston, in 1856.

Revivals, objections to

1 Cor. 4:17; 1 Tim. 1:2; 2 Tim. 1:2

A bishop once said to me: "We don't believe in revivals. We believe in taking them in childhood, like Timothy, and training them up in the church." But didn't Paul say Timothy was begotten by him? I have an idea that Timothy was converted in one of Paul's meetings.

Revivals, opposition to

Acts 24:25; Eph. 2:2; 2 Tim. 4:10; Jude 18

I want to say right here that the great reason so many Christians—so-called Christians—are against revivals, is because they are mixed up with the world. The world doesn't want revivals. When you mention revivals among worldly people, you will see a sneer and a scornful look. And for fear of being out of keeping with the world, a great many so-called Christians throw their influence against revivals.

Rewards for service

Matt. 25:21, 23; Luke 19:17

Our greatest reward will not be the sense of a lasting memorial on earth. That will be forgotten in the joy unspeakable of seeing his face and receiving his welcome. In Queen Victoria's jubilee procession in 1897, along the line of march there was a stand occupied by some old veteran officers of the army; they were men who had seen hardships and privations in the service of their land and monarch, but this had only strengthened their loyalty, and when at last the Queen came opposite their stand, they raised a rousing British cheer, which the Queen most graciously acknowledged. I am told that these old soldiers were so overcome by this mark of their sovereign's approval that they could not control their feelings, and these old warriors wept for joy at that token of royal favor.

We, too, are in a royal service infinitely more noble than any earthly monarch's army, and we, too, shall soon see our King, and if we are but loyal to his cause on earth we shall receive from him the welcome approval, "Well done, good and faithful servants."

Rewards, significance of

Matt. 5:10; 10:22; Mark 10:30; John 16:2, 33; Gal. 6:12; 2 Tim. 3:12; 1 Peter 4:12

If I understand things correctly, whenever you find a man or woman who is looking to be rewarded here for doing right, they are unqualified to work for God; because if they are looking for the applause of men, looking for the reward in this life, it will just disqualify them for the service of God, because they are all the while compromising truth. They are afraid of hurting someone's feelings. They are afraid that someone is going to say something against them, or there will be some articles written against them. Now, we must trample the world under our feet if we are going to get our reward hereafter.

If we live for God we must suffer persecution. The kingdom of darkness and the kingdom of light are at war, and have been, and will be as long as Satan is permitted to reign in this world, and as long as the kingdom of darkness is permitted to exist, there will be a conflict. If you want to be popular in the kingdom of God in heaven, and get a reward that shall last forever, you will have to be unpopular here.

Riches, dangers of

Ruth 3:10; Matt. 13:22; 19:24; Mark 4:19; 10:25; Luke 12:21; 18:25; 1 Tim. 6:17; Rev. 3:17

How many are worshiping gold today! Where war has slain its thousands, gain has slain its millions. Its history is the history of slavery and oppression in all ages. At this moment what an empire it has. The mine with its drudgery, the factory with its misery, the plantation with its toil, and the market and exchange with their haggard and care-worn faces—these are but specimens of its menial servants. Titles and honors are its rewards, and thrones are at its disposal. Among its counselors are kings, and many of the great and mighty of the earth are its subjects. This spirit of gain tries even to turn the globe itself into gold.

It is related that Tarpeia, the daughter of the governor of the fortress situated on the Capitoline Hill in Rome, was captivated with the golden bracelets of the Sabine soldiers, and agreed to let them into the fortress if they would give her what they wore upon their left arms. The contract was made; the Sabines kept their promise. Tatius, their commander, was the first to deliver his bracelets and shield. The coveted treasures were thrown upon the woman by each of the soldiers, till she sank beneath their weight and died. Thus does the weight of gold carry many down.

Riches, deceitfulness of

Ruth 3:10; Matt. 13:22; 19:24; Mark 4:19; 10:25; Luke 12:21; 18:25; 1 Tim. 6:17; Rev. 3:17

I heard of a man who had accumulated great wealth, and death came upon him suddenly and he realized, as the saying is, that "there was no bank in the shroud," that he couldn't take anything away with him; we may have all the money on earth, but we must leave it behind us. He called a lawyer in and commenced to will away his property before he went away. His little girl couldn't understand exactly where he was going, and she said, "Father, have you got a home in that land you are going to?" The arrow went down to his soul. "Got a home there?"

The rich man had hurled away God, and neglected to secure a home there for the sake of his money, and he found it was now too late. He was money mad, and he was money blind. It wouldn't be right for me to give names, but I could tell you a good many here in Chicago who are going on in this way spending all their lives in the accumulation of what they cannot take with them. This is going on while how many poor people are suffering for the necessaries of life. These men don't know they are blind—money is their god.

Riches, deceitfulness of; Life, brevity of

Ruth 3:10; Matt. 13:22; 19:24; Mark 4:19; 10:25; Luke 12:21; 18:25; 1 Tim. 6:17; Rev. 3:17

A friend of mine was once taken by an old man to see his riches. He took him to a splendid mansion, and said, "This is all mine." He pointed to a little town, "That is mine; it is called by my name." He pointed to a rolling prairie, "That is all mine; the sun never shone on a finer prairie than that, so fruitful and rich, and it's all mine." In another direction he showed him fertile farms extending for thirty miles, "These are all mine." He took him into his grand house, showed him his beautiful pictures, his costly gold plate, his jewels, and still he said, "These are all mine. This grand hall I have built; it is called by my name; there is my insignia on it. And yet I was once a poor boy. I have made it all myself."

My friend looked at him. "Well, you've all this on earth; but what have you got up there?" "Up where?" said the old man. "Up in heaven." "Well, I'm afraid I haven't got much up there." "Ah," said my friend, "but you've got to die, to leave this world; what will you take with you of all these things? You will die a beggar; for all these riches count as nothing in the kingdom of heaven. You will be a pauper; for you have no inheritance with the saints above." The poor old man (he was poor enough in reality, though rich in all the world's goods) burst into tears. He had no hope for the future. In four months' time he was dead: and where is he now? He lived and died without God, and without hope in this world or the next.

Riches, deceitfulness of; Wealth, snare of; Money, love of

Ruth 3:10; Matt. 13:22; 19:24; Mark 4:19; 10:25; Luke 12:21; 18:25; 1 Tim. 6:17; Rev. 3:17

The Bible speaks of the deceitfulness of two things—"the deceitfulness of sin" and "the deceitfulness of riches." Riches are like a mirage in the desert, which has all the appearance of satisfying, and lures on the traveler with the promise of water and shade; but he only wastes his strength in the effort to reach it. So riches never satisfy: the pursuit of them always turns out a snare.

Riches, nature of; Heaven, invest there

Ruth 3:10; Matt. 6:20; 13:22; 19:24; Mark 4:19; 10:25; Luke 12:21; 18:25; 1 Tim. 6:17; Rev. 3:17

Very few people are satisfied with earthly riches. Often the richer the individual the greater the poverty. Somebody has said that getting riches brings care; keeping them brings trouble; abusing them brings guilt; and losing them brings sorrow. It is a great mistake to make so much of riches as we do. But there are some riches that we cannot praise too much: that never pass away. They are the treasures laid up in heaven for those who truly belong to God.

Riches, true

Luke 12:33; 16:11; 18:22; 1 Peter 5:4; Rev. 3:18

It is a great mistake to make so much of riches as we do. But there are some riches that we cannot praise too much. They never pass away. They are the treasures laid up in heaven for those who truly belong to God. No matter how rich or elevated we may be here, there is always something that we want. The greatest advantage the rich have over the poor, is the one they enjoy the least—that of making themselves happy. Worldly riches never make anyone truly happy. We all know, too, that they often take wings and fly away. Money, like time, ought not to be wasted, but I pity those who have more of either than they know how to use.

There is no truer saying than that people by doing good with their money, stamp, as it were, the image of God upon it, and make it pass as currency for the merchandise of heaven; but all the wealth of the universe would not buy the way there. Salvation must be taken as a gift for the asking. There is no man so poor that he may not be a heavenly millionaire.

Prov. 10:22; 15:6

The Rev. John Newton one day called to visit a Christian family that had suffered the loss of all they possessed by fire. He found the wife and mother, and saluted her with: "I give you joy." Surprised, and ready to be offended, she exclaimed: "What! Joy that all my property is consumed?" "Oh no," he answered, "but joy that you have so much property that fire cannot touch." This allusion to her real treasures checked her grief and brought reconciliation. As it says in the 15th chapter of Proverbs: "In the house of the righteous is much treasure; but in the revenues of the wicked is trouble." I have never seen a dying saint who was rich in heavenly treasures who had any regret; I have never heard them say they had lived too much for God and heaven.

Riches, vanity of

Prov. 30:8; Eccles. 4:8; 6:2

No man thinks himself rich until he has all he wants. Very few people are satisfied with earthly riches. If they want anything at all that they cannot get, that is a kind of poverty. Sometimes the richer the man the greater the poverty.

Righteousness, fruit of

Ps. 85:10; Isa. 32:17; 48:18; Rom. 14:17; James 3:18

The only way to be happy is to be good. The man who steals from necessity sins because he is afraid of being unhappy, but for the moment he forgets all about how unhappy the sin is going to make him. Man is the best and noblest thing on earth, as bad as he is, and it is easy to understand how he fails to find true happiness in anything lower than himself. The only object better than ourselves is God, and that is all we can ever be satisfied with. Gold, that is mere dross dug up out of the earth, does not satisfy man. Neither does the honor and praise of other men. The human soul needs something more than that. Heaven is the only place it exists in full measure. No wonder that the angels who see God all the time are so happy.

Sabbath, observing; Commandment, fourth

Exod. 23:12; Deut. 5:13; Luke 13:10; Heb. 4:4

"Sabbath" means "rest," and the meaning of the word gives a hint as to the true way to observe the day. God rested after creation, and ordained the Sabbath as a rest for man. He blessed it and hallowed it. Remember the rest day to keep it holy. It is the day when the body may be refreshed and strengthened after six days of labor, and the soul drawn into closer fellowship with its Maker. True observance of the Sabbath may be considered under two general heads: cessation from ordinary secular work, and religious exercises.

A person ought to turn aside from ordinary employment one day in seven. There are many whose occupation will not permit them to observe Sunday, but they should observe some other day as a Sabbath. Saturday is my day of rest, because I generally preach on Sunday, and I look forward to Saturday as a boy does to a holiday. God knows what we need. No person should make another work seven days in the week. One day is demanded for rest. A person who has to work the seven days has nothing to look forward to, and life becomes humdrum. Many Christians are guilty in this respect.

But "rest" does not mean idleness. No one enjoys idleness for any length of time. When we go on a vacation, we do not lie around doing nothing all the time. Hard work at tennis, hunting, and other pursuits fills the hours. A healthy mind must find something to do. Hence the Sabbath rest does not mean inactivity. "Satan finds some mischief still for idle hands to do." The best way to keep off bad thoughts and to avoid temptation is to engage in active religious exercises.

But we must not mistake the means for the end. We must not think that the Sunday sabbatical is just for the sake of being able to attend meetings. There are some people who think they must spend the whole day at meetings or private devotions. The result is that at nightfall they are tired out, and the day has brought them no rest. That is a terrible mistake. The number of church services attended ought to be measured by the person's ability to enjoy them and get good from them, without being wearied.

Attending meetings is not the only way to observe the Sabbath. The Israelites were commanded to keep it in their dwellings as well as in holy convocation. The home, that center of so great influence over the life and character of the people, ought to be made the scene of true Sabbath observance.

Sabbath principle, importance of; Commandment, fourth

Exod. 23:12; Deut. 5:13; Luke 13:10; Heb. 4:4

Ministers and missionaries often tell me that they take no rest day; they do not need it because they are in the Lord's work. That is a mistake. When God was giving Moses instructions about the building of the tabernacle, he referred especially to the Sabbath, and gave injunctions for its strict observance; and later, when Moses was conveying the words of the Lord to the children of Israel, he interpreted them by saying that not even were sticks to be gathered on the Sabbath to kindle fires for smelting or other purposes. In spite of their zeal and haste to erect the tabernacle, the workmen were to have their day of rest. The command applies to ministers and others engaged in Christian work today as much as to those Israelite workmen of old. We need one day in seven as a day of rest to observe the Sabbath principle. Our ministry will be the better for it.

Sabbath rest activities; Commandment, fourth

Exod. 23:12; Deut. 5:13; Luke 13:10; Heb. 4:4

Apart from public and family observance on the day of Sabbath rest, the individual ought to devote a portion of the time to personal edification. Prayer, meditation, reading, ought not to be forgotten. Think of people devoting six days a week to their body, which will soon pass away, and begrudging one day to the soul, which will live on forever! Is it too much for God to ask for one day to be devoted to the growth and training of the spiritual senses, when the other senses are kept busy the other six days?

If your circumstances permit, engage in some definite Christian work, such as teaching in Sunday school, or visiting the sick. Do all the good you can. Sin keeps no Sabbath, and no more should good deeds. There is plenty of opportunity in this fallen world to perform works of mercy and religion. Make your Sabbath rest day down here a foretaste of the eternal Sabbath that is in store for believers.

You want power in your Christian life, do you? You want Holy Spirit power? You want the dew of heaven on your brow? You want to see people convicted and converted? I don't believe we shall ever have genuine conversions until we get straight on this fourth commandment.

Sabbath rest, importance of; Commandment, fourth

Exod. 23:12; Deut. 5:13; Luke 13:10; Heb. 4:4

"Our bodies are seven-day wind up clocks," says Talmage, "and they need to be wound up, and if they are not wound up they run down into the grave. No man can continuously break the Sabbath-rest principle and keep his physical and mental health. Ask aged men, and they will tell you they never knew men who continuously broke the Sabbath-rest principle who did not fail in mind, body, or moral rectitude."

Exod. 23:12; Deut. 5:13; Luke 13:10; Heb. 4:4

Parents, if you want your children to grow up and honor you, have them honor the Sabbath day principle by being in church on Sunday. Don't let them go off fishing and getting into bad company, or it won't be long before they will come home and curse you. I know few things more beautiful than to see a father and mother coming up the aisle with their children and sitting down together to hear the Word of God. It is a good thing to have the children, not in some remote loft or balcony, but in a good place, well in sight. Though they cannot understand the sermon now, when they get older they won't desire to break away, they will continue attending public worship in the house of God.

Exod. 23:12; Deut. 5:13; Luke 13:10; Heb. 4:4

Adam brought marriage and the Sabbath rest day with him out of Eden, and neither can be disregarded without suffering. When the children of Israel went into the Promised Land, God told them to let their land rest every seven years, and he would give them as much in six years as in seven. For four hundred and ninety years they disregarded that law. But mark you, Nebuchadnezzar came and took them off into Babylon, and kept them seventy years in captivity, and the land had its seventy Sabbaths of rest. Seven times seventy is four hundred and ninety. So they did not gain much by breaking this law. You can give God his day, or he will take it.

Sabbath rest principle; Commandment, fourth

Exod. 23:12; Deut. 5:13; Luke 13:10; Heb. 4:4

I used to think that I could work seven days a week, and I was an older man at thirty than I am now at sixty-two. I used to work so hard that the "spring" went out of me. When I saw that I was violating God's law of resting one day in seven, I repented and turned around. You can't get anything out of me on Saturday. I take the whole day of Saturday to rest, and on Sunday I am as fierce to get at an audience as I was at twenty. I read a paragraph in a newspaper the other day, that ministers are not wanted after they are fifty. That is the deadline. I don't believe ministers are worth much until they get to be fifty. People say the best is behind, that our heyday is the past. It is not so. I am growing younger day by day in my heart.

Exod. 23:12; Deut. 5:13; Luke 13:10; Heb. 4:4

You hear about ministers "overworking." Well, they do when they work seven days in the week. I believe that the professional man who works hardest with his brains is the pastor. Look at the sick he has to visit; at the funerals he has to attend and conduct. I would rather preach twelve sermons than attend one funeral. If he has a heart in him a funeral saps his life. Two sermons a week, and then the pastoral calls. His work is never done. I am sorry that most work seven days in the week; that is where they make a mistake. Give the body a rest. That is the Sabbath principle. Does anyone need it any more than a person engaged in Christian work? Let the brains have rest and you can keep going twelve months of the year.

Exod. 23:12; Deut. 5:13; Luke 13:10; Heb. 4:4

I give my horses a rest. If they have to work Sunday they get a rest on Monday. We have a good many horses connected with the Northfield farm. Our Boys' School is four miles from the church, and the teachers have to ride. It was a problem to be decided how they could be conveyed to church. I came to the conclusion that the Lord would make it up to us if we let some of our horses rest one day; and the horse that works Sunday gets his rest on Saturday or Thursday. The horses are fat, and fresh, and strong. Apply the Golden Rule to the horses that work for you. If you do, that will speak well of you and testify on your behalf.

Safety in God; Rocks, cleft of

Exod. 33:22; Deut. 33:12; Pss. 18:2; 55:6; 91:1; Song of Sol. 2:14; Jer. 48:28; Jude 24

There is a beautiful legend about a conference held by the doves to decide where they should make their home. One suggested that they should go to the forest but the objection was made that there they would be in danger from hawks; another mentioned the cities, but boys would stone them there, and drive them away or kill them. Presently some dove suggested that they go and hide in the clefts of the rocks, and there they were safe.

Safety, lack of; Security, lack of

Pss. 42:11; 73:25; Isa. 41:10; 54:4; John 6:40; 10:29; 11:25; Rom. 8:38; 9:33; 2 Tim. 4:17; 1 Peter 4:19

There is an old fable that a doe that had but one eye used to graze near the sea; and in order to be safe, she kept her blind eye toward the water, from which side she expected no danger, while with the good eye she watched the country. Some men, noticing this, took a boat and came upon her from the sea and shot her. With her dying breath, she said: "Oh! Hard fate! That I should receive my death wound from that side whence I expected no harm, and be safe in the part where I looked for most danger."

Saintliness, example of

Acts 5:41; 2 Cor. 1:4; 4:17; 7:4; 12:10

In England I was told of a lady who had been bedridden for years. She was one of those saints that God polishes up for the kingdom; for I believe that there are a good many saints in this world that we never hear about; we never see their names heralded through the press; they live very near the Master; they live very near heaven; and I think it takes a great deal more grace to suffer God's will than it does to do God's will; and if a person lies on a bed of sickness, and suffers cheerfully, it is just as acceptable to God as if they went out and worked in his vineyard.

Now, it was one of those saints, and a lady, who said that for a long time she used to have a great deal of pleasure in watching a bird that came to make its nest near her window. One year it came to make its nest, and it began to make it so low she was afraid something would happen to the young; and every day that she saw that bird busy at work making its nest, she kept saying, "O bird, build higher!" She could see that the bird was going to come to grief and disappointment.

At last the bird got its nest done, and laid its eggs and hatched its young; and every morning the lady looked out to see if the nest was there, and she saw the old bird bringing food for the little ones, and she took a great deal of pleasure in looking at it. But one morning she woke up and she looked out and she saw nothing but feathers scattered all around, and she said, "Ah, the cat has got the old bird and all its young."

It would have been a mercy to have torn that nest down so the bird could have started over higher up. That is what God does for us very often—just snatches things away before it is too late. Now, I think that is what we need to say to church people—that if you build for time you will be disappointed. God says: Build up higher.

Salvation, available to all

Isa. 55:1; Matt. 7:24; 10:32; Luke 6:47; John 7:37; Rev. 21:6; 22:17

Do you believe that Jesus Christ would send those men out to preach the gospel to every creature unless he wanted every creature to be saved? Do you believe he would tell them to preach it to people without giving people the power to accept it? Do you believe the God of heaven is mocking men by offering them his gospel and not giving them the power to take hold of it? Do you believe he will not give people power to accept this sal-

vation as a gift? Man might do that, but God never mocks men. And when he says, "Preach the gospel to every creature," every creature can be saved by simply trusting Christ.

Salvation, by grace

Rom. 3:24; 4:16; Eph. 2:5, 8–9

I remember when I was a boy and went to Boston, I went to the post office two or three times a day to see if there was a letter for me. I knew there was not, as there was but one mail a day. I had not had any employment and was very homesick, and so went constantly to the post office, thinking perhaps when the mail did come in my letter had been mislaid. At last, however, I got a letter. It was from my youngest sister, the first letter she ever wrote to me. I opened it with a light heart thinking there was some good news from home, but the burden of the whole letter was that she had heard there were pickpockets in Boston, and warned me to take care of them.

I thought I had better get some money in hand first, and then I might take care of pickpockets. And so you must take care to remember salvation is a gift. You don't work for salvation, but work day and night after you have got it. Get it first before you do anything, but don't try to get it yourself. We have all got to get into heaven the same way. We cannot work our way there; we have to take our salvation from God.

Salvation, by grace alone

Rom. 3:24; 4:16; Eph. 2:5, 8–9

A man got up in one of our meetings and said that he had been forty-two years learning three things. I said: "If I can learn three things in three minutes that you have taken all your life to learn, I'll be glad to listen." "First," he said, "I couldn't do anything to earn my salvation." "Well," said I to myself, "that is worth learning." "Second, the Lord didn't require me to do anything to earn my salvation." I said, "That's so; I tried it; I couldn't do anything." He continued, "Third, Jesus Christ had already done it all. When Christ cried, 'It is finished!'—all I had to do was to accept." Dear friends, let us learn this lesson; let us give up our struggling and striving, and accept salvation at once.

Salvation, date of

1 Peter 1:23

Some of you are troubled about sudden conversions, and say you don't know the exact hour when you were converted. It isn't worth going across the street to find out when it was; only ask yourselves if you have got the Spirit of Christ now.

Salvation, evidence of; Doubt, danger of

Luke 1:18–20

Now, I find a great many people who need some evidence that they have accepted the Son of God. My friends, if you need any evidence, take God's word for it. You can't find better evidence than that. You know that when the Angel Gabriel came down and told Zachariah he should have a son he wanted a further token than the angel's word. He asked Gabriel for it and the angel answered, "I am Gabriel, who stands in the presence of the Lord." He had never been doubted, and he thundered this out to Zachariah. But Zachariah wanted a further token, and Gabriel said, "You shall have a token: you shall not be able to talk until your son shall be given you."

Salvation for all; Regeneration, wonder of

Ps. 91:15; Joel 2:32; Luke 23:42; Rom. 10:13; 1 Cor. 1:2

Listen to the prodigal, "Father, I have sinned!" That was enough; the father took him right to his bosom. The past was blotted out at once. Look at the men on the day of Pentecost. Their hands were dripping with the blood of the Son of God; they had murdered Jesus Christ. And what did Peter say to them? "It shall come to pass, that whosoever shall call on the name of the Lord shall be saved."

Look at the penitent thief. It might have been that when a little boy, his mother taught him that same passage in Joel, "It shall come to pass, that whosoever shall call on the name of the Lord shall be saved." As he hung there on the cross, it flashed into his mind that this was the Lord of glory, and though he was on the very borders of hell, he cried out, "Lord, remember me," and the answer came right then and there, "This day thou shalt be with me in paradise." In the morning, as black as hell could make him; in the evening, not a spot or wrinkle. Why? Because he took God at his word. Why will men doubt God?

Salvation, free

Zech. 3:4; Acts 13:39; Rom. 1:17; 3:22; 4:5, 24; 5:2; Gal. 2:16

Take salvation freely, and then show your gratitude and love by working for Christ. "To him that worketh not, but believeth," says the apostle. Rowland Hill used to say that auctioneers worked hard to get people to bid up, but he worked hard to get them to bid down—to take salvation for nothing—for the asking.

Salvation, instantaneous

John 3:36; 20:31; 1 John 3:14; 5:1,11

One day I was walking through the streets of York, in England. I saw a little way ahead a soldier coming toward me. He had the red uniform on of the infantry—the dress of the army. I knew at once when I saw him that he was a soldier. When he came near me I stopped him. I said, "My good man, if you have no objection I would like to ask you a few questions." "Certainly, sir," said he.

"Well, then, I would like to know how you first became a soldier." "Yes, sir, I will tell you. You see, sir, I wanted to become a soldier, and the recruiting officer was in our town, and I went up to him and told him I wanted to enlist. 'Well, sir,' he said, 'All right,' and the first thing he did, sir, he took an English shilling out of his pocket, sir, and put it into my hand. The very moment, sir, a recruiting sergeant puts a shilling into your hand, sir, you are a soldier." I said to myself, "That is the very illustration I want."

That man was a free man at one time—he could go here and there; do just what he liked; but the moment the shilling was put into his hand he was subject to the rules of war, and Queen Victoria could send him anywhere and make him obey the rules and regulations of the army. He is a soldier the very minute he takes the shilling. He has not got to wait to put on the uniform. And when you ask me how a man may be converted at once, I answer, just the same as that man became a soldier. The citizen becomes a soldier in a minute, and from being a free man becomes subject to the command of others. The moment you take Christ into your heart, that moment your name is written in the roll of heaven.

Salvation, necessity of

James 2:10

I tell you if you break one commandment, you break the whole law, and you are a sinner in the sight of God. I was once reading of Whitefield being the guest of a very moral, upright man who was unsaved. Whitefield loved this man very much, and wished to talk with him about his soul, but he was a very hard man to approach. Whitefield tried many times to approach him, but could not succeed. He had to start away very early the next morning to take the coach and leave him, never to see him, perhaps, in this world again. So when he went into the man's study he saw his diamond ring there and took it and cut right into his drinking glass, "One thing thou lackest," and then he prayed God that night the man's heart might be softened, and that sometime his eyes might rest upon it and it might be the means of his conversion.

That writing was used of God and it did lead to the conversion of that man. I would to God that I could say something to you tonight that might cut down deep into your heart, and that you would never forget, that if you lack salvation, you lack everything. What's rank and position in this world when we come to die, if we haven't got salvation? It seems to me it would be better if we had never been born. If you had held a high position for twenty, thirty, forty, or fifty years—life is short—it seems it would be pretty empty if you hadn't got this one thing—salvation.

Salvation, time of

1 Peter 1:23

There are a great many people that the moment we speak of regeneration say: "These people can tell the very hour and the very minute that God met them. Now, I can't point back to the day that God met me and to the time when the old things passed away." And they are in trouble, and think because they cannot do this that they are not Christians. Now, let me say it is of little account where or how it took place, if you are only converted. Some people have been converted like the flash of a meteor, and others like the rising of the sun, gradually. But if you have the evidences, if you have the fruits of the Spirit, then you are children of God. It is not necessary that we should be able to tell where or how we have been converted, but it is important that we should be able to tell that we are converted.

Salvation without works; Thief on the cross

Luke 23:43; Rom. 4:5; 10:10; Gal. 2:16

The thief on the cross beside Jesus' cross had nails through both hands, so that he could not work; and nails through each foot, so that he could not run errands for the Lord; he could not lift a hand or a foot toward his salvation; and yet Christ offered him the gift of God, and he took it. He threw him a passport, and took him with him into paradise.

Samaritan, a good; Kindness, acts of

Exod. 2:6; Prov. 27:10; Matt. 18:33; Luke 10:33

I remember the first good Samaritan I ever saw. I had been in this world only three or four years when my father died a bankrupt, and the creditors came and swept away about everything we had. My widow mother had a cow and a few things, and it was a hard struggle to keep the wolf from the door. My brother went to Greenfield, and secured work in a store for his board, and went to school. It was so lonely there that he wanted me to get a place so as to be with him, but I didn't want to leave home. One cold day in November my brother came home and said he had a place for me. I said that I wouldn't go, but after it was talked over they decided I should go. I didn't want my brothers to know that I hadn't the courage to go, but that night was a long one.

The next morning we started. We went up on the hill, and had a last sight of the old house. We sat down there and cried. I thought that would be the last time I should ever see that old home. I cried all the way down to Greenfield. There my brother introduced me to an old man who was so old he couldn't milk his cows and do the chores, so I was to do his errands, milk his cows and go to school. I looked at the old man and saw that he was cross. I took a good look at the wife and thought that she was crosser than the old man. I stayed there an hour and it seemed like a week.

I went around then to my brother and said, "I am going home." "What are you going home for?" "I am homesick," I said. "Oh well, you will get over it in a few days." "I never will," I said. "I don't want to." He said, "You will get lost if you start for home now; it is getting dark." I was frightened then, as I was only about ten years old, and I said, "I will go at daybreak tomorrow morning."

He took me to a shop window, where they had some jackknives and other things, and tried to divert my mind. What did I care for those old jackknives? I wanted to get back home to my mother and brothers; it seemed as if my heart was breaking.

All at once my brother said, "Dwight, there comes a man that will give you a penny." "How do you know he will?" I asked. "Oh! He gives every new boy that comes to town a penny."

I brushed away the tears, for I wouldn't have him see me crying, and I got right in the middle of the sidewalk, where he couldn't help but see me, and kept my eyes right upon him. I remember how that old man looked as he came tottering down the sidewalk. Oh, such a bright, cheerful, sunny face he had! When he came opposite to where I was he stopped, took my hat off, put his hand on my head, and said to my brother, "This is a new boy in town, isn't it?" "Yes, sir, he is; just came today."

I watched to see if he would put his hand into his pocket. I was thinking of that penny. He began to talk to me so kindly that I forgot all about it. He told me that God had an only Son, and he sent him down here, and wicked men killed him, and he said he died for me. He only talked five minutes, but he took me captive. After he had given me this little talk, he put his hand in his pocket and took out a brand new penny, a copper that looked just like gold. He gave me that; I thought it was gold, and didn't I hold it tight! I never felt so rich before or since.

I don't know what became of that cent; I have always regretted that I didn't keep it; but I can feel the pressure of the old man's hand on my head today. Fifty years have rolled away, and I can hear those kind words ringing yet. I never shall forget that act. He put the money at interest; that penny has cost me a great many dollars. I have never walked up the streets of this country or the old country but down into my pocket goes my hand, and I take out some money and give it to every forlorn, miserable child I see.

I think how the old man lifted a load from me, and I want to lift a load from someone else. Do you want to be like Christ? Go and find someone who has fallen, and get your arm under him, and lift him up toward heaven. The Lord will bless you in the very act. May God help us to go and do like the good Samaritan!

Sanctification, process of; Growth, spiritual; Justification, nature of

Eph. 4:15; Col. 1:10; 3:10; 1 Peter 2:2; 5:10; 2 Peter 3:18

Although you may be born again, it will require time to become a fullgrown Christian. Justification is instantaneous, but sanctification is a lifework. We are to grow in wisdom. We are to add grace to grace. A tree may be perfect in its first year of growth, but it has not attained its maturity. So with the Christian: he may be a true child of God, but not a matured Christian.

Satan blamed for sin

Matt. 15:18; Mark 7:21; Rom. 7:11; Heb. 3:13; James 1:14; 4:1–2

You may have heard of the little child that went for berries when she had been told not to. Her mother said, "Why did you go into those berry bushes after I had said you mustn't?" "Well," said the child, "the devil pushed me right in." A good many people excuse themselves in that way. There's a battle that rages all the while between me and the temptations of the flesh, and I am either to overcome them or they will overcome me. That is the question for me to settle.

Satan, deception of

Matt. 13:19; Mark 4:15; Luke 8:12; 2 Cor. 2:11; 4:4; 11:3; 1 Peter 5:8; Rev. 20:8

How many men all over the world are being deceived by the god of this world? It has been asserted that during the late Franco-German war, German drummers and trumpeters used to give the French beats and calls in order to deceive their enemies. The command to "halt," or "cease firing" was often given by the Germans, it has been said, and the French soldiers were thus placed in positions where they could be shot down like cattle.

Satan is the archenemy of our souls, and he has often blinded our reason and deceived our conscience by his falsehoods. He has often come as an angel of light, concealing his hideousness under a borrowed cloak. He says to a young man, "Sow your wild oats. Time enough to be religious when you grow old." The young man yields himself to a life of extravagance and excess, under the false hope that he will obtain solid satisfaction, and it is well if he awakens to the deception before his appetites become tyrants, dragging him down into depths of want and woe. Satan promises great things to his victims in the indulgence of their lusts, but they never realize the promises. The promised pleasure turns out to be pain, the promised heaven a hell.

Satan, delusive tactics

Matt. 13:19; Mark 4:15; Luke 8:12; 2 Cor. 2:11; 4:4; 11:3; 1 Peter 5:8; Rev. 20:8

Satan puts straws across our path and magnifies it and makes us believe it is a mountain, but all the devil's mountains are mountains of smoke; when you come up to them they are not there.

Satan in church

Matt. 13:19; Mark 4:15; Luke 8:12; 2 Cor. 2:11; 4:4; 11:3; 1 Peter 5:8; Rev. 20:8

Many say, "Oh, yes, I am a Christian, I go to church every Sunday." There is no one who goes to church so regularly as Satan. He is always there before the minister and the last one out of church. There is not a church, or chapel, but he is a regular attendant of it. The idea that he is only in slums, and lanes, and public houses, is a false one.

Satan, opposition of

2 Cor. 2:11; 4:4; 11:3; 1 Peter 5:8; Rev. 20:8

When a man is truly born of God, it seems as if every influence of evil is arrayed against him, and unless the work is genuine he will not stand. I know of a certain temperance lecturer who was once a poor, wretched drunkard. A short time after his conversion he was asked to speak in his native town, and when he came on the stage it was found that liquor had been sprinkled about the floor in order that its fumes might tempt him to drink again. But he trusted God and held firm.

Satan, resisting of

Luke 22:32; Eph. 4:27; 6:11,13; James 4:7; 1 Peter 5:8;

A man in Manchester, England, had a greyhound dog that he was training for a race, and he had a large bet on him for a poor man, and he was anxious his dog should succeed. The day came, and the dog didn't run at all. He was so mad that he beat the greyhound. Then he took the dog down to the zoo and pushed it through a cage in which there was a lion. He cried out in anger, "That lion will make short work of him!" But the dog ran right up to the lion as though it wanted mercy, and instead of the lion eating it, began to lap it. By-and-by the man called to the dog to come out, but he would not come. Then he put his hand in, and the lion began to growl, and he took it out again. And some people went and told the keeper what the man had done and how he had ill-used the greyhound.

When the keeper came around, the man wanted him to get his dog out for him; and the keeper asked him how he got in there, and the man was ashamed to tell. At last the keeper said, "You put him in; you'd better go and get him out. I'll open the cage door for you." But the man went home and so the dog has remained there ever since. Now, that may be a homely illustration, but I hope it will fasten on our minds the idea that we are no match for Satan. He has had six thousand years experience. I always tremble when I hear a man talk about defying Satan, and I want to add "by the grace of God," for that is the only way. The lion of the tribe of Judah will take care of us if we will come to him.

Satan, strategy of

Matt. 13:19; Mark 4:15; Luke 8:12; 2 Cor. 2:11; 4:4; 11:3; 1 Peter 5:8; Rev. 20:8

Satan rules all men that are in his kingdom. Some he rules through lust. Some he rules through covetousness. Some he rules through appetite. Some he rules by their temper, but he rules them. And none will ever seek to be delivered until they get their eyes open and see that they have been taken captive.

Matt. 13:19; Mark 4:15; Luke 8:12; 2 Cor. 2:11; 4:4; 11:3; 1 Peter 5:8; Rev. 20:8

Satan has three lines of attack. First, he tries to keep men from becoming Christians. Then, if foiled here, he tries to keep them from being active and useful as Christians. And finally, as a last resort, he tries to blacken their characters. If any man will live godly in Christ Jesus, he will suffer persecution. If the world has nothing to say against us, it is likely that Christ has nothing to say for us. The world hates the crucified Savior, and all who bear his image. Men don't want to be troubled by the truth. They don't like pungent preaching. Some think over their business while in church, so as not to hear.

Satan, strategy of; Commandment, second

Matt. 13:19; Mark 4:15; Luke 8:12; 2 Cor. 2:11; 4:4; 11:3; 1 Peter 5:8; Rev 20:8

Satan tries to keep us from worshiping God properly, and from making him first in everything. If I let some image made by man get into my heart and take the place of God the Creator, it is a sin. I believe that Satan is willing to have us worship anything, however sacred—the Bible, the crucifix, the church—if only we do not worship God himself. You cannot find a place in the Bible where a man has been allowed to bow down and worship anyone but the triune God of heaven. In the book of Revelation when an angel came down to John, he was about to fall down and worship him, but the angel would not let him. If an angel from heaven is not to be worshiped, when you find people bowing down to pictures, to images, even when they bow down to worship the cross, it is a sin.

Satan, strategy of; Preaching, gain attention

Matt. 13:19; Mark 4:15; Luke 8:12; 2 Cor. 2:11; 4:4; 11:3; 1 Peter 5:8; Rev. 20:8

When you talk to people, get their attention at once. If you don't get their attention the first ten minutes, you have lost your audience. Satan tries to divert their minds, and if you don't get hold of their attention the very first thing, they will be thinking of business, making bargains, marrying wives, and roaming all over the world. Start out with some striking thought or some illustration that will seize their attention, and you will generally manage to hold it.

Satan, strategy of; Seed snatched away

Matt. 13:19; Mark 4:15; Luke 8:12; 2 Cor. 2:11; 4:4; 11:3; 1 Peter 5:8; Rev. 20:8

There was an architect in Chicago who was converted. In giving his testimony, he said he had been in the habit of attending church for a great many years, but he could not say that he had really heard a sermon all the time. He said that when the minister gave out the text and began to preach, he used to settle himself in the corner of the pew and work out the plans of some building. He could not tell how many plans he had prepared while the minister was preaching. He was the architect for one or two companies; and he used to do much of his planning in that way.

You see, Satan came in between him and the preacher, and caught away the good seed of the Word. I have often preached to people, and have been perfectly amazed to find they could hardly tell one solitary word of the sermon; even the text had completely gone from them.

Satan, victory over

Luke 22:32; Eph. 4:27; 6:11,13; James 4:7; 1 Peter 5:8

Martin Luther had a conflict with the devil, but when he said the blood of Christ cleanseth from all sin, Satan left him.

Satan, wiles of

Matt. 13:19; Mark 4:15; Luke 8:12; 2 Cor. 2:11; 4:4; 11:3; 1 Peter 5:8; Rev. 20:8

Now it seems as if there are three wiles of Satan against which we ought to be on our guard. In the first place, he moves all his kingdom to keep us away from Christ; then he devotes himself to get us into "Doubting Castle"; but if we have, in spite of him, a clear ringing witness for the Son of God, he will do all he can to blacken our characters and belie our testimony.

Satisfaction, inner; Worldliness, futility of; Sin, cleansing from

Jer. 2:13; 17:13; Joel 3:18; Zech. 13:1; John 7:37

How this world is thirsting for something that will satisfy! What fills the places of amusement, the dance houses, the music halls, and the theaters, night after night? Men and women are thirsting for something they don't have. The moment a man turns his back upon God, he begins to thirst; and that thirst will never be quenched until he returns to "the fountain of living waters." As the prophet Jeremiah tells us, we have forsaken the fountain of living waters, and hewn out for ourselves cisterns, broken cisterns, that can hold no water. There is a thirst this world can never quench: the more we drink of its pleasures, the thirstier we become. We cry out for more and more, and we are all the while being dragged down lower and lower. But there is a fountain opened to the house of David for sin and for uncleanness. Let us press up to it, and drink and live.

Scripture, disputed; Bible study, importance of

Deut. 29:29; Dan. 2:22; Matt. 13:35

There are many things in the Bible which were dark and mysterious to me five years ago, on which I have since had a flood of light; and I expect to be finding out something fresh about God throughout eternity. I make a point of not discussing disputed passages of Scripture. An old divine has said that some people, if they want to eat fish, commence by picking the bones. I leave such things till I have light on them. I am not bound to explain what I do not comprehend. "The secret things belong unto the Lord our God: but those things which are revealed belong unto us and to our children forever"; and these I take, and eat, and feed upon, in order to get spiritual strength.

Scripture, ignorance of; Shepherd, true

Ps. 23:1; Isa. 40:11; Luke 19:10; John 10:11

I tell you the true sheep know a true shepherd. I got up in Scotland once and quoted a passage of Scripture a little different from what it was in the Bible, and an old woman crept up and said: "Mr. Moody, you said—." I might make forty misquotations in an ordinary audience, and no one would tell me about them. Like two lawyers: one said in court that the other didn't know the Lord's Prayer. The other said he did: "Now I lay me down to sleep." "Well," the first said, "I give up. You do know it." Didn't either one of them know it, you see.

Secret sin, danger of

Gen. 44:16; Num. 32:23; Pss. 90:8; 140:11; Isa. 59:2,12

Do you want to know the reason why, every now and then, the church is scandalized by the exposure of some pastor, leading church member or Sunday school superintendent? It is not his Christianity, but his lack of it. Some secret sin has been eating at the heart of the tree, and in a critical moment it is blown down and its rottenness revealed.

Security, source of; Assurance, source of

Deut. 32:4,15; 1 Sam. 2:2; 2 Sam. 22:3, 32, 47; Pss. 18:2, 31, 46; 94:22; Isa. 17:10

Another writer says, "I have seen shrubs and trees grow out of the rocks, and overhang fearful precipices, roaring cataracts, and deep running waters; but they maintained their position, and threw out their foliage and branches as much as if they had been in the midst of a dense forest. It was their hold on the rock that made them secure; and the influences of nature that sustained their life. So believers are oftentimes exposed to the most horrible dangers in their journey to heaven; but, so long as they are 'rooted and grounded' in the Rock of Ages, they are perfectly secure."

Seek God's kingdom

1 Kings 3:11; 2 Chron. 31:21; Ps. 34:10; Matt. 5:6; 6:33; Luke 12:31; 18:29; John 6:27; Rom. 14:17

I am told that when the war broke out on the Gold Coast of Africa, though it was known that the climate was a very unhealthy one, and a great many who went there would never return, yet hundreds and thousands of men wanted to go. Why? They wanted to get wealth, and from wealth honor. And if there is a chance of going to India to do battle, no end of men are willing to go. To get a little honor they will sacrifice comfort, pleasure, health, and everything. What we want is to have men seeking the kingdom of God as they seek for honor and wealth.

Seeker trusts Christ

Matt. 19:16; Luke 10:25; 18:18; John 5:39; 6:27; Acts 16:30; 1 John 5:20

The other Sunday, when I was speaking on "Trust," a person came to me next day and said, "I want to tell you how I was saved. You remember you told about that lady who sought Christ three years and could not find him, and when you told that, it was I. I was in that same condition and through your story I got light." I don't think I have ever told it but what somebody got light and life. I will tell it again, for I would go up and down the world telling it if I could get a convert.

One night I was preaching, and happening to cast my eyes down during the sermon, I saw two eyes just riveted upon me. Every word that fell from my lips she just seemed to catch with her own lips, and I was very anxious to go down where she was. After the sermon I went to the pew and said, "My friend, are you a Christian?" "Oh, no," said she, "I wish I were. I have been seeking Christ three years and I cannot find him." Said I, "Oh, there is a great mistake about that." Says she, "Do you think I am not in earnest? Do you think, sir, I have not been seeking Christ?"

Said I, "I suppose you think you have, but Christ has been seeking you these twenty years, and it would not take an anxious sinner and an anxious Savior three years to meet, and if you had been really seeking him you would have found him long before this." She asked, "What would you do, then?" Said I, "Do nothing, only believe on the Lord Jesus Christ and thou shalt be saved."

"Oh," said she, "I have heard that till my head swims. Everybody says, 'believe! believe! believe!' and I am none the wiser. I don't know what you mean by it." "Very well," said I, "I will drop the word; but just trust the Lord Jesus Christ to save." "If I say I trust Jesus, will he save me?" "You may do a thousand things; but if you really trust Jesus Christ, he will save you." "Well," said she, "I trust him, but I don't feel any different." "Ah," said I, "I have found your difficulty. You have been hunting for feeling all these three years. You have not been looking for Christ."

Says she, "Christians tell how much joy they have got." "But," said I, "you want a Christian experience before you get one. Instead of trusting God, you are looking for Christian experience." Then I said, "Right here in this pew, just commit yourself to the Lord Jesus Christ, and trust him, and you will be saved," and I held her right to that word "trust," which is the same as the word "believe" in the Old Testament. "You know what it is to trust a friend. Cannot you trust God as a friend?"

She looked at me for five minutes, it seemed, and then said slowly, "Mr. Moody, I trust the Lord Jesus Christ this night to save my soul." Turning to the pastor of the church she took him by the hand and repeated the declaration. Turning to an elder in the church she said again the solemn words, and near the door, meeting another officer of the church, she repeated for the fourth time, "I am trusting Jesus," and went off home.

The next night when I was preaching I saw her right in front of me, "Eternity" written in her eyes, her face lighted up, and when I asked inquirers to go into the other room she was the first to go in. I wondered at it, for I could see in her face that she was in the joy of the Lord. But when I got in I found her with her arms around a young lady's neck, and I heard her say, "It is only just trusting. I stumbled over it for three years and found it all in trusting!" The three weeks I was there, she led more souls to Christ than anybody else. If I got a difficult case I would send it to her. Oh, my friends, won't you trust Jesus? Let us put our trust in him.

Self-control, importance of

Prov. 23:2; Gal. 5:16; Phil. 3:19; Titus 2:2; 2 Peter 2:10; 1 John 2:16

The lust of the flesh is appetite. I must either control my appetite or it will control me. Suppose a person has an appetite for opium, or for strong drink, or for anything that is injurious, and it has gained the mastery over his will, I can assert that no slave ever had a harder master than that man. The question is, have you got control of the appetite, or has it got control of you?

Paul admonishes us to be sound in faith, in patience, in love. You wouldn't have a preacher that was unsound in the faith. But if he was unsound in temper, or unsound in love, you might still call him a splendid man. There is the same responsibility to be sound in patience as there is to be sound in faith. If you begin to use discipline on church members who are not sound in patience, what would become of the church? You wouldn't have many members, and many ministers would be without pulpits.

Prov. 23:2; Gal. 5:16, 22; Phil. 3:19; Titus 2:2; 2 Peter 2:10; 1 John 2:16

The minister who hasn't patience and can't control his temper had better get out of the pulpit. I know lots of ministers who are not worth a snap of my finger; they can't control their tempers. They go into the pulpit and scold and find fault with their people, and lose their power and lose their influence. We must control ourselves if we ever expect to control our families, our enemies, or anyone else.

Self-control, importance of; Christ, reigning with

Prov. 23:2; Gal. 5:16, 22; Phil. 3:19; 2 Tim. 2:12; Titus 2:2; 2 Peter 2:10; 1 John 2:16; Rev. 5:10; 20:6; 22:5

Those that are able to rule themselves by God's grace are the ones that God can trust with power. Only those who can govern themselves are fit to govern other people. I have an idea that we are down here in training, that God is just polishing us for some higher service. I don't know where the kingdoms are, but if we are to be kings and priests we must have kingdoms to reign over.

Self-control, importance of; Sin, victory over

Ps. 91:14; 1 Cor. 10:13; Gal. 5:25; James 1:12

We all have some weak point in our character. When we would go forward, it drags us back, and when we would rise up into higher spheres of usefulness and the atmosphere of heaven, something drags us down. Now I have no sympathy with the idea that God puts us behind the blood and saves us, and then leaves us in Egypt to be under the old taskmaster. I believe God brings us out of Egypt into the promised land, and that it is the privilege of every child of God to be delivered from every foe, from every besetting sin. If there is some sin that is getting the mastery over you, you certainly can't be useful. You certainly can't bring forth fruit to the honor and glory of God until you get self-control.

Self-denial, influence of; Faithfulness, reward of

Neh. 2:5; Matt. 16:24; Mark 8:34; Luke 9:23

It meant a good deal for Nehemiah to give up the palace of Shushan and his high office, and identify himself with the despised and captive Jews. He was among the highest in the whole realm. Not only that, but he was a man of wealth, lived in ease and luxury, and had great influence at court. For him to go to Jerusalem and leave his position was like Moses turning his back on the palace of Pharaoh and identifying himself with the Hebrew slaves. Yet we might never have heard of either of them if they had not done this. They stooped to conquer; and when you get ready to stoop God will bless you. Plato, Socrates, and other Greek philosophers lived in the same century as Nehemiah. How few have heard of them and read their words compared with the hundreds of thousands who have heard and read of Nehemiah during the last two thousand years!

Self-denial, key to service

Matt. 16:24; Mark 8:34; Luke 9:23; 2 Tim. 2:3

The first step to a higher service is the end of self. God's way up is down. God never yet lifted up a man high that he did not cast him down first; never. Self must be annihilated. When we get to the end of our own power then it is that the power of God is manifested in us.

Selfishness, danger of; Doubts, cure for

Pss. 34:5; 123:2; Isa. 45:22; Heb. 12:2

If you want to scatter your doubts, look at the blood; and if you want to increase your doubts, look at yourself. You will get doubts enough for years by being occupied with yourself only a few days.

Selfishness, danger of; Pride, danger of

Gen. 3:5–6; 11:4; Num. 12:1; 16:3; 1 Kings 1:5; Ps. 49:11; Matt. 20:20; 23:6; Luke 9:25; 11:43; 22:3; 1 John 2:16; 3 John 1:9

If we preached down ourselves and exalted Christ, the world would soon be reached. The world is perishing today for the need of Christ. The church could do without our theories and pet views, but not without Christ; and when her ministers get behind the cross, so that Christ is held up, the people will come flocking to hear the gospel.

Selfishness is one of the greatest hindrances to the cause of Christ. Everyone wants the chief seat in the synagogue. One prides himself that he is pastor of this church, and another of that. Would to God we could get all this out of the way, and say, "He must increase, but I must decrease." We cannot do it, however, except we get down at the foot of the cross. Human nature likes to be lifted up; the grace of God alone can humble us.

Separation from world; Perseverance, value of

Ps. 1:1; Isa. 52:11; Acts 2:40; 2 Cor. 6:17; 7:1; Rev. 18:4

I believe that a Christian man should lead a separated life. The line between the church and the world is almost obliterated today. I have no sympathy with the idea that you must hunt up an old musty church record in order to find out whether a man is a member of the church or not. A man ought to live so that everybody will know he is a Christian. The Bible tells us to lead a separate life. You may lose influence, but you will gain it at the same time. I suppose Daniel was the most unpopular man in Babylon at a certain time, but, thank God, he has outlived all the other men of his day.

Sermon feedback

1 Peter 1:18

It is a good thing to question the people a little now and then, to see if they understand your sermons. A man said to me in Chicago: "I liked your sermon last Sunday." "Did you? What was the text?" "I can't remember." "What was the subject?" "I can't remember." "What do you remember?" "Well, I liked the way you talked." It was a lesson to me. If that is all people remember of what you say, you will not do them much good.

Sermons, length of

Acts 20:9

When a man has a reputation for being long, he had better get out of the ministry. Did you ever hear anyone complain that a minister's sermons and prayers were too short? But how often do you hear complaints that they are too long? Congregations are dwindling away for that reason when they ought to be increasing. Young people are falling away from the habit of attending church. Remember that we are living now in a fast age—a century of railroads and telegraphs. Men's minds move quicker than they used to. So let us say what we want to say in as striking a manner as we can, and then stop. Many men don't know just where to stop, and think they must round out a passage nicely so as to leave a good impression. But it is a great deal better to stop abruptly than to feel around for a good stopping place.

Service, do what you can; Talents, use of

Matt. 25:15; Rom. 12:6; 1 Cor. 12:31; 14:12; Eph. 4:11–12

The first two or three years that I attempted to talk in the meetings I saw that the older people did not like it. I had sense enough to know that I was a bore to them. Well, I went out upon the street and I got eighteen little children to follow me the first Sunday, and I led them into the Sunday school. I found that I had something to do. I was encouraged and I kept at that work. And if I am worth anything to the Christian church today, it is as much due to that work as anything else. I could not explain these scriptural passages to them for I did not then comprehend them; but I could tell them stories. I could tell them that Christ loved them and that he died for them. I did the best I could. I used the little talent I had, and God kept giving me more talents, and so, let me say, find some work.

See if you can get a Sunday school class to teach. If you cannot get that, go down into the dark lanes and byways of the city and talk to them and sing some gospel hymns; or, if you cannot sing, take someone with you who can sing some of these songs of praise. Sing or read the Twenty-third Psalm, or pray, and you can get a blessing in that way. When you have won one soul to Christ, you will want to win two; and when you get into the luxury of winning souls, it will be a new world to you, and you will not think of going back to the world at all.

Service, heart for

2 Chron. 15:15; Ps. 119:10; Isa. 6:8; Mark 12:33; Acts 22:21

There are but few now that say, "Here am I, Lord; send me"; the cry now is, "Send someone else. Send the minister, send the church officers, the churchwarden, the elders; but not me. I have not got the ability, the gifts, or the talents." Ah! honestly say you haven't got the heart; for if the heart is loyal God can use you. It is really all a matter of heart. It does not take God a great while to qualify a man for his work, if he only has the heart for it.

Service in Christ's power

Isa. 40:29; 41:10; John 15:5; 2 Cor. 3:5; 12:9; Eph. 3:16; 6:10; Phil. 4:13; Col. 1:11

Trying to be good without Christ is like trying to fill a tub that has no bottom with a bucket that is full of holes.

Service, invitation to

Gen. 12:1; Exod. 3:10; Isa. 6:8; Acts 22:21

There is no luxury like working for the Lord. He gives us something more than silver and gold. If the Mayor of Chicago were to issue a proclamation for 10,000 people, offering to give them a large wage, you would think it very good; but here is a proclamation from the throne of God that tens of thousands of men, women, and children can be used in the Lord's vineyard in gathering the treasures of life. The Lord can use the oldest, the youngest, and all between.

Service, key to

Num. 16:9; Deut. 21:5; 1 Kings 18:36; Ps. 75:1; Dan. 3:26

When I was in Scotland I heard a minister use an expression that struck me. He says, "God always uses the vessel that is nearest to him." It may be some man or woman in the pew that has got nearer to God than the man in the pulpit. What we professed Christians need is to get nearer to God, so that he will use us. It is the highest privilege to be used by God.

Service, nature of

1 Cor. 15:58; Col. 2:7; 1 Thess. 3:12; 2 Thess. 1:3; 2 Peter 3:18

I read some time ago of a man who took passage in a stagecoach. There were first, second, and third class passengers. But when he looked into the coach, he saw all the passengers sitting together without distinction. He could not understand it till by and by they came to a hill, and the coach stopped, and the driver called out, "First class passengers keep their seats, second-class passengers get out and walk, third-class passengers get behind and push."

Now in the church we have no room for first-class passengers—people who think that salvation means an easy ride all the way to heaven. We have no room for second-class passengers—people who are carried most of the time and who, when they must work out their own salvation, go trudging on giving never a thought to helping their fellows along. All church members ought to be third-class passengers—ready to dismount and push all together, and push with a will. That was John Wesley's definition of a church, "All at it, and always at it."

Service, persistence in; Obedience to God

Mark 14:8; John 12:7

I imagine when Mary of Bethany died, if God had sent an angel to write her epitaph, he couldn't have done better than to put over her grave what Christ said, "She hath done what she could." I would rather have that said over my grave, if it could honestly be said, than to have all the wealth of the Rothschilds. Christ raised a monument to Mary that is more lasting than the monuments raised to the Czar or Napoleon. Their monuments crumble away, but hers endures. Her name never appeared in print while she was on earth, but today it is famous in three hundred and fifty languages.

We may never be great. We may never be known outside our circle of friends; but we may, like Mary, do what we can. May God help each one of us to do what we can! Life will soon be over; it is short at the longest. Let us rise and follow in the footsteps of Mary of Bethany.

Service, power for; Holy Spirit, filling

Luke 11:13; Acts 1:8; 11:24; Eph. 5:18; Titus 2:14

We need the power the filling of the Holy Spirit gives us for the ministry of God's Word. Sin leaped into the world full-grown at the first leap. Without the power of God we can do nothing. When we enter the pulpit we want to know that we have got the witness of the Spirit along with us. In any efforts in the service of Christ we need the filling of God's Spirit.

Service, readiness for

2 Tim. 2:3–4

Now, I have found since I have been here in New York that there is not one out of a hundred of God's people ready to go when I ask them to go and speak to any person about his soul. Why, what is a fire escape good for if it is not ready when it is needed? What is a soldier good for if be is not ready for battle when called on? We should be like soldiers, ready to obey God's command, for God wants his children all ready. The trouble is that men are all the time getting ready. Suppose a man tumbled into the river, would you appoint a committee to consult about getting him out? We should be ready to plunge in and save him. I pray God today to make us ready.

Service, strength for; Obedience, empowerment for

Matt. 14:10; Mark 6:16; Luke 9:9; John 3:30; Acts 7:51

Sometimes it looks as if God's servants fail. When Herod beheaded John the Baptist, it looked as if John's mission was a failure. But was it? The voice that rang through the valley of the Jordan rings through the whole world today. You can hear its echo upon the mountains and the valleys yet, "I must decrease, but he must increase." He held up Jesus Christ and introduced him to the world, and Herod had not power to behead John until his life's work had been accomplished.

Stephen preached but one sermon that we know of and that was before the Sanhedrin; but how that sermon has been preached again and again all over the world! Out of his death probably came Paul, the greatest preacher the world has seen since Christ left this earth. If a man is sent by the Lord he may expect the Lord's strength to accomplish the work.

Service, vision for; Values, eternal

Luke 16:9; 2 Tim. 4:8; Heb. 6:10; Rev. 14:13

Think of Paul up yonder. People are going up to heaven every day and every hour, men and women who have been brought to Christ through his writings. He set streams in motion that have flowed on for almost two thousand years. I can imagine people going up to him and saying, "Paul, I thank you for writing that letter to the Ephesians; I found Christ in that." "Paul, I thank you for writing that epistle to the Corinthians." "Paul, I found Christ in that epistle to the Philippians." "I thank you, Paul, for that epistle to the Galatians; I found Christ in that." When Paul was put in prison he did not fold his hands and sit down in idleness! No, he began to write; and his epistles have come down through the ages and brought thousands on thousands to a knowledge of Christ crucified.

Service, wholehearted; Dedication, appeal to

Deut. 10:12; 11:13; Josh. 22:5; 1 Chron. 28:9

When I was in Glasgow, Scotland, one of the physicians of that city came up to the platform one day, and said, "I'm not used to speaking in public, but I'd like to say a word." "Glad to have you," I said. He was at the head of the medical profession of that country, greatly respected and getting on in years. He had passed three score years and ten, so he was living on borrowed time. He stood up, and there was a hush, and as it were a voice coming from heaven, from another world. He said, "I want to tell you of a great mistake made in my life. If I had my life to live over again, I wouldn't make it. I haven't served God with all my heart." There weren't any dry eyes there. I shall never forget that speech. What confession would you make right now as to how you have served God? Will you from this moment commit yourself to serving God with all your heart?

Sheep nature of Christians

Ps.119:176; Isa. 53:6; Jer. 23:1; John 10:14; 21:16; 1 Peter 2:25

In John chapter ten we have Christ the Good Shepherd. Someone has said that the Lord's sheep have three marks. First, they hear the voice of the Shepherd; second, they know the voice of the Shepherd; third, they follow the voice of the Shepherd. They hear, they know, and they follow. The Lord does not say they shall try to follow him but they do follow him.

Shepherd, follow voice of

Ps. 23:1; Isa. 40:11; Matt. 26:31; Luke 19:10; John 10:11; Heb. 13:7; 1 Peter 2:25; 5:4

Rev. Mr. Brown, an evangelist from Wisconsin, in one of the Chicago meetings, related the following incident: I have a friend who used to live in Syria, and he became very well acquainted with the shepherds of that country. One day as he was riding among the mountains he came to a spring of water, and stopped to rest awhile. Presently down one of the steep mountain paths a shepherd came, leading his flock of sheep. Not long after another shepherd with another flock came down to the water by another path, and after awhile a third. The three flocks mingled together, so that he began to wonder how each shepherd was ever going to find his own sheep again.

At last one of them rose up and called out, "Men-ah!" which in Arabic means "follow"; and his sheep came out from the great flock, and followed him back into the mountains. He did not even stop to count them. Then the second shepherd got up and called out to his sheep, "Men-ah!" and those of his flock left the others and followed him away.

My friend could speak Arabic very well; so one day he said to a shepherd, "I think I could make your sheep follow me."

"I think not," said the shepherd. "Give me your turban, and your cloak, and your crook," said my friend, "and we'll see." So he put on the shepherd's turban and his cloak, and took the crook in his hand, and stood up where the sheep could see him, and called out, "Men-ah! Men-ah!" But not a sheep would take any notice of him. They know not the voice of strangers.

My friend asked the shepherd if the sheep never followed anybody but him. "O yes; sometimes a sheep gets sick, and then it will follow a stranger." Just so with us Christians; we get sick and backslidden, and then we follow the devil.

Shepherd ministry of Christ; Sheep nature of mankind; Need of savior

Ps. 23:1; Isa. 40:11; 53:6; Matt. 18:12; 25:33; Mark 6:34; John 10:11; Heb. 13:7; 1 Peter 2:25; 5:4

A friend of mine was in Syria, and he found a shepherd that kept up the old custom of naming his sheep. My friend said he wouldn't believe that the sheep knew him when he called them by name. So he said to the shepherd, "I wish you would just call one or two." The shepherd said, "Neriah." The sheep stopped eating and looked up. The shepherd called out, "Come here." The sheep came, and stood looking up into his face.

He called another, and another, and there they stood looking up at the shepherd. "How can you tell them apart?" "Oh, there are no two alike. Don't you see? That sheep has lost a little bit of wool. That one is a little cross-eyed; this one is a little bow-legged; and that one over there turns his toes in; this sheep is a little bit squint-eyed; that sheep has a black spot on its nose." My friend found that he knew every one of his sheep by their faults and failings. He didn't have a perfect one in his flock.

I suppose that is the way the Lord knows you and me. There is a man that is covetous; he wants to grasp the whole world. He needs a shepherd to keep down that spirit. There is a woman down there who has an awful tongue; she keeps the whole neighborhood stirred up. There is a woman over there who is deceitful, terribly so. She needs the care of a shepherd to keep her from deceit, for she will ruin all her children; they will all turn out just like their mother. There is a father over there who wouldn't swear for all the world before his children, but sometimes he gets provoked in his business and swears before he knows it. Doesn't he need a shepherd's care?

I would like to know if there is a man or woman on earth who doesn't need the care of a shepherd. Haven't we all got failings? If you really want to know what your failings are, you can find someone who can point them out. God would never have sent Christ into the world if we didn't need his care. We are as weak and foolish as sheep.

Short accounts, keeping

Pss. 19:12; 51:2; Dan. 9:4; Acts 19:18; 1 John 1:7, 9

It is said that "short accounts make long friends." Keep short accounts with God. You should see the face of God every morning before you see the face of any human being. If you come to the cross every morning, you will never get but one day's journey from the cross. Just keep close to the cross and close to Jesus, and if anything has gone wrong during the day or evening, do not sleep until that account has been settled. Take your trouble to Christ and tell it right out to him, tell him you are sorry, and ask him to forgive you. He delights to forgive. That is what I mean by keeping a short account with God.

You know when you continue to buy a little something at a grocery store every few days, in a short time the grocer has a large bill against you. You are surprised, and perhaps say you never bought that much. Then you quarrel with the grocer, and you have a great deal of trouble over it. Perhaps if you kept short accounts you would remember what you owed. Keep short accounts or else you won't prosper.

Significance, eternal; Value, true; Vision, spiritual

Isa. 14:24; 46:10; Rom. 8:28; 9:11; Eph. 1:11; 3:11; 2 Tim. 1:9

A certain John Bacon, once a famous sculptor, left an inscription to be placed on his tomb in Westminster Abbey: "What I was as an artist seemed of some importance to me while I lived; but what I was as a believer in Jesus Christ is the only thing of importance to me now."

Sin blotted out

Pss. 51:9; 103:12; Isa. 1:18; 43:25; 44:22; Acts 3:19

God has promised to blot out our sins like a thick cloud. You see a cloud tonight, and you get up early in the morning, and it is gone. Can you find the cloud? Never. There may be other clouds, but that cloud will never appear in the history of the universe. God says he will blot sin out like a thick cloud.

Sin, confession of

Gen. 3:12; Ps. 32:3; Prov. 28:13; Matt. 23:35; Acts 26:20

"He that covereth his sins shall not prosper." He may be a man in the pulpit, a priest before the altar, a king on the throne; I don't care who he is. People have been trying it for six thousand years. Adam tried it, and failed. Moses tried it when he buried the Egyptian whom he killed, but he failed. "Be sure your sin will find you out." You cannot bury your sin so deep but it will have a resurrection by and by, if it has not been blotted out by the Son of God. What man has failed to do for six thousand years, we had better give up trying to do.

Lev. 10:17; 16:10; Isa. 53:12; Matt. 26:28; Heb. 9:28; 1 John 3:5

A great many people want to bring their faith, their works, their good deeds to Christ for salvation. Bring your sins, and he will bear them away into the wilderness of forgetfulness, and you will never see them again.

Matt. 18:15–17; James 5:20; 1 John 1:9

There are three kinds of confession. For instance, if I have been a public transgressor—if I have been known in the streets of Northfield as a public transgressor—I ought not only to confess my sins to God, but to the whole town. The confession ought to be just as public as the transgression was. I ought to be willing to confess in as public a manner as I can my sin, and let people know that I have changed my life. Then, there is another kind of confession. If I have done that man down there a wrong, and no one knows it but himself and myself, I ought to go to him and confess my sin to him and before God. If I have got too much pride to do that, I have got too much pride. Then there is a third kind of confession, and that is between me and my God alone. I go to him with all my sins that nobody knows anything about but myself, and confess them to him as we are instructed in 1 John 1:9.

Gen. 4:9; Lev. 26:40, 42; Job 31:33; Prov. 10:12; 28:13; 1 John 1:9

I met a man, aged 32 years, in Chicago, who, twelve years previously had fled from Canada because of a crime he had committed. For twelve years he had been trying to cover up his sin, but it pursued him night and day. Finally he asked me to advise him. I told him to make restitution of the money he had stolen, and to make an honest confession. You should have seen the tears of joy run down that man's face when he found that he could be forgiven and have his sin put away. What a terrible time he had been having those twelve years! He had been trying to cover his sin in man's way. If you want your sins blotted out completely, you must make a clean breast of them all.

Ps. 32:1; Isa. 55:7; Acts 2:38; 26:20; 1 John 1:9; Rev. 2:5

I read of an ex-prisoner who had secured a position as night watchman in a store. One of his prison associates came to him, and attempted to persuade the man to leave the doors open, so that he could rob the store. The watchman refused, and his former companion threatened to tell his employers about his past life. The watchman laughed in his tempter's face and replied: "Go and tell them. I have nothing to fear, for they knew all of my past life before they hired me." O, man, woman, confess your sins to God! Then you shall know what it is to have heaven in your soul. Blessed—happy—is the man whose transgression is forgiven, whose sin is covered.

Prov. 15:8; 28:9; Isa. 55:7; Matt. 3:8; Luke 3:8, 14; Eph. 4:7; 1 Peter 4:2; 2 Peter 1:5

There are a great many fathers and mothers who are concerned for the conversion of their children. I have had as many as fifty messages from parents come to me within a single week, wondering why their children are not saved, and asking prayer for them. I venture to say that, as a rule, the fault lies at our own door. There may be something in our own lives that stands in the way. It may be there is some secret sin that keeps back the blessing. David lived in the awful sin into which he

fell for many months before Nathan the prophet made his appearance.

As Matthew Henry says, "It was owing to themselves—they stood in their own light, they shut their own door. God was coming toward them in the way of mercy, and they hindered him. 'Your iniquities have kept good things from you.'" It is well for us to search our hearts, and find out why it is that our prayers are not answered.

Pss. 6:2; 31:10; 32:3; Prov. 28:13; Jer. 31:19; Hosea 7:14

Someone has said: "Unconfessed sin in the soul is like a bullet in the body." If you have no power, it may be there is some sin that needs to be confessed, something in your life that needs straightening out. There is no amount of psalm-singing, no amount of attending religious meetings, no amount of praying or reading your Bible that is going to cover up anything of that kind. It must be confessed, and if I am too proud to confess I need expect no mercy from God and no answers to my prayers.

Sin, confession of; Restitution, importance of

Luke 8:15; 2 Cor. 8:21; 13:7; Eph. 4:28; 1 Peter 2:12; Rev. 12:9

Go downtown and you will see in every window the announcement that "this is the cheapest store in town," and that you can buy goods cheaper there than anywhere else. It is very singular that you can buy them the cheapest at every store, and they say, "That is the very lowest, and we cannot get them any less." It seems to me there is a good deal of lying in business transactions, and we need a revival of honesty. Then the world will have confidence in their Christianity. Straighten out all these differences. If a man has defrauded another man, go and make restitution and people will have confidence in your piety; but to come here and pray and sing, and try to cover up these things by loud singing and praying, is not going to deceive the Almighty. You may deceive your neighbor, you may deceive yourselves, but you can't deceive God.

Sin, confession of; Worldliness, danger of

Prov. 23:20, 21; Mark 10:21–22; Luke 18:22; Rev. 2:4

I once heard of two men who were under the influence of liquor. They came down at night to where their boat was tied. They wanted to return home, so they got in and began to row. They pulled away hard all night, wondering why they never got to the other side of the bay. When the gray dawn of morning broke, behold! they had never loosed the mooring line or raised the anchor! That's just the way with many who are striving to enter the kingdom of heaven. They cannot believe, because they are tied to this world. Cut the cord! Confess and forsake your sins! Cut the cord! Set yourselves free from the clogging weight of earthly things, and you will soon rise heavenward.

Sin, consequences of; Retribution, certainty of

Gen 2:17; 2 Sam. 12:14; Ps. 95:10–11

God forgave the sins of Jacob and David, and the other Old Testament saints, yet there were certain consequences of those sins which those saints had to suffer after they were forgiven. If a man gets drunk, and goes out and breaks his leg, so that it must be amputated, God will forgive him if he asks it, but he will have to hop around on one leg all his life. A man may sow this-tle seed with grain seed in a moment of anger against his master, and the master may forgive him, but the man will have to reap the thistles with the grain.

Sin, conviction of; Habit, nature of

2 Tim. 4:2; Titus 1:13; Jude 15; Rev. 3:19

My wife was once teaching our little boy a Sunday school lesson. She was telling him to notice how sin grows till it becomes a habit and illustrating with examples from life. The little fellow thought it was coming too close to him, so he colored up, and finally said, "Mamma, I think you are getting a good way from the subject."

Sin, danger of

Gen. 3:19; Ezek. 18:4, 20; Rom. 6:23; James 1:15

Beware of sin. Its wages are death and these wages have never been reduced. While out walking one day a man saw a magnificent golden eagle soaring upward. He stopped and watched its flight. Soon he observed something was wrong. The eagle wavered in flight and began to fall. Soon it lay dead at his feet. Eager to know the reason of its death, he examined the eagle and found no trace of gunshot wound. But he saw in its talons a small weasel, which, in its flight, drawn near its body, had sucked the lifeblood from the eagle's breast. Such is the end of everyone who persistently clings to sin.

Sin, danger of; Habit, danger of

Prov. 26:11; 2 Peter 2:22

Polybius says that whereas man is held to be the wisest of all creatures, to him he seems to be the most foolish. Where other creatures have smarted, they will come no more; the fox returns not to the snare, nor the wolf to the pitfall. But man returns to the same sin and will not take warning until he is utterly ruined.

Sin, danger of; Sin, cleansing from

Rom. 6:18, 20, 22; 8:2

A number of years ago the mouth of the Mississippi River became so clogged that no vessels could pass through the channel. Much anxiety was felt, for the farmers along its banks depended upon the river for the transportation of their products. There were no great, overhanging rocks to fall into the stream and block the way of the vessels. No volcanic upheaval had changed its bed. The trouble was simply the deposit of sediment washings from the great Mississippi watershed and deposited on the bottom of the river. The deposits were so fine that a filter would hardly free the water from its impurity. These tiny specks, massed together, hindered the great river's flow to the ocean, for a time threatening the industries of the South and Central States.

We do not need some great sin in our lives to block the channel of blessing. Small sins will block the stream. Human ingenuity at last found a way to dredge the Mississippi and keep the channel open, but only Divine power can free our hearts from sin.

Sin, deliverance from

Rom. 6:18, 20, 22; 8:2; 1 Tim. 1:15

There is no sin in the whole catalog of sins you can name but Christ will deliver you from it perfectly. You say, "I am afraid I cannot hold out." Well, Christ will hold out for you. There is no mountain that he will not climb with you if you will ask him. He will deliver you from your besetting sin.

1 Cor. 15:22

Did any of you ever go down into a coal pit, fifteen hundred or two thousand feet, right down into the bowels of the earth? If you have, don't you know that it would be sheer madness to try to climb up the steep sides of that shaft and so get out of the pit? Of course, you couldn't leap out of it; in fact, you couldn't get out of it at all by yourself. But I'll tell you this—you could get out of a coal pit fifteen hundred feet deep a good deal quicker than you can get out of the pit that Adam took you into. When Adam went down into it, he took the whole human family with him. But the Lord can take us out.

Sin, deliverance from; Satan's strategy

1 Cor. 10:13; Eph. 6:11; 1 Peter 5:8–9

Satan goes about his work very slyly. He winds around us a golden spider's web, which we could blow away with a breath; then he binds us with a thread; and we say, "Oh, that is nothing; I can break that any time." But he goes on winding his threads around us, and they get larger and stronger all the time, until at last he has bound us hand and foot, and then he mocks our helpless sorrow and our vain struggles to get away. The Son of God has power to break every band and fetter, to deliver every captive, and to let the oppressed go free.

Sin, extent of; Righteousness, lack of

Rom. 3:10, 22–23

All have sinned and fall short of God's perfection. That is one of the hardest truths man has to learn. We are apt to think that others are a little better than ourselves. We go to work and try to pull them down to our level. If you want to find out who and what man really is, go to the third chapter of Romans, and there the whole story is told. "There are none righteous, no, not one." "All have sinned and come short." All! Some men like to have their lives written before they die. If you would like to read your biography, turn to this chapter, and you will find it already written.

Sin, freedom from

Gal. 5:1; Eph. 6:8; 2 Tim. 4:18; Heb. 2:15; 1 Peter 2:16

In the British Colonies, before the time of Wilberforce, there used to be a great many slaves; but that good man began to agitate the question of setting them free; and all the slaves in the colonies were anxious to know how he was getting along. But in those days there were no telegraphs and no steamships. The mails went by the slow sailing vessels. They would be from six to eight months in making a voyage to some of the colonies. The slaves used to watch for the British ships, hoping to hear good news, but fearing they might hear bad news. There was a ship which had sailed immediately after the Emancipation Act had been passed and signed by the king; and when she came within hailing distance of the boats which had put off from the shore at the port where she was bound, the captain could not wait to deliver the message officially, and have it duly promulgated by the government; but, seeing the poor anxious people standing up in their boats, eager for the news, he placed his trumpet to his mouth, and shouted with all his might, "Free! Free!"

Just so the angels shout when a poor bondsman is taken in hand by the Savior himself; delivered from the bondage of darkness, into the liberty of his dear Son; free—free from sin—free from the curse of the law.

Sin, hidden; Self-judgment, importance of

Gen. 18:25

There is nothing the world needs more than holy Christians. The cause of Christ is paralyzed because of sin—sin in believers. The natural man will always take sides against God when you press him closely and says, "God isn't going to punish sin. He wouldn't do this or that." But the new man ought always to justify God and take sides with him against sin. There ought to be that difference between God's children and the children of the world. When people say the punishment is severe and unjust, we should side with God and say, "Shall not the Judge of all the earth do right?" We should all condemn sin as God condemns it, the moment we see it in ourselves. It may be some hidden sin that keeps God from using us more.

Sin nature, danger of

Rom. 6:6; 2 Cor. 5:17; Eph. 4:22; Col. 3:9

A man in India once got a tiger cub and tamed it so that it became a pet. One day when it had grown up, it tasted blood, and the old tiger nature flashed out, and it had to be killed. So with the old nature in the believer. It never dies, though it is subdued; and unless he is watchful and prayerful, it will gain the upper hand and rush him into sin. Someone has pointed out that "I" is the center of S-I-N. It is the medium through which Satan acts.

Sin, penalty of; Retribution, certainty of; Harvest follows planting

Prov. 22:8; Jer. 12:13; Hosea 8:7; 10:12

Whenever I hear a young man talking in a flippant way about sowing his wild oats, I don't laugh. I feel more like crying, because I know he is going to make his gray-haired mother reap in tears; he is going to make his wife reap in shame; he is going to make his old father and his innocent children reap with him. Only ten or fifteen or twenty years will pass before he will have to reap his wild oats; no man has ever sowed them without having to reap them. Sow the wind and you reap the whirlwind.

Sin, preaching against; Ears, itching

Jer. 5:31; 6:16; John 8:45; Acts 17:21; 2 Tim. 3:1; 4:3; 2 Peter 2:1

A young minister took a church in Scotland, and began to preach about the sins of the present day, and those of the people who came to hear him. An older member came to him and said, "Young man, if you expect to hold this people you must be careful about preaching on modern sins. You can preach about the sins of Abraham, and Isaac, and Jacob, and the old Patriarchs, but don't you preach about the sins of the present day, because the people will not stand it."

Sin, remedy for

Isa. 3:11; John 5:24; Rom. 5:21; 6:23

Now, the great trouble is to make people believe they are sick but the moment you believe that you are, then it is that you willing to take the remedy. I remember some years ago a patent medicine came out, and the whole of the city was placarded about it. I could not turn my head but I saw "Paine's Pain Killer." On the walls, on the curbstones, everywhere was "pain killer," "pain killer." I felt disgusted at the sight of these bills constantly telling me about this patent medicine. But one day I had a terrible headache, so bad that I could hardly see, and was walking down streets and saw the billboards again, and went and bought some. When I was well I didn't care for it, but when I got sick, I found it was the very thing I wanted. If there is one here who feels the need of the Savior, remember the greater the sin the greater the need of the Savior.

Sin, reward of

Mark 4:7; Luke 8:14; John 4:36; Rom. 6:21; Phil. 1:22

I remember in the north of England a prominent citizen told a sad case that happened there in the city of Newcastle-on-Tyne. It was about a young boy. He was very young. He was an only child. The father and mother thought everything of him and did all they could for him. But he fell into bad ways. He took up with evil characters, and finally got to running with thieves. He didn't let his parents know about it. By and by the gang he was with broke into a house, and he with them. Yes, he had to do it all. They stopped outside of the building, while he crept in and started to rob the till. He was caught in the act, taken into court, tried, convicted, and sent to the penitentiary for ten years.

He was too ashamed to communicate with his parents. Time went on in the convict's cell, till at last his term was out. And at once he started for home. When he came back to the town, he started down the street where his father and mother used to live. He went to the house and rapped. A stranger came to the door and stared him in the face. "No, there is no such person lives here, and where your parents are I don't know," was the only welcome he received. Then he turned through the gate, and went down the street, asking even the children that he met about his folks, where they were living, and if they were well.

But everybody looked blank. Ten years had rolled by and though that seemed perhaps a short time, how many changes had taken place. There where he was born and brought up he was now an alien, and unknown even in the old haunts. But at last he found a couple of townsmen that remembered his father and mother, but they told him the old house had been deserted long years ago, that he had been gone but a few months before his father was confined to his house, and very soon after died broken-hearted, and that his mother had gone out of her mind.

He went to the asylum where his mother was, and went up to her and said, "Mother, mother, don't you know me? I am your son." But she raved and slapped him on the face and shrieked, "You're not my son," and then raved again and tore her hair. He left the asylum more dead than alive, so completely brokenhearted that he died in a few months. Yes, the fruit was long growing, but at the last it ripened to the harvest like a whirlwind.

Job. 4:8; Prov. 22:8; Hosea 10:13; Gal. 6:8

I was coming along North Clark Street in Chicago one evening when a man shot past me like an arrow. But he had seen me, and turned and seized me by the arm, saying eagerly, "Can I be saved tonight? The devil is coming to take me to hell at 1 o'clock tonight." "My friend, you are mistaken." I thought the man was sick. But he persisted that the devil had come and laid his hand upon him, and told him he might have till 1 o'clock, and said he: "Won't you go up to my room and sit with me?" I got some men up to his room to see to him. At 1 o'clock the devils came into that room, and all the men in that room could not hold him. He was reaping what he had sown. When the Angel of Death came and laid his cold hand on him, oh, how he cried for mercy.

Sin seen by God; Judgment, certainty of

Deut. 11:12; 2 Chron. 16:9; Ps. 11:4; Prov. 15:3; Zech. 4:10; 1 Peter 3:12

Leech, the celebrated artist and caricaturist, is said to have had an effective method of reprimanding his children. If their faces were distorted by anger, by rebellious temper, or a sullen mood, he took out his sketchbook, transferred their expressions to paper, and showed them, to their confusion, how ugly naughtiness was. Like children, grown-up people also dislike seeing themselves as others see them. And yet, whether we like it or not, all our words and deeds are set down in God's book of remembrance.

Sin, slavery to

Isa. 55:1; 61:3; Matt. 11:28–30; 2 Thess. 1:7

The path of the unjust grows blacker and blacker. Ask the drunkard if he has a hard time. I met a man on the street yesterday morning here in Boston. He had just crept out of one of the lodging houses, and he looked as if he had come from the pit of hell. I said, "The devil works you hard now, doesn't he?" He said, "That's so." Of course that's so. I pity the man who is the child of the devil, led captive by the devil, enslaved to do the devil's will. I thank God the fetters may be broken today. I want to say that my God isn't a hard Master. I want to drive that lie back to the pit of hell. Jesus said, "My yoke is easy and my burden is light."

Sin, unconfessed

Ps. 32:5; Hosea 13:12; Rom. 2:5

An unconfessed sin is an ever-present foe. It makes a man cowardly, suspicious, and malicious. One unconfessed wrong has oftentimes ruined a man's whole life, deprived him of its joys, destroyed his friendships, and clouded his entire course.

Sin, unpardonable

Matt. 12:31; Mark 3:29; Luke 12:10; 1 John 5:16

An aged minister fancied that he had committed the unpardonable sin. At last, after much conflict, he submitted to what he mistakably considered was the will of God, for him to be lost. Then something within him whispered, "Suppose there is a hell for you, what would you, with your disposition and habits, do there?" The quick answer was, "I would set up a prayer meeting," and with the words came the light of God to show him the absurdity of it all. The fact that one fears that he has committed this sin is the sure proof that he has not.

Matt. 12:31; Mark 3:29; Luke 12:10; 1 John 5:16

Almost everywhere we go we find people who think they have committed the unpardonable sin, that there was no hope for them in this life, nor in the life to come. Almost the first letter when we come to a new place is from a person who thinks they have committed that sin, and want to have me preach upon it. I have met a person here who thinks she has committed the unpardonable sin, and she is almost on the borders of insanity. It is no more that sin than light is darkness, and it is astonishing how people will go on for weeks and months, and sometimes years in darkness, when, if they only just turned to the Word of God, and looked carefully and prayerfully, they would find out what that sin is.

Blasphemy against the Holy Spirit is described as the unpardonable sin. To grieve the Spirit of God and resist the Holy Ghost is one thing, and to commit that awful sin, to blaspheme against the Holy Ghost, is another thing. If I have evil thoughts that come in my mind and evil desires, it is no sign that I have committed the unpardonable sin, but if I love these thoughts and harbor them, and love to think evil of God, and love to think that Jesus Christ was a blasphemer, and love to think that he did his earthly work in the power of Satan, then I am committing the unpardonable sin. I have never met anyone who would admit to doing that nor do I expect to do so.

Sin, warning of; Repentance, need of

Mark 6:18; John 8:45; Gal. 4:16

If your minister comes to you frankly, tells you of your sin, and warns you faithfully, thank God for him. He is your best friend; he is a heaven-sent man. But if your minister speaks smooth, oily words to you, tells you it is all right, when you know, and

he knows, that it is all wrong, and that you are living in sin, you may be sure that he is a devil-sent man. I want to say I have a contempt for a preacher that will tone his message down to suit someone in his audience; some senator, or big man whom he sees present. If the devil can get possession of such a minister and speak through him, he will do the work better than the devil himself. All the priests and ministers of all the churches can't save one soul that will not part with sin.

Sin's danger, warning of

Mark 6:18; John 8:45; Gal. 4:16; 1 Tim. 4:3

If I saw a blind man going to walk over a precipice and I did not warn him, would not the blood of that man be required at my hands? Would not I be guilty morally? There was danger that a train would be wrecked, and it seemed impossible that it could be warned in time. There was not time to go to the next station and warn the passengers of their danger. So they lighted three fires between the coming train and the dangerous place, and between these fires the people assembled; and when the train approached the first set of people they called out "Danger!" but the engineer did not heed their shouts; and at the second fire they did the same thing, but still the train went on; but at the third fire the engineer thought there must be something the matter and he paid attention to the cries of "Danger! danger!" and stopped the train just upon the verge of the precipice.

Do you think that these people were not the friends of the people upon that train? The person that warns you is the best friend that you have. Suppose I am going home at night, at midnight, and I see a building on fire and I pass along and say nothing about it, and the occupants are all asleep and I go right home and go to bed, and in the morning I find that fifteen people in that house died in the fire;

how you would condemn me! If in preaching the gospel I don't warn you about your danger, about your sins and God's punishment, what will you say to me when I meet you at the eternal throne?

Singing, importance of

Zeph. 3:17; Eph. 5:19; Col. 3:16; Rev. 5:9; 15:3

I can't sing. I couldn't start "Rock of Ages," but I suppose I have heard it once a day for six years. I can't sing with my lips. I can't get it out of these thick lips of mine, but way down in my heart I sing just as well as Mr. Sankey, and it is just as acceptable to God. But when we all get to heaven I expect to sing with Moses and the Lamb. A real Christian church is a church of song. I don't know all they do in heaven, but they sing there, and by and by we shall be there and join with them.

Singing, influence of

Pss. 33:3; 40:3; 144:9; Rev. 5:9; 14:3

Now, if we have got a "new tongue," we can sing the "new song." Psalm 40:3 says, "And he hath put a new song into my mouth." That's what we want. There's more said in the Bible about song than prayer. If we have been born again, we ought to sing the new song; and even I can sing that. Now, when I sing loudly, Mr. Sankey wants me to go to the other end of the platform; but when I get home to heaven, I'll sing as well as he. Larks sing on the wing, when they are soaring; they don't sing in their nests. And that's what has been the matter with some of the churches; they get into their comfortable nests, and get four people to do the singing, as far off as they can get, and then the church gets cold.

The Methodists sang religion into the hearts of the people. The world is after the best thing. If we can show them that religion is a joy, and a song in our hearts all the time, instead of speaking of our doubts and fears, they will get it.

Sinners, God's love for

Matt. 9:11; Luke 5:30; 7:34; 15:2; 1 John 1:7

Another young man told me last night that he was too great a sinner to be saved. Why, they are the very men Christ came after. The only charge they could bring against Christ down here was that he was receiving bad people. They are the very kind of people he is still willing to receive. All you have to do is to prove that you are a sinner, and I will prove that you have got a Savior. And the greater the sinner, the greater need you have of a Savior. You say your heart is hard; well, then, of course you want Christ to soften it. You cannot do it yourself. The harder your heart, the more need you have of Christ: the blacker you are, the more need you have of a Savior.

If your sins rise up before you like a dark mountain, bear in mind that the blood of Jesus Christ cleanses from all sin. There is no sin so big, or so black, or so corrupt and vile, but the blood of Christ can cover it.

Sinners, love for

Rom 5:8; 1 John 4:7, 10

My friends, don't forget that it was while we were yet sinners that Christ died for us. I have been into some homes in this city that were so vile and dirty that I couldn't stay there five minutes. But Jesus Christ waits to come into the heart of the vilest sinner and take up his residence there. It isn't because we are lovely, but because he is love, that Christ died for us, and offers to come and dwell with us. Love always grows as it descends. The mother loves her child more than the child loves its mother. Just so God loves us more than we can ever love him.

Sinners, need of pardon

Deut. 32:4; Pss. 45:7; 89:14; 97:2; 99:4; John 1:17

Suppose Queen Victoria did not like any man to be deprived of his liberty, and threw all her prisons open, and was so merciful that she could not bear anyone to suffer for guilt, how long would she hold the scepter? How long would she rule? Not twenty-four hours. Those very men who cry out about God being merciful would say, "We don't want such a queen." Well, God is merciful, but he is not going to take an unpardoned sinner into heaven.

Sins blotted out

Pss. 51:9; 103:12; Isa. 1:18; 43:25; 44:22; Acts 3:19

When I stand before God at the judgment day, he has promised not to remember one of my sins. If God blots out my sins, neither devil nor man can bring anything against me. The old Eastern merchants used to keep their accounts on tablets of wax, and when they were settled they were blotted out. And that's what God does with our sins.

Sins, covering for

Pss. 51:9; 103:12; Isa. 1:18; 43:25; 44:22; Micah 7:19; Acts 3:19

God has cast our sins into the depths of the sea. Let the devil go down there and get them if he can. It is a safe place to have them, in the depths of the sea. There are some parts of the sea which they never have been able to fathom. Bunyan says, "Thank God, it is a sea, not a river. If it was a river, it might dry up, and they might find them in the bed of the river, but the sea never dries up."

Sins, forgiveness of

Col. 3:12–14

The past sins of Christians are all forgiven as soon as they are confessed; and they are never to be mentioned. That is a question which is not to be opened up again. If our sins have been put away, that is the end of them. They are not to be remembered, and God will not mention them anymore.

This principle is recognized in courts of justice. A case came up in the courts in which a man had had trouble with his wife; but he forgave her, and then afterwards brought her into court for that for which he had forgiven her. And, when it was known that he had forgiven her, the judge said that the thing was settled. The judge recognized the soundness of the principle, that if a sin were once forgiven there was an end of it.

Skeptical persons, ministry to

Ps. 25:8; John 1:47; 7:17

I was in an inquiry meeting, some time ago, and I handed over to a Christian lady, whom I had known some time, one who was skeptical. On looking round soon after I noticed the inquirer marching out of the hall. I asked, "Why have you let her go?" "Oh, she is a skeptic!" was the reply. I ran to the door and got her to stop, and introduced her to another Christian worker, who spent over an hour in conversation and prayer with her. He visited her and her husband, and in the course of a week, that intelligent lady cast off her skepticism and came out an active Christian. It took time, tact, and prayer; but if a person like this is honest we ought to deal with such a one as the Master would have us.

Slander, sin of; Commandment, ninth; Murder, by tongue

Exod. 20:16; Ps. 101:5; Prov. 10:18; 11:13; Matt. 26:59; Acts 6:13; Eph. 4:25, 29; James 4:11

You don't like to have anyone bear false witness against you, or help to ruin your character or reputation; then why should you do it to others? How public men are slandered in this country! None escape, whether good or bad. Judgment is passed upon them, their family, their character by the press and by individuals who know little or nothing about them. If one-tenth that is said and written about our public men was true, half of them should be hung. Slander has been called "tongue murder." Slanderers are compared to flies that always settle on sores, but do not touch a man's healthy parts. If the archangel Gabriel should come down to earth and mix in human affairs, I believe his character would be assailed inside of forty-eight hours. Slanderers called Christ a gluttonous man and a winebibber. He claimed to be the Truth, but instead of worshiping him, men took him and crucified him.

Slander, sin of; Tongue, misuse of; Commandment, ninth

Acts 5:3; James 1:26; 3:2

Government of the tongue is made the test of true religion by James. Just as a doctor looks at the tongue to diagnose the condition of bodily health, so a person's words are an index of what is within. Truth will spring from a clean heart: falsehood and deceit from a corrupt one. When Ananias kept back part of the price of land, Peter asked him, "Why hath Satan filled thine heart to lie to the Holy Ghost?" (Acts 5:3). Satan is the father of lies and the promoter of lies.

Small things, importance of

Matt. 12:36; 18:16; 2 Cor. 5:10

We must learn that there is no such thing as a trifle on earth. When we realize that every thought and word and act has an eternal influence, and will come back to us in the same way as the seed returns in the harvest, we must perceive their responsibility, however trifling they may seem. We are apt to overlook the results that hinge on small things. The law of gravitation was suggested by the fall of an apple. It is said that some years ago a Harvard professor brought some gypsy moths to this country in the hope that they could with advantage be crossed with silkworms. The moths accidentally got away, and multiplied so enormously that the Commonwealth of Massachusetts has had to spend hundreds of thousands of dollars trying to exterminate them.

Small things, power of

Matt. 12:36; 18:16; 2 Cor. 5:10

When H. M. Stanley was pressing his way through the forests of darkest Africa, the most formidable foes that he encountered, those that caused most loss of life to his caravan and came the nearest to entirely defeating his expedition, were the little Wambutti dwarfs. So annoying were they that very slow progress could be made through their dwelling places.

These little men had only little bows and little arrows that looked like children's playthings, but upon these tiny arrows there was a small drop of poison which would kill an elephant or a man as quickly and as surely as a Winchester rifle. Their defense was by means of poison and traps. They would steal through the darkness of the forest and, waiting in ambush, let fly their deadly arrows before they could be discovered. They dug ditches and carefully covered them over with leaves. They fixed spikes in the ground and tipped them with the most deadly poison, and then covered them. Into these ditches and on these spikes man and beast would fall or step to their death.

You may think that your sins are little things but they are tipped with deadly poison. Sin is a deadly trap that destroys all who fall into it.

Smile, power of; Kindness, power of

1 Cor. 13:4; Eph. 4:32; Titus 1:8; Jude 22

In London one Sunday morning a minister said to me, "I want you to notice that family there in one of the front seats, and when we go home I want to tell you their story. When we got home I asked him for the story, and he said, "All that family were won by a smile." "Why," said I, "how's that?" "Well," said he, "as I was walking down a street one day I saw a child at a window; it smiled, and I smiled, and we bowed. So it was the second time; I bowed, she bowed. It was not long before there was another child, and I had got in a habit of looking and bowing, and pretty soon the group grew, and at last, as I went by, a lady was with them. I didn't know what to do. I didn't want to bow to her, but I knew the children expected it, and so I bowed to them all. And the mother thought I was a minister, because I carried a Bible every Sunday morning.

"So the children followed me the next Sunday and found I was a minister. And they thought I was the greatest preacher, and their parents must hear me. A minister who is kind to a child and gives him a pat on the head, why the children will think he is the greatest preacher in the world. Kindness goes a great way. And to make a long story short, the father and mother and five children were converted, and they are going to join our church next Sunday." Won to Christ by a smile! We must get the wrinkles out of our brows, and we must have smiling faces.

Son, a prodigal

Luke 15:12

A young man in New York City, whose father I knew, was a great prodigal, and had broken his mother's heart, and brought her down to the grave in sorrow. Every night he was out carousing with boon companions. The father's heart was nearly broken too, and one night a few weeks after the mother's death the young man was just starting out; the father said: "My son, I want one favor of you. I would like you to stay at home and spend one night with me." The young man said, "I don't want to stay, it is so gloomy here." "But," said the father, "will you not stay and gratify your aged father? You know your conduct killed your poor mother. My boy, won't you stay?" The old man pleaded with him, and even begged him to stay, but he said: "No, I am not going to stay at home."

The old father put forth one more effort to save his prodigal boy, and he threw himself down before him in the hall. What did that son do? He just leaped over his father's body, and went out to join his comrades. There is not one of you but would say, "That was an ungrateful wretch, not fit to live." Ah, sinner, what would you do with Christ in such a case? Why, many of you, I believe, if he were to throw himself down before you and plead with you, would step right over him. Will you not yield your heart to his tender love now?

Sorrow, made obsolete; Sighing

Isa. 35:10; Jer. 33:11; John 16:22; Rev. 21:4

Joseph Parker of London said something that I thought was splendid in regard to the thirty-fifth of Isaiah, where it says: "Sorrow and sighing shall flee away." Take up an old dictionary, he said, and once in a while you will come across a word marked "obsolete." The time is coming, he said, when those two words, "sorrow" and "sighing," shall be obsolete. Sighing and sorrow shall flee away, to be no more. Thank God for the outlook!

Soul insurance; Salvation, need of

Job 27:8; Matt. 16:26; Mark 8:36–37; Luke 9:25

"Pa," said a little boy as he climbed to his father's knee, and looked into his face as earnestly as if he understood the importance of the subject, "Pa, is your soul insured?" "What are you thinking about, my son?" replied the agitated father. "Why do you ask that question?" "Why, Pa, I heard Uncle George say that you have your house insured, and your life insured; but he didn't believe you had thought of your soul, and he was afraid you would lose it; won't you get it insured right away?"

The father leaned his head on his hand, and was silent. He owned broad acres of land that were covered with a bountiful produce; his barns were even now filled with plenty, his buildings were all well covered by insurance; and as if that would not suffice for the maintenance of his wife and only child in case of his death, he had the day before taken a life policy for a large amount, yet not one thought had he given to his own immortal soul. On that which was to waste away and become part and parcel of its native dust he had spared no pains; but for that which was to live on and on through the long ages of eternity he had made no provision.

Soul, value of

1 Cor. 9:22; James 5:20; Rev. 20:6

One afternoon I noticed a lady in the services whom I knew to be a Sunday school teacher who should have been teaching a class of boys. After the service I asked her where her class was. "Oh," said she, "I went to the school and found only a little boy, and so I came away." "Only a little boy!" said I. "Think of the value of one such soul! The fires of a reformation may be slumbering in that tow-headed boy; there may be a young Knox, or a Wesley, or a Whitefield in your class."

John 4:10

There is a bridge over the Niagara River. It is one of the great highways of the nation. Trains pass over it every few minutes of the day. When they began to make the bridge the first thing they did was to take a boy's kite and send a little thread across the river. It seemed a very small thing but it was the beginning of a great work. So if we only lead one soul to Christ, eternity alone may tell what the result will be. You may be the means of bringing someone to Christ who may become one of the most eminent individuals in the service of God that the world has ever seen.

Soul winning, greatest pleasure

Prov. 11:30; 1 Thess. 2:19

It is the greatest pleasure of living to win souls to Christ.

Soul winning, joy of; Witnessing, joy of

Luke 15:7, 10; 2 Cor. 6:1; 3 John 1:3

There is more than one kind of joy; there is the joy of one's own salvation. I thought, when I first tasted that, it was the most delicious joy I had ever known, and that I could never get beyond it. But I found, afterward, there was something more joyful than that, the joy of the salvation of others. Oh, the privilege, the blessed privilege, to be used of God to win a soul to Christ, and to see a man or woman being led out of bondage by some act of ours. To think that God should condescend to allow us to be co-workers with him! It is the highest honor we can have. It surpasses the joy of our own salvation, this joy of seeing others saved, and walking in the truth.

Soul winning, value of

Prov. 11:30; Matt. 16:26; Mark 8:37; 1 Thess. 2:19

We all want to shine—to be admired and praised; the mother wishes it for her boy, when she sends him to school; the father for his lad, when he goes off to college. God tells us who are the ones who will shine—it is not statesmen, nor warriors, nor such like, they shine but for a season—but those who will shine forever and ever are those who win souls to Christ; even the little boy or girl who persuades someone to come to Christ.

Sower, parable of

Matt. 13:18; Mark 4:3; Luke 8:5

Our Savior, as he sat by the seaside, saw a man go forth to sow his field; and pointing to him he gave his hearers a lesson about preaching the gospel. This parable classifies the hearers of the gospel. It is true now as it was then, and will be to the end of time. I am glad that Christ spoke this parable; for it keeps me from being discouraged when I see so many go back after they have been interested in the truth. Christ himself explains the parable, and we have only to apply it.

The first class are wayside hearers. They are impressed by the truth but the impression is transient. They like the meetings, the singing, and the crowd. They are sympathetically interested. But if they don't go further and become converted, they will get more harm than good. If the gospel doesn't soften, it hardens. The wayside was not in the condition to receive the seed because it was trampled hard. And so if a man's heart is full of business or amusements; if he only comes to the meetings now and then, with a preoccupied mind, they will do

him no good. Things not wrong in themselves may so engross the thoughts that the good seed cannot take root.

The second class are the stony ground hearers. Here the seed springs up quickly, and grows well for a time, but soon withers and dies. These hearers are like trees that blossom, but fail to perfect their fruit. There are a good many Christians of this class. They want to be religious, but they don't count the cost. They go with the crowd when it shouts "hosanna" to the Son of David today, and they will go with it when it cries "crucify him" tomorrow. A little opposition discourages them.

Sunshine is good. It makes the tree grow that is well rooted. But it withers the tree that has no root. Storms that will develop the vigor of trees in a deep soil, will blow down those that are in a shallow soil. And so it is in churches. When all is calm and the minister popular, etc., the shallow professor gets along pretty well. But when trials come he falls away. How easily some people are offended! If we are truly converted—if we are united to God and not merely to a church or a minister—we won't leave, whatever others may do or fail to do. What we need is a personal Savior. If we have him, all trials will only drive us nearer to him.

The third class presented in the parable are the unfruitful. Alas! how many such in all the churches. Stunted, useless, good for nothing, choked with worldly cares. It is not enough to plant good seed in a good soil. There must be cultivation. The weeds must be kept down. The richer the soil, the ranker will be the growth of weeds. This person will take no personal interest in the work of the church, or in the cause of missions. And so the God of this world will keep him from bearing fruit.

The fourth class, those whose hearts are good ground in the parable, do three things: hear the Word, receive it, and respond to it. The good seed in the good soil brought forth some thirty, some sixty, and some a hundredfold. We don't have to make the fruit, but only to receive and cultivate the seed. Christ says: "Let your light shine." You don't have to make the light. You don't have to shine. You are to let God shine in and through you. If I am a good hearer of the Word my life will be a success. I will grow and be useful.

There is a great difference between receiving a man's word and God's. There is power in the words of God. They are spirit, and they are life. Hence the sower must not scatter his opinions. Even if they were precious as gems, they would not grow. There is no life in them. They can produce no spiritual harvest. The sower must sow the Word. And if that seed falls into a good and honest heart it will grow and bear fruit. By a good heart is not meant a perfect one, but one that welcomes the truth. The gospel is not for the righteous, but for sinners.

Sowing and reaping

Gal. 6:7–8

Now I want to divide this text into four parts: First, when a man sows in the natural world he expects to reap. You will see the farmers out in their fields sowing, and they will all expect to reap. Secondly, they will expect to reap more than they sow. Thirdly, they will expect to reap the same as they sow. If they sow wheat they will expect to reap wheat. If they sow oats they won't expect to gather watermelons. If they plant an apple tree they don't look for peaches on it. If they plant a grapevine they expect to find grapes, not pumpkins. They will look for just the very seed they sow. Fourth, ignorance of what they sowed will make no difference in the reaping. It wouldn't do for a man to say, "I didn't know but what it was wheat I was sowing, when I sowed tares." That makes no difference. You have got to know. If I go out and sow tares thinking that it's wheat, I've got to gather tares all the

same. That is a universal law. If a man learns the carpenter's trade he doesn't expect to be a watchmaker, he expects to be a carpenter. Whatsoever a man or a nation sows he and they must reap.

Sowing to the flesh; Judgment, certainty of

Jer. 12:13; Hosea 10:13; Gal. 6:8

I was at the Paris Exhibition in 1867, and I noticed there a little oil painting, only about a foot square, and the face was the most hideous I have ever seen. On the paper attached to the painting were the words "Sowing the Tares." The face looked more like a demon's than a man's. As he sowed these tares, up came serpents and reptiles, and they were crawling up his body, and all around were woods with wolves and animals prowling them. I have seen that picture many times since. Ah! the reaping time is coming. If you sow to the flesh you must reap corruption.

Spiritism, avoidance of; Occult, avoidance of

Isa. 8:19

Any man, any woman who comes to us with any doctrine that is not according to the Bible, let us understand that they are from the evil one, and that they are enemies of righteousness. They have no light in them. You will find these people who are consulting familiar spirits, first and last, attack the Word of God. They don't believe it.

There is another passage which reads, "And when they shall say unto you, seek unto them that have familiar spirits, and unto wizards that peep and mutter: Should not a people seek unto their God? for the living to the dead?" What is that but table-rapping, and spiritism? If it was a message from God, do you think you would have to go into a dark room and put out all the lights? In secret my Master taught nothing. God is not in that movement, and we want, as children of God, to keep ourselves from this evil.

Spiritual gifts, use of; Assessment, personal

Rom. 12:6; 1 Cor. 12:1; 14:12; Eph. 1:3; 1 Tim. 4:14

Spurgeon preaches on an average eight times a week. Any man who can preach as Spurgeon can ought not to do any pastoral work. There are others that can do the pastoral work. The deacons can visit the sick. You can get godly, blessed women that will go from house to house. If a minister feels that he ought to be preaching all the time, that he has got a call to proclaim the glad tidings to a perishing world, by all means let him do it. If he can do more elsewhere than at home, let him go, and everyone ought to say, "God bless him." There is plenty of work in this country—plenty to do; and there is no room for this petty jealousy and bickering. Let each of us find out what is our own work, and then let us go and do it, and the work will be done.

Spiritual life, depth of; Sanctification, evidence of

Prov. 18:4; 20:5; 1 Cor. 2:11

It is not those who make the most noise who have the most piety. There is a brook, or a little "burn," as the Scotch call it, not far from where I live. After a heavy rain you can hear the rush of its waters a long way off; but let there come a few days of pleasant weather, and the brook becomes almost silent. But there is a river near my house, the flow of which I have never heard in my life, as it pours on in its deep and majestic course the year round. We should have so much of the love of God within us that its presence shall be evident without our loud proclamation of the fact.

Spiritual life, source of

Isa. 49:10; John 4:14; 7:38–39; 10:10; Rev. 7:16

Many are trying to give themselves spiritual life. You may galvanize yourselves and put electricity into yourselves, so to speak; but the effect will not last very long. Christ alone is the author of life. If you would have real spiritual life, get to know Christ. Many try to stir up spiritual life by going to meetings. That may be well enough; but it will be of no use, unless they get into contact with the living Christ. Then their spiritual life will not be a spasmodic thing, but will be perpetual; flowing on and on, and bringing forth fruit to God.

Spiritual power, nature of

John 4:14; 7:37–38

It seems to me we have got about three classes of Christians: the first class, in the third chapter of John, were those who had got to Calvary and there got life. They believed on the Son and were saved and there they rested satisfied. They did not seek anything higher. Then in the fourth chapter of John we come to a better class of Christians. There it was a well of living water bubbling up. There are a few of these but they are not a hundredth part of the first class. But the best class is in the seventh chapter of John: "Out of his belly shall flow rivers of living water." That is the kind of Christian we ought to be.

When I was a boy I used to have to pump water for the cattle. Ah, how many times I have pumped with that old right hand until it ached, and many times I used to pump when I could not get any water. I was taught that when the pump was dry I must pour a pail of water down the pump. That would prime it so I could get the water up. And that is what Christians want—a well of living water. We will have plenty of grace to spare—all we need ourselves and an abundance for others.

Now they have a way of digging artesian wells. They don't have to pump now to get the water. When they dig the well, they cut down through the gravel and through the clay perhaps 1,000 or 2,000 feet, not stopping when they can pump the water up, but they cut to a lower strata and the water flows up abundantly of itself. And so we ought every one of us to be like artesian wells. God has got grace enough for every one of us. It is the filling of the Holy Spirit that is the artesian well of power within us.

Spiritual warfare; Satan, strategy of

Eph. 6:12

The reason why so many Christians fail all through life is just this—they underestimate the strength of the enemy. We have a terrible enemy to contend with. Don't let Satan deceive us. Unless we are spiritually dead, it means warfare. Nearly everything around tends to draw us away from God. We do not step clear out of Egypt onto the throne of God. There is the wilderness journey, and there are enemies in the land.

Standing for right

Dan. 1:8

I have great respect for a man who can stand up for what he believes is right against all the world. A man who can stand alone is a hero. There are a good many times in college life when young people have got to go against some custom. Perhaps it is fashionable to drink wine, and you have conscientious scruples against drinking wine. You have got to take your stand, and you need all your courage. Suppose it is the custom for young men to do certain things you wouldn't like your mother to know of—things that your mother taught you were wrong. You may have to stand up alone

among all your companions. They will say: "You can't get away from your mother, eh? Tied to your mother's apron strings!"

But just you say: "Yes ! I have respect for my mother; she taught me what is right, and she is the best friend I have. I believe that is wrong, and I am going to stand for the right." What young men want to do is to take their stand for the right, and if they have got to stand alone, to stand.

Standing for righteousness; Sinner, mercy for

Ps. 25:7; Isa. 6:5; Jer. 31:19; Dan. 9:9; Luke 18:13

They were going to have a great celebration at the opening of a saloon and billiard hall in Chicago, in the northern part of the city, where I lived. It was to be a gateway to death and to hell, one of the worst places in Chicago. As a joke they sent me an invitation to go to the opening. I took the invitation, and went down and saw the two men who owned the saloon, and I said, "Is that a genuine invitation?" They said it was. "Thank you," I said; "I will be around, and if there is anything here I don't like I may have something to say about it."

They said, "You are not going to preach, are you?" "I may." "We don't want you. We won't let you in." "How are you going to keep me out?" I asked. "There is the invitation."

"We will put a policeman at the door." "What is the policeman going to do with that invitation?" "We won't let you in." "Well," I said, "I will be there." I gave them a good scare, and then I said, "I will compromise the matter; if you two men will get down here and let me pray with you, I will let you off."

I got those two rum sellers down on their knees, one on one side of me and the other on the other side, and I prayed God to save their souls and smite their business. One of them had a Christian mother, and he seemed to have some conscience left. After I had prayed, I said, "How can you do this business? How can you throw this place open to ruin the young men of Chicago?" Within three months the whole thing smashed up, and one of them was converted shortly after. I have never been invited to a saloon since.

One of these men later told me a story that touched my soul. He said when this business hadn't prospered he felt a failure, and went away to the Rocky Mountains. Life became a burden to him and he made up his mind that he would put an end to his days. He took a sharp knife which he proposed to drive into his heart. He sought a part of the mountains to kill himself. He had the knife ready to plunge into his heart, when he seemed to hear a voice—it was the voice of his mother. He remembered her words when she was dying, even though he was a boy. He heard her say, "Johnny, if you get into trouble, pray."

That knife dropped from his hand, and he asked God to be merciful to him. He was accepted, and he came back to Chicago and lifted up his voice for Christ. He may be in this tabernacle tonight. Just the moment he cried for mercy he got it. If you only cry, "God, be merciful to me a sinner," he will hear you.

Stealing, dealing with; Commandment, eighth

Lev. 19:35; Deut. 24:14; 25:13; Isa. 3:15; Ezek. 22:12; Amos 8:5; Micah 6:11; James 5:4

Extortioner, are you ready to step into the scales of the eighth commandment? Employer, are you guilty of abusing your employees? Have you defrauded the worker of his wages? Have you paid starvation wages? And you, employee, have you been honest with your employer? Have you robbed him of his due by wasting your time when he was not looking?

If God should summon you into his presence now, what would you say?

Let the merchant step into the scales. See if you will prove light when weighed against the law of God. Are you guilty of adulterating what you sell? Do you substitute inferior grades of goods? Are your advertisements deceptive? Are your cheap prices made possible by defrauding your customers either in quantity or in quality? Do you teach your clerks to put a French or an English tag on domestic manufactures, and then sell them as imported goods? Do you tell them to say that the goods are all wool when you know they are half cotton? Do you give short weight or measure?

Stealing, foolishness of; Theft, foolishness of; Commandment, eighth

Prov. 23:5; Jer. 17:11; 22:13; Luke 12:20; James 5:3

I heard of a boy who stole a cannonball from a navy yard. He watched his opportunity, sneaked into the yard, and secured it. But when he had it, he hardly knew what to do with it. It was heavy, and too large to conceal in his pocket, so he had to put it under his hat. When he got home with it, he dared not show it to his parents, because it would have led at once to his detection. He said in after years it was the last thing he ever stole.

Prov. 23:5; Jer. 17:11; 22:13; Luke 12:20; James 5:3

The story is told that a royal diamond valued at $600,000 was stolen from a window of a jeweler, to whom it had been given to set. A few months afterward a miserable man died a miserable death in a poor lodging house. In his pocket was found the diamond, and a letter telling how he had not dared to sell it, lest it should lead to his discovery and imprisonment. It never brought him anything but anxiety and pain.

Stealing, sin of; Commandment, eighth

Prov. 30:9; Jer. 7:9; Zech. 7:9; John 12:6; 1 Cor. 6:10

The value of the thing that is stolen has nothing to say to the guilt of the act. Two people were arguing on this point, and one said: "Will you contend that a theft of a pin and of a dollar are the same to God?" The reply came, "The value or amount is not what is to be considered, but whether the act is right or wrong. Part obedience is not enough: obedience must be entire." The little indulgences, the small transgressions are what drive character out of the soul. They lay the foundation for the grosser sins. If you give way to little temptations, you will be less able to resist when great temptations come to you.

Lev. 19:35; Deut. 24:14; 25:13; Isa. 3:15; Ezek. 22:12; Amos 8:5; Micah 6:11; James 5:4

"Show me a people whose trade is dishonest," said Froude, "and I will show you a people whose religion is a sham." Unless your religion can keep you honest in your business, it isn't worth much; it isn't the right kind. God is a God of righteousness, and no true follower of his can swerve one inch to the right or left without disobeying him.

Lev. 19:13; Prov. 11:21; 20:14; Amos 8:5; 1 Thess. 4:6

Perhaps it is not necessary to speak about the grosser violations of the eighth commandment, because the law of the land looks after that, but a man or woman can steal without cracking a safe and picking pockets. Many a person who would shrink from taking what belongs to another person thinks nothing of stealing from the government or from large public corporations. If you steal from a rich man it is as much a sin as stealing from a poor man. If you lie about the value of things you buy, are you not trying to defraud the storekeeper? "It is naught, it is naught, saith the buyer: but when he is gone his way, then he boasteth" (Prov. 20:14).

On the other hand, many a person who would not steal himself holds stock in companies that make dishonest profits; but "though hand join in hand, the wicked shall not go unpunished" (Prov. 11:21).

Stealing, sin of; Gambling, danger of; Commandment, eighth

Prov. 22:22; Isa. 1:23–24; Rom. 1:18; James 2:6

You can hardly take up a paper now without reading of some cashier of a bank who has become a defaulter, or of some large swindling operation that has ruined scores, or of some breach of trust, or fraudulent failure in business. These things are going on all over the land. I would to God that we could have all gambling swept away. If Christian men take the right stand they can check it and break it up in a great many places. In my mind it leads directly to stealing.

The stream generally starts at home and in the school. Parents are woefully lax in their condemnation and punishment of the sin of stealing. The child begins by taking sugar, it may be. The mother makes light of it at first, and the child's conscience is violated without any sense of wrong. By and by it is not an easy matter to check the habit, because it grows and multiplies with every new commission.

Subjection to God

Matt. 6:10; Luke 11:2; Acts 10:35; Rom. 14:8; 2 Cor. 5:9

It is reported of a woman, who, being sick, was asked whether she was willing to live or die, that she answered, "Which God pleases." "But," said one, "if God should refer it to you, which would you choose?" "Truly," replied she, "I would refer it to him again." Thus we obtain the will of God when our will is subjected to God.

Submission, example of

Deut. 6:18; 12:28; Matt. 11:26; Luke 10:21

Someone inquired of a deaf and dumb boy why he thought he was born deaf and dumb. Taking the chalk he wrote upon the board, "Even so, Father: for so it seemed good in thy sight."

Submission, prayer of

James 4:7; 1 Peter 5:5

In view of the difficulty of bringing our hearts to submission before God, we may well adopt Fenelon's prayer: "O God, take my heart, for I cannot give it; and when Thou hast it, keep it; for I cannot keep it for Thee; and save me in spite of myself."

Submit to one another

Eph. 5:21; Phil. 2:3; 1 Peter 5:5

We ought to endure and sacrifice much, rather than permit discord and division to prevail in our hearts. Martin Luther has said, "When two goats meet upon a narrow bridge over deep water, how do they behave? Neither of them can turn back again, neither can pass the other, because the bridge is too narrow; if they should thrust one another, they might both fall into the water and be drowned. Nature, then, has taught them that if the one lays himself down and permits the other to go over him, both remain unhurt. Even so people should rather endure to be trod upon than to fall into debate and discord one with another."

Substance abuse, danger of

Prov. 20:1; 23:29; Isa. 5:11; Luke 21:34

I was reading an account of snake worshiping in India. I thought it was a horrible thing. I read of a mother who saw a snake come into her home and coil itself around her little infant only six months old, and she thought that the reptile was such a sacred thing that she did not dare to touch it; and she saw that snake destroy her child; she heard its pitiful cries, but dared not rescue it. My soul revolted as I read it. But I do not know but we have things right here in America that are just as bad as that serpent in India. Serpents that are coming into many a Christian home, and coiling around many a son and daughter, binding them hand and foot, and the fathers and mothers seem to be asleep. How the devil blinds these moderate drinkers! I do not know of any sin more binding than the sin of intemperance; people are bound hand and foot by drinking before they know it.

Substitution, example of

Exod. 12:13; 32:30; Lev. 16:22; 17:11; Isa. 53:6; Matt. 8:17; 20:28; John 1:29; 1 Cor. 10:16; 15:3; 2 Cor. 5:21; Gal. 3:13; Eph. 2:13; 5:2; Titus 2:14; Heb. 9:28; 1 Peter 1:2, 19; 2:24; 3:18; 4:1; 1 John 1:7; 3:5; Rev. 1:5

There is a well-known story told of Napoleon the First's time. In one of the conscriptions, during one of his many wars, a man was balloted as a conscript who did not want to go, but he had a friend who offered to go in his place. His friend joined the regiment in his name, and was sent off to the war. By and by a battle came on, in which he was killed, and they buried him on the battlefield. Some time after, the Emperor wanted more men, and by some mistake the first man was balloted a second time. They went to take him, but he refused.

"You cannot take me." "Why not?" "I am dead," was the reply. "You are not dead; you are alive and well." "But I am dead," he said. "Why, man, you must be mad. Where did you die?" "At such a battle, and you left me buried on such a battlefield." "You talk like a madman," they cried; but the man stuck to his point that he had been dead and buried some months. "Look up your books," he said, "and see if it is not so." They looked, and found that he was right. They found the man's name entered as drafted, sent to the war, and marked off as killed.

"Look here," they said, "you didn't die; you must have got someone to go for you; it must have been your substitute." "You are correct," he said; "he died in my stead. You cannot touch me; I died in that man, and I go free. The law has no claim against me."

They would not recognize the doctrine of substitution, and the case was carried to the Emperor. He said that the man was right, that he was dead and buried in the eyes of the law, and that France had no claim against him. This story may or may not be true, but one thing I know is true: Jesus Christ suffered death for the sinner, and those who accept him are free from the Law.

Exod. 12:13; 32:30; Lev. 16:22; 17:11; Isa. 53:6; Matt. 8:17; 20:28; John 1:29; 1 Cor. 10:16; 15:3; 2 Cor. 5:21; Gal. 3:13; Eph. 2:13; 5:2; Titus 2:14; Heb. 9:28; 1 Peter 1:2, 19; 2:24; 3:18; 4:1; 1 John 1:7; 3:5; Rev. 1:5

An entire army was guilty of mutiny, and one of the laws of war is that all mutineers shall be put to death, but the generals did not want to lose their army, and yet they wanted to carry out their rules, so they ordered that every tenth man should be shot. Now, in the army there were a father and a son, and when the son saw that his father was to be one of the tenth he stepped behind him and took his place— the place of death. And is this not an illustration of what Christ has done for us? He opened the way of escape for us, and took our place and died for us.

Substitution, importance of; Blood of Christ; Passover, significance of

Exod. 12:13; 32:30; Lev. 16:22; 17:11; Isa. 53:6; Matt. 8:17; 20:28; John 1:29; 1 Cor. 10:16; 15:3; 2 Cor. 5:21; Gal. 3:13; Eph. 2:13; 5:2; Titus 2:14; Heb. 9:28; 1 Peter 1:2, 19; 2:24; 3:18; 4:1; 1 John 1:7; 3:5; Rev. 1:5

Some people say preach anything but the death of Christ; preach the life of Christ. You may preach that and you'll never reach a soul for salvation. It is not Christ's sympathy—his life—we preach, it is his sacrifice. That's what brings men out of darkness. I can imagine some proud Egyptians that day of the Passover, who when they heard the bleating of the lambs at the time of the first Passover— there must have been over 200,000 lambs—saying, "What an absurd performance. Every man has got a lamb, and they have got the best lambs out of the flock, too, and they are going to cover their houses with the blood." They looked upon this as a flaw in their character.

You may find a good many flaws in your character, but you cannot find a flaw in the Lamb of God. When the hour came you could see them all slaying their lamb, and putting the blood on the doorposts. To those Egyptians or to the men of the world how absurd it looked. They probably said, "Why are you disfiguring your houses in that way?" It was not upon the threshold. God didn't want that, but they were to put it upon the lintels and doorposts where God could see it that night as a token.

This blood was to be a substitution for death, and all who hadn't that token in the land of Egypt had their firstborn slain at midnight. There was a wail from Egypt from one end to the other. But death didn't come near the homes where the blood was. It was the death of the lambs that kept death out of the dwellings. It is the blood of the Lamb of God that will keep death out of your house.

Suffering, importance of; Trials, importance of

Phil. 1:29; 2 Tim. 2:12; 3:12; 1 Peter 3:17; 4:19; Rev. 2:10

When projected pictures are to be viewed by an audience, the projectionist darkens the room in which they sit, so that the pictures may be more fully seen. So God sometimes darkens our place on earth, puts out this light and that and then before our souls he makes to pass the splendors and glories of the better land.

Suicide, self-murder; Commandment, sixth

Judg. 16:29; 1 Sam. 31:4–5; 2 Sam. 17:23; 1 Kings 16:18; 1 Chron. 10:4–5; Matt. 27:5; Acts 1:18

There is that other kind of murder that is increasing at an appalling rate among us—suicide. There have been unbelievers in all ages who have advocated it as a justifiable means of release from trial and difficulty; yet thinking men, as far back as Aristotle, have generally condemned it as cowardly and unjustifiable under any conditions. No man has a right to take his own life from such motives any more than the life of another.

It has been pointed out that the Jewish race, the people of God, always counted length of days as blessing. The Bible does not mention one single instance of a good man committing suicide. In the four thousand years of Old Testament history it records only five suicides, and only one suicide in the New Testament. Samson, Saul, king of Israel, and his armor bearer, Ahithophel, Zimri and Judas Iscariot are the six cases. Look at the references in the Bible to see what kind of men they were.

Sympathy, need of; Understanding, need of

Hosea 1:7; Joel 2:18; Titus 3:4

A young man, just out of the penitentiary, came to see me, and after I had talked with him for some time he didn't seem to think I was in sympathy with him. I offered him a little money. "No," he said, "I don't want your money." "What do you want?" "I want someone to have confidence in me!" I knelt down and prayed with him, and in my prayer I called him "brother," and he shed tears the moment I called him my brother. If we are going to reach people we must make them believe we are one with them. We must put ourselves in their places.

Talents, use of; Handicaps, overcoming

Matt. 25:28

I was at a meeting in London, when I was there, and I heard a man speaking with wonderful power and earnestness. "Who is that man?" I asked. "That is Dr. Moon. He is a very learned minister. He is blind." I felt interest in this man, and at the close of the meeting, I sought an interview, and he told me that he had been stricken blind when very young. His mother took him to a doctor, and asked him about his sight. "You must give up all hope," the doctor said. "Your boy is blind, and will be forever." The mother took her boy to her bosom and cried, "Oh, my boy, who will take care of you when I am gone?" She forgot the faithfulness of that God she had taught him to love.

He became a servant of the Lord and was used to print the Bible in seventy-two different languages in Braille so that blind people could read the Scriptures themselves. He had a congregation of three million people, and I think that blind man was one of the happiest beings in all London. He was naturally blind, but he had eyes to his soul, and could see a bright eternity in the future. He had built his foundation upon the living God. We pity those who have not their natural sight; but how you should pity yourself if you are spiritually blind.

Talents, use of; Opportunity, use of

Prov. 11:24; 22:9; Eccles. 11:1; 2 Cor. 9:6,10; Gal. 6:10

An Eastern allegory runs thus: A merchant, going abroad for a time, gave respectively to two of his friends two sacks of wheat each, to take care of against his return. Years passed. When he came back, he asked for them again. The first took him into a storehouse, and showed him his sacks; but they were mildewed and worthless. The other led him out into the open country, and pointed to field after field of waving wheat, the produce of the two sacks given him. Said the merchant, "You have been a faithful friend. Give me two sacks of that wheat; the rest shall be yours." Let us put to good use the talents God has given us.

Talents, use of; Service, benefit of

Matt. 25:25; Luke 6:38; Heb. 6:10

I read of a man who had a thousand dollars. He hid it away, thinking he would in that way take care of it, and that when he was an old man he would have something to fall back upon. After keeping the deposit receipt for twenty years he took it to a bank and got just one thousand dollars for it. If he had put the money at interest in the usual way, he might have had three times the amount or more.

He made the mistake that a great many people are making today throughout Christendom, of not using their talents. My experience has been as I have gone about in the world and mingled with professing Christians, that those who find most fault with others are those who themselves do nothing. If a person is busy improving the talents that God has given him he will have too much to do to find fault and complain about others.

Temptation, avoiding; Prayer for deliverance

Matt. 6:13; 26:41; Mark 14:38; Luke 11:4; 22:40, 46; 1 Cor. 10:13; 2 Peter 2:9

A steamboat was stranded in the Mississippi River, and the captain could not get her free. Eventually a hard-looking fellow came on board, and said: "Captain, I understand you want a pilot to take you out of this difficulty?" The captain said, "Are you a pilot?" "Well, they call me one." "Do you know where the snags and sandbars are?" "No, sir." "Well, how do you expect to take me out of here if you don't know where the snags and sandbars are?" "I know where they ain't!" was the reply.

Beware of temptations. "Lead us not into temptation," our Lord taught us to pray; and again he said, "Watch and pray, lest ye enter into temptation." We are weak and sinful by nature, and it is a good deal better for us to pray for deliverance rather than to run into temptation and then pray for strength to resist.

Temptation, avoiding; Satan, strategy of

Matt. 6:13; 26:41; Mark 14:38; Luke 11:4; 22:40, 46; 1 Cor. 10:13; 2 Peter 2:9

There is a legend that the apostle John was much distressed over the fall of a young convert. He summoned Satan before him, and reproached him for ruining so good a youth. "I found your good youth on my ground," said Satan. "So I took him." The only safe course is to avoid places of known temptation altogether.

Temptation, common to all; Satan aims high

1 Cor. 10:13; Rev. 12:9

No person on earth is beyond the reach of the tempter. I used to think that when I got along a certain distance in my Christian life I would get beyond the tempter, and he would have no more influence over me. I have given that up. The tempter will follow you from the cradle to the grave, and the nearer you get to Christ, the hotter the fight will be. As someone has said, Satan aims high. When he wanted one to sell the Lord, he went to the treasurer of the company; and when he wanted one to deny him, he went to the chief apostle. Angels fell, even in heaven. Adam fell in Paradise. Think of it!

Temptation in life's stages

1 Cor. 10:12; 1 Tim. 3:6–7; Heb. 4:11; James 5:12; 2 Peter 3:17

Think of the periods of our aging as the four watches of life. Someone has said that the time a person is most liable to fall is in the second and the third watch. The first watch, I start out, and say, "I must be on my guard; I am weak." I realize my weakness, and keep my eye upon the Master, going to him daily and hourly for strength; and so I am not so liable to fall. But in the second and third watches I begin to feel my adulthood, and say, "I am strong now, and I can stand." So I begin to lean on the arm of flesh, then the peril comes, and the fall. As I get into the fourth watch, I am nearing home, and I begin to see this old world receding from my vision. I realize how weak the flesh is, because it has failed me so often, and I am on guard again. I am not so liable to fall if I have passed through the second and third watches, though I am always liable and must be on my guard.

Temptation of Christ;
Temptation, nature of

Gen. 3:15; Matt. 4:1; Mark 1:13; Luke 4:1; John 14:30; Heb. 2:18; 4:15

Now, notice, Christ was full of the Holy Spirit, and yet he was tempted. Temptation comes upon us with its strongest power when we are nearest to God. I used to believe it was just the reverse—that when I got near to God I would be free from temptation. But when you are very near to God, then it is that temptation makes its strongest attack upon you. When Jesus was anointed for service, then it was that the devil tempted him for forty days. As someone has said, the devil aims high. He got one apostle to curse and swear and say he didn't know Christ. Very few men have had such conflicts with the devil as Martin Luther had. Why? Because he was going to shake the very kingdom of hell.

Temptation, power of; Satan, strategy of

Ps. 1:3; Jer. 17:8; Ezek. 17:8; Matt. 7:24

The strength of a chain is in its weakest link. Mark that; in its weakest link. Few men can stand alone when the storm sweeps over them. Away they go! Have you ever been in a forest after a great storm has swept through it? Where the roots just run along on the surface and do not have any depth of earth, acres and acres of trees will be torn up. A friend from Scotland said to me, speaking of a place where I had been, "Some time ago they had a storm that blew down between four and five thousand of the finest trees on that old estate. Do you know why? Because the storm came in an unexpected direction. It had never come from that quarter before. It had blown in every direction but that one, and the forest wasn't prepared, and away the trees went."

Temptation, subtlety of

1 Cor. 10:12; 1 Tim. 3:6–7; Heb. 4:11; James 5:12; 2 Peter 3:17

It is said that Edinburgh Castle, in all the wars of Scotland, was never taken but once. Then the enemy came up the steep rocks at a place where the garrison thought it was so safe they needn't guard it. Very often temptation comes in an unexpected form or from an unexpected quarter, when you are off your guard; hence, the necessity of watching and praying, because if you are not on the alert, you will be tripped up by the tempter.

Temptations, danger of

1 Cor. 10:12; 1 Tim. 3:6–7; Heb. 4:11; James 5:12; 2 Peter 3:17

I remember when I was a young Christian I used to think that it would be easier after a time, and that when I had been a Christian fifteen or twenty years, I should have but few temptations and difficulties; but I find that the longer I live the more dangers I see surrounding me. Why, Samson judged Israel for twenty years and then fell into sin; and how many men there are who fall in their old age. I don't mean that they are finally lost, but they fall into sin. They make some mistake, or their old temper springs up, and they do some mean thing, and very often the church has not as much sympathy with such persons as it ought to have.

Too much is frequently expected of new Christians. There is a great difference between a person falling into sin and loving sin. If you fall into sin and all the time hate it, go and tell God all about it, for he is faithful and just to forgive us our sins and to cleanse us from all unrighteousness.

Ten Commandments, breaking of

Rom. 3:10, 23; 1 Tim. 1:9; 1 John 1:8

We sometimes hear people pray to be preserved from certain sins, as if they were in no danger of committing others. I firmly believe that if a person begins by willfully breaking one of these commandments it is much easier to break the others.

I know of a gentleman who had a confidential clerk and insisted on his going down Sunday morning to work on his books. The young man had a good deal of principle, and at first refused; but he was anxious to keep in the good graces of his employer and finally yielded. He had not done that a great while before he speculated in stocks with company money, and became a defaulter for one hundred and twenty thousand dollars.

The employer had him arrested and put in the penitentiary for ten years, but I believe he was just as guilty in the sight of God as that young man, for he led him to take the first step on the downward road. You remember the story of a soldier who was smuggled into a fortress in a load of hay, and opened the gates to his comrades. Every sin we commit opens the door for other sins.

Rom. 3:10, 23; 1 Tim. 1:9; 1 John 1:8

For fifteen hundred years man was under the law, and no one was equal to it. Christ came and showed that the commandments went beyond the mere letter; and can anyone since say that he has been able to keep them in his own strength? As the plummet line is held up, we see how much we are out of the perpendicular. As we measure ourselves by that holy standard, we find how much we are lacking. As a child said, when reproved by her mother and told that she ought to do right: "How can I do right when there is no 'right' in me?"

Testimony, Christian; Substance abuse, recovery from

Matt. 4:24; 8:17; 9:2, 6; Luke 4:40; 6:17; 7:21, 47–48; 9:1; Acts 19:12; 28:9; James 5:15–16

"Have you ever heard the gospel?" asked a missionary of a Chinese national, whom he had not seen in his mission before. "No," he replied, "but I have seen it. I know a man who used to be the terror of his neighborhood. He was a bad opium smoker and dangerous as a wild beast; but he became wholly changed when he became a Christian. He is now gentle and good and has left off opium."

Testimony, importance of; Public witness, importance of

Ps. 107:2; John 9:11; 2 Cor. 2:17; Phil. 1:14; 1 Thess. 1:8

The blind man Christ had healed told a straightforward story, just what the Lord had done for him. That is all. That is what a witness ought to do—tell what he knows, not what he does not know. He did not try to make a long speech. It is not the most flippant and fluent witness who has the most influence with a jury.

This man's testimony is what I call "experience." One of the greatest hindrances to the progress of the gospel today is that the narration of the experience of the church is not encouraged. There are a great many men and women who come into the church, and we never hear anything of the Lord's dealings with them. If we did, it would be a great help to others. It would stimulate faith and encourage the more feeble of the flock. The apostle Paul's experience has been recorded three times. I have no doubt that he told it everywhere he went: how God had met him; how God had opened his eyes and his heart; and how God had blessed him.

Testimony, value of; Doubts, remedy for

1 John 5:9–10; Rev. 3:14

Human affairs would come to a standstill if we did not take the testimony of men. How should we get on in the ordinary affairs of life, and how would commerce continue, if we disregarded men's testimony? Things social and commercial would come to a deadlock within forty-eight hours. This is the drift of the apostle's argument here. "If we receive the witness of men, the witness of God is greater." God has borne witness to Jesus Christ. And if man can believe his fellow men who are frequently telling untruths and whom we are constantly finding unfaithful, why should we not take God at his word and believe his testimony?

Faith is a belief in testimony. It is not a leap in the dark, as some tell us. That would be no faith at all. God does not ask any man to believe without giving him something to believe. You might as well ask a man to see without eyes; to hear without ears; and to walk without feet— as to bid him believe without giving him something to believe.

When I started for California I procured a guidebook. This told me, that after leaving the state of Illinois, I should cross the Mississippi, and then the Missouri; get into Nebraska; then go over the Rocky Mountains to the Mormon settlement at Salt Lake City, and proceed by the way of the Sierra Nevada into San Francisco. I found the guidebook all right as I went along; and I should have been a miserable skeptic if, having proved it to be correct three-fourths of the way, I had said that I would not believe it for the remainder of the journey.

Testimony, willingness for

Deut. 32:30; Josh. 23:10; Rom. 1:16

Somebody spoke once to a young convert who got up in the streets and tried to preach, and said, "You ought to be ashamed of yourself." "Well," he said, "I am, but I am not ashamed of my Savior." So let us be ashamed of ourselves, but not of Christ, but speak out in our business and in our homes, everywhere where we are for Christ. This is the way to have a true revival—work for Christ, talk for Christ, speak to those who are about you, and don't you see that if this whole audience here was full of holy enthusiasm, this community would feel our influence within twenty-four hours? "One shall chase a thousand and two shall put ten thousand to flight."

Thankfulness, example of; Cheerfulness, example of

Job 1:21; Ps. 34:1; Eph. 5:20; Phil. 4:6; Col. 3:17; 1 Thess. 5:18

I remember a man who was a carpenter, who used to belong to the same church that I did. He always wore a smile—not a forced smile, but a natural one. Every time he got up in prayer meeting a smile passed over the whole congregation. A smile was on his face before he said anything, and he always began by saying, "Bless the Lord!" It wasn't one of those insincere expressions that we hear sometimes, it was honest and hearty. While at work one day he cut his thumb so that it only held by a little piece of skin. I said to myself, the next time I see that man he probably won't smile or say, "Bless the Lord!" But at the next weekly prayer meeting he was there, and the first thing he said was: "Bless the Lord! I cut my thumb, but I didn't cut it clear off."

Most of us would have changed our shout into a wail, and it would have been a doleful sort of testimony. I would as soon get a blast of chilly east wind in March, right off the Maine seacoast, as to meet some of those Christians who are not thankful. Let us be cheerful, and bright, and sincere. If God has been good to us, let us give thanks.

Thanksgiving, example of

Job 1:21; Pss. 34:1; 147:1; 148:1; 149:1; Eph. 5:20; Phil. 4:6; Col. 3:17; 1 Thess. 5:18

The King of England, at the close of the Revolutionary War, appointed a day of thanksgiving. Not a day for the thirteen colonies lost, nor the money spent and the lives sacrificed, but to praise God that it was no worse. So we should look on the bright side. We would get more blessings if we were more thankful.

Theology without love

1 Cor. 13:1

I once went into a restaurant with a couple of professing Christians, and we sat there five minutes; and one of them—he was a prominent man in the community—called up the headwaiter, and said in a loud voice, "What does this mean, sir? We have been here half an hour waiting for someone to come," and he gave the head waiter a good blowing up. That man knew there was not a word of truth in it. We hadn't been there over five minutes. I was ashamed of the company I was in, and have been careful not to be caught with them again. Yet that man boasted of his sound theology. He lives on that.

What do I care for his theology? Theology without love is useless. A man's religion that has no love in it is like a clock without hands. It may have beautiful machinery, and you may put it in a fine case and stud it with diamonds, but it will not be worth anything as a timekeeper. A person has got to love, to win other people to Christ. If I am cross and peevish and disagreeable, I may be ever so sound in doctrine, but I shall not win anyone to accept it. They will hate me, and hate it, and despise it.

Thoughts, open to God; Heart, sinfulness of

Isa. 55:7

"Let the wicked forsake his way, and the unrighteous man his thoughts." Thoughts! The world doesn't see them, but God sees them. Even those of us who have been in the Christian life for years don't know what is in us. Years ago I thought I knew my own heart, but there are depths in it I know

293

nothing about. When I hear a man say he knows his own heart, I pity him. The best way is to get down on our faces before God, and honestly ask him to show us ourselves and our need of a Savior.

Times and seasons, knowledge of; Prophecy, biblical

Acts 1:7

Commenting on the text, "It is not for you to know the times or the seasons, which the Father hath put in His own power," Spurgeon said, "If I were introduced into a room where a large number of parcels were stored up, and I was told that there was something good for me, I should begin to look for that which had my name upon it, and when I came upon a parcel and I saw in pretty big letters, 'It is not for you,' I should leave it alone. Here, then, is a parcel of knowledge marked, 'It is not for you to know the times or the seasons, which the Father hath put in His own power.' Cease to meddle with matters which are concealed, and be satisfied to know the things which are clearly revealed."

Tobacco, use of

John 2:21; 1 Cor. 6:19

Is it best for a converted alcoholic to also give up tobacco? I would let that go with the whisky. It belongs to the old nature. It is clearly taught that our bodies are the temples for the Holy Spirit, and we ought to be careful to keep them pure. I do not think it is becoming for a son of the Most High to be using that filthy weed, and I have an idea that many a man that uses tobacco is led thereby to drinking. How is it with men that have no work using tobacco? I don't see how they can afford it. I do not think it keeps the body in a healthy state. I think we ought to be very careful about the body, because it is so identified with the soul.

Tongue, misuse of; Commandment, ninth

Pss. 52:2; 140:3; Prov. 10:11; 15:2; James 3:3

The tongue can be an instrument of untold good or incalculable evil. Someone has said that a sharp tongue is the only edged tool that grows keener with constant use. Bishop Hall said that the tongues of busybodies are like the tails of Samson's foxes—they carry firebrands and are enough to set the whole field of the world in flame. Blighted hopes and blasted reputations are witness to the tongue's awful power. In many cases the tongue has murdered its victims. Can we not all recall cases where men and women have died under the wounds of calumny and misrepresentation? History is full of such cases.

Tongues, new

Mark 16:17

I want now to call your attention to Mark 16:17, "And these signs shall follow them that believe; in my name shall they cast out devils; they shall speak with new tongues." With all these new things we get also new tongues. There is a great deal of mischief done by slanderous tongues. I think we don't preach enough about this. If our hearts are right with God, we will not go about backbiting people. Many a man has gone to the grave with a broken heart because of a few abusive words uttered by a professed friend.

Christ said to his disciples when he was leaving them: "These signs shall follow them; they shall speak with new tongues." I heard the story of a young man who abused his mother and finally knocked her down, because she would not give him money to gamble with. She did not mind this; she only prayed for him. She did not care for the money, but she did for his soul. He was converted, came back and asked his mother to forgive him, and she did it gladly, and he praised God, and he has erected a family altar. He had gotten a new tongue.

Transfiguration of Christ; Atonement, substitutionary

Matt. 17:2; Mark 9:2; John 17:22; Rom. 8:29–30; Col. 3:4; 2 Thess. 2:14; 1 Peter 5:10

What a dark night it would have been if our Lord and Master had been caught up with Moses and Elijah, and Christ had not died for our sins. Oh, how Jesus Christ has lit up this world! But suppose that he had gone up to heaven on the other side of Calvary, and had never finished his work. Suppose that God in his love for his Son had said, "I can't let those men spit upon you and smite you; I will take you back to my bosom." What darkness would have settled down on the world! But Moses disappeared, and Elijah disappeared, and Christ only was left, for Christ is all. The law and the prophets were honored and fulfilled in him.

Transfiguration of Christ; Salvation, fullness of

Matt. 17:2; Mark 9:2; John 17:22; Rom. 8:29–30; Col. 3:4; 2 Thess. 2:14; 1 Peter 5:10

I believe we don't learn the fringe of the subject of salvation down here. When our Master was on earth, he said he had many more things to say, but he could not reveal them to his disciples because they were not ready to receive them. But when we go yonder, where these mortal bodies have put on immortality, when our spiritual faculties are loosed from the power of the flesh, I believe we shall be able to take more in. God will lead us from glory to glory, and show us the fullness of our salvation. Don't you think Moses knew more at the Mount of Transfiguration than he did at Pisgah? Didn't Christ talk with him then about the death he was to accomplish at Jerusalem? He couldn't

have received this truth before, any more than the disciples, but when he had received his glorified body, Christ could show him everything.

Transgressor, way of; Sin, price of; Satan, hard taskmaster

Prov. 23:27; Isa. 24:20; James 2:11

"Mr. Moody, the way of the transgressor is pretty hard." It is a common expression. I have been with men in court and in prison who have said this. It is not a hard thing to serve God if you are born of God; but, my friends, it is a hard thing to serve Satan. The way of sin grows darker and harder to a man the longer he is in it. I took up a newspaper this morning, and the first thing I saw was an account of a Boston man who had forged, and it closed by saying his path was a hard, flinty one.

Now, take up any class of sinners in Chicago. We've representatives here tonight. Take the prostitute. Do you think her life is an easy one? It is very short. The average one is seven years. Just look at her as she comes up to the city from the home where she has left sisters and a mother as pure as the morning air. She came down to the city and is now in a low brothel. Sometimes her mind goes back to the pure home where her mother prayed for her; where she used to lay down her head on that mother's bosom, and she used to press the sweet face of her child to her own. She remembers when she went to Sunday school; remembers when her mother tried to teach her to serve God, and now she is an exile.

She doesn't want to go home. She is full of shame. She looks into the future and sees darkness before her. In a few short years she dies the death of a harlot, and she is laid away in an unknown grave. All the flattery of her lovers is hollow and false. Is her life a happy one? Ask a harlot tonight, and she will tell you the way of the transgressor is hard; and then ask the pure and virtuous if Christ is a hard master.

Acts 9:5; 26:14

There was a man whom I knew who was an inveterate drinker. He had a wife and children. He thought he could stop whenever he felt inclined, but he went the ways of most moderate drinkers. I had not been gone more than three years and, when I returned I found that his mother had gone down to her grave with a broken heart, and that man was the murderer of the wife of his bosom. His children have all been taken away from him, and he is now walking up and down those streets homeless. But four years ago he had a beautiful and a happy home with his wife and children around him. They are gone; probably he will never see them again. Perhaps he has come in here tonight. If he has, I ask him: "Is not the way of the transgressor hard?"

Don't believe the devil's lies; don't think God is a hard master. If you persist in wrong doing, you will find out the truth of what was said to Saul, "It is hard for thee to kick against the pricks."

Trinity, description of; Faith, saving

Matt. 28:19; John 15:26; Acts 17:29; 26:18; 2 Cor. 13:14; 1 John 5:7

It is not long ago, it just seems the other day, when my dear friend Dr. Mathieson, now in heaven, told me he was preaching the gospel in Scotland, and a minister told him he had in his congregation a little retarded boy. He did not know what to do with him; he had spoken to him many times, but the boy always said, "Ye must wait till I come to you, and when I come I'll sing ye a song and tell ye a story; but ye must wait till I come to ye." The minister heard that the boy was dying, and he went to him and said, "Sandy, you

promised me that you would sing me a song and tell me a story before you died; will you tell it now?"

"Yes, minister," replied the boy, "Three in one an' one in three, and Jesus Christ, he died for me; and that's it."

I tell you I would rather be a little retarded boy and know that, than be one of the mightiest and so-called wisest men in the city of Chicago, and not believe that Jesus took my place and died for me on Calvary's cross. The gospel is very simple; it is very easy to understand.

Trinity, nature of

Matt. 28:19; John 15:26; Acts 17:29; 2 Cor. 13:14; 1 John 5:7

By the Father is meant the first Person, Christ, the Word, is the second, and the Holy Spirit, perfectly fulfilling his own office and work in union with the Father and the Son, is the third. I find clearly presented in my Bible, that the One God who demands my love, service, and worship has there revealed himself, and that each of those three names of Father, Son and Holy Spirit has personality attached to them. Therefore we find some things ascribed to God as Father, some to God as Savior, and some to God as Comforter and Teacher. It has been remarked that the Father plans, the Son executes, and the Holy Spirit applies. But I also believe they plan and work together.

Trouble, dealing with; Trials, dealing with

Job 5:7; Pss. 50:15; 91:15; Matt. 6:34

We are apt to think that young children do not have any trouble, but if they haven't, there is one thing they can make sure of; that they are going to have trouble later. "Man is born unto trouble, as the sparks fly upward." Trouble is coming. No one is exempt. God has had one Son without sin, but he has never had one without sorrow. Jesus Christ, our Master, suffered as few men ever suffered, and he died very young. Ours is a path of sorrow and suffering, and it is so sweet to hear the Master say, "I will be with you in trouble." Don't think for a moment that you can get on without God. You may say now, "I can get on; I am in good health and prosperity," but the hour is coming when you will need him.

Trouble, refuge in

Pss. 9:9; 46:1; 59:16; 91:15

I was greatly depressed on the steamship *Spree* when told it was going to sink. My wife and children were in America. I had been away from my country a long time and was coming home. I just longed to get to my family. I was awake one Saturday morning, at daybreak, and the old boat shook. The lifeboats were swung into the water, and the life preservers were brought out on deck and we were told to put them on. It looked as if we were to leap into the ocean.

All that Saturday my heart was like a lump of lead. Sunday came. The moment you spoke to anyone about his soul, he would tremble like an aspen leaf; all thought they were going down. What an opportunity for doing good! But they were too much taken up with the great sorrow, of parting with their friends and loved ones, to think of anything else. Sunday afternoon came, and we got the people together and I read the Ninety-first Psalm.

When I got down to the verse, "I will be with him in the time of trouble," the burden rolled away and light burst in upon me, and from that hour I was as calm as if I were a babe in my mother's arms. I went to my berth and lay down and slept as soundly as ever, thinking, "I may be in heaven when I awake; but I may reach my home at Northfield. This boat can't go down without the will of God; and if it is his will that I should go down, his will be done."

God made that pillow as calm and peaceful as any pillow I ever had in my life. If a storm had burst on us any time during that time, we would have gone down, but God was with us in the time of trouble, and the burden was lifted. God in his providence rescued us but if he had not, I would have gone into his presence in peace.

Troubles, given to God

1 Peter 5:7

A great many people seem to embalm their troubles. I always feel like running away when I see them coming. They bring out their old mummy, and tell you in a sad voice, "You don't know the troubles I have!" My friends, if you go to the Lord with your troubles, he will take them away. Would you not rather be with the Lord and get rid of your troubles, than be with your troubles and without God? Let trouble come if it will drive us nearer to God. The Lord says, "Cast all your care on me. I want to carry your burdens and your troubles."

What we need is a joyful church, and we are not going to convert the world until we have it. We want to get this long-faced Christianity off the face of the earth. Take these people that have some great burden, and let them come into a meeting. If you can get their attention upon the singing or preaching, they will say, "Oh, wasn't it grand! I forgot all my cares." And they just drop their bundle at the end of the pew. But the moment the benediction is pronounced they grab the bundle again. You laugh, but you do it yourself. Cast your care on Christ.

Trust, example of

2 Chron. 32:7–8; Ps. 9:10; Matt. 4:22; 9:21; Mark 1:18; John 6:69; Acts 8:37; James 2:21–22

There's a story told that Alexander the Great had a favorite doctor who always went with him into battle. This doctor had another doctor envious of him, who wanted to get his position. One day the envious doctor wrote to Alexander, and told him that his personal physician was going to poison him; that the next morning when he took his wine, there would be death in the goblet. The emperor read the communication to himself and the next morning, when his doctor handed him the wine glass, he took it, held it in his hand, and then read the letter aloud. Before his doctor could deny the accusation, Alexander drank all the wine in the goblet.

He showed that he trusted his physician with all his heart. There was not a shadow of distrust between them. Is that the way you treat God? If you trust God in that way you'll have no clouds, no dark days, no blue days. It'll be better and better every day. I hope you have learned to fully trust God. I pity those people who live in Doubting Castle.

Trust in Christ; Security, basis of

Job 19:25; Ps. 23:4; Isa. 12:2; John 3:15; 5:24; 6:39; 10:28; Rom. 6:23; Phil. 1:6; 1 Peter 1:5; 1 John 3:2; Jude 24

I remember while in Europe I was traveling with friends. On one occasion we were journeying from London to Liverpool, and the question was put as to where we would stop. We said we would go to the "Northwestern," at Lime Street, as that was the hotel where Americans generally stayed. When we got there, the house was full and they could not let us in. Every room was engaged. But this friend said, "I am going to stay here. I engaged a room ahead. I sent a telegram on."

My friends, that is just what the Christians are doing—sending their names in ahead. They are sending a message up saying: "Lord Jesus, I want one of those mansions you are preparing; I want to be there." Every man and woman who wants one, if you have not already got one, had

better make up your mind. Send your names up now. I would rather a thousand times have my name written in the Lamb's Book than have all the wealth of the world rolling at my feet.

Trust, nature of

Pss. 27:5; 33:6; 91:1; Isa. 40:26; John 1:3; Acts 17:24; Rom. 1:19; 8:25; Gal. 5:6; 1 Peter 1:7; 2 Peter 3:5; Heb. 10:22, 39; 11:3, 6

A prominent and much loved minister died, one of those ministers who had had a large salary and had given it all to the poor where he lived. He was a public man struck down in the prime of life. As he lay on his dying bed, he thought of leaving his wife and children unprovided for, and there came a cloud over his mind. He was greatly depressed; he couldn't get above it. While he lay there, thinking of the sad lot of his loved ones, a little bird with a worm in its mouth lit on his windowsill. With that a warmness came into his heart, and the thought came into his mouth, "If God can take care of that bird, he can take care of my wife and children." At once the trust of a child came into his heart and the burden rolled away. He knew he could trust his family to God.

As they bore him away, the whole city was moved; the rich and the poor were there, and for miles up to the cemetery the streets were lined with people weeping. This poor man was hardly laid away in his grave before a friend rose and proposed that £5000 Sterling ($25,000) be raised for the widow and her children, and it was done. God took care of the trusting minister's widow and orphans.

Trust, nature of; Illustrations, value of

Exod. 15:2; 2 Sam. 7:28; 2 Chron. 32:7–8; Jer. 31:1; John 3:16; 13:35; Rom. 8:24; Heb. 11:1–2, 13; 1 Peter 1:8

When I was preaching in Baltimore in 1879, an infidel reporter, who believed I was a humbug, came to the meetings with the express purpose of catching me in my remarks. He believed that my stories and anecdotes were all made up, and he intended to expose me in his paper. One of the anecdotes I told was as follows:

A gentleman was walking down the streets of a city some time before. It was near Christmastime and many of the shop windows were filled with Christmas presents and toys. As this gentleman passed along, he saw three little girls standing before a shop window. Two of them were trying to describe to the third the things that were in the window. It aroused his attention, and he wondered what it could mean. He went back, and found that the middle one was blind— she had never been able to see—and her two sisters were endeavoring to tell her how the things looked.

The gentleman stood beside them for some time and listened; he said it was most interesting to hear them trying to describe the different articles to the blind child—they found it a difficult task. "That is just my position in trying to tell other men about Christ," I said. "I may talk about Christ; and yet they see no beauty in him that they should desire him. But if they will only come to him, he will open their eyes and reveal himself to them in all his loveliness and grace."

After the meeting this reporter came to me and asked where I got that story. I said I had read it in a Boston paper. He told me that it had happened right there in the streets of Baltimore, and that he was the gentleman referred to! It made such an impression on him that he accepted Christ and became one of the first converts in that city. Many and many a time I have found that when the sermon—and even the text—has been forgotten, some story has fastened itself in a hearer's mind, and has borne fruit. Anecdotes are like windows to let light in upon a subject. They have a useful ministry.

Trust, object of; Communion, meaning of

Gen. 15:6; Deut. 31:8; 2 Sam. 22:31; Neh. 4:14; Pss. 5:11; 7:1; 118:8–9; Isa. 26:4; Rom. 4:3; 1 Cor. 5:2; 1 Thess. 2:13; 1 Peter 2:6; James 2:23

Every child knows what it is to trust. But the important matter is, who to trust. The most restless people are those who trust in themselves, who are always thinking about themselves. It is not what I am to God, but what God is to me. Many go to the communion table to remember themselves; to think over and mourn over their sins. We ought to go there to remember Christ. When I want to get lifted up, I forget myself, and think about God. Love must have an object. Let the soul be stayed upon God, and it will have perfect peace.

Trust, wholehearted; Dedication, appeal to

Gen. 24:7; Josh. 1:9; 1 Sam. 17:37; 2 Kings 18:5; 2 Chron. 32:8; Jer. 24:7; Matt. 21:21; Luke 8:48; Rom. 6:17; 1 Tim. 1:19; Heb.11:11; James 1:6, 25

Oh, man, oh, woman, trust God with all your heart! How miserable you wives feel if you haven't full confidence in your husbands; or if your husbands don't trust you with all their hearts. And how the husband feels if the wife doesn't trust him with all her heart. What God wants is the whole heart.

Truth, carelessness about

Lev. 19:11; Col. 3:9

Dr. Johnson once said that it is more from carelessness regarding the truth than from intentional lying that there is so much falsehood in the world.

Truth, personal application of

John 5:39; 10:28; 17:3; 1 John 5:11

One thing I know—I cannot speak for others, but I can speak for myself; I cannot read other minds and other hearts; I cannot read the Bible and lay hold for others; but I can read for myself, and take God at his word. The great trouble is that people take everything in general, and do not take it to themselves. Suppose a man should say to me, "Moody, there was a man in Europe who died last week, and left five million dollars to a certain individual." "Well," I say, "I don't doubt that; it's rather a common thing to happen," and I don't think anything more about it.

But suppose he says, "But he left the money to you." Then I pay attention. I say, "To me?" "Yes, he left it to you." I become suddenly interested. I want to know all about it. So we are apt to think Christ died for sinners; he died for everybody, and for nobody in particular. But when the truth comes to me that eternal life is mine, and all the glories of heaven are mine, I begin to be interested. I say, "Where is the chapter and verse where it says I can be saved?" If I put myself among sinners, I take the place of the sinner, then it is that salvation is mine and I am sure of it for time and eternity.

Truth, standing for; Conviction, expression of

John 6:70; 8:44

R. A. Torrey, the American evangelist, said, "D. L. Moody was generally considered a broad man, and so he was. No matter how far astray a man might go in doctrine, D. L. Moody would do his best to reclaim him to the truth. But Mr. Moody was a plainspoken man as well as a broad man. One man whose views of the Bible were extremely lax used to make a good deal of Mr. Moody's friendship for him, and that Mr. Moody was friendly towards him there can be no doubt, but Mr. Moody told me that he told this man to his face that he was doing the devil's work. It was plain talking, but it was unquestionable truth."

Unbelief, hopelessness of

Matt. 13:58; Rom. 3:3; 11:20; Heb. 3:12

What does unbelief do for a man? "Why," said a dying infidel, "my principles have lost me my friends; they have sent my wife to her grave with a broken heart; they have made my children beggars, and I am going down to my grave without peace or consolation." I never heard of an infidel going down to the grave happily. How many young men are turned away from Christ by them? Let infidels remember that God will hold them responsible.

Unbelief of natural man

1 Cor. 2:14; Heb. 4:6, 11

I was in the inquiry room one night talking to a skeptical person. He didn't come in to inquire, but to have a discussion with someone. You know there are a great many people that are fond of discussing; and he said he didn't believe in the Bible. He didn't agree with it. I said: "Why, my dear friend, the Bible agrees with you. You and the Bible agree." He said: "Oh, no, I don't believe in it at all." "Why, yes you do. You have just agreed with the Bible. It says: 'The natural man cannot receive spiritual things.'" The poor fellow didn't know what to do, so he hung his head.

Unbelief, overcoming

Rom. 4:20; Phil. 4:13

We must keep battering away at unbelief. I remember when leaving Scotland I was told I couldn't expect much in Ireland where I was going; that the Irish were peculiar. I could expect good work in Scotland because the people understood their Bibles, and all I had to do was to sing and preach the gospel; but I found unbelief my difficulty there. I found just the same thing in Ireland, just the same old human nature. The same power of God was needed in Scotland, and we found the same hard work of surmounting unbelief in Ireland.

When we left Ireland to go to England, and especially Liverpool, where there are a great many drinking saloons, there was a great deal of opposition and unbelief. But the Spirit of God worked in Liverpool. When we went to London it was said we should certainly have defeat there. And starting from there for this country we were not to expect results here because you had singing and preaching here. But we found in Philadelphia and New York the gospel had effect upon the people.

When we left for Chicago this fall it was said we would surely be successful there, and when we got there we found Christian men and women we had worked with for years who did not believe we would be successful because Chicago was a peculiar city. When we came to Boston some people told me, "Mr. Moody, we must give you a little warning; you must remember that Boston is a peculiar place, and you cannot expect to do the same as elsewhere; there are a great many obstacles."

It is the same old story, the same old human nature. Boston is the same as these other places. They are all alike, but the enemy can't hinder God from working if we only have faith. With God all things are possible. This terrible unbelief God can shake in Boston as easy as a mother can shake her little child. We can do all things through his power and strength.

Unbelief, substitute gods; Commandment, first

Deut. 32:31; 1 Sam. 2:2; Dan. 6:26

There is the atheist. He says that he does not believe in God; he denies God's existence, but he can't help setting up some other god in his place. Voltaire said, "If there were no God, it would be necessary to invent one." So the atheist speaks of the Great Unknown, the First Cause, the Infinite Mind, etc. Then there is the deist. He is a man who believes in one God who caused all things; but he doesn't believe in revelation. He only accepts such truths as can be discovered by reason. He doesn't believe in Jesus Christ, or in the inspiration of the Bible. Then there is the pantheist, who says: "I believe that the whole universe is God. He is in the air, the water, the sun, the stars"; the liar and the thief included.

Unbelief, tragedy of; Doubt, sin of

John 3:36; Rom. 3:3; 2 Cor. 1:18; 1 John 5:10

You cannot offer a man a greater insult than to tell him he is a liar. Unbelief is telling God he is a liar. Suppose a man said, "Mr. Moody, I have no faith in you whatever." Don't you think it would grieve me? There is not anything that would wound a man much more than to be told that you do not have any faith in him. A great many men say, "Oh, I have profound reverence and respect for God." Yes, profound respect, but not faith. Why, it is a downright insult.

Suppose a man says, "Mr. Moody, I have profound respect for you, profound admiration for you, but I do not believe a word you say." I wouldn't give much for his respect or admiration; I wouldn't give much for his friendship. God wants us to put our faith in him. How it would wound a mother's feelings to hear her children say, "I do love mamma so much, but I don't believe what she says." How it would grieve that mother. And that is about the way a great many of God's professed children talk. Some men seem to think it is a great misfortune that they do not have faith. Bear in mind it is not a misfortune, but it is the damning sin of the world.

Unchurched, reaching the

1 Cor. 9:22

I remember in one country town where the people did not attend the meetings, they went out into the mountains and fields and had meetings there, and the church soon became four or five times larger than it was. That got people interested. If people will not come to the churches, why not send others out after them, and why not have meetings outside? Have prayer meetings in the homes. A good many mothers can't come out to church; but we can go down to their homes, and have four or five families come together, and pray with them and get them interested.

Unchurched, reaching the; New converts, work of

Matt. 28:19–20; Mark 16:15

The church makes a woeful mistake in not setting these young converts to work. Those men who have been drunkards, let them just set out and work among their old friends. No man can reach a drunkard better than one who has been a drunkard himself. I don't know any work so blessed in Chicago as the going out into the billiard saloons and preaching the gospel there. If they will not come to church, go down where they are, in the name of our God, and you will reach them. If you say, "Oh, they will put you out," I say, "No, I have never been turned out of a saloon in my life."

Go down in a saloon where there are thirty or forty men playing, and ask them if they don't want a little singing. They say, "Yes, we don't mind your singing." "Well, what will you have?" And perhaps they ask you to sing a comic song. "But we don't know any. We don't know how to sing comic songs. Wouldn't you like to have us sing the 'Star Spangled Banner,' or 'My Country, 'tis of Thee'?" And so you sing "My Country, 'tis of Thee," and they stop playing cards. "Now boys, wouldn't you like to have us sing a hymn our mothers taught us when we were boys?" And then you can sing,

> There is a fountain filled with blood,
> Drawn from Immanuel's veins;
> And sinners plunged beneath that flood
> Lose all their guilty stains.

Or give out "Rock of Ages, Cleft for Me," and it won't be long before the hats will be coming off, and they will remember how their mothers sung that to them once when they were in bed, and the tears will begin to run down their cheeks, and it won't be long before they will want you to read a few verses out of the Bible, and then they will ask you to pray with them, and you will be having a prayer meeting there before you know it. We took sixteen out of a saloon in that way one night and brought them to the meeting. Nine of them went into the inquiry room.

Unchurched, reaching the; Witness, lay

Pss. 22:27; 98:2; Luke 24:47–48

There was a man who came to Christ in Chicago who couldn't speak a word of English. We had to make use of an interpreter, and what to do with that man after he became a Christian I didn't know. He wanted to do something for the Lord, and, finally, I stationed him at the corner of Clark and Madison streets to give out handbills inviting people to hear me preach at the YMCA hall. And when the Lord converted him the man was so happy! His face was just lit up, and to every person that went by—and there were some pretty hard cases—he gave a handbill. And some thanked him and some swore at him, but he kept smiling all the time. He couldn't tell the difference between thanks and curses.

For two months he stood there, without a hat part of the time, and every night he was there. When it got to be dark in the short days, he would have a lantern all lighted up right there on the corner. There he stood for months and months, and the Lord gave him a good many souls. What could you do if you would only try?

Unequal yoke in business

Ezra 9:1; Ps. 106:35; 1 Cor. 10:21; 2 Cor. 6:14; James 4:4

A banker once came to me in great distress and said his two partners in business had made up their minds to do a very disreputable thing that would compromise his Christian character, and he was greatly agitated over it. I asked: "Will you tell me when you formed that partnership?" "Five years ago." "How long have you been a Christian?" "Twenty-five years." "And you took these ungodly men into partnership with you; did you read what the Bible says about that?" "Well," he said, "I thought I could make money faster, and have more to give to the Lord."

When godly men yoke themselves up with ungodly men because they can make money faster, they are sure to get into trouble. I told him he had tied himself to two ungodly men and he was going to suffer. And he did suffer. Today his testimony is gone and his influence has been swept away. A good many people think they are going to make more by forming ungodly alliances; but you can't find a case in the Bible where a man ever made anything by selling his principles; not one who gained by going against the Word of God.

Ungodliness, danger of; Backsliding, danger of

Gen. 19:14; Jer. 2:19

When I was in St. Louis, there was an old man who had been away off on the valley of an ungodly life, but in his early manhood he had known Christ. He came into the inquiry room, literally broken down. About midnight that old man came trembling before God and was saved. He wiped away his tears, and started home. Next night I saw him in the audience with a terrible look in his face. As soon as I finished preaching, I went to him and said: "My good friend, you haven't gone back into darkness again?" Said he: "Oh, Mr. Moody, it has been the most wretched day in my life." "Why so?"

"Well, this morning as soon as I got my breakfast, I started out. I have a number of children, married, and in this city, and they have families; and I have spent the day going around and telling them what God has done for me. I told them how I had tasted salvation, with the tears trickling down my face; and, Mr. Moody, I hadn't a child that didn't mock me!" That made me think of Lot down in Sodom. It is an awful thing for a man who has been a backslider to have his children mock him.

Unity, benefits of

Ps. 133:1; 1 Cor. 1:10; 12:12; Eph. 4:3,13; Phil. 2:2

One of the saddest things in the present day is the division in God's church. You notice that when the power of God came upon the early church, it was when they were "all of one accord." I believe the blessing of Pentecost never would have been given but for that spirit of unity. If they had been divided and quarreling among themselves, do you think the Holy Spirit would have come, and those thousands been converted? I have noticed in our work, that if we have gone to a town where three churches were united in it, we have had greater blessing than if only one church was in sympathy. And if there have been twelve churches united, the blessing has multiplied fourfold; it has always been in proportion to the spirit of unity that has been manifested. Where

303

there are bickerings and divisions, and where the spirit of unity is absent, there is very little blessing and praise.

Unity, importance of

Ps. 133:1; 1 Cor. 1:10; 12:12; Eph. 4:3,13; Phil. 2:2

I was in a little town some time ago, when one night as I came out of the meeting, I saw another building where the people were coming out. I said to a friend, "Have you got two churches here?" "Oh, yes." "How do you get on?" "Oh, we get on very well." "I am glad to hear that. Was your brother minister at the meeting?" "Oh, no, we don't have anything to do with each other. We find that is the best way." And they called that "getting on very well."

Oh, may God make us of one heart and of one mind! Let our hearts be like drops of water flowing together. Unity among the people of God is a sort of foretaste of heaven. There we shall not find any Baptists, or Methodists, or Congregationalists, or Episcopalians; we shall all be one in Christ. We leave all our party names behind us when we leave this earth. Oh that the Spirit of God may speedily sweep away all these miserable walls that we have been building up!

Ps. 133:1; 1 Cor. 1:10; 12:12; Eph. 4:3, 13; Phil. 2:2

If a church is divided, I don't care what has divided it; the first thing that a church that is divided ought to do is to get together and get that difficulty out of the way. If I were the minister of a church, and could not unite the church, if those that were dissatisfied would not fall in, I would want them either to go, or I would go myself. I think that there are a good many ministers in this country who are losing their time; they have lost, some of them, months and years, and yet have not seen any fruit, and they will not see any fruit, because they have got a divided church;

that church won't grow. I don't know what has divided them; that is not the question. The Spirit of God doesn't work where there is division, and what we need in all churches today is the spirit of unity so that the Lord may work.

Unity, importance of; Sectarian spirit, avoidance of

Num. 11:27–29; Ps. 133:1; 1 Cor. 1:10; 12:12; Eph. 4:3, 13; Phil. 2:2

Let us present a united front, and this sectarian spirit will soon begin to roll away. If our neighbor is trying to bring men from darkness to light, let us pray for him. Children of God, let us make haste and carry the torch of salvation amongst our fellows and not talk to them about this sect or that sect. There was no sectarian or party feeling on the day of Pentecost, and the Spirit of God fell upon them, and if we are of one mind in this city the Spirit of God will fall on us.

When the Spirit of the Lord fell on the elders of Israel, in the time of Moses, Joshua came and told him that Eldad and Medad prophesied. That is the only blot on the record of Joshua. Moses rebuked him, saying, "Would to God that all the Lord's people were prophets." That is the spirit we need now. When one of our Lord's disciples came and said, "Master, we saw one casting out devils in thy name, and he doesn't belong to our little party," the Lord rebuked him.

Oh, my friends, let the crowning of Christ as King be our aim, and do not do it for this creed or that creed. I remember hearing of Mrs. Comstock's work for the Master in India. Her sons had got to come back from that land to be educated. She brought them down to the vessel which was to take them back to her native land. She knelt on the dock and committed them to God. Her closing words were, "Lord Jesus, I do this for Thee." Let there be no room for jealousy. Oh, that the

Spirit of God may come on us this morning, that we may be of one spirit and one mind, with no self-seeking, but everything for the Lord Jesus.

Unity, power of

John 17:11, 22

Did you ever notice that the last prayer Jesus Christ made on earth, before they led him away to Calvary, was that his disciples might all be one? He could look down the stream of time, and see that divisions would come—how Satan would try to divide the flock of God. Nothing will silence critics so quickly as Christians everywhere being united. Then our testimony will have weight with the ungodly and the careless. But when they see how Christians are divided, they will not believe their testimony. The Holy Spirit is grieved; and there is little power where there is no unity. If I thought I had one drop of sectarian blood in my veins, I would let it out before I went to bed; if I had one sectarian hair in my head, I would pull it out. Let us get right to the heart of Jesus Christ; then our prayers will be acceptable to God, and showers of blessings will descend.

Value, lasting; Greed, danger of

Matt. 16:26; Mark 8:37

"What is the value of this estate?" said a gentleman to another, as they passed a fine mansion surrounded by fair and fertile fields. "I don't know what it is valued at but I know what it cost its last owner." "How much?" "His soul."

Values, assessment of; Vision, nature of; Purpose of life

Gen. 3:9

A man once said to me, "How do you know that God actually asked Adam, 'Where art thou?'" The best answer I can give is, "Because God has put the question to me many a time. I doubt whether there ever has been a son or a daughter of Adam who has not heard that voice ringing through the soul many a time. Who am I? What am I? Where am I going? So let us put the question to ourselves personally, Where am I? Not in the sight of man—that is of very little account; but where am I in the sight of God?"

Values, enduring; Vision, spiritual

Ps. 73:18; Isa. 57:20; Micah 2:2; Jude 12–13

This world that some think is heaven, is the home of sin, a hospital of sorrow, a place that has nothing in it to satisfy the soul. We go all over it and then want to get out of it. The more people see of the world the less they think of it. People soon grow tired of the best pleasures it has to offer. Someone has said that the world is a stormy sea, whose every wave is strewed with the wrecks of mortals that perish in it. Every time we breathe someone is dying. We all know that we are going to stay here but a very little while. Only the other life is enduring.

Values, eternal

Rev. 21:2

An old minister in Kentucky had a son in Chicago in the real estate business, and with the son it was "real estate," "real estate," morning, noon, and night. The old father came to visit him, and he found his boy's mind full of real estate. He had lost all his Christianity. He could talk of nothing but corner lots, corner lots, corner lots. He seemed to live on corner lots. The old gentleman was very much grieved. One day he went down to the office and his son said, "Father, I am going out for a few minutes, and if anyone comes in, you can tell them there is a very good lot here that is worth so

305

much; and here is another nice lot that is worth so much; and here is a good one that is worth so much" and so on.

The old gentleman didn't have much heart for the business; his thoughts were elsewhere. By and by a gentleman came in to inquire about a lot, and the old minister said, "My son says this lot is worth so much. And here's another one worth so much. I don't know anything about them, but I tell you, my friend, I would give more for standing room in the new Jerusalem than for all the corner lots in Chicago." And the son came in and found that his father had gone to preaching. You can tell where the heart is by what it is set upon. It is a good thing to be sure of standing room in the new Jerusalem.

Values, eternal; Perspective, accurate

2 Cor. 4:18; 5:1; Heb. 11:16

The heir to some great estate, while a child, thinks more of a dollar in his pocket than all his inheritance. So even some professing Christians are more elated by a passing pleasure than they are by their title to eternal glory.

Values, eternal; Sowing and reaping

Heb. 1:11; 1 Peter 1:7–8

A famous painter was well known for the careful manner in which he went about his work. When someone asked him why he took such pains, he replied, "Because I am painting for eternity." It is a solemn thing to think that the future will be the harvest of the present—that my condition in my dying hour may depend upon my actions today! Belief in a future life and in a coming judgment magnifies the importance of the present. Eternal issues depend upon it. The opportunity for sowing will not last forever; it is slipping through our fingers moment by moment;

and the future can only reveal the harvest of the seed sown now.

Victory in God's strength

2 Chron. 14:11; Hosea 1:7; Zech. 4:6; 1 Cor. 2:5; 2 Cor. 10:4–5

When at first the Christian receives the grace of salvation, he must not imagine for a moment that he has won the victory. He has only enlisted as a soldier of the cross, and the battles are yet to come. So enlisting in the army of the Lord and fighting the enemy of our souls are altogether distinct. He who relies upon his own strength to overcome his evil propensities will fail. You might as well hope to turn the Pacific Ocean into a ball of fire, as to hope to overcome in your own strength. Everything human failed from the days of Adam down.

Vision, broadness of; Burden bearing

2 Tim. 3:17; Titus 2:14

I tell you if a man has got his heart full of the word of God, he will not be interested in one little corner of the world alone, but he will take a wide field. "Thoroughly furnished to all good works." If he is a Baptist he will be glad to hear of a glorious work among the Methodists, or that the Presbyterians are having a good revival. He gets out of all narrow sectarian fields and takes a broad one. Not only that, but he is ready to do everything he can to carry on the work—not simply to build up his own little party, but to contribute to every good work. A good many aching hearts can be relieved if we only watch to do good. Our prayer should be every morning: "Help me to lift some burden today; help me to wipe away the tears of someone today." If we are going to help that widow or that fatherless child we must do it here, for we cannot do it hereafter.

Vision, failed; Planning without God

Ps. 39:5; James 1:10; 4:14; 1 Peter 1:24; 1 John 2:17

Men will tell how they came to Chicago poor boys, how by hard work, by incessant toiling, they have gained what they have now, taking all the glory to themselves instead of giving it to God. Look at him! If a man cheated him out of $5 how he would resent it. Shrewd, practical, businessman; and yet the devil was cheating him out of his soul. That is the way today. They are just living for time. They don't want to take death into their plans. "In every man's garden there is a sepulcher." My friends, in every man's home there is a sepulcher. Death is inevitable, and is not a man mad who does not take it into his plans?

Vision focused on Christ

Micah 7:7; Matt. 20:28; John 8:56; 12:32; Acts 5:31; Phil. 3:20; Titus 2:13; Heb. 2:10; 5:9; 9:28; 10:14; 12:2–3; 1 Peter 2:21; Rev. 1:8, 11, 17; 2:8

When I was a boy, I used to try to describe a straight path through the snow in the fields by looking down at my feet. The way to make a straight path would be to look at an object beyond; so in this passage we are directed to have our eyes on the mark at the right hand of the Master.

Vision, force of; Mission focus

Phil. 3:13–14

I made up my mind that I would go on as if there were not another man in the world but me to do the work. I knew I had to give an account of stewardship. I suppose they say of me, "Oh! he's a fanatic, he's a radical. He has only one idea." Well, it's a glorious idea. I would rather have that said of me, than to be a man of ten thousand ideas, and do nothing with them.

Vision, importance of; Focus, importance of

Phil. 3:13–14

I remember when I was in Chicago before the fire, I was on some ten or twelve committees. My hands were full. If a man came to me to talk about his soul I would say I haven't time; got a committee to attend to. But now I have turned my back on everything—turned my attention to saving souls, and God has blessed me and made me an instrument to save more souls during the last four or five years than during all my previous life. And so if a minister will devote himself to this undivided work, God will bless him. Take that motto of Paul's: "One thing I do, forgetting those things which are behind, and reaching forth unto those things which are before, I press toward the mark for the prize of the high calling of God in Christ Jesus."

Vision, necessity of

Ps. 27:4; Luke 10:42; 1 Cor. 9:24; Heb. 12:1

I pity the people who are trying to live on their past experience, when there is glory before them.

Vision, power for; Mission, strength for

James 5:17–18

God knows and you know what he has sent you to do. God sent Moses to Egypt to bring three millions of bondsmen up out of the house of bondage into the promised land. Did he fail? It looked, at first, as if he were going to. But did he? God sent Elijah to stand before Ahab, and it was a bold thing for him to say there should be neither dew nor rain: but did God not lock up the heavens for three years and six months? But did he fail? And you cannot find any place in Scripture where a man was ever sent by God to do a work in which he failed as he trusted in him.

Vision, power of; Purpose, importance of; Mission statement

Rom. 12:1–2

It was Henry Varley who said, "It remains to be seen what God will do with a man who gives himself up wholly to Him." D. L. Moody said, "By the grace of God I intend to be that man."

Vision, spiritual

2 Cor. 12:9–10

Chloe Lankton has been forty years bedridden, and a great sufferer. Yet she is one of the happiest women in New England, and hundreds go to see her to learn how a Christian can suffer and yet be happy. Those that God does the most for in temporal things generally think the least of him. Thank God for the grace that takes us to glory. Grace is glory militant; glory is grace triumphant. If we live looking up, we will die looking up.

Vision, spiritual; Affections, set above; Heavenly minded

Ps. 27:4; Luke 10:42; 1 Cor. 9:24; 2 Cor. 5:16; Phil. 3:8, 13, 20; Heb. 12:2

The moment we become heavenly minded and get our hearts and affections set on things above, then life becomes beautiful, the light of heaven shines across our pathway and we don't have to be all the time lashing ourselves and upbraiding ourselves because we are not more with Christ. Someone asked a Scotchman if he was on the way to heaven, and he said, "Why, man, I live there; I am not on the way." We need to live in heaven. While we are walking in this world it is our privilege to have our hearts and affections there.

Vision, spiritual; Upward look

Matt. 14:30; Mark 14:38; 2 Tim. 4:17

Someone has said, "There are three ways to look. If you want to be wretched, look within; if you wish to be distracted, look around; but if you would have peace, look up." Peter looked away from Christ, and he immediately began to sink. He had God's eternal Word, which was sure footing, and better than either marble, granite or iron; but the moment he took his eyes off Christ down he went.

Walk circumspectly

Exod. 23:13; Eph. 5:15; Phil. 1:27; Col. 4:5; James 3:13; 1 Peter 1:22

One word more to the new converts: Be sure that you don't disgrace "the old family name," as Dr. Bonar puts it. Some of the people of New York are very proud of their old family names: and let us remember that the family to which you now belong has a history reaching back eighteen hundred years. You are called the sons and daughters of God; a high calling—a wonderful calling. Walk circumspectly; walk as daughters of heaven, as the sons of a king.

Walk, nature of; Manner of life; Behavior, circumspect

Exod. 23:13; Eph. 5:15; Phil. 1:27; Col. 4:5; James 3:13; 1 Peter 1:22

I said to someone the other day, "That man must have been in the army or in a military school." He said, "Yes, he is an army veteran. How did you know?" I said, "By the way he walks." There are some people that you can tell have been with Jesus Christ by their walk. An old divine, trying to illustrate this passage in Ephesians, "walking circumspectly," describes a cat walking on a brick wall covered with sharp pieces of glass. The cat goes along, putting his feet down very cautiously, so as not to cut his paws. Let us keep in mind that the eyes of the world are upon our acts so let our walk be very circumspect.

Walk worthy

Phil. 3:14; 1 Thess. 2:12; 2 Thess. 1:11; Rev. 3:4

When Lincoln was called to be President of the United States it was a very high calling, and he walked differently from what he did before. When General Grant was called to the head of the American Army, and afterwards to the White House, he walked worthy of the positions which he held. I heard one person say that it would be impossible for Grant to do it but he did do it. But your call and mine is very much higher than Lincoln's, much higher than Grant's, much higher than that of any king or potentate, for we are called to represent the King of Kings and Lord of Lords. Therefore let us walk worthy of our vocation.

Warfare, Christian

2 Cor. 10:4; Eph. 6:12; 1 Tim. 1:18

It is said of Napoleon, after his army had gained a great victory, he was so pleased that he had a medal made, on one side of which was the date, and on the other these words: "I was there." It is said of these old veterans that long years afterwards they would bring out these medals and show them. As they would tell of the battle their faces would light up. They would show the medal, and say, "I was there." My friends, a great battle is now going on between the kingdom of heaven and the powers of darkness, and God wants all of us to do what we can. By and by up yonder we shall talk of the battle we fought in this dark world, and be joyful to say, "I was there."

Warfare, spiritual; Depression, cure for; Satan, strategy of

2 Cor. 10:4; Eph. 6:12; 1 Tim. 1:18

The story is told that Frederick Douglass, the great slave orator, once said in a mournful speech when things looked dark for his race, "The white man is against us, governments are against us, the spirit of the times is against us. I see no hope for the colored race. I am full of sadness." Just then a poor old black woman rose in the audience, and said, "Frederick, is God dead?"

It makes a difference when you count God in. Now, many a young believer is discouraged and disheartened when he realizes this warfare. He begins to think that God has forsaken him, that Christianity is not all that it professes to be. But he should rather regard it as an encouraging sign. No sooner has a soul escaped from his snare than Satan takes steps to ensnare it again. He puts forth all his powers to recapture his lost prey. The fiercest attacks are made on the strongest forts, and the fiercer the battle the young believer is called on to wage, the surer evidence it is of the work of the Holy Spirit in his heart. God will not desert him in his time of need.

Warnings, importance of

Matt. 24:4; 1 Cor. 10:6, 12; Col. 1:27–28

A pilot guiding a steamer down the Cumberland River saw a light, apparently from a small craft, in the middle of the narrow channel. His impulse was to disregard the signal and run down the boat. As he came near, a voice shouted: "Keep off, keep off." In great anger he cursed what he supposed to be a boatman in his way as he adjusted his course. On arriving at his next landing he learned that a huge rock had fallen from the mountain into the bed of the stream, and that a signal was placed there to warn the coming boats of the unknown danger. Alas! many regard God's warnings in the same way, and are angry with any who tell them of the destructive rocks in their course. They will understand better at the end of the way.

Watch and pray

Matt. 26:41; Mark 14:38; Luke 21:36; 22:46

The devil can do most anything with a man when he gets asleep spiritually. A man dreamt he was traveling, and came to a little church, and on the cupola of that church there was a devil fast asleep. He went along further, and came to a log cabin, and it was surrounded by devils all wide awake. He asked one of them what it meant; said the devil: "I will tell you. The fact is, that whole church is asleep and one devil can take care of all the people, but here are a man and woman who pray, and they have more power than that whole church." When Christ tells us to watch, we must do it.

Watchfulness, importance of

Matt. 26:41; Mark 14:38; Luke 21:36; 22:46

The Persians had an annual festival when they killed all the snakes and venomous creatures they could find; but they allowed them to swarm as fast and freely as ever until the festival came round once more. It was poor policy. Sins, like serpents, breed quickly, and need to be constantly watched.

And we ought to watch on every side. Many a man has fallen at the very point where he thought he was safest. The meekness of Moses has passed into a proverb. Yet he lost the Promised Land, because he allowed the children of Israel to provoke him, and "he spake unadvisedly with his lips." Peter was the most zealous and defiant of the disciples, bold and outspoken; yet he degenerated for a short time into a lying, swearing, sneaking coward, afraid of a maid.

Water of life, abundance of

John 3:5; 4:10, 14; 10:10

A good many people have life, but that is all; they haven't this living water in abundance. They are satisfied with their present attainment, and the water doesn't flow out. They are not fruit-bearing Christians at all; they have very little power. The poor Samaritan woman drank deeper than Nicodemus of the water of life. She turned her whole town upside down—no, right side up. Nicodemus got a pitcher of living water, but this woman got a whole well full.

Water of life, need of; Holy Spirit filling

John 3:5; 4:10; 1 John 5:6

I have been in some churches and have met a member as dry as a dry brook, with no spiritual life or growth, while right alongside of him has been one who was all the time bringing forth fruit. What is the secret? One was under the fountain and the other was not.

Weakness apart from God

1 Kings 18:38; 19:2–4; 1 Cor. 10:12

Elijah was noted for his boldness. He stood on Carmel and called on the four hundred prophets of the Grove and four hundred and fifty of Baal, and it looked as if every man was keen against him. He stood there alone, the boldest man on the face of the earth. But he got his eyes off the Master, and when he received a message from the queen, he fled and hid under a juniper tree, and wished himself dead. That bold man of Carmel tumbled. Perhaps he had been elated with his successes. It was all to prove to himself how weak he was away from God. We are all as weak as water. "Let him that thinketh he standeth take heed lest he fall."

Weakness into strength

Deut. 33:25; Isa. 40:29; Zech. 10:12; Rom. 4:17; 1 Cor. 1:28; 2 Cor. 12:9; Phil. 4:13; Col. 1:11

Notice that all the men whom Christ called around him were weak men in a worldly sense. They were all men without rank, without title, without position, without wealth or culture. Nearly all of them were fishermen and unlettered men; yet Christ chose them to build up his kingdom. When God wanted to bring the children of Israel out of bondage, he did not send an army; he sent one solitary man. So in all ages God has used the weak things of the world to accomplish his purposes.

Weakness, significance of

Deut. 33:25; Isa. 40:29; Zech. 10:12; Rom. 4:17; 1 Cor. 1:28; 2 Cor. 12:9; Phil. 4:13; Col. 1:11

People say that they haven't got strength. That is all right. We don't want any of our own strength. We need his strength. He has plenty of strength for us. The weaker we are, the better for us, for then we lay hold of God's strength.

Wealth, danger of

Ps. 39:6; Prov. 11:4; Acts 8:20; 1 Tim. 6:9; 2 Peter 2:3

We read in 1 Timothy 6:9: "They that will be rich fall into temptation, and a snare." How many young men started out as active Christians. But they grew rich, and riches choked their piety. When they became millionaires they found that instead of their having got riches, riches had got them. They are slaves to their money, and it will ruin their children. He who sows to the wind must reap the whirlwind. What sad wrecks are all around us! How many have turned away from God and the Bible in order to get rich, and have found their ill-gotten gains a curse! They give up everything good. They gain nothing, and incur the danger of losing their souls.

Wealth, danger of; Riches, danger of

Prov. 11:4; Luke 12:20; 16:23; Acts 8:20; 1 Tim. 6:9; 2 Peter 2:3

Wealth to most men proves nothing more or less than a great rock upon which their eternity is wrecked.

Wealth, futility of

Ps. 39:6; Prov. 11:4; Eccles. 5:14; Acts 8:20; 1 Tim. 6:9; 2 Peter 2:3

Not long ago the only daughter of a wealthy friend of mine sickened and died. The father and mother stood by her dying bed. He had spent all his time in accumulating wealth for her; she had been introduced into a gay and fashionable society; but she had been taught nothing of Christ. As she came to the brink of the river of death, she said, "Won't you help me; it is very dark, and the stream is bitter cold." They wrung their hands in grief, but could do nothing for her; and the poor girl died in darkness and despair. What was their wealth to them then?

Wealth, spiritual

Rom. 8:17; Heb. 6:17; James 2:5

You ask me how much I am worth today? I don't know. I can't calculate it. I am a joint-heir with Jesus Christ, and you must find out how much he is worth in order to find out my wealth.

Welfare and grace

Prov. 20:4; 21:25; 24:30; 2 Thess. 3:10

A great many people think it is time enough to seek the kingdom of God after they have attended to everything else. What God puts first you put last, and what he puts last you put first. But someone will say: "Ah, Mr. Moody, that is well enough for talk, but you just get where I am—out of work, no money, no friends, a stranger in the city—and you would tell a different story." My friends, I know just what that means. I have walked the streets of Boston out of work, out of money, and not knowing what I was going to do for a living. The whole of my early life was one long struggle with poverty; but I have no doubt it was God's way of bringing me to himself.

And since I began to seek first the kingdom of God, I have never lacked anything: God has added all other things unto me. But it will not do to seek Christ because of what you hope to make by it. I used to make a mistake on that point. When I was at work in the City Relief Society in Chicago, before the fire, I used to go to a poor sinner with the Bible in one hand and a loaf of bread in the other.

Dr. Chalmers used to forbid his missionaries giving away money or supplies. He said those things ought to come by other hands, and I thought he was all wrong. My idea was that I could open a poor man's heart by giving him a load of wood or a ton of coal when the winter was coming on, but I soon found out that he wasn't any more interested in the gospel on that account.

Instead of thinking how he could come to Christ, he was thinking how long it would be before he got another load of wood. If I had the Bible in one hand and a loaf in the other the people always looked first at the loaf; and that was just contrary to the order laid down in the gospel.

Wholeheartedness, importance of; Seekers for Christ

Deut. 4:29; 1 Kings 2:4; Ps. 119:2; Isa. 55:6; Jer. 24:7; 29:13; Hosea 5:15; Joel 2:12; Amos 5:4; Acts 8:37; Rom. 10:10

These are the people who find Christ—those who seek for him with all their heart. I am tired and sick of halfheartedness. You don't like a half-hearted man,

you don't care for anyone to love you with a half-heart and the Lord won't have it. If we are going to seek for him and find him, we must do it with all our heart. I believe the reason why so few people find Christ is because they are not terribly in earnest about their soul's salvation. God is in earnest; everything he has done proves that he is in earnest about the salvation of men's souls. What is Calvary but a proof of that? And the Lord wants us to be in earnest when it comes to this great question of the soul's salvation. I never saw men seeking Christ with all their hearts but they soon found him.

Whosoever includes me; Promises of God for all

Acts 2:21; 10:43; Rom. 9:33; 10:13; 1 John 4:15; 5:1; Rev. 22:17

Every one of God's proclamations is connected with that word "whosoever," "whosoever believeth," "whosoever will." Richard Baxter said he thanked God for that "whosoever." He would a good deal rather have that word "whosoever" there than Richard Baxter; for if it was Richard Baxter, he should have thought it was some other Richard Baxter who had lived and died before him; but "whosoever" he knew included him.

I heard of a woman once that thought there was no promise in the Bible for her; she thought the promises were for someone else, not for her. There are a good many of these people in the world. They think it is too good to be true that they can be saved for nothing. This woman one day got a letter, and when she opened it she found it was not for her at all; it was meant for another woman that had the same name; and she had her eyes opened to the fact that if she should find some promise in the Bible directed to her name, she would not know whether it meant her or someone else that bore her name. But you know the word "whosoever" includes everyone in the wide world.

Will of God, importance of

Matt. 6:10; 26:42; Luke 11:2; Acts 21:14

I learned a lesson once from my little girl. She was always teasing me for a great big doll. She had a lot of dolls around the house without heads, some without arms, some without legs, but she wanted a great big doll. You know if a man has an only daughter he is rather soft (and they find it out, you know), so she was determined to get that big doll. One day I had a good streak come over me and I took her to a toy shop to get her a doll, but as we went in the door we saw a basket of little china dolls. "Oh, papa, isn't that the cutest little doll you ever saw?" "Yes, yes." "Well, won't you buy it?" "Well, now Emma, let me choose this time." "Oh, no, papa, I just want this little doll." I paid for the doll and took her home.

After the newness had worn off the doll was left with all the others. I said, "Emma, do you know what I was going to do that day when I took you into the toy shop and you selected that little china doll?" "No, papa." "Well, I was going to buy you one of those great big dolls." "You were, why didn't you do it?" "Because you wouldn't let me. You remember you wanted that little doll and you would have it." Emma saw the point and she bit her lips and did not say anything more.

From that day to this I cannot get her to say what she wants. When I was going to Europe the last time I asked her what she wanted me to bring her, and she said, "Anything you like." It is far better to let God choose for us than to choose for ourselves. Let us learn to say, "Thy will, not mine, be done."

Willingness, power of; Vision, power of

Isa. 1:19

Someone has said that there are three classes of people: the "wills," the "won'ts,"
and the "can'ts." The first accomplish everything, the second oppose everything, and the third fail in everything.

Witness of child, example of

Luke 1:48; Acts 12:14

A little girl who had attended one of our meetings went home and climbed upon her father's knees and said, "Papa, you have been drinking again." It troubled him. If his wife had spoken to him, he might have got mad and gone out into some shop or saloon and got more liquor, but that little child acted like an angel. He came down here with her to the meeting and he found out how he might be saved, and now that home is a little heaven. There is many a home that can be made happy when fathers trust Christ.

Matt. 19:14; Mark 10:14; Luke 18:16

A little child at one of the meetings was seen talking so earnestly to a companion that a lady sat by her to hear what she was saying, and found that the dear child was telling how much Jesus loved her, and how she loved him, and asked her little companion if she would not love him too. The lady was so much impressed by the child's words that she spoke to a concerned soul that very night for the first time in her life. And so "a little child shall lead them."

Witness of life

Matt. 5:16; Eph. 2:10; 5:8; Phil. 2:15–16; 1 Peter 2:9

Even though you cannot talk about Christ, you can live him. A young lady, a daughter of one of the wealthiest merchants in London, felt that she could not speak much for Christ, but I learned that every Sunday afternoon she stole out from that magnificent home of hers and went to an old man who could not speak the English language, but could only speak Gaelic. This girl could read that language, and every Sunday afternoon she went and read to him, because that was the time of all the week when he was tempted to get drunk, and she wanted to save him.

Witness of women

Matt. 5:16; Eph. 2:10; 5:8; Phil. 2:15–16; 1 Peter 2:9

I want to say to young ladies, perhaps you have a godless father or mother, a skeptical brother, who is going down through drink, and perhaps there is no one who can reach them but you. How many times a godly, pure young lady has taken the light into some darkened home! Many a home might be lit up with the gospel if the mothers and daughters would only speak the word.

Witnessing, aggressive

Isa. 6:8; Luke 14:23; 2 Cor. 5:11, 20; 6:1; 2 Tim. 4:2

Is it not time for us to launch out into the deep? I have never seen people go out into the lanes and alleys, into the hedges and highways, and try to bring the people in, but the Lord gave his blessing. If a man has the courage to go right to his neighbor and speak to him about his soul, God is sure to smile upon the effort. The person who is spoken to may wake up angry, but that is not always a bad sign; he may write a letter next day and apologize. At any rate it is better to wake him up in this way than that he should continue to slumber on to death and ruin.

Witnessing, aggressive; Vision, large; Mission, sense of

Isa. 6:8; Luke 14:23; 2 Cor. 5:11, 20; 6:1; 2 Tim. 4:2

If we have known Jesus Christ for years, and have not been able to introduce an anxious soul to him, there has been something wrong somewhere. If we were

full of grace, we should be ready for any call that comes to us. Paul said, when he had that famous interview with Christ on the way to Damascus, "Lord, what will you have me to do?" Isaiah said, "Here am I, send me." No man can tell what he can do until he moves forward. If we do that in the name of God, instead of there being a few scores or hundreds converted, there will be thousands flocking into the kingdom of God. Remember that we honor God when we ask for great things. It is a humiliating thing to think that we are satisfied with very small results.

Witnessing, be ready to

Isa. 6:8; Luke 14:23; 2 Cor. 5:11, 20; 6:1; 2 Tim. 4:2

There was a Christian lady in London who got into one of the buses, and a person in the bus saw her get in and saw she had a Bible in her hand. This person was sitting on the other side of the bus and she got up from the seat where she was sitting and sat right down alongside the Christian and said to her, "Are you a Christian?" "Yes, I am." "I thought you were because you had a Bible. I am very concerned about my soul. Can you tell me what I must do to be saved?" She trusted Christ right there on the bus. There are many who want to learn the ways of life, and there ought to be a good many Christians ready to point these souls the way to God.

Witnessing, blessing of

Acts 2:47; 4:33; 11:24; 13:48

An old man—a minister in Glasgow, Scotland—was one of the most active in our meetings. When he would be preaching elsewhere he would drive up in a cab, with his Bible in his hand. It made no difference what part of Glasgow he was preaching in, he managed to attend nearly every one of our services. The old man would come in and tenderly speak to those assembled, and help one soul after another see the light of the gospel. His congregation was comparatively small when we got there, but, by his painstaking efforts to minister to those in search of the Word, when we left Glasgow his church could not hold the people who sought admission.

Witnessing, consistency in; Sowing wisely

Matt. 9:9; John 3:2; 4:5; Acts 9:5; 16:14, 31

No two persons are converted in just the same way. How different the conversion of Matthew and that of Saul of Tarsus. Compare the accounts of the woman of Sychar, of Lydia, and the jailer at Philippi with that of Nicodemus. We are to sow in all kinds of soil, and if we do so wisely and prayerfully, God will give the increase.

Witnessing, courage in

Pss. 40:9; 71:15; Rom. 1:16; 15:29

I heard a story about two young men who came to New York City from the country on a visit. They went to the same board-inghouse to stay and took a room together. Well, when they came to go to bed each felt ashamed to go down on his knees before his companion first. So they sat watching each other. In fact, to express the situation in one word, they were both cowards, yes, cowards! But at last one of them mustered up a little courage, and with burning blushes, as if he was about to do something wrong and wicked, he sunk down on his knees to say his prayers. As soon as the second saw that, he also knelt. And then, after they had said their prayers, each waited for the other to get up. When they did manage to get up one said to the other: "I really am glad to see that you knelt; I was afraid of you." "Well," said the other, "and I was afraid of you."

So it turned out that both were Christians, and yet they were afraid of each other. You smile at that, but how many times have you done the same thing, perhaps not in that way, but the same thing in effect. Henceforth, then, be not ashamed, but let everyone know you are his.

Witnessing, importance of; Evangelism, importance of

Ezek. 3:17; 33:6; Hosea 9:8; Acts 26:23; Rom. 15:16

I remember hearing of two men who had charge of a revolving light in a lighthouse on a stormbound rocky coast. Somehow the machinery went wrong, and the light did not revolve. They were so afraid that those at sea should mistake it for some other light, that they worked all the night through to keep the light moving round. Let us keep our lights in the proper place, so that the world may see that the religion of Christ is not a sham but a reality.

Witnessing, importance of; Resurrection, light of

Prov. 4:18; Matt. 5:14; John 5:35; 12:36; Phil. 2:15; Rev. 1:20

God has left us down here to shine. We are not here to buy and sell and get gain, to accumulate wealth, to acquire worldly position. This earth, if we are Christians, is not our home; it is yonder. God has sent us into the world to shine for him—to light up this dark world. Christ came to be the Light of the world, but men put out that light. They took it to Calvary, and blew it out. But an even more brilliant light shone forth from the empty tomb when Christ rose from the dead. Before Christ went up on high, he said to his disciples: "Ye are the light of the world. Ye are my witnesses. Go forth and carry the gospel to the perishing nations of the earth."

Witnessing, importance of; Testimony, public

Ps. 51:15; Prov. 4:18; Matt. 5:14; John 5:35; 12:36; Phil. 2:15; Rev. 1:20

It is a very sad thing that so many of God's children are silent about their faith; yet it is true. Parents would think it a great calamity to have their children born unable to ever speak; they would mourn over it, and weep, and well they might; but did you ever think of the many dumb children God has? The churches are full of them. They can talk about politics, art, and science; they can speak well enough and fast enough about the fashions of the day; but they have no voice for the Son of God.

Dear friend, if Christ is your Savior, confess him. Every follower of Jesus should bear testimony for him. How many opportunities each one has in society and in business to speak a word for Christ! How many opportunities occur daily wherein every Christian might be "instant in season and out of season" in pleading for Jesus! In so doing we receive blessing for ourselves, and also become a means of blessing to others.

Witnessing in love

1 Cor. 13:1; Gal. 5:6; 1 Tim. 1:5; 1 Peter 4:8

When in London, Dr. William Arnott came down from Edinburgh to one of our meetings, and he told those people something—I don't think the Londoners understood him, but if they knew of farm life as I did, they would have known what he meant. He said: "When I was on my father's farm, when they wanted to teach a calf to drink, they would bring it to the pail and a man would dip his finger into the milk and put it into the calf's mouth and submerging it in the milk, then draw his hand slowly away, and before you knew it the calf was drinking itself. And so," he said, "if you want to win people to Christ you have to go lovingly to them

and lead them gradually to him." If you do not make people love you, you need not talk to them. Oh that God may show you this truth tonight, that the great lever of the Christian is love.

Witnessing, kindness in; Salvation of drunken woman

1 Cor. 13:1; Gal. 5:6; 1 Tim. 1:5; 1 Peter 4:8

A lady came into the office of the New York City Mission, and said that, although she did not think she could do very much of active work for the Lord, yet she should like to distribute a few tracts. One day she saw a policeman taking a poor drunken woman to jail—a miserable object, ragged, dirty, with hair disordered; but the lady's heart went out in sympathy toward her. She found the woman after she came out of jail, and just went and folded her arms around her, and kissed her. The woman exclaimed, "My God! what did you do that for?" She replied, "I don't know, but I think Jesus sent me to do it." The woman said, "Oh, don't kiss me anymore; you'll break my heart. Why, nobody has kissed me since my mother died." But that kiss brought the woman to the feet of the Savior, and for the last three years she has been living a godly Christian life, won to God by a kiss.

Witnessing, need of

Matt. 28:19–20; Mark 16:15; Luke 24:47; Acts 2:39; 13:47

Some people have said that I made the statement that "nine-tenths of the church members haven't got power." I didn't say that to hurt any feelings; but I refer to a good many Christians who lack power to reach out to the unsaved. Christ says, "Go and disciple the world!" Am I uncharitable when I say that there's not more than one out of ten who is doing that kind of work? I don't want to slander the church. I would never preach again as long as I live if I thought I was hurting the church. I pray God day and night to help me to awake the church. I don't say they are not Christians, by a good deal. I never dreamed such a thing. Many are good, converted people, but they haven't got "converting power." There's the trouble.

Witnessing, opportunities for; Witnessing, vision for

Matt. 28:19–20; Mark 16:15; Luke 24:47; Acts 2:39; 13:47

I remember a good many years ago I resolved I wouldn't let a day pass without talking to someone about their soul's salvation. And it was in that school God qualified me to speak the gospel. If we were faithful over small things God will promote us. If God says: "Speak to that young man," obey the word, and you will be given by and by plenty of souls.

Witnessing, parental influence

2 Tim. 1:5

When I was in London, there was one lady dressed in black up in the balcony. All the rest were ministers. I wondered who that lady could be. At the close of the meeting I stepped up to her, and she asked me if I did not remember her. I did not, but she told me who she was, and her story came to my mind. When we were preaching in Dundee, Scotland, a mother came up with her two sons, 16 and 17 years old. She said to me, "Will you talk to my boys?" I asked her if she would talk to the inquirers, and told her there were more inquirers than workers. She said she was not a good enough Christian—was not prepared enough. I told her I could not talk to her then.

Next night she came to me and asked me again, and the following night she repeated her request. Five hundred miles she journeyed to get God's blessing for her boys. Would to God we had more

mothers like her. She came to London, and the first night I was there, I saw her in the Agricultural Hall. She was accompanied by only one of her boys—the other had died.

Towards the close of the meetings I received this letter from her: "Dear Mr. Moody: For months I have never considered the day's work ended unless you and your work had been specially prayed for. Now it appears before us more and more. What in our little measure we have found has no doubt been the happy experience of many others in London. My husband and I have sought as our greatest privilege to take unconverted friends one by one to the Agricultural Hall, and I thank God that, with a single exception, those brought under the preaching from your lips have accepted Christ as their Savior, and are rejoicing in his love."

That lady was a lady of wealth and position. She lived a little way out of London; gave up her beautiful home and took lodgings near the Agricultural Hall, so as to be useful in the inquiry room. When we went down to the Opera House she was there; when we went down to the east end there she was again, and when I left London she had the names of all who had accepted Christ through her work in the inquiry room.

Some said that our work in London was a failure. Ask her if the work was a failure, and she will tell you. We need thousands of such mothers. Go and bring your friends, here to the meetings. Think of the privilege, my friends, of leading a soul to Christ. If we are going to work for good we must be up and about it. Men say, "I have not the time." Take it. Ten minutes every day for Christ will give you good wages. There is many a person who is working for you or with you. Take them by the hand.

Witnessing, persistence in; Sowing and reaping

Matt. 4:19; Mark 1:17; John 12:32

God uses the weak things of this world to confound the mighty. God's promise is better than a bank note—"I promise to pay so-and-so"—and here is one of Christ's promissory notes, "If you follow me, I will make you fishers of men." Will you not lay hold of the promise, and trust it, and follow him now? If we present the gospel, and present it faithfully, we ought to expect results then and there. I believe it is the privilege of God's children to reap the fruit of their labor three hundred and sixty-five days in the year.

"Well, but," say some, "is there not a sowing time as well as harvest?" Yes, it is true, there is; but then, you can sow with one hand and reap with the other. What would you think of a farmer who went on sowing all the year round and never thought of reaping? I repeat it, we want to sow with one hand and reap with the other; and if we look for the fruit of our labors, we shall see it. "I, if I be lifted up, will draw all men unto me." We must lift Christ up and then seek men out and bring them to him.

Witnessing, power of

Matt. 28:19–20; Mark 16:15; Luke 24:47; Acts 2:39; 13:47

A lady once writing to a young man in the Navy who was almost a stranger, thought, "Shall I close this as anybody would, or shall I say a word for my Jesus?" and, lifting up her heart in prayer for a moment, she wrote, telling him that his constant change of scene and place was an apt illustration of the scripture, "Here we have no continuing city," and asked if he could say, "I seek one to come." Tremblingly she folded it and sent it off.

Back came the answer. "Thank you so much for those kind words. I am an orphan, and no one has spoken to me like that since my mother died, long years ago." The arrow shot at venture hit home, and the young man shortly after rejoiced in the fullness of the blessing of the gospel of peace.

Witnessing, primary need in

Matt. 26:58; Mark 14:54; Luke 22:54

You don't gain anything by following the Lord afar off. When a man follows the Lord afar off, he cannot testify for Jesus Christ. If I wanted to introduce a man to another man, and the man was away up at the upper end of the balcony, I wouldn't say, "Dr. Schofield, I want to introduce you to a gentleman away up there." You've got to be near the Lord to introduce others to him.

Witnessing, readiness for

Ezek. 3:17; 33:6; Hosea 9:8; Acts 26:23; Rom. 15:16

I don't know of anything that impressed me so in England as to see the Christians with their Bibles in the meetings looking at them to see if what was said was according to the Word of God. Then after the meeting, instead of grabbing their hats and trying to get out before the benediction was pronounced, as you do here sometimes, they were already at work for God and trying to find someone to talk to about Christ instead of rushing out. We tried to drive the nail and they endeavored to clinch it. If all the Christians here this morning were watching for souls and talked to someone near them, what an influence they would have. You can generally tell who are Christians by their eyes and manners—their faces shine, or if there is a Christian in doubting castle, have your Bible and be ready to give them God's promises, and see how blessed this week would be and see how many you could lead to Christ.

Witnessing, sharing light

Ezek. 3:17; 33:6; Hosea 9:8; Acts 26:23; Rom. 15:16

When a theater in Vienna was on fire a few years ago, a man in one of the corridors was hurrying out. Many others of the people were trying to find their way out so as to escape from the fire. The fire was in another part of the building and the theater was dark, but this man had a single match in his pocket. He struck the match, and by doing so he was able to save twenty lives. He did what he could. Are you doing what you can do?

Witnessing, shine your light

Ezek. 3:17; 33:6; Hosea 9:8; Acts 26:23; Rom. 15:16

Away out in the prairie regions, when meetings are held at night in the log schoolhouses, the announcement of the meeting is given out in this way: "A MEETING WILL BE HELD BY CANDLE-LIGHT." The first man who comes brings a tallow candle with him. It is perhaps all he has; but he brings it and sets it on the desk. It does not light the building much; but it is better than nothing. The next brings a candle; and the next family bring theirs. By the time the house is full, there is plenty of light.

So if we all shine a little, there will be a good deal of light. That is what God wants us to do. If we cannot all be light-houses, any one of us can at any rate be a tallow candle. A little light will sometimes do a great deal. The city of Chicago was set on fire by a cow kicking over a lamp, and a hundred thousand people were burned out of house and home. Don't let Satan get the advantage of you and make you think that because you cannot do any great thing you cannot do anything at all. Jesus commands, "Let Your Light Shine." Remember that we are to let our light shine. It does not say,

"Make your light shine." You do not have to make light shine; all you have to do is to let your God-given light shine.

Witnessing to neighbor

Exod. 4:12; Jer. 1:7; John 15:16; Acts 9:15; Rom. 1:13; Eph. 3:7

Now, we send a lot of people abroad as missionaries, and God forbid that I should say one word against missions. God bless the missionaries! I wish we had thousands more going round the world for Christ. But don't let us forget the people at our own doors. What are we doing for them? Shouldn't we have some enthusiasm to go and reach these people who are right here by our side?

Witnessing to prostitutes

Luke 7:37; John 4:18; 8:11

You think you can't do much. If you are the means of saving one soul, that person may be instrumental in reaching a hundred more. I remember when we were in England ten years ago, there was a woman in the city where we labored who got stirred up to do what she could. She had been a nominal Christian for a good many years, but she had not thought that she had any particular mission in the world. I am afraid that is the condition of many professed Christians.

This woman began to look about her to see what she could do. She thought she would try to do something for her fallen sisters in that city. She went out and began to talk kindly to prostitutes she met on the street. She rented a house and invited them to come and meet her there. When we went back to that city about a year or so ago, she had rescued over three hundred of these fallen ones, and had restored them to their parents and homes. She is now corresponding with many of them. She did what she could. How she will rejoice when she

319

hears the Master say, "Well done, good and faithful servant."

Witnessing, wisdom of; Affirmation, importance of

Prov. 11:30

"He that winneth souls is wise." Do you want to win men? Do not drive or scold them. Do not try to tear down their prejudices before you begin to lead them to the truth. Some people think they have to tear down the scaffolding before they begin on the building. An old minister once invited a young brother to preach for him. The latter scolded the people, and when he got home, asked the old minister how he had done. He said he had an old cow, and when he wanted a good supply of milk, he fed the cow; he did not scold her.

Witnessing with enthusiasm

John 10:11; 2 Cor. 1:6; 12:14–15; 1 Thess. 2:8; 2 Tim. 2:10

Oh, may God awaken us, and may every child of God go forth into the vineyard and work for him with enthusiasm. Let us not be afraid of enthusiasm, or to carry it into the work of the Lord. Why should we be afraid of it? Christ died for us. Shall not we be ready to live for him and work for him?

Witnessing, work of all

Matt. 28:19–20; Mark 16:15; Luke 24:47; Acts 2:39; 13:47

Winning souls to God is a work that anyone can do. A little girl only eleven years old came to me in a Sunday school and said: "Won't you please pray that God will make me a winner of souls?" I felt so proud of her, and my pride was justified, for she has become one of the best winners of souls in this country. Suppose she lives sixty years, and goes on winning four or five souls every year; at the end of her journey there will be three hundred souls on the way to glory. And how long will it be before that little company swells to a great army?

Don't you see how that little mountain stream keeps swelling till it carries everything before it? Little trickling streams have run into it, till now, a mighty river, it has great cities on its banks, and the commerce of nations floating on its waters. So when a single soul is won to Christ you cannot see the result. A single one multiplies to a thousand, and that into ten thousand. Perhaps a million shall be the fruit; we cannot tell. We only know that the Christian who has turned so many to righteousness shall indeed shine for ever and ever. Look at those poor fishermen, Jesus' disciples, how unlettered. They were not learned men, but great in winning souls. Any Christian can work for God.

Matt. 28:19–20; Mark 16:15; Luke 24:47; Acts 2:39; 13:47

I remember Mr. Spurgeon making this remark: When Moses went to tell the king of Egypt that he would call up the plague of frogs upon the land, the pharaoh may have said: "Your God is the God of frogs, is he? I am not afraid of frogs. Bring them on. I am not concerned about a few frogs!" Says Moses: "But there are a good many of them, O king." And so he found out.

So we may be weak and contemptible individually, but there are a good many Christians scattered all over the land, and we can accomplish a great deal when we all get busy for Christ. Supposing each one who loves the Lord Jesus were to resolve today, by God's help, to try and lead one soul to Christ this week. Is there a professing Christian who cannot lead some soul into the kingdom of God? If you cannot I want to tell you that there is something wrong in your life. You had better have it straightened out at once. If you have not an influence for good over some one of your friends or neighbors, there is something in your life that needs to be put right. May God show it to you today so that you may get your heart right and get to work in Christ's service.

Witnessing, work of all;
Evangelism, work of all

Matt. 28:19–20; Mark 16:15; Luke 24:47; Acts 1:8; 2:39; 13:47

I have little sympathy with the idea that Christian men and women have to live for years before they can have the privilege of leading anyone out of the darkness of this world into the kingdom of God. I do not believe, either, that all God's work is going to be done by ministers, and other officers in the churches. This lost world will never be reached and brought back to loyalty to God until the children of God wake up to the fact that they have a mission in the world. If we are true Christians we shall all be missionaries. Christ came down from heaven on a mission, and if we have his Holy Spirit in us we will be missionaries too. If we have no desire to see the world discipled, to see men brought back to God, there is something very far wrong in our religion.

Women's ministries

Mark 15:41; Luke 8:3; 24:10; Acts 16:14; 18:26

The women in the inquiry meetings here are of great help. A women's meeting is held every day at the close of the noon prayer meeting, and their inquiry room is always nearly full. No one can visit so well as a woman. The time is coming when there will be ten women missionaries for one we have now. A woman can go into the kitchen and sit right down and talk with a woman at work there. The poor woman will tell a person of her own sex her troubles, when she will not converse with a man. What a blessing it would be if in this city, as in London, ladies of wealth and position would visit the poor.

Women's rights, need for;
Commandment, fifth

Lev. 19:3; Prov. 1:8; 20:20; 23:22; 28:24; 30:17; Eph. 6:1; Col. 3:20

The fifth commandment commands honor for the mother and yet in eastern countries in the present day a woman is held of little account. When I was in Palestine a few years ago, the prettiest girl in Jericho was sold by her father in exchange for a donkey. In many ancient nations, just as in certain parts of the world today, the parents are killed off as soon as they become old and feeble. Can't we see the hand of God in this fifth commandment, raising the woman to her rightful position of honor out of the degradation into which she had been dragged by pagan cultures?

Work, earthly opportunity only

John 9:4; 1 Cor. 3:9; 2 Cor. 5:8–9; 6:1; Heb. 3:13,15

If I am to wipe a tear from the cheek of that fatherless boy, I must do it down here. It is not said in Scripture that we will have the privilege of doing that hereafter. If I am going to help some fallen man up that has been overtaken by sin, I must do it here. We are not taught anywhere in Scripture that we are going to have the glorious privilege of working for God in the world to come. We are not told that we are going to have the privilege of being coworkers with God in the future but we know that is our privilege today. We may not have it tomorrow. It may be taken from us tomorrow; but we can enter into the vineyard and do something today before the sun goes down and before we go to glory.

Work, evidence of faith;
Welfare, discussion of

Prov. 19:15; Eccles. 10:18; Matt. 7:16–17; 12:33; Luke 6:43; John 8:39; 1 Cor. 3:2; 2 Thess. 3:10; Heb. 11:31; James 2:18; 3:12

What should you do with men that will not work? I think Paul has it right. If a man will not work, he shall not eat. I think we are doing these men a great injury if we help them when they won't work. Some of these men have professed faith; but there is a difference between profession and regeneration. If they will not work, it is a pretty good sign that they have not been born of God. When I was President of the Young Men's Christian Association in Chicago, we used to have those men coming in all the time. They would tell about their suffering, and how they had no work and wanted help.

At last I got two or three hundred cords of wood and put it in a vacant lot, and got some saws and axes and kept them out of sight. A man would come and ask for help. "Why don't you work?" "Can't get any." "Would you do it if you could get any?" "Oh, yes, anything." "Would you really work in the street?" "Yes." "Would you chop wood?" "Yes." "All right." Then we'd bring out the saw and ax and send them out. But we would have a boy to watch and see that they did not steal the saw and ax.

Then the fellow would say: "I will go home and tell my wife I have got some work." That would be the last we would see of him. Out of the whole winter I never got more than three or four cords of wood worked on. If you are always showering money on these men, and giving them clothing and raiment, they will live in idleness, and not only ruin themselves, but their children. It is not charity at all to help them when they will not work. If a man will not work, let him starve. They never die. I never heard of them really starving to death. You may say that is harsh, but we need a little of that now.

Work, importance of

Neh. 4:17; Matt. 6:33; Luke 12:43; Eph. 4:28; Col. 3:22; 1 Thess. 4:11; 2 Thess. 3:12

When I first went to Boston I was what you might call a tramp; I was in that city without a place to lay my head; my money was all gone, and in my extremity I cried out to God on the streets; I promised that I would serve him. And I had work inside of an hour. I have never known what it was to want from that day to this. I have had plenty of work right along. I pity a man that has nothing to do, even if he is worth his million. Seek the kingdom of God first, and you will have plenty to do; no fiction about that.

Work, involvement in

1 Cor. 15:58; 1 Thess. 2:14; 3:6; Rev. 2:19

If you want to get church members to work you have got to work with them privately and personally. A great many persons would work if they were shown what to do, and there are a good many others of executive ability in the church who could set them about it. Suppose the politicians wanted to carry New York; they would know how every man would vote. The most precious hours I ever spent were employed going from house to house preaching Christ. There is plenty of work, the fields are already white for the harvest.

Works, greater than Christ; Holy Spirit, power of

Matt. 21:21; Mark 11:13; 16:17; Luke 10:17; John 14:12; Acts 2:41; 3:6; 4:33; 9:40; 16:18

Jesus said, "The works that I do shall ye do also, and greater works than these shall ye do because I go to the Father." I used to stumble over that. I didn't understand it. I thought, what greater work could any man do than Christ had done? How could anyone raise a dead man who had been laid away in the sepulcher for days, and who had already begun to turn back to dust; how with a word could he call him forth?

But the longer I live the more I am convinced it is a greater thing to influence a man's will; a man whose will is set against God; to have that will broken and brought into subjection to God's will or, in other words, it is a greater thing to have power over a living, sinning, God-hating man, than to quicken the dead. He who could create a world could speak a dead soul into life; but I think the greatest miracle this world has ever seen was the miracle at Pentecost.

Here were men who surrounded the apostles, full of prejudice, full of malice, full of bitterness, their hands, as it were, dripping with the blood of the Son of God, and yet an unlettered man, a man whom they detested, a man whom they hated, stands up there and preaches the gospel in the power of the Holy Spirit, and three thousand of them are immediately convicted and converted, become disciples of the Lord Jesus Christ, and are willing to lay down their lives for him.

Works, importance of

Matt. 25:35; Luke 16:25; 1 Cor. 15:58; Gal. 6:7–8; Rev. 14:13

Now, death may rob us of money. Death may rob us of position. Death may rob us of our friends; but there is one thing death can never do, and that is, rob us of the work that we do for God. That will live on forever. "Their works will follow them." How much are we doing? Anything that we do outside of ourselves, and not with a mean and selfish motive, that is going to live. We have the privilege of setting in motion streams of activity that will flow on when we are dead and gone.

Matt. 25:35; Luke 16:25; 1 Cor. 15:58; Gal. 6:7–8; Rev. 14:13

Martin Luther lives more today than he did centuries ago, when he was living in Germany. He only lived one life for a while. But now, look at the hundreds and thousands and millions of lives that he is living. There are between fifty and sixty millions of people that profess to be followers of the Lord Jesus Christ, as taught by Martin Luther, that bear his name. He is dead in the sight of the world, but his "works do follow him." He still lives.

Matt. 25:35; Luke 16:25; 1 Cor. 15:58; Gal. 6:7–8; Rev. 14:13

If a man lives a mean, selfish life, he goes down in the grave, and his name and everything goes down in the grave with him. If he is ambitious to leave a record behind him, with a selfish motive, his name rots with his body. But if a man just gets outside of himself and begins to work for God, his name will live forever. Why, you may go to Scotland today, and you will find the influence of John Knox over every mountain in Scotland. It seems as if you could almost feel the breath of that man's prayer in Scotland today. His influence still lives. "Blessed are the dead who die in the Lord. They rest from their labors and their works do follow them." Blessed rest is in store; we will rest by and by; but we don't want to talk about rest down here.

World, separation from; Compromise, danger of

John 15:19–20; 17:14; 1 John 4:5

Now mark you, no man can be true for God, and live for him, without at some time or other being unpopular in this world. Those people who are trying to live for both worlds make a wreck of it; for at some time or other the collision is sure to come.

World, separation from; Holy Spirit filling, source of

John 15:19–20; 17:14; 1 John 4:5

When you want to fill a man with electricity without killing him, you have to put him on a chair with glass legs and insulate him from the earth, and then pour the electricity into him until the sparks flame from him. And if you want to get filled with the power of heaven, you'll have to get separated from the world. It is easy enough to lead your children into Sodom, but it is mighty hard to get them out. It is easy enough for the father and mother to take their children in the way of temptation, but when they want to get them away, it is a different thing. You must be separated from the world if you want power.

Worldliness, danger of

John 15:19; 1 John 2:15; 3:1

Some time ago I was on the ocean liner *Spree* and it went along all right until they knocked a hole in it and water began to come in and the boat began to sink. Then it was all wrong. The ship was made for the water, but when the water gets into the ship down it goes. There are a lot of Christians in the world about waist deep, and then they wonder why they haven't any power or influence. Man or woman, get out of the world and keep out of it, if you want power!

John 15:19; 1 John 2:15; 3:1

Do not be deceived by the attractiveness of this world. It will cheat you and destroy you. "The Redoubtable" was the name of a French ship that Lord Nelson spared twice from destruction; and it was from the rigging of that very ship that the fatal ball that killed him was fired. The devil administers many a sin in honey; but there is poison mixed with it. The truest pleasures spring from the good seed of righteousness—none else are profitable.

John 15:19; 1 John 2:15; 3:1

A disciple in the world is one thing, but the world in a disciple is quite a different thing. It is all right to have the ship in the water, but when the water gets into the ship you want to get out, don't you? I was very comfortable on my voyage home to my family on board the steamer *Spree* while the water was outside the boat; but when a hole was made in the bottom and the ship began to sink, so that we were afraid it was going down, we wanted to get off.

That is the problem with many Christians; they get waterlogged with worldliness and have to be towed. We waited forty-eight hours on the *Spree* before we saw a steamer coming to tow us into Boston, and when it started to take us into port there was a joyful time, although we had to be towed in. There are lots of Christians that have to be towed in, and ministers have all they can do to keep them from sinking. Let's keep the world out of our hearts.

Worldliness ruins peace

Ps. 85:10; Isa. 32:17; 48:18; Rom. 14:17; James 3:18

If you want real peace and rest to your soul, keep separate from the world. I remember when I was a boy in Northfield, Massachusetts, right near the old red schoolhouse there was an apple tree that bore the earliest apples of any tree in town. They had a law in that town that fruit on a tree overhanging the street belonged to the public, and any fruit on the other side of the fence belonged to the property holders. Half that apple tree was over in the street, and it got more old brooms and brickbats and handles than any other tree in town. We boys used to watch to see when an apple was getting red. I never got a ripe apple from that tree in my life, and I don't believe anyone else ever did. You never went by that tree that you didn't see a lot of broom handles and clubs up there.

Now, take a lot of Christians who want to live right on the line, with one foot in the world and one foot in the church. They get more clubs than anyone else. The world clubs them. They say, "I don't believe in that man's religion." And the church clubs them. They get clubs on both sides. It is a good deal better to keep just as far from the line as you can if you want power.

Worship, abuse of; Commandment, second

Exod. 32:1; Lev. 26:1; Deut. 4:23; 27:15; Isa. 42:8; Ezek. 8:10; Acts 17:29

I would a great deal sooner have five minutes spiritual communion with Christ than spend years before pictures and images of him. Whatever comes between my soul and my Maker is not a help to me, but a hindrance. God has given different means of grace by which we can approach him. Let us use these, and not seek for other things that he has distinctly forbidden.

Dr. Dale says that in his college days he had an engraving of our Lord hanging over his mantelpiece. "The calmness, the dignity, the gentleness, and the sadness of the face represented the highest conceptions which I had in those days of the human presence of Christ. I often looked at it, and seldom without being touched by it. I discovered in the course of a few months that the superstitious sentiments were gradually clustering about it, which are always created by the visible representations of the divine. The engraving was becoming to me the shrine of God manifest in the flesh, and I understood the growth of idolatry. The visible symbol is at first a symbol and nothing more; it assists thought; it stirs passion. At last it is identified with the God whom it represents. If, every day, I bow before a crucifix in prayer, if I address it as though it were Christ, though I know it is not, I shall come to feel for it a reverence and love which are of the very essence of idolatry."

Exod. 32:1; Lev. 26:1; Deut. 4:23; 27:15; Isa. 42:8; Ezek. 8:10; Acts 17:29

Did you ever stop to think that the world has not a single picture of Christ that has been handed down to us from his disciples? Who knows what he was like? The Bible does not tell us how he looked, except in one or two isolated general expressions as when it says, "His visage was so marred more than any man, and his form more than the sons of men." We don't know anything definite about his features, the color of his hair and eyes, and the other details that would help to give a true representation. What artist can tell us? He left no keepsakes to his disciples. His clothes were seized by the Roman soldiers who crucified him. Not a solitary thing was left to be handed down among his followers. Doesn't it look as if Christ left no relics lest they should be held sacred and worshiped?

History tells us further that the early Christians shrank from making pictures and statues of any kind of Christ. They knew him as they had seen him after his resurrection, and had promises of his continued presence that pictures could not make any more real. I have seen very few pictures of Christ that do not repel me more or less. I sometimes think that it is wrong to have pictures of him at all.

Exod. 32:1; Lev. 26:1; Deut. 4:23; 27:15; Isa. 42:8; Ezek. 8:10; Acts 17:29

Speaking of the crucifix Dr. Dale says: "It makes our worship and our prayer unreal. We are adoring a Christ who does not exist. He is not on the cross now, but on the throne. His agonies are past forever. He has risen from the dead. He is at the right hand of God. If we pray to a dying Christ, we are praying not to Christ himself, but to a mere remembrance of him. The injury which the crucifix has inflicted on the religious life of Christendom, in encouraging a morbid and unreal devotion, is absolutely incalculable. It has given us a dying Christ instead of a living Christ, a Christ separated from us by many centuries instead of a Christ nigh at hand."

Worship, centrality of; Commandment, first

Exod. 20:2–3; Acts 17:23

Even the most primitive races of mankind reach out beyond the world of matter to a superior Being. It is as natural for human beings to feel after God as it is for the ivy to feel after a support. Hunger and thirst drive man to seek for food, and there is a hunger of the soul that needs satisfying, too. Man does not need to be commanded to worship, as there is not a race so high or so low in the scale of civilization but has some kind of god. What he needs is to be directed correctly.

This is what the first commandment is for. Before we can worship intelligently, we must know what or whom to worship. God does not leave us in ignorance. When Paul went to Athens, he found an altar dedicated to "The Unknown God," and he proceeded to tell of him whom we worship. When God gave the commandments to Moses, he commenced with a declaration of his own character, and demanded exclusive recognition.

Isa. 45:22; 46:9; Jer. 35:15; Matt. 4:10; Rev. 22:9

Dr. Dale explained the significance of the first commandment: "The Jews knew Jehovah as the God who had held back the waves like a wall while they fled across the sea to escape the vengeance of their enemies; they knew him as the God who had sent thunder, and lightning, and hail, plagues on cattle, and plagues on men, to punish the Egyptians and to compel them to let the children of Israel go; they knew him as the God whose angel had slain the firstborn of their oppressors, and filled the land from end to end with death, and agony, and terror. He was the same God, so Moses and Aaron told them, who by visions and voices, in promises and precepts, had revealed himself long before to Abraham, Isaac, and Jacob.

"We learn what men are from what they say and from what they do. A biography of Luther gives us a more vivid and trustworthy knowledge of the man than the most philosophical essay on his character and creed. The story of his imprisonment and of his journey to Worms, his Letters, his Sermons, and his Table Talk, are worth more than the most elaborate speculations about him. The Jews learned what God is, not from theological dissertations on the Divine attributes, but from the facts of a Divine history. They knew him for themselves in his own acts and in his own words."

Isa. 45:22; 46:9; Jer. 35:15; Matt. 4:10; Rev. 22:9

We may learn a lesson from the way a farmer deals with the little shoots that spring up around the trunk of an apple tree. They look promising, and one who has not learned better might welcome their growth. But the farmer knows that they will draw the life sap from the main tree, injuring its prospects so that it will produce inferior fruit. He therefore takes his ax and his hoe, and cuts away these suckers. The tree then gives a more plentiful and finer crop. "Thou shalt have no other gods before me" is the pruning knife that God uses. From beginning to end, the Bible calls for wholehearted allegiance to the true God. There is to be no compromise with other gods.

Isa. 45:22; 46:9; Jer. 35:15; Matt. 4:10; Rev. 22:9

This is one matter in which no toleration can be shown. Religious liberty is a good thing, within certain limits. But it is one thing to show toleration to those who agree on essentials, and another, to those who differ on fundamental beliefs. They were willing to admit any god to the Roman Pantheon. One reason the early Christians were persecuted was that they would not accept a place for Jesus Christ there. They would not place the true God as a peer with the gods of this world. Napoleon is said to have entertained the idea of having separate temples in Paris for every known religion, so that every stranger should have a place of worship when attracted toward that city. Such plans are directly opposed to the divine one. God sounded no uncertain note in this commandment. It is plain, unmistakable, uncompromising.

Worship, centrality of; Values, primary; Commandment, first

Isa. 45:22; 46:9; Jer. 35:15; Matt. 4:10; Rev. 22:9

If people were true to the first commandment, obedience to the remaining nine would follow naturally. It is because they are unsound in this that they break the others.

Worship, ceremonialism; Commandment, second

Matt. 18:20; 1 John 5:21

No one can say that we have any need of visual representations of Christ like the crucifix. If Christ is in our hearts, why need we set a representation of him before our eyes? "Where two or three are gathered together in my name, there am I in the midst of them." If we take hold of that promise by faith, what need is there of outward symbols and reminders? If the King is present, why need we bow down before statues supposed to represent him? To fill his place with an image, someone has said, is like blotting the sun out of the heavens and substituting some other light in its place.

You cannot see Christ through the chinks of ceremonialism; or through the blind eyes of erring man; or by images graven with art and man's device; or in cunningly devised fables of artificial and perverted theology. Nay, seek him in his own Word, in the revelation of himself which he gives to all who walk in his ways. So you will be able to keep that admonition of the last word of all the New Testament revelation: "Little children, keep yourselves from idols."

Worship, formalism; Commandment, second

John 4:24

I believe the second commandment is a call for spiritual worship. It is in line with Christ's declaration to that Samaritan woman, "God is a Spirit: and they that worship him must worship him in spirit and in truth" (John 4:24). This is precisely what is difficult for men to do. The apostles were hardly in their graves before people began to put up images of them, and to worship relics. People have a desire for something tangible, something that they can see. That is why there is a demand for ritualism. Some people are born Puritans; they want a simple form of worship. Others think they cannot get along without forms and ceremonies that appeal to the senses. And many a one whose heart is not sincere before God takes refuge in these forms, and eases his conscience by making an outward show of religion.

Worship, importance of; Commandment, first

Ps. 115:4; Isa. 2:8; 37:19; 57:5; Jer. 2:28; Hosea 13:2; Rom. 1:25

There are very few who in their hearts do not believe in God, but what they will not do is give him exclusive right of way. Missionaries tell us that they could easily get converts if they did not require them to be baptized, thus publicly renouncing their idols. Many a person in our land would become a Christian if the gate was not so straight. Christianity is too strict for them. They are not ready to promise full allegiance to God alone. Many a professing Christian is a stumbling block because his worship is divided. On Sunday he worships God; on weekdays God has little or no place in his thoughts.

You don't have to go to heathen lands today to find false gods. America is full of them. Whatever you make most of is your god. Whatever you love more than God is your idol. Many a man's heart is like some Sheiks' huts, so full of idols that there is hardly room to turn around. Rich and poor, learned and unlearned, all classes of men and women are guilty of this sin. A man may make a god of himself, of a child, of a mother, of some precious gift that God has bestowed upon him. He may forget the Giver and let his heart go out in adoration toward the gift.

Worship, priority of; Commandment, first

Job 31:24; Isa. 47:8; Matt. 6:24; Luke 16:13; 2 Tim. 3:4; Heb. 11:25; James 4:3; 2 Peter 2:13

Many make a god of pleasure; that is what their hearts are set on. If some old Greek or Roman came to life again and saw man in a drunken debauch, would he believe that the worship of Bacchus had died out? If he saw the streets of our large cities filled with harlots, would he believe that the worship of Venus had ceased? Others take fashion as their god. They give their time and thought to dress. They fear what others will think of them. Do not let us flatter ourselves that all idolaters are in heathen countries.

With many it is the god of money. We haven't got through worshiping the golden calf yet. If a man will sell his principles for gold, isn't he making it a god? If he trusts in his wealth to keep him from want and to supply his needs, are not riches his god? Many a man says, "Give

me money, and I will give you heaven. What care I for all the glories and treasures of heaven? Give me treasures here! I don't care for heaven! I want to be a successful businessman now."

Zeal, examples of; Wealth, search for; Witnessing, importance of

John 2:17; Rom. 10:2; 2 Cor. 9:2; Phil. 3:6; Col. 4:13; 1 Tim. 6:10

Look how men search for wealth. Men say they cannot come to these meetings and wait half an hour; they cannot leave their families; but let them think they can accumulate a little wealth and they can leave their families six months, and six years if need be. Men sacrifice honor and home in pursuit of wealth, and yet people never accuse them of being mad. Look how earnest the politicians become during election time. Men have got hold of me on the street and tried to drag me to the polls to vote their ticket—democratic and republican both. They do not know me, but it makes no difference. They are in earnest. But when we become earnest to save souls, we are called fanatics.

Zeal, importance of; Earnestness, importance of

John 2:17; Rom. 10:2; 2 Cor. 9:2; Phil. 3:6; Col. 4:13; 1 Tim. 6:10

A man may talk in his sleep, and it seems to me that there is a good deal of that kind of thing now in the Lord's work. A man may even preach in his sleep. A friend of mine sat up in his bed one night and preached a sermon right through. He was sound asleep all the time. Next morning his wife told him all about it. He preached the same sermon in his church the next Sabbath morning; I have it in print, and a good sermon it is. So a man may not only talk but actually preach in his sleep.

There are many preachers in these days who are fast asleep.

There is one thing, however, that we must remember; a man cannot work in his sleep. There is no better way to wake up a church than to set it to work. One man will wake up another in waking himself up. Of course the moment we begin a work of aggression, and declare war with the world, the flesh, and the devil, some wise head will begin to shake, and there will be the cry, "Zeal without knowledge!" I think I have heard that objection ever since I commenced the Christian life. Let us be up and at the work. There is no power on earth that can stand before the onward march of God's people when they are in dead earnest.

Zeal, power of; Dedication, power of

John 2:17; Rom. 10:2; 2 Cor. 9:2; Phil. 3:6; Col. 4:13; 1 Tim. 6:10

There's a story told in history in the ninth century, I believe, of a young man that came up with a little handful of men to attack a king who had a great army of three thousand men. The young man had only five hundred, and the king sent a messenger to the young man, saying that he need not fear to surrender, for he would treat him mercifully. The young man called up one of his soldiers and said: "Take this dagger and drive it to your heart"; and the soldier took the dagger and drove it to his heart. And calling up another, he said to him, "Leap into yonder chasm," and the man leaped into the chasm.

The young man then said to the messenger, "Go back and tell your king I have got five hundred men like these. We will die, but we will never surrender. And tell your king another thing; that I will have him chained with my dog inside of half a day." And when the king heard that he did not dare to meet them, and his army fled before them like chaff before the wind,

and within twenty-four hours he had that king chained with his dog. That is the kind of zeal we need. "We will die, but we will never surrender." We will work until Jesus comes, and then we will rise with him.

Zeal, power of; Dedication, power of; Persistence, power of

John 2:17; Rom. 10:2; 2 Cor. 9:2; Phil. 3:6; Col. 4:13; 1 Tim. 6:10

A young woman was about to go to China as the wife of a missionary. She had a large Sunday school class in the city and succeeded in being a blessing to many of her scholars. She was very anxious to get someone who would look after her little flock and take care of them while she was gone. She had a brother who was not a Christian, and her heart was set on his being converted and taking her place as leader of the class. The young man refused to accept Christ, but away in her closet alone she pleaded with God that her brother might be converted and take her place. She wanted to reproduce herself.

That is what every Christian ought to do—get somebody else converted to take up your work. Well, the last morning came, and around the family altar as the moment drew near for the lady's departure, and they did not know when they should see her again, the father broke down, and the boy went upstairs. Just before she left for the train the boy came down, and putting his arms around his sister's neck, said to her, "My dear sister, I will take your Savior for mine, and I will take care of your class for you." The young man took her class and learned God's truth while he taught it. The last I heard of him he was still filling her place. There was a young lady established in good work.

Bibliography

Adams, Charles Francis, ed. *Life and Sermons of Dwight Lyman Moody.* Chicago: M. A. Donohue, 1902.

Albertson, Charles C., ed. *Gems of Truth and Beauty.* Chicago: Rhodes & McClure, 1890.

Albus, Harry J. *A Treasury of Dwight L. Moody.* Grand Rapids: Eerdmans, 1949.

Atkins, Gaius Glenn, ed. *Master Sermons of the Nineteenth Century.* New York: Willett, Clark, 1940.

Bailey, Faith Coxe. *D. L. Moody.* Chicago: Moody Press, 1959.

Chapman, J. Wilbur. *The Life and Work of D. L. Moody.* Chicago: John C. Winston, 1900.

Cook, Richard B., ed. *Life, Work, and Sermons of Dwight L. Moody.* Baltimore: R. H. Woodward, 1900.

Daniels, Rev. W. H., ed. *Moody: His Words, Work and Workers.* New York: Nelson & Phillips, 1877.

DeMaster, Beth, and Walter Osborn. *Subject Index to D. L. Moody's Sermons.* Chicago: Moody Bible Institute, 1991.

Dunn, James B., ed. *Moody's Talks on Temperance.* New York: National Temperance Society & Publication House, 1877.

Erdman, Charles R. *D. L. Moody, His Message for Today.* New York: Revell, 1928.

Fitt, Arthur Percy. *The Shorter Life of D. L. Moody.* Chicago: Moody Press, 1890.

Goodspeed, Edgar Johnson, ed. *A Full History of the Wonderful Career of Moody and Sankey, in Great Britain and America.* Chicago: Thompson & Wakefield, 1876.

Gunther, Peter F., comp. *Great Sermons by Great Preachers.* Chicago: Moody Press, 1960.

Herford, Brook. *Revival Extravagance Caused by Respectable Indifference.* Boston: American Unitarian Assn., 1900.

Hutson, Curtis, comp. *The Friend of the Sorrowing.* Murfreesboro, Tenn.: Sword of the Lord Publishers, 1990.

———. *Great Preaching on Comfort.* Murfreesboro, Tenn.: Sword of the Lord Publishers, 1990.

———. *Great Preaching on Soul Winning.* Murfreesboro, Tenn.: Sword of the Lord Publishers, 1989.

———. *True Wisdom—Soul Winning.* Murfreesboro, Tenn.: Sword of the Lord Publishers, 1990.

Moody, D. L. *Addresses by D. L. Moody.* Chicago: n.p., n.d.

———. *Arrows and Anecdotes.* London: Christian Age, 1876.

———. *The Best of Dwight L. Moody.* Grand Rapids: Baker, 1990.

———. *Bible Readings Delivered in San Francisco and Oakland*. San Francisco: Bacon, Book and Job Printers, 1881.

———. *Calvary's Cross*. Grand Rapids: Baker, 1966.

———. *Crowning Glory*. Chicago: Laird & Lee Publishers, 1893.

———. *D. L. Moody on the Ten Commandments*. Chicago: Moody Press, 1977.

———. *Dwight Lyman Moody, the Great Evangelist of the Nineteenth Century*. Chicago: Thompson & Thomas, 1900.

———. *The D. L. Moody Year Book: A Living Daily Message from the Words of D. L. Moody*. New York: Revell, 1900.

———. *Echoes from the Pulpit and Platform*. Hartford, Conn.: A. D. Worthington, 1900.

———. *Evenings with Moody and Sankey*. Philadelphia: John C. Winston, 1877.

———. *Faith*. Chicago: Great Commission Prayer League, 1879.

———. *The Faith Which Overcomes and Other Addresses*. London: Marshall, Morgan & Scott, 1932.

———. *Finding God*. Chicago: Moody Press, 1958.

———. *50 Evenings at the Great Revival Meetings Conducted by Moody and Sankey*. Philadelphia: C. H. Yost, 1876.

——— *Fifty Sermons and Evangelistic Talks*. Cleveland: F. M. Barton, 1899.

———. *The Fullness of the Gospel*. Chicago: Revell, 1908.

———. *Gems from Northfield*. Chicago: Revell, 1881.

———. *Glad Tidings. Comprising Sermons and Prayer-Meeting Talks*. New York: E. B. Treat, 1876.

———. *The Gospel Awakening*. 30th ed. Chicago: Fairbanks & Palmer Publishing, 1887.

———. *The Gospel Awakening*. Cleveland: C. C. Wick, 1877.

———. *Grace, Prayer, and Work*. London: Morgan & Scott, n.d.

———. *Great Joy. Comprising Sermons and Prayer-Meeting Talks Delivered at the Chicago Tabernacle*. New York: E. B. Treat, 1877.

———. *The Great Redemption*. Chicago: J. Fairbanks, 1880.

———. *The Gospel Tidings*. New York: F. O. Evans, 1878.

———. *Heaven: Where It Is, Its Inhabitants, and How to Get There*. Chicago, Ill.: F. H. Revell, 1880.

———. *Holding the Fort*. Philadelphia: Chas. H. Yost, Bible Publisher, 1877.

———. *Holding the Fort*. Cincinnati: United States Book and Bible, 1879.

———. *The Home Work of D. L. Moody*. Chicago: Revell, 1886.

———. *The London Discourses of Mr. D. L. Moody*. London: J. Clarke, 1875.

———. *Men of the Bible*. Chicago: Bible Institute Colportage Assn., 1898.

———. *Moody's Anecdotes*. Chicago: Revell, 1898.

———. *Moody and Sankey in Hartford*. Hartford: W. H. Goodrich, 1878.

———. *Moody's Child Stories*. Milwaukee: Rhodes & McClure, 1902.

———. *Moody's Gospel Sermons*. Chicago: Rhodes & McClure, 1896.

———. *Moody's Gospel Sermons Delivered in Europe and America*. Two Volumes. Chicago: Rhodes & McClure, 1891.

———. *Moody's Great Sermons*. Chicago: Laird & Lee, 1899.

———. *Moody's Latest Sermons*. Chicago: Revell, 1900.

———. *Moody's Stories*. Chicago: The Bible Institute Colportage Assn., 1899.

———. *Narrative of Messrs. Moody and Sankey's Labors in Great Britain and Ireland*. New York: A. D. F. Randolph, 1875.

———. *The New Sermons, Addresses and Prayers.* Chicago: H. S. Goodspeed Publisher, 1877.

———. *The New Sermons of Dwight Lyman Moody.* New York: Goodspeed, 1880.

———. *The Old Gospel.* London: Morgan and Scott, n.d.

———. *The Overcoming Life: And Other Sermons.* Chicago: Moody Press, 1896.

———. *Prevailing Prayer: What Hinders It?* Chicago: Moody Press, 1913.

———. *The Prodigal.* Chicago: Moody Press, 1896.

———. *Salvation for All.* London: Morgan & Scott, 1877.

———. *Saviour and Sinner.* n.p., n.d.

———. *The Second Coming of Christ.* Chicago: The Bible Institute Colportage Assn., 1896.

———. *Secret Power.* Ventura, Calif.: Regal Books, 1987.

———. *Select Sermons by D. L. Moody.* Chicago: Revell, 1881.

———. *Sermons and Addresses, Question Drawer, and Other Proceedings of the Christian Convention, September 18th to 20th, 1883.* Chicago: Fairbanks, Palmer, 1884.

———. *Short Talks.* Chicago: The Bible Institute Colportage Assn., 1900.

———. *Sovereign Grace: Its Source, Its Nature, and Its Effects.* Chicago: Revell, 1891.

———. *Sowing and Reaping.* London: Morgan & Scott, 1896.

———. *Stand Up for Jesus.* London: J. E. Hawkins, 1870.

———. *Success in the Christian Life.* Grand Rapids: Baker, 1972.

———. *Ten Days with Moody.* New York: J. S. Ogilvie, 1886.

———. *Thou Fool! and Eleven Other Sermons Never Before Published.* New York: The Christian Herald, 1911.

———, ed. *Thoughts for the Quiet Hour.* Eugene, Ore.: Harvest House, 1994.

———. *To All People.* New York: E. B. Treat, 1877.

———. *To the Work, To the Work: Exhortations to Christians.* Chicago: Revell, 1884.

———. *Twelve Penny Addresses.* London: Morgan & Scott, 1884.

———. *Twelve Select Sermons.* Chicago: Revell, 1881.

———. *Twelve Sermons.* London: John Snow, 1875.

———. *The Way to God.* Springdale, Penn.: Whitaker House, 1893.

———. *The Way Home.* Chicago: The Bible Institute Colportage Assn., 1904.

———. *Weighed in the Balances. Addresses on the Ten Commandments.* London & Edinburgh: Marshall, Morgan & Scott, n.d.

———. *Weighed and Wanting: Addresses on the Ten Commandments.* Chicago: Revell, 1898.

———. *Wondrous Love and Other Gospel Addresses.* London: Pickering & Inglis, 1876.

Moody, D. L., and Ira David Sankey, *Evenings with Moody and Sankey.* Philadelphia: Porter & Coates, 1877.

Moody, William R. *The Life of Dwight L. Moody.* Chicago: Revell, 1900.

Morrow, Abbie Clemens, ed. *Best Thoughts and Discourses of D. L. Moody.* New York: N. Tibbals, 1876.

Northrop, Henry Davenport. *Life and Labors of D. L. Moody, the Great Evangelist.* Cincinnati: Forshee, 1899.

Ogilvie, J. S., ed. *Life and Sermons of Dwight L. Moody.* New York: J. S. Ogilvie, 1900.

Remlap, L. T., ed. *The Gospel Awakening.* Chicago: Fairbanks, Palmer, 1883.

Rhodes, Richard S., ed. *Dwight Lyman Moody's Life Work and Gospel Sermons.* Chicago: Rhodes & McClure, 1900.

———, ed. *Dwight Lyman Moody's Life Work and Latest Sermons.* Chicago: Rhodes & McClure, 1900.

Rost, Stephen, ed. *Dwight L. Moody: The Best from All His Works.* Nashville: T. Nelson Publishers, 1989.

Rowe, A. T. *D. L. Moody, the Soul-Winner.* Anderson, Ind.: Gospel Trumpet, 1927.

Shanks, T. J., ed. *A College of Colleges.* Vol. 1. Chicago: Revell, 1887.

———, ed. *A College of Colleges.* Vol. 2. Chicago: Revell, 1888.

———, ed. *A College of Colleges.* Vol. 3. Chicago: Revell, 1889.

Simons, M. Laird, ed. *Evenings with Moody and Sankey.* Philadelphia: Porter & Coates, 1877.

Smith, Wilbur M., ed. *The Best of D. L. Moody.* Chicago: Moody Press, 1971.

Sunderland, Jabez Thomas. *Orthodoxy and Revivalism.* New York: Miller, 1877.

Turnbull, Ralph, ed. *The Best of Dwight L. Moody.* Grand Rapids: Baker, 1979.

Wharton, H. M. *A Month with Moody in Chicago.* Baltimore: Wharton & Barron, 1894.

Subject Index

Abilities, use of, 119
Abstinence, importance of, 9
Acceptance, power of, 9
Adam's sin, result of, 9–10
Adoration of God, 10
Adultery
  curse of, 10, 11
  danger of, 11–12
  defilement of, 12
  nature of, 12
  recovery from, 12–13
  sin of, 13
Adversity, strength for, 180
Advertising church services, 13
Affections, set above, 308
Affliction(s)
  blessings of, 14
  comfort in, 38–39
  strength for, 126
  submission in, 13–14
Affirmation, importance of, 320
Aging
  gracefully, 14
  proper perspective, 87
Alcoholism
  healing from, 14
  help in recovery, 15
  recovery from, 15, 153
Ambition, controlling, 15–16
Anger, control of, 16
Animal rights, 196
Anxiety, cure of, 16–17
Appetite, spiritual, 17
Application to self, 134
Approval, God's, 17
Arguments, futility of, 17–18
Ark, Noah's, 36
Assessment, personal, 282
Assurance
  basis of, 18–19
  example of, 19–20
  hope of, 20
  importance of, 20–21
  lack of, 21
  misunderstanding of, 21
  scope of, 22
  source of, 22–23, 259

Atheism
  cure for, 23
  failure of, 23–24
  hopelessness of, 24
Atonement
  importance of, 24
  power of, 24
  substitutionary, 25, 295
Availability to God, 25–26

Backsliders
  condition of, 26
  influence of, 26
  restored, 26–27
  restoring, 27
  return of, 27
  unhappiness of, 27–28
Backsliding
  cure of, 28
  danger of, 303
  process of, 28
Bad habits, danger of, 28
Behavior, circumspect, 308
Belief
  aspects of, 93
  before works, 93
  content of, 95
  definition of, 96
  elements of, 96
  example of, 97
  exercise of, 98
  grounds of, 98
  joy of, 99
  lack of, 98
  nature of, 97, 99
  object of, 100
  possibility of, 105
  power of, 102, 103
  reasonableness of, 104
  result of, 104
  reward of, 104
  in testimony, 98
  and works, 93
Bible
  denial of, 28
  depth of, 28–29
  Jesus' endorsement of, 29
  knowledge of, 29
  misjudgment of, 29–30

power of, 30–31, 67
relevancy of, 31
standard of truth, 65
tried and proven, 33
value of, 198–99
Bible study
  depth of, 31
  diligence in, 31
  importance of, 31–32, 258
  interest in, 32
  method of, 32
  value of, 32–33
Blood, covering for sin, 33–34
Blood of Christ, 287
  atonement by, 34–35
  cleansing power, 174
  importance of, 35
  power of, 35–36
  source of salvation, 36
Boasting excluded, 36
Body, temple of Holy Spirit, 37
Broken hearts
  cure of, 37–38
  healing for, 38–39
Brotherhood, universal, 39
Brotherly love, 183
Burden bearing, 306
Burdens
  bear one another's, 39
  help for, 61
  provision for, 16–17
  put on God, 39
Burial of Christians, 39–40

Call to preach, 117
Calvary, wonder of, 40
Care, pastoral, 182–83
Cares, help with, 45–46
Change, resistance to, 170
Character
  enduring power of, 162
  importance of, 40, 64, 70–71, 92
  influence of, 40
  proof of confession, 40–41
  ruin of, 41

vindication of, 41–42
Chastening
    of God, 42
    importance of, 42
Cheating, danger of, 170
Cheerfulness, example of, 293
Child
    death of, 42
    influence of on conversion, 42–43
Child rearing, strength for, 153
Childhood spiritual education, 43
Children
    conversion of, 44
    and covenants, 43–44
    discipline of, 14
    of God, 197
    instruction of, 185
    prayer for, 44
Choice, importance of, 44
Christ
    and Adam, 44–45
    burden bearer, 45–46
    comfort from, 46
    compassion of, 46
    confession of, 46–47
    confidence in, 47–48
    dedication to, 48
    deity of, 48–49
    description of, 49
    fellowship with, 50
    God and man, 50
    good Shepherd, 56–57
    great physician, 50
    and his parents, 205
    last act of, 50
    liberty in, 50–51
    new creation in, 51
    new life in, 51
    no room for, 51–52
    not ashamed of, 52
    our advocate, 52–53
    our helper, 53
    our pioneer leader, 53
    our rock, 110
    personality of, 53
    pleasing, 53–54
    redemption by, 54–55
    reign of, 244
    reigning with, 260–61
    saves, not doctrine, 55
    second coming of, 55
    seeking sinners, 56–57
    as Shepherd, 45
    sin bearer, 57

sinlessness of, 57
spoke clearly, 57
time of second coming, 57–58
trust in, 58
water of life, 58
worth hearing, 58
wrong views of, 58
Christ's second coming
    anticipating, 59
    and evangelism, 59
Christianity, proof of, 96
Christians
    classes of, 146
    as lights, 59
Christlikeness, our opportunity, 59
Church
    effectiveness, key to, 60
    getting it to work, 60
    how to fill a, 60–61
    importance of, 61
    membership, necessity of, 61
    a place for work, 59–60
Circumstances, victory over, 228
Citizenship in heaven, 76
Comfort, source of, 61
Commandment(s)
    eighth, 284–85
    eleventh, 120–21
    fifth, 108, 156, 191–93, 205–7, 321
    first, 49, 301, 326–28
    fourth, 247–450
    ninth, 106–7, 187, 276–77, 277, 294
    for our good, 61–62
    second, 58–59, 105–6, 161–62, 187–88, 243, 257, 325–26, 327
    seventh, 10, 11–13
    sixth, 195–96, 288
    tenth, 70–75, 174
    third, 225–26
Commitment, power of, 79
Communion
    with God, 82
    meaning of, 299
Complaint, danger of, 75
Compromise, danger of, 323
Concern for others, 62–63
Confession
    importance of, 63, 234, 237
    power of, 63
    public, 63–64

of sin, 63, 113
vs. profession, 64
Confidence
    based on Scripture, 64
    in God, 101
Conflict resolution, 64, 166
Confrontation, spiritual, 64–65
Conscience
    awaking of, 65
    education of, 65
    nature of, 65
    power of, 65–66
    searing of, 135
    weakness of, 151
Consecration, fruit of, 66
Contentment, importance of, 66
Contrition, importance of, 67
Conversion(s)
    example of, 67
    impact of, 145
    of infidel, 97–98
    instantaneous, 67–68
    meaning of, 68
    of older woman, 57
    of saloonkeeper, 219
    of skeptical woman, 68
    of skeptics, 68
    thorough, 69–70
    work of God, 23, 69
    of youth, 68–69
Converts, work of, 69
Conviction
    expression of, 300
    importance of, 69
    lack of, 69
    power of, 107–8
    of sin, importance of, 69–70
Correction, divine, 42
Corruption, inner, 135
Courage, source of, 102
Covetousness
    control of, 70
    danger of, 70–71
    deceitfulness of, 71–72
    defilement of, 72
    evil of, 72–73
    example of, 73
    extent of, 73–74
    folly of, 74
    greed of, 74
    sin of, 74–75
Creation
    evidence of God, 75
    old and new, 75

revelation of deity, 196–97
Creator, God as, 75
Criticism, danger of, 75
Cross, importance of, 76
Culture
    importance of, 231–32
    inadequate to regenerate,
        76

Daughter, prodigal, 10
Death
    certainty of, 76–77
    Christ's victory over, 77
    of Christian, 77–78
    conquered by Christ, 77
    facing, 126
    as gain, 76
    victory over, 78, 239
    view of, 78
Debt of sin, canceled,
    170–71
Deception, futility of, 79
Decision, importance of, 79
Dedication
    appeal to, 265, 299
    evidence of, 79
    example of, 79–80, 107
    importance of, 48, 83
    need of all, 80, 146
    power of, 80, 87, 329
Deliverance from sin, 230
Denial of spiritual need, 69
Depression
    cure for, 309
    victory over, 80–81
Desire, object of, 112
Despair, victory over, 80–81
Devotional life, importance
    of, 81
Diligence, reward of, 81–82
Discipline
    based on love, 82
    parental, 193
Discord, danger of, 82
Discouragement, overcom-
    ing, 84–85
Disobedience, danger of,
    200
Dispute, danger of, 82
Doctrines, limits of, 82
Doubt(s)
    cure for, 82, 261
    danger of, 82, 252
    futility of, 75
    remedy for, 83, 292
    sin of, 301
Doubter converted, 219–20
Dreams, unable to save, 83

Earnestness
    importance of, 83, 328–29
    need for, 146
Ears, itching, 271–72
Education, early childhood,
    90, 201–2
Election
    doctrine of, 83–84
    proof of, 84
Encouragement
    importance of, 84
    power of, 84–86
    for service, 84
End times, faithfulness in, 86
Enemies of righteousness,
    202–3
Enthusiasm
    example of, 79–80
    need of, 86–87
    power of, 87, 91
    in preaching, 165
Envy, danger of, 166
Eternal life
    gate to, 166–67
    importance of, 87
    nature of, 88
Eternity, length of, 88
Evangelism
    call to, 88
    of children, 90
    church-wide, 88
    importance of, 315
    individual, 88
    kindness in, 88–89
    lay, 89
    lostness of men, 89
    through love, 185
    necessity of, 89–90
    need for, 90
    patience in, 90–91
    of peers, 90
    united effort, 91
    vision for, 91
    work of all, 91, 321
Evangelistic meetings, time
    of, 91
Evangelize your world of
    influence, 91–92
Evil, association with, 92
Exaggeration, sin of, 92
Example, importance of, 92
Excesses, fruit of, 28
Excuses
    abundance of, 92
    inadequacy of, 92
    weakness of, 92
Existence of God, evidence
    of, 93

Exultation of believers, 167

Failure, recovery from, 235
Faith
    aspects of, 93
    before works, 93
    bond of society, 93
    childlike, 93–95, 227
    content of, 95
    courageous, 95–96
    credentials of, 96
    definition of, 96
    elements of, 96
    enemies of, 96–97
    example of, 97–98
    exercise of, 98
    not feelings, 100
    fervent, 98
    fruit of, 22–23
    grounds of, 98
    lack of, 98–99
    little, 99
    naturalness of, 99
    nature of, 99–100
    object of, 100–101
    pilgrim nature of, 101–2
    power of, 102, 103
    practical, 103
    prayer of, 103
    reasonableness of, 103–4
    result of, 104
    reward of, 104
    saving, 104, 105, 296
    simplicity of, 105
    submission in, 221
    in testimony, 98
    vs. feeling, 105–6
    and works, 93
Faithfulness, reward of, 261
False god, business, 187–88
False witness
    danger of, 106
    dealing with, 106
    sin of, 106–7
Family, time with, 108
Family altar
    example of, 107
    importance of, 107, 108
    significance of, 107–8
Family leadership, 161
Father
    honoring, 108
    as leader, 107
    responsibility of, 108
Father's example, power of,
    109
Father's influence, 109
Fatherhood of God, 183–84

Fathering, importance of, 108
Fault-finders, cure of, 109–10
Fault-finding
  cure of, 131
  futility of, 110
Favor, unmerited, 124
Fear, cure for, 82
Feed people well, 110
Feelings, unable to save, 105, 110
Fellowship
  of believers, 111
  encouragement of, 110
  with God, 111
  importance of, 140
Finishing
  importance of, 111
  well, 111
Fitness for service, 20–21
Flesh
  struggling against, 111–12
  walking after the, 112
  weakness of, 112
Focus
  importance of, 307
  positive, 112
Followers of Christ or Satan, 112–13
Forgiveness
  accepting, 113
  and church growth, 113
  before service, 114
  extent of, 114
  importance of, 114–15
  repeated, 15
  and retribution, 113
  of son, 115–16
  true, 116
Formalism, danger of, 116
Freedom from sin, 50–51
Freshness, spiritual, 116
Friendliness, church, 116
Friendship
  with Christ, 28
  Christian, 116–17
Fruit, source of, 93
Fruit bearing, importance of, 117
Fruit of the Spirit, 117
Fruitfulness
  evidence of call, 190
  importance of, 117
  source of, 102, 117–18
Funeral sermons, 77
Future, glorious, 118

Gambling, danger of, 285
Generosity, nature of, 118
Gifts
  use of, 118–19
  variety of, 119
Giving
  blessing of, 119–20
  joy of, 120
  to the poor, 48, 215
  treasures in heaven, 120–21
God
  abundant love of, 122
  the Father's love, 121
  is love, 121, 185–86
  mercy of, 122
  as seeker, 121
  view of, 121
  works through people, 121–22
God's will
  doing, 122
  importance of, 122
  surrender to, 122–23
Good works, encouragement to, 123
Gospel
  danger of rejecting, 189
  good news, 123
  need for clarity, 123
  power of, 52
  source of liberty, 77
Gospels, simplicity of, 123
Gossip, dealing with, 106
Grace
  abundance of, 124
  abundant, 124, 129
  availability of, 124–25
  crowning act, 36
  daily, 125
  dying, 125–26
  for forgiveness, 126
  free, 126–27
  free to all, 127
  to the Gentiles, 129
  and glory contrasted, 124
  growing in, 127
  growth in, 127–28
  for living, 126
  for needs, 126
  obtaining, 128
  overflowing, 128
  redeeming, 179–80
  for service, 126
  sufficient, 128–29
  sufficient for need, 128
  unlimited, 129–30
  using daily, 130

Gray areas, test of, 130
Greatness
  path to, 130
  true, 130–31
Greed
  danger of, 305
  nature of, 74–75
Growth
  Christian, 131
  spiritual, 31, 255
Grumblers, church of, 131
Grumbling
  cure of, 131
  uselessness of, 131–32
Guilty, all people, 132
Guns, use of, 133

Habit(s)
  danger of, 269
  nature of, 269
  power of, 133
  sinful, 133–34
Handicaps, overcoming, 288
Happiness, nature of, 169–70
Harvest
  certainty of, 240–41
  follows planting, 271
  result of sowing, 134
Hearing
  for others, 134
  spiritual, 134
Heart(s)
  cleansing of, 134
  deceitful, 55, 134–35
  hardening of, 135
  preparation of, 135
  searcher of, 71
  sinfulness of, 293–94
  value of a good, 136
Heart searching, need of, 135–36
Heaven
  certainty of, 136–37, 141
  description of, 137
  as home, 136
  hope of, 137
  without hypocrites, 140
  identity retained in, 138
  inhabitants of, 141
  information concerning, 138
  interest in, 138
  invest there, 246–47
  nature of, 111, 138–39
  new song of, 141–42
  only way to, 139
  people in heaven, 142
  perfections of, 142–43

place of God's presence, 139
place of joy, 139
place of song, 139–40
place of triumph, 136
residents of, 231
and service, 136
society of, 140
surprises in, 143
without tears, 122
treasures in, 140
way to, 24, 140
worth living for, 141
Heavenly minded, 143, 308
Heavenly perspective, 143
Hell, despair of, 143–44
Help, source of, 144
Holiness, influence of, 144
Holy Spirit
  brings hope, 145
  convicting power of, 145
  conviction, 145–46
  filling, 150–51, 159–60, 264, 310
    availability of, 146
    commanded, 146
    evidence of, 146
    experience of, 146–47
    importance of, 148
    method of, 148–49
    need of, 149
    power of, 149–50
    price of, 150
    for service, 147–48
    significance of, 150
    source of, 323–24
  as fire, 145
  fullness of, 169
  guidance, 151
  illumination of, 151–53
  leadership of, 153
  need of, 153
  power, 191, 239–40, 322–23
    importance of, 154
    need of, 154
  and prayer, 145
  quenching of, 154
  quickening, 154–55
  sealing of, 155
  source of love, 180
  striving, 121
  use of Scripture by, 30–31
  witness of, 155
  work of, 155
Holy Spirit-filled woman, 146

Home, importance of, 155–56
Home life, importance of, 40–41
Honor from above, 17
Hope, power of, 85
Humanism, danger of, 156
Humility
  based in holiness, 156
  detection of, 157
  evidence of, 157
  example of, 157–58
  fruit of, 158
  before God, 156–57
  importance of, 158–59
  nature of, 159
  power of, 159–60
  source of fruitfulness, 160
  source of peace, 160
  spirit of, 131
Hunger, spiritual, 160
Husbands, sensitivity of, 160
Hymns, singing new, 160–51
Hypocrisy
  danger of, 152, 161
  problem of, 161
  source of, 161
Hypocritical spirit, 143

Idol worship, 161–62
Illustrations
  use of, 203
  value of, 298–99
Impossible task for God, 36
Impure thoughts, control of, 162
Impurity, curse of, 11
Indifference, danger of, 162
Infallibility of Bible, proof of, 162
Influence
  enduring nature of, 162
  evil, danger of, 162–63
  power of, 163
Inheritance of the saints, 163
Inner city
  evangelism, 164
  ministry, 164–65
Inspiration, spiritual, 165
Integrity, power of, 165–66
Intimacy with God, 116
Introducing others to God, 166
Invitation to salvation, 83–84

Jealousy
  cure of, 166
  danger of, 166

Jesus
  importance of name, 166–67
  as physician, 58
Joint-heirs with Christ, 167–68
Joy
  of Christianity, 169
  continuing, 168
  definition of, 168
  source of, 17, 169
  strength of, 169–70
Judgment
  accuracy of, 170
  certainty of, 170, 273, 281
  nature of, 92
  nearness of, 170
Justice, nature of, 170
Justification
  meaning of, 170–71
  nature of, 255

Kindness
  acts of, 254–55
  power of, 171, 278
Knowing Christ intimately, 186
Knowledge
  act on, 171
  partial on earth, 171

Law
  and grace
    contrasted, 171–72
    differences, 172
  perfect nature of, 172–73
  power of, 173, 174
  reveals sin, 174
  still current, 174–75
  vs. grace, 175
Lay ministry, importance of, 175
Lay volunteers, work of, 176
Lay witness, 47
  importance of, 88, 176
Laziness
  brings leanness, 243–44
  cure for, 226
  danger of, 176–77
  problem of, 82, 177–78
Leaders, failure of, 153
Leadership, lay, 178
Life
  brevity of, 178, 246
  purpose of, 179
  wasted, 179
Love
  in action, 183

active, 179
badge of Christian, 179
begets love, 64
brotherly, 179
Christ's forgiving, 179–80
covers sins, 180
crowning act, 36
dimensions of, 180
generosity of, 180
for God, 180
of God, 184–85
God's for sinners, 181–82
and God's law, 179
God's unchangeable, 182
importance of, 117, 182–83
language of, 183
nature of, 183–84
nature of God, 184
not duty, 184
power of, 182, 183, 185–86
produces love, 186
real (negative example), 186
sign of new birth, 186–87
Lust, danger of, 11–12
Lying, sin of, 92, 187

Manner of life, 308
Marriage to unbeliever, 187
Materialism, danger of, 187–88
Maturity, spiritual, 188
Meditation, importance of, 188
Memory, power of, 188–89
Mercy, cry for, 189
Message more than ministers, 189
Millennium, views of, 190
Ministers, prayer for, 190
Ministry
    call to, 190
    lay, 190–91
    power for, 191
    worthless without love, 191
Mission
    focus, 307
    sense of, 314
    statement, 308
    strength for, 307
    work of all, 91
Money
    love of, 246
    use of, 191
Mother
    faithfulness of, 192

heart of, 193
honoring, 191–92
importance of, 138–39
influence of, 193–94
love of, 194
    example of, 194–95
Mother's heart, 227
Motivation, inner, 195
Motives, nature of, 195
Murder
    from carelessness, 196
    definition of, 196
    by evil conduct, 195–96
    nature of, 196
    by tongue, 276–77

Nature
    old, 196
    witness to God, 196–97
Natures, two, 111–12, 197
Need(s)
    of savior, 266
    supply of, 124, 126
Neglect, danger of, 197
New birth, 231–32
    fruit of, 197
    importance of, 197–98
New converts
    advice to, 198
    treatment of, 225
    witness of, 198
    work of, 198, 302
New creation, law of, 237
New man, example of, 198
No, just say, 198
Nourishment, spiritual, 198–99

Obedience
    continual, 130
    empowerment for, 264
    examples of, 199
    fruit of, 199
    to God, 264
    importance of, 199–200
    joy of, 200
    pleases God, 200
    power of, 119, 200–201
    source of, 159
    source of harmony, 201
Obstacles, look beyond the, 201
Occult, avoidance of, 281–82
Old man vs. new man, 201
Opinions of others, 201
Opportunity
    lost, 201–2
    nature of, 202
    use of, 289

Opposition to work, 202–3
Optimism, example of, 209
Organization, importance of, 203
Overcoming the world, 53–54

Parables, teaching in, 203
Pardon
    joy of, 204
    for sins, 203
Parental correction, 204
Parental discipline, importance of, 61–62
Parental influence, 156, 204–5
Parents
    honor of, 205–7
    treatment of, 207
Passover, 25
    blood, 33–34
    power of, 24
    significance of, 287
Patience, example of, 111
Peace
    benediction, 207
    enemies of, 207
    gift of Christ, 207–8
    marred by sin, 208
    a source of, 32, 84, 199, 208, 229–30
Peculiar people, 208
Perfectionism, danger of, 208
Perseverance
    basis of, 209
    example of, 209
    importance of, 209
    value of, 262
Persistence
    example of, 209
    importance of, 209
    power of, 329
Personal holiness, power of, 210
Perspective, accurate, 306
Petition, persistence in, 214
Planning without God, 307
Pleasing God, process of, 199
Power, inner, 210
Praise
    blessing of, 131–32
    in church, 211
    for health, 210
    heaven's occupation, 210
    importance of, 210–11
    naturalness of, 211

power of, 211
source of, 146
Pray, too busy to, 211–12
Prayer
answer to, 212
answered, 212–13
asking, 213
attitude in, 214
of Christ, 218
cold, 222
conditions for answers, 214
in crisis, 216
delayed answers, 214
for deliverance, 289
earnestness in, 214
fervency, 214–15
focus in, 215
importance of, 216
importunity in, 216
influence of, 216
influence of unconfessed sin, 217
intensity in, 217
for ministers, 215
mother's, 217, 222
mother's influence, 217–18
partnership with God, 218
petitions, 218
power of, 98, 110, 218–20
public, 220
sinner's, 220
submission in, 220, 221
unanswered, 221
for unbelieving husband, 215–16
understood by God, 221
vital nature of, 221–22
for workers, 85–86
Preach(ing)
to convict, 223
for effect, 223
gain attention, 257
to inspire, 224
maintain interest, 223
naturalness in, 223–24
power in, 224
the text, 222
to be understood, 222–23
use of humor, 224
use of surprise, 224
word choice, 224–25
Pride
danger of, 225, 261–62
deceitfulness of, 225
futility of, 225

Priorities of life, 211–12
Prodigal(s)
losses of, 26
unhappy, 27
Profanity
cure for, 175, 225–26
excuses for, 226
Progress, importance of, 208
Promises of God
for all, 312
availability of, 226
best of, 226
faithfulness of, 226
number of, 226–27
surety of, 33
trusting, 227
Promises of man, unfulfilled, 227
Prophecy, biblical, 294
Prostitute(s)
ministry to, 227
salvation of, 227
Providence
consequences of, 227–28
of God, 228
Provision
daily, 125
of God, 21
God's abundant, 66, 213, 228
Public witness, importance of, 292
Purpose
importance of, 308
of life, 228, 305
spiritual, 228–29

Questionable practices
guidelines, 229
handling, 229

Raikes, Robert, conversion of, 42–43
Reaping
not fainting, 177
result of sowing, 134, 163, 170, 241, 242–43
Rebellion
against God, 9–10
God's love in spite of, 229
Reconciliation
extent of, 229–30
to others, 230
Redemption, power of, 230
Regeneration
doctrine of, 197–98
evidence of, 186–87, 231
by faith alone, 230–31

importance of, 231
nature of, 231–32
power of, 152–53
wonder of, 252
Religion, sensual, 105–6
Religious education of children, 68–69, 232
Renewal, spiritual, 149, 154–55, 232
Repentance
example of, 80–81
and faith, 232–33
is not conviction, 233
is not praying, 233
lack of, 233
nature of, 233–34
need of, 234, 274
not breaking from sin, 234
true, 234–35
Resentment, danger of, 166
Rest
in Christ, 226
in heaven, 235
lack of, 235–36
seeking, 236
source of, 236
Restitution
example of, 66
help from, 236–37
importance of, 67–68, 268–69
necessity of, 237
requirement for, 237
Resurrection
of believers, 39–40
disbelief in, 237–38
doctrine of, 238
hope of, 76, 140, 238, 239
importance of, 239
light of, 315
power of, 240
Resurrection body, nature of, 237
Resurrection power, 239–40
Retribution
certainty of, 240–42, 269, 271
degree of, 242
examples of, 242–43
nature of, 243
Return of Christ, 55
Return of the Lord, 55–56
time of, 57–58
Reverence
false, 103
importance of, 67

Subject Index

Revival(s)
  cost of, 243
  effectiveness of, 244
  importance of, 243
  Jonathan and David, 244
  necessity of, 244
  need for, 243
  objections to, 244
  opposition to, 244
  time of, 243–44
Rewards
  desire for, 195
  for service, 244–45
  significance of, 245
Riches
  danger of, 245, 311
  deceitfulness of, 245–46
  nature of, 246–47
  true, 247
  vanity of, 247
Righteousness
  fruit of, 247
  lack of, 270
Rivalry, cure of, 166
Rocks, cleft of, 250

Sabbath, observing, 247–48
Sabbath principle, importance of, 248
Sabbath rest
  activities, 248–49
  importance of, 249
  principle, 249–50
Safety
  in God, 250
  lack of, 250
Saintliness, example of, 250–51
Salvation
  available to all, 251
  for all, 50, 252
  basis of, 110
  date of, 252
  divine activity, 23, 69
  of drunken woman, 316
  evidence of, 252
  free, 252
  fullness of, 295
  by grace, 251–52
  importance of, 178
  instantaneous, 232, 252–53
  necessity of, 253
  need of, 279
  rewards of, 167–68
  time of, 253–54
  without works, 254

Samaritan
  a good, 254–55
  true, 118
Sanctification
  evidence of, 282
  process of, 255
Satan
  aims high, 289–90
  blamed for sin, 255
  in church, 256
  deception of, 255–56
  delusive tactics, 256
  hard taskmaster, 295–96
  influence on children, 43
  opposition of, 256
  resisting of, 256
  strategy of, 128–29, 133–34, 185, 256–57, 270, 283, 289, 290, 309
  victory over, 53, 258
  wiles of, 258
Satisfaction
  inner, 258
  true, 180
Scarlet thread, 35
Scripture
  critics of, 29–30
  disputed, 258
  ignorance of, 258
  power of, 67
Secret sin, danger of, 258–59
Sectarian spirit, avoidance of, 304–5
Security
  basis of, 18–21, 22–23, 298
  of believer, 36
  grounded in Bible, 64
  lack of, 250
  source of, 23, 259
Seed snatched away, 257
Seek God's kingdom, 259
Seeker trusts Christ, 259–60
Seekers for Christ, 312
Seeking higher life, 66
Self-control
  importance of, 260–61
  need of, 16, 133
Self-denial
  influence of, 261
  key to service, 261
Self-defense, 196
Self-discipline, importance of, 128
Self-judgment, importance of, 271
Self-protection, basis of, 133
Self-sacrifice

  power of, 39
  strength of, 150
Selfishness, danger of, 261–62
Selflessness, power of, 87
Separation from world, 262
Sermon feedback, 262
Sermons, length of, 262
Service
  benefit of, 289
  in Christ's power, 263
  do what you can, 262–63
  heart for, 263
  invitation to, 263
  key to, 263
  nature of, 263–64
  persistence in, 264
  power for, 264
  power of, 149
  readiness for, 264
  reasons for, 195
  self-sacrificial, 130
  strength for, 264
  vision for, 86, 265
  wholehearted, 265
  willingness for, 216
Sheep nature
  of Christians, 265
  of mankind, 266
Shepherd
  Christ as, 22
  follow voice of, 265–66
  ministry of Christ, 266
  true, 258
Short accounts, keeping, 266–67
Sighing, 278
Significance, eternal, 267
Sin(s)
  blotted out, 267, 276
  cleansing from, 258, 269–70
  confession of, 235, 267–69
  consequences of, 269
  conviction of, 160, 269
  covering for, 276
  danger of, 269–70
  debt of paid, 127
  deliverance from, 270
  extent of, 270
  forgiveness of, 276
  freedom from, 133–34, 270–71
  hidden, 271
  penalty of, 174, 271
  power of, 112
  preaching against, 271–72
  price of, 27–28, 295–96

342

remedy for, 57, 272
remission of, 34–35
reward of, 272–73
seen by God, 273
slavery to, 273
unconfessed, 221, 273
unpardonable, 273–74
victory over, 261
warning of, 274
Sin nature, danger of, 271
Sin's danger, warning of, 274–75
Sincerity, 195
Singing
  importance of, 275
  influence of, 275
Sinners
  God's love for, 275
  love for, 275
  mercy for, 283–84
  need of pardon, 276
Skeptical persons, ministry to, 276
Skepticism, weakness of, 31
Slander, sin of, 276–77
Small things
  importance of, 277
  power of, 277
Smile, power of, 278
Son, a prodigal, 278
Sorrow, made obsolete, 278
Soul
  ear of, 134
  value of, 279
Soul insurance, 279
Soul winning
  greatest pleasure, 279
  joy of, 279–80
Sower, parable of, 280–81
Sowing
  to the flesh, 281
  and reaping, 240–42, 281, 306, 318
  wisely, 315
Spiritism, avoidance of, 281–82
Spiritual gifts, use of, 282
Spiritual growth, hindrances to, 53–54
Spiritual life
  depth of, 282
  source of, 282
Spiritual power, nature of, 282–83
Spiritual warfare, 283
Spurgeon's power, 150–51
Standing for right, 283

Standing for righteousness, 283–84
Stealing
  dealing with, 284
  foolishness of, 284–85
  sin of, 285
Strangers on earth, 101–2
Subjection to God, 285–86
Submission
  example of, 286
  to God, 42
  importance of, 199–200
  prayer of, 286
Submit to one another, 286
Substance abuse
  danger of, 286
  recover from, 291–92
Substitution
  example of, 286–87
  importance of, 287
Suffering, importance of, 288
Suicide, self-murder, 288
Swearing, excuses for, 226
Sword of the Spirit, 29
Sympathy, need of, 288

Talents, use of, 262–63, 288, 289
Temper, control of, 16
Temperance, importance of, 9
Temptation(s)
  avoiding, 289
  of Christ, 290
  common to all, 289–90
  danger of, 291
  in life's stages, 290
  nature of, 290
  power of, 290
  resisting, 128–29
  strength in, 101
  subtlety of, 290–91
Ten commandments, breaking of, 41, 291
Testimony
  Christian, 291–92
  importance of, 99, 292
  loss of, 162–63
  need of, 155
  power of, 40
  public, 316
  value of, 292
  willingness for, 292–93
Thankfulness, example of, 293
Thanksgiving
  blessing of, 131–32

  example of, 293
  value of, 211
Theft, foolishness of, 284–85
Theology without love, 293
Thief on the cross, 254
Thoughts, open to God, 293–94
Times and seasons, knowledge of, 294
Tobacco, use of, 294
Tongue(s)
  misuse of, 277, 294
  new, 294–95
Tranquility, source of, 207
Transfiguration of Christ, 239, 295
Transgressor, way of, 295–96
Transparency, importance of, 187
Trials
  dealing with, 296–97
  importance of, 288
  ministry of, 46
  strength for, 126
  strength in, 101, 186
Trinity
  description of, 296
  nature of, 296
Trouble(s)
  dealing with, 296–97
  given to God, 297
  refuge in, 297
Trust
  in Christ, 298
  example of, 297–98
  nature of, 298–99
  object of, 299
  wholehearted, 299
Truth
  avoidance of, 28
  carelessness about, 299
  personal application of, 299–300
  standing for, 300

Unbelief
  cruelty of, 239
  danger of, 98–99, 102, 170
  failure of, 103
  hopelessness of, 300
  of natural man, 300
  nature of, 99–100
  overcoming, 300–301
  substitute gods, 301
  tragedy of, 301
Unchurched, reaching the, 302–3
Understanding, need of, 288

Unequal yoke in business, 303
Ungodliness, danger of, 303
Unity
    benefits of, 303–4
    importance of, 304–5
    power of, 305
    source of, 179, 201
    working in, 119
Upward look, 308
Value
    lasting, 305
    true, 267
Values
    assessment of, 305
    enduring, 305
    eternal, 118, 163, 168, 265, 305–6
    importance of, 228
    primary, 211–12, 327
Victory in God's strength, 306
Vision
    broadness of, 306
    eternal, 118
    failed, 307
    focused on Christ, 307
    force of, 307
    importance of, 95–96, 111, 168, 228, 307
    lack of, 179
    large, 314
    nature of, 305
    necessity of, 307
    power of, 78, 201, 307, 308, 313
    spiritual, 66, 228–29, 267, 305, 308

Waiting on God, 154
Walk
    circumspectly, 308
    nature of, 308
    worthy, 309
Warfare
    Christian, 309
    spiritual, 309
Warnings, importance of, 309
Watch and pray, 310
Watchfulness, importance of, 310

Water of life
    abundance of, 310
    need of, 310
Weakness
    apart from God, 310
    significance of, 311
    into strength, 310–11
Wealth
    of Christians, 163
    danger of, 311
    futility of, 311
    search for, 328
    snare of, 246
    spiritual, 311
Welfare, 177–78
    discussion of, 321–22
    and grace, 311–12
Wholeheartedness, importance of, 312
Whosoever includes me, 312
Wickedness, fruit of, 208
Will, power of, 199–200
Will of God, importance of, 313
Willingness
    advantages of, 123
    power of, 313
    to work, 164
Witness
    of child, example of, 313
    consistent, 64–65
    importance of, 163
    lay, 60–61, 302–3
    of life, 313–14
    of a pure life, 210
    of women, 314
Witnessing
    aggressive, 314
    blessing of, 314–15
    consistency in, 315
    cost of, 145–46
    courage in, 315
    with enthusiasm, 320
    importance of, 155, 315, 316, 328
    joy of, 279–80
    kindness in, 316
    in love, 316
    need of, 154–55, 316–17
    to neighbor, 319
    opportunities for, 317
    parental influence, 317

persistence in, 318
    power of, 318
    primary need in, 318
    to prostitutes, 319–20
    readiness for, 318
    be ready to, 314
    sharing light, 319
    shine your light, 319
    value of, 280
    vision for, 317
    wisdom of, 320
    work of all, 91, 320–21
Women, ministry of, 47, 321
Women's rights, need for, 321
Work
    earthly opportunity only, 321
    evidence of faith, 321–22
    importance of, 322
    involvement in, 322
    spirit of, 177
Works
    greater than Christ, 322–23
    importance of, 323
World, separation from, 323–24
Worldliness
    danger of, 86, 269, 324
    futility of, 258
    ruins peace, 324–25
Worship
    abuse of, 325–26
    centrality of, 326–27
    ceremonialism, 327
    formalism, 327
    importance of, 327–28
    priority of, 328
Worry
    answers for, 16–17
    lack of, 17
Worship, human need for, 160

Yieldedness to God, 148–49

Zeal
    example of, 79–80, 328
    importance of, 48, 83, 328–29
    power of, 80, 83, 87, 329

Scripture Index

Genesis

1:11   76
2:17   269
2:24   160
3:1   182
3:5–6   15, 261
3:6   73, 74, 134
3:8–9   9, 44, 45, 111
3:9   305
3:10   69
3:12   100, 105, 110, 267
3:15   9, 44, 45, 111, 290
3:17   9, 44, 45, 111
3:19   76, 269
3:21   9, 44, 45, 111
4:5   16
4:7   53
4:8   188, 230
4:9   62, 267
6:5   55, 135
6:7   234
6:8   84, 124, 126, 128, 130
6:9   25
6:14   36
9:6   196
9:21   235
11:4   15, 261
12:1   263
12:4   25
13:11   44, 71
13:12   28
15:6   93, 101, 299
15:15   14
16:2   100, 105, 110
17:7   14, 95, 96, 98, 103, 104
17:18   44
18:14   122
18:17   50
18:19   107, 108, 155, 156, 170
18:25   271
19:14   27, 303
19:32   235
23:4   101, 102
24:5   109
24:7   95, 98, 299
25:8   14
27:41   195, 196
28:17   10

28:20–22   10
30:1   221
31:49   110
32:7   16, 17
34:25   16
35:2   243
35:5   25
39:12   12
41:42   41
44:16   258
44:21   109
46:29   206
47:9   101, 102
47:12   206
50:20   227, 228

Exodus

2:6   254
2:21   66
3:1   83
3:10   263
3:14   228
4:12   319
6:6   54
12:13   24, 25, 33, 34, 35, 36, 286, 287
12:26   107, 108, 155, 156
13:8   43
15:2   95, 96, 98, 103, 104, 298
15:16   40
15:26   200
16:2   131
17:3   131
17:11–12   215
18:21   70, 203
18:24   70
19:5   208
19:6   40
20:2–3   326
20:4   105
20:4–6   161
20:6   122
20:7   225, 226
20:12   61, 191, 192, 205, 206
20:13   196
20:14   11, 13
20:16   187, 276
20:17   72, 73

22:1   236, 237
22:2   196
23:4   39
23:12   247, 248, 249, 250
23:13   308
28:3   148
31:3   148
32:1   325
32:30   24, 25, 33, 34, 35, 36, 286, 287
33:11   57
33:13   129
33:17   128
33:22   250
34:9   203
35:31   148
40:34–35   148, 154

Leviticus

6:4   236, 237
10:9   9
10:16   267
16:10   267
16:21   63
16:22   24, 25, 33, 34, 35, 36, 174, 286, 287
17:11   24, 25, 33, 34, 35, 36, 174, 286, 287
19:3   321
19:11   299
19:13   285
19:35   284, 285
25:23   101, 102
26:1   325
26:33   26
26:40   27, 28, 267
26:42   26, 267

Numbers

5:7   236, 237
6:3–4   9
6:23   207
11:1   131
11:27–29   304
12:1   15, 261
12:11   69
13:30   179
16:3   15, 261

345

16:9   263
20:10   64
22:7   73
22:28   75
23:19   98
32:33   258

Deuteronomy

4:9   28, 155, 156, 232
4:23   325
4:29   312
5:11   225, 226
5:13   247, 248, 249, 250
5:16   192
6:2   14
6:6   43
6:7   107, 108, 155, 156, 232
6:18   286
7:6   40
7:25   243
8:5   42, 82
10:12 265
11:12 273
11:13 265
11:18 29
11:19 43
11:29 107, 108
12:7   130
12:28 286
14:2   208
15:7   116, 120
16:19 189
21:5   263
24:14 284, 285
25:13 284, 285
26:18 208
27:15 325
27:26 174
29:18 44
29:29 258
31:8   93, 101, 299
32:4   259, 276
32:15 110, 259
32:30 292
32:31 301
33:12 250
33:25 126, 128, 130, 310,
       311

Joshua

1:6   86
1:7   223
1:8   188
1:9   95, 98, 124, 299
5:4   244
6:5   119
7:1   73

7:20   69
7:21   73
7:25   73
8:35   43
22:5   135, 265
23:10 292
23:12 92
24:15 44, 243
24:24 25
24:27 26

Judges

2:11   162
3:7   162
4:1   162
6:1   162
6:11   83
7:20   224
9:5   205, 206
10:6   162
10:16 243
13:1   162
13:5   9
16:1   12
16:29 288
16:30 26

Ruth

1:16   44
1:17   123
1:18   165, 209
2:2   126, 127
3:1   193, 194
3:9   54, 203
3:10   245, 246
3:13   230
4:14   203

1 Samuel

1:10   39
1:11   217, 222
1:15   16, 17, 146
1:18   124, 125
1:24   232
2:2   259, 301
2:19   193, 194
2:22   10, 11, 12
2:34   28
7:3   243
7:3–6 244
7:5   110
8:3   74
9:2   200
15:11 234
15:14 235
15:22 169, 200, 201

15:26 200
16:7   71
17:32 25
17:37 86, 95, 98
17:49 157
18:4   131
23:25 86
30:6   16, 17, 39
31:4–5 288

2 Samuel

7:14   42, 82
7:28   95, 96, 98, 103, 104,
       298
11:2   72
11:3   71
11:4   10, 11, 12
12:5   64, 225
12:10 13
12:13 63, 235
12:13–14 12, 113
12:14 269
12:16 44
12:23 42
14:1   233
17:23 288
17:37 299
18:33 205, 206, 233
22:3   19, 259
22:31 93, 101, 299
22:32 259
22:47 110, 259
24:10 107, 108, 235

1 Kings

1:5   15, 261
2:2   223
2:4   312
3:11   235, 259
3:27   194
5:5   123
8:23   10
8:35   68
10:9   170
11:6   162
16:18 288
17:21 78
18:21 41, 44, 79
18:36 263
18:38 310
19:2–4 310
19:4   221, 243
19:19 83

2 Kings

4:33   78

4:34   42
5:14   199
5:23   73
5:27   73
7:9   42
8:13   112
10:31   116
17:14   204
18:5   95, 98, 299
19:19   218
20:1–2 218
22:19   156

1 Chronicles

10:4–5 288
22:12   44
22:19   143, 179
28:9   71, 265
29:2   179
29:15   101, 102
29:19   44
29:28   188

2 Chronicles

6:24   68
7:14   10, 26, 27, 28, 50, 68,
    243, 244
12:1   41
12:7   156
12:14   135
14:11   306
15:15   263
16:9   273
19:3   135
19:7   189
21:6   162
29:30   110
30:7   204
31:21   235, 259
32:7   104
32:7–8 58, 86, 95, 96, 97, 98,
    103, 297, 298
32:8   95, 98, 299
32:20   16, 17
32:26   159
32:27   159
33:12   16, 17, 157, 159
33:26   157

Ezra

6:16   26
7:10   92, 135
9:1   303
9:8   124

Nehemiah

1:4   214
1:5   10
1:6   63, 216
2:5   261
4:14   93, 101, 299
4:17   322
5:9   113
8:10   168, 169
9:4   10
9:13   170
9:32   10

Esther

2:17   126
3:5   225
8:2   115
8:15   41
10:3   9, 207

Job

1:5   44
1:6   25
1:21   70, 293
2:2   202
2:10   64
4:8   134, 273
5:2   166
5:7   296
5:18   50
5:26   14
13:15   105
14:1   178
15:3   17
15:31   134
16:3   17
19:25   18, 19, 77, 298
20:8   83
23:12   17, 28, 31, 32, 33
25:6   67
27:8   279
27:9   216
29:12   121
29:16   121
30:23   76
31:24   328
31:33   9, 44, 45, 111, 267
32:7   14
35:10   131
42:6   121, 234
42:9   9

Psalms

1:1   92, 198, 262
1:2   31, 32, 33

1:3   117, 290
3:8   18, 19, 20, 21
5:11   93, 101, 299
6:2   268
6:5   179
6:9   221
7:1   93, 101, 299
7:9   71
7:17   110
8:3   75
9:9   297
9:10   18, 19, 20, 21, 58, 97,
    98, 297
10:3   70
10:17   221
11:4   273
12:1   221
13:2   90
16:9   85
16:10   39
16:26   15
18:2   19, 110, 250, 259
18:30   102, 103, 104
18:31   259
18:46   259
19:1   75, 196
19:7   172
19:8   30
19:10   17
19:12   266
20:20   15
21:4   87
22:1   217
22:9   85
22:26   210
22:27   91, 302
23:1   22, 45, 56, 258, 265,
    266
23:4   18, 19, 77, 239, 298
23:6   15
25:7   283
25:8   276
25:11   203
27:3   18, 19
27:4   19, 20, 21, 307, 308
27:5   20, 21, 298
27:14   39
29:2   10
30:5   80
31:10   268
31:24   85
32:1   268
32:3   267, 268
32:4   26, 42
32:5   12, 27, 28, 50, 63, 107,
    108, 235, 273
32:6   26
32:10   26

33:1   211
33:3   141, 160, 275
33:6   96, 99, 226, 298
34:1   293
34:5   261
34:8   162
34:10   235, 259
34:11   43
34:12   188
34:15   144
34:18   67
37:5   39
37:7   214
38:18   235
39:3   190
39:5   178, 307
39:6   311
39:12   101, 102
40:3   141, 160, 275
40:8   122
40:9   315
40:9–10   13, 52
41:4   50
42:1   81
42:5   210
42:11   19, 21, 23, 133, 250
43:5   133
44:3   9
44:21   135
44:26   230
45:7   111, 276
46:1   297
46:11   18, 19, 20, 21
49:11   15, 261
49:15   54
49:16–17   70
50:2   10
50:15   50, 296
50:23   17
51:1   134, 235, 244
51:2   50, 134, 266
51:3   12, 27, 28
51:4   63, 69
51:7   134
51:9   267, 276
51:10   40, 51, 75, 136, 232, 237
51:14   26
51:15   316
51:17   26, 67, 200, 201
52:2   294
53:1   23, 24
55:6   250
55:17   16, 17, 218
55:22   45, 209
56:3   39
56:9   18, 19
57:1   189

57:9   210
59:1   133
59:16   297
61:1   217
62:6   133
62:7   110
63:1   81
64:9   83
65:2   218
66:18   221
71:6   210
71:9   14
71:15   13, 315
71:18   14
72:3   208
73:1   136
73:18   305
73:19   70
73:20   83
73:24   18, 19
73:25   18, 19, 20, 21, 23, 250
73:28   27, 28
74:8   107, 108
74:21   210, 211
75:1   263
77:6   131
78:1   134
78:4   155, 156
78:30   70
78:37   161
78:57   204
78:72   183
84:2   81
84:11   124
85:6   243
85:10   9, 208, 247, 324
88:1   217
89:14   276
89:15   199
89:26   110
89:47   178
89:48   76
90:4   88
90:5   178
90:8   258
91:1   84, 250, 298
91:14   17, 261
91:15   252, 296, 297
91:16   14, 87
92:14   117
94:22   259
95:10   98, 110
95:10–11   269
96:1   141, 160
96:6   10
96:9   10
97:2   276
98:1   141, 160

98:2   302
99:4   276
99:6   162, 163
101:5   276
102:3   178
103:8   16
103:12   267, 276
104:4   165
106:35   303
107:2   198, 292
107:19   216
107:28   216
112:5   180
115:4   327
115:17–18   210
116:15   42
116:19   210
118:8–9   93, 101, 299
118:19   210
119:2   312
119:10   263
119:11   209
119:18   30
119:19   101, 102
119:36   73
119:46   13, 52
119:62   131
119:71   42
119:75   42
119:97   29, 31, 32, 33, 188
119:100   28
119:103   17, 162
119:105   30
119:106   165
119:111   17, 44
119:115   165
119:130   30, 67, 134
119:132   189
119:165   32, 33, 207
119:176   265
123:2   261
125:1   102, 103, 104
125:5   26
126:1   80
127:2   16, 17
128:5   188
130:1   217
133:1   303, 304
137:2   210
137:4   80
138:6   159
138:7   243
139:23   135
140:3   294
140:11   258
142:7   86
143:6   81
144:9   141, 160, 275

145:4   14
146:1   211
146:9   101, 102
147:1   211, 293
148:1   293
149:1   160, 293

Proverbs

1:3   170
1:5   31, 32, 33
1:8   191, 192, 205, 206, 321
1:9   73
1:19   70
1:28   222
1:31   134
1:33   25
2:17   26
3:2   87
3:4   125
3:10   17
3:12   42, 82
3:16   14
3:27   118
3:34   160
3:35   163
4:1   155, 156
4:18   315, 316
4:23   135, 136
5:5   12
5:15   160
5:18   12
6:6   176, 177
6:9   176, 177
6:14   82
6:17   106
6:19   82
6:26   12
6:29   11
6:31   236, 237
6:32   11, 12
7:24   223, 224
8:34   58
9:6   198
9:18   12
10:11   294
10:12   267
10:18   276
10:22   247
11:4   311
11:13   276
11:18   134
11:21   285
11:24   289
11:30   92, 279, 280, 320
12:19   106
13:4   176, 177
13:7   69

13:12   82
13:22   14
13:24   42, 204
14:17   16
14:29   16
14:30   166
15:2   294
15:3   273
15:6   247
15:8   221, 268
15:18   16
15:23   91
15:27   70
15:33   160
16:1   116
16:7   207
16:18   225
16:28   82
16:32   16, 64
17:22   224
18:4   282
18:10   64
19:11   16
19:15   321
19:17   48, 180
19:18   204
19:19   16
19:22   187
19:24   176, 177
20:1   286
20:4   176, 177, 311
20:5   282
20:9   136
20:14   285
20:20   191, 192, 205, 321
21:3   170, 200, 201
21:6   106
21:13   222
21:25   176, 177, 311
22:4   160
22:6   14, 43, 232
22:8   240, 241, 242, 243,
    271, 273
22:9   180, 289
22:13   176, 177
22:15   204
22:16   48
22:22   285
23:2   260
23:5   236, 284
23:13   204
23:17   166
23:20   9, 269
23:21   269
23:22   14, 205, 321
23:24   169
23:27   11, 12, 295
23:29   235, 286

23:31–32   9
24:30   311
25:28   16
26:11   26, 269
27:8   41
27:10   254
28:5   102, 103, 104
28:9   217, 268
28:13   107, 108, 234, 243,
    244, 267, 268
28:24   321
28:26   55, 135
29:2   41
29:3   12
29:17   204
29:23   157, 160
29:25   102, 103, 104
30:8   247
30:9   26, 285
30:11   191, 192
30:17   191, 192, 205, 321
30:20   234
30:24   32

Ecclesiastes

2:26   41
3:4   80
3:20   76
4:8   247
5:8   170
5:10   236
5:14   311
5:18   188
6:2   247
7:9   16
9:3   135
9:7   224
9:10   179
10:18   177, 321
11:1   289
11:6   240, 241, 242, 243
12:14   79

Song of Solomon

2:4   179
2:14   250
8:7   184

Isaiah

1:3   73
1:15   217, 221
1:17   170
1:18   50, 267, 276
1:19   199, 313
1:23–24   285
2:3   42

2:5   199
2:8   327
2:11   156, 225
2:17   157
3:11   272
3:15   284, 285
5:11   235, 286
6:3   67
6:5   283
6:8   25, 263, 314
6:10   233
8:14   76
8:19   281
8:20   28
9:6   46, 229
9:7   170
9:15   106
11:6   42
12:2   18, 19, 20, 21, 133, 298
14:24   267
17:10   110, 259
24:20   295
25:1   69
25:4   78, 133
25:8   78
26:3   102, 103, 104
26:3–4   100, 208
26:4   93, 101, 299
26:9   81
27:5   208
28:9–10   43
28:23   223, 224
29:13   41, 116
30:15   28
30:29   131
32:15   46
32:17   20, 21, 208, 247, 324
33:17   141
34:16   31, 32, 33
35:2   169
35:4   104, 124, 230, 232
35:10   278
37:19   327
38:18   179
40:1   61
40:11   42, 44, 45, 56, 110,
    183, 258, 265, 266
40:18   161
40:26   75, 93, 96, 99, 196,
    226, 298
40:29   125, 126, 210, 263,
    310, 311
40:30   125
40:31   13, 14, 37, 38, 232
41:1   232
41:10   19, 21, 23, 250, 263
41:13   124, 126, 128
42:1   9, 57, 126

42:8   105, 325
42:10   141, 160
42:13   79
43:2   104, 124, 230, 232
43:10   190
43:25   267, 276
44:8   190, 207
44:22   267, 276
45:17   51, 75
45:22   201, 261, 326, 327
46:4   14
46:5   161
46:9   326, 327
46:10   267
47:8   328
48:16   49
48:18   247, 324
49:10   58, 282
50:4   91, 190
51:11   83
52:7   198
52:11   198, 262
53:4   57, 124
53:5   34
53:6   24, 25, 33, 34, 35, 36,
    87, 174, 265, 266, 286, 287
53:11   50
53:12   267
54:4   19, 21, 23, 250
54:13   46
54:17   149, 150
55:1   17, 58, 251, 273
55:6   50, 124, 312
55:7   268, 293
55:10   76
55:11   67
56:11   70, 74
57:5   327
57:13   102, 103, 104
57:15   67, 156, 160, 243
57:19   46, 50, 208
57:20   27, 208, 305
58:8   103
59:2   258
59:4   106
59:12   258
59:21   146
60:1   179
61:3   273
61:10   115
61:11   210
62:7   88, 89
63:9   185
65:24   50, 89
66:2   67
66:19   198

Jeremiah

1:7   319
1:8   126
2:13   258
2:19   303
2:28   327
3:15   110, 119
3:22   50
4:3   135
5:8   74
5:14   30
5:31   271
6:16   271
6:17   223, 224
7:9   285
7:11   74
7:23   200, 201
9:3   106
10:24   42
11:11   222
12:5   133
12:13   271, 281
15:16   17, 30, 169, 190
15:21   54
17:7   16, 17, 103, 104, 133
17:7–8   102
17:8   117, 290
17:9   55, 134
17:9–10   135
17:10   135
17:11   70, 284
17:13   92, 258
17:14   50
20:9   190
20:13   211
22:13   284
23:1   265
23:16   201, 227
23:24   160
23:29   30, 31, 67, 190
24:7   95, 98, 299, 312
29:8   83
29:13   312
31:1   95, 96, 98, 103, 104,
    298
31:19   268, 283
32:19   9, 44, 45, 111
33:11   278
33:15   326, 327
35:6   9
36:2   29
42:11   104, 230, 232
46:28   204
48:28   250
50:6   90
51:10   83

Lamentations

1:7 189
5:21 232

Ezekiel

1:3 29
3:9 147, 150
3:17 88, 89, 315, 318, 319
8:10 325
11:19 40, 51, 75, 136
14:6 234
16:9 115
17:8 290
18:4 269
18:20 269
18:27 68
18:30 234
18:31 51, 75, 237
20:39 44
22:12 284, 285
22:25 74
33:6 315, 318, 319
33:7 198
33:15 236, 237
33:31 90, 161
34:2 183
34:16 90, 110, 121
34:26 91
36:24 95, 98
36:25 134, 162, 229
36:26 51, 75, 237
37:4 243

Daniel

1:8 9, 25, 123, 165, 283
1:17 41
2:22 258
2:23 211
2:44 53
2:44–45 244
3:16 16, 17
3:26 263
4:30 225
4:36 17
4:37 157
5:1 70
5:2 28
5:14 41
5:22 157, 225
6:5 75
6:10 211
6:26 301
7:14 244
9:4 10, 63, 214, 266
9:7 10
9:9 283

9:16 10
12:2 79
12:3 17, 92
12:4 156

Hosea

1:7 288, 306
4:2 106
4:6 26
4:10 28
4:11 11, 12
5:15 312
6:1 50, 234
6:5 30
6:6 200, 201
7:8 41
7:14 268
8:7 82, 271
9:8 315, 318, 319
10:12 135, 271
10:13 73, 273, 281
11:4 185
12:8 69
13:2 327
13:12 273
13:14 54, 78
14:4 185
14:7 17
14:9 83

Joel

1:3 43
2:12 312
2:18 288
2:32 252
3:18 258

Amos

5:4 312
8:5 284, 285

Obadiah

1:3 225

Jonah

1:5 233
2:4 27, 28
2:10 240

Micah

2:2 305
3:8 153
4:10 54

6:8 170
6:11 284, 285
7:7 53, 307
7:9 69
7:18 50
7:19 276
7:20 10

Nahum

1:7 20, 21

Habakkuk

3:2 243

Zephaniah

1:12 135
3:17 104, 230, 232, 275

Haggai

1:12 199

Zechariah

1:6 30
3:2 53, 112
3:4 252
4:6 153, 306
4:10 273
7:9 285
7:11 233
8:8 163
10:12 310, 311
12:10 40, 145
13:1 134, 162, 258

Malachi

3:6 182
3:7 27, 28
4:2 57

Matthew

1:21 166
2:2 58, 97, 98
2:11 193, 194
3:1 25
3:2 234
3:3 159
3:8 268
3:11 145
3:17 57
4:1 290
4:10 112, 326, 327
4:17 234
4:19 318

4:22   58, 97, 98, 297
4:24   14, 15, 291
5:6   235, 259
5:8   136, 141
5:10   245
5:11   13, 14, 37, 38
5:11–12   124
5:13   27, 28
5:13–14   59
5:14   315, 316
5:16   103, 152, 313, 314
5:19   135, 174
5:22   16
5:24   114, 115, 230
5:28   11, 12
5:40   169
6:2   195
6:5   224
6:8   183
6:9   220
6:10   220, 221, 285, 313
6:12   114
6:13   289
6:15   113
6:20   120, 138, 140, 246
6:21   228
6:24   41, 79, 328
6:25   16, 17, 93, 94, 95, 99,
       102, 105, 227
6:32   183
6:33   45, 144, 187, 235, 259,
       322
6:34   39, 93, 94, 95, 99, 102,
       105, 208, 227, 296
7:3–5   225
7:7   213, 214, 215, 219
7:12   64
7:16–17   93, 321
7:20   117, 231
7:21   58
7:22–23   143
7:23   92
7:24   64, 251, 290
7:29   57
8:2   93, 94, 95, 99, 102, 105,
       219, 227
8:11   138
8:16   50
8:17   14, 15, 24, 25, 33, 34,
       35, 36, 57, 174, 286, 287,
       291
9:2   14, 15, 291
9:6   14, 15, 291
9:9   109, 315
9:11   275
9:12   58
9:13   56, 57, 66, 121

9:20   93, 94, 95, 99, 102, 105,
       227
9:21   58, 97, 98, 297
9:22   102, 103, 104
9:29   102
9:36   46
10:3   159
10:6   89, 90
10:19 13, 14, 37, 38
10:20 149, 150
10:22 245
10:32 46, 47, 63, 69, 251
10:40 16, 17
11:11 140
11:12 202
11:15 134
11:26 286
11:28 45, 136, 167, 168,
       226, 235, 236
11:28–30   273
12:11 16
12:25 26
12:31 273, 274
12:33 40, 93, 321
12:34 228
12:35 228
12:36 17, 277
12:39–40   240
13:3   76
13:5   199
13:15 233
13:18 280
13:19 255, 256, 257, 258
13:22 28, 71, 72, 245, 246
13:23 28, 31, 32, 33
13:35 258
13:38 39
13:58 98, 300
14:10 264
14:11 202
14:14 46, 50
14:20 104
14:27 207
14:30 308
14:31 82
15:4   191, 192, 205
15:4–5   108
15:5   205
15:5–6   206
15:6   205
15:9   136
15:18 255
15:19 55
15:25 219
15:32 46
16:4   240
16:8   98
16:17 30

16:23 64, 183
16:24 27, 261
16:26 279, 280, 305
17:2   138, 157, 239, 295
17:5   49, 57
17:8   93, 94, 95, 99, 102, 105
17:17 109
17:19 95
17:19–20   93, 94, 99, 102,
       105, 227
17:20 99
17:21 103
18:3   90, 123
18:4   44
18:7   113
18:9   143
18:10 44
18:11 56, 57, 66, 89, 121
18:12 266
18:15 92, 114, 115, 230
18:15–17   267
18:16 277
18:18 113
18:20 327
18:21–22   114
18:33 254
18:35 92
19:2   50
19:14 68, 123, 136, 167,
       168, 313
19:14–15   44
19:16 259
19:21 120, 140
19:24 245, 246
19:29 163
20:16 50
20:19 240
20:20 130, 261
20:28 24, 25, 33, 34, 35, 36,
       53, 174, 286, 287, 307
20:34 46
21:21 82, 95, 98, 103, 104,
       299, 322
21:21–22   102
21:22 218
21:35 202
22:29 28
22:39 179
23:5   195
23:6   261
23:12 157, 159
23:15 57
23:23 115
23:25 74
23:35 267
23:37 46
23:39 55, 56, 57, 59
24:4   309

24:9   131
24:12   26
24:14   58
24:22   83
24:24   201
24:25   91
24:35   64
24:43   196
25:4   111
25:15   119, 262
25:21   168, 169, 244
25:23   168, 169, 244
25:25   289
25:28   288
25:33   266
25:34   163
25:35   323
25:41   92
25:46   141
26:14   188
26:28   267
26:31   45, 265
26:32   237
26:38   50
26:41   112, 289, 310
26:42   200, 212, 218, 220, 221, 313
26:45   116
26:56   29, 111
26:58   318
26:59   276
26:67   131
26:73   144
26:74   225
26:75   189
27:3   73
27:5   233, 288
27:18   166
27:29–30   131, 179
27:34   40
27:63   237
28:18   57
28:18–20   175
28:19   49, 91, 121, 296
28:19–20   302, 316, 317, 318, 320, 321
28:20   125

Mark

1:3   159
1:13   290
1:14   46
1:15   234
1:17   318
1:18   58, 97, 98, 297
1:27   57
1:35   218

1:40   93, 94, 95, 99, 102, 105, 219, 227
3:10   50
3:11   49
3:29   273, 274
4:3   280
4:5   199
4:7   272
4:9   134
4:15   112, 255, 256, 257, 258
4:19   71, 72, 245, 246
4:21   103
4:31   99
4:39   207
5:12   93, 94, 95, 99, 102, 105
5:20   90
5:27   22
5:28   93, 94, 95, 99, 102, 105, 227
5:41   42, 78
6:7   22
6:13   50
6:16   264
6:18   274
6:19   16
6:28   202
6:34   46, 266
6:43   104
6:50   207
7:2   109, 110
7:10   108
7:11   205, 206
7:21   55, 135, 136, 255
7:21–22   135
7:22   13
8:2   46
8:19   104
8:34   27, 261
8:36–37   279
8:37   280, 305
8:38   13, 28, 52
9:2   138, 157, 239, 295
9:19   98, 109
9:24   23, 24
9:31   240
9:34–35   130
9:37   44
9:47   143
9:50   26
10:14   68, 123, 136, 167, 168, 313
10:14–15   90
10:16   44
10:17   90
10:21–22   269
10:25   245, 246
10:30   245
10:34   240

10:37   130
10:44   130
10:48   58, 97, 98
11:13   322
11:23   82, 95
11:23–24   93, 94, 99, 102, 105, 227
11:24   215
11:26   113
12:30–31   174
12:33   263
13:31   64
14:8   264
14:10   188
14:28   237
14:35   218
14:36   122, 200, 212
14:37   116
14:38   112, 289, 308, 310
14:54   318
14:72   189
15:10   166
15:17   131, 179
15:19   131, 179
15:22   40
15:41   321
16:14   98
16:15   91, 121, 176, 302, 316, 317, 318, 320, 321
16:16   23, 24
16:17   294, 322
16:20   48
18:16   167, 168

Luke

1:15   9, 146, 193, 194
1:16–17   48
1:17   149, 150
1:18–20   252
1:28   9
1:33   244
1:35   153
1:41   146
1:44   146
1:48   313
1:52   159
1:72   10
1:77   30
2:7   51
2:14   46, 229
2:17   42
2:19   209
2:23   193, 194
2:35   135
2:40   127, 130
2:41   148
2:42   42

2:51   205, 206, 217
2:52   50
3:4   159
3:8   268
3:14   66, 268
4:1   290
4:12   15
4:14   148
4:18   50, 57, 191
4:40   14, 15, 291
5:6   58, 97, 98
5:12   219
5:16   218
5:17   50
5:20   97
5:24   219
5:30   275
5:32   56, 57, 66, 121
6:17   14, 291
6:17–19   15
6:22   168
6:23   204
6:24   69
6:32   131
6:35   169, 180
6:38   289
6:41–42   225
6:43   93, 321
6:47   251
7:13   46
7:21   14, 15, 291
7:28   140
7:33   9
7:34   275
7:37   227, 319
7:47   122, 185
7:47–48   14, 15, 291
8:3   321
8:5   76, 280
8:6   199
8:8   134
8:12   255, 256, 257, 258
8:14   92, 272
8:15   268
8:44   93, 94, 95, 99, 102, 105, 227
8:48   95, 98, 102, 103, 104, 299
8:54   42, 78
9:1   14, 15, 291
9:9   264
9:17   104
9:23   27, 261
9:25   15, 261, 279
9:26   13, 52
9:41   98, 109
9:42   50
9:46   130

9:62   111
10:17   22, 322
10:19   176
10:21   286
10:25   259
10:33   254
10:39   58, 81, 188
10:41   236
10:42   307, 308
11:1   216
11:2   220, 221, 285, 313
11:4   133, 289
11:5   218
11:8   216
11:9   213, 214, 215, 219
11:13   264
11:26   26
11:27   57
11:29–30   240
11:33   103
11:39   74
11:43   15, 261
11:46   39
12:4   46
12:5   143, 201
12:8   46, 47, 63, 69
12:10   273, 274
12:11–12   149, 150
12:15   73
12:17   236
12:18   74
12:20   70, 187, 284
12:21   245, 246
12:22   39
12:23   138
12:30   144, 183
12:31   235, 259
12:32   93, 94, 95, 99, 102, 105, 136, 140, 167, 168, 227
12:33   120, 247
12:39   196
12:43   322
12:58   114
13:3   234
13:5   234
13:10   247, 248, 249, 250
13:19   99
13:34   46
14:11   158
14:13   164
14:18   23, 24
14:18–19   92
14:21   164
14:23   314
14:32   208
15:2   275
15:4   56, 57, 66, 89, 90, 121
15:7   279

15:10   279
15:11   176, 203
15:12   278
15:16   26
15:18   27, 63, 69
15:20   50
15:21   63
15:22   115
15:24   89, 204
16:9   143, 265
16:11   247
16:13   328
16:14   72
16:15   71, 135, 195, 234
16:22   70
16:23   143
16:25   188, 189, 323
16:29   28
17:3   92, 234
17:6   93, 94, 95, 99, 102, 105, 227
17:12   199
17:29   29
17:32   29, 111
18:1   217, 218
18:5   218
18:7   122
18:11   69, 225
18:13   189, 220, 283
18:14   158
18:15–16   44
18:16   68, 123, 136, 167, 168, 313
18:16–17   90
18:18   259
18:20   207
18:22   120, 140, 247, 269
18:24   92
18:25   245, 246
18:29   235, 259
18:31   29
18:33   240
18:38   58, 97, 98
19:6   67
19:7   209
19:8   67
19:10   45, 50, 56, 57, 66, 89, 90, 121, 258, 265
19:17   244
20:35   39, 209
21:33   64
21:34   236, 286
21:36   222, 310
22:3   15, 261
22:24   130
22:32   133, 256, 258
22:40   289
22:41   218

22:42 122, 212
22:44 217
22:46 116, 133, 289, 310
22:47 195
22:48 188
22:54 318
22:61 189
23:33 40
23:34 179
23:42 22, 252
23:43 50, 254
24:7 40, 240
24:8 189
24:9 46, 47
24:10 321
24:25 98
24:27 29, 164
24:28 163
24:39 23, 24
24:44 29
24:45 88
24:47 91, 316, 317, 318, 320, 321
24:47–48 302
24:48 88, 121

John

1:1–2 49
1:3 96, 99, 226, 298
1:4 171
1:9 93
1:11 51
1:12 17, 23, 24
1:13 231
1:16 127, 128, 129
1:17 124, 125, 126, 171, 172, 175, 276
1:23 159
1:29 24, 25, 33, 34, 35, 36, 57, 174, 286, 287
1:33 191
1:41 46, 47
1:41–42 42
1:45 31, 32, 33, 42, 91, 166
1:46 69
1:47 276
2:5 217
2:17 79, 328, 329
2:21 294
3:2 315
3:3 39, 161, 197, 231
3:5 162, 310
3:10 40
3:14 29
3:15 298
3:16 55, 95, 96, 98, 103, 104, 121, 181, 184, 298

3:19 28, 134
3:30 53, 131, 157, 264
3:36 18, 19, 23, 24, 252, 301
4:5 315
4:10 116, 279, 310
4:14 17, 58, 146, 149, 282, 310
4:18 227, 319
4:23 149
4:24 327
4:29 42, 46, 47, 90
4:34 57, 122
4:36 272
5:15 50
5:23 49
5:24 18, 19, 20, 21, 136, 167, 168, 232, 272, 298
5:26 49
5:29 79
5:30 57
5:35 158, 315, 316
5:39 28, 29, 31, 32, 33, 259, 299
5:46 29
6:13 104
6:20 207
6:26 161
6:27 235, 259
6:33 17
6:34 125
6:35 58
6:38 57
6:39 20, 21, 80, 298
6:40 19, 21, 23, 250
6:51 198
6:54 88
6:63 112, 134
6:64 161
6:67 26
6:68 44
6:69 58, 97, 98, 297
6:70 39, 300
7:15 144
7:17 276
7:29 228
7:37 17, 45, 167, 168, 251, 258
7:37–38 282
7:38 58, 116
7:38–39 146, 282
8:7 225
8:11 227, 319
8:12 199
8:20 51
8:21 140
8:29 57
8:31 58
8:32 50

8:36 50
8:39 93, 321
8:40 50
8:42 185
8:44 39, 106
8:45 271, 274
8:51 17, 239
8:56 53, 58, 97, 98, 201, 307
8:58 49
9:4 321
9:7 199
9:10 69
9:11 292
9:41 179
10:1 36, 166
10:7 166
10:9 139
10:10 282, 310
10:11 45, 56, 258, 265, 266, 320
10:14 265
10:15 52
10:27 18, 19, 20, 21
10:28 20, 21, 80, 298, 299
10:28–30 22
10:29 19, 21, 23, 250
10:30 49, 50
10:33 50
11:4 46
11:25 19, 21, 23, 46, 77, 238, 239, 250
11:39 218
11:43 42, 78
12:6 74, 285
12:7 264
12:22 166
12:24 50, 237
12:26 17, 141, 142
12:27 212
12:32 53, 185, 307, 318
12:36 315, 316
12:42 64
12:43 195
12:50 134
13:4 130
13:14 39
13:34 186
13:34–35 116, 179, 183
13:35 95, 96, 98, 103, 104, 185, 298
14:2 137
14:3 46, 50, 138, 142
14:6 20, 21, 52, 139, 166
14:9 49
14:12 322
14:17 23, 24
14:23 136, 167, 168
14:26 151

14:27   46, 207, 208
14:30   290
15:3   31
15:4   210
15:5   40, 263
15:6   28
15:8   117
15:12   186
15:14   28
15:15   50
15:16   117, 212, 214, 319
15:19   324
15:19–20   323
15:26   151, 296
15:27   88
16:2   245
16:8   145
16:9   98
16:13   151, 152
16:14   155
16:20   80
16:22   278
16:23   212, 214
16:24   213, 218
16:33   46, 207, 208, 245
17:1   220
17:3   93, 299
17:4   57
17:7   88
17:11   18, 19, 305
17:12   18, 19, 20, 21
17:13   20, 21
17:14   323
17:17   162
17:19   59
17:21   49, 183
17:22   295, 305
17:23   59
17:24   141, 142, 185
17:26   50
19:2   131, 179
19:17   40
19:24   29
19:34   179
20:21   207, 208
20:27   23, 24, 27, 28, 82, 98
20:28   26, 98, 99
20:31   31, 252
21:16   265
21:16–17   110, 182
21:25   43

Acts

1:7   294
1:8   88, 91, 148, 154, 175, 190, 210, 264
1:14   217, 222

1:16   29
1:18   288
1:24   71
2:3   145
2:4   147, 148, 150, 154, 191
2:14   151
2:21   312
2:23   40
2:24   95, 96, 98, 103, 104
2:31–34   39
2:32   176
2:38   268
2:39   68, 316, 317, 318, 320, 321
2:40   262
2:41   322
2:42   111
2:47   314
3:6   166, 322
3:15   163
3:16   102, 103, 104
3:17   29
3:19   233, 267, 276
3:23   88
4:8   147, 148, 150
4:12   139, 166
4:13   48, 144
4:31   30, 148
4:32   183
4:33   126, 176, 314, 322
4:36   9, 84
5:3   106, 112, 277
5:4   74
5:5   73
5:10   73
5:15   99, 227
5:30   57
5:31   53, 307
5:32   163, 176
5:41   209, 250
5:42   48
6:5   147, 150
6:7   199
6:8   58, 97, 98, 126, 153, 176
6:10   41, 149, 150
6:13   276
7:10   41
7:51   264
7:56   22
8:3   200
8:4   48
8:5   91
8:18   161
8:20   311
8:26   90
8:30   88, 166
8:35   88
8:37   58, 97, 98, 297, 312

8:39   147, 150, 153
9:5   296, 315
9:6   67, 68, 200
9:15   83, 319
9:27   9, 84
9:36   40
9:40   218, 322
10:19   89, 153
10:35   9, 53, 285
10:36   46
10:39   57, 176
10:43   312
11:1   31, 32, 33
11:12   89, 153
11:23   44, 165
11:24   146, 264, 314
11:28   153
12:5   85
12:14   313
13:4   153
13:10   39
13:14   145
13:18   98
13:27   28, 29
13:36   14
13:39   252
13:43   126
13:45   166
13:46   121
13:47   316, 317, 318, 320, 321
13:48   314
14:2   145
14:17   160
14:22   208
14:27   91
15:17   160
15:28   153
16:5   61
16:7   153
16:14   315, 321
16:15   80
16:18   322
16:25   102, 131
16:30   259
16:31   315
17:3   88
17:5   145
17:11   31, 32, 33, 111
17:13   145
17:21   31, 135, 271
17:23   190, 326
17:24   96, 99, 226, 298
17:27   160
17:29   58, 105, 161, 296, 325
18:5   153
18:12   145
18:25   48

18:26   321
19:12   14, 15, 291
19:18   92, 266
19:21   153
19:26   161
20:9   262
20:24   87, 168, 169
20:28   91, 110, 183
20:32   127
20:33   70
21:4   153
21:5   86
21:8   88, 89
21:9   146
21:14   313
22:3   172
22:15   176
22:21   263
23:1   65
24:14   63, 69, 86
24:16   65
24:25   90, 170, 244
24:26   191
26:14   296
26:18   30, 53, 104, 112, 230,
    232, 234, 296
26:20   267, 268
26:23   77, 239, 315, 318, 319
26:25   79, 86
26:28   90
27:25   98
28:9   14, 15, 291
28:15   86
28:27   233

Romans

1:13   319
1:16   48, 51, 52, 75, 76, 104,
    230, 232, 237, 292, 315
1:17   252
1:18   28, 285
1:19   96, 99, 226, 298
1:19–20   75, 93
1:20   160, 196
1:23   105, 161
1:25   327
1:27   11, 12
1:29   72
1:30   205
1:32   170
2:5   170, 273
2:11   189
2:15   65, 66
2:29   195
3:3   300, 301
3:4   99, 132
3:9   132

3:10   270, 291
3:22   252
3:22–23   270
3:23   69, 132, 291
3:24   126, 127, 128, 203, 251
3:27   36
3:31   174
4:2   36, 104, 230, 232
4:3   93, 101, 299
4:4   82
4:5   252, 254
4:7   113
4:10   100, 105, 110
4:16   127, 128, 129, 175, 251
4:17   310, 311
4:20   14, 23, 24, 98, 300
4:24   252
4:25   170
5:1   46, 100, 104, 105, 110,
    207, 208, 230, 232
5:2   124, 139, 252
5:3   131
5:5   18, 19, 20, 21, 180, 225,
    226
5:8   87, 185, 275
5:12   76, 132
5:14   9, 44, 45, 111
5:15   124
5:16   170
5:17   244
5:18   170
5:20   175
5:20–21   126
5:21   88, 172, 272
6:1   68
6:5   238, 239
6:6   26, 196, 197, 201, 271
6:13   28
6:14   126, 127, 128, 172, 175
6:16   79
6:17   95, 98, 199, 299
6:18   50, 269, 270
6:19   112
6:20   269, 270
6:21   272
6:22   50, 269, 270
6:23   18, 19, 132, 269, 272,
    298
7:7   73, 132
7:10–11   173
7:11   255
7:18   112
8:2   50, 269, 270
8:4   112
8:5   53
8:9   40, 111
8:11   77, 239
8:13   112

8:15   39, 115, 197
8:17   136, 167, 168, 311
8:21   39
8:24   95, 96, 98, 103, 104,
    298
8:25   96, 99, 141, 226, 298
8:26   103, 145, 221
8:28   227, 228, 267
8:29   59
8:29–30   295
8:33   83, 113, 170
8:34   80, 219
8:38   19, 20, 21, 23, 250
8:38–39   202
8:39   80, 121
9:1   65
9:11   267
9:26   95, 96, 98, 103, 104
9:30   129
9:32   104, 230, 232
9:33   19, 21, 23, 76, 250, 312
10:2   328, 329
10:8   222, 224
10:9   46, 47
10:9–10   234
10:10   254, 312
10:13   23, 24, 252, 312
10:14   89, 198
10:17   100, 134
11:6   36, 128
11:8   28, 29, 116
11:14   222
11:20   225, 300
11:33   28
12:1–2   308
12:2   60
12:6   118, 119, 126, 127,
    262, 282
12:9   186
12:10   179, 183, 190
12:11   179
12:12   222
12:18   114
13:2   202
13:5   65
13:7   118
13:8   179, 185
13:9   73
13:10   64, 174, 179
13:11   116
13:11–12   243, 244
13:12   243
14:1   117
14:7–8   40
14:8   285
14:11   46, 47
14:17   145, 208, 235, 247,
    259, 324

14:21   64
15:1   39, 75, 110, 117
15:4   29, 84
15:5   61
15:9   46, 47, 63
15:11   210
15:13   145, 207, 208
15:16   315, 318, 319
15:19   52
15:29   52, 315
15:30   85
15:31   9
16:18   161
16:20   53, 112

1 Corinthians

1:2   252
1:3   207, 208
1:7   55, 56, 57, 59
1:8   76
1:10   303, 304
1:17   90
1:18   23, 24
1:23   76, 88
1:24   123
1:28   310, 311
1:29   36
1:30   204
2:2   52
2:4   149, 150
2:5   306
2:8   29
2:10   150, 151
2:11   282
2:14   156, 300
3:2   17, 93, 321
3:9   191, 321
3:11   166
3:14   81
3:16   37, 148, 154
4:2   80
4:5   17, 79, 92, 210
4:8   69
4:17   80, 244
4:21   109, 110
5:2   299
5:9   92
5:11   74
6:7   109, 110, 114
6:8   115
6:9   134
6:10   74
6:11   134, 162
6:15   19, 21, 23
6:19   37, 294
6:19–20   154
7:3   160

7:35   223, 224
7:37   123, 165
8:7   65, 66
8:10   285
9:19   92
9:22   222, 279, 302
9:24   112, 307, 308
9:25   163
9:26   179
9:27   53
10:6   26, 28, 309
10:8   26
10:10   131
10:12   28, 290, 291, 309, 310
10:13   13, 14, 37, 38, 53, 124, 133, 261, 270, 289
10:16   24, 25, 33, 34, 35, 36, 174, 286, 287
10:21   79, 303
10:30   91
10:31   130, 202
11:22   113
11:31   63
11:34   203
12:1   118, 282
12:7   118
12:9   119, 128
12:12   303, 304
12:28   119
12:31   119, 262
13:1   191, 293, 316
13:3   185
13:4   166, 171, 278
13:7   180
13:12   171, 196
13:13   186
14:1   118
14:12   118, 262, 282
14:40   203
15:1   123
15:3   24, 25, 33, 34, 35, 36, 174, 286, 287
15:3–4   34, 68, 239
15:8   239
15:9   158
15:10   124, 126
15:12–23   239
15:14   68, 237, 238
15:22   9, 44, 45, 77, 111, 239, 270
15:23   55, 56, 57, 59
15:26   78
15:42   238, 239
15:42–44   39
15:45   9, 44, 45, 111
15:49   76, 141, 142
15:50   39
15:52   39

15:55   77, 239
15:58   59, 60, 209, 263, 322, 323
16:2   119

2 Corinthians

1:3   61
1:4   13, 14, 37, 38, 85, 250
1:6   84, 320
1:11   85
1:12   65
1:18   301
1:20   226
1:22   155
2:10   113
2:11   255, 256, 257, 258
2:14   136
2:17   292
3:2   210
3:5   13, 14, 37, 38, 124, 210, 263
3:6   134
3:7   144, 173
3:13   157
3:15   28
3:18   59, 171
4:2   90
4:3   89
4:4   28, 29, 202, 255, 256, 257, 258
4:15–16   125
4:17   125, 250
4:17–18   141
4:18   118, 306
5:1   18, 22, 137, 306
5:7   140, 171
5:8–9   321
5:9   9, 53, 285
5:10   17, 277
5:11   314
5:13   79
5:14   40, 180, 184, 185
5:16   308
5:17   40, 51, 75, 136, 198, 225, 226, 237, 271
5:18–19   229
5:20   113, 314
5:21   24, 25, 33, 34, 35, 36, 40, 174, 286, 287
6:1   191, 279, 314, 321
6:2   9
6:6   180, 186
6:14   79, 92, 187, 303
6:15   112
6:17   111, 198, 229, 262
7:1   198, 226, 262
7:4   250

7:7   83, 146
8:1   119
8:9   126
8:12   120
8:18   211
8:21   268
9:2   79, 328, 329
9:5   119
9:6   240, 241, 242, 243, 289
9:7   120
9:8   59, 60
9:10   76, 289
10:1   109, 110
10:3   112
10:4   309
10:4–5   306
10:7   71
11:3   74, 182, 255, 256, 257,
    258
11:22   86
11:30   13, 14, 37, 38, 124
12:5   13, 14, 37, 38, 124
12:7   139
12:8   217
12:9   124, 263, 310, 311
12:9–10   124, 308
12:10   250
12:11   86
12:14–15   320
12:20   26
12:21   13
13:4   180
13:5   19, 21, 23
13:7   268
13:14   49, 296

Galatians

1:6   26, 123
2:8   104
2:9   111
2:16   252, 254
2:20   40, 80, 182
2:21   175
3:3   100, 105, 110
3:10   132, 174
3:13   24, 25, 33, 34, 35, 36,
    40, 54, 57, 230, 286, 287
3:16   197
3:22   132
3:24   82, 104, 174, 230, 232
3:26   136, 167, 168
4:6   197
4:7   136, 167, 168
4:16   274
5:1   50, 270
5:4   175
5:6   96, 99, 226, 298, 316

5:7   178
5:13   39, 190
5:14   64, 179, 186
5:16   11, 12, 112, 260
5:18   153, 172
5:19   12, 13
5:20   16
5:21   235
5:22   117, 146, 169, 231, 260
5:22–23   117
5:23   109, 110
5:24   112
5:25   146, 261
6:1   27, 109, 110, 225
6:2   39, 116, 117
6:7   134
6:7–8   240, 241, 242, 243,
    281, 323
6:8   273, 281
6:9   91, 209
6:10   118, 169, 201, 202, 289
6:12   245
6:14   132
6:15   51, 75, 237

Ephesians

1:3   282
1:4   17, 40, 51, 75, 237
1:6   9, 53, 124
1:7   203
1:11   59, 267
1:13   140, 155
1:14   204
1:17–18   30
1:18   59, 138, 186
2:2   244
2:4   121, 182
2:5   69, 251
2:8   103
2:8–9   36, 104, 129, 230,
    232, 251
2:10   40, 51, 75, 237, 313,
    314
2:13   24, 25, 33, 34, 35, 36,
    174, 229, 286, 287
2:14   207, 208
2:15   51, 75, 237
2:17   208
2:18   52
3:6   136, 167, 168
3:7   319
3:8   129, 158
3:11   267
3:16   13, 14, 37, 38, 124, 210,
    263
3:18–19   180
4:2   190

4:3   303, 304
4:7   118, 268
4:11   119
4:11–12   262
4:12   59, 60, 119
4:13   303, 304
4:15   255
4:17   60, 187
4:22   196, 197, 201, 271
4:24   59, 111, 229
4:25   106, 276
4:26   16
4:27   256, 258
4:28   268, 322
4:29   276
4:30   150, 155
4:31   187
4:32   113, 171, 278
5:2   24, 25, 33, 34, 35, 36,
    174, 180, 182, 286, 287
5:3   12, 72
5:5   12
5:6   134, 201, 227
5:8   59, 103, 146, 199, 313,
    314
5:9   117, 146
5:11   92, 223
5:14   243
5:15   144, 308
5:16   179
5:18   147, 148, 150, 235, 264
5:18–20   146
5:19   275
5:20   293
5:21   286
5:25   160
5:26   162
6:1   321
6:1–3   205
6:2   108, 207
6:4   155, 156, 232
6:8   270
6:10   223, 263
6:11   256, 258, 270
6:12   202, 283, 309
6:13   133, 256, 258
6:18   217, 221
6:19   189, 190

Philippians

1:3   201, 202
1:6   18, 19, 298
1:11   211
1:14   292
1:19   85
1:20   18, 19, 20, 21
1:21   76

1:22   272
1:23   142
1:27   308
1:27–28   48
1:29   288
2:1   46
2:2   303, 304
2:3   130, 209, 286
2:10   199
2:11   46, 47
2:12   93
2:12–13   177
2:15   48, 59, 103, 315, 316
2:15–16   313, 314
2:20   59, 60
3:3   112
3:6   328, 329
3:8   186, 308
3:9   161
3:10   186
3:12   171
3:13   112, 308
3:13–14   307
3:14   48, 309
3:19   72, 260
3:20   53, 76, 137, 138, 307,
   308
3:21   39
4:6   16, 17, 39, 45, 124, 293
4:7   46, 207, 208
4:10   201, 202
4:11   66
4:13   13, 14, 37, 38, 53, 124,
   210, 263, 300, 310, 311
4:15   119
4:19   124, 125, 126, 129

Colossians

1:5   138
1:10   59, 60, 117, 255
1:11   13, 14, 37, 38, 124, 263,
   310, 311
1:12–13   22
1:18   49, 53, 77, 239
1:20   46, 207, 208, 229
1:27–28   309
2:3   113
2:4   201
2:5   209
2:7   209, 263
2:8   201
3:1   40
3:1–2   143
3:3   80
3:4   17, 295
3:5   70, 72
3:8   16

3:9   106, 196, 197, 201, 271,
   299
3:10   111, 229, 255
3:12–14   276
3:13   75, 92, 114, 179
3:14   179
3:16   188, 275
3:17   130, 293
3:19   160
3:20   205, 321
3:21   155, 156
3:22   322
3:23   179
4:2   222
4:3   85
4:5   308
4:6   17
4:7   80
4:13   87, 328, 329

1 Thessalonians

1:3   59, 60, 209
1:4   84
1:5   202
1:6   31, 32, 33, 123, 168, 169
1:7–8   210
1:8   198, 292
1:9   234
1:10   55, 56, 57, 59
2:2   202
2:3   140
2:4   60
2:5   70, 72
2:8   320
2:11   67, 87
2:12   309
2:13   28, 31, 32, 33, 93, 101,
   123, 299
2:14   61, 322
2:19   55, 56, 57, 59, 279, 280
2:20   169
3:3–4   208
3:6   322
3:12   263
3:13   55, 56, 57, 59
4:3   10, 11, 13
4:6   285
4:9   179, 183, 190
4:11   322
4:15   55, 56, 57, 59
4:16   190
4:17   142
5:6   116
5:14   39
5:15   109
5:17   131, 214, 222
5:18   293

5:19   150, 154
5:28   110

2 Thessalonians

1:3   209, 263
1:4   61
1:7   17, 273
1:9   122
1:11   309
2:1   55, 56, 57, 59
2:10   28, 71
2:14   118, 295
2:16   182
3:1   198
3:3   133
3:9   109
3:10   311, 321
3:12   322
3:13   209
3:14   92

1 Timothy

1:2   244
1:4   17
1:5   64, 98, 179, 316
1:9   65, 66, 291
1:10   187
1:13   29
1:14   13, 14, 37, 38, 124
1:15   65, 158, 164, 270
1:18   309
1:19   95, 98, 299
2:3   74
2:5   52, 166
2:10   40
2:14   9, 44, 45, 111
3:1   59, 60, 80
3:3   70, 74, 191
3:6   225
3:6–7   290, 291
3:8   191
4:1   28
4:2   65, 66, 106, 135, 187
4:3   274
4:7   17
4:14   282
5:10   59, 60
5:18   81
5:20   223
6:4   17
6:6   70
6:7   70
6:8   66, 70
6:9   72, 74, 236, 311
6:10   72, 73, 202, 328, 329
6:17   120, 245, 246
6:18   40, 169

2 Timothy

1:2   244
1:5   68, 155, 156, 193, 194, 217, 317
1:8   13, 52
1:9   36, 267
1:10   78
1:12   20, 21, 52
1:15   111
1:16   52
2:2   163
2:3   261
2:3–4   264
2:10   320
2:12   260, 288
2:13   122
2:14   17
2:16   17, 31
2:19   84, 133, 155
2:23   17
2:25   109, 110
3:1   271
3:2   205
3:4   86, 328
3:5   31, 32, 33
3:12   245, 288
3:15   155, 156
3:17   306
4:2   91, 222, 224, 269, 314
4:3   271
4:5   59, 60, 88, 89, 198
4:8   17, 163, 201, 265
4:10   111, 244
4:11   9
4:14   162
4:16   111
4:17   19, 21, 23, 250, 308
4:18   18, 19, 20, 21, 270

Titus

1:2   187
1:5   203
1:6   229
1:7   191
1:8   171, 278
1:9   223
1:11   74
1:13   223, 269
1:14   17
2:1   125
2:2   260
2:7   40
2:11   124, 125, 126
2:13   49, 53, 307
2:14   24, 25, 33, 34, 35, 36, 40, 48, 54, 162, 174, 208, 230, 264, 286, 287, 306

3:1   59, 60, 82, 202
3:4   288
3:5   36, 162
3:7   136, 167, 168
3:8   40
3:9   17
3:15   127, 128

Philemon

7   84

Hebrews

1:3   25
1:7   165
1:8   244
1:11   306
2:1   69, 146
2:3   197
2:9   128, 129
2:10   53, 201, 307
2:12   211
2:15   50, 270
2:18   290
3:1   47
3:12   135, 300
3:13   26, 71, 255, 321
3:13–14   124
3:14   209
3:15   28, 321
3:19   102, 104
4:2   98
4:4   247, 248, 249, 250
4:6   300
4:9   59, 60, 235
4:10   235
4:11   23, 24, 290, 291, 300
4:12   30, 67, 198
4:13   71
4:15   57, 219, 290
4:16   13, 14, 37, 38, 53, 124
5:7   122, 217
5:8–9   200
5:9   53, 307
5:12   17
6:10   59, 60, 82, 265, 289
6:11   20, 21
6:17   311
6:18   85
6:19   18, 19, 20, 21, 133
7:25   18, 19, 50, 52, 80, 219
7:26   57, 171
9:14   134
9:22   34
9:24   52
9:27   76, 170

9:28   24, 25, 33, 34, 35, 36, 53, 57, 174, 267, 286, 287, 307
10:14   53, 307
10:22   19, 21, 23, 96, 99, 226, 298
10:24   40, 86
10:28   197
10:34   48, 140
10:35   98
10:38   98
10:39   96, 99, 226, 298
11:1   104
11:1–2   95, 96, 98, 103, 298
11:3   96, 99, 226, 298
11:6   23, 24, 96, 99, 226, 298
11:7   84
11:10   83, 137, 138
11:11   14, 98, 299
11:13   95, 98, 101, 102, 103, 104, 298
11:16   306
11:21   76, 139
11:25   141, 328
11:26   81
11:31   23, 24, 93, 321
11:32   162, 163
11:34   101, 102
12:1   307
12:2   100, 112, 261, 308
12:2–3   53, 201, 307
12:3   131, 202
12:6   42, 82
12:7   155, 156, 204
12:9   61
12:13   110, 117
12:14   141
12:15   125
12:22   137, 138
12:23–24   141, 142
12:25   178
12:28   53, 137
12:29   131
13:1   179, 183
13:2   101, 102
13:4   10, 11, 13
13:5   16, 17, 66, 72, 191, 208
13:5–6   70
13:6   39, 45, 144
13:7   265, 266
13:8   182
13:9   127, 128, 130
13:12   40
13:14   137, 138
13:15   211
13:16   169
13:17   169
13:18   110, 151

James

1:5   132, 219, 229
1:6   23, 24, 95, 98, 102, 103, 104, 215, 222, 299
1:8   41
1:9   156, 159
1:10   178, 307
1:12   17, 42, 261
1:14   255
1:15   269
1:17   182
1:18   30, 231
1:19   16
1:21   31, 32, 33
1:22   58
1:23   156, 171
1:25   59, 60, 95, 98, 299
1:26   277
1:27   231
2:5   164, 311
2:6   285
2:8   39, 64, 179, 185
2:10   174, 253
2:11   295
2:13   75
2:18   93, 321
2:20   64
2:21   25, 58, 97, 98
2:21–22   297
2:23   93, 101, 299
2:24   50
2:25   58, 97, 98
3:2   277
3:3   294
3:12   93, 321
3:13   308
3:15   74
3:17   186
3:18   208, 247, 324
4:1   111
4:1–2   255
4:3   212, 221, 222, 328
4:4   303
4:5   166
4:6   126, 127, 130
4:7   256, 258, 286
4:8   243, 244
4:10   156, 157, 158
4:11   187, 276
4:14   70, 178, 307
4:17   169
5:3   284
5:4   284, 285
5:9   120
5:10   162, 163
5:11   42, 46
5:12   290, 291
5:15   103
5:15–16   14, 15, 291
5:16   63, 92, 214, 215, 217
5:16–18   215
5:17–18   307
5:19   117
5:20   92, 180, 267, 279

1 Peter

1:1   101, 102
1:2   33, 35, 36, 174, 286, 287
1:3   77, 80, 85, 231, 238, 239
1:4   39, 120, 163
1:5   20, 21, 298
1:6–7   133
1:7   99, 226, 298
1:7–8   306
1:8   298
1:14   199
1:17   82
1:18   262
1:19   33, 35, 36, 174, 286, 287
1:19–20   34
1:22   40, 186, 308
1:23   67, 231, 252, 253
1:24   178, 307
2:2   17, 31, 255
2:3   162
2:4   15
2:6   93, 101, 299
2:7   23, 24, 96
2:9   40, 103, 187, 208, 313, 314
2:10   124, 140
2:11   101, 102
2:12   40, 268
2:16   270
2:21   53, 57, 307
2:24   24, 25, 33, 34, 35, 36, 40, 50, 57, 174, 286, 287
2:25   45, 56, 265, 266
3:2   84
3:7   114, 160
3:10   188
3:11   169
3:12   273
3:15   69
3:16   65
3:17   288
3:18   33, 35, 36, 87, 174, 239, 286, 287
4:1   33, 35, 36, 174, 286, 287
4:2   229, 268
4:7   222
4:8   180, 316
4:9   120
4:10   118
4:11   130, 211
4:12   245
4:13–14   13, 14, 37, 38
4:16   52
4:17   178
4:19   19, 21, 23, 250, 288
5:2   70, 110, 183
5:4   17, 118, 163, 247, 265, 266
5:5   126, 127, 158, 286
5:6   130, 157, 159, 160
5:7   16, 17, 39, 45, 53, 61, 144, 168, 169, 297
5:8   255, 256, 257, 258
5:8–9   270
5:10   255, 295
5:12   123

2 Peter

1:1   95, 96, 98, 103, 104
1:3   118
1:4   59, 111, 209, 226, 229
1:5   268
1:8   95, 96, 98, 103, 104
1:9   28, 31, 32, 33, 69
1:10   84
1:19   28, 30
2:1   271
2:3   311
2:4   143
2:9   133, 170, 289
2:10   12, 260
2:13   328
2:14   12, 41, 72, 73
2:15   73, 111
2:22   269
3:2   162, 163
3:3–4   57
3:4   209
3:5   96, 99, 226, 298
3:8   88
3:9   89
3:16   41
3:17   290, 291
3:18   17, 127, 255, 263

1 John

1:1   162
1:2   190
1:3   42, 50, 88, 111
1:7   33, 35, 36, 111, 174, 199, 266, 275, 286, 287
1:8   107, 108, 132, 291
1:9   113, 134, 179, 266, 267, 268
2:1   27, 52, 57

2:3   171, 186
2:5   19, 21, 23, 186
2:12   113
2:15   96, 143, 324
2:16   15, 20, 21, 260, 261
2:17   12, 20, 21, 307
2:19   135
2:20   151
2:25   226
2:27   151
2:28   47
3:1   324
3:1–2   197
3:2   17, 18, 19, 59, 141, 298
3:3   142
3:5   33, 35, 36, 174, 267, 286, 287
3:8   39
3:9   68
3:10   183
3:12   187
3:13   53
3:14   186, 252
3:15   195, 196
4:4   53
4:5   323
4:7   186, 275
4:8   121, 184, 185
4:9   180
4:10   87, 122, 182, 275
4:13   19, 21, 23
4:14   87
4:15   46, 47, 69, 312
4:16   121, 184, 185
4:18   19, 21, 23, 83, 185
4:19   122
4:21   39
5:1   197, 252, 312
5:4   53, 111
5:5   111
5:6   310
5:7   49, 296
5:9–10   292
5:10   23, 24, 301
5:11   252, 299
5:12   23, 24
5:13   18, 19, 20, 21
5:14   47
5:16   273, 274
5:19   110
5:20   49, 259
5:21   327

3 John

1:3   279
1:9   261
4   169
5   82
9   15

Jude

7   122
11   73
12   117
12–13   305
14   55, 56, 57, 59
15   223, 269
16   131
18   244
20   221
21   122, 201
22   278
24   20, 21, 52, 250, 298

Revelation

1:5   33, 35, 36, 77, 122, 174, 239, 286, 287
1:7   55, 56, 57, 59
1:8   53, 307
1:11   53, 307
1:17   53, 307
1:18   143
1:20   315, 316
2:4   28, 269
2:5   27, 28, 63, 162, 234, 268
2:8   53, 307
2:10   288
2:11   163
2:14   73
2:16   234
2:19   322
3:3   234
3:4   309
3:5   64, 138, 143
3:12   142
3:14   292
3:16   162
3:17   69, 245, 246
3:18   247
3:19   42, 48, 64, 82, 113, 223, 234, 269
3:21   53
4:8   67

5:6   139
5:9   54, 139, 141, 160, 230, 275
5:10   260
5:12   10
5:13   210
5:14   10
7:12   10
7:14   141, 142
7:16   282
11:15   53, 243, 244
12:9   182, 268, 289
12:11   185
14:3   139, 160, 275
14:13   42, 265, 323
14:14   141, 142
15:3   275
15:4   67
18:4   262
19:5   210
19:6   211
19:9   164
19:11   55, 56, 57, 59
20:2   53
20:4   190
20:6   238, 239, 243, 260, 279
20:8   255, 256, 257, 258
20:10   136
20:12   79, 92
20:14   143
20:15   22, 138
21:2   305
21:3   138, 139
21:3–4   139
21:4   78, 122, 136, 137, 278
21:5   136
21:6   251
21:7   163
21:8   106, 140
21:18   78
21:22   137
22:2   117
22:3   136, 137, 138
22:4   141
22:5   260
22:9   326, 327
22:11   140, 210
22:12   81, 195
22:15   140
22:17   17, 45, 83, 136, 139, 167, 168, 251, 312

John W. Reed has served as a pastor and faculty member at Dallas Theological Seminary. He is co-author of The Power Sermon.